SQL Server 2012 T-SQL Recipes

A Problem-Solution Approach

Jason Brimhall
David Dye
Jonathan Gennick
Andy Roberts
Wayne Sheffield

Apress

SQL Server 2012 T-SQL Recipes: A Problem-Solution Approach

ISBN-13 (pbk): 978-1-4302-4200-0

ISBN-13 (electronic): 978-1-4302-4201-7

President and Publisher: Paul Manning
Lead Editor: Jonathan Gennick
Developmental Editor: Douglas Pundick
Technical Reviewers: Jay Visnansky, Alastair Aitchison, Joseph Sack
Editorial Board: Steve Anglin, Ewan Buckingham, Gary Cornell, Louise Corrigan, Morgan Ertel, Jonathan Gennick, Jonathan Hassell, Robert Hutchinson, Michelle Lowman, James Markham, Matthew Moodie, Jeff Olson, Jeffrey Pepper, Douglas Pundick, Ben Renow-Clarke, Dominic Shakeshaft, Gwenan Spearing, Matt Wade, Tom Welsh
Coordinating Editors: Brent Dubi and Kevin Shea
Copy Editor: Kim Wimpsett
Compositor: SPi Global
Indexer: SPi Global
Artist: SPi Global
Cover Designer: Anna Ishchenko

Distributed to the book trade worldwide by Springer Science+Business Media New York, 233 Spring Street, 6th Floor, New York, NY 10013. Phone 1-800-SPRINGER, fax (201) 348-4505, e-mail `orders-ny@springer-sbm.com`, or visit `www.springeronline.com`.

For information on translations, please e-mail `rights@apress.com`, or visit `www.apress.com`.

Apress and friends of ED books may be purchased in bulk for academic, corporate, or promotional use. eBook versions and licenses are also available for most titles. For more information, reference our Special Bulk Sales–eBook Licensing web page at `www.apress.com/bulk-sales`.

Any source code or other supplementary materials referenced by the author in this text is available to readers at `www.apress.com`. For detailed information about how to locate your book's source code, go to `www.apress.com/source-code`.

Contents at a Glance

Contents

About the Authors

Jason Brimhall is first and foremost a family man. He has 15+ years of experience in IT and has worked with SQL Server starting with SQL Server 6.5. He has worked for both large and small companies in varied industries. He has experience in performance tuning, high transaction environments, large environments, and VLDBs. He is currently a database architect and an MCITP for SQL 2008. Jason regularly volunteers for PASS and is the VP of the Las Vegas User Group (SSSOLV). You can read more from Jason on his blog at `http://jasonbrimhall.info`.

David Dye is a Microsoft SQL Server MVP, instructor, and author specializing in relational database management systems, business intelligence systems, reporting solutions, and Microsoft SharePoint. For the past nine years David's expertise has been focused on Microsoft SQL Server development and administration. His work has earned him recognition as a Microsoft MVP in 2009 and 2010, as a moderator for the Microsoft Developer Network for SQL Server forums, as an Innovator of the Year runner-up in 2009 by SQL Server Magazine, and in the Training Associates Technical Trainer Spotlight in April 2011. David currently serves as a technical reviewer and coauthor for Apress in the SQL Server 2012 series and as an author with Packt Publishing.

Jonathan Gennick is an Apress assistant editorial director with responsibility for database topics. He is line-leader for Apress's Oracle and SQL Server lines. He publishes carefully chosen database books of a general nature. He maintains a keen interest in books across all lines that touch upon relational databases.

Andy Roberts is a data platform technology specialist (TS) for Microsoft in the Northeast district. Prior to his life as a TS, Andy spent 12 years as a consultant for Microsoft Consulting Services. As a consultant, Andy assisted customers in implementing mission-critical OLTP and DW/BI solutions on SQL Server. Andy wore many hats as a consultant including application developer, solution architect, mentor to development teams, mentor to DBAs, BI lead, SCRUM master, and guy-that-knows-a-bunch-of-stuff-about-Microsoft.

When not basking behind the glow of his laptop, Andy enjoys volunteering as a ski instructor at Maine Adaptive Sports, golfing, biking, and, of course, trying to reverse engineer his five-month-old son, Max, to see what makes him work.

Wayne Sheffield started working with databases in the late 1980s, using DBase, Foxbase, and FoxPro. With more than 20 years in the IT industry, he has worked with SQL Server database systems (starting from version 6.5) since the late 1990s in various development and administration roles, with an emphasis in performance tuning. He is author of several articles at `www.sqlservercentral.com` and enjoys sharing his knowledge by presenting at various SQL PASS events and posting on his blog at `http://blog.waynesheffield.com/wayne`.

About the Technical Reviewers

Alastair Aitchison is an independent developer, consultant, and trainer, specializing in spatial data reporting and analysis. His work has been used by the House of Lords, various police forces, political parties, and media agencies.

Alastair is an active contributor to the development community; he is a moderator and one of the top answerers on the MSDN spatial and Bing Maps forums, he speaks at conferences, and he maintains a blog about all things to do with spatial data at `http://alastaira.wordpress.com`. He holds a number of certifications and has twice been awarded the Most Valuable Professional (MVP) award from Microsoft.

He lives in Norwich, England, with his wife and children.

Joseph Sack is a principal consultant with SQL skills. He has worked as a SQL Server professional since 1997 and has supported and developed for SQL Server environments in financial services, IT consulting, manufacturing, retail, and the real estate industry. Prior to joining SQLskills, he worked at Microsoft as a Premier Field Engineer supporting very large enterprise customer environments. He was responsible for providing deep SQL Server advisory services, training, troubleshooting, and ongoing solutions guidance. His areas of expertise include performance tuning, scalability, T-SQL development, and high availability. In 2006 Joe earned the Microsoft Certified Master: SQL Server 2005 certification, and in 2008, he earned the Microsoft Certified Master: SQL Server 2008 certification. In 2009 he took over responsibility for the SQL Server Microsoft Certified Master program and held that post until 2011. He is the author of a few books and white papers, including most recently *SQL Server 2008 Transact-SQL Recipes* (Apress, 2008). Joe's blog is at `www.SQLskills.com/blogs/joe`, and he can be reached at `joe@SQLskills.com`.

Jay Visnansky is a veteran developer with more than a decade of web development experience specializing in the design, development, and implementation of GIS mapping solutions using the Google and Microsoft Bing mapping APIs. The last four years he has been involved with implementing various marketing and routing applications utilizing SQL Server 2008 spatial features and, more recently, SQL Server 2012. Jay's technical knowledge includes ASP.NET C#, JavaScript, and SQL Server. Jay welcomes any questions or feedback and can be contacted at `jjvisnansky@hotmail.com`.

Acknowledgments

I've enjoyed very much my small contribution to this work. I'm thus grateful first to my coauthors—Jason Brimhall, David Dye, Wayne Sheffield, and Andy Roberts—for tolerating my presence in their book. I love the magic of working in SQL but as an editor don't often get the chance to go hands-on. Thanks, guys, for allowing me that chance once again.

Gratitude also is due to Donna, Jeff, and Jenny Gennick; Justin Miller; Karl and Ryan Olson; Lizzy Olson; Elijah Nieman; and Larry Treul. These are my family and friends who endured (sometimes unknowingly so!) the fallout from my spending time on the book. I'm grateful to Jeremiah Wilton for answering some questions about Amazon Web Services, which I made use of in the writing of this book. Thanks finally to technical reviewers Alastair Aitchison, Joe Sack, and Jay Visnansky for their consistent good help in reading the chapters, testing the code, and providing feedback to improve the work.

–Jonathan Gennick

I am grateful for the opportunity to have worked on this book. I appreciate very much the opportunity to work with my coauthors—Jonathan Gennick, David Dye, Wayne Sheffield, and Andy Roberts. I love working with SQL Server and doing what I can to share that enthusiasm with fellow SQL Server professionals.

Much gratitude is due to my wife, Krista, and our children. Krista and ATW Photography were gracious enough to provide photography services to me for this book—thank you! I am thankful to Jerry and Sheila Hurst who were influential to me. Many thanks to extended family and friends who also contributed in many different ways while I worked on this book (mostly unknowingly)!

Thanks finally to technical reviewers Alastair Aitchison, Joe Sack, and Jay Visnansky for their hard work in reading the chapters, testing the code, and providing feedback to improve the work.

–Jason Brimhall

I deeply appreciate the opportunity to have worked on this book. The entire team, from the other coauthors (Jason Brimhall, David Dye, Jonathan Gennick, and Andy Roberts), the technical reviewers (Alastair Aitchison, Joe Sack, and Jay Visnansky), and all of the Apress staff working diligently behind the scenes, contributed to make this book the fine finished product you are now reading. It was indeed a pleasure to work with all of these professionals.

To my wife, Karen—the words "thank you" are so insufficient for all of the hours that this project took me away from you. I guess I owe you that cruise.

–Wayne Sheffield

I would like to thank the team for this chance to contribute to such a great book. It has been fun to revisit some old concepts and think about how to apply some of the new features of SQL Server to problems that we all face every day. I would also like to thank Tim Roberts, who one day in 1996 dropped 1,200 pages of SQL Server reference material on my desk and said, "I need to you be a SQL Expert tomorrow." One long night of reading and 16 years of practice later, here I am.

–Andy Roberts

Introduction

Sometimes all one wants is a good example. That's our motivation for accepting the baton from Joe Sack and revising his excellent work to cover the very latest edition of Microsoft's database engine—SQL Server 2012.

T-SQL is fundamental to working with SQL Server. Almost everything you do, from querying a table to creating indexes to backing up and recovering, ultimately comes down to T-SQL statements being issued and executed. Sometimes it's a utility executing statements on your behalf. Other times you must write them yourself.

And when you have to write them yourself, you're probably going to be in a hurry. Information technology is like that. It's a field full of stress and deadlines, and don't we all just want to get home for dinner with our families?

We sure do want to be home for dinner, and that brings us full circle to the example-based format you'll find in this book. If you have a job to do that's covered in this book, you can count on a clear code example and very few words to waste your time. We put the code first! And explain it afterward. We hope our examples are clear enough that you can just crib from them and get on with your day, but the detailed explanations are there if you need them.

We've missed a few dinners from working on this book. We hope it helps you avoid the same fate.

Who This Book Is For

SQL Server 2012 T-SQL Recipes is aimed at developers deploying applications against Microsoft SQL Server 2012. The book also helps database administrators responsible for managing those databases. Any developer or administrator valuing good code examples will find something of use in this book.

Conventions

Throughout the book, we've tried to keep to a consistent style for presenting SQL and results. Where a piece of code, a SQL reserved word, or a fragment of SQL is presented in the text, it is presented in fixed-width Courier font, such as this example:

```
SELECT * FROM HumanResources.Employee;
```

Where we discuss the syntax and options of SQL commands, we use a conversational style so you can quickly reach an understanding of the command or technique. We have chosen not to duplicate complex syntax diagrams that are best left to the official, vendor-supplied documentation. Instead, we take an example-based approach that is easy to understand and adapt.

Downloading the Code

The code for the examples shown in this book is available on the Apress web site, `www.apress.com`. A link can be found on the book's information page (`www.apress.com/9781430242000`) on the Source Code/Downloads tab. This tab is located in the Related Titles section of the page.

CHAPTER 1

Getting Started with SELECT

by Jonathan Gennick

The SELECT command is the cornerstone of the Transact-SQL language, allowing you to retrieve data from a SQL Server database (and more specifically from database objects within a SQL Server database). Although the full syntax of the SELECT statement is enormous, the basic syntax can be presented in a more boiled-down form:

```
SELECT select_list
FROM table_list
WHERE predicates
ORDER BY sort_key_columns;
```

The `select_list` argument is the list of columns that you wish to return in the results of the query. The `table_list` arguments are the actual tables and/or views from which the data will be retrieved. Write predicates in your WHERE clause to restrict results to rows of interest, and specify sort key columns control the ordering of results.

Note All examples in this chapter make use of the AdventureWorks database. Be sure to execute a `USE AdventureWorks` command to switch to that database before executing any of the examples in this chapter. If you don't already have it, you'll find the `AdventureWorks` example database in Microsoft's repository at www.codeplex.com. The specific URL for the SQL Server version is currently: `http://msftdbprodsamples.codeplex.com/`.

1-1. Connecting to a Database

Problem

You are running SQL Server Management Studio to execute ad hoc SQL statements. You wish to connect to a specific database, such as the example database.

Solution

Execute the USE command, and specify the name of your target database. For example, we executed the following command to attach to the example database used during work on this book:

```
USE AdventureWorks2008R2;
```

```
Command(s) completed successfully.
```

The success message indicates a successful connection. You may now execute queries against tables and views in the database without having to qualify those object names by specifying the database name each time.

How It Works

When you first launch SQL Server Management Studio you are connected by default to the master database. That's usually not convenient, and you shouldn't be storing your data in that database. You can query tables and views in other databases provided you specify fully qualified names. For example, you can specify a fully qualified name in the following, `database.schema.object` format:

```
AdventureWorks2008R2.HumanResources.Employee
```

The `USE` statement in the solution enables you to omit the database name and refer to the object using the shorter and simpler, `schema.object` notation. For example:

```
HumanResources.Employee
```

It's cumbersome to specify the database name—`AdventureWorks2008R2` in this case—with each object reference. Doing so ties your queries and program code to a specific database, reducing flexibility by making it difficult or impossible to run against a different database in the future. Examples in this book generally assume that you are connected to the `AdventureWorks` example database that you can download from www.codeplex.com.

1-2. Retrieving Specific Columns

Problem

You have a table or a view. You wish to retrieve data from specific columns.

Solution

Write a `SELECT` statement. List the columns you wish returned following the `SELECT` keyword. The following example demonstrates a very simple `SELECT` against the `AdventureWorks` database, whereby three columns are returned, along with several rows from the `HumanResources.Employee` table.

```
SELECT NationalIDNumber,
    LoginID,
    JobTitle
FROM  HumanResources.Employee;
```

The query returns the following abridged results:

```
NationalIDNumber    LoginID                     JobTitle
----------------    ------------------------    ----------------------------
295847284           adventure-works\ken0        Chief Executive Officer
245797967           adventure-works\terri0      Vice President of Engineering
509647174           adventure-works\roberto0    Engineering Manager
112457891           adventure-works\rob0        Senior Tool Designer
695256908           adventure-works\gail0       Design Engineer
...
```

How It Works

The first few lines of code define which columns to display in the query results:

```
SELECT NationalIDNumber,
    LoginID,
    JobTitle
```

The next line of code is the FROM clause:

```
FROM  HumanResources.Employee;
```

The FROM clause specifies the data source, which in this example is a table. Notice the two-part name of HumanResources.Employee. The first part (the part before the period) is the *schema,* and the second part (after the period) is the actual table name. A schema contains the object, and that schema is then owned by a user. Because users own a schema, and the schema contains the object, you can change the owner of the schema without having to modify object ownership.

1-3. Retrieving All Columns

Problem

You are writing an ad hoc query. You wish to retrieve all columns from a table or view without having to type all the column names.

Solution

Specify an asterisk (*) instead of a column list. Doing so causes SQL Server to return all columns from the table or view. For example:

```
SELECT *
FROM  HumanResources.Employee;
```

The abridged column and row output are shown here:

```
BusinessEntityID   NationalIDNumber   LoginID                    OrganizationNode ...
----------------   ----------------   ------------------------   ---------------- ...
1                  295847284          adventure-works\ken0       0x          ...
2                  245797967          adventure-works\terri0     0x58         ...
3                  509647174          adventure-works\roberto0   0x5AC0        ...
...
```

How It Works

The asterisk symbol (*) returns all columns of the table or view you are querying. All other details are as explained in the previous recipe.

Please remember that, as good practice, it is better to reference the columns you want to retrieve explicitly instead of using SELECT *. If you write an application that uses SELECT *, your application may expect the same columns (in the same order) from the query. If later on you add a new column to the underlying table or view, or if you reorder the table columns, you could break the calling application, because the new column in your result set is unexpected.

Using SELECT * can also negatively affect performance, as you may be returning more data than you need over the network, increasing the result set size and data retrieval operations on the SQL Server instance. For applications requiring thousands of transactions per second, the number of columns returned in the result set can have a nontrivial impact.

1-4. Specifying the Rows to Be Returned

Problem

You do not want to return all rows from a table or a view. You want to restrict query results to only those rows of interest.

Solution

Specify a WHERE clause giving the conditions that rows must meet in order to be returned. For example, the following query returns only rows in which the person's title is "Ms."

```
SELECT Title,
   FirstName,
   LastName

FROM  Person.Person
WHERE  Title = 'Ms.';
```

This example returns the following (abridged) results:

```
Title    FirstName    LastName
-----    ---------    -----------
Ms.      Gail         Erickson
Ms.      Janice       Galvin
Ms.      Jill         Williams
...
```

You may combine multiple conditions in a WHERE clause through the use of the keywords AND and OR. The following query looks specifically for Ms. Antrim's data:

```
SELECT Title,

   FirstName,
   LastName

FROM Person.Person
WHERE Title = 'Ms.' AND
   LastName = 'Antrim';
```

The result from this query will be the following single row:

```
Title    FirstName    LastName
-----    ---------    --------
Ms.      Ramona       Antrim
```

How It Works

In a SELECT query, the WHERE clause restricts rows returned in the query result set. The WHERE clause provides search conditions that determine the rows returned by the query. Search conditions are written as predicates, which are expressions that evaluate to one of the Boolean results of TRUE, FALSE, or UNKNOWN. Only rows for which the final evaluation of the WHERE clause is TRUE are returned. Table 1-1 lists some of the common operators available.

Table 1-1. *Operators*

Operator	Description
`!=`	Tests two expressions not being equal to each other.
`!>`	Tests whether the left condition is less than or equal to (i.e., not greater than) the condition on the right.
`!<`	Tests whether the left condition is greater than or equal to (i.e., not less than) the condition on the right.
`<`	Tests the left condition as less than the right condition.
`<=`	Tests the left condition as less than or equal to the right condition.
`<>`	Tests two expressions not being equal to each other.
`=`	Tests equality between two expressions.
`>`	Tests the left condition being greater than the expression to the right.
`>=`	Tests the left condition being greater than or equal to the expression to the right.

■ **Tip** Don't think of a WHERE clause as going out and retrieving rows that match the conditions. Think of it as a fishnet or a sieve. All the possible rows are dropped into the net. Unwanted rows fall on through. When a query is done executing, the rows remaining in the net are those that match the predicates you listed. Database engines will optimize execution, but the fishnet metaphor is a useful one when initially crafting a query.

In this recipe's first example, you can see that only rows where the person's title was equal to "Ms." were returned. This search condition was defined in the WHERE clause of the query:

```
WHERE Title = 'Ms.'
```

You may combine multiple search conditions by utilizing the AND and OR logical operators. The AND logical operator joins two or more search conditions and returns rows only when each of the search conditions is true. The OR logical operator joins two or more search conditions and returns rows when any of the conditions are true. The second solution example shows the following AND operation:

```
WHERE Title = 'Ms.' AND
    LastName = 'Antrim'
```

Both search conditions must be true for a row to be returned in the result set. Thus, only the row for Ms. Antrim is returned.

Use the OR operator to specify alternate choices. Use parentheses to clarify the order of operations. For example:

```
WHERE Title = 'Ms.' AND
   (LastName = 'Antrim' OR LastName = 'Galvin')
```

Here, the OR expression involving the two LastName values is evaluated first, and then the Title is examined. UNKNOWN values can make their appearance when NULL data is accessed in the search condition. A NULL value doesn't mean that the value is blank or zero, only that the value is unknown. Recipe 1-7 later in this chapter shows how to identify rows having or not having NULL values.

1-5. Renaming the Output Columns

Problem

You don't like the column names returned by a query. You wish to change the names for clarity in reporting, or to be compatible with an already written program that is consuming the results from the query.

Solution

Designate column aliases. Use the AS clause for that purpose. For example:

```
SELECT BusinessEntityID AS "Employee ID",
   VacationHours AS "Vacation",
   SickLeaveHours AS "Sick Time"
FROM  HumanResources.Employee;
```

Results are as follows:

```
Employee ID     Vacation        Sick Time
-----------     --------        ---------
1               99              69
2               1               20
3               2               21
...
```

How It Works

Each column in a result set is given a name. That name appears in the column heading when you execute a query ad hoc using management studio. The name is also the name by which any program code must reference the column when consuming the results from a query. You can specify any name you like for a column via the AS clause. The name you specify is termed a *column alias*.

The solution query places column names in double quotes. Follow that approach when your new name contains spaces or other nonalphabetic or nonnumeric characters, or when you wish to specify lowercase characters and have the database configured to use an uppercase collation. For example:

```
BusinessEntityID AS "Employee ID",
```

If your new name has no spaces or other unusual characters, then you can omit the double quotes:

```
VacationHours AS Vacation,
```

You may also choose to omit the AS keyword:

```
VacationHours Vacation,
```

Well-chosen column aliases make ad hoc reports easier to comprehend. Column aliases also provide a way to insulate program code from changes in column names at the database level. They are especially helpful in that regard when you have columns that are the results of expressions. See Recipe 1-6 for an example.

SQUARE BRACKETS OR QUOTES? AS OR NOT-AS?

Recipe 1-5 shows the ISO standard syntax for handling spaces and other special characters in alias names. SQL Server also supports a proprietary syntax involving square brackets. Following are two examples that are equivilant in meaning:

```
BusinessEntityID AS "Employee ID",
BusinessEntityID AS [Employee ID],
```

Recipe 1-5 also shows that you can take or leave the AS keyword when specifying column aliases. In fact, SQL Server also supports its own proprietary syntax. Here are three examples that all mean the same thing:

```
VacationHours AS Vacation,
VacationHours Vacation,
Vacation = VacationHours,
```

I prefer to follow the ISO standard, so I write enclosing quotes whenever I must deal with unusual characters in a column alias. I also prefer the clarity of specifying the `AS` keyword. I avoid SQL Server's proprietary syntax in these cases.

1-6. Building a Column from an Expression

Problem

You are querying a table that lacks the precise bit of information you need. However, you are able to write an expression to generate the result that you are after. For example, you want to report on total time off available to employees. Your database design divides time off into separate buckets for vacation time and sick time. You, however, wish to report a single value.

Solution

Write the expression. Place it into the SELECT list as you would any other column. Provide a column alias by which the program executing the query can reference the column.

Following is an example showing an expression to compute the total number of hours an employee might be able to take off from work. The total includes both vacation and sick time.

```
SELECT BusinessEntityID AS EmployeeID,
   VacationHours + SickLeaveHours AS AvailableTimeOff
FROM  HumanResources.Employee;
```

```
EmployeeID      AvailableTimeOff
----------      ----------------
1               168
2               21
3               23
...
```

How It Works

Recipe 1-5 introduces column aliases. It's especially important to provide them for computed columns. That's because if you don't provide them, you get no name at all. For example, you can omit the AvailableTimeOff alias as follows:

```
SELECT BusinessEntityID AS EmployeeID,
   VacationHours + SickLeaveHours
FROM  HumanResources.Employee;
```

Do so, and you'll be rewarded by a result set having a column with no name:

```
EmployeeID
-------     ------
1           168
2           21
3           23
```

What is that second column? Will you remember what it is on the day after? How does program code refer to the column? Avoid these pesky questions by providing a stable column alias that you can maintain throughout the life of the query.

1-7. Providing Shorthand Names for Tables

Problem

You are writing a query and want to qualify all your column references by indicating the source table. Your table name is long. You wish for a shorter nickname by which to refer to the table.

Solution

Specify a table alias. Use the AS keyword to do that. For example:

```
SELECT E.BusinessEntityID AS "Employee ID",
   E.VacationHours AS "Vacation",
   E.SickLeaveHours AS "Sick Time"
FROM  HumanResources.Employee AS E;
```

How It Works

Table aliases work much like column aliases. Specify them using an AS clause. Place the AS clause immediately following the table name in your query's FROM clause. The solution example provides the alternate name E for the table HumanResources.Employee. As far as the rest of the query is concerned, the table is now named E. In fact, you may no longer refer to the table as HumanResources.Employee. If you try, you will get the following error:

```
SELECT HumanResources.Employee.BusinessEntityID AS "Employee ID",
   E.VacationHours AS "Vacation",
   E.SickLeaveHours AS "Sick Time"
FROM HumanResources.Employee AS E
```

```
Msg 4104, Level 16, State 1, Line 1
The multi-part identifier "HumanResources.Employee.BusinessEntityID" could not be bound.
```

Table aliases make it much easier to fully qualify your column names in a query. It is much easier to type:

```
E.BusinessEntityID
```

...than it is to type:

```
HumanResources.Employee.BusinessEntityID
```

You may not see the full utility of table aliases now, but their benefits become readily apparent the moment you begin writing queries involving multiple tables. Chapter 4 makes extensive use of table aliases in queries involving joins and subqueries.

1-8. Negating a Search Condition

Problem

You are finding it easier to describe those rows that you do not want rather than those that you do want.

Solution

Describe the rows that you do not want. Then use the NOT operator to essentially reverse the description so that you get those rows that you do want. The NOT logical operator negates the expression that follows it.

For example, you can retrieve all employees having a title of anything but "Ms." or "Mrs." Not having yet had your morning coffee, you prefer not to think through how to translate that requirement into a conjunction of two, not-equal predicates, preferring instead to write a predicate more in line with how the problem has been described. For example:

```
SELECT Title,
   FirstName,
   LastName FROM Person.Person
WHERE NOT (Title = 'Ms.' OR Title = 'Mrs.');
```

This returns the following (abridged) results:

```
Title    FirstName      LastName
-----    -----------    -----------------
Mr.      Jossef         Goldberg
Mr.      Hung-Fu        Ting
Mr.      Brian          Welcker
Mr.      Tete           Mensa-Annan
Mr.      Syed           Abbas
Mr.      Gustavo        Achong
Sr.      Humberto       Acevedo
Sra.     Pilar          Ackerman
Ms       Alyssa         Moore
...
```

How It Works

This example demonstrated the NOT operator:

```
WHERE NOT (Title = 'Ms.' OR Title = 'Mrs.');
```

NOT specifies the reverse of a search condition, in this case specifying that only rows that don't have the Title equal to "Ms."or "Mrs." be returned. Rows that do represent "Ms." or "Mrs." are excluded from the results. You can also choose to write the query using a conjunction of two not-equal predicates. For example:

```
SELECT Title,
   FirstName,
   LastName FROM Person.Person
WHERE Title != 'Ms.' AND Title != 'Mrs.';
```

There is generally no right or wrong choice to be made here. Rather, your decision will most often come down to your own preference and how you tend to approach and think about query problems.

KEEPING YOUR WHERE CLAUSE UNAMBIGUOUS

You can write multiple operators (AND, OR, NOT) in a single WHERE clause, but it is important to make your intentions clear by properly embedding your ANDs and ORs in parentheses. The NOT operator takes precedence (is evaluated first) before AND. The AND operator takes precedence over the OR operator. Using both AND and OR operators in the same WHERE clause without parentheses can return unexpected results. For example, the following query may return unintended results:

```
SELECT Title,
   FirstName,
   LastName
FROM Person.Person
WHERE Title = 'Ms.' AND
   FirstName = 'Catherine' OR
   LastName = 'Adams'
```

Is the intention to return results for all rows with a Title of "Ms.", and of those rows, only include those with a FirstName of Catherine or a LastName of Adams? Or did the query author wish to search for all people named "Ms." with a FirstName of Catherine, as well as anyone with a LastName of Adams?

It is good practice to use parentheses to clarify exactly what rows should be returned. Even if you are fully conversant with the rules of operator precedence, those who come after you may not be. Make judicious use of parentheses to remove all doubt as to your intentions.

1-9. Specifying A Range of Values

Problem

You wish to specify a range of values as a search condition. For example, you are querying a table having a date column. You wish to return rows having dates only in a specified range of interest.

Solution

Write a predicate involving the BETWEEN operator. That operator allows you to specify a range of values, in this case of date values. For example, to find sales orders placed between the dates July 23, 2005 and July 24, 2005:

```
SELECT SalesOrderID,
   ShipDate
FROM  Sales.SalesOrderHeader
WHERE  ShipDate BETWEEN '2005-07-23T00:00:00'
       AND   '2005-07-24T23:59:59';
```

The query returns the following results:

```
SalesOrderID    ShipDate
------------    -----------------------
43758           2005-07-23 00:00:00.000
43759           2005-07-23 00:00:00.000
43760           2005-07-23 00:00:00.000
43761           2005-07-23 00:00:00.000
43762           2005-07-24 00:00:00.000
43763           2005-07-24 00:00:00.000
43764           2005-07-24 00:00:00.000
43765           2005-07-24 00:00:00.000
```

How It Works

This recipe demonstrates the BETWEEN operator, which tests whether a column's value falls between two values that you specify. The value range is inclusive of the two endpoints.

The WHERE clause in the solution example is written as:

```
WHERE ShipDate BETWEEN '2005-07-23T00:00:00' AND '2005-07-24T23:59:59'
```

Notice that we designate the specific time in hours, minutes, and seconds as well. The time-of-day defaults to 00:00:00, which is midnight at the start of a date. In this example, we wanted to include all of July 24, 2005. Thus we specify the last possible minute of that day.

1-10. Checking for NULL Values

Problem

Some of the values in a column might be NULL. You wish to identify rows having or not having NULL values.

Solution

Make use of the IS NULL and IS NOT NULL tests to identify rows having or not having NULL values in a given column. For example, the following query returns any rows for which the value of the product's weight is unknown:

```
SELECT ProductID,
   Name,
   Weight
FROM  Production.Product
WHERE  Weight IS NULL;
```

This query returns the following (abridged) results:

```
ProductID   Name                   Weight
---------   --------------------   ------
1           Adjustable Race        NULL
2           Bearing Ball           NULL
3           BB Ball Bearing        NULL
4           Headset Ball Bearings  NULL
...
```

How It Works

NULL values cannot be identified using operators such as = and <> that are designed to compare two values and return a TRUE or FALSE result. NULL actually indicates the absence of a value. For that reason, neither of the following predicates can be used to detect a NULL value:

```
Weight = NULL yields the value UNKNOWN, which is neither TRUE nor FALSE
Weight <> NULL also yields UNKNOWN
```

IS NULL however, is specifically designed to return TRUE when a value is NULL. Likewise, the expression IS NOT NULL returns TRUE when a value is not NULL. Predicates involving IS NULL and IS NOT NULL enable you to filter for rows having or not having NULL values in one or more columns.

■ **Caution** NULL values and their improper handling are one of the most prevelant sources of query mistakes. See Chapter 3 for guidance and techniques that can help you avoid trouble and get the results you want.

1-11. Providing a List of Values

Problem

You are searching for matches to a specific list of values. You could write a string of predicates joined by OR operators. But you prefer a more easily readable and maintainable solution.

Solution

Create a predicate involving the IN operator, which allows you to specify an arbitrary list of values. For example, the IN operator in the following query tests the equality of the Color column to a list of expressions:

```
SELECT ProductID,
   Name,
   Color
FROM  Production.Product
WHERE  Color IN ('Silver', 'Black', 'Red');
```

This returns the following (abridged) results:

```
ProductID  Name             Color
---------  ---------------  ------
317        LL Crankarm      Black
318        ML Crankarm      Black
319        HL Crankarm      Black
320        Chainring Bolts  Silver
321        Chainring Nut    Silver
...
```

How It Works

Use the IN operator any time you have a specific list of values. You can think of IN as shorthand for multiple OR expressions. For example, the following two WHERE clauses are semantically equivalent:

```
WHERE Color IN ('Silver', 'Black', 'Red')
```

```
WHERE Color = 'Silver' OR Color = 'Black' OR Color = 'Red'
```

You can see that an IN list becomes less cumbersome than a string of OR'd together expressions. This is especially true as the number of values grows.

■ **Tip** You can write NOT IN to find rows having values other than those that you list.

1-12. Performing Wildcard Searches

Problem

You don't have a specific value or list of values to find. What you do have is a general pattern, and you want to find all values that match that pattern.

Solution

Make use of the LIKE predicate, which provides a set of basic pattern-matching capabilities. Create a string using so-called *wildcards* to serve as a search expression. Table 1-2 shows the wildcards available in SQL Server 2012.

Table 1-2. *Wildcards for the LIKE predicate*

Wildcard	Usage
%	The percent sign. Represents a string of zero or more characters
_	The underscore. Represents a single character
[...]	A list of characters enclosed within square brackets. Represents a single character from among any in the list. You may use the hyphen as a shorthand to translate a range into a list. For example, [ABCDEF]-flatcan be written more succinctly as[A-F]-flat.You can also mix and match single characters and ranges. The expressions[A-CD-F]-flat, [A-DEF]-flat, and [ABC-F]-flat all mean the same thing and ultimately resolve to [ABCDEF]-flat.
[^...]	A list of characters enclosed within square brackets and preceeded by a caret. Represents a single character from among any *not* in the list.

The following example demonstrates using the LIKE operation with the % wildcard, searching for any product with a name beginning with the letter B:

```
SELECT ProductID,
   Name
FROM  Production.Product
WHERE  Name LIKE 'B%';
```

This query returns the following results:

```
ProductID    Name
---------    ---------------------
3            BB Ball Bearing
2            Bearing Ball
877          Bike Wash - Dissolver
316          Blade
```

What if you want to search for the literal % (percentage sign) or an _ (underscore) in your character column? For this, you can use an ESCAPE operator. The ESCAPE operator allows you to search for a wildcard symbol as an actual character. First modify a row in the Production.ProductDescription table, adding a percentage sign to the Description column:

```
UPDATE Production.ProductDescription
SET   Description = 'Chromoly steel. High % of defects'
WHERE  ProductDescriptionID = 3;
```

Next, query the table, searching for any descriptions containing the literal percentage sign:

```
SELECT ProductDescriptionID,
    Description
FROM  Production.ProductDescription
WHERE  Description LIKE '%/%%' ESCAPE '/';
```

Notice the use of /% in the middle of the search string passed to LIKE. The / is the ESCAPE operator. Thus, the characters /% are interpreted as %, and the LIKE predicate will identify strings containing a % in any position. The query given will return the following row:

```
ProductDescriptionID    Description
--------------------    ---------------------------------
3                       Chromoly steel. High % of defects
```

How It Works

Wildcards allow you to search for patterns in character-based columns. In the example from this recipe, the % percentage sign represents a string of zero or more characters:

```
WHERE Name LIKE 'B%'
```

If searching for a literal that would otherwise be interpreted by SQL Server as a wildcard, you can use the ESCAPE clause. The example from this recipe searches for a literal percentage sign in the Description column:

```
WHERE Description LIKE '%/%%' ESCAPE '/'
```

A slash embedded in single quotes was put after the ESCAPE command. This designates the slash symbol as the escape character for the preceding LIKE expression string. Any wildcard preceded by a slash is then treated as just a regular character.

1-13. Sorting Your Results

Problem

You are executing a query, and you wish the results to come back in a specific order.

Solution

Write an ORDER BY clause into your query. Specify the columns on which to sort. Place the clause at the very end of your query.

This next example demonstrates ordering the query results by columns ProductID and EndDate:

```
SELECT p.Name,
   h.EndDate,
   h.ListPrice
FROM  Production.Product AS p
   INNER JOIN Production.ProductListPriceHistory AS h
     ON p.ProductID = h.ProductID
ORDER BY p.Name,
   h.EndDate;
```

This query returns results as follows:

```
Name                      EndDate                   ListPrice
----------------------    -----------------------   ---------
All-Purpose Bike Stand    NULL                      159.00
AWC Logo Cap              NULL                      8.99
AWC Logo Cap              2006-06-30 00:00:00.000   8.6442
AWC Logo Cap              2007-06-30 00:00:00.000   8.6442
Bike Wash - Dissolver     NULL                      7.95
Cable Lock                2007-06-30 00:00:00.000   25.00
...
```

Notice the results are first sorted on Name. Within Name, they are sorted on EndDate.

How It Works

Although queries sometimes appear to return data properly without an ORDER BY clause, you should never depend upon any ordering that is accidental. You must write an ORDER BY into your query if the order of the result set is critical. You can designate one or more columns in your ORDER BY clause, as long as the columns do not exceed 8,060 bytes in total.

■ **Caution** We can't stress enough the importance of ORDER BY when order matters. Grouping operations and indexing sometimes make it seem that ORDER BY is superfluous. It isn't. Trust us: there are enough corner cases that sooner or later you'll be caught out. If the sort order matters, then say so explicitly in your query by writing an ORDER BY clause.

In the solution example, the Production.Product and Production.ProductListPriceHistory tables are queried to view the history of product prices over time. The query involves an inner join, and there is more about those in Chapter 4. The following line of code sorted the results first alphabetically by product name, and then by the end date:

```
ORDER BY p.Name, h.EndDate
```

The default sort order is an ascending sort. NULL values sort to the top in an ascending sort.

■ **Note** Need a descending sort? No problem. Just drop into the next recipe for an example.

1-14. Specifying Sort Order

Problem

You do not want the default, ascending-order sort. You want to sort by one or more columns in descending order.

Solution

Make use of the keywords ASC and ASCENDING, or DESC and DESCENDING, to specify the sort direction. Apply these keywords to each sort column as you desire.

This next example sorts on the same two columns as Recipe 1-13's query, but this time in descending order for each of those columns:

```
SELECT p.Name,
   h.EndDate,
   h.ListPrice
FROM  Production.Product AS p
   INNER JOIN Production.ProductListPriceHistory AS h
     ON p.ProductID = h.ProductID
ORDER BY p.Name DESC,
   h.EndDate DESC;
```

Following are some of the results:

```
Name                 EndDate                   ListPrice
-----------------    ----------------------    ---------
Women's Tights, S    2007-06-30 00:00:00.000   74.99
Women's Tights, M    2007-06-30 00:00:00.000   74.99
```

```
Women's Tights, L       2007-06-30 00:00:00.000   74.99
...
Sport-100 Helmet, Red   2007-06-30 00:00:00.000   33.6442
Sport-100 Helmet, Red   2006-06-30 00:00:00.000   33.6442
Sport-100 Helmet, Red   NULL                      34.99
...
```

How It Works

Use the keywords ASC and DESC on a column-by-column basis to specify whether you want an ascending or descending sort on that column's values. If you prefer it, you can spell out the words as ASCENDING and DESCENDING.

You need not specify the same sort order for all columns listed in the ORDER BY clause. How each column's values are sorted is independent of the other columns. It is perfectly reasonable, for example, to specify an ascending sort by product name and a descending sort by end date.

NULL values in a descending sort are sorted to the bottom. You can see that in the solution results. The NULL value for the Sport-100 Helmet's end date is at the end of the list for that helmet.

1-15. Sorting by Columns Not Selected

Problem

You want to sort by columns not returned by the query.

Solution

Simply specify the columns you wish to sort by. They do not need to be in your query results. For example, you can return a list of product names sorted by color without returning the colors:

```
SELECT p.Name
FROM   Production.Product AS p
ORDER BY p.Color;
```

Results from this query are:

```
Name
--------------------
Guide Pulley
LL Grip Tape
ML Grip Tape
HL Grip Tape
Thin-Jam Hex Nut 9
Thin-Jam Hex Nut 10
...
```

How It Works

You can sort by any column. It doesn't matter whether that column is in the SELECT list. What does matter is that the column must be available to the query. The solution query is against the Product table. Color is a column in that table, so it is available as a sort key.

One caveat when ordering by unselected columns is that ORDER BY items must appear in the SELECT list if SELECT DISTINCT is specified. That's because the grouping operation used internally to eliminate duplicate rows from the result set has the effect of disassociating rows in the result set from their original underlying rows in the table. That behavior makes perfect sense when you think about it. A deduplicated row in a result set would come from what originally were two or more table rows. And which of those rows would you go to for the excluded column? There is no answer to that question, and hence the caveat.

1-16. Forcing Unusual Sort Orders

Problem

You wish to force a sort order not directly supported by the data. For example, you wish to retrieve only the colored products, and you further wish to force the color red to sort first.

Solution

Write an expression to translate values in the data to values that will give the sort order you are after. Then order your query results by that expression. Following is one approach to the problem of retrieving colored parts and listing the red ones first:

```
SELECT p.ProductID,
   p.Name,
   p.Color
FROM  Production.Product AS p
WHERE  p.Color IS NOT NULL
ORDER BY CASE p.Color
    WHEN 'Red' THEN NULL
    ELSE p.Color
    END;
```

Results will be as follows:

```
ProductID      Name                       Color
---------      -----------------------    -------
706            HL Road Frame - Red, 58    Red
707            Sport-100 Helmet, Red      Red
725            LL Road Frame - Red, 44    Red
726            LL Road Frame - Red, 48    Red
...
790            Road-250 Red, 48           Red
791            Road-250 Red, 52           Red
792            Road-250 Red, 58           Red
793            Road-250 Black, 44         Black
794            Road-250 Black, 48         Black
...
```

How It Works

The solution takes advantage of the fact that SQL Server sorts nulls first. The CASE expression returns NULL for red-colored items, thus forcing those first. Other colors are returned unchanged. The result is all the red items first in the list, and then red is followed by other colors in their natural sort order.

You don't have to rely upon nulls sorting first. Here is another version of the query to illustrate that and one other point:

```
SELECT p.ProductID,
   p.Name,
   p.Color
FROM  Production.Product AS p
WHERE  p.Color IS NOT NULL
ORDER BY CASE LOWER(p.Color)
    WHEN 'red' THEN ' '
    ELSE LOWER(p.Color)
   END;
```

This version of the query returns the same results as before. The value 'Red' is converted into a single space, which sorts before all the spelled-out color names. The CASE expression specifies `LOWER(p.Color)` to ensure 'Red,' 'RED,' 'red,' and so forth are all treated the same. Other color values are forced to lowercase to prevent any case-sensitivity problems in the sort.

1-17. Paging Through A Result Set

Problem

You wish to present a result set to an application user N rows at a time.

Solution

Make use of the query paging feature that is brand new in SQL Server 2012. Do this by adding `OFFSET` and `FETCH` clauses to your query's `ORDER BY` clause. For example, the following query uses `OFFSET` and `FETCH` to retrieve the first 10 rows of results:

```
SELECT ProductID, Name
FROM Production.Product
ORDER BY Name
OFFSET 0 ROWS FETCH NEXT 10 ROWS ONLY;
```

Results from this query will be the first 10 rows, as ordered by product name:

```
ProductID    Name
---------    -----------------------
1            Adjustable Race
879          All-Purpose Bike Stand
712          AWC Logo Cap
3            BB Ball Bearing
2            Bearing Ball
877          Bike Wash - Dissolver
316          Blade
```

```
843           Cable Lock
952           Chain
324           Chain Stays
```

Changing the offset from 0 to 8 will fetch another 10 rows. The offset will skip the first eight rows. There will be a two-row overlap with the preceding result set. Here is the query:

```
SELECT ProductID, Name
FROM Production.Product
ORDER BY Name
OFFSET 8 ROWS FETCH NEXT 10 ROWS ONLY;
```

And here are the results:

```
ProductID   Name
---------   ----------------
952         Chain
324         Chain Stays
322         Chainring
320         Chainring Bolts
321         Chainring Nut
866         Classic Vest, L
865         Classic Vest, M
864         Classic Vest, S
505         Cone-Shaped Race
323         Crown Race
```

Continue modifying the offset each time, paging through the result until the user is finished.

How It Works

OFFSET and FETCH turn a SELECT statement into a query fetching a specific window of rows from those possible. Use OFFSET to specify how many rows to skip from the beginning of the possible result set. Use FETCH to set the number of rows to return. You can change either value as you wish from one execution to the next.

You must specify an ORDER BY clause! OFFSET and FETCH are actually considered as part of that clause. If you don't specify a sort order, then rows can come back in any order. What does it mean to ask for the second set of 10 rows returned in random order? It doesn't really mean anything.

Be sure to specify a deterministic set of sort columns in your ORDER BY clause. Each SELECT to get the next page of results is a separate query and a separate sort operation. Make sure that your data sorts the same way each time. Do not leave ambiguity.

■ **Note** The word *deterministic* means that the same inputs always give the same outputs. Specify your sort such that the same set of input rows will always yield the same ordering in the query output.

Each execution of a paging query is a separate execution from the others. Consider executing sequences of paging queries from within a transaction providing a snapshot or serializable isolation. Chapter 12 discusses transactions in detail. However, you can begin and end such a transaction as follows:

```
SET TRANSACTION ISOLATION LEVEL SNAPSHOT;
BEGIN TRANSACTION;
… /* Queries go here */
COMMIT;
```

Anomalies are possible without isolation. For example:

- You might see a row twice. In the solution example, if another user inserted eight new rows with names sorting earlier than "Adjustable Race," then the second query results would be the same as the first.
- You might miss rows. If another user quickly deleted the first eight rows, then the second solution query would miss everything from "Chainring" to "Crown Race."

You may decide to risk the default isolation level. If your target table is read-only, or if it is updated in batch-mode only at night, then you might be justified in leaving the isolation level at its default because the risk of change during the day is low to non-existent. Possibly you might choose not to worry about the issue at all. However, make sure that whatever you do is the result of thinking things through and making a conscious choice.

■ **Note** It may seem rash for us to even hint at not allowing the possibility of inconsistent results. We advocate making careful and conscious decisions. Some applications—Facebook is a well-known example—trade away some consistency in favor of performance. (We routinely see minor inconsistencies on our Facebook walls.) We are not saying you should do the same. We simply acknowledge the possibility of such a choice.

CHAPTER 2

Elementary Programming

by Jonathan Gennick

In this chapter, you'll find recipes showing several of the basic programming constructs available in T-SQL. The chapter is not a complete tutorial to the language. You'll need to read other books for that. A good tutorial, if you need one that begins with first-principles, is *Beginning T-SQL 2012* by Scott Shaw and Kathi Kellenberger (Apress, 2012). What you will find in this chapter, though, are fast examples of commonly used constructs such as IF and CASE statements, WHILE loops, and T-SQL cursors.

2-1. Declaring Variables

Problem

You want to declare a variable and use it in subsequent T-SQL statements. For example, you want to build a search string, store that search string into a variable, and reference the string in the WHERE clause of a subsequent query.

Solution

Execute a DECLARE statement. Specify the variable and the data type. Optionally provide an initial value.

The following example demonstrates using a variable to hold a search string. The variable is declared and initialized to a value. Then a SELECT statement finds people with names that include the given string.

```
DECLARE @AddressLine1 nvarchar(60) = 'Heiderplatz';
SELECT AddressID, AddressLine1
FROM Person.Address
WHERE AddressLine1 LIKE '%' + @AddressLine1 + '%';
```

The query in this example returns all rows with an address containing the search string value.

```
AddressID   AddressLine1
----------- ---------------
20333       Heiderplatz 268
17062       Heiderplatz 268
24962       Heiderplatz 662
15742       Heiderplatz 662
27109       Heiderplatz 772
23496       Heiderplatz 772
...
```

How It Works

Throughout the book you'll see examples of variables being used within queries and module-based SQL Server objects (stored procedures, triggers, and more). Variables are objects you can create to temporarily contain data. Variables can be defined across several different data types and then referenced within the allowable context of that type.

The solution query begins by declaring a new variable that is prefixed by the @ symbol and followed by the defining data type that will be used to contain the search string. Here's an example:

```
DECLARE @AddressLine1 nvarchar(60)
```

Next and last in the declaration is the initial value of the variable:

```
DECLARE @AddressLine1 nvarchar(60) = 'Heiderplatz';
```

You can also specify a value by executing a SET statement, and prior to SQL Server 2008, you are *required* to do so. Here's an example:

```
DECLARE @AddressLine1 nvarchar(60);
SET @AddressLine1 = 'Heiderplatz';
```

Next the solution executes a query referencing the variable in the WHERE clause, embedding it between the % wildcards to find any row with an address containing the search string:

```
WHERE AddressLine1 LIKE '%' + @AddressLine1 + '%'
```

It's possible to declare a variable without assigning a value. In that case, the variable is said to be *null*. Here's an example:

```
DECLARE @AddressLine1 nvarchar(60);
SELECT @AddressLine1;
Results from this query are as follows:
--------------------------------------
NULL
(1 row(s) affected)
```

It is the same with a variable as with a table column. A null column is one having no value. Likewise, a null variable is one having no value.

2-2. Retrieving a Value into a Variable

Problem

You want to retrieve a value from the database into a variable for use in later T-SQL code.

Solution

Issue a query that returns zero or one rows. Specify the primary key, or a unique key, of the target row in your WHERE clause. Assign the column value to the variable, as shown in the following example:

```
DECLARE @AddressLine1 nvarchar(60);
DECLARE @AddressLine2 nvarchar(60);
SELECT @AddressLine1 = AddressLine1, @AddressLine2 = AddressLine2
FROM Person.Address
WHERE AddressID = 66;
SELECT @AddressLine1 AS Address1, @AddressLine2 AS Address2;
```

The results are as follows:

```
Address1        Address2
--------------  ----------
4775 Kentucky   Dr. Unit E
```

How It Works

The solution query retrieves the two address lines for address #66. Because AddressID is the table's primary key, there can be only one row with ID #66. A query such as in the example that can return at most one row is sometimes termed a *singleton select.*

■ **Caution** It is critical when using the technique in this recipe to make sure to write queries that can return at most one row. Do that by specifying either a primary key or a unique key in the WHERE clause.

The key syntax aspect to focus on is the following pattern in the SELECT list for assigning values returned by the query to variables that you declare:

```
@VariableName = ColumnName
```

The solution query contains two such assignments: @AddressLine1 = AddressLine1 and @AddressLine2 = AddressLine2. They assign the values from the columns AddressLine1 and AddressLine2, respectively, into the variables @AddressLine1 and @AddressLine2.

What if your query returns no rows? In that case, your target variables will be left unchanged. For example, execute the following query block:

```
DECLARE @AddressLine1 nvarchar(60) = '101 E. Varnum'
DECLARE @AddressLine2 nvarchar(60) = 'Ambulance Desk'
SELECT @AddressLine1 = AddressLine1, @AddressLine2 = AddressLine2
FROM Person.Address
WHERE AddressID = 49862;
SELECT @AddressLine1, @AddressLine2;
```

You will get the following results:

```
------------- --------------
101 E. Varnum Ambulance Desk
```

Now you have a problem. How do you know whether the values in the variables are from the query or whether they are left over from prior code? One solution is to test the global variable @@ROWCOUNT. Here's an example:

```
DECLARE @AddressLine1 nvarchar(60) = '101 E. Varnum'
DECLARE @AddressLine2 nvarchar(60) = 'Ambulance Desk'
SELECT @AddressLine1 = AddressLine1, @AddressLine2 = AddressLine2
FROM Person.Address
WHERE AddressID = 49862;
IF @@ROWCOUNT = 1
  SELECT @AddressLine1, @AddressLine2
```

```
ELSE
  SELECT 'Either no rows or too many rows found.';
```

If @@ROWCOUNT is 1, then our singleton select is successful. Any other value indicates a problem. A @@ROWCOUNT of zero indicates that no row was found. A @@ROWCOUNT greater than zero indicates that more than one row was found. If multiple rows are found, you will arbitrarily be given the values from the last row in the result set. That is rarely desirable behavior and is the reason for our strong admonition to query by either the primary key or a unique key.

2-3. Writing an IF...THEN...ELSE Statement

Problem

You want to write an IF...THEN...ELSE statement so that you can control which of two possible code paths is taken.

Solution

Write your statement using the following syntax:

```
IF Boolean_expression
{ sql_statement | statement_block }
[ ELSE
{ sql_statement | statement_block } ]
```

For example, the following code block demonstrates executing a query conditionally based on the value of a local variable:

```
DECLARE @QuerySelector int = 3;
IF @QuerySelector = 1
BEGIN
 SELECT TOP 3 ProductID, Name, Color
 FROM Production.Product
 WHERE Color = 'Silver'
 ORDER BY Name
END
 ELSE
BEGIN
 SELECT TOP 3 ProductID, Name, Color
 FROM Production.Product
 WHERE Color = 'Black'
 ORDER BY Name
END;
```

This code block returns the following results:

```
ProductID    Name                    Color
---------    --------------------    ------
322          Chainring               Black
863          Full-Finger Gloves, L   Black
862          Full-Finger Gloves, M   Black
```

How It Works

In this recipe, an integer local variable is created called @QuerySelector. That variable is set to the value of 3. Here is the declaration:

```
DECLARE @QuerySelector int = 3;
```

The IF statement begins by evaluating whether @QuerySelector is equal to 1:

```
IF @QuerySelector = 1
```

If @QuerySelector were indeed 1, the next block of code (starting with the BEGIN statement) would be executed:

```
BEGIN
 SELECT TOP 3 ProductID, Name, Color
 FROM Production.Product
 WHERE Color = 'Silver'
 ORDER BY Name
END
```

Because the @QuerySelector variable is not set to 1, the second block of T-SQL code is executed, which is the block after the ELSE clause:

```
BEGIN
 SELECT TOP 3 ProductID, Name, Color
 FROM Production.Product
 WHERE Color = 'Black'
 ORDER BY Name
END;
```

Your IF expression can be any expression evaluating to TRUE, FALSE, or NULL. You are free to use AND, OR, and NOT; parentheses for grouping; and all the common operators that you are used to using for equality, greater than, less than, and so forth. The following is a somewhat contrived example showing some of the possibilities:

```
IF (@QuerySelector = 1 OR @QuerySelector = 3) AND (NOT @QuerySelector IS NULL)
```

Execute the solution example using this version of the IF statement, and you'll get the silver color parts:

```
ProductID      Name                Color
---------      ---------           --------
952            Chain               Silver
320            Chainring Bolts     Silver
321            Chainring Nut       Silver
```

Because the solution example is written with only one statement in each block, you can omit the BEGIN...END syntax. Here's an example:

```
DECLARE @QuerySelector int = 3;
IF @QuerySelector = 1
  SELECT TOP 3 ProductID, Name, Color
  FROM Production.Product
  WHERE Color = 'Silver'
  ORDER BY Name
ELSE
  SELECT TOP 3 ProductID, Name, Color
  FROM Production.Product
```

```
WHERE Color = 'Black'
ORDER BY Name;
```

BEGIN is optional for single statements following IF, but for multiple statements that must be executed as a group, BEGIN and END *must* be used. As a best practice, it is easier to use BEGIN...END for single statements, too, so that you don't forget to do so if/when the code is changed at a later time.

2-4. Writing a Simple CASE Expression

Problem

You have a single expression, table column, or variable that can take on a well-defined set of possible values. You want to specify an output value for each possible input value. For example, you want to translate department names into conference room assignments.

Solution

Write a CASE expression associating each value with its own code path. Optionally, include an ELSE clause to provide a code path for any unexpected values.

For example, the following code block uses CASE to assign departments to specific conference rooms. Departments not specifically named are lumped together by the ELSE clause into Room D.

```
SELECT DepartmentID AS DeptID, Name, GroupName,
   CASE GroupName
    WHEN 'Research and Development' THEN 'Room A'
    WHEN 'Sales and Marketing' THEN 'Room B'
    WHEN 'Manufacturing' THEN 'Room C'
   ELSE 'Room D'
   END AS ConfRoom
FROM HumanResources.Department
```

Results from this query show the different conference room assignments as specified in the CASE expression.

```
DeptID  Name                        GroupName                             ConfRoom
------  --------------------------  ------------------------------------  --------
1       Engineering                 Research and Development              Room A
2       Tool Design                 Research and Development              Room A
3       Sales                       Sales and Marketing                   Room B
4       Marketing                   Sales and Marketing                   Room B
5       Purchasing                  Inventory Management                  Room D
6       Research and Development    Research and Development              Room A
7       Production                  Manufacturing                         Room C
8       Production Control          Manufacturing                         Room C
9       Human Resources             Executive General and Administration  Room D
10      Finance                     Executive General and Administration  Room D
11      Information Services        Executive General and Administration  Room D
12      Document Control            Quality Assurance                     Room D
13      Quality Assurance           Quality Assurance                     Room D
14      Facilities and Maintenance  Executive General and Administration  Room D
15      Shipping and Receiving      Inventory Management                  Room D
16      Executive                   Executive General and Administration  Room D
```

How It Works

Use a CASE expression whenever you need to translate one set of defined values into another. In the case of the solution example, the expression translates group names into a set of conference room assignments. The effect is essentially a mapping of groups to rooms.

The general format of the CASE expression in the example is as follows:

```
CASE ColumnName
  WHEN OneValue THEN AnotherValue
  ...
ELSE CatchAllValue
END AS ColumnAlias
```

The ELSE clause in the expression is optional. In the example, it's used to assign any unspecified groups to Room D.

The result from a CASE expression in a SELECT statement is a column of output. It's good practice to name that column by providing a column alias. The solution example specifies AS ConfRoom to give the name ConfRoom to the column of output holding the conference room assignments, which is the column generated by the CASE expression.

2-5. Writing a Searched CASE Expression

Problem

You want to evaluate a series of expressions. When an expression is true, you want to specify a corresponding return value.

Solution

Write a so-called searched CASE expression, which you can loosely think of as similar to multiple IF statements strung together. The following is a variation on the query from Recipe 2-4. This time, the department name is evaluated in addition to other values, such as the department identifier and the first letter of the department name.

```
SELECT DepartmentID, Name,
   CASE
    WHEN Name = 'Research and Development' THEN 'Room A'
    WHEN (Name = 'Sales and Marketing' OR DepartmentID = 10) THEN 'Room B'
    WHEN Name LIKE 'T%'THEN 'Room C'
   ELSE 'Room D' END AS ConferenceRoom
FROM HumanResources.Department;
```

Execute this query, and your results should look as follows:

```
DepartmentID   Name                        ConferenceRoom
------------   -------------------------   --------------
12             Document Control            Room D
1              Engineering                 Room D
16             Executive                   Room D
14             Facilities and Maintenance  Room D
10             Finance                     Room B
```

```
9              Human Resources            Room D
11             Information Services       Room D
4              Marketing                  Room D
7              Production                 Room D
8              Production Control         Room D
5              Purchasing                 Room D
13             Quality Assurance          Room D
6              Research and Development   Room A
3              Sales                      Room D
15             Shipping and Receiving     Room D
2              Tool Design                Room C
```

How It Works

CASE offers an alternative syntax that doesn't use an initial input expression. Instead, one or more Boolean expressions are evaluated. (A Boolean expression is most typically a comparison expression returning either true or false.) The general form as used in the example is as follows:

```
CASE
 WHEN Boolean_expression_1 THEN result_expression_1
 ...
 WHEN Boolean_expression_n THEN result_expression_n
 ELSE CatchAllValue
END AS ColumnAlias
```

Boolean expressions are evaluated in the order you list them until one is found that evaluates as true. The corresponding result is then returned. If none of the expressions evaluates as true, then the optional ELSE value is returned. The ability to evaluate Boolean expressions of arbitrary complexity in this flavor of CASE provides additional flexibility above the simple CASE expression from the previous recipe.

2-6. Writing a WHILE Statement

Problem

You want to write a WHILE statement to execute a block of code so long as a given condition is true.

Solution

Write a WHILE statement using the following example as a template. In the example, the system stored procedure sp_spaceused is used to return the table space usage for each table in the @AWTables table variable.

```
-- Declare variables
DECLARE @AWTables TABLE (SchemaTable varchar(100));
DECLARE @TableName varchar(100);

-- Insert table names into the table variable
INSERT @AWTables (SchemaTable)
  SELECT TABLE_SCHEMA + '.' + TABLE_NAME
  FROM INFORMATION_SCHEMA.tables
  WHERE TABLE_TYPE = 'BASE TABLE'
  ORDER BY TABLE_SCHEMA + '.' + TABLE_NAME;
```

```
-- Report on each table using sp_spaceused
WHILE (SELECT COUNT(*) FROM @AWTables) > 0
BEGIN
  SELECT TOP 1 @TableName = SchemaTable
  FROM @AWTables
  ORDER BY SchemaTable;

  EXEC sp_spaceused @TableName;
  DELETE @AWTables
  WHERE SchemaTable = @TableName;
END;
```

Execute this code, and you will get multiple result sets—one for each table—similar to the following:

```
name            rows   reserved   data      index_size   unused
--------------  ----   --------   ----      ----------   ------
AWBuildVersion  1      16 KB      8 KB      8 KB         0 KB

name            rows   reserved   data      index_size   unused
-----------     ----   --------   -------   ----------   ------
DatabaseLog     1597   6656 KB    6544 KB   56 KB        56 KB

name            rows   reserved   data      index_size   unused
--------        ----   --------   ----      ----------   ------
ErrorLog        0      0 KB       0 KB      0 KB         0 KB
```

How It Works

The example in this recipe demonstrates the WHILE statement, which allows you to repeat a specific operation or batch of operations while a condition remains true. The general form for WHILE is as follows:

```
WHILE Boolean_expression
BEGIN
  { sql_statement | statement_block }
END;
```

WHILE will keep the T-SQL statement or batch processing while the Boolean expression remains true. In the case of the example, the Boolean expression tests the result of a query against the value zero. The query returns the number of values in a table variable. Looping continues until all values have been processed and no values remain.

In the example, the table variable @AWTABLES is populated with all the table names in the database using the following INSERT statement:

```
INSERT @AWTables (SchemaTable)
  SELECT TABLE_SCHEMA + '.' + TABLE_NAME
  FROM INFORMATION_SCHEMA.tables
  WHERE TABLE_TYPE = 'BASE TABLE'
  ORDER BY TABLE_SCHEMA + '.' + TABLE_NAME;
```

The WHILE loop is then started, looping as long as there are rows remaining in the @AWTables table variable:

```
WHILE (SELECT COUNT(*) FROM @AWTables) > 0
```

Within the WHILE, the @TableName local variable is populated with the TOP 1 table name from the @AWTables table variable:

```
SELECT TOP 1 @TableName = SchemaTable
FROM @AWTables
ORDER BY SchemaTable;
```

Then EXEC sp_spaceused is executed on against that table name:

```
EXEC sp_spaceused @TableName;
```

Lastly, the row for the reported table is deleted from the table variable:

```
DELETE @AWTables
WHERE SchemaTable = @TableName;
```

WHILE will continue to execute sp_spaceused until all rows are deleted from the @AWTables table variable.

Two special statements that you can execute from within a WHILE loop are BREAK and CONTINUE. Execute a BREAK statement to exit the loop. Execute the CONTINUE statement to skip the remainder of the current iteration. For example, the following is an example of BREAK in action to prevent an infinite loop:

```
WHILE (1=1)
BEGIN
  PRINT 'Endless While, because 1 always equals 1.';
  IF 1=1
   BEGIN
     PRINT 'But we won''t let the endless loop happen!';
     BREAK; --Because this BREAK statement terminates the loop.
   END;
END;
```

And next is an example of CONTINUE:

```
DECLARE @n int = 1;
WHILE @n = 1
BEGIN
  SET @n = @n + 1;
  IF @n > 1
   CONTINUE;
  PRINT 'You will never see this message.';
END;
```

This example will execute with one loop iteration, but no message is displayed. Why? It's because the first iteration moves the value of @n to greater than 1, triggering execution of the CONTINUE statement. CONTINUE causes the remainder of the BEGIN...END block to be skipped. The WHEN condition is reevaluated. Because @n is no longer 1, the loop terminates.

2-7. Returning from the Current Execution Scope

Problem

You want to discontinue execution of a stored procedure or T-SQL batch, possibly including a numeric return code.

Solution #1: Exit with No Return Value

Write an IF statement to specify the condition under which to discontinue execution. Execute a RETURN in the event the condition is true. For example, the second query in the following code block will not execute because there are no pink bike parts in the Product table:

```
IF NOT EXISTS
  (SELECT ProductID
   FROM Production.Product
   WHERE Color = 'Pink')
BEGIN
   RETURN;
END;

SELECT ProductID
FROM Production.Product
WHERE Color = 'Pink';
```

Solution #2: Exit and Provide a Value

You have the option to provide a status value to the invoking code. First, create a stored procedure along the following lines. Notice particularly the RETURN statements.

```
CREATE PROCEDURE ReportPink AS
IF NOT EXISTS
  (SELECT ProductID
   FROM Production.Product
   WHERE Color = 'Pink')
BEGIN
  --Return the value 100 to indicate no pink products
  RETURN 100;
END;

SELECT ProductID
FROM Production.Product
WHERE Color = 'Pink';

--Return the value 0 to indicate pink was found
RETURN 0;
```

With this procedure in place, execute the following:

```
DECLARE @ResultStatus int;
EXEC @ResultStatus = ReportPink;
PRINT @ResultStatus;
```

You will get the following result:

```
100
```

This is because no pink products exist in the example database.

How It Works

RETURN exits the current Transact-SQL batch, query, or stored procedure immediately. RETURN exits only the code executing in the current scope; if you have called stored procedure B from stored procedure A and if stored procedure B issues a RETURN, stored procedure B stops immediately, but stored procedure A continues as though B had completed successfully.

The solution examples show how RETURN can be invoked with or without a return code. Use whichever approach makes sense for your application. Passing a RETURN code does allow the invoking code to determine why you have returned control, but it is not always necessary to allow for that.

The solution examples also show how it sometimes makes sense to invoke RETURN from an IF statement and other times makes sense to invoke RETURN as a stand-alone statement. Again, use whichever approach best facilitates what you are working to accomplish.

2-8. Going to a Label in a Transact-SQL Batch

Problem

You want to label a specific point in a T-SQL batch. Then you want the ability to have processing jump directly to that point in the code that you have identified by label.

Solution

Create a label using the following syntax, which is simply to provide a label name followed by a colon:

```
LabelName:
```

Then write a GOTO statement to branch directly to the point in the code that you have labeled. Here's an example:

```
GOTO LabelName;
```

The following is an example that checks whether a department name is already in use by an existing department. If so, the INSERT is bypassed using GOTO. If not, the INSERT is performed.

```
DECLARE @Name nvarchar(50) = 'Engineering';
DECLARE @GroupName nvarchar(50) = 'Research and Development';
DECLARE @Exists bit = 0;

IF EXISTS (
  SELECT Name
  FROM HumanResources.Department
  WHERE Name = @Name)
BEGIN
  SET @Exists = 1;
  GOTO SkipInsert;
END;

INSERT INTO HumanResources.Department
  (Name, GroupName)
  VALUES(@Name , @GroupName);

SkipInsert: IF @Exists = 1
BEGIN
  PRINT @Name + ' already exists in HumanResources.Department';
END
```

```
ELSE
BEGIN
 PRINT 'Row added';
END;
```

There is, in fact, a department named Engineering defined in the example database. So if you execute this code example, you should get the following result:

```
Engineering already exists in HumanResources.Department
```

How It Works

In this recipe's example, two local variables are declared and set to values in preparation for those values being inserted into the HumanResources.Department table:

```
DECLARE @Name nvarchar(50) = 'Engineering';
DECLARE @GroupName nvarchar(50) = 'Research and Development';
```

Another variable is defined to hold a bit value. This value acts as a flag to mark whether a row already exists in the table.

```
DECLARE @Exists bit = 0;
```

Next, an IF statement checks for the existence of any row with the same department name as the local variable. If such a row exists, the bit variable is set to 1 and the GOTO command is invoked. GOTO references the label name that you want to skip to, in this case called SkipInsert:

```
IF EXISTS (
  SELECT Name
  FROM HumanResources.Department
  WHERE Name = @Name)
BEGIN
  SET @Exists = 1;
  GOTO SkipInsert;
END;
```

The target label appears in the code as follows:

```
SkipInsert: IF @Exists = 1
...
```

It is also possible to, and perfectly reasonable to do so, write the label on a line by itself:

```
SkipInsert:
IF @Exists = 1
...
```

Following the label is another IF statement. If the bit flag is enabled, a PRINT statement gives a message stating that the row already exists:

```
SkipInsert: IF @Exists = 1
BEGIN
  PRINT @Name + ' already exists in HumanResources.Department';
END
```

Otherwise, a message is printed that the row was successfully added:

```
ELSE
BEGIN
 PRINT 'Row added';
END;
```

As a best practice, when given a choice between using GOTO and other control-of-flow methods, you should choose something other than GOTO. GOTO can decrease the clarity of the code, because you'll have to jump around the batch or stored procedure code in order to understand the original intention of the query author.

■ **Tip** Going to a label at the end of a block can be a useful way to exit a block. This is especially the case when you have cleanup code that must be executed. In such a case, put the cleanup code following the exit label and then jump to that label whenever you need to exit the block.

2-9. Pausing Execution for a Period of Time

Problem

You want to pause execution for an amount of time or until a given time of day.

Solution

Execute the WAITFOR statement. With it you can delay a specific amount of time, or you can halt until a specific moment in time is reached.

The following is an example showing how to delay for a specific number of hours:minutes:seconds. The example delays for ten seconds and then executes the query following:

```
WAITFOR DELAY '00:00:10';
BEGIN
 SELECT TransactionID, Quantity
 FROM Production.TransactionHistory;
END;
```

Next is another example showing how to wait until a specific time is reached. The subsequent statement will execute at 12:22 p.m.

```
WAITFOR TIME '12:22:00';
BEGIN
 SELECT COUNT(*)
 FROM Production.TransactionHistory;
END;
```

How It Works

WAITFOR provides for two options: DELAY and TIME. Specify DELAY when you want to pause for a duration of time. Specify TIME when you want to pause until a given time of day is reached. For example, DELAY '12:22:00' pauses execution for 12 hours and 22 minutes. TIME '12:22:00' pauses execution until the next time it is 12:22 p.m.

■ **Caution** If you specify `TIME '12:22:00'` at, say 12:24 p.m., then you will be waiting almost 24 hours until execution resumes. Because the time is already in the past in the current day, execution will pause until the given time is reached the next day.

Waiting for a certain amount of time is useful when you know another operation must execute asynchronously while your current batch process must wait. For example, if you have kicked off an asynchronous SQL Server Agent job using the `sp_start_job` system stored procedure, control is returned immediately to the batch after the job starts to execute. If you know that the job you just kicked off takes at least five minutes to run and your consecutive tasks are dependent on the completion of the job, `WAITFOR` can be used to delay processing until the job is complete.

Waiting until a specific time of day is handy when an operation must occur during a specific time period in the day. For example, say you have a stored procedure that performs data warehouse aggregations from transaction-processing tables. The aggregations may take a couple of hours to complete, but you don't want to load the finished data from the staging to the production tables until after business hours. Using `WAITFOR TIME` in the procedure, you can stop the final load of the tables until nonbusiness hours.

2-10. Creating and Using Cursors

Problem

You need to implement row-by-row processing in your application. You don't want to fire off a single `UPDATE` or `SELECT` statement and let the database engine do the work. Instead, you want to "touch" each row and process it individually.

Solution

Implement cursor-based processing. A T-SQL cursor allows you to write row-by-row processing into your application, giving you full control over exactly what is one.

■ **Caution** Cursors can eat up instance memory, reduce concurrency, decrease network bandwidth, lock resources, and often require an excessive amount of code compared to a set-based alternative. Transact-SQL is a set-based language, meaning that it excels at manipulating and retrieving sets of rows, rather than performing single row-by-row processing. Before implementing a cursor, think carefully about whether you can avoid the need for a cursor by taking a set-based approach to the problem at hand.

Although we recommend avoiding cursors whenever possible, using cursors for ad hoc, periodic database administration information gathering, as demonstrated in this next example, is usually perfectly justified.

The following code block demonstrates a cursor that loops through each session ID currently active on the SQL Server instance. The block executes `SP_WHO`on each session to see each session's logged-in user name and other data.

```
-- Do not show rowcounts in the results
SET NOCOUNT ON;

DECLARE @session_id smallint;
```

```
-- Declare the cursor
DECLARE session_cursor CURSOR FORWARD_ONLY READ_ONLY FOR
  SELECT session_id
  FROM sys.dm_exec_requests
  WHERE status IN ('runnable', 'sleeping', 'running');

-- Open the cursor
OPEN session_cursor;

-- Retrieve one row at a time from the cursor
FETCH NEXT
  FROM session_cursor
  INTO @session_id;

-- Process and retrieve new rows until no more are available
WHILE @@FETCH_STATUS = 0
BEGIN
  PRINT 'Spid #: ' + STR(@session_id);
  EXEC ('sp_who ' + @session_id);

  FETCH NEXT
   FROM session_cursor
   INTO @session_id;
END;

-- Close the cursor
CLOSE session_cursor;

-- Deallocate the cursor
DEALLOCATE session_cursor
```

Execute the code block. You'll get output as follows:

```
Spid #:     10
spid    ecid status     loginame          ...
------  -----------     --------          ...
10      0 sleeping      sa       ...
...
Spid #:     52
spid    ecid status     loginame                      ...
-----   -----------     ----------------------        ...
10      0 runnable      Jonathan-T410\Jonathan        ...
```

This output indicates that I have no security access to view buffers connected to session 27. However, session 52 is my own session, and I am allowed to see my own buffer.

How It Works

Query authors with programming backgrounds are often more comfortable using Transact-SQL cursors than the set-based alternatives for retrieving or updating rows. For example, a programmer may decide to loop through one row at a time, updating rows in a singleton fashion, instead of updating an entire set of rows in a single operation. Often it's better to find a set-based solution, but there are some cases, as in the example, in which using a cursor is justifiable.

The code example illustrates the general life cycle of a T-SQL cursor, which is as follows:

1. A cursor variable is declared and associated with a SQL statement.

```
DECLARE session_cursor CURSOR FORWARD_ONLY READ_ONLY FOR
  SELECT session_id
  FROM sys.dm_exec_requests
  WHERE status IN ('runnable', 'sleeping', 'running');
```

2. The cursor is then opened for use.

```
OPEN session_cursor;
```

3. Rows can then be fetched one at a time.

```
FETCH NEXT
  FROM session_cursor
  INTO @session_id;
```

4. Typically a `WHILE` loop is used to process and fetch as long as rows remain.

```
WHILE @@FETCH_STATUS = 0
BEGIN
  … Processing goes here …

  FETCH NEXT
   FROM session_cursor
   INTO @session_id;
END;
```

5. The cursor is then closed.

```
CLOSE session_cursor;
```

6. And finally, you should deallocate the cursor and associated memory.

```
DEALLOCATE session_cursor;
```

The `@@FETCH_STATUS` function used in the example returns a code indicating the results from the preceding `FETCH`. Possible result codes are as follows:

> `0`: The fetch operation was successful. You now have a row to process.
>
> `-1`: You have fetched beyond the end of the cursor or otherwise have attempted to fetch a row not included in the cursor's result set.
>
> `-2`: You have fetched what should be a valid row, but the row has been deleted since you have first opened the cursor, or the row has been modified such that it is no longer part of the cursor's query results.

Most often when doing row-by-row processing, you'll just process and fetch until the status is no longer zero. That's the precise approach taken in the solution example. The other codes come into play when you are executing variations on `FETCH` that allow you to specify specific result set rows by their absolute or relative positions in the set.

The difference between closing and deallocating a cursor is that closing a cursor retains the definition. You are able to reopen the cursor. Once you deallocate a cursor, the definition and resources are gone, as if you had never declared it in the first place.

CHAPTER 3

NULLs and Other Pitfalls

by Andy Roberts

A NULL value represents the absence of data, in other words, data that is missing or unknown. When coding queries, stored procedures, or any other T-SQL, it is important to keep in mind the nullability of data because it will affect many aspects of your logic. For example, the result of any operator (for example, +, -, AND, and OR) when either operand is NULL is NULL.

- NULL + 10 = NULL
- NULL OR TRUE = NULL
- NULL OR FALSE = NULL

Many functions will also return NULL when an input is NULL. This chapter discusses how to use SQL Server's built-in functions and other common logic to overcome some of the hurdles associated with working with NULL values. Table 3-1 describes some of the functions that SQL Server provides to work with NULL values.

Table 3-1. NULL *Functions*

Function	Description
ISNULL	ISNULL validates whether an expression is NULL and, if so, replaces the NULL value with an alternate value.
COALESCE	The COALESCE function returns the first non-NULL value from a provided list of expressions.
NULLIF	NULLIF returns a NULL value when the two provided expressions have the same value. Otherwise, the first expression is returned.

These next few recipes will demonstrate these functions in action.

3-1. Replacing NULL with an Alternate Value

Problem

You are selecting rows from a table, and your results contain NULL values. You would like to replace the NULL values with an alternate value.

Solution

ISNULLvalidates whether an expression is NULL and, if so, replaces the NULL value with an alternate value. In this example, any NULL value in the CreditCardApprovalCode column will be replaced with the value 0:

```
SELECT h.SalesOrderID,
    h.CreditCardApprovalCode,
    CreditApprovalCode_Display = ISNULL(h.CreditCardApprovalCode,
                      '**NO APPROVAL**')
FROM  Sales.SalesOrderHeader h ;
```

This returns the following (abridged) results:

```
SalesOrderID    CreditCardApprovalCode      CreditApprovalCode_Display
43735           1034619Vi33896              1034619Vi33896
43736           1135092Vi7270               1135092Vi7270
43737           NULL                        **NO APPROVAL**
43738           631125Vi62053               631125Vi62053
43739           NULL                        **NO APPROVAL**
43740           834624Vi94036               834624Vi94036
```

How It Works

In this example, the column CreditCardApprovalCode contains NULL values for rows where there is no credit approval. This query returns the original value of CreditCardApprovalCode in the second column. In the third column, the query uses the ISNULL function to evaluate each CreditCardApprovalCode. If the value is NULL, the value passed to the second parameter of ISNULL—**NO APPROVAL**'—is returned.

It is important to note that the return type of ISNULL is the same as the type of the first parameter. To illustrate this, view the following SELECT statements and their results. The first statement attempts to return a string when the first input to ISNULL is an integer:

```
SELECT ISNULL(CAST(NULL AS INT), 'String Value') ;
```

This query returns the following:

```
Msg 245, Level 16, State 1, Line 1
Conversion failed when converting the varchar value 'String Value' to data type int.
```

The second example attempts to return a string that is longer than the defined length of the first input:

```
SELECT ISNULL(CAST(NULL AS CHAR(10)), '20 characters*******') ;
```

This query returns the following:

```
----------
20 charact
```

Note that the 20-character string is truncated to 10 characters. This behavior can be tricky because the type of the second parameter is not checked until it is used. For example, if the first example is modified so that the non-NULL value is supplied in the first parameter, no error is generated.

```
SELECT ISNULL(1, 'String Value') ;
```

This query returns the following:

```
-----------
1
```

No error is generated in this query because the second parameter is not used. When testing your use of ISNULL, it is important both to test the conditions where NULL and non-NULL values are supplied to the first parameter and to take note that any string values are not truncated.

3-2. Returning the First Non-NULL Value from a List

Problem

You have a list of values that may contain NULLs, and you would like to return the first non-NULL value from your list.

Solution

The COALESCE function returns the first non-NULL value from a provided list of expressions. The syntax is as follows:

```
COALESCE ( expression [ ,…n ] )
```

This recipe demonstrates how to use COALESCE to return the first occurrence of a non-NULL value:

```
SELECT c.CustomerID,
    SalesPersonPhone = spp.PhoneNumber,
    CustomerPhone = pp.PhoneNumber,
    PhoneNumber = COALESCE(pp.PhoneNumber, spp.PhoneNumber, '**NO PHONE**')
FROM  Sales.Customer c
   LEFT OUTER JOIN Sales.Store s
     ON c.StoreID = s.BusinessEntityID
   LEFT OUTER JOIN Person.PersonPhone spp
     ON s.SalesPersonID = spp.BusinessEntityID
   LEFT OUTER JOIN Person.PersonPhone pp
     ON c.CustomerID = pp.BusinessEntityID
ORDER BY CustomerID ;
```

This returns the following (abridged) results:

```
CustomerID     SalesPersonPhone    CustomerPhone    PhoneNumber
-----------    -----------------   -------------    -------------
1              340-555-0193        697-555-0142     697-555-0142
2              740-555-0182        819-555-0175     819-555-0175
3              517-555-0117        212-555-0187     212-555-0187
…
292            517-555-0117        NULL             517-555-0117
293            330-555-0120        747-555-0171     747-555-0171
294            883-555-0116        NULL             883-555-0116
…
```

```
CustomerID      SalesPersonPhone     CustomerPhone      PhoneNumber
-----------     -----------------    -------------      -------------
11000           NULL                 608-555-0117       608-555-0117
11001           NULL                 637-555-0123       637-555-0123
11002           NULL                 683-555-0161       683-555-0161
...
20778           NULL                 NULL               **NO PHONE**
20779           NULL                 NULL               **NO PHONE**
20780           NULL                 NULL               **NO PHONE**
...
```

How It Works

In this recipe, you know that a customer is either a customer in the Person table or the SalesPerson associated with a Store. You would like to return the PhoneNumber associated with all of your customers. You use the COALESCE function to return the customer's PhoneNumber if it exists; otherwise, you return the SalesPerson's PhoneNumber. Note that a third value was added to the COALESCE function: '** NO PHONE **'. The COALESCE function will not return a non-NULL value and will raise an error if all choices evaluate to NULL. It is good practice when using COALESCE in conjunction with an OUTER JOIN or NULLABLE columns to add a known non-NULL value to the list of choices for COALESCE to choose from.

3-3. Choosing Between ISNULL and COALESCE in a SELECT Statement

Problem

You are coding a SELECT statement, and the calling application expects that NULL values will be replaced with non-NULL alternates. You know that you can choose between ISNULL and COALESCE to perform the operation but cannot decide which option is best.

Solution

There are generally two camps when it comes to making one's mind up between ISNULL and COALESCE:

- ISNULL is easier to spell, and the name makes more sense; use COALESCE only if you have more than two arguments and even then consider chaining your calls to ISNULL to avoid COALESCE, like so: ISNULL(value1, ISNULL(value2, ISNULL(value3, ''))).
- COALESCE is more flexible and is part of the ANSI standard SQL so is a more portable function if a developer is writing SQL on more than one platform.

At their core, both functions essentially accomplish the same task; however, the functions have some subtle differences, and being aware of them may assist in debugging efforts.

On the surface, ISNULL is simply a version of COALESCE that is limited to two parameters; however, ISNULL is a function that is built into the SQL Server engine and evaluated at query-processing time, and COALESCE is expanded into a CASE expression during query compilation.

One difference between the two functions is the data type returned by the function when the parameters are different data types. Take the following example:

```
DECLARE @sql NVARCHAR(MAX) = '
  SELECT ISNULL(''5'', 5),
      ISNULL(5, ''5''),
      COALESCE(''5'', 5),
      COALESCE(5, ''5'') ;
  ' ;

EXEC sp_executesql @sql ;

SELECT column_ordinal,
   is_nullable,
   system_type_name
FROM  master.sys.dm_exec_describe_first_result_set(@sql, NULL, 0) a ;
```

■ **Note** This example introduces some concepts that have not yet been discussed in this book. In the example, we would like to execute a query but also retrieve metadata about the query. The procedure `sp_executesql` accepts an `NVARCHAR` parameter and executes that string as a T-SQL batch. This is a useful tactic when building and executing dynamic queries in your applications. For further information on `sp_executesql`, please refer to the SQL Server Books Online at `http://msdn.microsoft.com/en-us/library/ms188001.aspx`.

To describe the results of the query, we use the table-valued function `dm_exec_describe_first_result_set`. Table-valued functions are described in Chapter 18, and this function in particular is documented in SQL Server Books Online at `http://msdn.microsoft.com/en-us/library/ff878236.aspx`.

The following is the result of this set of statements:

```
----   -----------  -----------  -----------
5      5            5            5

column_ordinal      is_nullable   system_type_name
--------------      -----------   ----------------
1                   0             varchar(1)
2                   0             int
3                   1             int
4                   0             int
```

Note that the type returned from ISNULL changes depending on the order of the input parameters, while COALESCE returns the data type of highest precedence regardless of argument order. So long as an implicit conversion exists between the value selected by the ISNULL or COALESCE function and the return type selected, the function will implicitly cast the return value to the return type. However, be aware that if an implicit conversion does not exist between the return type and value to be returned, SQL Server will raise an error.

■ **Note** For a complete list of data types in SQL Server listed in order of precedence, refer to SQL Server Books Online at `http://msdn.microsoft.com/en-us/library/ms190309(v=sql.110).aspx`.

```
SELECT COALESCE('five', 5) ;
```

This returns the following:

```
Msg 245, Level 16, State 1, Line 1
Conversion failed when converting the varchar value 'five' to data type int.
```

```
DECLARE @i INT = NULL ;
SELECT ISNULL(@i, 'five') ;
```

This returns the following:

```
Msg 245, Level 16, State 1, Line 2
Conversion failed when converting the varchar value 'five' to data type int.
```

The nullability of the return value may be different as well. Take the case where an application requests LastName, FirstName, and MiddleName from a table. The application expects the NULL values in the MiddleName columns to be replaced with an empty string. The following SELECT statement uses both ISNULL and COALESCE to convert the values, so the differences can be observed by describing the result set.

```
DECLARE @sql NVARCHAR(MAX) = '
SELECT TOP 10
   FirstName,
   LastName,
   MiddleName_ISNULL = ISNULL(MiddleName, ''''),
   MiddleName_COALESCE = COALESCE(MiddleName, '''')
FROM  Person.Person ;
      ' ;

EXEC sp_executesql @sql ;

SELECT column_ordinal,
   name,
   is_nullable
FROM  master.sys.dm_exec_describe_first_result_set(@sql, NULL, 0) a ;
```

The preceding statements return the two result sets:

```
FirstName      LastName       MiddleName_ISNULL    MiddleName_COALESCE
----------     ------------   -----------------    --------------------
Syed           Abbas          E                    E
Catherine      Abel           R.                   R.
Kim            Abercrombie
Kim            Abercrombie
Kim            Abercrombie    B                    B
Hazem          Abolrous       E                    E
Sam            Abolrous
Humberto       Acevedo
Gustavo        Achong
Pilar          Ackerman
```

```
column_ordinal  name                is_nullable
--------------  ------------------  -----------
1               FirstName           0
2               LastName            0
3               MiddleName_ISNULL   0
4               MiddleName_COALESCE 1
```

The nullability of ISNULL will always be false if at least one of the inputs is not nullable. COALESCE's nullability will be false only if all inputs are not nullable.

■ **Tip** This is a fairly subtle difference and may or may not affect you. Where I have seen these differences creep up is in application code where you may have a data access library or object relational mapping layer that makes data type decisions based on the nullability of columns in your result set.

How It Works

It is important to understand the nuances of the function you are using and how the data returned from ISNULL and COALESCE will be used. To eliminate the confusion that may occur with implicit type conversions, type precedence rules, and nullability rules, it is good practice to explicitly cast all inputs to the same type prior to input to ISNULL or COALESCE.

■ **Note** There are a number of discussions regarding the performance of ISNULL vs. COALESCE. For most uses of these functions, the performance differences are negligible. There are some cases when using correlated subqueries where ISNULL and COALESCE will cause the query optimizer to generate different query plans with COALESCE generating a suboptimal plan compared to ISNULL.

3-4. Looking for NULLs in a Table

Problem

You have a table with a nullable column. You would like to return rows where that column is NULLor where the column is not NULL.

Solution

The first hurdle to overcome when working with NULLs is to remove this WHERE clause from your mind: WHERE SomeColumn = NULL. The second hurdle is to remove this clause: WHERE SomeCol <> NULL. NULL is an "unknown" value. Because the value is unknown, SQL Server cannot evaluate any operator where an input to the operator is unknown.

- What is NULL + 1? NULL?
- What is NULL * 5? NULL?
- Does NULL = 1? NULL?
- Is NULL <> 1? NULL?

To search for NULL values, use the unary operators IS NULL and IS NOT NULL. Specifically, IS NULL returns true if the operand is NULL, and IS NOT NULL returns true if the operand is defined. Take the following statement:

```
DECLARE @value INT = NULL;

SELECT CASE WHEN @value = NULL THEN 1
     WHEN @value <> NULL THEN 2
     WHEN @value IS NULL THEN 3
     ELSE 4
    END ;
```

This simple CASE statement demonstrates that the NULL value stored in the variable @value cannot be evaluated with traditional equality operators. The IS NULL operator evaluates to true, and the result of the statement is the following:

```
3
```

So, how does this apply to searching for NULL values in a table? Say an application requests all rows in the Person table with an NULL MiddleName.

```
SELECT TOP 5
   LastName, FirstName, MiddleName
FROM  Person.Person
WHERE  MiddleName IS NULL ;
```

The result of this statement is as follows:

```
LastName        FirstName    MiddleName
-----------     ---------    -----------
Abercrombie     Kim          NULL
Abercrombie     Kim          NULL
Abolrous        Sam          NULL
Acevedo         Humberto     NULL
Achong          Gustavo      NULL
```

How It Works

The IS NULL operator evaluates one operand and returns true if the value is unknown. The IS NOT NULL operator evaluates on operand and returns true if the value is defined.

Previous recipes in this chapter introduced the ISNULL and COALESCE functions. The ISNULL function is often confused with the IS NULL operator. After all, the names differ by only one space. Functionally, the ISNULL operator may be used in a WHERE clause; however, there are some differences in how the SQL Server query plan optimizer decides how to execute statements with IS NULL vs. ISNULL used as a predicate in a SELECT statement.

Look at the following three statements that query the JobCandidate table and return the JobCandidate rows that have a non-NULL BusinessEntityID. All three statements return the same rows, but there is a difference in the execution plan.

The first statement uses ISNULL to return 1 for NULL values and returns all rows where ISNULL does not return 1.

```
SET SHOWPLAN_TEXT ON ;
GO

SELECT JobCandidateID,
   BusinessEntityID
```

```
FROM   HumanResources.JobCandidate
WHERE  ISNULL(BusinessEntityID, 1) <> 1 ;
GO

SET SHOWPLAN_TEXT OFF ;
```

```
|--Index Scan(OBJECT:([AdventureWorks2008R2].[HumanResources].[JobCandidate].
[IX_JobCandidate_BusinessEntityID]),
WHERE:(isnull([AdventureWorks2008R2].[HumanResources].[JobCandidate].
[BusinessEntityID],(1))<>(1)))
```

The execution plan contains an index scan. In this case, SQL Server will look at every row in the index to satisfy the results. Maybe the reason for this is the inequality operator (<>). The query may be rewritten as follows:

```
SET SHOWPLAN_TEXT ON ;
GO

SELECT JobCandidateID,
   BusinessEntityID
FROM   HumanResources.JobCandidate
WHERE  ISNULL(BusinessEntityID, 1) = BusinessEntityID ;
GO

SET SHOWPLAN_TEXT OFF ;
```

```
|--Index Scan(OBJECT:([AdventureWorks2008R2].[HumanResources].[JobCandidate].
[IX_JobCandidate_BusinessEntityID]),
WHERE:(isnull([AdventureWorks2008R2].[HumanResources].[JobCandidate].[BusinessEntityID],(1))=
[AdventureWorks2008R2].[HumanResources].[JobCandidate].[BusinessEntityID]))
```

Again, the query optimizer chooses to use an index scan to satisfy the query. What happens when the `IS NULL` operator is used instead of the `ISNULL` function?

```
SET SHOWPLAN_TEXT ON ;
GO

SELECT JobCandidateID,
   BusinessEntityID
FROM   HumanResources.JobCandidate
WHERE  BusinessEntityID IS NOT NULL ;
GO

SET SHOWPLAN_TEXT OFF ;
```

```
|--Index Seek(OBJECT:([AdventureWorks2008R2].[HumanResources].[JobCandidate].
[IX_JobCandidate_BusinessEntityID]), SEEK:([AdventureWorks2008R2].[HumanResources].
[JobCandidate].[BusinessEntityID] IsNotNull) ORDERED FORWARD)
```

By using the `IS NULL` operator, SQL Server is able to seek on the index instead of scan the index. ISNULL() is a function, when a column is passed into a function SQL Server must evaluate that function for every row and is not able to seek on an index to satisfy the `WHERE` clause.

3-5. Removing Values from an Aggregate

Problem

You are attempting to understand production delays and have decided to report on the average variance between ActualStartDate and ScheduledStartDate of operations in your production sequence. You would like to understand the following:

- What is the variance for all operations?
- What is the variance for all operations where the variance is not 0?

Solution

NULLIF returns a NULL value when the two provided expressions have the same value; otherwise, the first expression is returned.

```
SELECT r.ProductID,
   r.OperationSequence,
   StartDateVariance = AVG(DATEDIFF(day, ScheduledStartDate,
                       ActualStartDate)),
   StartDateVariance_Adjusted = AVG(NULLIF(DATEDIFF(day,
                                ScheduledStartDate,
                                ActualStartDate), 0))
FROM  Production.WorkOrderRouting r
GROUP BY r.ProductID,
   r.OperationSequence
ORDER BY r.ProductID,
   r.OperationSequence ;
```

The query returns the following results (abridged):

```
ProductID  OperationSequence  StartDateVariance    StartDateVariance_Adjusted
514        6                  4                    8
514        7                  4                    8
515        6                  0                    NULL
515        7                  0                    NULL
516        6                  4                    8
...
```

How It Works

The query includes two columns that use the aggregate function AVG to return the average difference in days between the scheduled and actual start dates of a production sequence for a given product. The column StateDateVariance includes all of the rows in the aggregate. The column StartDateVariance_Adjusted eliminates rows where the variance is 0 by using the NULLIF function. The NULLIF function accepts the result of DATEDIFF as the first parameter and compares this result to the value 0 that we passed to the second parameter. If DATEDIFF returns 0,NULLIF returnsNULL, and theNULL value is eliminated from theAVG aggregate.

3-6. Enforcing Uniqueness with NULL Values

Problem

You have a table that contains a column that allows NULLs. There may be many rows with NULL values, but any non-NULL value must be unique.

Solution

For this recipe, create a table Product where CodeName may be NULL.

```
CREATE TABLE Product
   (
    ProductId INT NOT NULL
            CONSTRAINT PK_Product PRIMARY KEY CLUSTERED,
    ProductName NVARCHAR(50) NOT NULL,
    CodeName NVARCHAR(50)
   ) ;
GO
```

Create a unique nonclustered index on CodeName.

```
CREATE UNIQUE INDEX UX_Product_CodeName ON Product (CodeName) ;
GO
```

Test the unique index by adding some rows to the table.

```
INSERT INTO Product
    (ProductId, ProductName, CodeName)
VALUES (1, 'Product 1', 'Shiloh') ;

INSERT INTO Product
    (ProductId, ProductName, CodeName)
VALUES (2, 'Product 2', 'Sphynx');

INSERT INTO Product
    (ProductId, ProductName, CodeName)
VALUES (3, 'Product 3', NULL);

INSERT INTO Product
    (ProductId, ProductName, CodeName)
VALUES (4, 'Product 4', NULL);

GO
```

Here is the result of the insert statements:

```
(1 row(s) affected)

(1 row(s) affected)

(1 row(s) affected)
Msg 2601, Level 14, State 1, Line 13
```

```
Cannot insert duplicate key row in object 'dbo.Product' with unique index
'UX_Product_CodeName'. The duplicate key value is (<NULL>).

The statement has been terminated.
```

A unique index may be built on a nullable column; however, the unique index can contain only one NULL. SQL Server allows filtered indexes where the index is created only for a subset of the data in the table. Drop the unique index created earlier and create a new unique, nonclustered, filtered index on CodeName to index (and enforce uniqueness) only on rows that have a defined CodeName.

```
DROP INDEX Product.UX_Product_CodeName;
GO

CREATE UNIQUE INDEX UX_Product_CodeName ON Product (CodeName) WHERE CodeName IS NOT NULL
GO
```

Test the new index by adding some rows.

```
INSERT INTO Product
    (ProductId, ProductName, CodeName)
VALUES (4, 'Product 4', NULL);

INSERT INTO Product
    (ProductId, ProductName, CodeName)
VALUES (5, 'Product 5', NULL);
```

The results show two rows added successfully:

```
(1 row(s) affected)

(1 row(s) affected)
```

If a row is added that violates the unique constraint on the CodeName, a constraint violation will be raised:

```
INSERT INTO Product
    (ProductId, ProductName, CodeName)
VALUES (6, 'Product 6', 'Shiloh');
```

Here are the results:

```
Msg 2601, Level 14, State 1, Line 1

Cannot insert duplicate key row in object 'dbo.Product' with unique index
'UX_Product_CodeName'. The duplicate key value is (Shiloh).

The statement has been terminated.
```

A select from the table will show that multiple nulls have been added to the CodeName table; however, uniqueness has been maintained on defined CodeName values.

```
SELECT *
FROM  Product
```

The SELECT statement yields the following:

```
ProductId       ProductName     CodeName
---------       -----------     --------
1               Product 1       Shiloh
2               Product 2       Sphynx
3               Product 3       NULL
4               Product 4       NULL
5               Product 5       NULL
```

How It Works

Unique constraints and unique indexes will, by default, enforce uniqueness the same way with respect to NULL values. Indexes allow for the use of index filtering, and the filter will be created only on the rows that meet the filter criteria. There are many benefits to filtered indexes, as discussed in Chapter 17.

3-7. Enforcing Referential Integrity on Nullable Columns

Problem

You have a table with a foreign key defined to enforce referential integrity. You want to enforce the foreign key where values are defined but allow NULLvalues into the foreign key column.

Solution

The default behavior of a foreign key constraint is to enforce referential integrity on non-NULL values but allow NULL values even though there may not be a corresponding NULL value in the primary key table. This example uses a Category table and an Item table. The Item table includes a nullable CategoryId column that references the CategoryId of the Category table.

First, create the Category table and add some values.

```
CREATE TABLE Category
    (
     CategoryId INT NOT NULL
            CONSTRAINT PK_Category PRIMARY KEY CLUSTERED,
     CategoryName NVARCHAR(50) NOT NULL
    ) ;
GO

INSERT INTO Category
   (CategoryId, CategoryName)
VALUES (1, 'Category 1'),
   (2, 'Category 2'),
   (3, 'Category 3') ;
GO
```

Next, create the Item table and add the foreign key to the Category table.

```
CREATE TABLE Item
   (
   ItemId INT NOT NULL
         CONSTRAINT PK_Item PRIMARY KEY CLUSTERED,
   ItemName NVARCHAR(50) NOT NULL,
   CategoryId INT NULL
   ) ;
GO

ALTER TABLE Item ADD CONSTRAINT FK_Item_Category FOREIGN KEY (CategoryId) REFERENCES
Category(CategoryId) ;
GO
```

Attempt to insert three rows into the Item table. The first row contains a valid reference to the Category table. The second row will fail with a foreign key violation. The third row will insert successfully because the CategoryId is NULL.

```
INSERT INTO Item
   (ItemId, ItemName, CategoryId)
VALUES (1, 'Item 1', 1) ;

INSERT INTO Item
   (ItemId, ItemName, CategoryId)
VALUES (2, 'Item 2', 4) ;

INSERT INTO Item
   (ItemId, ItemName, CategoryId)
VALUES (3, 'Item 3', NULL) ;
```

The insert statements generate the following results:

```
(1 row(s) affected)
Msg 547, Level 16, State 0, Line 5

The INSERT statement conflicted with the FOREIGN KEY constraint “FK_Item_Category”. The conflict
occurred in database “AdventureWorks2012”, table “dbo.Category”, column 'CategoryId'.

The statement has been terminated.

(1 row(s) affected)
```

How It Works

If a table contains a foreign key reference on a nullable column, NULLvalues are allowed in the foreign key table. To enforce the referential integrity on all rows, the foreign key column must be declared as non-nullable. Foreign keys are discussed in detail in Chapter 15.

3-8. Joining Tables on Nullable Columns

Problem

You need to join two tables but have NULLvalues in one or both sides of the join.

Solution

When joining on a nullable column, remember that the equality operator returns false for NULL = NULL. Let's see what happens when you have NULL values on both sides of a join. Create two tables with sample data.

```
CREATE TABLE Test1
   (
   TestValue NVARCHAR(10) NULL
   );
CREATE TABLE Test2
   (
   TestValue NVARCHAR(10) NULL
   ) ;
GO

INSERT INTO Test1
VALUES ('apples'),
   ('oranges'),
   (NULL),
   (NULL) ;

INSERT INTO Test2
VALUES (NULL),
   ('oranges'),
   ('grapes'),
   (NULL) ;
GO
```

If an inner join is attempted on these tables, like so:

```
SELECT t1.TestValue,
   t2.TestValue
FROM  Test1 t1
   INNER JOIN Test2 t2
     ON t1.TestValue = t2.TestValue ;
```

the query returns the following:

```
TestValue    TestValue
---------    ---------
oranges      oranges
```

How It Works

Predicates in the join condition evaluate NULLs the same way as predicates in the WHERE clause. When SQL Server evaluates the condition t1.TestValue = t2.TestValue, the equals operator returns false if one or both of the operands is NULL; therefore, the only rows that will be returned from an INNER JOIN are rows where neither side of the join is NULL and those non-NULL values are equal.

CHAPTER 4

Querying from Multiple Tables

by Jonathan Gennick

It is the rare database that has all its data in a single table. Data tends to be spread over multiple tables in ways that optimize storage and ensure consistency and integrity. Part of your job when writing a query is to deploy and link together T-SQL operations that can operate across tables in order to generate needed business results.

Building blocks at your disposal include:

> **Joins**. Imagine holding two spreadsheets side by side. A *join* takes two rowsets and combines the rows from each to create a single rowset having the combined columns. Look towards a join when you want to correlate data from two tables into a single result set. For example, you can combine a list of paychecks with information about the employees being paid.
>
> **Unions**. Now imagine holding the two spreadsheets vertically, one atop the other. The result is a rowset having the same number of columns. A *union* allows you to combine two rowsets into one when rows from those two rowsets represent instances of the same thing. For example, you can combine a list of customer names with a list of employee names to generate a single list of person names.
>
> **Subqueries**. Think about looking at a single row in one spreadsheet, and then consulting all the rows in a second spreadsheet for some bit of relevant information. Subqueries provide the analogous functionality in T-SQL.

These are not rigorous definitions. Their imagery provides only a beginning to help you understand the operations. The recipes that follow go deeper and show how to combine these building blocks, along with other basic T-SQL functionality, to generate business results.

4-1. Correlating Parent and Child Rows

Problem

You want to bring together data from parent and child tables. For example, you have a list of people in a parent table named `Person`, and a list of phone numbers in a child table named `PersonPhone`. Each person may have zero, one, or several phone numbers. You want to return a list of each person having at least one phone number, along with all their numbers.

Note It is also possible to return *all* persons, including those having zero phone numbers. You would do that by making the phone number side of the join optional, using the method from Recipe 4-3.

Solution

Write an *inner join* to bring related information from two tables together into a single result set. Begin with a FROM clause and one of the tables:

```
FROM Person.Person
```

Add the keywords INNER JOIN followed by the second table:

```
FROM  Person.Person
   INNER JOIN Person.PersonPhone
```

Follow with an ON clause to specify the *join condition*. The join condition identifies the row combinations of interest. It is the BusinessEntityID that identifies a person. That same ID identifies the phone numbers for a person. For this example, you want all combinations of Person and PersonPhone rows sharing the same value for BusinessEntityID. The following ON clause gives that result:

```
FROM  Person.Person
   INNER JOIN Person.PersonPhone
     ON Person.BusinessEntityID = PersonPhone.BusinessEntityID
```

Specify the columns you wish to see in the output. All columns from both tables are available. The following final version of the query returns two columns from each table:

```
SELECT PersonPhone.BusinessEntityID,
   FirstName,
   LastName,
   PhoneNumber
FROM  Person.Person
   INNER JOIN Person.PersonPhone
     ON Person.BusinessEntityID = PersonPhone.BusinessEntityID
ORDER BY LastName,
   FirstName,
   Person.BusinessEntityID;
```

The ORDER BY clause sorts the results so that all phone numbers for a given person fall together. Results are as follows:

```
BusinessEntityID    FirstName     LastName       PhoneNumber
----------------    ----------    ------------   -------------
285                 Syed          Abbas          926-555-0182
293                 Catherine     Abel           747-555-0171
38                  Kim           Abercrombie    208-555-0114
295                 Kim           Abercrombie    334-555-0137
2170                Kim           Abercrombie    919-555-0100
211                 Hazem         Abolrous       869-555-0125
2357                Sam           Abolrous       567-555-0100
297                 Humberto      Acevedo        599-555-0127
...
```

How It Works

The inner join is one of the most fundamental operations to understand. Imagine the following, very simplified two tables:

```
Person                                                  PersonPhone
BusinessEntityID      FirstName     LastName     BusinessEntityID     PhoneNumber
----------------      ----------    --------     ----------------     ------------
285                   Syed          Abbas        285                  926-555-0182
293                   Catherine     Abel         293                  747-555-0171
```

From a conceptual standpoint, an inner join begins with all possible combinations of rows from the two tables. Some combinations make sense. Some do not. The set of all possible combinations is called the *Cartesian product.* Notice the bold rows in the following Cartesian product.

```
BusinessEntityID   FirstName    LastName   BusinessEntityID   PhoneNumber
----------------   ----------   --------   ----------------   ------------
285                Syed         Abbas      285                926-555-0182
285                Syed         Abbas      293                747-555-0171
293                Catherine    Abel       293                747-555-0171
293                Catherine    Abel       285                926-555-0182
```

It makes sense to have Syed's name in the same row as his phone number. Likewise, it is sensible to list Catherine with her phone number. There's no logic at all in listing Syed's name with Catherine's number, or vice versa. Thus, the join condition is very sensibly written to specify the case in which the two BusinessEntityID values are the same:

```
ON Person.BusinessEntityID = PersonPhone.BusinessEntityID
```

The Cartesian product gives all possible results from an inner join. Picture the Cartesian product in your mind. Bring in the fishnet analogy from Recipe 1-4. Then write join conditions to trap the rows that you care about as the Cartesian product falls through your net.

■ **Note** Database engines do not materialize the entire Cartesian product when executing an inner join. There are more efficient approaches for SQL Server to take. However, regardless of approach, the results will always be in line with the conceptual description given here in this recipe.

THE TERM "RELATIONAL"

One sometimes hears the claim that the word "relational" in *relational database* refers to the fact that one table can "relate" to another in the sense that one joins the two tables together as described in Recipe 4-1. That explanation sounds so very plausible, yet it is wrong.

The term *relation* comes from set theory, and you can read in detail about what a relation is by visiting Wikipedia's article on *finitary relations*:

`http://en.wikipedia.org/wiki/Finitary_relation`

The key statement from the current version of this article reads as follows (emphasis mine).

> Typically, the property [a relation] describes a possible connection *between the components of a k-tuple.*

The words "between the components of" tell the tale. A tuple's analog is the row. The components of a tuple are its values, and thus the database analog would be the values in a row. The term *relation* speaks to a relationship, not between tables, but between the values in a row.

We encourage you to read the Wikipedia article. Then if you really want to dive deep into set theory and how it can help you work with data, we recommend the book *Applied Mathematics for Database Professionals* by Lex de Haan and Toon Koppelaars (Apress, 2007).

4-2. Querying Many-to-Many Relationships

Problem

You have a many-to-many relationship with two detail tables on either side of an intersection table. You want to resolve the relationship across all three tables.

Solution

String two inner joins together. The following example joins three tables in order to return discount information on a specific product:

```
SELECT p.Name,
   s.DiscountPct
FROM  Sales.SpecialOffer s
   INNER JOIN Sales.SpecialOfferProduct o
     ON s.SpecialOfferID = o.SpecialOfferID
   INNER JOIN Production.Product p
     ON o.ProductID = p.ProductID
WHERE  p.Name = 'All-Purpose Bike Stand';
```

The results of this query are as follows:

```
Name                      DiscountPct
-----------------------   -----------
All-Purpose Bike Stand    0.00
```

How It Works

A join starts after the first table in the FROM clause. In this example, three tables are joined together: Sales.SpecialOffer, Sales.SpecialOfferProduct, and Production.Product. Sales.SpecialOffer, the first table referenced in the FROM clause, contains a lookup of sales discounts:

```
FROM Sales.SpecialOffer s
```

Notice the letter s that trails the table name. This is a *table alias*. Once you begin using more than one table in a query, it is important to identify the data source of the individual columns explicitly. If the same column names exist in two different tables, you can get an error from the SQL compiler asking you to clarify which column you really want to return.

As a best practice, it is a good idea to use aliases whenever column names are specified in a query. For each of the referenced tables, an alias is used to symbolize the table name, saving you the trouble of spelling it out each time. This query uses a single character as a table alias, but you can use any valid identifier. A table alias, aside from allowing you to shorten or clarify the original table name, allows you to swap out the base table name if you ever have to replace it with a different table or view, or if you need to self-join the tables. Table aliases are optional, but recommended when your query has more than one table. (Because table aliases are optional, you can instead specify the entire table name every time you refer to the column in that table.)

Getting back to the example, the INNER JOIN keywords follow the first table reference, and then the table being joined to it, followed by its alias:

```
INNER JOIN Sales.SpecialOfferProduct o
```

After that, the ON keyword prefaces the column joins:

```
ON
```

This particular INNER JOIN is based on the equality of two columns, one from the first table and another from the second:

```
s.SpecialOfferID = o.SpecialOfferID
```

Next, the Production.Producttable is inner joined too:

```
INNER JOIN Production.Product p
  ON o.ProductID = p.ProductID
```

Lastly, a WHERE clause is used to filter rows returned in the final result set:

```
WHERE  p.Name = 'All-Purpose Bike Stand';
```

■ **Tip** As a query performance best practice, try to avoid having to convert data types of the columns in your join clause (using CONVERT or CAST, for example). Opt instead for modifying the underlying schema to match data types (or convert the data beforehand in a separate table, temp table, table variable, or common table expression [CTE]). Also, allowing implicit data type conversions to occur for frequently executed queries can cause significant performance issues (for example, converting nchar to char).

4-3. Making One Side of a Join Optional

Problem

You want rows returned from one table in a join even when there are no corresponding rows in the other table. For example, you want to list states and provinces and their tax rates. Sometimes no tax rate is on file. In those cases, you still want to list the state or province.

Solution

Write an *outer join* rather than the inner join that you have seen in the recipes so far. You can designate an outer join as either *left* or *right*. Following is a left outer join to produce a list of all states and provinces, including tax rates when they are available.

```
SELECT s.CountryRegionCode,
   s.StateProvinceCode,
   t.TaxType,
   t.TaxRate
FROM  Person.StateProvince s
   LEFT OUTER JOIN Sales.SalesTaxRate t
     ON s.StateProvinceID = t.StateProvinceID;
```

This returns the following (abridged) results.

```
CountryRegionCode    StateProvinceCode   TaxType    TaxRate
-----------------    -----------------   -------    -------
CA                   AB                  1          14.00
CA                   AB                  2          7.00
US                   AK                  NULL       NULL
US                   AL                  NULL       NULL
US                   AR                  NULL       NULL
AS                   AS                  NULL       NULL
US                   AZ                  1          7.75
CA                   BC                  3          7.00
...
```

How It Works

A left outer join causes the table named first to become the nonoptional, or anchor table. The word "left" derives from the fact that English is written left to right. The left outer join in the solution makes `StateProvince` the anchor table, so all states are returned. The sales tax side of the join is then the optional side, and the database engine supplies nulls for the sales tax columns when no corresponding row exists for each state in question.

Change the join type in the solution from `LEFT OUTER` to `INNER`, and you'll get only those rows for states having tax rates defined in the `SalesTaxRate` table. That's because an inner join requires a row from each table involved. By making the join a left outer join, you make the right-hand table optional. Rows from the left-hand table are returned regardless of whether corresponding rows exist in the other table. Thus, you get *all* states and provinces; lack of a tax rate does not prevent a state or province from appearing in the results.

It is common to write outer joins with one optional table as left outer joins. However, you do have the option of looking at things from the other direction. For example:

```
FROM  Sales.SalesTaxRate t
   RIGHT OUTER JOIN Person.StateProvince s
```

This right outer join will yield the same results as the left outer join in the solution example. That's because the order of the tables has been flipped. `StateProvince` is now on the right-hand side, and it is the anchor table once again because this time a right outer join is used.

■ **Tip** Experiment! Take time to execute the solution query. Then change the join clause to read `INNER JOIN`. Note the difference in results. Then change the entire `FROM` clause to use a right outer join with the `StateProvince` table on the right-hand side. You should get the same results as from the solution query.

4-4. Making Both Sides of a Join Optional

Problem

You want the effect of a left and a right outer join at the same time.

Solution

Write a full outer join. Do that using the keywords `FULL OUTER JOIN`.

For example:

```
SELECT soh.SalesOrderID,
   sr.SalesReasonID,
   sr.Name
FROM  Sales.SalesOrderHeader soh
   FULL OUTER JOIN Sales.SalesOrderHeaderSalesReason sohsr
     ON soh.SalesOrderID = sohsr.SalesOrderID
   FULL OUTER JOIN Sales.SalesReason sr
     ON sr.SalesReasonID = sohsr.SalesReasonID;
```

This query follows the same pattern as that in Recipe 4-3 on querying many-to-many relationships. Only the join type and tables are different.

How It Works

The solution query returns sales orders and their associated reasons. The full outer join in the query guarantees the following:

- All the results from an inner join
- One additional row for each order not associated with a sale
- One additional row for each sales reason not associated with an order

The additional rows have nulls from one side of the join or the other. If there is no order associated with a reason, then there is no value available for the `SalesOrderID` column in the result, and the value is null. Likewise, the `SalesReasonID` and `Name` values are null in the case of an order having no reason.

Results are as follows for orders associated with reasons:

```
SalesOrderID    SalesReasonID    Name
------------    -------------    ------------
43697           5                Manufacturer
43697           9                Quality
43702           5                Manufacturer
...
```

Any reasons not associated with an order will come back with nulls in the order columns:

```
SalesOrderID    SalesReasonID    Name
------------    -------------    ----------------------
NULL            3                Magazine Advertisement
NULL            7                Demo Event
NULL            8                Sponsorship
...
```

Any orders not given a reason will likewise come back with nulls in the reason columns:

```
SalesOrderID  SalesReasonID  Name
------------  -------------  ----
45889         NULL           NULL
48806         NULL           NULL
51723         NULL           NULL
...
```

All the preceding results will come back as a single result set.

■ **Tip** Consider adding a `WHERE` clause to hone in on the special-case rows in the result set. By itself, the sample query returns a great many rows, most of them having data from both sides of the join. You can hone in on the rows having only reasons by appending the clause `WHERE soh.SalesOrderID IS NULL` to the end of the query. Likewise, append `WHERE sr.SalesReasonID IS NULL` to see rows having only data from the sales side of the join.

4-5. Generating All Possible Row Combinations

Problem

You want to generate all possible combinations of rows from two tables. You want to generate the Cartesian product described in Recipe 4-1.

Solution

Write a *cross join*. In this example, the `Person.StateProvince` and `Sales.SalesTaxRate` tables are cross joined to generate all possible combinations of rows from the two tables:

```
SELECT s.CountryRegionCode,
   s.StateProvinceCode,
   t.TaxType,
   t.TaxRate
FROM  Person.StateProvince s
   CROSS JOIN Sales.SalesTaxRate t;
```

This returns the following (abridged) results:

```
CountryRegionCode  StateProvinceCode  TaxType  TaxRate
-----------------  -----------------  -------  -------
CA                 AB                 1        14.00
US                 AK                 1        14.00
US                 AL                 1        14.00
...
```

How It Works

A cross join is essentially a join with no join conditions. Every row from one table is joined to every row in the other table, regardless of whether the resulting combination of values makes any sense. The result is termed a *Cartesian product.*

The solution results show StateProvince and SalesTaxRate information that doesn't logically go together. Because the Person.StateProvince table had 181 rows, and the Sales.SalesTaxRate had 29 rows, the query returned 5249 rows.

4-6. Selecting from a Result Set

Problem

You find it easier to think in terms of selecting a set of rows, and then selecting again from that result.

Solution

Create a *derived table* in your FROM clause by enclosing a SELECT statement within parentheses. For example, the following query joins SalesOrderHeader to the results from a query against SalesOrderDetail:

```
SELECT DISTINCT
   s.PurchaseOrderNumber
FROM  Sales.SalesOrderHeader s
   INNER JOIN (SELECT SalesOrderID
          FROM  Sales.SalesOrderDetail
          WHERE  UnitPrice BETWEEN 1000 AND 2000
          ) d
      ON s.SalesOrderID = d.SalesOrderID;
```

This returns the following abridged results:

```
PurchaseOrderNumber
-------------------
PO10962177551
PO11571175810
PO10469158272
PO10237188382
PO17661178081
...
```

How It Works

Derived tables are SELECT statements that act as tables in the FROM clause. A derived table is a separate query in itself, and doesn't require the use of a temporary table to store its results. Thus, queries that use derived tables can sometimes perform significantly better than the process of building a temporary table and querying from it, as you eliminate the steps needed for SQL Server to create and allocate a temporary table prior to use.

This example's query searches for the PurchaseOrderNumber from the Sales.SalesOrderHeader table for any order containing products with a UnitPrice between 1000 and 2000. The query joins a table to a derived table using an inner join operation. The derived table query is encapsulated in parentheses and is followed by a table alias.

4-7. Testing for the Existence of a Row

Problem

You are writing a WHERE clause. You want to return rows from the table you are querying based upon the existence of related rows in some other table.

Solution

One solution is to write a subquery in conjunction with the EXISTS predicate:

```
SELECT DISTINCT
   s.PurchaseOrderNumber
FROM  Sales.SalesOrderHeader s
WHERE  EXISTS ( SELECT SalesOrderID
         FROM  Sales.SalesOrderDetail
         WHERE UnitPrice BETWEEN 1000 AND 2000
            AND SalesOrderID = s.SalesOrderID );
```

This returns the following abridged results.

```
PurchaseOrderNumber
-------------------
PO10962177551
PO11571175810
PO10469158272
PO10237188382
...
```

How It Works

The critical piece in the solution example is the subquery in the WHERE clause, which checks for the existence of SalesOrderIDs that have products with a UnitPrice between 1000 and 2000. A JOIN is essentially written into the WHERE clause of the subquery by stating SalesOrderID = s.SalesOrderID. The subquery uses the SalesOrderID from each returned row in the outer query.

The subquery in this recipe is known as a *correlated subquery*. It is called such because the subquery accesses values from the parent query. It is certainly possible to write an EXISTS predicate with a noncorrelated subquery, however, it is unusual to do so.

Look back at Recipe 4-6. It solves the same problem and generates the same results, but using a derived table in the FROM clause. Often you can solve such problems multiple ways. Pick the one that performs best. If performance is equal, then pick the approach with which you are most comfortable.

4-8. Testing Against the Result from a Query

Problem

You are writing a WHERE clause and wish to write a predicate involving the result from another query. For example, you wish to compare a value in a table against the maximum value in a related table.

Solution

Write a *noncorrelated* subquery. Make sure it returns a single value. Put the query where you would normally refer to the value. For example:

```
SELECT BusinessEntityID,
    SalesQuota CurrentSalesQuota
FROM  Sales.SalesPerson
WHERE  SalesQuota = (SELECT  MAX(SalesQuota)
           FROM   Sales.SalesPerson
           );
```

This returns the three salespeople who had the maximum sales quota of 300,000:

```
BusinessEntityID   CurrentSalesQuota
----------------   ---------------------
275                300000.00
279                300000.00
284                300000.00
Warning: Null value is eliminated by an aggregate or other SET operation.
```

How It Works

There is no WHERE clause in the subquery, and the subquery does not reference values from the parent query. It is therefore not a correlated subquery. Instead, the maximum sales quota is retrieved once. That value is used to evaluate the WHERE clause for all rows tested by the parent query.

Ignore the warning message in the results. That message simply indicates that some of the SalesQuota values fed into the MAX function were null. You can avoid the message by adding WHERE SalesQuota IS NOT NULL to the subquery. You can also avoid the message by issuing the command set ANSI_WARNINGS OFF. However, there is no real need to avoid the message at all unless it offends your sense of tidiness to see it.

4-9. Comparing Subsets of a Table

Problem

You have two subsets in a table, and you want to compare values between them. For example, you want to compare sales data between two calendar years.

Solution

One solution is to join the table with itself through the use of table aliases. In this example, the Sales.SalesPersonOuotaHistory table is referenced twice in the FROM clause, once for 2008 sales quota data and again for 2007 sales quota data:

```
SELECT s.BusinessEntityID,
   SUM(s2008.SalesQuota) Total_2008_SQ,
   SUM(s2007.SalesQuota) Total_2007_SQ
FROM  Sales.SalesPerson s
   LEFT OUTER JOIN Sales.SalesPersonQuotaHistory s2008
     ON s.BusinessEntityID = s2008.BusinessEntityID
       AND YEAR(s2008.QuotaDate) = 2008
```

```
    LEFT OUTER JOIN Sales.SalesPersonQuotaHistory s2007
      ON s.BusinessEntityID = s2007.BusinessEntityID
        AND YEAR(s2007.QuotaDate) = 2007
GROUP BY s.BusinessEntityID;
```

This returns the following (abridged) results:

```
BusinessEntityID  Total_2008_SQ  Total_2007_SQ
----------------  -------------  -------------
274               1084000.00     1088000.00
275               6872000.00     9432000.00
276               8072000.00     9364000.00
...
```

How It Works

Sometimes you may need to treat the same table as two separate tables. This may be because the table contains nested hierarchies of data (for example, a table containing employee records has a manager ID that is a foreign key reference to the employee ID), or perhaps you wish to reference the same table based on different time periods (comparing sales records from the year 2008 versus the year 2007).

This recipe queries the year 2008 and year 2007 sales quota results. The `FROM` clause includes an anchor to all salesperson identifiers:

```
FROM Sales.Salesperson s
```

The query then left outer joins the first reference to the sales quota data, giving it an alias of `S2008`:

```
LEFT OUTER JOIN Sales.SalesPersonQuotaHistory s2008
  ON s.BusinessEntityID = s2008.BusinessEntityID
    AND YEAR(s2008.QuotaDate) = 2008
```

Next, another reference was created to the same sales quota table, however, this time aliasing the table as `S2007`:

```
LEFT OUTER JOIN Sales.SalesPersonQuotaHistory s2007
  ON s.BusinessEntityID = s2007.BusinessEntityID
    AND YEAR(s2007.QuotaDate) = 2007
```

As demonstrated here, you can reference the same table multiple times in the same query as long as you give each reference a unique table alias to differentiate it from the others.

■ **Tip** When you find yourself using the technique in Recipe 4-9, step back and consider whether you can rethink your approach and apply window function syntax instead. The article "H.G. Wells and SQL: Travelling in the Second Dimension" at `http://gennick.com/windowss02.html` describes a scenario similar to this recipe's solution in which values are compared across time. Window functions often solve such problems with better performance than the self-join technique given in this recipe. Chapter 7 includes examples covering this useful and expressive class of functions.

4-10. Stacking Two Row Sets Vertically

Problem

You are querying the same data from two different sources. You wish to combine the two sets of results. For example, you wish to combine current with historical sales quotas.

Solution

Write two queries. Glue them together with the UNION ALL operator. For example:

```
SELECT BusinessEntityID,
    GETDATE() QuotaDate,
    SalesQuota
FROM  Sales.SalesPerson
WHERE  SalesQuota > 0
UNION ALL
SELECT BusinessEntityID,
    QuotaDate,
    SalesQuota
FROM  Sales.SalesPersonQuotaHistory
WHERE  SalesQuota > 0
ORDER BY BusinessEntityID DESC,
    QuotaDate DESC;
```

Results are as follows.

```
BusinessEntityID   QuotaDate                 SalesQuota
----------------   -----------------------   ----------
290                2012-02-09 00:04:39.420    250000.00
290                2008-04-01 00:00:00.000    908000.00
290                2008-01-01 00:00:00.000    707000.00
290                2007-10-01 00:00:00.000   1057000.00
...
```

How It Works

The solution query appends two result sets into a single result set. The first result set returns the BusinessEntityID, the current date, and the SalesQuota. Because GETDATE() is a function, it doesn't naturally generate a column name, so a QuotaDate column alias was used in its place:

```
SELECT BusinessEntityID,
   GETDATE() QuotaDate,
   SalesQuota
FROM  Sales.SalesPerson
```

The WHERE clause filters data for those salespeople with a SalesQuota greater than zero:

```
WHERE  SalesQuota > 0
```

The next part of the query is the UNION ALL operator, which appends all results from the second query:

```
UNION ALL
```

The second query pulls data from the Sales.SalesPersonQuotaHistory, which keeps the history for a salesperson's sales quota as it changes through time:

```
SELECT BusinessEntityID,
   QuotaDate,
   SalesQuota
FROM  Sales.SalesPersonQuotaHistory
```

The ORDER BY clause sorts the result set by BusinessEntityID and QuotaDate, both in descending order. The ORDER BY clause, when needed, must appear at the bottom of the entire statement. In the solution query, the clause is:

```
ORDER BY BusinessEntityID DESC,
   QuotaDate DESC;
```

You cannot write individual ORDER BY clauses for each of the SELECTs that you UNION together. ORDER BY can only appear once at the end, and applies to the combined result set.

Column names in the final, combined result set derive from the first SELECT in the overall statement. Thus, the ORDER BY clause should only refer to column names from the *first* result set.

■ **Tip** UNION ALL is more efficient than UNION (described in the next recipe), because UNION ALL does not force a sort or similar operation in support of duplicate elimination. Use UNION ALL whenever possible, unless you really do need duplicate rows in the result set to be eliminated.

4-11. Eliminating Duplicate Values from a Union

Problem

You are writing a UNION query and prefer not to have duplicate rows in the results. For example, you wish to generate a list of unique surnames from among employees and salespersons.

Solution

Write a union query, but omit the ALL keyword and write just UNION instead. For example:

```
SELECT P1.LastName
FROM  HumanResources.Employee E
   INNER JOIN Person.Person P1
     ON E.BusinessEntityID = P1.BusinessEntityID
UNION
SELECT P2.LastName
FROM  Sales.SalesPerson SP
   INNER JOIN Person.Person P2
     ON SP.BusinessEntityID = P2.BusinessEntityID;
```

Results are as follows.

```
LastName
-----------
Abbas
Abercrombie
Abolrous
Ackerman
Adams
...
```

How It Works

The behavior of the UNION operator is to remove all duplicate rows. The solution query uses that behavior to generate a list of unique surnames from among the combined group of employees and salespersons.

For large result sets, deduplication can be a very costly operation. It very often involves a sort. If you don't need to deduplicate your data, or if your data is naturally distinct, write UNION ALL instead and your queries will run more efficiently. (See Recipe 4-10 for an example of UNION ALL.)

■ **Caution** Do you need your results sorted? Then be sure to write an ORDER BY clause. The solution results appear sorted, but that is a side effect from the deduplication operation. You should not count on such a side effect. The database engine might not drive the sort to completion. Other deduplication logic can be introduced in a future release and break your query. If you need ordering, write an ORDER BY clause into your query.

4-12. Subtracting One Row Set from Another

Problem

You want to subtract one set of rows from another. For example, you want to subtract component ID numbers from a list of product ID numbers to find those products that are at the top of the heap and are not themselves part of some larger product.

Solution

Write a union query involving the EXCEPT operator. Subtract products that are components from the total list of products, leaving only those products that are not components. For example:

```
SELECT P.ProductID
FROM   Production.Product P
EXCEPT
SELECT BOM.ComponentID
FROM   Production.BillOfMaterials BOM;
```

```
ProductID
-----------
378
710
879
856
...
```

How It Works

EXCEPT begins with the first query and eliminates any rows that are also found in the second. It is considered to be a union operator, although the operation is along the lines of a subtraction.

In the Adventure Works database, the `BillOfMaterials` table describes products that are made up of other products. The component products are recorded in the `ComponentID` column. Thus, subtracting the `ComponentID` values from the `ProductID` values in the `Product` table leaves only those products that are at the top and are not themselves part of some larger product.

■ **Note** The `EXCEPT` operator implicitly deduplicates the final result set.

4-13. Finding Rows in Common Between Two Row Sets

Problem

You have two queries. You want to find which rows are returned by both. For example, you wish to find products that have incurred both good and poor reviews.

Solution

Write a union query using the `INTERSECT` keyword. For example:

```
SELECT PR1.ProductID
FROM  Production.ProductReview PR1
WHERE  PR1.Rating >= 4
INTERSECT
SELECT PR1.ProductID
FROM  Production.ProductReview PR1
WHERE  PR1.Rating <= 2;
```

Results from this query show the one product having both good and bad reviews:

```
ProductID
---------
937
```

How It Works

The `INTERSECT` operator finds rows in common between two row sets. The solution example defines a good review as one with a rating of 4 and above. A bad review is a rating of 2 and lower. It's easy to write a separate query to identify products falling into each case. The INTERSECT operator takes the results from both those simple queries and returns a single result set showing the products—just one in this case—that both queries return.

■ **Note** Like the EXCEPT operator, INTERSECT implicitly deduplicates the final results.

Sometimes you'll find yourself wanting to include other columns in an INTERSECT query, and those columns cause the intersection operation to fail because that operation is performed taking all columns into account. One solution is to treat the intersection query as a derived table and join it to the Product table. For example:

```
SELECT PR3.ProductID,
   PR3.Name
FROM  Production.Product PR3
   INNER JOIN (SELECT PR1.ProductID
         FROM  Production.ProductReview PR1
         WHERE  PR1.Rating >= 4
         INTERSECT
         SELECT PR1.ProductID
         FROM  Production.ProductReview PR1
         WHERE  PR1.Rating <= 2
         ) SQ
     ON PR3.ProductID = SQ.ProductID;
```

```
ProductID   Name
---------   -----------------
937         HL Mountain Pedal
```

Another approach is to move the intersection subquery into the WHERE clause and use it to generate an in-list using a technique similar to that shown earlier in Recipe 4-8. For example:

```
SELECT ProductID,
   Name
FROM  Production.Product
WHERE  ProductID IN (SELECT  PR1.ProductID
          FROM   Production.ProductReview PR1
          WHERE   PR1.Rating >= 4
          INTERSECT
          SELECT  PR1.ProductID
          FROM   Production.ProductReview PR1
          WHERE   PR1.Rating <= 2);
```

```
ProductID  Name
---------  -----------------
937        HL Mountain Pedal
```

In this version of the query, the subquery generates a list of product ID numbers. The database engine then treats that list as input into the IN predicate. There is only one product in this case, so you can think loosely in terms of the database engine ultimately executing a statement such as the following:

```
SELECT ProductID,
   Name
FROM  Production.Product
WHERE  ProductID IN (937);
```

You can actually write an IN predicate giving a list of hard-coded values. Or you can choose to generate that list of values from a SELECT, as in this recipe.

4-14. Finding Rows That Are Missing

Problem

You want to find rows in one table or result set that have no corresponding rows in another. For example, you want to find all products in the Product table having no corresponding special offers.

Solution

Different approaches are possible. One approach is to write a query involving EXCEPT:

```
SELECT ProductID
FROM  Production.Product
EXCEPT
SELECT ProductID
FROM  Sales.SpecialOfferProduct;
```

```
ProductID
-----------
1
2
3
...
```

If you want to see more than just a list of ID numbers, you can write a query involving NOT EXISTS and a correlated subquery. For example:

```
SELECT P.ProductID,
   P.Name
FROM  Production.Product P
WHERE  NOT EXISTS ( SELECT *
         FROM  Sales.SpecialOfferProduct SOP
         WHERE SOP.ProductID = P.ProductID );
```

```
ProductID  Name
---------  ---------------
1          Adjustable Race
2          Bearing Ball
3          BB Ball Bearing
...
```

How It Works

The solution involving EXCEPT is simple to write and easy to understand. The top query generates a list of all possible products. The bottom query generates a list of products that have been given special offers. EXCEPT subtracts the second list from the first and returns a list of products having no corresponding rows in SpecialOfferProduct. The downside is that the approach of using EXCEPT limits the final results to just a list of ID numbers.

The second solution involves a NOT EXISTS predicate. You first read about EXISTS in Recipe 4-7. NOT EXISTS is a variation on that theme. Rather than testing for existence, the predicate tests for nonexistence. The parent query then returns all product rows not having corresponding special offers. You are able to include any columns from the Product table in the query results that you desire.

4-15. Comparing Two Tables

Problem

You have two copies of a table. You want to test for equality. Do both copies have the same rows and column values?

Solution

Begin by creating a copy of a table, in this case the Password table:

```
SELECT *
INTO  Person.PasswordCopy
FROM  Person.Password;
```

Then execute the following union query to compare the data between the two tables and report on the differences.

```
SELECT *,
   COUNT(*) DupeCount,
   'Password' TableName
FROM  Person.Password P
GROUP BY BusinessEntityID,
   PasswordHash,
   PasswordSalt,
   rowguid,
   ModifiedDate
HAVING NOT EXISTS ( SELECT *,
             COUNT(*)
          FROM  Person.PasswordCopy PC
          GROUP BY BusinessEntityID,
            PasswordHash,
            PasswordSalt,
            rowguid,
            ModifiedDate
          HAVING PC.BusinessEntityID = P.BusinessEntityID
              AND PC.PasswordHash = P.PasswordHash
              AND PC.PasswordSalt = P.PasswordSalt
              AND PC.rowguid = P.rowguid
              AND PC.ModifiedDate = P.ModifiedDate
              AND COUNT(*) = COUNT(ALL P.BusinessEntityID))
```

```
UNION
SELECT *,
    COUNT(*) DupeCount,
    'PasswordCopy' TableName
FROM  Person.PasswordCopy PC
GROUP BY BusinessEntityID,
    PasswordHash,
    PasswordSalt,
    rowguid,
    ModifiedDate
HAVING NOT EXISTS ( SELECT *,
            COUNT(*)
        FROM  Person.Password P
        GROUP BY BusinessEntityID,
            PasswordHash,
            PasswordSalt,
            rowguid,
            ModifiedDate
        HAVING PC.BusinessEntityID = P.BusinessEntityID
            AND PC.PasswordHash = P.PasswordHash
            AND PC.PasswordSalt = P.PasswordSalt
            AND PC.rowguid = P.rowguid
            AND PC.ModifiedDate = P.ModifiedDate
            AND COUNT(*) = COUNT(ALL PC.BusinessEntityID) );
```

Results from this query will be zero rows. That is because the tables are unchanged. You've made a copy of Password, but haven't changed values in either table.

Now make some changes to the data in the two tables. BusinessEntityID numbers are in the range 1, . . . , 19972. Following are some statements to change data in each table, and to create one duplicate row in the copy:

```
UPDATE Person.PasswordCopy
SET   PasswordSalt = 'Munising!'
WHERE  BusinessEntityID IN (9783, 221);

UPDATE Person.Password
SET   PasswordSalt = 'Marquette!'
WHERE  BusinessEntityID IN (42, 4242);

INSERT INTO Person.PasswordCopy
    SELECT *
    FROM  Person.PasswordCopy
    WHERE  BusinessEntityID = 1;
```

Having changed the data, reissue the previous union query to compare the two tables. This time there are results indicating the differences just created:

```
BusinessEntityID  PasswordHash    ...  PasswordSalt   ...  DupeCount  TableName
----------------  -------------   ...  ------------   ...  ---------  ------------
1                 pbFwXWE99vobT   ...  bE3XiWw=       ...  1          Password
42                HSLAA7MxklY4d   ...  Marquette!     ...  1          Password
221               DFSEDLoy3em1I   ...  5nzaMoQ=       ...  1          Password
4242              YITAXaCQCapPi   ...  Marquette!     ...  1          Password
9783              1gvO8vLyjlhQY   ...  YcAxsQQ=       ...  1          Password
```

```
1       pbFwXWE99vobT  ...  bE3XiWw=   ...  2  PasswordCopy
42      HSLAA7MxklY4d  ...  uTuRBuI=   ...  1  PasswordCopy
221     DFSEDLoy3em1I  ...  Munising!  ...  1  PasswordCopy
4242    YITAXaCQCapPi  ...  mj6TQG4=   ...  1  PasswordCopy
9783    gvO8vLyjlhQY   ...  Munising!  ...  1  PasswordCopy
```

These results indicate rows from each table that are not found in the other. They also indicate differences in duplication counts.

How It Works

The solution query is intimidating at first, and it is a lot to type. But it is a rote query once you get the hang of it, and the two halves are essentially mirror images of each other.

The grouping and counting is there to handle the possibility of duplicate rows. Each of the queries on either side of the union begins by grouping on all columns and generating a duplication count. For example, the second subquery examines PasswordCopy:

```
SELECT *,
    COUNT(*) DupeCount,
    'PasswordCopy' TableName
FROM  Person.PasswordCopy PC
GROUP BY BusinessEntityID,
    PasswordHash,
    PasswordSalt,
    rowguid,
    ModifiedDate;
```

```
BusinessEntityID    PasswordHash    ...  DupeCount  TableName
----------------    -------------   ...  ---------  ------------
1                   pbFwXWE99vobT   ...  2          PasswordCopy
2                   bawRVNrZQYQ05   ...  1          PasswordCopy
```

Here you can see that there are two rows containing the same set of values. Both rows are associated with BusinessEntityID 1. The DupeCount for that ID is 2.

Next comes a subquery in the HAVING clause to restrict the results to only those rows not also appearing in the Password table:

```
HAVING NOT EXISTS ( SELECT *,
              COUNT(*)
           FROM  Person.PasswordCopy PC
           GROUP BY BusinessEntityID,
              PasswordHash,
              PasswordSalt,
              rowguid,
              ModifiedDate
           HAVING PC.BusinessEntityID = P.BusinessEntityID
              AND PC.PasswordHash = P.PasswordHash
              AND PC.PasswordSalt = P.PasswordSalt
              AND PC.rowguid = P.rowguid
              AND PC.ModifiedDate = P.ModifiedDate
              AND COUNT(*) = COUNT(ALL P.BusinessEntityID) )
```

This HAVING clause is tedious to write, but it is conceptually simple. It compares all columns for equality. It compares row counts to check for differences in the number of times a row is duplicated in either of the tables. The results are a list of rows in PasswordCopy that do not also exist the same number of times in Password.

Both queries do the same thing from different directions. The first query in the union finds rows in Password that are not also in PasswordCopy. The second query reverses things and finds rows in PasswordCopy that are not also in Password. Both queries will detect differences in duplication counts.

In the solution results there is one row that is reported because it occurs twice in the copy and once in the original:

```
BusinessEntityID   PasswordHash    …  PasswordSalt  …  DupeCount   TableName
----------------   ------------    …  ------------  …  ---------   ------------
1                  pbFwXWE99vobT   …  bE3XiWw=      …  1           Password
…
1                  pbFwXWE99vobT   …  bE3XiWw=      …  2           PasswordCopy
…
```

The TableName column lets you see that Password contains just one row for BusinessEntityID 1. That makes sense, because that column is the primary key. The PasswordCopy table, however, has no primary key. Somehow, someone has duplicated the row for BusinessEntityID 1. That table has two copies of the row. Because the number of copies is different, the tables do not compare as being equal.

The solution query reports differences between the two tables. An empty result set indicates that the two tables contain the same rows, having the same values, and occurring the same number of times.

CHAPTER 5

Grouping and Summarizing

by Wayne Sheffield

Grouping is primarily performed in SQL Server by using the GROUP BY clause in a SELECT query to determine in which groups rows should be put. Data is summarized by using the SUM function. The simplified syntax is as follows:

```
SELECT Column1, SUM(Column2)
FROM table_list
[WHERE search_conditions]
GROUP BY Column1
```

GROUP BY follows the optional WHERE clause and is most often used when aggregate functions are being utilized in the SELECT statement (aggregate functions are reviewed in more detail in Chapter 7).

5-1. Summarizing a Result Set

Problem

You need to know the total number of items in your warehouse.

Solution

Use the SUM function to add up the Quantity column values in your inventory table.

```
SELECT SUM(i.Quantity) AS Total
FROM   Production.ProductInventory i;
```

This query returns the following result set:

```
Total
------
335974
```

How It Works

The entire Production.ProductInventory table is scanned, and the Quantity column values are added up, and a sum is returned.

5-2. Creating Summary Groups

Problem

You need to summarize one column for every change in a second column. For example, you want to report the total amount due by an order date from the sales table. There are many orders per day, and you want to report only the total per day.

Solution

Group your detail data in the OrderDate column. Then apply the SUM function to the TotalDue column to generate a total due per date. This example uses the GROUP BY clause to summarize the total amount due by the order date from the Sales.SalesOrderHeader table:

```
SELECT OrderDate,
       SUM(TotalDue) AS TotalDueByOrderDate
FROM   Sales.SalesOrderHeader
WHERE  OrderDate >= '2005-07-01T00:00:00'
       AND OrderDate < '2005-08-01T00:00:00'
GROUP BY OrderDate;
```

This query returns the following (abridged) result set:

```
OrderDate               TotalDueByOrderDate
----------------------- -------------------
2005-07-01 00:00:00.000 567020.9498
2005-07-02 00:00:00.000 15394.3298
2005-07-03 00:00:00.000 16588.4572
2005-07-30 00:00:00.000 15914.584
2005-07-31 00:00:00.000 16588.4572
```

How It Works

To determine the groups that rows should be put in, the GROUP BY clause is used in a SELECT query. Stepping through the first line of the query, the SELECT clause designates that the OrderDate should be returned, as well as the SUM total of values in the TotalDue column. SUM is an aggregate function. An aggregate function performs a calculation against a set of values (in this case TotalDue), returning a single value (the total of TotalDue by OrderDate):

```
SELECT OrderDate,
       SUM(TotalDue) AS TotalDueByOrderDate
```

Notice that a column alias for the SUM(TotalDue) aggregation is used. A column alias returns a different name for a calculated, aggregated, or regular column. In the next part of the query, the Sales.SalesOrderHeader table is referenced in the FROM clause.

```
FROM   Sales.SalesOrderHeader
```

Next, the OrderDate is qualified to return rows for the month of July and the year 2005.

```
WHERE  OrderDate >= '2005-07-01T00:00:00'
       AND OrderDate < '2005-08-01T00:00:00'
```

The result set is grouped by OrderDate (note that grouping can occur against one or more combined columns).

```
GROUP BY OrderDate;
```

If the GROUP BY clause were to have been left out of the query, using an aggregate function in the SELECT clause would have raised the following error:

```
Msg 8120, Level 16, State 1, Line 1
Column 'Sales.SalesOrderHeader.OrderDate' is invalid in the select list because
it is not contained in either an aggregate function or the GROUP BY clause.
```

This error is raised because any column that is not used in an aggregate function in the SELECT list must be listed in the GROUP BY clause.

5-3. Restricting a Result Set to Groups of Interest

Problem

You do not want to return all of the rows being returned by an aggregation; instead, you want only the rows where the aggregation itself is filtered. For example, you want to report on the reasons that the product was scrapped, but only for the reasons that have more than 50 occurrences.

Solution

Specify a HAVING clause, giving the conditions that the aggregated rows must meet in order to be returned.

This example queries two tables, Production.ScrapReason and Production.WorkOrder. The Production.ScrapReason table is a lookup table that contains manufacturing failure reasons, and the Production.WorkOrder table contains the manufacturing work orders that control which products are manufactured in the quantity and time period in order to meet inventory and sales needs. A report is needed that shows which of the "failure reasons" have occurred more than 50 times.

```
SELECT s.Name,
       COUNT(w.WorkOrderID) AS Cnt
FROM   Production.ScrapReason s
       INNER JOIN Production.WorkOrder w
           ON s.ScrapReasonID = w.ScrapReasonID
GROUP BY s.Name
HAVING COUNT(*) > 50;
```

This query returns the following result set:

```
Name                            Cnt
------------------------------  ---
Gouge in metal                  54
Stress test failed              52
Thermoform temperature too low  63
Trim length too long            52
Wheel misaligned                51
```

How It Works

The HAVING clause of the SELECT statement allows you to specify a search condition on a query using GROUP BY and/or an aggregated value. The syntax is as follows:

```
SELECT select_list
FROM table_list
[ WHERE search_conditions ]
[ GROUP BY group_by_list ]
[ HAVING search_conditions ]
```

The HAVING clause is used to qualify the results after the GROUP BY has been applied. The WHERE clause, in contrast, is used to qualify the rows that are returned *before* the data is aggregated or grouped. HAVING qualifies the aggregated data *after* the data has been grouped or aggregated.

In this recipe, the SELECT clause requests a count of WorkOrderIDs by failure name:

```
SELECT s.Name,
       COUNT(w.WorkOrderID) AS Cnt
```

Two tables are joined by the ScrapReasonID column:

```
FROM   Production.ScrapReason s
       INNER JOIN Production.WorkOrder w
          ON s.ScrapReasonID = w.ScrapReasonID
```

Because an aggregate function is used in the SELECT clause, the nonaggregated columns must appear in the GROUP BY clause:

```
GROUP BY s.Name
```

Lastly, using the HAVING query determines that, of the selected and grouped data, only those rows in the result set with a count of more than 50 will be returned:

```
HAVING COUNT(*)>50
```

5-4. Removing Duplicates from the Detailed Results

Problem

You need to know the quantity of unique values per date.

Solution

Add the DISTINCT clause to the COUNT function.

```
SELECT [RateChangeDate],
       COUNT([Rate]) AS [Count],
       COUNT(DISTINCT Rate) AS [DistinctCount]
FROM   [HumanResources].[EmployeePayHistory]
WHERE  RateChangeDate >= '2003-01-01T00:00:00.000'
       AND RateChangeDate < '2003-01-10T00:00:00.000'
GROUP BY RateChangeDate;
```

This query returns the following result set:

```
RateChangeDate            Count    DistinctCount
-----------------------   -----    -------------
2003-01-02 00:00:00.000   2        2
2003-01-03 00:00:00.000   3        2
2003-01-04 00:00:00.000   1        1
2003-01-05 00:00:00.000   3        3
2003-01-06 00:00:00.000   1        1
2003-01-07 00:00:00.000   2        2
2003-01-08 00:00:00.000   5        3
2003-01-09 00:00:00.000   2        2
```

How It Works

The previous query utilizes two COUNT functions; the second one also uses the DISTINCT clause. This forces the COUNT function to count only the distinct values in the specified column, in this case the Rate column.

5-5. Creating Summary Cubes

Problem

You need to return a data set with the detail data and with the data summarized on each combination of columns specified in the GROUP BY clause.

Solution

You need to include the CUBE argument after the GROUP BY clause. This example uses the CUBE argument to produce subtotal lines at the Shelf and LocationID levels, as well as a grand total.

```
SELECT i.Shelf,
       i.LocationID,
       SUM(i.Quantity) AS Total
FROM   Production.ProductInventory i
GROUP BY CUBE(i.Shelf, i.LocationID);
```

This query produces several levels of totals, the first being by LocationID. The abridged result set is as follows:

```
Shelf    LocationID   Total
-----    ----------   -----
A        1            2727
C        1            13777
D        1            6551
…
J        1            5051
K        1            6751
L        1            7537
NULL     1            72899
```

Later in this result set, you will see totals by shelf and then across all shelves and locations.

```
Shelf       LocationID   Total
-----       ----------   ------
...
T           NULL         10634
U           NULL         18700
V           NULL         2635
W           NULL         2908
Y           NULL         437
NULL        NULL         335974
```

How It Works

By using the CUBE argument, the query groups by the specified columns, and it creates additional rows that provide totals for each combination of the columns specified in the GROUP BY clause.

CUBE uses a slightly different syntax from previous versions of SQL Server: CUBE is after the GROUP BY clause, instead of trailing the GROUP BY clause with a WITH CUBE. Notice also that the column lists are contained within parentheses.

■ **Note** The GROUP BY WITH CUBE feature does not follow the ISO standard, and it will be removed in a future version of Microsoft SQL Server. You should avoid using this feature in any new development work, and you should modify any applications that currently use this feature to use the CUBE argument.

5-6. Creating Hierarchical Summaries

Problem

You need to return a data set with the detail data and with subtotals and grand total rows based upon the GROUP BY clause.

Solution

You need to include the ROLLUP argument after the GROUP BY clause. This example uses the ROLLUP argument to produce subtotal lines at the Shelf level, as well as a grand-total line.

```
SELECT i.Shelf,
       p.Name,
       SUM(i.Quantity) AS Total
FROM   Production.ProductInventory i
       INNER JOIN Production.Product p
           ON i.ProductID = p.ProductID
GROUP BY ROLLUP(i.Shelf, p.Name);
```

This query returns the following abridged result set:

```
Shelf       Name               Total
-----       ---------------    ------
A           Adjustable Race    761
A           BB Ball Bearing    909
A           Bearing Ball       791
A           NULL               26833
...
B           Adjustable Race    324
B           BB Ball Bearing    443
B           Bearing Ball       318
B           NULL               12672
...
Y           HL Spindle/Axle    228
Y           LL Spindle/Axle    209
Y           NULL               437
NULL        NULL               335974
```

How It Works

The order you place the columns in the GROUP BY ROLLUP clause affects how data is aggregated. ROLLUP in this query aggregates the total quantity for each change in Shelf. Notice the row with shelf A and the NULL name; this holds the total quantity for shelf A. Also notice that the final row is the grand total of all product quantities. Whereas CUBE creates a result set that aggregates all combinations for the selected columns, ROLLUP generates the aggregates for a hierarchy of values.

```
GROUP BY ROLLUP (i.Shelf, p.Name)
```

ROLLUP aggregated a grand total and totals by shelf. Totals were not generated for the product name but would have been had CUBE been designated instead.

Just as CUBE does, ROLLUP uses slightly different syntax from previous versions of SQL Server. ROLLUP is after the GROUP BY, instead of trailing the GROUP BY clause with a WITH ROLLUP. Notice also that the column lists are contained within parentheses.

■ **Note** The GROUP BY WITH ROLLUP feature does not follow the ISO standard, and it will be removed in a future version of Microsoft SQL Server. You should avoid using this feature in any new development work, and you should modify any applications that currently use this feature to use the ROLLUP argument.

5-7. Creating Custom Summaries

Problem

You need to have one result set with multiple custom aggregations.

Solution

You need to include the GROUPING SETS argument after the GROUP BY clause and include each of the custom aggregations that you want performed.

SQL Server gives you the ability to define your own grouping sets within a single query result set without having to resort to multiple UNION ALLs. GROUPING SETS also provides you with more control over what is aggregated, compared to the previously demonstrated CUBE and ROLLUP operations. This is performed by using the GROUPING SETS operator.

First, I demonstrate by defining an example business requirement for a query. Let's assume I want a single result set to contain three different aggregate quantity summaries. Specifically, I would like to see quantity totals by shelf, quantity totals by shelf and product name, and then also quantity totals by location and name.

To achieve this in previous versions of SQL Server, you would have needed to use the UNION ALL operator.

```
SELECT   NULL AS Shelf,
         i.LocationID,
         p.Name,
         SUM(i.Quantity) AS Total
FROM     Production.ProductInventory i
         INNER JOIN Production.Product p
             ON i.ProductID = p.ProductID
WHERE    Shelf IN ('A', 'C')
         AND Name IN ('Chain', 'Decal', 'Head Tube')
GROUP BY i.LocationID,
         p.Name
UNION ALL
SELECT   i.Shelf,
         NULL,
         NULL,
         SUM(i.Quantity) AS Total
FROM     Production.ProductInventory i
         INNER JOIN Production.Product p
             ON i.ProductID = p.ProductID
WHERE    Shelf IN ('A', 'C')
         AND Name IN ('Chain', 'Decal', 'Head Tube')
GROUP BY i.Shelf
UNION ALL
SELECT   i.Shelf,
         NULL,
         p.Name,
         SUM(i.Quantity) AS Total
FROM     Production.ProductInventory i
         INNER JOIN Production.Product p
             ON i.ProductID = p.ProductID
WHERE    Shelf IN ('A', 'C')
         AND Name IN ('Chain', 'Decal', 'Head Tube')
GROUP BY i.Shelf,
         p.Name;
```

This query returns the following result set:

```
Shelf    LocationID   Name        Total
-----    ----------   ---------   -----
NULL     1            Chain       236
NULL     5            Chain       192
NULL     50           Chain       161
NULL     20           Head Tube   544
A        NULL         NULL        897
C        NULL         NULL        236
A        NULL         Chain       353
C        NULL         Chain       236
A        NULL         Head Tube   544
```

You can save yourself all that extra code by using the GROUPING SETS operator to define the various aggregations you would like to have returned in a single result set:

```
SELECT  i.Shelf,
        i.LocationID,
        p.Name,
        SUM(i.Quantity) AS Total
FROM    Production.ProductInventory i
        INNER JOIN Production.Product p
            ON i.ProductID = p.ProductID
WHERE   Shelf IN ('A', 'C')
        AND Name IN ('Chain', 'Decal', 'Head Tube')
GROUP BY GROUPING SETS((i.Shelf),
                       (i.Shelf, p.Name),
                       (i.LocationID, p.Name));
```

This returns the same result set as the previous query (only ordered a little differently):

```
Shelf    LocationID   Name        Total
-----    ----------   ---------   -----
NULL     1            Chain       236
NULL     5            Chain       192
NULL     50           Chain       161
NULL     20           Head Tube   544
A        NULL         Chain       353
A        NULL         Head Tube   544
A        NULL         NULL        897
C        NULL         Chain       236
C        NULL         NULL        236
```

How It Works

The new GROUPING SETS operator allows you to define varying aggregate groups in a single query while avoiding having multiple queries attached together using the UNION ALL operator. The core of this recipe's example is the following two lines of code:

```
GROUP BY GROUPING SETS
((i.Shelf), (i.Shelf, p.Name), (i.LocationID, p.Name))
```

Notice that unlike a regular aggregated query, the GROUP BY clause is not followed by a list of columns. Instead, it is followed by GROUPING SETS. GROUPING SETS is then followed by parentheses and the groupings of column names, each also encapsulated in parentheses.

5-8. Identifying Rows Generated by the GROUP BY Arguments

Problem

You need to differentiate between the rows that actually have stored NULL data and the rows generated by the GROUP BY arguments that have a NULL generated for that column.

Solution

You need to utilize the GROUPING function in your query.

The following query uses a CASE statement to evaluate whether each row is a total by shelf, total by location, grand total, or regular noncubed row:

```
SELECT   i.Shelf,
         i.LocationID,
         CASE WHEN GROUPING(i.Shelf) = 0
                   AND GROUPING(i.LocationID) = 1 THEN 'Shelf Total'
              WHEN GROUPING(i.Shelf) = 1
                   AND GROUPING(i.LocationID) = 0 THEN 'Location Total'
              WHEN GROUPING(i.Shelf) = 1
                   AND GROUPING(i.LocationID) = 1 THEN 'Grand Total'
              ELSE 'Regular Row'
         END AS RowType,
         SUM(i.Quantity) AS Total
FROM     Production.ProductInventory i
WHERE    LocationID = 2
GROUP BY CUBE(i.Shelf, i.LocationID);
```

This query returns the following result set:

```
Shelf    LocationID   RowType          Total
-----    ----------   --------------   -----
B        2            Regular Row      900
C        2            Regular Row      1557
D        2            Regular Row      3092
NULL     2            Location Total   5549
NULL     NULL         Grand Total      5549
B        NULL         Shelf Total      900
C        NULL         Shelf Total      1557
D        NULL         Shelf Total      3092
```

How It Works

You may have noticed that the rows grouped in the previous recipes have NULL values in the columns that aren't participating in the aggregate totals. For example, when shelf C is totaled up in Recipe 5-6, the location and product name columns are NULL:

```
C NULL NULL 236
```

The NULL values are acceptable if your data doesn't explicitly contain NULLs; however, what if it does? How can you differentiate "stored" NULLs from those generated in the rollups, cubes, and grouping sets? To address this issue, you can use the GROUPING function.

The GROUPING function allows you to differentiate and act upon those rows that are generated automatically for aggregates using CUBE, ROLLUP, and GROUPING SETS. In this example, the SELECT statement starts off normally, with the Shelf and Location columns:

```
SELECT i.Shelf, i.LocationID,
```

Following this is a CASE statement that would evaluate the combinations of return values for the GROUPING statement.

■ **Tip** For more on CASE, see Chapter 2.

When GROUPING returns a 1 value (true), it means the column NULL is not an actual data value but is a result of the aggregate operation, standing in for the value all. So, for example, if the shelf value is not NULL and the location ID is NULL because of the CUBE aggregation process and not the data itself, the string Shelf Total is returned:

```
CASE WHEN GROUPING(i.Shelf) = 0
          AND GROUPING(i.LocationID) = 1 THEN 'Shelf Total'
```

This continues with similar logic, only this time if the shelf value is NULL because of the CUBE aggregation process but the location is not null, a location total is provided:

```
WHEN GROUPING(i.Shelf) = 1
     AND GROUPING(i.LocationID) = 0 THEN 'Location Total'
```

The last WHEN defines when both shelf and location are NULL because of the CUBE aggregation process, which means the row contains the grand total for the result set:

```
WHEN GROUPING(i.Shelf) = 1
     AND GROUPING(i.LocationID) = 1 THEN 'Grand Total'
```

GROUPING returns only a 1 or a 0; however, in SQL Server, you also have the option of using GROUPING_ID to compute grouping at a finer grain, as I demonstrate in the next recipe.

5-9. Identifying Summary Levels

Problem

You need to identify which columns are being considered in the grouping rows added to the result set.

Solution

You need to utilize the GROUPING_ID function in your query.

The following query uses the GROUPING_ID function to return those columns used in the grouping of that particular row:

```
SELECT   i.Shelf,
         i.LocationID,
         i.Bin,
         CASE GROUPING_ID(i.Shelf, i.LocationID, i.Bin)
           WHEN 1 THEN 'Shelf/Location Total'
           WHEN 2 THEN 'Shelf/Bin Total'
           WHEN 3 THEN 'Shelf Total'
           WHEN 4 THEN 'Location/Bin Total'
           WHEN 5 THEN 'Location Total'
           WHEN 6 THEN 'Bin Total'
           WHEN 7 THEN 'Grand Total'
           ELSE 'Regular Row'
         END AS GroupingType,
         SUM(i.Quantity) AS Total
FROM     Production.ProductInventory i
WHERE    i.LocationID IN (3)
         AND i.Bin IN (1, 2)
GROUP BY CUBE(i.Shelf, i.LocationID, i.Bin)
ORDER BY i.Shelf,
         i.LocationID,
         i.Bin;
```

The result set returned from this query has descriptions of the various aggregations CUBE resulted in.

```
Shelf   LocationID   Bin    GroupingType           Total
-----   ----------   ----   --------------------   -----
NULL    NULL         NULL   Grand Total            90
NULL    NULL         1      Bin Total              49
NULL    NULL         2      Bin Total              41
NULL    3            NULL   Location Total         90
NULL    3            1      Location/Bin Total     49
NULL    3            2      Location/Bin Total     41
A       NULL         NULL   Shelf Total            90
A       NULL         1      Shelf/Bin Total        49
A       NULL         2      Shelf/Bin Total        41
A       3            NULL   Shelf/Location Total   90
A       3            1      Regular Row            49
A       3            2      Regular Row            41
```

How It Works

■ **Note** This recipe assumes an understanding of the binary/base-2 number system.

Identifying which rows belong to which type of aggregate becomes progressively more difficult for each new column you add to the GROUP BY clause and for each unique data value that can be grouped and aggregated. For example, this query shows the quantity of products in location 3 within bins 1 and 2:

```
SELECT i.Shelf,
       i.LocationID,
```

```
        i.Bin,
        i.Quantity
FROM    Production.ProductInventory i
WHERE   i.LocationID IN (3)
        AND i.Bin IN (1, 2);
```

This query returns only two rows:

```
Shelf  LocationID  Bin  Quantity
-----  ----------  ---  --------
A      3           2    41
A      3           1    49
```

Now what if we needed to report aggregations based on the various combinations of Shelf, Location, and Bin? We could use CUBE to give summaries of all these potential combinations:

```
SELECT   i.Shelf,
         i.LocationID,
         i.Bin,
         SUM(i.Quantity) AS Total
FROM     Production.ProductInventory i
WHERE    i.LocationID IN (3)
         AND i.Bin IN (1, 2)
GROUP BY CUBE(i.Shelf, i.LocationID, i.Bin)
ORDER BY i.Shelf,
         i.LocationID,
         i.Bin;
```

Although the query returns the various aggregations expected from CUBE, the results are difficult to decipher.

```
Shelf   LocationID  Bin    Total
-----   ----------  ----   -----
NULL    NULL        NULL   90
NULL    NULL        1      49
NULL    NULL        2      41
NULL    3           NULL   90
NULL    3           1      49
NULL    3           2      41
A       NULL        NULL   90
A       NULL        1      49
A       NULL        2      41
A       3           NULL   90
A       3           1      49
A       3           2      41
```

This is where GROUPING_ID comes in handy. Using this function, we can determine the level of grouping for the row. This function is more complicated than GROUPING, however, because GROUPING_ID takes one or more columns as its input and then returns the integer equivalent of the base-2 (binary) number calculation on the columns.

In analyzing the query in the solution, GROUPING_ID takes a column list and returns the integer value of the base-2 binary column list calculation. Stepping through this, the query started off with the list of the three nonaggregated columns to be returned in the result set:

```
SELECT i.Shelf,
       i.LocationID,
       i.Bin,
```

Next, a CASE statement evaluates the return value of GROUPING_ID for the list of the three columns:

```
CASE GROUPING_ID(i.Shelf, i.LocationID, i.Bin)
```

To illustrate the base-2 conversion to integer concept, let's focus on a single row, namely, the row that shows the grand total for shelf A generated automatically by CUBE:

```
Shelf   LocationID      Bin     Total
-----   ----------      ----    -----
NULL    NULL            NULL    90
```

Now envision another row beneath it that shows the bit values being enabled or disabled based on whether the column is a grouping column. Both Location and Bin from GROUPING_ID's perspective have a bit value of 1 because neither of them is a grouping column for this specific row. For this row, Shelf is the grouping column. Let's also add a third row that shows the integer value beneath the flipped bits:

```
Shelf   LocationID   Bin
-----   ----------   ----
A       NULL         NULL
0       1            1
4       2            1
```

Because only the location and bin have enabled bits, we add 1 and 2 to get a summarized value of 3, which is the value returned for this row by GROUPING_ID. So, the various grouping combinations are calculated from binary to integer. In the CASE statement that follows, 3 translates to a shelf total.

Because there are three columns, the various potential aggregations are represented in the following WHENs/THENs:

```
CASE GROUPING_ID(i.Shelf,i.LocationID, i.Bin)
     WHEN 1 THEN 'Shelf/Location Total'
     WHEN 2 THEN 'Shelf/Bin Total'
     WHEN 3 THEN 'Shelf Total'
     WHEN 4 THEN 'Location/Bin Total'
     WHEN 5 THEN 'Location Total'
     WHEN 6 THEN 'Bin Total'
     WHEN 7 THEN 'Grand Total'
ELSE 'Regular Row'
END,
```

Each potential combination of aggregations is handled in the CASE statement. The rest of the query involves using an aggregate function on quantity and then using CUBE to find the various aggregation combinations for the shelf, location, and bin:

```
       SUM(i.Quantity) AS Total
 FROM  Production.ProductInventory i
 WHERE i.LocationID IN (3)
   AND i.Bin IN (1, 2)
 GROUP BY CUBE (i.Shelf, i.LocationID, i.Bin)
 ORDER BY i.Shelf, i.LocationID, i.Bin;
```

CHAPTER 6

Advanced Select Techniques

by Wayne Sheffield

It's easy to return data from a table. What's not so easy is to get the data you need how you need it, utilizing fast, set-based methods. This chapter will show you some of the advanced techniques that can be used when selecting data.

6-1. Avoiding Duplicate Results

Problem

You need to see all of the dates where any employee was hired. However, you have hired multiple employees on the same dates, and you want to see the date only once.

Solution #1

Utilize the DISTINCT clause of the SELECT statement to remove duplicate values.

```
SELECT DISTINCT HireDate
FROM   HumanResources.Employee
ORDER BY HireDate;
```

This query returns the following abridged result set:

```
HireDate
----------
2000-07-31
2001-02-26
2001-12-12
...
2006-05-18
2006-07-01
2006-11-01
2007-04-15
2007-07-01
```

Solution #2

Utilize the GROUP BY clause of the SELECT statement to remove duplicate values.

```
SELECT HireDate
FROM   HumanResources.Employee
GROUP BY HireDate
ORDER BY HireDate;
```

This query returns the same result set.

How It Works

The default behavior of a SELECT statement is to use the ALL keyword (however, because it is the default, you'll rarely see this being used in a query), meaning that all rows will be retrieved and displayed if they exist. Using the DISTINCT keyword instead of ALL allows you to return only unique rows (across columns selected) in your results.

When utilizing the GROUP BY clause, all unique values are grouped together. If all columns in the query are in the GROUP BY clause, the output will not have any duplicate rows.

6-2. Returning the Top *N* Rows

Problem

You want to return only the last five dates where any employee was hired.

Solution

Utilize the TOP clause of the SELECT statement, together with an ORDER BY clause, to return the five most recent dates where an employee was hired.

```
SELECT TOP (5) HireDate
FROM   HumanResources.Employee
GROUP BY HireDate
ORDER BY HireDate DESC;
```

This query returns the following result set:

```
HireDate
----------
2007-07-01
2007-04-15
2006-11-01
2006-07-01
2006-05-18
```

How It Works

The TOP keyword allows you to return the first *n* number of rows from a query based on the number of rows or percentage of rows that you define. The first rows returned are also impacted by how your query is ordered. In this example, we are ordering the results by HireDate descending, so only the first five most recent dates are returned.

The TOP keyword also allows returning a percentage. To return the top 5 percent of the most recent dates any employee was hired, add the PERCENT keyword to the previous query.

```
SELECT TOP (5) PERCENT HireDate
FROM   HumanResources.Employee
GROUP BY HireDate
ORDER BY HireDate DESC;
```

This query returns the following result set:

```
HireDate
----------
2007-07-01
2007-04-15
2006-11-01
2006-07-01
2006-05-18
2005-07-01
2005-03-28
2005-03-18
2005-03-17
```

■ **Note** The parentheses surrounding the expression are required in INSERT, UPDATE, DELETE, and MERGE statements. To maintain backward compatibility, they are optional in SELECT statements, though it is recommended that they be used in order to be consistent across all of the statements in which they are used.

6-3. Renaming a Column in the Output

Problem

Your query has a column that is the result of a function, and you need to assign the column a name. Or, your query joins multiple tables together, and you are returning a column from multiple tables that have the same name.

Solution

Utilize a column alias to specify an alternate name for a column in the result set.

```
SELECT ss.name AS SchemaName,
       TableName = st.name,
       st.object_id ObjectId
FROM sys.schemas AS ss
     JOIN sys.tables st
       ON ss.schema_id = st.schema_id
ORDER BY SchemaName, TableName;
```

This query returns the following abridged result set:

```
SchemaName TableName       ObjectId
---------- --------------- ----------
dbo        AWBuildVersion  469576711
dbo        DatabaseLog     245575913
dbo        ErrorLog        277576027
dbo        MyTestTable     1159675179
dbo        Person          1975678086
dbo        PersonPhone     2039678314
dbo        PhoneNumberType 2007678200
```

■ **Note** The `ObjectId` values returned may be different on your server.

How It Works

In this example, two system views are being queried. Each system view contains a name column. To prevent ambiguity, each column is supplied a column alias.

Note that two methods are shown for providing a column alias. In the first line, the column is aliased by specifying the column being returned, followed by the optional AS keyword, and then followed by the column alias. In the second line, the column alias is specified first, followed by an equals sign, which is followed by the column being returned. The third column utilizes the first method without the optional AS keyword. Either method will work in SQL Server. It should be noted that the AS method is the ANSI standard for column aliases.

6-4. Retrieving Data Directly into Variables

Problem

You need to retrieve data with a query directly into a variable for subsequent use.

Solution

Utilize the SELECT statement to retrieve data from a table and populate a variable with that data.

```
DECLARE @FirstHireDate DATE,
        @LastHireDate DATE;

SELECT @FirstHireDate = MIN(HireDate),
       @LastHireDate = MAX(HireDate)
FROM    HumanResources.Employee;

SELECT @FirstHireDate AS FirstHireDate,
       @LastHireDate AS LastHireDate;
```

This query returns the following result set:

```
FirstHireDate  LastHireDate
-------------  ------------
2000-07-31     2007-07-01
```

How It Works

The variables are initially declared. The first query retrieves the first and last hire dates and populates the variables with these values. The final query returns these variables to be displayed.

6-5. Creating a New Table with the Results from a Query

Problem

You have a query where you need to have the result set from it put into a new table.

Solution

Utilize the INTO clauses of the SELECT statement to create and populate a new table with the results from this query.

```
SELECT *
INTO   #Sales
FROM   Sales.SalesOrderDetail
WHERE  ModifiedDate = '2005-07-01T00:00:00';

SELECT COUNT(*) AS QtyOfRows
FROM   #Sales;
```

This query returns the following result set:

```
QtyOfRows
---------
357
```

How It Works

The SELECT ... INTO statement creates a new table in the default filegroup and then inserts the result set from the query into it. In the previous example, the rows from the Sales.SalesOrderDetail table that were modified on July 1, 2005, are put into the new local temporary table #Sales. You can use a three-part naming sequence to create the table in a different database on the same SQL Server instance. The columns created are in the order of the columns returned in the query, and they have the name of the column as specified in the query (meaning that if you use a column alias, the column alias will be the name of the column). The data types for the columns will be the data type of the underlying column.

There are some limitations with the use of this syntax.

- You cannot create a new table on a different instance or server.
- You cannot create a table variable or a partitioned table.
- Only data and columns are copied; indexes, constraints, and triggers are not copied.
- Use of the ORDER BY clause does not guarantee that the rows will be inserted in that order.
- If a computed column is selected, the column in the new table will not be a computed column. The data in this column will be the result of the computed column.
- New columns that originate from a sparse column will not have the sparse property set.

- The Identity property of a column is applied to the new column, unless one of the following conditions is true:
  - Multiple select statements are joined by using UNION.
  - More than one column in the result set has a column with the Identity property set.
  - The identity column is listed more than once in the select list.
  - The SELECT statement contains a join, contains a GROUP BY, or uses an aggregate function.
  - The identity column is from a remote data source.

If the database is in the simple or bulk-logged recovery model, then the SELECT... INTO statement is minimally logged. For more information about minimally logged operations, see http://msdn.microsoft.com/en-us/library/ms190925.aspx#MinimallyLogged.

6-6. Filtering on the Results from a Subquery

Problem

You need to filter the results from one query based upon the results from another query. For instance, you want to retrieve all of the purchase order numbers for any order where there is a line item unit price between 1,900 and 2,000.

Solution

Utilize a query with a subquery, where the subquery has the results that will be used to be filtered upon by the outer query.

```
SELECT s.PurchaseOrderNumber
FROM   Sales.SalesOrderHeader s
WHERE  EXISTS ( SELECT SalesOrderID
                FROM   Sales.SalesOrderDetail
                WHERE  UnitPrice BETWEEN 1900 AND 2000
                       AND SalesOrderID = s.SalesOrderID );
```

This query returns the following result set:

```
PurchaseOrderNumber
-------------------
PO12586178184
PO10440182311
PO13543119495
PO12586169040
PO2146113582
PO7569171528
PO5858172038
```

How It Works

In this example, the PurchaseOrderNumber column is retrieved from the Sales.SalesOrderHeader table. The individual line items for each order are in the Sales.SalesOrderDetail table. The subquery returns a row if there is a Sales.SalesOrderDetail record with a UnitPrice between 1,900 and 2,000 for the SalesOrderId. If a record exists in the subquery, the outer query will return the PurchaseOrderNumber for that order. If you look at the last line of the subquery, you can see that the SalesOrderId is being related to the SalesOrderId column from the Sales.SalesOrderHeader table. This is an example of a correlated subquery: the values returned depend upon the values of the outer query.

Subqueries can frequently be rewritten into a query with a JOIN condition. You should evaluate each query to see which method achieves the best performance. For instance, the example shown in this recipe can be rewritten to the following format, which returns the same result set:

```
SELECT DISTINCT sh.PurchaseOrderNumber
FROM Sales.SalesOrderHeader AS sh
     JOIN Sales.SalesOrderDetail AS sd
     ON sh.SalesOrderID = sd.SalesOrderID
WHERE sd.UnitPrice BETWEEN 1900 AND 2000;
```

6-7. Selecting from the Results of Another Query

Problem

You have a query that needs to be used as a data source input into another query.

Solution

Make the query into a derived table, and use it in the FROM clause of the second query.

```
SELECT DISTINCT
        s.PurchaseOrderNumber
FROM    Sales.SalesOrderHeader s
        INNER JOIN (SELECT  SalesOrderID
                    FROM    Sales.SalesOrderDetail
                    WHERE   UnitPrice BETWEEN 1900 AND 2000
                   ) dt
            ON s.SalesOrderID = dt.SalesOrderID;
```

This query returns the following result set:

```
PurchaseOrderNumber
-------------------
PO10440182311
PO12586169040
PO12586178184
PO13543119495
PO2146113582
PO5858172038
PO7569171528
```

How It Works

This example's query searches for the PurchaseOrderNumber from the Sales.SalesOrderHeader table for any order that contains products in the Sales.SalesOrderDetails table with a UnitPrice between 1,900 and 2,000. The query joins the Sales.SalesOrderHeader table to a derived table (which is itself a query), which is encapsulated in parentheses and is followed by a table alias (dt).

Since the derived table doesn't require a temporary table to store the results, it can frequently perform better than using temporary tables since you eliminate the steps that SQL Server takes to create, allocate, populate, and destroy the temporary table.

6-8. Passing Rows Through a Function

Problem

You have a table-valued function that you want to utilize in your query.

Solution

Use the APPLY operator in the FROM clause of a query to invoke a table-valued function.

```
CREATE FUNCTION dbo.fn_WorkOrderRouting (@WorkOrderID INT)
RETURNS TABLE
AS
RETURN
       SELECT  WorkOrderID,
               ProductID,
               OperationSequence,
               LocationID
       FROM    Production.WorkOrderRouting
       WHERE   WorkOrderID = @WorkOrderID;
GO

SELECT TOP (5)
       w.WorkOrderID,
       w.OrderQty,
       r.ProductID,
       r.OperationSequence
FROM   Production.WorkOrder w
       CROSS APPLY dbo.fn_WorkOrderRouting(w.WorkOrderID) AS r
ORDER BY w.WorkOrderID,
         w.OrderQty,
         r.ProductID;
```

This query returns the following result set:

```
WorkOrderID OrderQty  ProductID OperationSequence
----------- --------  --------- -----------------
13          4         747       1
13          4         747       2
13          4         747       3
13          4         747       4
13          4         747       6
```

How It Works

First, a table-valued function is created that returns work order routing information for the WorkOrderId passed to it. The query then selects the first five records from the Production.WorkOrder table with two columns from the table-valued function. The next part of the SELECT statement is the key piece of this recipe: in the FROM clause, for each row from the Production.WorkOrder table, the WorkOrderId column is passed to the new fn_WorkOrderRouting function with the CROSS APPLY operator.

Both the left and right operands of the APPLY operator are table sources; the difference is that the right operand can be a table-valued function that accepts a parameter from the left operand. (The left operand can be a table-valued function, but it cannot accept an input to a parameter from the right operand.) The APPLY operator works by applying the right operand against each row of the left operand. Similar to the JOIN operators, the columns being returned from the left operand will be duplicated for each row returned by the right operand.

The CROSS and OUTER clauses of the APPLY operator are used to control how rows are returned in the final result of the two operands when the APPLY operator does not return any rows. Similar to an INNER JOIN, if CROSS APPLY is utilized and the right operand does not return any rows, then that row from the left operand is removed from the result set. And like an OUTER JOIN, if OUTER APPLY is utilized and the right operand does not return any rows, then that row from the left operand is returned with the values of the columns that come from the right operand being set to NULL.

To illustrate the difference between CROSS APPLY and OUTER APPLY, let's add a record to the Production.WorkOrder table.

```
INSERT  INTO Production.WorkOrder
        (ProductID,
         OrderQty,
         ScrappedQty,
         StartDate,
         EndDate,
         DueDate,
         ScrapReasonID,
         ModifiedDate)
VALUES  (1,
         1,
         1,
         GETDATE(),
         GETDATE(),
         GETDATE(),
         1,
         GETDATE());
```

Because this is a new row and the Production.WorkOrder table has an IDENTITY column for the WorkOrderId, the new row will have the maximum WorkOrderId value in the table. Additionally, the new row will not have an associated value in the Production.WorkOrderRouting table because it was just added.

Next, the previous CROSS APPLY query is executed, filtering it to return data for the newly inserted row only.

```
SELECT w.WorkOrderID,
       w.OrderQty,
       r.ProductID,
       r.OperationSequence
FROM   Production.WorkOrder AS w
       CROSS APPLY dbo.fn_WorkOrderRouting(w.WorkOrderID) AS r
WHERE  w.WorkOrderID IN (SELECT  MAX(WorkOrderID)
                         FROM    Production.WorkOrder);
```

This query returns the following result set:

```
WorkOrderID OrderQty ProductID OperationSequence
----------- -------- --------- -----------------
```

Since there isn't a row in the `Production.WorkOrderRouting` table, a row isn't returned by the function. Since a `CROSS APPLY` is being utilized, the absence of a row from the function removes the row from the left operand, resulting in no rows being returned by the query.

Now, change the `CROSS APPLY` to an `OUTER APPLY`.

```
SELECT w.WorkOrderID,
       w.OrderQty,
       r.ProductID,
       r.OperationSequence
FROM   Production.WorkOrder AS w
       OUTER APPLY dbo.fn_WorkOrderRouting(w.WorkOrderID) AS r
WHERE  w.WorkOrderID IN (SELECT  MAX(WorkOrderID)
                         FROM    Production.WorkOrder);
```

This query returns the following result set:

```
WorkOrderID OrderQty ProductID OperationSequence
----------- -------- --------- -----------------
72592       1        NULL      NULL
```

You may have noticed that I have described the left and right operands of the `APPLY` operator as a table source. This means that you do not have to utilize a table-valued function for the right operand; you can use anything that returns a table, such as another `SELECT` statement. For example, the following query returns the same result set as the first example in this recipe without the use of the table-valued function:

```
SELECT TOP (5)
        w.WorkOrderID,
        w.OrderQty,
        r.ProductID,
        r.OperationSequence
FROM    Production.WorkOrder w
        CROSS APPLY (SELECT WorkOrderID,
                            ProductID,
                            OperationSequence,
                            LocationID
                     FROM   Production.WorkOrderRouting
                     WHERE  WorkOrderID = w.WorkOrderId
                    ) AS r
```

```
ORDER BY  w.WorkOrderID,
          w.OrderQty,
          r.ProductID;
```

In this example, we are utilizing the CROSS APPLY operator against a correlated subquery instead of a table-valued function. The only difference in the correlated subquery is that the variable in the WHERE clause has been replaced with the column from the table that was being passed into the table-valued function.

6-9. Returning Random Rows from a Table

Problem

You want to return a sampling of rows from a table.

Solution

Utilize the TABLESAMPLE clause of the SELECT statement.

```
SELECT FirstName,
       LastName
FROM   Person.Person
TABLESAMPLE SYSTEM (2 PERCENT);
```

This query returns the following abridged result set:

```
FirstName    LastName
---------    -----------
Madeline     King
Marcus       King
Maria        King
Anton        Kirilov
Anton        Kirilov
Sandra       Kitt
Christian    Kleinerman
Christian    Kleinerman
Andrew       Kobylinski
Reed         Koch
Reed         Koch
Reed         Koch
```

■ **Note** Because of the random nature of this clause, you will see different results from what is shown.

How It Works

TABLESAMPLE allows you to extract a sampling of rows from a table in the FROM clause. This sampling can be based on a percentage of a number of rows. You can use TABLESAMPLE when only a sampling of rows is necessary for the application instead of a full result set. TABLESAMPLE also provides you with a somewhat randomized result set. Because of this, if you rerun the previous example, you will get different results.

TABLESAMPLE works by extracting a sample of rows from the query result set. In this example, 2 percent of rows were sampled from the Person.Person table. However, don't let the "percent" fool you. That percentage is the *percentage of the table's data pages*. Once the sample pages are selected, all rows for the selected pages are returned. Since the fill state of pages can vary, the number of rows returned will also vary—you'll notice this in the row count returned. If you designate the number of rows, this is actually converted by SQL Server into a percentage, and then the same method used by SQL Server to identify the percentage of data pages is used.

6-10. Converting Rows into Columns

Problem

Your database stores information about your employees, including what department they are assigned to and what shift they work in. You need to produce a report that shows how many employees by department are assigned to each shift for selected departments, with each department being a separate column in the result set.

Solution

Use the PIVOT operator to pivot the department column into columns for each department, and count the employees in each department by shift.

How It Works

We start off this example by first examining the data before it is pivoted.

```
SELECT s.Name AS ShiftName,
       h.BusinessEntityID,
       d.Name AS DepartmentName
FROM   HumanResources.EmployeeDepartmentHistory h
       INNER JOIN HumanResources.Department d
           ON h.DepartmentID = d.DepartmentID
       INNER JOIN HumanResources.Shift s
           ON h.ShiftID = s.ShiftID
WHERE  EndDate IS NULL
       AND d.Name IN ('Production', 'Engineering', 'Marketing')
ORDER BY ShiftName;
```

This query returns the following (abridged) result set:

```
ShiftName  BusinessEntityID  DepartmentName
---------  ----------------  --------------
Day        6                 Engineering
Day        14                Engineering
Day        15                Engineering
Day        16                Marketing
Day        17                Marketing
Day        18                Marketing
Day        25                Production
Day        27                Production
Day        28                Production
...
```

```
Evening    145             Production
Evening    146             Production
Evening    147             Production
...
Night      71              Production
Night      72              Production
Night      73              Production
```

In this result set, we can see that all of the departments are listed in one column. The next step is to pivot the department values returned from this query into columns, along with a count of employees by shift.

```
SELECT ShiftName,
       Production,
       Engineering,
       Marketing
FROM   (SELECT s.Name AS ShiftName,
               h.BusinessEntityID,
               d.Name AS DepartmentName
        FROM   HumanResources.EmployeeDepartmentHistory h
               INNER JOIN HumanResources.Department d
                   ON h.DepartmentID = d.DepartmentID
               INNER JOIN HumanResources.Shift s
                   ON h.ShiftID = s.ShiftID
        WHERE EndDate IS NULL
               AND d.Name IN ('Production', 'Engineering', 'Marketing')
        ) AS a
PIVOT
(
 COUNT(BusinessEntityID)
 FOR DepartmentName IN ([Production], [Engineering], [Marketing])
)  AS b
ORDER BY ShiftName;
```

This query returns the following result set:

```
ShiftName  Production  Engineering  Marketing
---------  ----------- -----------  ---------
Day        79          6            9
Evening    54          0            0
Night      46          0            0
```

In this second query, we utilized the PIVOT operator to shift the specified departments into columns, while simultaneously performing a COUNT aggregation by the shift. The syntax for the PIVOT operator is as follows:

```
FROM table_source
PIVOT  ( aggregate_function ( value_column )
       FOR pivot_column
       IN ( <column_list>)
       ) table_alias
```

Table 6-1 shows the arguments for the PIVOT operator.

Table 6-1. *PIVOT Arguments*

Argument	Description
table_source	The table where the data will be pivoted.
aggregate_function	The aggregate function that will be used against the specified column. COUNT(*) is not allowed.
value_column	The column that will be used in the aggregate function.
pivot_column	The column that will be used to create the column headers.
column_list	The values to pivot from the pivot column.
table_alias	The table alias of the pivoted result set.

Prior to the introduction of the PIVOT operator, a pivot would be performed through aggregations, calculated columns, and the GROUP BY operator. The previous query with the PIVOT operator can be replicated using this method:

```
SELECT s.Name AS ShiftName,
       SUM(CASE WHEN d.Name = 'Production' THEN 1 ELSE 0 END) AS Production,
       SUM(CASE WHEN d.Name = 'Engineering' THEN 1 ELSE 0 END) AS Engineering,
       SUM(CASE WHEN d.Name = 'Marketing' THEN 1 ELSE 0 END) AS Marketing
FROM   HumanResources.EmployeeDepartmentHistory h
       INNER JOIN HumanResources.Department d
           ON h.DepartmentID = d.DepartmentID
       INNER JOIN HumanResources.Shift s
           ON h.ShiftID = s.ShiftID
WHERE  h.EndDate IS NULL
       AND d.Name IN ('Production', 'Engineering', 'Marketing')
GROUP BY s.Name;
```

This query returns the same result set as the query utilizing the PIVOT operator.

One key item to point out in using these pivoting queries is that the values being pivoted must be known in advance. If the values are not known in advance, then the queries have to be constructed dynamically. In looking at the query utilizing the PIVOT operator, the dynamically generated name needs to be used in two places: in the column_list from the outer query and then again in the PIVOT operator; and in this second place the value needs to have the [] brackets for qualifying a name. In the second example (that doesn't utilize the PIVOT operator), the value is used twice, in the same line. When constructing a dynamic pivot, many developers find it easier to work with the second example than the first. (This comparison ignores the department names hard-coded in the WHERE clause in both examples; if the values aren't known, then you would not be utilizing the values.)

6-11. Converting Columns into Rows

Problem

You have a table that has multiple columns for the various phone numbers. You want to normalize this data by converting the columns into rows.

Solution

Utilize the UNPIVOT operator to convert multiple columns of a row to a row for each column.

```
CREATE TABLE dbo.Contact
       (
       EmployeeID INT NOT NULL,
       PhoneNumber1 BIGINT,
       PhoneNumber2 BIGINT,
       PhoneNumber3 BIGINT
       )
GO

INSERT dbo.Contact
       (EmployeeID, PhoneNumber1, PhoneNumber2, PhoneNumber3)
VALUES (1, 2718353881, 3385531980, 5324571342),
       (2, 6007163571, 6875099415, 7756620787),
       (3, 9439250939, NULL, NULL);

SELECT EmployeeID,
       PhoneType,
       PhoneValue
FROM   dbo.Contact c
UNPIVOT
(
 PhoneValue
 FOR PhoneType IN ([PhoneNumber1], [PhoneNumber2], [PhoneNumber3])
)  AS p;
```

This query returns the following result set:

```
EmployeeID  PhoneType     PhoneValue
----------- ------------ ----------
1           PhoneNumber1 2718353881
1           PhoneNumber2 3385531980
1           PhoneNumber3 5324571342
2           PhoneNumber1 6007163571
2           PhoneNumber2 6875099415
2           PhoneNumber3 7756620787
3           PhoneNumber1 9439250939
```

How It Works

The UNPIVOT operator does *almost* the opposite of the PIVOT operator by changing columns into rows. It uses the same syntax as the PIVOT operator, only UNPIVOT is used instead of PIVOT.

This example utilizes UNPIVOT to remove column-repeating groups frequently found in denormalized tables. The first part of this example creates and populates a denormalized table, which has incrementing phone number columns.

The UNPIVOT operator is then utilized to convert the numerous phone number columns into a more normalized form of reusing a single PhoneValue column and having a PhoneType column to identify the type of phone number, instead of repeating the phone number column multiple times.

The UNPIVOT operator starts off with an opening parenthesis. A new column called PhoneValue is created to hold the values from the specified columns. The FOR clause specifies the pivot column (PhoneType) that will be created, and its value will be the name of the column. This is followed by the IN clause, which specifies the columns from the original table that will be consolidated into a single column. Finally, a closing parenthesis is specified, and the UNPIVOT operation is aliased with an arbitrary table alias.

6-12. Reusing Common Subqueries in a Query

Problem

You have a query that utilizes the same subquery multiple times. You have noticed that changes to the subquery are becoming problematic because you occasionally miss making a change to one of the subqueries.

Solution

Utilize a common table expression to define the query once, and reference it in place of the subqueries in your query.

```
WITH cte AS
(
SELECT SalesOrderID
FROM   Sales.SalesOrderDetail
WHERE  UnitPrice BETWEEN 1900 AND 2000
)
SELECT s.PurchaseOrderNumber
FROM   Sales.SalesOrderHeader s
WHERE  EXISTS (SELECT SalesOrderID
               FROM   cte
               WHERE  SalesOrderID = s.SalesOrderID );
```

This query returns the following result set:

```
PurchaseOrderNumber
-------------------
PO12586178184
PO10440182311
PO13543119495
PO12586169040
PO2146113582
PO7569171528
PO5858172038
```

How It Works

A common table expression, commonly referred to by its acronym CTE, is similar to a view or derived query, allowing you to create a temporary query that can be referenced within the scope of a SELECT, INSERT, UPDATE, DELETE, or MERGE statement. Unlike a derived query, you don't need to copy the query definition multiple times for each time it is used. You can also use local variables within a CTE definition—something you can't do in a view definition. The syntax for a CTE is as follows:

```
WITH expression_name [ ( column_name [ , ... n ] ) ] AS ( CTE_query_definition ) [ , ... n ]
```

The arguments of a CTE are described in the Table 6-2.

Table 6-2. *CTE Arguments*

Argument	Description
expression_name	The name of the common table expression
column_name [, ... n]	The unique column names of the expression
CTE_query_definition	The SELECT query that defines the common table expression

There are two forms of CTEs: a *recursive* CTE is one where the query for the CTE references itself. A recursive CTE will be shown in the next recipe. A *nonrecursive* CTE does not reference itself.

In this example, a nonrecursive CTE is created that selects the SalesOrderId column from all records from the Sales.SalesOrderDetail table that have a UnitPrice between 1,900 and 2,000. Later in the query, this CTE is referenced in the EXISTS clause. If this query had used this subquery multiple times, you would simply reference the CTE where necessary while the logic for the subquery is contained just once in the definition of the CTE.

Each time a CTE is referenced, the entire query that makes up the CTE is executed; a CTE does not perform the action once and have the results available for all references to the CTE. If you desire this capability, investigate the Temporary Storage options discussed in Recipe 13-23. To illustrate that CTEs are called each time that they are referenced, let's look at the following queries:

```
SET STATISTICS IO ON;
RAISERROR('CTE #1', 10, 1) WITH NOWAIT;
WITH VendorSearch(RowNumber, VendorName, AccountNumber) AS
(
SELECT  ROW_NUMBER() OVER (ORDER BY Name) RowNum,
        Name,
        AccountNumber
FROM    Purchasing.Vendor
)
SELECT *
FROM VendorSearch;

RAISERROR('CTE #2', 10, 1) WITH NOWAIT;
WITH VendorSearch(RowNumber, VendorName, AccountNumber) AS
(
SELECT  ROW_NUMBER() OVER (ORDER BY Name) RowNum,
        Name,
        AccountNumber
FROM    Purchasing.Vendor
)
SELECT  RowNumber,
        VendorName,
        AccountNumber
FROM    VendorSearch
WHERE   RowNumber BETWEEN 1 AND 5
UNION
SELECT  RowNumber,
        VendorName,
        AccountNumber
```

```
FROM      VendorSearch
WHERE     RowNumber BETWEEN 100 AND 104;
SET STATISTICS IO OFF;
```

In this example, I/O statistics are turned on, and then the same CTE is used in two queries. In the first query, the CTE is referenced once. In the second CTE, it is referenced twice. A message is also displayed at the start of each query. Ignoring the returned result sets, the I/O statistics returned are as follows:

```
CTE #1

Table 'Vendor'. Scan count 1, logical reads 4, physical reads 0, read-ahead reads 0, lob
logical reads 0, lob physical reads 0, lob read-ahead reads 0.

CTE #2

Table 'Vendor'. Scan count 2, logical reads 8, physical reads 0, read-ahead reads 0, lob
logical reads 0, lob physical reads 0, lob read-ahead reads 0.
```

As shown, the first CTE scans the Vendor table once, for four logical reads. The second CTE scans the Vendor table twice, for eight logical reads.

Multiple CTEs can be utilized within one WITH clause; they just need to be separated from each other with a comma. Optionally, column aliases can be defined for the CTE with the definition of the CTE. If column aliases are not defined, then the column names from the query will be utilized. A CTE can reference previously defined CTEs.

■ **Caution** If the CTE is not the first statement in a batch of statements, the previous statement must be terminated with a semicolon.

■ **Note** Terminating a SQL statement with a semicolon is part of the ANSI specifications. Currently, SQL Server does not require most statements to be terminated with a semicolon; however, this practice is deprecated, and its usage will be required in a future version of SQL Server.

6-13. Querying Recursive Tables

Problem

You have a table with hierarchal data where one column references another column in the same table on a different row. You need to query the data to return data for each record from the parent row. For instance, the following builds a company table that contains an entry for each company in a (hypothetical) giant mega-conglomerate:

```
CREATE TABLE dbo.Company
       (
       CompanyID  INT NOT NULL
                  PRIMARY KEY,
       ParentCompanyID INT NULL,
       CompanyName VARCHAR(25) NOT NULL
       );
```

```
INSERT dbo.Company
       (CompanyID, ParentCompanyID, CompanyName)
VALUES (1, NULL, 'Mega-Corp'),
       (2, 1, 'Mediamus-Corp'),
       (3, 1, 'KindaBigus-Corp'),
       (4, 3, 'GettinSmaller-Corp'),
       (5, 4, 'Smallest-Corp'),
       (6, 5, 'Puny-Corp'),
       (7, 5, 'Small2-Corp');
```

Solution

Utilize a *recursive* CTE to create the hierarchy tree.

```
WITH CompanyTree(ParentCompanyID, CompanyID, CompanyName, CompanyLevel) AS
(
SELECT  ParentCompanyID,
        CompanyID,
        CompanyName,
        0 AS CompanyLevel
FROM    dbo.Company
WHERE   ParentCompanyID IS NULL
UNION ALL
SELECT  c.ParentCompanyID,
        c.CompanyID,
        c.CompanyName,
        p.CompanyLevel + 1
FROM    dbo.Company c
        INNER JOIN CompanyTree p
            ON c.ParentCompanyID = p.CompanyID
)
SELECT ParentCompanyID,
       CompanyID,
       CompanyName,
       CompanyLevel
FROM   CompanyTree;
```

This query returns the following result set:

```
ParentCompanyID  CompanyID   CompanyName         CompanyLevel
---------------  ----------- ------------------  ------------
NULL             1           Mega-Corp           0
1                2           Mediamus-Corp       1
1                3           KindaBigus-Corp     1
3                4           GettinSmaller-Corp  2
4                5           Smallest-Corp       3
5                6           Puny-Corp           4
5                7           Small2-Corp         4
```

How It Works

A recursive CTE is created by creating an *anchor* member and then performing a UNION ALL of the *anchor* member to the *recursive* member. The anchor member defines the base of the recursion, in this case, the top level of the corporate hierarchy. The anchor definition is defined first, and this query is joined to the next query through a UNION ALL set operation.

In this example, the anchor definition includes three columns from the Company table and a CompanyLevel column to display how many levels deep a particular company is in the company hierarchy.

The recursive query is defined next. The same three columns are returned from the Company table. The recursion is next; the query is joined to the anchor member by referencing the name of the CTE and specifying the join condition. In this case, the join condition is the expression c.ParentCompanyID = p.CompanyId. Finally, in the column list for this query, the CompanyLevel from the CTE is incremented for the hierarchy level.

After the recursive CTE has been defined, the columns from the CTE are returned in the final query.

Multiple anchor members and recursive members can be defined. All anchor members must be defined before any recursive members. Multiple anchor members can utilize the UNION, UNION ALL, INTERSECT, and EXCEPT set operators. The UNION ALL set operator must be used between the last anchor member and the first recursive member. All recursive members must use the UNION ALL set operator.

If the recursive member contains a value in the joining column that is in the anchor member, then an infinite loop is created. You can utilize the MAXRECURSION query hint to limit the depth of recursions. By default, the serverwide recursion depth default is 100 levels. The value you utilize in the query hint should be based upon your understanding of the data. For example, if you know that your data should not go beyond ten levels deep, then set the MAXRECURSION query hint to that value.

6-14. Hard-Coding the Results from a Query

Problem

In your query, you have a set of constant values that you want to use as a source of data.

Solution

Utilize the VALUES clause to create a table value constructor.

How It Works

The VALUES clause can be used as a source of data in INSERT statements, as the source table in the MERGE statement, and as a derived table in a SELECT statement. An example of using the VALUES clause in an INSERT statement can be seen in the previous recipe when populating the Company table.

An example of using the VALUES clause in a SELECT statement would be if you always referred to the first ten presidents of the United States:

```
SELECT *
FROM (VALUES ('George', 'Washington'),
             ('Thomas', 'Jefferson'),
             ('John', 'Adams'),
             ('James', 'Madison'),
             ('James', 'Monroe'),
             ('John Quincy', 'Adams'),
             ('Andrew', 'Jackson'),
             ('Martin', 'Van Buren'),
```

```
        ('William', 'Harrison'),
        ('John', 'Tyler')
    ) dtPresidents(FirstName, LastName);
```

This query returns the following result set:

```
FirstName     LastName
-----------   ----------
George        Washington
Thomas        Jefferson
John          Adams
James         Madison
James         Monroe
John Quincy   Adams
Andrew        Jackson
Martin        Van Buren
William       Harrison
John          Tyler
```

The syntax for the VALUES clause is as follows:

```
VALUES ( <row value expression list> ) [ , ... n ]

<row value expression list> ::=
    {<row value expression> } [ , ... n ]

<row value expression> ::=
    { DEFAULT | NULL | expression }
```

The VALUES keyword introduces the row value expression list. Each list must start and end with a parenthesis, and multiple lists must be separated with a comma. The maximum number of rows that can be constructed using a table value constructor is 1,000. The table value constructor is equivalent to each list being a separate SELECT statement that is subsequently used with the UNION ALL set operator to make a single result set out of multiple SELECT statements. The number of values specified in each list must be the same, and they follow the data type conversion properties of the UNION ALL set operator, for which unmatched data types between rows are implicitly converted to a type of the next higher precedence. If the conversion cannot be implicitly converted, then an error is returned.

CHAPTER 7

Aggregations and Windowing

by Wayne Sheffield

In this chapter, we will look at several of the built-in functions that are frequently used when querying data for reporting purposes. We'll start off with the aggregate functions in their nonwindowed form. We'll then explore the windowing functions: aggregate functions, ranking functions, analytic functions, and the `NEXT VALUE FOR` sequence generation function.

Aggregate Functions

Aggregate functions are used to perform a calculation on one or more values, resulting in a single value. If your query has any columns with any nonwindowed aggregate functions, then a `GROUP BY` clause is required for the query. Table 7-1 shows the various aggregate functions.

***Table 7-1.** Aggregate Functions*

Function Name	Description
`AVG`	The `AVG` aggregate function calculates the average of non-`NULL` values in a group.
`CHECKSUM_AGG`	The `CHECKSUM_AGG` function returns a checksum value based on a group of rows, allowing you to potentially track changes to a table. For example, adding a new row or changing the value of a column that is being aggregated will usually result in a new checksum integer value. The reason I say "usually" is because there is a possibility that the checksum value does not change even if values are modified.
`COUNT`	The `COUNT` aggregate function returns an integer data type showing the count of rows in a group, including rows with `NULL` values.
`COUNT_BIG`	The `COUNT_BIG` aggregate function returns a `bigint` data type showing the count of rows in a group, including rows with `NULL` values.
`GROUPING`	The `GROUPING` function returns `1` (`True`) or `0` (`False`) depending on whether a `NULL` value is due to a `CUBE`, `ROLLUP`, or `GROUPING SETS` operation. If `False`, the column expression `NULL` value is from the natural data. See Recipe 5-8 for usage of this function.
`MAX`	The `MAX` aggregate function returns the highest value in a set of non-`NULL` values.
`MIN`	The `MIN` aggregate function returns the lowest value in a group of non-`NULL` values.

(*continued*)

***Table 7-1.** (continued)*

Function Name	Description
STDEV	The STDEV function returns the standard deviation of all values provided in the expression based on a sample of the data population.
STDEVP	The STDEVP function also returns the standard deviation for all values in the provided expression, based upon the entire data population.
SUM	The SUM aggregate function returns the summation of all non-NULL values in an expression.
VAR	The VAR function returns the statistical variance of values in an expression based upon a sample of the provided population.
VARP	The VARP function returns the statistical variance of values in an expression based upon the entire data population.

With the exception of the COUNT, COUNT_BIG, and GROUPING functions, all of the aggregate functions have the same syntax (the syntax and usage of the GROUPING function is discussed in Recipe 5-8; the syntax for the COUNT and COUNT_BIG functions is discussed in Recipe 7-2).

```
function_name ( { [ [ ALL | DISTINCT ] expression ] } )
```

where expression is typically the column or calculation that the function will be calculated over. If the optional keyword DISTINCT is used, then only distinct values will be considered. If the optional keyword ALL is used, then all values will be considered. If neither is specified, then ALL is used by default. Aggregate functions and subqueries are not allowed for the expression parameter.

The next few recipes demonstrate these aggregate functions.

7-1. Computing an Average

Problem

You want to see the average rating of your products.

Solution

Use the AVG function to determine an average.

```
SELECT ProductID,
       AVG(Rating) AS AvgRating
FROM   Production.ProductReview
GROUP  BY ProductID;
```

This query produces the following result set:

```
ProductID   AvgRating
---------   ---------
709         5
798         5
937         3
```

How It Works

The AVG aggregate function calculates the average of non-NULL values in a group. To demonstrate the use of DISTINCT, let's compare the columns returned from the following query:

```
SELECT StudentId,
       AVG(Grade) AS AvgGrade,
       AVG(DISTINCT Grade) AS AvgDistinctGrade
FROM  (VALUES (1, 100),
              (1, 100),
              (1, 100),
              (1, 99),
              (1, 99),
              (1, 98),
              (1, 98),
              (1, 95),
              (1, 95),
              (1, 95)
       ) dt (StudentId, Grade)
GROUP BY StudentID;
```

This query produces the following result set:

```
StudentId  AvgGrade  AvgDistinctGrade
---------  --------  ----------------
1          97        98
```

In this example, we have a student with 10 grades. The average of all 10 grades is 97. Within these 10 grades are 4 distinct grades. The average of these distinct grades is 98.

When utilizing the AVG function, the expression parameter must be one of the numeric data types.

7-2. Counting the Rows in a Group

Problem

You want to see the number of products you have in inventory on each shelf for your first five shelves.

Solution

Utilize the COUNT or COUNT_BIG function to return the count of rows in a group.

```
SELECT TOP (5)
       Shelf,
       COUNT(ProductID) AS ProductCount,
       COUNT_BIG(ProductID) AS ProductCountBig
FROM   Production.ProductInventory
GROUP  BY Shelf
ORDER  BY Shelf;
```

This query returns the following result set:

```
Shelf ProductCount ProductCountBig
----- ------------ ---------------
A     81           81
B     36           36
C     55           55
D     50           50
E     85           85
```

How It Works

The COUNT and COUNT_BIG functions are utilized to return a count of the number of items in a group. The only difference between them is the data type returned: COUNT returns an INTEGER, while COUNT_BIG returns a BIGINT. The syntax for these functions is as follows:

```
COUNT | COUNT_BIG ( { [ [ ALL | DISTINCT ] expression ] | * } )
```

The difference between this syntax and the other aggregate functions is the optional asterisk (*) that can be specified. When COUNT(*) is utilized, this specifies that all rows should be counted to return the total number of rows within a table without getting rid of duplicates. COUNT(*) does not use any parameters, so it does not use any information about any column.

When utilizing the COUNT or COUNT_BIG function, the expression parameter can be of any data type except for the text, image, or ntext data type.

7-3. Summing the Values in a Group

Problem

You want to see the total due by account number for orders placed.

Summary

Utilize the SUM function to add up a column.

```
SELECT TOP (5)
       AccountNumber,
       SUM(TotalDue) AS TotalDueByAccountNumber
FROM   Sales.SalesOrderHeader
GROUP BY AccountNumber
ORDER BY AccountNumber;
```

This code returns the following result set:

```
AccountNumber   TotalDueByAccountNumber
--------------  -----------------------
10-4020-000001  95924.0197
10-4020-000002  28309.9672
10-4020-000003  407563.0075
10-4020-000004  660645.9404
10-4020-000005  97031.2173
```

How It Works

The SUM function returns the total of all values in the column being totaled. If the DISTINCT keyword is specified, the total of the distinct values in the column will be returned.

When utilizing the SUM function, the expression parameter must be one of the exact or approximate numeric data types, except for the bit data type.

7-4. Finding the High and Low Values in a Group

Problem

You want to see the highest and lowest ratings given on your products.

Solution

Utilize the MAX and MIN functions to return the highest and lowest ratings.

```
SELECT MIN(Rating) MinRating,
       MAX(Rating) MaxRating
FROM   Production.ProductReview;
```

This query returns the following result set:

```
MinRating  MaxRating
---------  ---------
2          5
```

How It Works

The MAX and MIN functions return the highest and lowest values from the expression being evaluated. Since nonaggregated columns are not specified, a GROUP BY clause is not required.

When utilizing the MAX and MIN functions, the expression parameter can be of any of the numeric, character, uniqueidentifier, or datetime data types.

7-5. Detecting Changes in a Table

Problem

You need to determine whether any changes have been made to the data in a column.

Solution

Utilize the CHECKSUM_AGG function to detect changes in a table.

```
SELECT StudentId,
       CHECKSUM_AGG(Grade) AS GradeChecksumAgg
FROM   (VALUES (1, 100),
               (1, 100),
```

```
                (1, 100),
                (1, 99),
                (1, 99),
                (1, 98),
                (1, 98),
                (1, 95),
                (1, 95),
                (1, 95)
      ) dt (StudentId, Grade)
GROUP BY StudentID;

SELECT StudentId,
       CHECKSUM_AGG(Grade) AS GradeChecksumAgg
FROM   (VALUES (1, 100),
                (1, 100),
                (1, 100),
                (1, 99),
                (1, 99),
                (1, 98),
                (1, 98),
                (1, 95),
                (1, 95),
                (1, 90)
        ) dt (StudentId, Grade)
GROUP BY StudentID;
```

These queries return the following result sets:

```
StudentId  GradeChecksumAgg
---------  ----------------
1          59

StudentId  GradeChecksumAgg
---------  ----------------
1          62
```

How It Works

The CHECKSUM_AGG function returns the checksum of the values in the group, in this case the Grade column. In the second query, the last grade is changed, and when the query is rerun, the aggregated checksum returns a different value.

When utilizing the CHECKSUM_AGG function, the expression parameter must be an integer data type.

■ **Note** Because of the hashing algorithm being used, it is possible for the CHECKSUM_AGG function to return the same value with different data. You should use this only if your application can tolerate occasionally missing a change.

7-6. Finding the Statistical Variance in the Values of a Column

Problem

You need to find the statistical variance of the data values in a column.

Solution

Utilize the VAR or VARP functions to return statistical variance.

```
SELECT VAR(TaxAmt) AS Variance_Sample,
       VARP(TaxAmt) AS Variance_EntirePopulation
FROM   Sales.SalesOrderHeader;
```

This query returns the following result set:

```
Variance_Sample   Variance_EntirePopulation
----------------  -------------------------
1177342.57277401  1177305.15524429
```

How It Works

The VAR and VARP functions return the statistical variance of all the values in the specified expression. VAR returns the value based upon a sample of the data population; VARP returns the value based upon the entire data population.

When utilizing the VAR or VARP functions, the expression parameter must be one of the exact or approximate numeric data types, except for the bit data type.

7-7. Finding the Standard Deviation in the Values of a Column

Problem

You need to see the standard deviation of the data values in a column.

Solution

Utilize the STDEV and STDEVP functions to obtain standard deviation values.

```
SELECT STDEV(UnitPrice) AS StandDevUnitPrice,
       STDEVP(UnitPrice) AS StandDevPopUnitPrice
FROM   Sales.SalesOrderDetail;
```

This query returns the following result set:

```
StandDevUnitPrice StandDevPopUnitPrice
----------------- --------------------
751.885080772954  751.881981921885
```

How It Works

The STDEV or STDEVP functions return the standard deviation of all the values in the specified expression. STDEV returns the value based upon a sample of the data population; STDEVP returns the value based upon the entire data population.

When utilizing the STDEV or STDEVP functions, the expression parameter must be one of the exact or approximate numeric data types, except for the bit data type.

Windowing Functions

SQL Server is designed to work best on sets of data. By definition, sets of data are unordered; it is not until the final ORDER BY clause that the final results of the query become ordered. Windowing functions allow your query to look at only a subset of the rows being returned by your query to apply the function to. In doing so, they allow you to specify an order to your unordered data set before the final result is ordered. This allows for processes that previously required self-joins, use of inefficient inequality operators, or non-set-based row-by-row processing to use set-based processing.

The key to windowing functions is in controlling the order that the rows are evaluated in, when the evaluation is restarted, and what set of rows within the result set to consider for the function (the window of the data set that the function will be applied to). These actions are performed with the OVER clause.

There are four groups of functions that the OVER clause can be applied to; in other words, there are four groups of functions that can be windowed. These groups are the aggregate functions, the ranking functions, the analytic functions, and the sequence function.

The syntax for the OVER clause is as follows:

```
OVER (
    [ <PARTITION BY clause> ]
    [ <ORDER BY clause> ]
    [ <ROW or RANGE clause> ]
   )

<PARTITION BY clause> ::=
PARTITION BY value_expression , ... [ n ]

<ORDER BY clause> ::=
ORDER BY order_by_expression
  [ COLLATE collation_name ]
  [ ASC | DESC ]
  [ ,... n ]

<ROW or RANGE clause> ::=
{ ROWS | RANGE } <window frame extent>

<window frame extent> ::=
{  <window frame preceding>
 | <window frame between>
}

<window frame between> ::=
 BETWEEN <window frame bound> AND <window frame bound>

<window frame bound> ::=
{  <window frame preceding>
 | <window frame following>
}
```

```
<window frame preceding> ::=
{
  UNBOUNDED PRECEDING
 | <unsigned_value_specification> PRECEDING
 | CURRENT ROW
}

<window frame following> ::=
{
  UNBOUNDED FOLLOWING
 | <unsigned_value_specification> FOLLOWING
 | CURRENT ROW
}

<unsigned value specification> ::=
{ <unsigned integer literal> }
```

Table 7-2 explains each of these parameters.

Table 7-2. OVER *Clause Parameters*

Function Name	Description
PARTITION BY	Divides the query result set into partitions. The window function is applied to each partition separately, and computation restarts for each partition.
value_expression	Specifies the column by which the row set is partitioned. value_expression can refer only to columns made available by the FROM clause. value_expression cannot refer to expressions or aliases in the select list. value_expression can be a column expression, scalar subquery, scalar function, or user-defined variable.
ORDER BY clause	Defines the logical order of the rows within each partition of the result set. That is, it specifies the logical order in which the window function calculation is performed. Using the ORDER BY clause in the OVER clause does not control the ordering of the final result set. To guarantee the order of the final result set, you must utilize the ORDER BY clause of the SELECT statement.
order_by_expression	Specifies a column or expression on which to sort. order_by_expression can only refer to columns made available by the FROM clause. An integer cannot be specified to represent a column name or alias.
ROWS | RANGE	Further limits the rows within the partition by specifying start and end points within the partition. This is done by specifying a range of rows with respect to the current row by either logical association or physical association. Physical association is achieved by using the ROWS clause. 1. The ROWS clause limits the rows within a partition by specifying a fixed number of rows preceding or following the current row. Alternatively, the RANGE clause logically limits the rows within a partition by specifying a range of values with respect to the value in the current row. Preceding and following rows are defined based on the ordering in the ORDER BY clause. The window frame RANGE … CURRENT ROW … includes all rows that have the same values in the ORDER BY expression as the current row. For example, ROWS BETWEEN 2 PRECEDING AND CURRENT ROW means that the window of rows that the function operates on is three rows in size, starting with two rows preceding until and including the current row.

(*continued*)

Table 7-2. (*continued*)

Function Name	Description
UNBOUNDED PRECEDING	Specifies that the window starts at the first row of the partition. UNBOUNDED PRECEDING can be specified only as a window starting point.
unsigned value specification PRECEDING	Indicates the number of rows or values to precede the current row. This specification is not allowed for RANGE.
CURRENT ROW	Specifies that the window starts or ends at the current row when used with ROWS or the current value when used with RANGE. CURRENT ROW can be specified as both a starting and ending point.
BETWEEN <window frame bound > AND <window frame bound >	Used with either ROWS or RANGE to specify the lower (starting) and upper (ending) boundary points of the window. <window frame bound> defines the boundary starting point, and <window frame bound> defines the boundary end point. The upper bound cannot be smaller than the lower bound.
UNBOUNDED FOLLOWING	Specifies that the window ends at the last row of the partition. UNBOUNDED FOLLOWING can be specified only as a window end point. For example, RANGE BETWEEN CURRENT ROW AND UNBOUNDED FOLLOWING defines a window that starts with the current row and ends with the last row of the partition.
<unsigned value specification> FOLLOWING	Specified with <unsigned value specification> to indicate the number of rows or values to follow the current row. When <unsigned value specification> FOLLOWING is specified as the window starting point, the ending point must be <unsigned value specification> FOLLOWING. For example, ROWS BETWEEN 2 FOLLOWING AND 10 FOLLOWING defines a window that starts with the second row that follows the current row and ends with the tenth row that follows the current row. This specification is not allowed for RANGE.
unsigned integer literal	Is a positive integer literal (including 0) that specifies the number of rows or values to precede or follow the current row or value. This specification is valid only for ROWS.

Each of the functions allows for and requires various clauses of the OVER clause.

Windowed Aggregate Functions

With the exception of the GROUPING function, all of the aggregate functions can be windowed through the OVER clause. Additionally, the new ROWS | RANGE clause allows you to perform *running aggregations* and *sliding aggregations.*

Most of the recipes in the "Windowed Aggregate Functions" section utilize the following table and data:

```
CREATE TABLE #Transactions
    (
    AccountId INTEGER,
    TranDate DATE,
    TranAmt NUMERIC(8, 2)
    );
INSERT INTO #Transactions
SELECT *
FROM  ( VALUES ( 1, '2011-01-01', 500),
```

```
        ( 1, '2011-01-15', 50),
        ( 1, '2011-01-22', 250),
        ( 1, '2011-01-24', 75),
        ( 1, '2011-01-26', 125),
        ( 1, '2011-01-28', 175),
        ( 2, '2011-01-01', 500),
        ( 2, '2011-01-15', 50),
        ( 2, '2011-01-22', 25),
        ( 2, '2011-01-23', 125),
        ( 2, '2011-01-26', 200),
        ( 2, '2011-01-29', 250),
        ( 3, '2011-01-01', 500),
        ( 3, '2011-01-15', 50 ),
        ( 3, '2011-01-22', 5000),
        ( 3, '2011-01-25', 550),
        ( 3, '2011-01-27', 95 ),
        ( 3, '2011-01-30', 2500)
    ) dt (AccountId, TranDate, TranAmt);
```

7-8. Calculating Totals Based Upon the Prior Row

Problem

You need to calculate the total of a column where the total is the sum of the column through the current row. For instance, for each account, calculate the total transaction amount to date in date order.

Solution

Utilize the SUM function with the OVER clause to perform a running total.

```
SELECT AccountId,
       TranDate,
       TranAmt,
       -- running total of all transactions
       RunTotalAmt = SUM(TranAmt) OVER (PARTITION BY AccountId ORDER BY TranDate)
FROM   #Transactions AS t
ORDER BY AccountId,
       TranDate;
```

This query returns the following result set:

```
AccountId TranDate   TranAmt RunTotalAmt
--------- ---------- ------- -----------
1         2011-01-01 500.00  500.00
1         2011-01-15 50.00   550.00
1         2011-01-22 250.00  800.00
1         2011-01-24 75.00   875.00
1         2011-01-26 125.00  1000.00
1         2011-01-28 175.00  1175.00
2         2011-01-01 500.00  500.00
```

```
2          2011-01-15 50.00    550.00
2          2011-01-22 25.00    575.00
2          2011-01-23 125.00   700.00
2          2011-01-26 200.00   900.00
2          2011-01-29 250.00   1150.00
3          2011-01-01 500.00   500.00
3          2011-01-15 50.00    550.00
3          2011-01-22 5000.00 5550.00
3          2011-01-25 550.00   6100.00
3          2011-01-27 95.00    6195.00
3          2011-01-30 2500.00 8695.00
```

How It Works

The OVER clause, when used in conjunction with the SUM function, allows us to perform a running total of the transaction. Within the OVER clause, the PARTITION BY clause is specified to restart the calculation every time the AccountId value changes. The ORDER BY clause is specified to determine in which order the rows should be calculated. Since the ROWS | RANGE clause is not specified, the default RANGE BETWEEN UNBOUNDED PRECEDING AND CURRENT ROW is utilized. When the query is executed, the TranAmt column from all of the rows prior to and including the current row is summed up and returned.

Running aggregations can be performed over the other aggregate functions also. In this next example, the query is modified to perform running averages, counts, and minimum/maximum calculations.

```
SELECT AccountId,
       TranDate,
       TranAmt,
       -- running average of all transactions
       RunAvg = AVG(TranAmt) OVER (PARTITION BY AccountId ORDER BY TranDate),
       -- running total # of transactions
       RunTranQty = COUNT(*) OVER (PARTITION BY AccountId ORDER BY TranDate),
       -- smallest of the transactions so far
       RunSmallAmt = MIN(TranAmt) OVER (PARTITION BY AccountId ORDER BY TranDate),
       -- largest of the transactions so far
       RunLargeAmt = MAX(TranAmt) OVER (PARTITION BY AccountId ORDER BY TranDate),
       -- running total of all transactions
       RunTotalAmt = SUM(TranAmt) OVER (PARTITION BY AccountId ORDER BY TranDate)
FROM   #Transactions AS t
ORDER BY AccountId,
         TranDate;
```

This query returns the following result set:

```
AccountId TranDate   TranAmt RunAvg     RunTranQty  RunSmallAmt RunLargeAmt RunTotalAmt
--------- ---------- ------- ---------- ----------  ----------- ----------- -----------
1         2011-01-01 500.00  500.000000 1           500.00      500.00      500.00
1         2011-01-15 50.00   275.000000 2           50.00       500.00      550.00
1         2011-01-22 250.00  266.666666 3           50.00       500.00      800.00
1         2011-01-24 75.00   218.750000 4           50.00       500.00      875.00
1         2011-01-26 125.00  200.000000 5           50.00       500.00      1000.00
1         2011-01-28 175.00  195.833333 6           50.00       500.00      1175.00
2         2011-01-01 500.00  500.000000 1           500.00      500.00      500.00
```

```
2          2011-01-15  50.00    275.000000  2         50.00      500.00     550.00
2          2011-01-22  25.00    191.666666  3         25.00      500.00     575.00
2          2011-01-23  125.00   175.000000  4         25.00      500.00     700.00
2          2011-01-26  200.00   180.000000  5         25.00      500.00     900.00
2          2011-01-29  250.00   191.666666  6         25.00      500.00     1150.00
3          2011-01-01  500.00   500.000000  1         500.00     500.00     500.00
3          2011-01-15  50.00    275.000000  2         50.00      500.00     550.00
3          2011-01-22  5000.00  1850.000000 3         50.00      5000.00    5550.00
3          2011-01-25  550.00   1525.000000 4         50.00      5000.00    6100.00
3          2011-01-27  95.00    1239.000000 5         50.00      5000.00    6195.00
3          2011-01-30  2500.00  1449.166666 6         50.00      5000.00    8695.00
```

7-9. Calculating Totals Based Upon a Subset of Rows

Problem

When performing these aggregations, you want only the current row and the two previous rows to be considered for the aggregation.

Solution

Utilize the ROWS clause of the OVER clause.

```
SELECT AccountId,
       TranDate,
       TranAmt,
       -- average of the current and previous 2 transactions
       SlideAvg = AVG(TranAmt)
                  OVER (PARTITION BY AccountId
                            ORDER BY TranDate
                             ROWS BETWEEN 2 PRECEDING AND CURRENT ROW),
       -- total # of the current and previous 2 transactions
       SlideQty = COUNT(*)
                   OVER (PARTITION BY AccountId
                             ORDER BY TranDate
                              ROWS BETWEEN 2 PRECEDING AND CURRENT ROW),
       -- smallest of the current and previous 2 transactions
       SlideMin = MIN(TranAmt)
                   OVER (PARTITION BY AccountId
                            ORDER BY TranDate
                             ROWS BETWEEN 2 PRECEDING AND CURRENT ROW),
       -- largest of the current and previous 2 transactions
       SlideMax = MAX(TranAmt)
                  OVER (PARTITION BY AccountId
                            ORDER BY TranDate
                             ROWS BETWEEN 2 PRECEDING AND CURRENT ROW),
       -- total of the current and previous 2 transactions
       SlideTotal = SUM(TranAmt)
                    OVER (PARTITION BY AccountId
                              ORDER BY TranDate
```

```
                                    ROWS BETWEEN 2 PRECEDING AND CURRENT ROW)
FROM  #Transactions AS t
ORDER BY AccountId,
      TranDate;
```

This query returns the following result set:

AccountId	TranDate	TranAmt	SlideAvg	SlideQty	SlideMin	SlideMax	SlideTotal
1	2011-01-01	500.00	500.000000	1	500.00	500.00	500.00
1	2011-01-15	50.00	275.000000	2	50.00	500.00	550.00
1	2011-01-22	250.00	266.666666	3	50.00	500.00	800.00
1	2011-01-24	75.00	125.000000	3	50.00	250.00	375.00
1	2011-01-26	125.00	150.000000	3	75.00	250.00	450.00
1	2011-01-28	175.00	125.000000	3	75.00	175.00	375.00
2	2011-01-01	500.00	500.000000	1	500.00	500.00	500.00
2	2011-01-15	50.00	275.000000	2	50.00	500.00	550.00
2	2011-01-22	25.00	191.666666	3	25.00	500.00	575.00
2	2011-01-23	125.00	66.666666	3	25.00	125.00	200.00
2	2011-01-26	200.00	116.666666	3	25.00	200.00	350.00
2	2011-01-29	250.00	191.666666	3	125.00	250.00	575.00
3	2011-01-01	500.00	500.000000	1	500.00	500.00	500.00
3	2011-01-15	50.00	275.000000	2	50.00	500.00	550.00
3	2011-01-22	5000.00	1850.000000	3	50.00	5000.00	5550.00
3	2011-01-25	550.00	1866.666666	3	50.00	5000.00	5600.00
3	2011-01-27	95.00	1881.666666	3	95.00	5000.00	5645.00
3	2011-01-30	2500.00	1048.333333	3	95.00	2500.00	3145.00

How It Works

The ROWS clause is added to the OVER clause of the aggregate functions to specify that the aggregate functions should look only at the current row and the previous two rows for their calculations. As you look at each column in the result set, you can see that the aggregation was performed over just these rows (the window of rows that the aggregation is applied to). As the query progresses through the result set, the window slides to encompass the specified rows relative to the current row.

7-10. Using a Logical Window

Problem

You want the rows being considered by the OVER clause to be affected by the value in the column instead of the physical ordering.

Solution

In the OVER clause, utilize the RANGE clause instead of the ROWS option.

```
DECLARE @Test TABLE
        (
         RowID INT IDENTITY,
         FName VARCHAR(20),
         Salary SMALLINT
        );

INSERT INTO @Test (FName, Salary)
VALUES ('George',    800),
       ('Sam',      950),
       ('Diane',     1100),
       ('Nicholas',  1250),
       ('Samuel',    1250),
       ('Patricia',  1300),
       ('Brian',     1500),
       ('Thomas',    1600),
       ('Fran',     2450),
       ('Debbie',    2850),
       ('Mark',     2975),
       ('James',     3000),
       ('Cynthia',   3000),
       ('Christopher', 5000);

SELECT RowID,
       FName,
       Salary,
       SumByRows = SUM(Salary)
                   OVER (ORDER BY Salary
                         ROWS UNBOUNDED PRECEDING),
       SumByRange = SUM(Salary)
                    OVER (ORDER BY Salary
                          RANGE UNBOUNDED PRECEDING)
FROM  @Test
ORDER BY RowID;
```

This query returns the following result set:

```
RowID      FName          Salary       SumByRows     SumByRange
-----      -----------    ------       ---------     ----------
1          George         800          800           800
2          Sam            950          1750          1750
3          Diane          1100         2850          2850
4          Nicholas       1250         4100          5350
5          Samuel         1250         5350          5350
6          Patricia       1300         6650          6650
7          Brian          1500         8150          8150
8          Thomas         1600         9750          9750
9          Fran           2450         12200         12200
10         Debbie         2850         15050         15050
11         Mark           2975         18025         18025
12         James          3000         21025         24025
13         Cynthia        3000         24025         24025
14         Christopher    5000         29025         29025
```

How It Works

When utilizing the RANGE clause, the SUM function adjusts its window based upon the values in the specified column. The previous example shows the salary of your employees, and the SUM function is performing a running total of the salaries in order of the salary. For comparison purposes, the running total is being calculated with both the ROWS and RANGE clauses. There are two groups of employees that have the same salary: RowIDs 4 and 5 are both 1,250, and 12 and 13 are both 3,000. When the running total is calculated with the ROWS clause, you can see that the salary of the current row is being added to the prior total of the previous rows. However, when the RANGE clause is used, all of the rows that contain the value of the current row are totaled and added to the total of the previous value. The result is that for rows 4 and 5, both employees with a salary of 1,250 are added together for the running total (and this action is repeated for rows 12 and 13).

Ranking Functions

Ranking functions allow you to return a ranking value associated to each row in a partition of a result set. Depending on the function used, multiple rows may receive the same value within the partition, and there may be gaps between assigned numbers. Table 7-3 describes the four ranking functions.

Table 7-3. *Ranking Functions*

Function	Description
ROW_NUMBER	ROW_NUMBER returns an incrementing integer for each row within a partition of a set.
RANK	Similar to ROW_NUMBER, RANK increments its value for each row within a partition of the set. The key difference is if rows with tied values exist within the partition, they will receive the same rank value, and the next value will receive the rank value as if there had been no ties, producing a gap between assigned numbers.
DENSE_RANK	The difference between DENSE_RANK and RANK is that DENSE_RANK doesn't have gaps in the rank values when there are tied values; the next value has the next rank assignment.
NTILE	NTILE divides the result set into a specified number of groups, based on the ordering and optional partition clause.

The syntax of the ranking functions is as follows:

```
ROW_NUMBER ( ) | RANK ( ) | DENSE_RANK ( ) | NTILE (integer_expression)
    OVER ( [ PARTITION BY value_expression , ... [ n ] ] order_by_clause )
```

where the optional PARTITION BY clause is a list of columns that control when to restart the numbering. If the PARTITION BY clause isn't specified, all of the rows in the result set are treated as one partition. The ORDER BY clause determines the order in which the rows within a partition are assigned their unique row number value. For the NTILE function, the integer_expression is a positive integer constant expression.

7-11. Generating an Incrementing Row Number

Problem

You need to have a query return total sales information. You need to assign a row number to each row in order of the date of the order, and the numbering needs to start over for each account number.

Solution

Utilize the ROW_NUMBER function to assign row numbers to each row.

```
SELECT TOP 10
       AccountNumber,
       OrderDate,
       TotalDue,
       ROW_NUMBER() OVER (PARTITION BY AccountNumber ORDER BY OrderDate) AS RN
FROM   Sales.SalesOrderHeader
ORDER BY AccountNumber;
```

This query returns the following result set:

```
AccountNumber   OrderDate                TotalDue      RN
--------------  -----------------------  -----------   --
10-4020-000001  2005-08-01 00:00:00.000  12381.0798    1
10-4020-000001  2005-11-01 00:00:00.000  22152.2446    2
10-4020-000001  2006-02-01 00:00:00.000  31972.1684    3
10-4020-000001  2006-05-01 00:00:00.000  29418.5269    4
10-4020-000002  2006-08-01 00:00:00.000  8727.1055     1
10-4020-000002  2006-11-01 00:00:00.000  4682.6908     2
10-4020-000002  2007-02-01 00:00:00.000  1485.918      3
10-4020-000002  2007-05-01 00:00:00.000  1668.3751     4
10-4020-000002  2007-08-01 00:00:00.000  3478.1096     5
10-4020-000002  2007-11-01 00:00:00.000  3941.9843     6
```

How It Works

The ROW_NUMBER function is utilized to generate a row number for each row in the partition. The PARTITION_BY clause is utilized to restart the number generation for each change in the AccountNumber column. The ORDER_BY clause is utilized to order the numbering of the rows in the order of the OrderDate column.

You can also utilize the ROW_NUMBER function to create a virtual *numbers*, or *tally*, table.

Note A numbers, or tally, table is simply a table of sequential numbers, and it can be utilized to eliminate loops. Use your favorite Internet search tool to find information about what the numbers or tally table is and how it can replace loops. One excellent article is at www.sqlservercentral.com/articles/T-SQL/62867/.

For instance, the sys.all_columns system view has more than 8,000 rows. You can utilize this to easily build a numbers table with this code:

```
SELECT ROW_NUMBER() OVER (ORDER BY (SELECT NULL)) AS RN
FROM   sys.all_columns;
```

This query will produce a row number for each row in the sys.all_columns view. In this instance, the ordering doesn't matter, but it is required, so the ORDER BY clause is specified as "(SELECT NULL)". If you need more records than what are available in this table, you can simply cross join this table to itself, which will produce more than 64 million rows.

In this example, a table scan is required. Another method is to produce the numbers or tally table by utilizing constants. The following example creates a one million row virtual tally table without incurring any disk I/O operations:

```
WITH
TENS      (N) AS (SELECT 0 UNION ALL SELECT 0 UNION ALL SELECT 0 UNION ALL
                  SELECT 0 UNION ALL SELECT 0 UNION ALL SELECT 0 UNION ALL
                  SELECT 0 UNION ALL SELECT 0 UNION ALL SELECT 0 UNION ALL SELECT 0),
THOUSANDS (N) AS (SELECT 1 FROM TENS t1 CROSS JOIN TENS t2 CROSS JOIN TENS t3),
MILLIONS  (N) AS (SELECT 1 FROM THOUSANDS t1 CROSS JOIN THOUSANDS t2),
TALLY     (N) AS (SELECT ROW_NUMBER() OVER (ORDER BY (SELECT 0)) FROM MILLIONS)
SELECT N
FROM   TALLY;
```

7-12. Returning Rows by Rank

Problem

You want to rank your salespeople based upon their sales quota.

Solution

Utilize the RANK function to rank your salespeople.

```
SELECT BusinessEntityID,
       QuotaDate,
       SalesQuota,
       RANK() OVER (ORDER BY SalesQuota DESC) AS RANK
FROM   Sales.SalesPersonQuotaHistory
WHERE  SalesQuota BETWEEN 266000.00 AND 319000.00;
```

This query returns the following result set:

```
BusinessEntityID   QuotaDate                 SalesQuota   RANK
----------------   -----------------------   ----------   ----
280                2007-07-01 00:00:00.000   319000.00    1
284                2007-04-01 00:00:00.000   304000.00    2
280                2006-04-01 00:00:00.000   301000.00    3
282                2007-01-01 00:00:00.000   288000.00    4
283                2007-04-01 00:00:00.000   284000.00    5
284                2007-01-01 00:00:00.000   281000.00    6
278                2008-01-01 00:00:00.000   280000.00    7
283                2006-01-01 00:00:00.000   280000.00    7
283                2006-04-01 00:00:00.000   267000.00    9
278                2006-01-01 00:00:00.000   266000.00    10
```

How It Works

RANK assigns a ranking value to each row within a partition. If multiple rows within the partition tie with the same value, they are assigned the same ranking value (see rank 7 in the example). When there is a tie, the following value has a ranking value assigned as if none of the previous rows had ties. If there are no ties in the partition, the ranking value assigned is the same as if the ROW_NUMBER function had been used with the same OVER clause definition.

7-13. Returning Rows by Rank Without Gaps

Problem

You want to rank your salespeople based upon their sales quota without any gaps in the ranking value assigned.

Solution

Utilize the DENSE_RANK function to rank your salespeople without gaps.

```
SELECT BusinessEntityID,
       QuotaDate,
       SalesQuota,
       DENSE_RANK() OVER (ORDER BY SalesQuota DESC) AS DENSERANK
FROM   Sales.SalesPersonQuotaHistory
WHERE  SalesQuota BETWEEN 266000.00 AND 319000.00;
```

This query returns the following result set:

```
BusinessEntityID   QuotaDate                 SalesQuota   DENSERANK
----------------   -----------------------   ----------   ---------
280                2007-07-01 00:00:00.000   319000.00    1
284                2007-04-01 00:00:00.000   304000.00    2
280                2006-04-01 00:00:00.000   301000.00    3
282                2007-01-01 00:00:00.000   288000.00    4
283                2007-04-01 00:00:00.000   284000.00    5
284                2007-01-01 00:00:00.000   281000.00    6
278                2008-01-01 00:00:00.000   280000.00    7
283                2006-01-01 00:00:00.000   280000.00    7
283                2006-04-01 00:00:00.000   267000.00    8
278                2006-01-01 00:00:00.000   266000.00    9
```

How It Works

DENSE_RANK assigns a ranking value to each row within a partition. If multiple rows within the partition tie with the same value, they are assigned the same ranking value (see rank 7 in the example). When there is a tie, the following value has the next ranking value assigned. If there are no ties in the partition, the ranking value assigned is the same as if the ROW_NUMBER function had been used with the same OVER clause definition.

7-14. Sorting Rows into Buckets

Problem

You want to split your salespeople up into four groups based upon their sales quota.

Solution

Utilize the NTILE function, and specify the number of groups to divide the result set into.

```
SELECT BusinessEntityID,
       QuotaDate,
       SalesQuota,
       NTILE(4) OVER (ORDER BY SalesQuota DESC) AS [NTILE]
FROM   Sales.SalesPersonQuotaHistory
WHERE  SalesQuota BETWEEN 266000.00 AND 319000.00;
```

This query produces the following result set:

```
BusinessEntityID  QuotaDate                SalesQuota  NTILE
----------------  -----------------------  ----------  -----
280               2007-07-01 00:00:00.000  319000.00   1
284               2007-04-01 00:00:00.000  304000.00   1
280               2006-04-01 00:00:00.000  301000.00   1
282               2007-01-01 00:00:00.000  288000.00   2
283               2007-04-01 00:00:00.000  284000.00   2
284               2007-01-01 00:00:00.000  281000.00   2
278               2008-01-01 00:00:00.000  280000.00   3
283               2006-01-01 00:00:00.000  280000.00   3
283               2006-04-01 00:00:00.000  267000.00   4
278               2006-01-01 00:00:00.000  266000.00   4
```

How It Works

The NTILE function divides the result set into the specified number of groups based upon the partitioning and ordering specified in the OVER clause. Notice that the first two groups have three rows in that group, and the final two groups have two. If the number of rows in the result set is not evenly divisible by the specified number of groups, then the leading groups will have one extra row assigned to that group until the remainder has been accommodated.

7-15. Grouping Logically Consecutive Rows Together

Problem

You need to group logically consecutive rows together so that subsequent calculations can treat those rows identically. For instance, your manufacturing plant utilizes RFID tags to track the movement of your products. During the manufacturing process, a product may be rejected and sent back to an earlier part of the process to be corrected. You want to track the number of trips that a tag makes to an area. However, you have multiple sensors to detect the tags in your larger areas, so multiple consecutive hits from different sensors can be entered in the system. These consecutive entries need to be considered together based upon the time in the same area and should be treated as the same trip in your results.

This recipe will utilize the following data:

```
DECLARE @RFID_Location TABLE (
    TagId INTEGER,
    Location VARCHAR(25),
    SensorDate DATETIME);
INSERT INTO @RFID_Location
        (TagId, Location, SensorDate)
VALUES  (1, 'Room1', '2012-01-10T08:00:01'),
        (1, 'Room1', '2012-01-10T08:18:32'),
        (1, 'Room2', '2012-01-10T08:25:42'),
        (1, 'Room3', '2012-01-10T09:52:48'),
        (1, 'Room2', '2012-01-10T10:05:22'),
        (1, 'Room3', '2012-01-10T11:22:15'),
        (1, 'Room4', '2012-01-10T14:18:58'),
        (2, 'Room1', '2012-01-10T08:32:18'),
        (2, 'Room1', '2012-01-10T08:51:53'),
        (2, 'Room2', '2012-01-10T09:22:09'),
        (2, 'Room1', '2012-01-10T09:42:17'),
        (2, 'Room1', '2012-01-10T09:59:16'),
        (2, 'Room2', '2012-01-10T10:35:18'),
        (2, 'Room3', '2012-01-10T11:18:42'),
        (2, 'Room4', '2012-01-10T15:22:18');
```

Solution

Utilize two `ROW_NUMBER` functions, differing only in that the last column in the `PARTITION BY` clause has an extra column. The difference between these results will group logically consecutive rows together.

```
WITH cte AS
(
SELECT TagId, Location, SensorDate,
       ROW_NUMBER()
       OVER (PARTITION BY TagId
                   ORDER BY SensorDate) -
       ROW_NUMBER()
       OVER (PARTITION BY TagId, Location
             ORDER BY SensorDate) AS Grp
FROM  @RFID_Location
)
SELECT TagId, Location, SensorDate, Grp,
       DENSE_RANK()
       OVER (PARTITION BY TagId, Location
                   ORDER BY Grp) AS TripNbr
FROM   cte
ORDER BY TagId, SensorDate;
```

This query returns the following result set:

```
TagId   Location   SensorDate                Grp    TripNbr
-----   --------   -----------------------   ---    -------
1       Room1      2012-01-10 08:00:01.000   0      1
1       Room1      2012-01-10 08:18:32.000   0      1
1       Room2      2012-01-10 08:25:42.000   2      1
1       Room3      2012-01-10 09:52:48.000   3      1
1       Room2      2012-01-10 10:05:22.000   3      2
1       Room3      2012-01-10 11:22:15.000   4      2
1       Room4      2012-01-10 14:18:58.000   6      1
2       Room1      2012-01-10 08:32:18.000   0      1
2       Room1      2012-01-10 08:51:53.000   0      1
2       Room2      2012-01-10 09:22:09.000   2      1
2       Room1      2012-01-10 09:42:17.000   1      2
2       Room1      2012-01-10 09:59:16.000   1      2
2       Room2      2012-01-10 10:35:18.000   4      2
2       Room3      2012-01-10 11:18:42.000   6      1
2       Room4      2012-01-10 15:22:18.000   7      1
```

How It Works

The first ROW_NUMBER function partitions the result set by the TagId and assigns the row number as ordered by the SensorDate. The second ROW_NUMBER function partitions the result set by the TagId and Location and assigns the row number as ordered by the SensorDate. The difference between these will assign consecutive rows in the same location as the same Grp number. The previous results show that consecutive entries in the same location are assigned the same Grp number. The following query breaks the ROW_NUMBER functions down into individual columns so that you can see how this is performed:

```
WITH cte AS
(
SELECT TagId, Location, SensorDate,
       ROW_NUMBER()
       OVER (PARTITION BY TagId
                 ORDER BY SensorDate) AS RN1,
       ROW_NUMBER()
       OVER (PARTITION BY TagId, Location
                 ORDER BY SensorDate) AS RN2
FROM   @RFID_Location
)
SELECT TagId, Location, SensorDate,
       RN1, RN2, RN1-RN2 AS Grp
FROM   cte
ORDER BY TagId, SensorDate;
```

This query returns the following result set:

```
TagId  Location  SensorDate               RN1  RN2  Grp
------ --------  -----------------------  ---  ---  ---
1      Room1     2012-01-10 08:00:01.000  1    1    0
1      Room1     2012-01-10 08:18:32.000  2    2    0
1      Room2     2012-01-10 08:25:42.000  3    1    2
1      Room3     2012-01-10 09:52:48.000  4    1    3
1      Room2     2012-01-10 10:05:22.000  5    2    3
1      Room3     2012-01-10 11:22:15.000  6    2    4
1      Room4     2012-01-10 14:18:58.000  7    1    6
2      Room1     2012-01-10 08:32:18.000  1    1    0
2      Room1     2012-01-10 08:51:53.000  2    2    0
2      Room2     2012-01-10 09:22:09.000  3    1    2
2      Room1     2012-01-10 09:42:17.000  4    3    1
2      Room1     2012-01-10 09:59:16.000  5    4    1
2      Room2     2012-01-10 10:35:18.000  6    2    4
2      Room3     2012-01-10 11:18:42.000  7    1    6
2      Room4     2012-01-10 15:22:18.000  8    1    7
```

With this query, you can see that for each TagId, the RN1 column is sequentially numbered from 1 to the number of rows for that TagId. For the RN2 column, the Location is added to the PARTITION BY clause, resulting in the assigned row numbers being restarted every time the location changes. By looking at this result set, you can see that subtracting RN2 from RN1 returns a number where each trip to a location has a higher number than the previous trip, and consecutive reads in the same location are treated the same. It doesn't matter that the calculated Grp column is not consecutive; it is the fact that it increases from the prior trip to this location that is critical. To handle calculating the trips, the DENSE_RANK function is utilized so that there will not be any gaps. The following query takes the first example and adds in the RANK function to illustrate the difference.

```
WITH cte AS

(
SELECT TagId, Location, SensorDate,
       ROW_NUMBER()
       OVER (PARTITION BY TagId
                 ORDER BY SensorDate) -
       ROW_NUMBER()
       OVER (PARTITION BY TagId, Location
                 ORDER BY SensorDate) AS Grp
FROM  @RFID_Location
)

SELECT TagId, Location, SensorDate, Grp,
       DENSE_RANK()
       OVER (PARTITION BY TagId, Location
                 ORDER BY Grp) AS TripNbr,
       RANK()
       OVER (PARTITION BY TagId, Location
                 ORDER BY Grp) AS TripNbrRank
FROM   cte
ORDER BY TagId, SensorDate;
```

This query returns the following result set:

```
TagId  Location  SensorDate               Grp  TripNbr  TripNbrRank
-----  --------  -----------------------  ---  -------  -----------
1      Room1     2012-01-10 08:00:01.000  0    1        1
1      Room1     2012-01-10 08:18:32.000  0    1        1
1      Room2     2012-01-10 08:25:42.000  2    1        1
1      Room3     2012-01-10 09:52:48.000  3    1        1
1      Room2     2012-01-10 10:05:22.000  3    2        2
1      Room3     2012-01-10 11:22:15.000  4    2        2
1      Room4     2012-01-10 14:18:58.000  6    1        1
2      Room1     2012-01-10 08:32:18.000  0    1        1
2      Room1     2012-01-10 08:51:53.000  0    1        1
2      Room2     2012-01-10 09:22:09.000  2    1        1
2      Room1     2012-01-10 09:42:17.000  1    2        3
2      Room1     2012-01-10 09:59:16.000  1    2        3
2      Room2     2012-01-10 10:35:18.000  4    2        2
2      Room3     2012-01-10 11:18:42.000  6    1        1
2      Room4     2012-01-10 15:22:18.000  7    1        1
```

In this query, you can see how the RANK function returns the wrong trip number for TagId 2 for the second trip to Room1 (the fourth and fifth rows for this tag).

Analytic Functions

New to SQL Server 2012 are the analytic functions. Analytic functions compute an aggregate value on a group of rows. In contrast to the aggregate functions, they can return multiple rows for each group. Table 7-4 describes the analytic functions.

Table 7-4. *Analytic Functions*

Function	Description
CUME_DIST	CUME_DIST calculates the cumulative distribution of a value in a group of values. The cumulative distribution is the relative position of a specified value in a group of values.
FIRST_VALUE	Returns the first value from an ordered set of values.
LAG	Retrieves data from a previous row in the same result set as specified by a row offset from the current row.
LAST_VALUE	Returns the last value from an ordered set of values.
LEAD	Retrieves data from a subsequent row in the same result set as specified by a row offset from the current row.
PERCENTILE_CONT	Calculates a percentile based on a continuous distribution of the column value. The value returned may or may not be equal to any of the specific values in the column.
PERCENTILE_DISC	Computes a specific percentile for sorted values in the result set. The value returned will be the value with the smallest CUME_DIST value (for the same sort specification) that is greater than or equal to the specified percentile. The value returned will be equal to one of the values in the specific column.
PERCENT_RANK	Computes the relative rank of a row within a set.

The analytic functions come in complementary pairs and will be discussed in this manner.

7-16. Accessing Values from Other Rows

Problem

You need to write a sales summary report that shows the total due from orders by year and quarter. You want to include a difference between the current quarter and prior quarter, as well as a difference between the current quarter of this year and the same quarter of the previous year.

Solution

Aggregate the total due by year and quarter, and utilize the LAG function to look at the previous records.

```
WITH cte AS
(
SELECT DATEPART(QUARTER, OrderDate) AS Qtr,
       DATEPART(YEAR, OrderDate) AS Yr,
       TotalDue
FROM   Sales.SalesOrderHeader
), cteAgg AS
(
SELECT Yr,
       Qtr,
       SUM(TotalDue) AS TotalDue
FROM   cte
GROUP BY Yr, Qtr
)
SELECT Yr,
       Qtr,
       TotalDue,
       TotalDue - LAG(TotalDue, 1, NULL)
                  OVER (ORDER BY Yr, Qtr) AS DeltaPriorQtr,
       TotalDue - LAG(TotalDue, 4, NULL)
                  OVER (ORDER BY Yr, Qtr) AS DeltaPriorYrQtr
FROM   cteAgg
ORDER BY Yr, Qtr;
```

This query returns the following result set:

```
Yr      Qtr    TotalDue        DeltaPriorQtr    DeltaPriorYrQtr
----    ---    -------------   -------------    ---------------
2005    3      5203127.8807    NULL             NULL
2005    4      7490122.7457    2286994.865      NULL
2006    1      6562121.6796    -928001.0661     NULL
2006    2      6947995.43      385873.7504      NULL
2006    3      11555907.1472   4607911.7172     6352779.2665
2006    4      9397824.1785    -2158082.9687    1907701.4328
2007    1      7492396.3224    -1905427.8561    930274.6428
2007    2      9379298.7027    1886902.3803     2431303.2727
```

```
2007   3      15413231.8434   6033933.1407     3857324.6962
2007   4      14886562.6775   -526669.1659     5488738.499
2008   1      12744940.3554   -2141622.3221    5252544.033
2008   2      16087078.2305   3342137.8751     6707779.5278
2008   3      56178.9223      -16030899.3082   -15357052.9211
```

How It Works

The first CTE is utilized to retrieve the year and quarter from the `OrderDate` column and to pass the `TotalDue` column to the rest of the query. The second CTE is used to aggregate the `TotalDue` column, grouping on the extracted `Yr` and `Qtr` columns. The final `SELECT` statement returns these aggregated values and then makes two calls to the `LAG` function. The first call retrieves the `TotalDue` column from the previous row in order to compute the difference between the current quarter and the previous quarter. The second call retrieves the `TotalDue` column from four rows prior to the current row in order to compute the difference between the current quarter and the same quarter one year ago.

The `LEAD` function works in a similar manner. In this example, a table is created that has gaps in the column. The table is then queried, comparing the value in the current row to the value in the next row. If the difference is greater than 1, then a gap exists and is returned in the result set. This solution is based on a method that I learned from Itzik Ben-Gan.

```
DECLARE @Gaps TABLE (col1 int PRIMARY KEY CLUSTERED);

INSERT INTO @Gaps (col1)
VALUES (1), (2), (3),
       (50), (51), (52), (53), (54), (55),
       (100), (101), (102),
       (500),
       (950), (951), (952),
       (954);

-- Compare the value of the current row to the next row.
-- If > 1, then there is a gap.
WITH cte AS
(
SELECT col1 AS CurrentRow,
       LEAD(col1, 1, NULL)
       OVER (ORDER BY col1) AS NextRow
FROM   @Gaps
)
SELECT cte.CurrentRow + 1 AS [Start of Gap],
       cte.NextRow - 1 AS [End of Gap]
FROM   cte
WHERE  cte.NextRow - cte.CurrentRow > 1;
```

This query returns the following result set:

```
Start of Gap  End of Gap
------------  ----------
4             49
56            99
103           499
501           949
953           953
```

The syntax for the LAG and LEAD functions is as follows:

```
LAG | LEAD (scalar_expression [,offset] [,default])
    OVER ( [ partition_by_clause ] order_by_clause )
```

Where scalar_expression is an expression of any type that returns a scalar value (typically a column), offset is the number of rows to offset the current row by, and default is the value to return if the value returned is NULL. The default value for offset is 1, and the default value for default is NULL.

7-17. Accessing the First or Last Value from a Partition

Problem

You need to write a report that shows, for each customer, the date that they placed their least and most expensive orders.

Solution

Utilize the FIRST_VALUE and LAST_VALUE functions.

```
SELECT DISTINCT TOP (5)
       CustomerID,
       FIRST_VALUE(OrderDate)
       OVER (PARTITION BY CustomerID
                 ORDER BY TotalDue
                  ROWS BETWEEN UNBOUNDED PRECEDING
                          AND UNBOUNDED FOLLOWING) AS OrderDateLow,
       LAST_VALUE(OrderDate)
       OVER (PARTITION BY CustomerID
                 ORDER BY TotalDue
                  ROWS BETWEEN UNBOUNDED PRECEDING
                          AND UNBOUNDED FOLLOWING) AS OrderDateHigh
FROM   Sales.SalesOrderHeader
ORDER BY CustomerID;
```

This query returns the following result set for the first five customers:

```
CustomerID  OrderDateLow             OrderDateHigh
----------- ----------------------- -----------------------
11000       2007-07-22 00:00:00.000 2005-07-22 00:00:00.000
11001       2008-06-12 00:00:00.000 2005-07-18 00:00:00.000
11002       2007-07-04 00:00:00.000 2005-07-10 00:00:00.000
11003       2007-07-09 00:00:00.000 2005-07-01 00:00:00.000
11004       2007-07-26 00:00:00.000 2005-07-26 00:00:00.000
```

How It Works

The FIRST_VALUE and LAST_VALUE functions are used to return the OrderDate for the first and last rows in the partition. The window is set to a partition of the CustomerID, ordered by the TotalDue, and the ROWS clause is used to specify all of the rows for the partition (CustomerId). The syntax for the FIRST_VALUE and LAST_VALUE functions is as follows:

```
FIRST_VALUE ( scalar_expression )
    OVER ( [ partition_by_clause ] order_by_clause [ rows_range_clause ] )
```

where scalar_expression is an expression of any type that returns a scalar value (typically a column).

7-18. Calculating the Relative Position or Rank of a Value in a Set of Values

Problem

You want to know the relative position and rank of a customer's order by the total of the order in respect to the total of all the customers' orders.

Solution

Utilize the CUME_DIST and PERCENT_RANK functions to obtain the relative position of a value and the relative rank of a value.

```
SELECT CustomerID,
       CUME_DIST()
       OVER (PARTITION BY CustomerID
                 ORDER BY TotalDue) AS CumeDistOrderTotalDue,
       PERCENT_RANK()
       OVER (PARTITION BY CustomerID
                 ORDER BY TotalDue) AS PercentRankOrderTotalDue
FROM   Sales.SalesOrderHeader
ORDER BY CustomerID;
```

This code returns the following abridged result set:

```
CustomerID   CumeDistOrderTotalDue      PercentRankOrderTotalDue
----------   ---------------------      ------------------------
30116        0.25                       0
30116        0.5                        0.333333333333333
30116        0.75                       0.666666666666667
30116        1                          1
30117        0.0833333333333333         0
30117        0.166666666666667          0.0909090909090909
30117        0.25                       0.181818181818182
30117        0.333333333333333          0.272727272727273
30117        0.416666666666667          0.363636363636364
30117        0.5                        0.454545454545455
30117        0.583333333333333          0.545454545454545
30117        0.666666666666667          0.636363636363636
30117        0.75                       0.727272727272727
30117        0.833333333333333          0.818181818181818
30117        0.916666666666667          0.909090909090909
30117        1                          1
```

```
30118       0.125              0
30118       0.25               0.142857142857143
30118       0.375              0.285714285714286
30118       0.5                0.428571428571429
30118       0.625              0.571428571428571
30118       0.75               0.714285714285714
30118       0.875              0.857142857142857
30118       1                  1
```

How It Works

The CUME_DIST function returns the relative position of a value in a set of values, while the PERCENT_RANK function returns the relative rank of a value in a set of values. The syntax of these functions is as follows:

```
CUME_DIST() | PERCENT_RANK( )
    OVER ( [ partition_by_clause ] order_by_clause )
```

The result returned by these functions will be a float(53) data type, with the value being greater than 0 and less than or equal to 1 (0 < x <= 1). When utilizing these functions, NULL values will be included, and the value returned will be the lowest possible value.

7-19. Calculating Continuous or Discrete Percentiles

Problem

You want to see the median salary and the 75 percentile salary for all employees per department.

Solution

Utilize the PERCENTILE_CONT and PERCENTILE_DISC functions to return percentile calculations based upon a value at a specified percentage.

```
DECLARE @Employees TABLE
        (
        EmplId INT PRIMARY KEY CLUSTERED,
        DeptId INT,
        Salary NUMERIC(8, 2)
        );

INSERT INTO @Employees
VALUES (1, 1, 10000),
       (2, 1, 11000),
       (3, 1, 12000),
       (4, 2, 25000),
       (5, 2, 35000),
       (6, 2, 75000),
       (7, 2, 100000);

SELECT EmplId,
       DeptId,
       Salary,
       PERCENTILE_CONT(0.5)
```

```
          WITHIN GROUP (ORDER BY Salary ASC)
          OVER (PARTITION BY DeptId) AS MedianCont,
        PERCENTILE_DISC(0.5)
          WITHIN GROUP (ORDER BY Salary ASC)
          OVER (PARTITION BY DeptId) AS MedianDisc,
        PERCENTILE_CONT(0.75)
          WITHIN GROUP (ORDER BY Salary ASC)
          OVER (PARTITION BY DeptId) AS Percent75Cont,
        PERCENTILE_DISC(0.75)
          WITHIN GROUP (ORDER BY Salary ASC)
          OVER (PARTITION BY DeptId) AS Percent75Disc,
        CUME_DIST()
          OVER (PARTITION BY DeptId
                    ORDER BY Salary) AS CumeDist
FROM   @Employees
ORDER BY DeptId, EmplId;
```

This query returns the following result set:

```
EmplId DeptId Salary      MedianCont MedianDisc  Percent75Cont Percent75Disc CumeDist
------ ------ --------    ---------- ----------  ------------- ------------- -----------------
1      1      10000.00    11000      11000.00    11500         12000.00      0.333333333333333
2      1      11000.00    11000      11000.00    11500         12000.00      0.666666666666667
3      1      12000.00    11000      11000.00    11500         12000.00      1
4      2      25000.00    55000      35000.00    81250         75000.00      0.25
5      2      35000.00    55000      35000.00    81250         75000.00      0.5
6      2      75000.00    55000      35000.00    81250         75000.00      0.75
7      2      100000.00   55000      35000.00    81250         75000.00      1
```

How It Works

PERCENTILE_CONT calculates a percentile based upon a continuous distribution of values of the specified column. This is performed by using the specified percentile value (SP) and the number of rows in the partition (N) and by computing the row number of interest (RN) after the ordering has been applied. The row number of interest is computed from the formula RN = (1 + (SP * (N- 1))). The result returned is the linear interpolation (essentially an average) between the values from the rows at CEILING(RN) and FLOOR(RN). The value returned may or may not exist in the partition being analyzed.

PERCENTILE_DISC calculates a percentile based upon a discrete distribution of the column values. For the specified percentile (P), the values of the partition are sorted, and the value returned will be from the row with the smallest CUME_DIST value (with the same ordering) that is greater than or equal to P. The value returned will exist in one of the rows in the partition being analyzed. Since the result for this function is based on the CUME_DIST value, that function was included in the previous query in order to show its value.

The syntax for these functions is as follows:

```
PERCENTILE_CONT ( numeric_literal) | PERCENTILE_DISC ( numeric_literal )
    WITHIN GROUP ( ORDER BY order_by_expression [ ASC | DESC ] )
    OVER ( [ <partition_by_clause> ] )
```

In the example, PERCENTILE_CONT(0.5) is utilized to obtain the median value. For DeptId = 1, there are three rows, so the median value is the value from the middle row (after sorting). For DeptId = 2, there are four rows, so the median value is the average of the two middle rows. This value does not exist in this partition.

PERCENTILE_DISC returns a value that exists in the partition, based upon the CUME_DIST value. By specifying PERCENTILE_DISC(0.5), the row in each partition that has a CUME_DIST value of .5, or the next row that is greater than .5, is utilized, and the salary for that row is returned.

Sequences

Sequences are used to create an incrementing number. While similar to an identity column, they are not bound to any table, can be reset, and can be used across multiple tables. Sequences are discussed in detail in Recipe 13-22. Sequences are assigned by calling the NEXT VALUE FOR function, and multiple values can be assigned simultaneously. The order of these assignments can be controlled by use of the optional OVER clause of the NEXT VALUE FOR function.

7-20. Assigning Sequences in a Specified Order

Problem

You are inserting multiple student grades into a table. Each record needs to have a sequence assigned, and you want the sequences to be assigned in order of the grades.

Solution

Utilize the OVER clause of the NEXT VALUE FOR function, specifying the desired order.

```
IF EXISTS (SELECT 1
           FROM sys.sequences AS seq
                JOIN sys.schemas AS sch
                  ON seq.schema_id = sch.schema_id
           WHERE sch.name = 'dbo'
           AND  seq.name = 'CH7Sequence')
   DROP SEQUENCE dbo.CH7Sequence;

CREATE SEQUENCE dbo.CH7Sequence AS INTEGER START WITH 1;

DECLARE @ClassRank TABLE
        (
         StudentID TINYINT,
         Grade TINYINT,
         SeqNbr INTEGER
        );
INSERT INTO @ClassRank (StudentId, Grade, SeqNbr)
SELECT StudentId,
       Grade,
       NEXT VALUE FOR dbo.CH7Sequence OVER (ORDER BY Grade ASC)
FROM  (VALUES (1, 100),
              (2, 95),
              (3, 85),
              (4, 100),
              (5, 99),
              (6, 98),
              (7, 95),
              (8, 90),
```

```
        (9, 89),
        (10, 89),
        (11, 85),
        (12, 82)) dt(StudentId, Grade);

SELECT StudentId, Grade, SeqNbr
FROM   @ClassRank;
```

This query returns the following result set:

```
StudentID  Grade  SeqNbr
---------  -----  ------
12         82     1
3          85     2
11         85     3
10         89     4
9          89     5
8          90     6
7          95     7
2          95     8
6          98     9
5          99     10
1          100    11
4          100    12
```

How It Works

The optional OVER clause of the NEXT VALUE FOR function is utilized to specify the order that the sequence should be applied. The syntax is as follows:

```
NEXT VALUE FOR [ database_name . ] [ schema_name . ] sequence_name
   [ OVER (<over_order_by_clause>) ]
```

CHAPTER 8

Inserting, Updating, Deleting

by Andy Roberts

In this chapter, I review how to modify data using the Transact-SQL INSERT, UPDATE, DELETE, and MERGE statements. I'll review the basics of each statement and cover specific techniques such as inserting data from a stored procedure and outputting the affected rows of a data modification.

Before going into the new features, let's start the chapter off by reviewing basic INSERT concepts.

The simplified syntax for the INSERT command is as follows:

```
INSERT [ INTO]
table_or_view_name [ ( column_list ) ] VALUES (({DEFAULT | NULL | expression } [ ,...n ]) [ ,...n ])
```

Table 8-1 describes the arguments of this command.

Table 8-1. *INSERT Command Arguments*

Argument	Description
table_or_view_name	The name of the table or updateable view into which you are inserting the data.
column_list	The explicit comma-separated list of columns on the insert table that will be populated with values.
({DEFAULT | NULL | expression }[,...n])	The comma-separated list of values to be inserted as a row into the table. You can insert multiple rows in a single statement. Each value can be an expression, NULL value, or DEFAULT value (if a default was defined for the column).

8-1. Inserting a New Row

Problem

You need to insert one row into a table using a set of defined values.

Solution

A simple use of the INSERT statement accepts a list of values in the VALUES clause that are mapped to a list of columns specified in the INTO clause. In this recipe, we will add a new row to the Production.Location table.

```
INSERT INTO Production.Location
       (Name, CostRate, Availability)
VALUES ('Wheel Storage', 11.25, 80.00) ;
```

This returns the following:

```
(1 row(s) affected)
```

To verify the row has been inserted correctly, let's query the Location table for the new row:

```
SELECT Name,
       CostRate,
       Availability
FROM   Production.Location
WHERE  Name = 'Wheel Storage' ;
```

This returns the following:

```
Name           CostRate  Availability
-------------  --------  ------------
Wheel Storage  11.25     80.00
```

How It Works

In this recipe, a new row was inserted into the Production.Location table. The query begins with the INSERT statement and the name of the table that will receive the inserted data (the INTO keyword is optional):

```
INSERT INTO Production.Location
```

Next, we explicitly list the columns of the destination table that will receive the supplied values:

```
(Name, CostRate, Availability)
```

A comma must separate each column. Columns don't need to be listed in the same order as they appear in the base table, but the values supplied in the VALUES clause must exactly match the order of the column list. Column lists are not necessary if the VALUES clause specifies values for all of the columns in the base table and these values are specified in the same order as they are defined in that table. However, using column lists is recommended because explicitly listing columns allows you to add new columns to the base table without changing your insert statements (assuming the new column has a default value).

The next line of code is the VALUES clause and contains a comma-separated list of values (expressions) to insert:

```
VALUES ('Wheel Storage', 11.25, 80.00)
```

The values in this list must be provided in the same order as the listed columns, or if no columns are listed, the VALUES clause must contain values for all of the table's columns in the same order as they appear in the table definition.

8-2. Specifying Default Values

Problem

You need to insert one row into a table, and you want to use a table's default values for some columns.

Solution

In the previous recipe, we inserted a row into the `Production.Location` table. The `Production.Location` table has two other columns that are not explicitly referenced in the `INSERT` statement. If you look at the definition of `Production.Location` listed in Table 8-2, you will see that there is also a `LocationID` column and a `ModifiedDate` column that we did not include in the `INSERT` statement.

Table 8-2. *`Production.Location` Table Definition*

Column Name	Data Type	Nullability	Default Value	Identity Column?
`LocationID`	`smallint`	`NOT NULL`		Yes
`Name`	`dbo.Name` (user-defined data type)	`NOT NULL`		No
`CostRate`	`smallmoney`	`NOT NULL`	0.00	No
`Availability`	`decimal(8,2)`	`NOT NULL`	0.00	No
`ModifiedDate`	`datetime`	`NOT NULL`	`GETDATE()` (function to return the current date and time)	No

---

■ **Note** See Chapter 15 for more information on the `CREATE TABLE` command, `IDENTITY` columns, and `DEFAULT` values.

The `ModifiedDate` column has a default value of `GETDATE()`. If an `INSERT` statement does not explicitly supply a value for the `ModifiedDate` column of a new row in the `Production.Location` table, SQL Server will execute the `GETDATE()` function to populate the column with the current date and time. The `INSERT` could have been written to supply a value and override the default value. Here's an example:

```
INSERT Production.Location
       (Name,
        CostRate,
        Availability,
        ModifiedDate)
VALUES ('Wheel Storage 2',
        11.25,
        80.00,
        '4/1/2012') ;
```

When a column has a default value specified, you can use the `DEFAULT` keyword in the `VALUES` clause to explicitly use the default value. Here's an example:

```
INSERT Production.Location
       (Name,
        CostRate,
        Availability,
        ModifiedDate)
VALUES ('Wheel Storage 3',
        11.25,
        80.00,
        DEFAULT) ;
```

When a column has no default value specified, you can use the DEFAULT keyword in the VALUES clause to explicitly use the default of the column's type. Here's an example:

```
INSERT INTO Person.Address
       (AddressLine1,
        AddressLine2,
        City,
        StateProvinceID,
        PostalCode)
VALUES ('15 Wake Robin Rd',
        DEFAULT,
        'Sudbury',
        30,
        '01776') ;
```

In this case, the Person.Address table has no default value specified for the AddressLine2 column, so SQL Server uses the default value for the NVARCHAR type, which is NULL.

If each column in the table uses defaults for all columns, you can trigger an insert that inserts a row using only the defaults by including the DEFAULT VALUES option. Here's an example:

```
INSERT dbo.ExampleTable DEFAULT VALUES ;
```

How It Works

The DEFAULT keyword allows you to explicitly set a column's default value in an INSERT statement. If all columns are to be set to their default values, the DEFAULT VALUES keywords can be used. If the table definition contains no default value for a column, the type's default value will be used.

The LocationID column from the Production.Location table, however, is an IDENTITY column (not a defaulted column). An IDENTITY property on a column causes the value in that column to automatically populate with an incrementing numeric value. Because LocationID is an IDENTITY column, the database manages inserting the values for this row, so an INSERT statement cannot normally specify a value for an IDENTITY column. If you want to specify a certain value for an IDENTITY column, you need to follow the procedure outlined in the next recipe.

8-3. Overriding an IDENTITY Column

Problem

You have a table with an IDENTITY column defined. You need to override the IDENTITY property and insert explicit values into the IDENTITY column.

Solution

A column using an IDENTITY property automatically increments based on a numeric seed and increment value for every row inserted into the table. IDENTITY columns are often used as surrogate keys (a *surrogate key* is a unique primary key generated by the database that holds no business-level significance other than to ensure uniqueness within the table).

In data load or recovery scenarios, you may find that you need to manually insert explicit values into an IDENTITY column. For example, a row with the key value of 4 is deleted accidentally, and you need to manually reconstruct that row and preserve the original value of 4 with the original business information.

To explicitly insert a numeric value into a column defined with an IDENTITY property, you must use the SET IDENTITY_INSERT command. The syntax is as follows:

```
SET IDENTITY_INSERT [database_name.[schema_name].]table { ON | OFF }
```

Table 8-3 shows the arguments of this command.

Table 8-3. *SET IDENTITY_INSERT Command*

Argument	Description
[database_name.[schema_name].] table	The optional database name, optional schema name, and required table name for which an insert statement will be allowed to explicitly specify IDENTITY values...
ON | OFF	When set ON, explicit value inserts are allowed. When set OFF, explicit value inserts are *not* allowed.

This recipe will demonstrate how to explicitly insert the value of an IDENTITY column into a table. The following query demonstrates what happens if you try to explicitly insert into an IDENTITY column without first using IDENTITY_INSERT:

```
INSERT INTO HumanResources.Department (DepartmentID, Name, GroupName)
VALUES (17, 'Database Services', 'Information Technology')
```

This returns an error, keeping you from inserting an explicit value for the IDENTITY column:

```
Msg 544, Level 16, State 1, Line 2
Cannot insert explicit value for identity column in table 'Department' when
IDENTITY_INSERT is set to OFF.
```

Using SET IDENTITY_INSERT removes this barrier:

```
SET IDENTITY_INSERT HumanResources.Department ON

INSERT HumanResources.Department (DepartmentID, Name, GroupName)
VALUES (17, 'Database Services', 'Information Technology')

SET IDENTITY_INSERT HumanResources.Department OFF
```

How It Works

In the recipe, IDENTITY_INSERT was set ON prior to the INSERT:

```
SET IDENTITY_INSERT HumanResources.Department ON ;
```

The INSERT was then performed using a value of 17. When inserting into an IDENTITY column, you must also explicitly list the column names after the INSERT table_name clause:

```
INSERT HumanResourcesDepartment
       (DepartmentID,
        Name,
        GroupName)
VALUES (17,
        'Database Services',
        'Information Technology') ;
```

If the inserted value is greater than the current IDENTITY value, new inserts to the table will automatically use this new value as the IDENTITY seed.

IDENTITY_INSERT should be set OFF once you are finished explicitly inserting values:

```
SET IDENTITY_INSERT HumanResources.Department OFF;
```

Once you are finished inserting into a table with IDENTITY_INSERT set to ON, you should set the property to OFF. Only one table in a session can have IDENTITY_INSERT ON at a time. If you were to explicitly insert IDENTITY values into multiple tables, the pattern would look something like the following:

```
SET IDENTITY_INSERT TableA ON ;
INSERT INTO TableA (...) VALUES (...);
INSERT INTO TableA (...) VALUES (...);
INSERT INTO TableA (...) VALUES (...);
SET IDENTITY_INSERT TableA OFF ;

SET IDENTITY_INSERT TableB ON ;
INSERT INTO TableB (...) VALUES (...);
INSERT INTO TableB (...) VALUES (...);
INSERT INTO TableB (...) VALUES (...);
SET IDENTITY_INSERT TableB OFF ;

SET IDENTITY_INSERT TableC ON ;
INSERT INTO TableC (...) VALUES (...);
INSERT INTO TableC (...) VALUES (...);
INSERT INTO TableC (...) VALUES (...);
SET IDENTITY_INSERT TableC OFF ;
```

Closing a connection will reset the IDENTITY_INSERT property to OFF for any table on which it is currently set to ON.

8-4. Generating a Globally Unique Identifier (GUID)

Problem

A column in your table is defined with the type UNIQUEIDENTIFIER. You need to insert a new row into the table and generate a new GUID for the row you are inserting.

■ **Note** For further information regarding the UniqueIdentifier data type, please refer to the SQL Server product documentation at http://msdn.microsoft.com/en-us/library/ms187942.aspx.

Solution

The NEWID system function generates a new GUID that can be inserted into a column defined with UNIQUEIDENTIFIER.

```
INSERT Purchasing.ShipMethod
       (Name,
        ShipBase,
        ShipRate,
        rowguid)
VALUES ('MIDDLETON CARGO TS1',
        8.99,
        1.22,
        NEWID()) ;


SELECT rowguid,
       Name
FROM   Purchasing.ShipMethod
WHERE  Name = 'MIDDLETON CARGO TS1'
```

This returns the following (note that your rowguid value will be different from this example):

```
rowguid                              Name
------------------------------------ --------------------
02F47979-CC55-4C4B-B4AA-ECD3F5CC85AF MIDDLETON CARGO TS1
```

How It Works

The rowguid column in the Purchasing.ShipMethod table is a UNIQUEIDENTIFIER data type column. Here is an excerpt from the table definition:

```
rowguid uniqueidentifier ROWGUIDCOL NOT NULL DEFAULT (newid()),
```

To generate a new uniqueidentifier data type value for this inserted row, the NEWID() function was used in the VALUES clause:

```
VALUES('MIDDLETON CARGO TS1', 8.99, 1.22, NEWID())
```

Selecting the new row that was just created, the rowguid was given a uniqueidentifier value of 174BE850-FDEA-4E64-8D17-C019521C6C07 (although when you test it yourself, you'll get a different value because NEWID creates a new value each time it is executed).

Note that the table is defined with a default value of newid(). If a value is not specified for the rowguid column, SQL Server will use the NEWID function to generate a new GUID for the row.

8-5. Inserting Results from a Query

Problem

You need to insert multiple rows into a table based on the results of a query.

Solution

The previous recipes show how to insert a single row of data. This recipe demonstrates how to insert multiple rows into a table using the INSERT..SELECT form of the INSERT statement. The syntax for performing an INSERT...SELECT is as follows:

```
INSERT [INTO]
table_or_view_name[(column_list)] SELECT column_list FROM data_source
```

The syntax for using INSERT...SELECT is almost identical to inserting a single row. Instead of using the VALUES clause, designate a SELECT query formatted to return rows with a column definition that matches the column list specified in the INSERT INTO clause of the statement. The SELECT query can be based on one or more data sources, so long as the column list conforms to the expected data types of the destination table.

For the purposes of this example, this recipe creates a new table for storing the result of a query. The example populates values from the HumanResources.Shift table into the new dbo.Shift_Archive table:

```
CREATE TABLE [dbo].[Shift_Archive]
       (
        [ShiftID] [tinyint] NOT NULL,
        [Name] [dbo].[Name] NOT NULL,
        [StartTime] [datetime] NOT NULL,
        [EndTime] [datetime] NOT NULL,
        [ModifiedDate] [datetime] NOT NULL
                                DEFAULT (GETDATE()),
        CONSTRAINT [PK_Shift_ShiftID] PRIMARY KEY CLUSTERED ([ShiftID] ASC)
        ) ;
GO
```

Next, an INSERT..SELECT is performed:

```
INSERT INTO dbo.Shift_Archive
       (ShiftID,
        Name,
        StartTime,
        EndTime,
        ModifiedDate)
       SELECT ShiftID,
              Name,
              StartTime,
              EndTime,
              ModifiedDate
    FROM      HumanResources.Shift
    ORDER BY ShiftID ;
```

The results show that three rows were inserted:

```
(3 row(s) affected)
```

Next, a query is executed to confirm the inserted rows in the Shift_Archive table:

```
SELECT ShiftID,
    Name
FROM  Shift_Archive ;
```

This returns:

```
ShiftID  Name
-------  -------
1        Day
2        Evening
3        Night
```

How It Works

The INSERT...SELECT form of the INSERT statement instructs SQL Server to insert multiple rows into a table based on a SELECT query. Just like regular, single-value INSERTs, you begin by using INSERT INTO table_name and specify the list of columns to be inserted:

```
INSERT INTO Shift_Archive (ShiftID, Name, StartTime, EndTime, ModifiedDate)
```

The next clause is the query used to populate the table. The SELECT statement must return columns in the same order as the columns appear in the INSERT column list, and these columns must have data type compatibility with the associated columns in the column list:

```
SELECT ShiftID
     , Name
     , StartTime
     , EndTime
     , ModifiedDate
 FROM  HumanResources.Shift
 ORDER BY ShiftID
```

When the column lists aren't designated, the SELECT statement must provide values for *all* the columns of the table into which the data is being inserted.

8-6. Inserting Results from a Stored Procedure

Problem

You want to insert multiple rows into a table based on the results of a stored procedure.

Solution

A *stored procedure* groups one or more Transact-SQL statements into a logical unit and stores it as an object in a SQL Server database. Stored procedures allow for more sophisticated result set creation (for example, you can use several intermediate result sets built in temporary tables before returning the final result set). Stored procedures that return a result set can be used with the INSERT...EXEC form of the INSERT statement.

This recipe demonstrates how to add rows to a table based on the output of a stored procedure. A stored procedure can be used in this manner if it returns data via a SELECT statement from within the procedure definition and the result set (or multiple result sets) matches the column list specified in the INSERT INTO clause of the INSERT statement.

■ **Note** For more information on stored procedures, see Chapter 19.

The syntax for inserting data from a stored procedure is as follows:

```
INSERT [INTO] table_or_view_name [(column_list)] EXEC stored_procedure_name
```

The syntax is almost identical to the INSERT...EXEC form, only this time the data is populated via a stored procedure execution and not a SELECT statement.

For this example, create a stored procedure that returns rows from the Production.TransactionHistory table where the begin and end dates are between the values passed to the stored procedure as parameters and the row does not already exist in the archive table:

```
CREATE PROCEDURE dbo.usp_SEL_Production_TransactionHistory
    @ModifiedStartDT DATETIME,
    @ModifiedEndDT DATETIME
AS
    SELECT  TransactionID,
            ProductID,
            ReferenceOrderID,
            ReferenceOrderLineID,
            TransactionDate,
            TransactionType,
            Quantity,
            ActualCost,
            ModifiedDate
    FROM    Production.TransactionHistory
    WHERE   ModifiedDate BETWEEN @ModifiedStartDT
               AND   @ModifiedEndDT
        AND TransactionID NOT IN (
        SELECT TransactionID
        FROM   Production.TransactionHistoryArchive) ;
GO
```

Test the stored procedures to check that the results are returned as expected:

```
EXEC dbo.usp_SEL_Production_TransactionHistory '2007-09-01', '2007-09-02'
```

This returns 4,171 rows based on the date range passed to the procedure. Next, use this stored procedure to insert the 4,171 rows into the Production.TransactionHistoryArchive table:

```
INSERT Production.TransactionHistoryArchive
      (TransactionID,
       ProductID,
       ReferenceOrderID,
       ReferenceOrderLineID,
       TransactionDate,
       TransactionType,
       Quantity,
       ActualCost,
       ModifiedDate)
      EXEC dbo.usp_SEL_Production_TransactionHistory '2007-09-01',
           '2007-09-02' ;
```

Executing this statement yields the following results:

```
(4171 row(s) affected)
```

How It Works

This example demonstrates using a stored procedure to populate a table using INSERT and EXEC. The INSERT begins with the name of the table into which rows are to be inserted:

```
INSERT Production.TransactionHistoryArchive
```

Next is the list of columns to be inserted into:

```
(TransactionID,
 ProductID,
 ReferenceOrderID,
 ReferenceOrderLineID,
 TransactionDate,
 TransactionType,
 Quantity,
 ActualCost,
 ModifiedDate)
```

Finally, the EXEC statement executes the stored procedure with the supplied parameters:

```
EXEC dbo.usp_SEL_Production_TransactionHistory '2007-09-01', '2007-09-02'
```

8-7. Inserting Multiple Rows at Once

Problem

You are creating a script that adds multiple rows into a table one at a time. You want to optimize the size and speed of the script by reducing the number of statements executed.

Solution

SQL Server includes the ability to insert multiple rows using a single INSERT statement without requiring a subquery or stored procedure call. This allows the application to reduce the code required to add multiple rows and also reduce the number of individual statements executed by the script. The VALUES clause is repeated once for each row inserted:

First, create a table to receive the rows:

```
CREATE TABLE HumanResources.Degree
    (
    DegreeID INT NOT NULL
                IDENTITY(1, 1)
                PRIMARY KEY,
    DegreeName VARCHAR(30) NOT NULL,
    DegreeCode VARCHAR(5) NOT NULL,
    ModifiedDate DATETIME NOT NULL
    ) ;
```

```
GO
```

Next, insert multiple rows into the new table:

```
INSERT INTO HumanResources.Degree
       (DegreeName, DegreeCode, ModifiedDate)
VALUES ('Bachelor of Arts', 'B.A.', GETDATE()),
     ('Bachelor of Science', 'B.S.', GETDATE()),
     ('Master of Arts', 'M.A.', GETDATE()),
     ('Master of Science', 'M.S.', GETDATE()),
     ('Associate'' s Degree', 'A.A.', GETDATE()) ;
GO
```

This returns the following query output:

```
(5 row(s) affected)
```

How It Works

This recipe demonstrates inserting multiple rows from a single INSERT statement. Start by creating a new table to contain college degree types. Then insert rows using the standard INSERT...VALUES form of the INSERT statement. The column list is specified like in all forms of the INSERT statement:

```
INSERT HumanResources.Degree (DegreeName, DegreeCode, ModifiedDate)
```

Next, in the VALUES clause, I designated a new row for each degree type. Each row had three columns, and these columns were encapsulated in parentheses:

```
VALUES ('Bachelor of Arts', 'B.A.', GETDATE()),
   ('Bachelor of Science', 'B.S.', GETDATE()),
   ('Master of Arts', 'M.A.', GETDATE()),
   ('Master of Science', 'M.S.', GETDATE()),
   ('Associate'' s Degree', 'A.A.', GETDATE()) ;
```

This feature allows a developer or DBA to insert multiple rows without needing to retype the initial INSERT table name and column list. This is a great way to populate the lookup tables of a database with a set of initial values. Rather than hand-code 50 INSERT statements in your setup script, create a single INSERT with multiple rows. Not only does this help the script development, but this also optimizes the script execution because there is only one statement to compile and execute instead of 50.

8-8. Inserting Rows and Returning the Inserted Rows

Problem

You are inserting a row into a table, and that table contains some default values. You want to return the resulting values to the calling application to update the user interface.

Solution

The OUTPUT clause adds a result set to the INSERT statement containing a specified set of columns and the set of rows that were inserted. For example, add three rows to the Purchasing.ShipMethod table:

```
INSERT Purchasing.ShipMethod
       (Name, ShipBase, ShipRate)
OUTPUT INSERTED.ShipMethodID, INSERTED.Name
VALUES ('MIDDLETON CARGO TS11', 10, 10),
       ('MIDDLETON CARGO TS12', 10, 10),
       ('MIDDLETON CARGO TS13', 10, 10) ;
```

The output of the previous insert statement will be as follows:

```
ShipMethodID Name
------------ --------------------
15           MIDDLETON CARGO TS11
16           MIDDLETON CARGO TS12
17           MIDDLETON CARGO TS13
```

Note that the results contain values for ShipMethodID, rowgui, and ModifiedDate, three columns for which the query did not specify values explicitly.

How It Works

The OUTPUT clause of the INSERT statement is added directly after the column_list of the INSERT statement (or the table_name if the column_list is not specified explicitly). As rows are inserted into the table, they are exposed to the OUTPUT clause through the virtual table inserted. In this example, the query outputs all columns from the inserted virtual table and returns them as a result set.

```
INSERT Purchasing.ShipMethod (Name, ShipBase, ShipRate)
OUTPUT inserted.*
VALUES
('MIDDLETON CARGO TS11', 10, 10)
, ('MIDDLETON CARGO TS12', 10, 10)
, ('MIDDLETON CARGO TS13', 10, 10) ;
```

It is also possible to output information from the INSERT statement to a table or table variable for further processing. In this case, maybe it is required that the IDs of the inserted rows be output to a table variable. If there was a table variable named @insertedShipMethodIDs defined prior to the INSERT statement (this query will return an error because this table variable is not defined):

```
INSERT Purchasing.ShipMethod (Name, ShipBase, ShipRate)
OUTPUT inserted.ShipMethodID INTO @insertedShipMethodIDs
VALUES
('MIDDLETON CARGO TS11', 10, 10)
, ('MIDDLETON CARGO TS12', 10, 10)
, ('MIDDLETON CARGO TS13', 10, 10) ;
```

These examples use value lists to perform the INSERT operations. The OUTPUT clause will work with any form of INSERT statement such as INSERT... SELECT and INSERT... EXEC.

8-9. Updating a Single Row or Set of Rows

Problem

You need to modify a set of columns in rows that already exist in a table.

Solution

The UPDATE statement modifies data that already exists in a table. The UPDATE statement applies changes to a single or multiple columns of a single or multiple rows.

The basic syntax for the UPDATE statement is as follows:

```
UPDATE <table_or_view_name>
SET  column_name = {expression | DEFAULT | NULL} [ ,...n ]
WHERE <search_condition>
```

Table 8-4 describes the arguments of this command.

Table 8-4. *UPDATE Command Arguments*

Argument	Description
table_or_view_name	The table or updateable view containing data to be updated.
column_name = {expression | DEFAULT | NULL}	The name of the column or columns to be updated. Followed by the expression to assign to the column. Instead of an explicit expression, DEFAULT or NULL may be specified.
search_condition	The search condition that defines *what* rows are modified. If this isn't included, all rows from the table or updateable view will be modified.

In this example, a single row is updated by designating the SpecialOfferID, which is the primary key of the table (for more on primary keys, see Chapter 15).

Before performing the update, first query the specific row that the update statement will modify:

```
SELECT DiscountPct
FROM   Sales.SpecialOffer
WHERE  SpecialOfferID = 10 ;
```

This returns the following:

```
DiscountPct
-----------
0.50
```

Next, perform the modification:

```
UPDATE Sales.SpecialOffer
SET    DiscountPct = 0.15
WHERE  SpecialOfferID = 10 ;
```

Querying the modified row after the update confirms that the value of DiscountPct was indeed modified:

```
SELECT DiscountPct
FROM   Sales.SpecialOffer
WHERE  SpecialOfferID = 10 ;
```

This returns the following:

```
DiscountPct
------------
0.15
```

How It Works

In this example, the query started off with UPDATE and the table name Sales.SpecialOffer:

```
UPDATE Sales.SpecialOffer
```

Next, the SET clause was used, followed by a list of column assignments:

```
SET DiscountPct = 0.15
```

Had this been the end of the query, *all* rows in the Sales.SpecialOffer table would have been modified. Just as a SELECT statement with no WHERE clause returns all the rows in a table, an UPDATE statement with no WHERE clause will update all rows in a table. But the intention of this query was to update the discount percentage for only a specific product. The WHERE clause was used in order to achieve this:

```
WHERE SpecialOfferID = 10 ;
```

After executing this query, only one row is modified. Had there been multiple rows that met the search condition in the WHERE clause, those rows would have been modified as well.

```
UPDATE Sales.SpecialOffer
SET    DiscountPct = 0.15
WHERE  SpecialOfferID IN (10, 11, 12) ;
```

Tip Performing a SELECT query with the FROM and WHERE clauses of an UPDATE, prior to the UPDATE, allows you to see what rows you will be updating (an extra validation that you are updating the proper rows). This is also a good opportunity to use a transaction to allow for rollbacks in the event that your modifications are undesired. For more on transactions, see Chapter 13.

8-10. Updating with a Second Table as the Data Source

Problem

You need to update rows in a table, but either your filter condition requires a second table or you need to use data from a second table as the source of your update.

Solution

The UPDATE statement can modify rows based on a FROM clause and associated WHERE clause search conditions. The basic syntax for this form of the UPDATE statement follows:

```
UPDATE <table_or_view_name | table_or_view_alias>
SET    column_name = {expression | DEFAULT | NULL} [ ,...n ]
FROM   <table_source>
WHERE  <search_condition>
```

The FROM and WHERE clauses are not mandatory; however, you will find that they are almost always implemented in order to specify exactly which rows are to be modified based on joins against one or more tables.

In this example, assume that a specific product, "Full-Finger Gloves, M," from the Production.Product table has a customer purchase limit of two units per customer. For this query's requirement, any shopping cart with a quantity of more than two units for this product should immediately be adjusted back to the limit of 2:

```
UPDATE Sales.ShoppingCartItem
SET    Quantity = 2,
       ModifiedDate = GETDATE()
FROM   Sales.ShoppingCartItem c
       INNER JOIN Production.Product p
          ON c.ProductID = p.ProductID
WHERE  p.Name = 'Full-Finger Gloves, M '
       AND c.Quantity > 2 ;
```

How It Works

Stepping through the code, the first line shows the alias of the table to be updated:

```
UPDATE Sales.ShoppingCartItem
```

Next, the columns to be updated are designated in the SET clause:

```
SET Quantity =2,
    ModifiedDate = GETDATE()
```

Next comes the FROM clause where the Sales.ShoppingCartltem and Production.Product tables are joined by ProductID. When joining multiple tables, the object to be updated must be referenced in the FROM clause:

```
FROM   Sales.ShoppingCartltem c
INNER JOIN Production.Product p
ON     c.ProductID = p.ProductID
```

Using the updated table in the FROM clause allows joins between multiple tables. Presumably, the joined tables will be used to filter the updated rows or to provide values for the updated rows.

The WHERE clause specifies that only the "Full-Finger Gloves, M" product in the Sales.ShoppingCartltem should be modified and only if the Quantity is greater than 2 units:

```
WHERE p.Name = 'Full-Finger Gloves, M '
AND   c.Quantity > 2 ;
```

8-11. Updating Data and Returning the Affected Rows

Problem

You are required to audit rows that have changed in a given table. Each time the DiscountPct is updated on the Sales.SpecialOffer table, the SpecialOfferID as well as the old and new values of the DiscountPct column should be recorded.

Solution

The OUTPUT clause adds a result set to the UPDATE statement containing a specified set of columns for the set of rows that were updated. For example, say all Customer discounts are increased by 5 percent:

```
UPDATE Sales.SpecialOffer
SET    DiscountPct *= 1.05
OUTPUT inserted.SpecialOfferID,
       deleted.DiscountPct AS old_DiscountPct,
       inserted.DiscountPct AS new_DiscountPct
WHERE  Category = 'Customer' ;
```

This update statement returns the following result:

```
SpecialOfferID  old_DiscountPct  new_DiscountPct
--------------  ---------------  ---------------
10              0.15             0.1575
15              0.50             0.525
```

How It Works

The OUTPUT clause of the UPDATE statement is added directly after the SET clause of the UPDATE statement. As rows are updated in the table, they are exposed to the OUTPUT clause through the virtual tables inserted and deleted. In this example, the query outputs all old and new DiscountPct column values for a changed SpecialOrderID and returns them as a result set:

```
UPDATE Sales.SpecialOffer
SET    DiscountPct *= 1.05
OUTPUT inserted.SpecialOfferID,
       deleted.DiscountPct AS old_DiscountPct,
       inserted.DiscountPct AS new_DiscountPct
WHERE  Category = 'Customer' ;
```

For columns that do not change (SpecialOfferID) in this case, either the inserted or deleted table can be used to retrieve values.

It is also possible to output information from the UPDATE statement to a table or table variable for further processing. If there was a table variable named @updatedOffers defined prior to the UPDATE statement (this query will return an error because this table variable is not defined):

```
UPDATE Sales.SpecialOffer
SET    DiscountPct *= 1.05
OUTPUT inserted.SpecialOfferID,
       deleted.DiscountPct AS old_DiscountPct,
       inserted.DiscountPct AS new_DiscountPct
       INTO @updatedOffers
WHERE  Category = 'Customer' ;
```

8-12. Updating Large-Value Columns

Problem

You have a large data type column and want to update a portion of the data in that column without updating the entire column.

Solution

Updates can be made to large-value data type column values without rewriting the entire column value. SQL Server introduced new large-value data types in SQL Server 2005, which are intended to replace the deprecated `text`, `ntext`, and `image` data types. These data types include the following:

- `varchar(max)`, which holds non-Unicode variable-length data
- `nvarchar(max)`, which holds Unicode variable-length data
- `varbinary(max)`, which holds variable-length binary data

These data types can store up to 2^31-1 bytes of data.

■ **Note** For more information on using large-value types in SQL Server, see the SQL Server product documentation at `http://msdn.microsoft.com/en-us/library/ms130896.aspx`.

A major drawback of `text` and `image` data types is that they require separate functions such as `WRITETEXT` and `UPDATETEXT` to manipulate the image/text data. The new large-value data types allow modification through standard `INSERT` and `UPDATE` statements.

The syntax for inserting a large-value data type is no different from a regular `INSERT`. To update a large-value data type, the `UPDATE` statement executes the `WRITE` method of the large-value data type.

```
UPDATE <table_or_view_name>
SET    column_name.WRITE (expression, (@Offset , @Length)
FROM   <table_source>
WHERE  <search_condition>
```

Table 8-5 describes the parameters of the `WRITE` method.

Table 8-5. *`UPDATE` Command with `WRITE` Method in the `SET` Clause*

Argument	Description
`Expression`	The expression defines the chunk of text to be placed in the column.
`@Offset`	`@Offset` determines the starting position in the existing column value where the new text should be placed. If `@Offset` is `NULL`, the new expression will be appended to the end of the column (also ignoring the second `@Length` parameter).
`@Length`	`@Length` determines the length of the section to overlay.

Create a new table called `RecipeChapter` to hold the large-value data type:

```
CREATE TABLE dbo.RecipeChapter
       (
       ChapterID INT NOT NULL,
       Chapter VARCHAR(MAX) NOT NULL
       ) ;
GO
```

Next, insert a row into the table. Notice that there is nothing special about the string being inserted into the `Chapter` column:

```
INSERT INTO dbo.RecipeChapter
        (ChapterID,
         Chapter)
VALUES (1,
         At the beginning of each chapter you will notice
that basic concepts are covered first.') ;
```

Next, update the inserted row by adding a sentence to the end of the column value:

```
UPDATE   RecipeChapter
SET      Chapter.WRITE(' In addition to the basics, this chapter will also provide
recipes that can be used in your day to day development and administration.',
                       NULL, NULL)
WHERE  ChapterID = 1 ;
```

Replace the phrase "day to day" with the single word "daily":

```
UPDATE RecipeChapter
SET    Chapter.WRITE('daily', CHARINDEX('day to day', Chapter) - 1,
                       LEN('day to day'))
WHERE  ChapterID = 1 ;
```

For further information on `CHARINDEX` and `LEN`, please see Chapter 9.

Finally, review the resulting string:

```
SELECT Chapter
FROM   RecipeChapter
WHERE  ChapterID = 1
```

This returns the following:

```
Chapter
-----------------------------------------------------------------------------------------
At the beginning of each chapter you will notice that basic concepts are covered first. In
addition to the basics, this chapter will also provide recipes that can be used in your daily
development and administration.
```

How It Works

The recipe begins by creating a table where book chapter descriptions will be held. The `Chapter` column uses a `varchar(max)` data type.

```
CREATE TABLE dbo.RecipeChapter
       (
       ChapterID INT NOT NULL,
       Chapter VARCHAR(MAX) NOT NULL
       ) ;
GO
```

Next, a new row is inserted. Notice that the syntax for inserting a large-object data type doesn't differ from inserting data into a regular non-large-value data type.

```
INSERT INTO dbo.RecipeChapter
       (ChapterID,
        Chapter)
VALUES (1,
        'At the beginning of each chapter you will notice
that basic concepts are covered first.') ;
```

An UPDATE is performed against the RecipeChapter table to add a second sentence after the end of the first sentence.

```
UPDATE RecipeChapter
```

The SET clause is followed by the name of the column to be updated (Chapter) and the new .WRITE method. The .WRITE takes three parameters. The first parameter is the sentence to be appended. The second and third parameters are null, indicating that the new text should be appended to the column and not inserted into the middle.

```
SET     Chapter.WRITE (' In addition to the basics, this chapter will also provide
recipes that can be used in your day to day development and administration.'
                    , NULL, NULL)
```

The WHERE clause specifies that the Chapter column for a single row matching ChapterlD = 1 is to be modified:

```
WHERE ChapterlD = 1 ;
```

The next example of .WRITE demonstrates replacing data within the body of the column. In the example, the expression "day to day" was replaced with "daily." The bigint value of @Offset and @Length are measured in bytes for the varbinary(max) and varchar(max) data types. For nvarchar(max), these parameters measure the actual number of characters. For this example, .WRITE has a value for @Offset (181 bytes into the text) and @Length (10 bytes long):

```
UPDATE RecipeChapter
SET    Chapter.WRITE('daily', CHARINDEX('day to day', Chapter) - 1,
                    LEN('day to day'))
WHERE  ChapterID = 1 ;
```

In the recipe example, string functions are used to find the required offset and length. These values may also be specified explicitly if they are known.

```
UPDATE RecipeChapter
SET   Chapter .WRITE('daily', 181, 10)
WHERE ChapterlD = 1 ;
```

To build on this recipe, consider the case of inserting data or removing data from the column value instead of replacing a set of characters.

```
-- insert the string '*test value* ' before the word 'beginning'
UPDATE RecipeChapter
SET    Chapter.WRITE('*test value* ', 7, 0)
WHERE  ChapterID = 1 ;
```

The following select statement will show the string "*test value*" inserted into the chapter text.

```
SELECT Chapter
FROM   RecipeChapter ;
```

This query returns the following:

```
Chapter
-------------------------------------------------------------------------------------------
At the *test value* beginning of each chapter you will notice that basic concepts are covered
first. In addition to the basics, this chapter will also provide recipes that can be used in
your daily development and administration.
```

Because a length of 0 is specified, no data in the original column will be overlaid by the string that is to be inserted.

```
-- remove the string '*test value* ' before the word 'beginning'
UPDATE RecipeChapter
SET    Chapter.WRITE('', 7, 13)
WHERE  ChapterID = 1 ;
```

The following `SELECT` statement will show the string `'*test value*'` removed from the chapter text.

```
SELECT Chapter
FROM   RecipeChapter ;
```

This query returns the following:

```
Chapter
-------------------------------------------------------------------------------------------
At the beginning of each chapter you will notice that basic concepts are covered first. In
addition to the basics, this chapter will also provide recipes that can be used in your daily
development and administration.
```

Because the empty string `''` is used and a length of `13,` 13 characters in the source value will be replaced by the empty string, effectively deleting 13 characters from the column.

■ **Note** So, why not update the entire value of the column? Let's say that instead of a 200- or 300-character string, the column contains 10MB or 1GB of data. By updating just the few bytes that need to change, only the changed pages will be required to be logged. If the entire value is updated, the entire value will be logged, which would be much less efficient.

8-13. Deleting Rows

Problem

You need to remove one or more rows from a table.

Solution

The DELETE statement removes one or more rows from a table. First, create an example table and populate it with rows:

```
SELECT *
INTO   Production.Example_ProductProductPhoto
FROM   Production.ProductProductPhoto ;
```

```
(504 row(s) affected)
```

■ **Note** The SELECT...INTO <table_name> form of the SELECT statement creates a new table with the name <table_name> and column definitions that conform to the columns returned from the SELECT clause. In the case of a SELECT * from a single table, the resulting table will have the same column definitions as the base table; however, no defaults, constraints, indexes, or keys are copied from the base table.

Next, delete all rows from the table.

```
DELETE Production.Example_ProductProductPhoto ;
```

This returns the following.

```
(504 row(s) affected)
```

Next, use a DELETE statement with a WHERE clause. Let's say the relationship of keys between two tables was dropped, and the users were able to delete data from the primary key table, but the data in the foreign key tables is not deleted (see Chapter 15 for a review of primary and foreign keys). We now need to delete rows in the foreign key tables that are missing a corresponding entry in the Product table. In this example, no rows meet this criteria:

```
-- Repopulate the Example_ProductProductPhoto table
INSERT Production.Example_ProductProductPhoto
       SELECT *
       FROM   Production.ProductProductPhoto ;

DELETE Production.Example_ProductProductPhoto
WHERE  ProductID NOT IN (SELECT  ProductID
                         FROM    Production.Product) ;
```

The INSERT followed by the DELETE returns the following:

```
(504 row(s) affected)
(0 row(s) affected)
```

This third example demonstrates the same functionality of the previous example; only the DELETE has been rewritten to use a FROM clause instead of a subquery:

```
DELETE
FROM    ppp
FROM    Production.Example_ProductProductPhoto ppp
        LEFT OUTER JOIN Production.Product p
           ON ppp.ProductID = p.ProductID
WHERE   p.ProductID IS NULL ;
```

```
This delete statement returns: (0 row(s) affected)
```

How It Works

In the first example of the recipe, all rows are deleted from the Example_ProductProductPhoto table:

```
DELETE Production.Example_ProductProductPhoto
```

This is because there was no WHERE clause to specify which rows would be deleted. In the second example, the WHERE clause is used to specify rows to be deleted based on a subquery lookup to another table:

```
WHERE ProductID NOT IN (SELECT ProductID FROM Production.Product)
```

The third example uses a LEFT OUTER JOIN instead of a subquery, joining the ProductID of the two tables:

```
DELETE
FROM  ppp -- the alias of the table to be modified
--
-- use a from clause and join to specify the table to be modified
-- and any joins used to filter the delete
--
FROM  Production.Example_ProductProductPhoto ppp
    LEFT OUTER JOIN Production.Product p
      ON ppp.ProductID = p.ProductID
--
-- and filters to select the rows to be deleted from the table to be modified
--
WHERE p.ProductID IS NULL ;
```

Because a LEFT OUTER JOIN was used, if any rows did *not* match between the left and right tables, the fields selected from the right table would be represented by NULL values. To show rows in Production.Example_ProductProductPhoto that do not have a matching ProductID in the Production.Product table, you can qualify the Production.Product as follows:

```
WHERE p.ProductID IS NULL
```

Any rows without a match to the Production.Product table will be deleted from the Production.Example_ProductProductPhoto table.

8-14. Deleting Rows and Returning the Deleted Rows

Problem

You need to delete a number of rows from a table and return the ID of the deleted rows to the client application.

Solution

A DELETE statement may contain an output clause. The OUTPUT clause of the DELETE statement instructs SQL Server to return specified columns from the deleted rows.

First, create a sample table.

```
SELECT *
INTO   HumanResources.Example_JobCandidate
FROM   HumanResources.JobCandidate ;
```

This statement will output the following:

```
(13 row(s) affected)
```

Next, delete rows from the table and return the ID of the deleted rows.

```
DELETE
FROM   HumanResources.Example_JobCandidate
OUTPUT deleted.JobCandidateID
WHERE  JobCandidateID < 5 ;
```

The DELETE statement returns these results:

```
JobCandidateID
--------------
1
2
3
4
```

How It Works

The OUTPUT clause adds a result set to the DELETE statement containing the columns in the OUTPUT clause. The DELETE, FROM, WHERE, and any of the JOIN clauses work the same as any other DELETE statement. The OUTPUT clause allows access to the deleted virtual table. The virtual table is a temporary view of the rows affected by the DELETE statement.

```
DELETE
FROM  HumanResources.Example_JobCandidate
OUTPUT deleted.JobCandidateID
WHERE JobCandidateID < 5
```

The output may be redirected to a destination table or table variable using the OUTPUT ... INTO form of the OUTPUT clause. For example, if a table variable @deletedCandidates had been declared in a stored procedure or script, the output of the DELETE statement would be inserted in the table variable with the statement.

```
DELETE
 FROM HumanResources.Example_JobCandidate
OUTPUT deleted.JobCandidateID INTO @deletedCandidates
 WHERE JobCandidateID < 5
```

8-15. Deleting All Rows Quickly (Truncating)

Problem

You need to remove all rows from a table quickly with minimal logging.

Solution

The TRUNCATE statement deletes all rows from a table in a minimally logged fashion that results in a much quicker delete than a standard DELETE statement if you have very large tables. The DELETE statement should be used for operations that must be fully logged; however, for test or throwaway data, this is a fast technique for removing large amounts of data from the database. "Minimal logging" refers to how much recoverability information is written to the database's transaction log (see Chapter 33). The syntax for TRUNCATE is as follows:

```
TRUNCATE TABLE table_name ;
```

This statement takes just the table name to truncate. Since TRUNCATE always removes *all* rows from a table, there is no FROM or WHERE clause.

First populate a sample table.

```
SELECT *
INTO  Production.Example_TransactionHistory
FROM  Production.TransactionHistory ;
```

The INSERT statement returns the following.

```
(113443 row(s) affected)
```

Next, truncate ALL rows from the example table.

```
TRUNCATE TABLE Production.Example_TransactionHistory ;
```

Next, the table's row count is queried:

```
SELECT COUNT(*)
FROM  Production.Example_TransactionHistory ;
```

This returns the following:

```
0
```

How It Works

The TRUNCATE TABLE statement, like the DELETE statement, can delete rows from a table. TRUNCATE TABLE deletes rows faster than DELETE, because it is minimally logged. Unlike DELETE, however, the TRUNCATE TABLE always removes ALL rows in the table (there is never a WHERE clause).

Although TRUNCATE TABLE is a faster way to delete rows, you cannot use it if the table columns are referenced by a foreign key constraint (see Chapter 15 for more information on foreign keys), if the table is published using transactional or merge replication, or if the table participates in an indexed view (see Chapter 16 for more information). Also, if the table has an IDENTITY column, keep in mind that the column will be reset to the seed value defined for the column (if no seed was explicitly set, it is set to 1).

8-16. Merging Data (Inserting, Updating, or Deleting Values)

Problem

You have a table that contains the ID of the last order placed by a customer. Each time a customer places an order, you need to either insert a new record if this is the first order placed by that customer or update an existing row if the customer had placed an order previously.

Solution

The MERGE statement accepts a row or set of rows and, for each row, determines whether that row exists in a target table. The statement allows different actions to be taken based on this determination. The basic syntax for the MERGE statement is as follows:

```
MERGE
     [ INTO ] <target_table> [ [ AS ] table_alias ]
     USING <table_source> [ [ AS ] table_alias ]
     ON <merge_search_condition>
     [ WHEN MATCHED [ AND <clause_search_condition> ]
       THEN <merge_matched> ] [ ...n ]
     [ WHEN NOT MATCHED [ BY TARGET ] [ AND <clause_search_condition> ]
         THEN <merge_not_matched> ]
     [ WHEN NOT MATCHED BY SOURCE [ AND <clause_search_condition> ]
         THEN <merge_matched> ] [ ...n ]
```

Table 8-6 describes the elements of the MERGE statement:

Table 8-6. MERGE *Statement*

Argument	Definition
target_table	The table or updateable view that the MERGE statement will update, insert into, or delete from.
table_source	The data source that will be matched to the target table. The MERGE statement will execute updates, inserts, or deletes against the target table based on the result of this match.
merge_search_condition	Specifies the conditions by which the source table will be matched against the target table.
clause_search_condition	The MERGE statement can choose from multiple WHEN MATCHED and WHEN NOT MATCHED clauses. If, for example, multiple WHEN MATCHED clauses exist, the MERGE statement will choose the first WHEN MATCHED clause found that matches the search condition specified.

(*continued*)

Table 8-6. (*continued*)

Argument	Definition
merge_matched	Specifies an UPDATE or DELETE to be executed against the target_table. In the case where the MERGE statement will update a row, this looks like this: UPDATE SET column_name = {expression | DEFAULT | NULL} [,...n } } [,...n] Note, this looks just like the update statement's column assignment list. There is no WHERE clause or table name specified here because this context has already been set previously in target_table and merge_search_condition. When the MERGE statement should execute a delete, the syntax is simply DELETE.
merge_not_matched	Specifies an INSERT to be executed against the target_table. The INSERT operation looks like this: INSERT [(column_list)] ({DEFAULT | NULL | expression }[,...n]) Note, the arguments to this statement follow the same rules as the INSERT statement syntax described in Table 8-1.

This example will track the latest customer order information in the following table:

```
CREATE TABLE Sales.LastCustomerOrder
       (
        CustomerID INT,
        SalesorderID INT,
        CONSTRAINT pk_LastCustomerOrder PRIMARY KEY CLUSTERED (CustomerId)
        ) ;
```

Executing this CREATE TABLE statement returns the following:

```
Command(s) completed successfully.
```

The following statements will declare variables representing the customer and order IDs and then use the MERGE statement to INSERT into or UPDATE the Sales.LastCustomerOrder table.

```
DECLARE @CustomerID INT = 100,
        @SalesOrderID INT = 101 ;

MERGE INTO Sales.LastCustomerOrder AS tgt
  USING
      (SELECT @CustomerID AS CustomerID,
              @SalesOrderID AS SalesOrderID
      ) AS src
  ON tgt.CustomerID = src.CustomerID
  WHEN MATCHED
      THEN UPDATE
```

```
      SET        SalesOrderID = src.SalesOrderID
    WHEN NOT MATCHED
      THEN INSERT (
                 CustomerID,
                 SalesOrderID
                 )
      VALUES     (src.CustomerID,
                  src.SalesOrderID) ;
```

Executing these statements will return the following:

```
(1 row(s) affected)
```

Check to see whether the record was inserted successfully.

```
SELECT *
FROM  Sales.LastCustomerOrder ;
```

This SELECT statement returns the following:

```
CustomerID  SalesorderID
----------- ------------
100         101
```

Using the following table, substitute values for the variables @CustomerID and @SalesOrderID. For each row in the table, update the script with the appropriate values and rerun the DECLARE and MERGE statements.

@CustomerID	@SalesOrderID
101	101
100	102
102	103
100	104
101	105

Now rerun the SELECT statement to check the results.

```
SELECT *
FROM   Sales.LastCustomerOrder ;
```

The SELECT statement returns the following:

```
CustomerID  SalesorderID
----------- ------------
100         104
101         105
102         103
```

As new orders are created for a customer, a new row is added to the table if this is the first order for that customer; however, if that customer had already placed an order, the existing row is updated.

A new requirement has arrived, and not only do we need to track the `LastCustomerOrder`, but we need to track the `LargestCustomerOrder`. We need to populate a new table and insert a row for the first order a customer places but update the row only if a new order from that customer is larger than the previously recorded order.

First, create a table to track the order information.

```
CREATE TABLE Sales.LargestCustomerOrder
       (
       CustomerID INT,
       SalesorderID INT,
              TotalDue MONEY,
       CONSTRAINT pk_LargestCustomerOrder PRIMARY KEY CLUSTERED (CustomerId)
       ) ;
```

Executing this `CREATE TABLE` statement returns the following:

```
Command(s) completed successfully.
```

The following statements will declare variables representing the customer and order IDs as well as the `TotalDue` for the order and then use the `MERGE` statement to `INSERT` into or `UPDATE` the `Sales.LastCustomerOrder` table.

```
DECLARE @CustomerID INT = 100,
        @SalesOrderID INT = 101 ,
        @TotalDue MONEY = 1000.00

MERGE INTO Sales.LargestCustomerOrder AS tgt
    USING
        (SELECT @CustomerID AS CustomerID,
                @SalesOrderID AS SalesOrderID,
                @TotalDue AS TotalDue
        ) AS src
    ON tgt.CustomerID = src.CustomerID
    WHEN MATCHED AND tgt.TotalDue < src.TotalDue
         THEN UPDATE
         SET    SalesOrderID = src.SalesOrderID
                , TotalDue = src.TotalDue
  WHEN NOT MATCHED
    THEN INSERT (
                 CustomerID,
                 SalesOrderID,
                 TotalDue
                 )
     VALUES      (src.CustomerID,
                  src.SalesOrderID,
                  src.TotalDue) ;
```

Check to see whether the record was inserted successfully.

```
SELECT *
FROM  Sales.LargestCustomerOrder ;
```

This `SELECT` statement returns the following:

```
CustomerID  SalesorderID  TotalDue
----------  ------------  --------
100         101           1000.00
```

Using the following table, substitute values for the variables `@CustomerID` and `@SalesOrderID and @ TotalDue`. For each row in the table, update the script with the appropriate values and rerun the `DECLARE` and `MERGE` statements.

@CustomerID	@SalesOrderID	@TotalDue
101	101	1000.00
100	102	1100.00
100	104	999.00
101	105	999.00

Now rerun the `SELECT` statement to check the results.

```
SELECT *
FROM  Sales.LargestCustomerOrder ;
```

The `SELECT` statement returns the following:

```
CustomerID   SalesorderID   TotalDue
----------   -------------  --------
100          102            1100.00
101          101            1000.00
```

Note that the final two orders did not update any rows, and the results indicate the correct largest orders of 1,100.00 and 1,000.00.

How It Works

In this example, we use the `MERGE` statement to insert new rows into a table or update rows that already exist in that table. The basic structure of the two examples is the same, so let's look at the elements of the `Sales.LargestCustomerOrder` example, which adds one twist.

The first two statements in the example create a table to hold the customer order information and declare variables that are used in the `MERGE` statement. The meat of the example is the `MERGE` statement itself.

First, we specify the table that will be the "target" of the `MERGE` statement, in this case `Sales.LargestCustomerOrder`. We alias this table `tgt` for reference throughout the statement. We are merging into a table in this case, but we could also specify an updateable view.

```
MERGE INTO Sales.LargestCustomerOrder AS tgt
```

Next, we specify the data that we will merge into the target table. In this case, we use a `SELECT` statement as a derived table, but this clause can take a number of forms. We could use one of the following:

- Table or view
- Row set function such as `OPENROWSET`
- User-defined table function
- Call to OPENXML
- Derived table

The `USING` clause may also include inner and outer joins to involve multiple tables and sources.

In the example we use a derived table that returns one row by mapping variable values to columns in our result set. This is a common pattern when using the MERGE statement with the stored procedure parameter values as the source of the merge.

```
USING
    (SELECT @CustomerID AS CustomerID,
            @SalesOrderID AS SalesOrderID,
            @TotalDue AS TotalDue
    ) AS src
```

Now that we have specified a source and target, we need to instruct the MERGE statement how to match the source row(s) with the rows in the target table. This is effectively a JOIN condition between the source and target.

```
ON tgt.CustomerID = src.CustomerID
```

For each source row processed by the MERGE statement, it may either:

- Exist in both the source and target (MATCHED)
- Exist in the source but not the target (NOT MATCHED)
- Exist in the target but not the source (NOT MATCHED BY SOURCE)

In this example, we use WHEN MATCHED with a filter so that only rows that meet the join condition and the filter condition are updated in the target table. For these rows, we update the TotalDue column of the target table.

```
WHEN MATCHED AND tgt.TotalDue < src.TotalDue
  THEN UPDATE
   SET           SalesOrderID = src.SalesOrderID
                 , TotalDue = src.TotalDue
```

The WHEN NOT MATCHED clause indicates that a row exists in the source that does not exist in the target. In this example, we would like to insert a new row in the target when this occurs.

```
WHEN NOT MATCHED
  THEN INSERT (
               CustomerID,
               SalesOrderID,
               TotalDue
              )
   VALUES     (src.CustomerID,
               src.SalesOrderID,
               src.TotalDue) ;
```

The MERGE statement accommodates multiple instances of the WHEN MATCHED, WHEN NOT MATCHED, and WHEN NOT MATCHED BY SOURCE clauses. Let's say that we would like to track the last customer order and the largest customer order in the same table. We may have these clauses:

```
WHEN MATCHED AND tgt.TotalDue < src.TotalDue
  THEN UPDATE
   SET           SalesOrderID = src.SalesOrderID
                 , TotalDue = src.TotalDue
WHEN MATCHED
  THEN UPDATE
   SET           SalesOrderID = src.SalesOrderID
```

The order of these clauses is important. The MERGE statement will choose the first clause that evaluates true. In this case, if the MERGE statement finds a match that had a TotalDue that is greater than the existing largest

TotalDue for a customer, then the first clause is chosen. The second clause is chosen for all other matches. If we reversed the order of these clauses, then the WHEN MATCHED with no filter would execute for all matched rows, and the filtered clause would never be chosen.

Like the INSERT, UPDATE, and DELETE statements described earlier, the MERGE statement contains an OUTPUT clause. The only difference is the MERGE statement adds a new $ACTION keyword that indicates whether an INSERT, UPDATE, or DELETE operation occurred against the target table. This T-SQL batch is the same as the batch described throughout this chapter; however, the OUTPUT clause with the $ACTION column has been added to the MERGE statement:

```
DECLARE @CustomerID INT = 100,
        @SalesOrderID INT = 201 ,
        @TotalDue MONEY = 1200.00

MERGE INTO Sales.LargestCustomerOrder AS tgt
  USING
      (SELECT @CustomerID AS CustomerID,
              @SalesOrderID AS SalesOrderID,
              @TotalDue AS TotalDue
       ) AS src
  ON tgt.CustomerID = src.CustomerID
  WHEN MATCHED AND tgt.TotalDue < src.TotalDue
    THEN UPDATE
     SET          SalesOrderID = src.SalesOrderID
                , TotalDue = src.TotalDue
  WHEN NOT MATCHED
    THEN INSERT (
                CustomerID,
                SalesOrderID,
                TotalDue
                )
     VALUES     (src.CustomerID,
                 src.SalesOrderID,
                 src.TotalDue)
  OUTPUT
      $ACTION,
      DELETED.*,
      INSERTED.* ;
```

This merge statement returns the following:

```
$ACTION  CustomerID  SalesorderID TotalDue  CustomerID  SalesorderID TotalDue
-------  ----------- ------------ --------- ----------- ------------ --------
UPDATE   100         102          1100.00   100         201          2000.00
```

The $ACTION keyword indicates that this set of values resulted in an update to the target table, and the columns that follow represent the version of the record before and after the update.

CHAPTER 9

Working with Strings

by Andy Roberts

This next set of recipes demonstrates SQL Server's string functions. String functions provide a multitude of uses for your Transact-SQL programming, allowing for string cleanup, conversion between ASCII and regular characters, pattern searches, removal of trailing blanks, and much more. Table 9-1 lists the different string functions available in SQL Server.

Table 9-1. *String Functions*

Function Name(s)	Description
CONCAT	The CONCAT function concatenates a variable list of string values into one larger string.
ASCII and CHAR	The ASCII function takes the leftmost character of a character expression and returns the ASCII code. The CHAR function converts an integer value for an ASCII code to a character value instead.
CHARINDEX and PATINDEX	The CHARINDEX function is used to return the starting position of a string within another string. The PATINDEX function is similar to CHARINDEX, except that PATINDEX allows the use of wildcards when specifying the string for which to search.
DIFFERENCE and SOUNDEX	The two functions DIFFERENCE and SOUNDEX both work with character strings to evaluate those that sound similar. SOUNDEX assigns a string a four-digit code, and DIFFERENCE evaluates the level of similarity between the SOUNDEX outputs for two separate strings.
LEFT and RIGHT	The LEFT function returns a part of a character string, beginning at the specified number of characters from the left. The RIGHT function is like the LEFT function, only it returns a part of a character string beginning at the specified number of characters from the right.
LEN and DATALENGTH	The LEN function returns the number of characters in a string expression, excluding any blanks after the last character (trailing blanks). DATALENGTH, on the other hand, returns the number of bytes used for an expression.
LOWER and UPPER	The LOWER function returns a character expression in lowercase, and the UPPER function returns a character expression in uppercase.
LTRIM and RTRIM	The LTRIM function removes leading blanks, and the RTRIM function removes trailing blanks.

(continued)

***Table 9-1.** continued*

Function Name(s)	Description
NCHAR and UNICODE	The UNICODE function returns the Unicode integer value for the first character of the character or input expression. The NCHAR function takes an integer value designating a Unicode character and converts it to its character equivalent.
REPLACE	The REPLACE function replaces all instances of a provided string within a specified string with a new string.
REPLICATE	The REPLICATE function repeats a given character expression a designated number of times.
REVERSE	The REVERSE function takes a character expression and outputs the expression with each character position displayed in reverse order.
SPACE	The SPACE function returns a string of repeated blank spaces, based on the integer you designate for the input parameter.
STUFF	The STUFF function deletes a specified length of characters and inserts a designated string at the specified starting point.
SUBSTRING	The SUBSTRING function returns a defined chunk of a specified expression.

The next few recipes will demonstrate examples of how string functions are used.

9-1. Concatenating Multiple Strings

Problem

You have a set of string values that you would like to concatenate into one string value. This is often a requirement when formatting names or addresses. In the database the name may be stored as separate first, middle and last names; however, you may wish to execute a query that returns "Last Name, First Name" and add the middle initial if it exists.

Solution

For this example, create a FullName column from the FirstName, MiddleName and LastName columns of the Person.Person table.

```
SELECT TOP 5
   FullName = CONCAT(LastName, ', ', FirstName, ' ', MiddleName)
FROM  Person.Person p ;
```

The result of this query is:

```
FullName
-----------------------------------
Abbas, Syed E
Abel, Catherine R.
Abercrombie, Kim
Abercrombie, Kim
Abercrombie, Kim B
```

How it Works

The CONCAT function accepts a variable list of string values (at least two are required) and concatenates them into one string. A difference between the CONCAT function and using the + operator is how nulls are handled. The operator + will return NULL if either the left or right side of the operator is NULL. The CONCATfunction will convert NULL arguments to an empty string prior to the concatenation.

Take the following select statement that concatenates a FullName with three different approaches:

```
SELECT TOP 5
   FullName = CONCAT(LastName, ', ', FirstName, ' ', MiddleName),
               FullName2 = LastName + ', ' + FirstName + ' ' + MiddleName,
               FullName3 = LastName + ', ' + FirstName +
                 IIF(MiddleName IS NULL, '', ' ' + MiddleName)
FROM Person.Person p
WHERE MiddleName IS NULL ;
```

This query yields the following results:

```
FullName             FullName2   FullName3
----------------     ---------   ------------------------
Abercrombie, Kim     NULL        Abercrombie, Kim
Abercrombie, Kim     NULL        Abercrombie, Kim
Abolrous, Sam        NULL        Abolrous, Sam
Acevedo, Humberto    NULL        Acevedo, Humberto
Achong, Gustavo      NULL        Achong, Gustavo
```

The FullName Column used the CONCAT function as seen in the recipe. FullName2 uses the + operator. The + operator will always return NULL if one of its operands is NULL - because MiddleName is NULL for all rows then FullName2 is NULLfor all rows. Finally, the FullName3 column shows the logic that is encapsulated in the CONCATfunction. In this recipe's example, 3 columns and two string literals are concatenated together using the CONCAT function. The MiddleName column is NULL for some rows in the table but no additional NULL handling logic is required when using CONCAT to generate the FullName string.

9-2. Finding a Character's ASCII Value

Problem

Your application requires the ASCII values of a string's characters or passes you ASCII values that you must assemble into a string.

Solution

This first example demonstrates how to convert characters into the integer ASCII value:

```
SELECT  ASCII('H'),
   ASCII('e'),
   ASCII('l'),
   ASCII('l'),
   ASCII('o') ;
```

This returns:

```
72        101        108        108        111
```

Next, the CHAR function is used to convert the integer values back into characters again:

```
SELECT  CHAR(72),
   CHAR(101),
   CHAR(108),
   CHAR(108),
   CHAR(111) ;
```

This returns:

```
H  e  l  l  o
```

How it Works

The ASCII function takes the leftmost character of a character expression and returns the ASCII code. The CHAR function converts the integer value of an ASCII code to a character value. The ASCII function only converts the first character of the supplied string. If the string is empty or NULL, ASCII will return NULL (although a blank, single-space value is represented by a value of 32).

In this recipe, the word "Hello" is deconstructed into 5 characters and then converted into the numeric ASCII values using the ASCII function. In the second T-SQL statement the processis reversed and the ASCII values are converted back into characters using the CHAR function.

9-3. Returning Integer and Character Unicode Values

Problem

Your application requires the Unicode values of a string's characters or passes you Unicode values that you must assemble into a string.

Solution

The UNICODE function returns the Unicode integer value for the first character of the character or input expression. The NCHAR function takes an integer value designating a Unicode character and converts it to its character equivalent.

This first example converts single characters into an integer value representing the Unicode standard character code:

```
SELECT  UNICODE('G'),
   UNICODE('o'),
   UNICODE('o'),
   UNICODE('d'),
   UNICODE('!') ;
```

This returns:

```
71           111           111           100           33
```

Next, the Unicode integer values are converted back into characters:

```
SELECT  NCHAR(71),
   NCHAR(111),
   NCHAR(111),
   NCHAR(100),
   NCHAR(33) ;
```

This returns

```
G    o    o    d    !
```

How it Works

In this example, the string "Good!" is deconstructed one character at a time and then each character is converted into an integer value using the UNICODE function. In the second example, the integer values are reversed back into characters by using the NCHAR function.

9-4. Locating a Substring

Problem

You need to find out where a string segment or character pattern starts within the context of a larger string. For example, you need to find all of the street addresses that match a pattern you are looking for.

Solution

This example demonstrates how to find the starting position of a string within another string:

```
SELECT CHARINDEX('string to find','This is the bigger string to find something in.');
```

This returns

```
20
```

That is, the first character of the first instance of the string "string to find" is the 20th character of the string that we are searching.

In some cases a character pattern must be found within a string. The following example returns all rows from the address table that contain the digit 0 preceding the word "Olive"

```
SELECT TOP 10
   AddressID,
   AddressLine1,
   PATINDEX('%[0]%Olive%', AddressLine1)
FROM     Person.Address
WHERE    PATINDEX('%[0]%Olive%', AddressLine1) > 0 ;
```

The results of this statement:

```
AddressID        AddressLine1
---------        ------------------    ---
29048            1201 Olive Hill       3
11768            1201 Olive Hill       3
15417            1206 Olive St         3
24480            1480 Oliveria Road    4
19871            1480 Oliveria Road    4
12826            1803 Olive Hill       3
292              1803 Olive Hill       3
29130            2309 Mt. Olivet Ct.   3
23767            2309 Mt. Olivet Ct.   3
23875            3280 Oliveria Road    4
```

How it Works

The CHARINDEX function is used to return the starting position of a string within another string. The syntax is as follows:

```
CHARINDEX ( expressionToFind ,expressionToSearch[ , start_location ] )
```

CHARINDEX will sefrarch the string passed to expressionToSearch for the first instance of expressionToFind that exists after the optionally specified start_location.

This function returned the starting character position, in this case the 20th character, where the first argument expression was found in the second expression. Wildcards are not supported with CHARINDEX.

To use wildcards when searching for a substring use the PATINDEX function. Similar to CHARINDEX, PATINDEX allows the use of wildcards in the string you are searching for. The syntax for PATINDEX is as follows:

```
PATINDEX ( '%pattern%' ,expression )
```

PATINDEX returns the start position of the first occurrence of the search pattern, but unlike CHARINDEX, it does not contain a starting position option. Both CHARINDEX and PATINDEX return 0 if the search expression is not found in the expression to be searched.

■ **Note** In this example we showed the a small set of the wild card searches that may be used within PATINDEX. PATINDEX supports the same wildcard functionality as the LIKE operator. For further information see the Performing Wildcard Searches recipe in Chapter 1.

9-5. Determining the Similarity of Strings

Problem

You are designing a call center application and the agents look up customers by last name while speaking with the customer on the phone. The agents would like to guess at the spelling of the name to narrow the search results and then work with the customer to determine the appropriate spelling.

Solution

The two functions SOUNDEXand DIFFERENCE both work with character strings and evaluate the strings based on English phonetic rules.

Take the example where an agent hears the name "Smith". SOUNDEX may be used to return all of the names that contain the same SOUNDEX value of the string "Smith".

```
SELECT  DISTINCT
SOUNDEX(LastName),
    SOUNDEX('Smith'),
    LastName
FROM    Person.Person
WHERE   SOUNDEX(LastName) = SOUNDEX('Smith') ;
```

This query returns the results:

```
                LastName
-----   -----   -----------
S530    S530    Schmidt
S530    S530    Smith
S530    S530    Smith-Bates
S530    S530    Sneath
```

Note that "Smith" is returned, but also a number of names that may sound like the last name "Smith".

Another way to look at the data would be to view the names that had the "least difference" from the search expression. The SQL Server DIFFERENCE function evaluates the phonetic similarity of two strings and returns a value from 0 (low similarity) to 4 (high similarity). If we look for last names with a phonetic similarity to "Smith"

```
SELECT  DISTINCT
   SOUNDEX(LastName),
   SOUNDEX('smith'),
   DIFFERENCE(LastName, 'Smith'),
   LastName
FROM    Person.Person
WHERE   DIFFERENCE(LastName, 'Smith') = 4 ;
```

This query returns:

```
                     LastName
-----   -----   -    -----------
S530    S530    4    Smith
S530    S530    4    Smith-Bates
S530    S530    4    Sneath
S550    S530    4    Simon
S553    S530    4    Samant
S553    S530    4    Swaminathan
```

Note that the name "Schmidt" contains the same SOUNDEX value so is returned from the first query but is absent from the second result.

How it Works

The SOUNDEX function follows a set of rules originally created to categorize names based on the phonetic characteristics of the name rather than the spelling of that name. The soundex of a name consists of a letter – the first letter of that name – followed by three representing the predominant consonant sounds of that name.

Difference uses a variation of the soundex algorithm to return a rather course determination of the phonetic similarity of two strings - a range of 0 representing very low similarity to 5 representing very high similarity. Taking the Leftmost or Rightmost Part of a String

9-6. Returning the Left-Most Portion of a String

Problem

You have a string value and only need the first or last part of the string. For example, you have a report that will list a set of products but you only have room on the report to display the first 10 characters of the product name.

Solution

This recipe demonstrates how to return a subset of the leftmost and rightmost parts of a string. First take the leftmost (first) 10 characters of a string:

```
SELECT LEFT('I only want the leftmost 10 characters.', 10) ;
```

This returns:

```
I only wan
```

Next, take the rightmost (last) 10 characters of a string:

```
SELECT RIGHT('I only want the rightmost 10 characters.', 10) ;
```

This returns:

```
haracters.
```

The example in the problem statement describes taking the left 10 characters of the product name for a report. The following query is an example of how to accomplish this.

```
SELECT TOP 5
   ProductNumber,
   ProductName = LEFT(Name, 10)
FROM    Production.Product ;
```

This query yields the following:

```
ProductNumber   ProductName
-------------   -----------
AR-5381         Adjustable
BA-8327         Bearing Ba
BE-2349         BB Ball Be
BE-2908         Headset Ba
BL-2036         Blade
```

It is common that a string needs to be "padded" on one side or another. For example, the AccountNumber column in the Sales.Customer table is 10 characters consisting of "AW" plus 8 digits. The 8 digits include the CustomerID column padded with 0's. A customer with the CustomerID 123 would have the account number "AW00000123".

```
SELECT TOP 5
   CustomerID,
   AccountNumber = CONCAT('AW', RIGHT(REPLICATE('0', 8)
                   + CAST(CustomerID AS VARCHAR(10)), 8))
FROM    Sales.Customer ;
```

This returns:

```
CustomerID      AccountNumber
----------      -------------
1               AW00000001
2               AW00000002
7               AW00000007
19              AW00000019
20              AW00000020
```

How it Works

The LEFT function returns the segment of the supplied character string that starts at the beginning of the string and ends at the specified number of characters from the beginning of the string. The RIGHT function returns the segment of the supplied character string that starts at the specified number of characters from the end of the string and ends at the end of the string.

This recipe demonstrates three examples of using LEFT and RIGHT. The first two examples demonstrate how to return the leftmost or the rightmost characters of a string value. The third example demonstrates how to the pad a string in order to conform to some expected business or reporting format.

When presenting data to end users or exporting data to external systems, you may sometimes need to preserve or add leading values, such as leading zeros to fixed-length numbers or spaces to varchar fields. CustomerID was zero-padded by first concatenating 8 zeros in a string to the converted varchar(10) value of the CustomerID. Then, outside of this concatenation, RIGHT was used to grab the last 8 characters of the concatenated string (thus taking leading zeros from the left side with it, when the CustomerID fell short of 8 digits).

9-7. Returning Part of a String

Problem

You are creating a call-center report that includes aggregations of data by area code and exchange of phone numbers in the system. You need to look at characters 1-3 and 5-7 of a phone number string. Solution

Use the left and substring functions to pull out the desired characters of the phone number.

```
SELECT TOP 3
   PhoneNumber,
   AreaCode = LEFT(PhoneNumber, 3),
   Exchange = SUBSTRING(PhoneNumber, 5, 3)
FROM    Person.PersonPhone
WHERE   PhoneNumber LIKE '[0-9][0-9][0-9]-[0-9][0-9][0-9]-[0-9][0-9][0-9][0-9]' ;
```

```
PhoneNumber     AreaCode    Exchange
-----------     --------    --------
100-555-0115    100         555
100-555-0124    100         555
100-555-0137    100         555
```

How it Works

The SUBSTRING function returns a defined segment of a specified string expression. The syntax is as follows:

```
SUBSTRING ( expression, start, length )
```

The first argument of this function is the character expression that contains the desired segment. The second argument defines the starting position within "expression" of the segment to return. The third argument is the length, in characters, of the segment to be returned.

In this recipe, the SUBSTRING function is used to extract digits 5-7 from a longer phone number. The first parameter is the phone number. The second parameter is the starting position of the string - the 5th character in the string. The third parameter indicates how many characters to extract - 3.

There are multiple phone number formats stored in the database and we are only interested in the format XXX-XXX-XXXX. The WHERE clause of the SELECT statement uses wildcards with the LIKE operator to filter the results to only numbers that meet this format.

9-8. Counting Characters or Bytes in a String

Problem

Your application requires you to return the length or size (in bytes) of strings that you return from a stored procedure.

Solution

This first example returns the number of characters in the Unicode string (Unicode data takes two bytes for each character, whereas non-Unicode takes only one):

```
SELECT LEN(N'She sells sea shells by the sea shore.  ') ;
```

This returns

```
38
```

This next example returns the number of bytes in the Unicode string:

```
SELECT DATALENGTH(N'She sells sea shells by the sea shore.  ') ;
```

This returns

```
80
```

How it Works

The LEN function returns the number of characters in a string expression excluding any blanks after the last character (trailing blanks). DATALENGTH returns the number of bytes used for an expression (including trailing blanks.

This recipe uses a Unicode string defined by prefixing the string with an N:

```
N'She sells sea shells by the sea shore.  '
```

The number of characters for this string is 38 according to LEN as there are 38 characters starting with the "S" in "She" and ending with the ".". The spaces following the "." are not counted by LEN. DATALENGTH returns 80 bytes. SQL Server uses the Unicode UCS-2 encoding form, which consumes 2 bytes per character stored and the trailing spaces are counted - (38 + 2) * 2.

■ **Note** We typically use DATALENGTH to find the number of bytes in a string; however, DATALENGTH will determine the length of any data type. Take the follow query for example:

```
SELECT  DATALENGTH(123),
   DATALENGTH(123.0),
   DATALENGTH(GETDATE()) ;
```

We pass an int, a numeric and a datetime value into DATALENGTH and DATALENGTH returns 4, 5, and 8 respectively.

9-9. Replacing Part of a String

Problem

You need to replace all instances of a string value within a larger string value. For example, the name of a product has changed and you must update product descriptions with the new product name.

Solution

This example replaces all instances of the string "Classic" with the work "Vintage":

```
SELECT REPLACE('The Classic Roadie is a stunning example of the bikes that AdventureWorks
have been producing for years - Order your classic Roadie today and experience AdventureWorks
history.', 'Classic', 'Vintage');
```

This returns:

```
The Vintage Roadie is a stunning example of the bikes that AdventureWorks have been producing
for years - Order your Vintage Roadie today and experience AdventureWorks history.
```

How it Works

The REPLACE function searches a source string for all instances of a provided search pattern and replaces them with the supplied replacement string. A strength of REPLACE is that unlike PATINDEX and CHARINDEX that return one location where a pattern is found, REPLACE finds and replaces all instances of the search string within a specific character string. The syntax for REPLACE is as follows:

```
REPLACE ( string_expression , search_string , replacement_string );
```

The first argument, string_expression, is the string that will be searched. The second argument, search_string, is the string to be removed from the original string. The third argument, replacement_string, is the string to use as a replacement to the search string.

In this example we searched the product description for all instances of the string "Classic" and replaced them with the string "Vintage".

REPLACE can also be used to remove portions of a string. If the replacement_string parameter is an empty string (''), REPLACE will remove search_string from string_expression and replace it with 0 characters. Note, in this case this is an empty string ('') not a NULL value. If replacement_string is NULL the the output of REPLACE will always be NULL.

9-10. Stuffing a String into a String

Problem

You need to insert a string into another string.

Solution

This example replaces a part of a string and inserts a new expression into the string body:

```
SELECT STUFF ( 'My cat''s name is X. Have you met him?', 18, 1, 'Edgar' );
```

This returns:

```
My cat's name is Edgar. Have you met him?
```

■ **Note** Do you notice the two single quotes in the query above? This is not double quote but an "escaped" apostrophe. String literals in SQL Server are identified by single quotes. To specify an apostrophe in a string literal you need to "escape" the apostrophe by placing two apostrophe's next to each other. As you can see in the results listing: "cat''s" is displayed as "cat's".

How it Works

The STUFF function deletes a specified length of characters and inserts a designated string at the specified starting point. The syntax is as follows:

```
STUFF ( character_expression, start, length, character_expression )
```

The first argument of this function is the character expression to be modified. The second argument is the starting position of the string to be inserted. The third argument is the number of characters to delete within the string in the first argument. The fourth argument is the actual character expression that you want to insert.

The first character expression in this recipe is "My cat's name is X. Have you met him?". The start value is 18, meaning the replacement will occur at the 18th character in the string ("X"). The length parameter is 1 meaning only one character at position 18 will be deleted. The last character expression is Edgar. This is the value to stuff into the string.

If a 0 length parameter is specified the STUFF function simply inserts the second string into the first string before the character specified with the start argument. For example:

```
SELECT STUFF ( 'My cat''s name is X. Have you met him?', 18, 0, 'Edgar' );
```

This returns:

```
My cat's name is EdgarX. Have you met him?
```

If an empty string ('') is specified for the second character expression the STUFF function deletes the characters starting with the character specified with the start argument and continuing for the number of characters specified in the length argument. For example:

```
SELECT STUFF ( 'My cat''s name is X. Have you met him?', 18, 8, '' );
```

This returns:

```
My cat's name is you met him?
```

9-11. Changing Between Lower- and Uppercase

Problem

You have some text that, for reporting purposes, you would like to return as all upper case or all lower case.

Solution

The following query shows the value of DocumentSummary for a specific row in the Production.Document table:

```
SELECT  DocumentSummary
FROM    Production.Document
WHERE   FileName = 'Installing Replacement Pedals.doc';
```

This returns the following sentence-case value:

```
DocumentSummary
----------------------------------- Detailed instructions for replacing pedals with Adventure
Works Cycles replacement pedals. Instructions are applicable to all Adventure Works Cycles
bicycle models and replacement pedals. Use only Adventure Works Cycles parts when replacing
worn or broken components.
```

This first example demonstrates setting values to lowercase:

```
SELECT  LOWER(DocumentSummary)
FROM    Production.Document
WHERE   FileName = 'Installing Replacement Pedals.doc';
```

This returns:

```
detailed instructions for replacing pedals with adventure works cycles replacement pedals.
instructions are applicable to all adventure works cycles bicycle models and replacement
pedals. use only adventure works cycles parts when replacing worn or broken components.
```

Now for uppercase:

```
SELECT  UPPER(DocumentSummary)
FROM    Production.Document
WHERE   FileName = 'Installing Replacement Pedals.doc';
```

This returns:

```
DETAILED INSTRUCTIONS FOR REPLACING PEDALS WITH ADVENTURE WORKS CYCLES REPLACEMENT PEDALS.
INSTRUCTIONS ARE APPLICABLE TO ALL ADVENTURE WORKS CYCLES BICYCLE MODELS AND REPLACEMENT
PEDALS. USE ONLY ADVENTURE WORKS CYCLES PARTS WHEN REPLACING WORN OR BROKEN COMPONENTS.
```

How it Works

The LOWER function returns a character expression in lowercase, and the UPPER function returns a character expression in uppercase. If a character in the string is not case-convertible the character is returned with no conversion. For example, look at the string with Thai characters used earlier in this chapter:

```
SELECT UPPER (N'เป็นสายอักขระ unicode');
```

This returns:

```
เป็นสายอักขระ UNICODE
```

Because there is no upper and lower case distinction for the Thai characters, UPPER and LOWER produce no affect on them.

■ **Tip** There is not a proper case function built into SQL Server; however, Chapter 20 discusses scalar user-defined functions. Using a user defined function would be a great technique to create a proper case function.

The first example demonstrates the LOWER function and returns a character expression in lowercase. The second example demonstrates the UPPER function and returns a character expression in uppercase. In both cases the function takes a single argument: the character expression containing the case to be converted to either upper- or lowercase.

9-12. Removing Leading and Trailing Blanks

Problem

You have text entered through an application that may contain leading or trailing blanks and you would like to remove these blanks before storing the data.

Solution

This first example demonstrates removing leading blanks from a string:

```
SELECT CONCAT('''', LTRIM('     String with leading and trailing blanks.     '), '''' );
```

This returns:

```
'String with leading and trailing blanks.     '
```

This second example demonstrates removing trailing blanks from a string:

```
SELECT CONCAT('''', RTRIM('     String with leading and trailing blanks.     '), '''' );
```

This returns:

```
'     String with leading and trailing blanks.'
```

The final example shows that LTRIM and RTRIM may be used together to remove blanks from both ends of a string

```
SELECT CONCAT('''', LTRIM(RTRIM('   String with leading and trailing blanks    ')), '''' );
```

This returns:

```
'String with leading and trailing blanks'
```

How it Works

Both `LTRIM` and `RTRIM` take a single argument—a character expression that is to be trimmed. The function then trims the leading or trailing blanks. Note that there is not a `TRIM` function (as seen in other programming languages) that can be used to remove both leading and trailing characters. To do this, you must use both `LTRIM` and `RTRIM` in the same expression.

9-13. Repeating an Expression N Times

Problem

Often when testing an application's user interface you will need to populate sample data into a database that fills the database columns to the maximum length of character data to ensure that the UI will properly display larger strings. Generally the character 'W' is used as it is a wide character.

Solution

Use the replicate function to produce a string of 30 character W's.

```
SELECT REPLICATE ('W', 30) ;
```

This returns

```
WWWWWWWWWWWWWWWWWWWWWWWWWWWWWW
```

Use the replicate function to produce a string of 30 repetitions of the string 'Z_'.

```
SELECT REPLICATE ('W_', 30) ;
```

This returns:

```
W_W_W_W_W_W_W_W_W_W_W_W_W_W_W_W_W_W_W_W_W_W_W_W_W_W_W_W_W_W_
```

How it Works

The REPLICATE function repeats a given character expression a designated number of times. The syntax is as follows:

```
REPLICATE ( character_expression,integer_expression )
```

The first argument is the character expression to be repeated. The second argument is the integer value representing the number of times the character expression is to be repeated.

In this recipe's first example the letter 'W' is supplied as the character expression and is as repeated 30 times. The second example shows that REPLICATE can repeat string values and not only single characers. Use REPLICATE to repeat values rather than having to enter the string literals manually.

9-14. Repeating a Blank Space N Times

Problem

You are formatting a set of values for display and you would like the values to be returned as a one column result set and aligned in 20 character columns.

Solution

This example demonstrates how to repeat a blank space a defined number of times to align the values onto 20-character boundaries:

```
DECLARE @string1 NVARCHAR(20) = 'elephant',
        @string2 NVARCHAR(20) = 'dog',
        @string3 NVARCHAR(20) = 'giraffe' ;

SELECT  *
FROM    ( VALUES
        ( CONCAT(@string1, SPACE(20 - LEN(@string1)), @string2,
                SPACE(20 - LEN(@string2)), @string3,
                SPACE(20 - LEN(@string3))))
 ,
        ( CONCAT(@string2, SPACE(20 - LEN(@string2)), @string3,
                SPACE(20 - LEN(@string3)), @string1,
                SPACE(20 - LEN(@string1)))) ) AS a (formatted_string) ;
```

This returns:

```
formatted_string
------------------------------------elephant            dog                 giraffe
dog                 giraffe             elephant
```

How it Works

The SPACE function returns a string of repeated blank spaces, based on the integer you designate for the input parameter. This is the same functionality as the REPLICATE function only the character to replicate is a constant.

In this recipe there are values that should be returned in one column of text aligned to 20 character boundaries. Each values is concatenated with a number of spaces equal to 20 - the length of the string.

The maximum return value for the SPACE function is 8,000 bytes.

9-15. Reversing the order of Characters in a String

Problem

You have the fully qualified file name and would like to split the string into path and filename.

Solution

In this example the files in the current database are broken out into paths and filenames. Find the last backslash ('\') character in the string and use that position as the basis for the boundary between path and filename.

```
SELECT  Path = LEFT(filename, LEN(filename) - CHARINDEX('\', REVERSE(filename)) + 1),
   FileName = RIGHT(filename, CHARINDEX('\', REVERSE(filename)) - 1)
FROM    sys.sysfiles ;
```

This example returns the following results (In this example the paths and filenames will differ depending on the database file names and locations.)

```
Path                    FileName
----------------        ---------------------------
E:\SqlDatabases\        AdventureWorks2012_Data.mdf
E:\SqlDatabases\        AdventureWorks2012_log.ldf
```

How it Works

The REVERSE function takes a character expression and outputs the expression with each character position displayed in reverse order.

By using CHARINDEX on the reversed string, instead of finding the first occurrence of the character the last occurrence is returned. LEFT and RIGHT are used to split the string at the identified location.

CHAPTER 10

Working with Dates and Times

by Wayne Sheffield

SQL Server has several different date and time data types, with varying levels of range and precision (and a corresponding varying level of storage requirement space). SQL Server also has numerous functions to retrieve, modify, and validate the data from these data types in various formats. This chapter focuses on these functions. Table 10-1 shows the various date/time data types.

Table 10-1. *SQL Server Date/Time Data Types*

Data Type	Format	Range	Accuracy	Storage Size (Bytes)
Time	hh:mm:ss[.nnnnnnn]	00:00:00.0000000 through 23:59:59.9999999	100 nanoseconds	3 to 5
Date	YYYY-MM-DD	0001-01-01 through 9999-12-31	1 day	3
Smalldatetime	YYYY-MM-DD hh:mm:ss	1900-01-01 through 2079-06-06	1 minute	4
Datetime	YYYY-MM-DD hh:mm:ss[.nnn]	1753-01-01 through 9999-12-31	0.00333 second	8
datetime2	YYYY-MM-DD hh:mm:ss[.nnnnnnn]	0001-01-01 00:00:00.0000000 through 9999-12-31 23:59:59.9999999	100 nanoseconds	6 to 8
Datetimeoffset	YYYY-MM-DD hh:mm:ss[.nnnnnnn] [+|-]hh:mm	0001-01-01 00:00:00.0000000 through 9999-12-31 23:59:59.9999999 (in UTC)	100 nanoseconds	8 to 10

10-1. Returning the Current Date and Time

Problem

You need to use the current date and time in your query.

Solution

Use the `GETDATE`, `GETUTCDATE`, `CURRENT_TIMESTAMP`, `SYSDATETIME`, `SYSUTCDATETIME`, or `SYSDATETIMEOFFSET` function to return the current time.

```
SELECT 'GETDATE()' AS [Function],          GETDATE() AS [Value];
SELECT 'CURRENT_TIMESTAMP'AS [Function],    CURRENT_TIMESTAMP AS [Value];
SELECT 'GETUTCDATE()' AS [Function],        GETUTCDATE() AS [Value];
SELECT 'SYSDATETIME()' AS [Function],       SYSDATETIME() AS [Value];
SELECT 'SYSUTCDATETIME()' AS [Function],    SYSUTCDATETIME() AS [Value];
SELECT 'SYSDATETIMEOFFSET()' AS [Function], SYSDATETIMEOFFSET() AS [Value];
```

This query returns the following results (with the redundant headers omitted):

```
Function                Value
-------------------     ---------------------------------
GETDATE()               2012-02-10 21:27:20.070
CURRENT_TIMESTAMP       2012-02-10 21:27:20.070
GETUTCDATE()            2012-02-11 02:27:20.070
SYSDATETIME()           2012-02-10 21:27:20.0700370
SYSUTCDATETIME()        2012-02-11 02:27:20.0700370
SYSDATETIMEOFFSET()     2012-02-10 21:27:20.0700370 -05:00
```

■ **Note** This recipe calls one or more functions that return a value based upon the current date and time. When you run this recipe on your system, you will get a different result that will be based upon the date and time as set on the computer running your instance of SQL Server.

How It Works

The GETDATE and CURRENT_TIMESTAMP functions return the local date and time, in a datetime data type. The GETUTCDATE function returns UTC time, also in a datetime data type. SYSDATETIME returns the local date and time in a datetime2 data type. SYSUTCDATETIME returns UTC time, also in a datetime2 data type. Finally, SYSDATETIMEOFFSET returns the local time, plus the number of hours and minutes offset from UTC, in a datetimeoffset data type.

10-2. Converting Between Time Zones

Problem

You need to convert a date/time value from one time zone to another.

Solution

Use the SWITCHOFFSET function to convert date/time values in one time zone to a different time zone.

```
SELECT SWITCHOFFSET('2007-08-12T09:43:25-05:00', '+03:00');
```

This query returns the following result:

```
2007-08-12 17:43:25.0000000 +03:00
```

How It Works

The SWITCHOFFSET function converts a datetimeoffset value (or a value that can be implicitly converted to a datetimeoffset value) to a different time zone, adjusting the date, hours, and minutes as necessary. The returned value will be the same UTC time as the supplied value.

■ **Note** The SWITCHOFFSET function is not aware of daylight saving time (DST). As such, the conversions it makes are not adjusted for DST.

10-3. Converting a Date/Time Value to a Datetimeoffset Value

Problem

You need to convert a date/time value to a datetimeoffset value for use in the SWITCHOFFSET function.

■ **Note** A datetimeoffset is a data type introduced in SQL Server 2008. It is based upon a 24-hour clock and is aware of the time zone, and it has the same precision as a datetime2 data type. See Table 10-1 for more information.

Solution

Use the TODATETIMEOFFSET function. This example converts the system's current date/time value to the current time in the Eastern Time Zone (without DST adjustments) and displays both that time and the current system time in a datetimeoffset format.

```
SELECT TODATETIMEOFFSET(GETDATE(), '-05:00') AS [Eastern Time Zone Time],
       SYSDATETIMEOFFSET() [Current System Time];
```

This query returns the following result:

```
Eastern Time Zone Time                Current System Time
------------------------------        ----------------------------------
2012-02-13 21:33:36.517 -05:00        2012-02-13 21:33:36.5200068 -05:00
```

How It Works

The TODATETIMEOFFSET function converts a datetime2 value (or a value that can be implicitly converted into a datetime2 value) to a datetimeoffset value of the specified time zone.

■ **Note** This recipe calls one or more functions that return a value based upon the current date and time. When you run this recipe on your system, you will get a different result that will be based upon the date and time as set on the computer running your instance of SQL Server.

■ **Note** The TODATETIMEOFFSET function is not aware of DST. As such, the conversions it makes are not adjusted for DST.

10-4. Incrementing or Decrementing a Date's Value

Problem

You need to add an interval to a date or time portion of a date/time value.

Solution

Use the DATEADD function to add any quantity of any portion of a date or time value.

```
SELECT DATEADD(YEAR, -1, '2009-04-02T00:00:00');
```

This query returns the following result:

```
2008-04-02 00:00:00.000
```

How It Works

The DATEADD function has three parameters. The first parameter is the part of the date to modify, and it can be any of the names or abbreviations shown in Table 10-2.

Table 10-2. *Datepart Boundaries*

Datepart	Abbreviations
Year	yy, yyyy
quarter	qq, q
month	mm, m
dayofyear	dy, y
Day	dd, d
week	wk, ww
weekday	dw, w
hour	hh
minute	mi, n
second	ss, s
millisecond	ms
microsecond	mcs
nanosecond	ns

The second parameter is a numeric value for the number of datepart units that you are adding to the date. If the value is negative, these units will be subtracted from the date. Finally, the third parameter is the date being modified.

10-5. Finding the Difference Between Two Dates

Problem

You need to calculate the difference between two dates.

Solution

Use the DATEDIFF function to calculate the difference between any two dates.

```
SELECT TOP (5)
       ProductID,
       GETDATE() AS Today,
       EndDate,
       DATEDIFF(MONTH, EndDate, GETDATE()) AS ElapsedMonths
FROM   Production.ProductCostHistory
WHERE  EndDate IS NOT NULL;
```

This query returns the ProductID, the current date/time, the product's EndDate, and the number of months between the EndDate and today's date. The first five records in this table are as follows:

```
ProductID Today                   EndDate                 ElapsedMonths
--------- ----------------------- ----------------------- -------------
707       2012-02-11 08:16:08.663 2006-06-30 00:00:00.000 68
707       2012-02-11 08:16:08.663 2007-06-30 00:00:00.000 56
708       2012-02-11 08:16:08.663 2006-06-30 00:00:00.000 68
708       2012-02-11 08:16:08.663 2007-06-30 00:00:00.000 56
709       2012-02-11 08:16:08.663 2006-06-30 00:00:00.000 68
```

■ **Note** This recipe calls one or more functions that return a value based upon the current date and time. When you run this recipe on your system, you will get a different result that will be based upon the date and time as set on the computer running your instance of SQL Server.

How It Works

The DATEDIFF function accepts three parameters; the first is the datepart (from Table 10-2) to identify whether you are counting the difference in terms of days, hours, minutes, months etc. The last two parameters are the two dates you want to compare.

Notice that the DATEDIFF function returns the number of datepart boundaries crossed; this is not the same as the elapsed time between the two dates. For instance, for the following query, each column returns the quantity of one datepart boundary crossed for each of the specified dateparts, even though the difference between these two date/time values is 100 nanoseconds (.000001 seconds).

```
WITH cteDates (StartDate, EndDate) AS
(
SELECT CONVERT(DATETIME2, '2010-12-31T23:59:59.9999999'),
       CONVERT(DATETIME2, '2011-01-01T00:00:00.0000000')
)
```

```
SELECT StartDate,
       EndDate,
       DATEDIFF(YEAR, StartDate, EndDate) AS Years,
       DATEDIFF(QUARTER, StartDate, EndDate) AS Quarters,
       DATEDIFF(MONTH, StartDate, EndDate) AS Months,
       DATEDIFF(DAY, StartDate, EndDate) AS Days,
       DATEDIFF(HOUR, StartDate, EndDate) AS Hours,
       DATEDIFF(MINUTE, StartDate, EndDate) AS Minutes,
       DATEDIFF(SECOND, StartDate, EndDate) AS Seconds,
       DATEDIFF(MILLISECOND, StartDate, EndDate) AS Milliseconds,
       DATEDIFF(MICROSECOND, StartDate, EndDate) AS MicroSeconds
FROM   cteDates;
```

10-6. Finding the Elapsed Time Between Two Dates

Problem

You need to find the elapsed time between two dates.

Solution

You need to calculate the number of datepart boundaries crossed at the smallest precision level that you are interested in and then calculate the higher datepart boundaries from that number. For example, the following code determines the elapsed time down to the seconds:

```
DECLARE @StartDate DATETIME2 = '2012-01-01T18:25:42.9999999',
        @EndDate   DATETIME2 = '2012-06-15T13:12:11.8675309';

WITH cte AS
(
SELECT DATEDIFF(SECOND, @StartDate, @EndDate) AS ElapsedSeconds,
       DATEDIFF(SECOND, @StartDate, @EndDate)/60 AS ElapsedMinutes,
       DATEDIFF(SECOND, @StartDate, @EndDate)/3600 AS ElapsedHours,
       DATEDIFF(SECOND, @StartDate, @EndDate)/86400 AS ElapsedDays
)
SELECT @StartDate AS StartDate,
       @EndDate AS EndDate,
       CONVERT(VARCHAR(10), ElapsedDays) + ':' +
          CONVERT(VARCHAR(10), ElapsedHours%24) + ':' +
          CONVERT(VARCHAR(10), ElapsedMinutes%60) + ':' +
          CONVERT(VARCHAR(10), ElapsedSeconds%60) AS [ElapsedTime (D:H:M:S)]
FROM   cte;
```

This query returns the following result:

```
StartDate                    EndDate                      ElapsedTime (D:H:M:S)
---------------------------  ---------------------------  ---------------------
2012-01-01 18:25:42.9999999  2012-06-15 13:12:11.8675309  165:18:46:29
```

How It Works

Since we are interested in knowing the elapsed time down to the second, we start off by getting the number of SECOND datepart boundaries that are crossed between these two dates. There are 60 seconds in a minute, so we then take the number of seconds and divide by 60 to get the number of minutes. There are 3,600 seconds in an hour (60 x 60), so we then divide the number of seconds by 3,600 to get the number of hours. And there are 86,400 seconds in a day (60 x 60 x 24), so we divide the number of seconds by 86,400 to get the number of hours.

However, these are not quite the numbers we are looking for; we need to express this as the number of that particular datepart boundary after the next highest boundary, for example the number of hours past the number of whole days. So, we then use the modulo operator to get the remaining number of hours that don't make up an entire day (Hours modulo 24), the remaining number of minutes that don't make up an entire hour (Minutes modulo 60), and the remaining number of seconds that don't make up an entire minute (Seconds modulo 60). Since all of these divisions are occurring with an integer, the fractional remainder will be truncated, so we do not have to worry about this floating down to the next lower datepart boundary calculation.

You can easily adapt this method for a finer precision (milliseconds, and so on). However, to get a less fine precision (for example, years), you now need to start looking at whether a year is a leap year, so you will need to be applying leap year criteria to your calculation.

10-7. Displaying the String Value for Part of a Date

Problem

You need to return the name of the month and day of the week for a specific date.

Solution

Use the DATENAME function to get the name of the datepart portion of the date.

```
SELECT TOP (5)
       ProductID,
       EndDate,
       DATENAME(MONTH, EndDate) AS MonthName,
       DATENAME(WEEKDAY, EndDate) AS WeekDayName
FROM   Production.ProductCostHistory
WHERE  EndDate IS NOT NULL;
```

This query returns the following results:

```
ProductID     EndDate                    MonthName    WeekDayName
---------     -----------------------    ---------    -----------
707           2006-06-30 00:00:00.000    June         Friday
707           2007-06-30 00:00:00.000    June         Saturday
708           2006-06-30 00:00:00.000    June         Friday
708           2007-06-30 00:00:00.000    June         Saturday
709           2006-06-30 00:00:00.000    June         Friday
```

How It Works

The DATENAME function returns a character string representing the datepart specified. While any of the dateparts listed in Table 10-2 can be used, only the month and weekday dateparts convert to a name; the other dateparts return the value as a string.

10-8. Displaying the Integer Representations for Parts of a Date

Problem

You need to separate a date into different columns for year, month, and date.

Solution

Use the DATEPART function to retrieve the datepart specified from a date as an integer.

```
SELECT TOP (5)
       ProductID,
       EndDate,
       DATEPART(YEAR, EndDate) AS [Year],
       DATEPART(MONTH, EndDate) AS [Month],
       DATEPART(DAY, EndDate) AS [Day]
FROM   Production.ProductCostHistory
WHERE  EndDate IS NOT NULL;
```

This query returns the following results:

```
ProductID   EndDate                    Year     Month    Day
---------   -----------------------    ----     -----    ---
707         2006-06-30 00:00:00.000    2006     6        30
707         2007-06-30 00:00:00.000    2007     6        30
708         2006-06-30 00:00:00.000    2006     6        30
708         2007-06-30 00:00:00.000    2007     6        30
709         2006-06-30 00:00:00.000    2006     6        30
```

How It Works

The DATEPART function retrieves the specified datepart from the date as an integer. Any of the dateparts in Table 10-2 can be utilized.

■ **Note** The YEAR, MONTH, and DAY functions are synonyms for the DATEPART function with the appropriate datepart specified.

10-9. Determining Whether a String Is a Valid Date

Problem

You need to determine whether the value of a string is a valid date.

Solution

You need to utilize the ISDATE function in your query.

```
SELECT MyData ,
       ISDATE(MyData) AS IsADate
FROM   (VALUES('IsThisADate'),
              ('2012-02-14'),
              ('2012-01-01T00:00:00'),
              ('2012-12-31T23:59:59.9999999')) dt(MyData);
```

This query returns the following results:

```
MyData                       IsADate
---------------------------  -------
IsThisADate                  0
2012-02-14                   1
2012-01-01T00:00:00          1
2012-12-31T23:59:59.9999999  0
```

How It Works

The ISDATE function checks to see whether the expression passed to it is a valid date, time, or datetime value. If the expression is a valid date, a true (1) will be returned; otherwise, a false (0) will be returned. Because the last record is a datetime2 data type, it does not pass this check.

10-10. Determining the Last Day of the Month

Problem

You need to determine what the last day of the month is for a date you are working with.

Solution

Use the EOMONTH function to determine the last day of the month for a given date.

```
SELECT MyData,
       EOMONTH(MyData) AS LastDayOfThisMonth,
       EOMONTH(MyData, 1) AS LastDayOfNextMonth
FROM   (VALUES ('2012-02-14T00:00:00' ),
               ('2012-01-01T00:00:00'),
               ('2012-12-31T23:59:59.9999999')) dt(MyData);
```

This query returns the following results:

```
MyData                          LastDayOfThisMonth   LastDayOfNextMonth
---------------------------     ------------------   ------------------
2012-02-14T00:00:00             2012-02-29           2012-03-31
2012-01-01T00:00:00             2012-01-31           2012-02-29
2012-12-31T23:59:59.9999999     2012-12-31           2013-01-31
```

How It Works

The EOMONTH function returns the last day of the month for the specified date. It has an optional parameter that will add the specified number of months to the specified date.

■ **Note** Prior to this function being added to SQL Server 2012, you would have to first determine the first day of the month that the specified date is in (see Recipe 10-12), add one month (see Recipe 10-4), and finally subtract one day (see Recipe 10-4) to obtain the last day of the month.

10-11. Creating a Date from Numbers

Problem

You need to create a date from numbers representing the various parts of the date. For example, you have data for the year, month, and day parts of a day, and you need to make a date out of those numbers.

Solution

Use the DATEFROMPARTS function to build a date from the numbers representing the year, month, and day.

```
SELECT 'DateFromParts' AS ConversionType,
       DATEFROMPARTS(2012, 8, 15) AS [Value];
SELECT 'TimeFromParts' AS ConversionType,
       TIMEFROMPARTS(18, 25, 32, 5, 1) AS [Value];
SELECT 'SmallDateTimeFromParts' AS ConversionType,
       SMALLDATETIMEFROMPARTS(2012, 8, 15, 18, 25) AS [Value];
SELECT 'DateTimeFromParts' AS ConversionType,
       DATETIMEFROMPARTS(2012, 8, 15, 18, 25, 32, 450) AS [Value];
SELECT 'DateTime2FromParts' AS ConversionType,
       DATETIME2FROMPARTS(2012, 8, 15, 18, 25, 32, 5, 7) AS [Value];
SELECT 'DateTimeOffsetFromParts' AS ConversionType,
       DATETIMEOFFSETFROMPARTS(2012, 8, 15, 18, 25, 32, 5, 4, 0, 7) AS [Value];
```

This query returns the following result set (with redundant headers removed):

```
ConversionType             Value
--------------             ----------
DateFromParts              2012-08-15
TimeFromParts              18:25:32.5
```

```
SmallDateTimeFromParts       2012-08-15 18:25:00
DateTimeFromParts            2012-08-15 18:25:32.450
DateTime2FromParts           2012-08-15 18:25:32.0000005
DateTimeOffsetFromParts      2012-08-15 18:25:32.0000005 +04:00
```

How It Works

The functions demonstrated earlier build an appropriate date/time value in the specified data type from the parts that make up that data type.

The TIMEFROMPARTS, DATETIME2FROMPARTS, and DATETIMEOFFSETFROMPARTS functions have a fraction parameter and a precision parameter. For the latter two, the fraction is the seventh parameter (in the previous example, the 5), and the precision parameter is the last parameter (the 7). For the TIMEFROMPARTS function, these parameters are the last two parameters. These parameters work together to control what precision the fraction is applied to. This is best demonstrated with the following query:

```
SELECT TIMEFROMPARTS(18, 25, 32, 5, 1);
SELECT TIMEFROMPARTS(18, 25, 32, 5, 2);
SELECT TIMEFROMPARTS(18, 25, 32, 5, 3);
SELECT TIMEFROMPARTS(18, 25, 32, 5, 4);
SELECT TIMEFROMPARTS(18, 25, 32, 5, 5);
SELECT TIMEFROMPARTS(18, 25, 32, 5, 6);
SELECT TIMEFROMPARTS(18, 25, 32, 5, 7);
SELECT TIMEFROMPARTS(18, 25, 32, 50, 2);
SELECT TIMEFROMPARTS(18, 25, 32, 500, 3);
```

These queries return the following result set (with the header lines removed):

```
18:25:32.5
18:25:32.05
18:25:32.005
18:25:32.0005
18:25:32.00005
18:25:32.000005
18:25:32.0000005
18:25:32.50
18:25:32.500
```

■ **Note** These functions are new to SQL Server 2012.

10-12. Finding the Beginning Date of a Datepart

Problem

You need to determine what the first day of a datepart boundary is for a specified date. For example, you want to know what the first day of the current quarter is for the specified date.

Solution #1

Use the DATEADD and DATEDIFF functions to perform this calculation.

```
DECLARE @MyDate DATETIME2 = '2012-01-01T18:25:42.9999999',
        @Base   DATETIME = '1900-01-01T00:00:00',
        @Base2  DATETIME = '2000-01-01T00:00:00';

-- Solution 1
SELECT  MyDate,
        DATEADD(YEAR,   DATEDIFF(YEAR,    @Base, MyDate), @Base) AS [FirstDayOfYear],
        DATEADD(MONTH,  DATEDIFF(MONTH,   @Base, MyDate), @Base) AS [FirstDayOfMonth],
        DATEADD(QUARTER,DATEDIFF(QUARTER, @Base, MyDate), @Base) AS [FirstDayOfQuarter]
FROM    (VALUES ('1981-01-17T00:00:00'),
                ('1961-11-23T00:00:00'),
                ('1960-07-09T00:00:00'),
                ('1980-07-11T00:00:00'),
                ('1983-01-05T00:00:00'),
                ('2006-11-27T00:00:00')) dt (MyDate);

SELECT 'StartOfHour' AS ConversionType,
       DATEADD(HOUR,   DATEDIFF(HOUR,   @Base, @MyDate), @Base) AS DateResult
UNION ALL
SELECT 'StartOfMinute',
       DATEADD(MINUTE, DATEDIFF(MINUTE, @Base, @MyDate), @Base)
UNION ALL
SELECT 'StartOfSecond',
       DATEADD(SECOND, DATEDIFF(SECOND, @Base2, @MyDate), @Base2);
```

This query returns the following:

```
MyDate               FirstDayOfYear           FirstDayOfMonth          FirstDayOfQuarter
-------------------  -----------------------  -----------------------  -----------------------
1981-01-17T00:00:00  1981-01-01 00:00:00.000  1981-01-01 00:00:00.000  1981-01-01 00:00:00.000
1961-11-23T00:00:00  1961-01-01 00:00:00.000  1961-11-01 00:00:00.000  1961-10-01 00:00:00.000
1960-07-09T00:00:00  1960-01-01 00:00:00.000  1960-07-01 00:00:00.000  1960-07-01 00:00:00.000
1980-07-11T00:00:00  1980-01-01 00:00:00.000  1980-07-01 00:00:00.000  1980-07-01 00:00:00.000
1983-01-05T00:00:00  1983-01-01 00:00:00.000  1983-01-01 00:00:00.000  1983-01-01 00:00:00.000
2006-11-27T00:00:00  2006-01-01 00:00:00.000  2006-11-01 00:00:00.000  2006-10-01 00:00:00.000

ConversionType  DateResult
--------------  -----------------------
StartOfHour     2012-01-01 18:00:00.000
StartOfMinute   2012-01-01 18:25:00.000
StartOfSecond   2012-01-01 18:25:42.000
```

Solution #2

Break the date down into the appropriate parts, and then use the DATETIMEFROMPARTS function to build a new date with the parts being truncated set to 1 (for months/dates) or zero (for hours/minutes/seconds/milliseconds).

```
SELECT MyDate,
       DATETIMEFROMPARTS(ca.Yr, 1,     1, 0, 0, 0, 0) AS FirstDayOfYear,
       DATETIMEFROMPARTS(ca.Yr, ca.Mn, 1, 0, 0, 0, 0) AS FirstDayOfMonth,
       DATETIMEFROMPARTS(ca.Yr, ca.Qt, 1, 0, 0, 0, 0) AS FirstDayOfQuarter
FROM   (VALUES ('1981-01-17T00:00:00'),
               ('1961-11-23T00:00:00'),
               ('1960-07-09T00:00:00'),
               ('1980-07-11T00:00:00'),
               ('1983-01-05T00:00:00'),
               ('2006-11-27T00:00:00')) dt (MyDate)
CROSS APPLY (SELECT DATEPART(YEAR, dt.MyDate) AS Yr,
                    DATEPART(MONTH, dt.MyDate) AS Mn,
                    ((CEILING(MONTH(dt.MyDate)/3.0)*3)-2) AS Qt
            ) ca;

WITH cte AS
(
SELECT DATEPART(YEAR, @MyDate) AS Yr,
       DATEPART(MONTH, @MyDate) AS Mth,
       DATEPART(DAY, @MyDate) AS Dy,
       DATEPART(HOUR, @MyDate) AS Hr,
       DATEPART(MINUTE, @MyDate) AS Mn,
       DATEPART(SECOND, @MyDate) AS Sec
)
SELECT 'StartOfHour' AS ConversionType,
       DATETIMEFROMPARTS(cte.Yr, cte.Mth, cte.Dy, cte.Hr, 0, 0, 0) AS DateResult
FROM   cte
UNION ALL
SELECT 'StartOfMinute',
       DATETIMEFROMPARTS(cte.Yr, cte.Mth, cte.Dy, cte.Hr, cte.Mn, 0, 0)
FROM cte
UNION ALL
SELECT 'StartOfSecond',
       DATETIMEFROMPARTS(cte.Yr, cte.Mth, cte.Dy, cte.Hr, cte.Mn, cte.Sec, 0)
FROM cte;
```

Solution #3

Use the FORMAT function to format the date, using default values for the parts to be truncated.

```
SELECT CONVERT(CHAR(10), ca.MyDate, 121) AS MyDate,
       CAST(FORMAT(ca.MyDate, 'yyyy-01-01') AS DATETIME) AS FirstDayOfYear,
       CAST(FORMAT(ca.MyDate, 'yyyy-MM-01') AS DATETIME) AS FirstDayOfMonth
FROM   (VALUES ('1981-01-17T00:00:00'),
               ('1961-11-23T00:00:00'),
               ('1960-07-09T00:00:00'),
```

```
               ('1980-07-11T00:00:00'),
               ('1983-01-05T00:00:00'),
               ('2006-11-27T00:00:00')) dt (MyDate)
CROSS APPLY (SELECT CAST(dt.MyDate AS DATE)) AS ca(MyDate);

SELECT 'StartOfHour' AS ConversionType,
       FORMAT(@MyDate, 'yyyy-MM-dd HH:00:00.000') AS DateResult
UNION ALL
SELECT 'StartOfMinute',
       FORMAT(@MyDate, 'yyyy-MM-dd HH:mm:00.000')
UNION ALL
SELECT 'StartOfSecond',
       FORMAT(@MyDate, 'yyyy-MM-dd HH:mm:ss.000');
```

How It Works #1

In the first solution, for the datepart boundary that you are interested in, you use the DATEDIFF function to return the number of boundaries between a known date and the date that you are comparing to. You then use the DATEADD function to add this number of boundaries back to the known date. Remember that the DATEDIFF returns an integer; choose your known date so that you won't cause a numeric overflow. This can become problematic when you work with the SECOND datepart boundary (or one of the fractional second datepart boundaries).

How It Works #2

In the second solution, the year, month, and beginning month of the quarter are calculated in the CROSS APPLY operator. The parts to keep are passed in to the DATETIMETOPARTS function, and default values are passed in for the remaining parts to generate the desired dates. For the second part of this solution, the year, month, day, hour, minute, and second parts are extracted, and then the desired parts are passed in to the DATETIMETOPARTS function, with the parts of the time to be truncated set to zero. This solution produces the same results as Solution #1.

How It Works #3

In the third solution, the FORMAT function utilizes the .NET 4.0 formatting capabilities to format the date as a string, and then the CAST function is utilized to change the string back into a datetime data type. The parts of the time that are to be truncated are set to zero, while for the first day of calculations, the day and month are set to 1 where appropriate. With the exception of FirstDayOfQuarter, this solution returns the same results as Solution #1.

■ **Tip** In my performance testing of these solutions, Solution #1 is the fastest. Solution #2 (as coded earlier where the date/time parts need to be extracted) takes about twice the time to run as Solution #1; however, if the parts of the dates are already available, then this solution is slightly faster than Solution #1. Solution #3 is by far the slowest, coming in at about 100 times slower than either of the other solutions.

10-13. Include Missing Dates

Problem

You are producing a report that breaks down expenses by category and that sums up the expenses at the month level. One of your categories does not have expenses for every month, so those months are missing values in the report. You want those missing months to be reported with a value of zero for the expense amount.

Solution

Utilize a calendar table to generate the missing months.

```
DECLARE @Base DATETIME = '1900-01-01T00:00:00';
WITH cteExpenses AS
(
SELECT  ca.FirstOfMonth,
        SUM(ExpenseAmount) AS MonthlyExpenses
FROM      ( VALUES ('2012-01-15T00:00:00', 1250.00),
                   ('2012-01-28T00:00:00', 750.00),
                   ('2012-03-01T00:00:00', 1475.00),
                   ('2012-03-23T00:00:00', 2285.00),
                   ('2012-04-01T00:00:00', 1650.00),
                   ('2012-04-22T00:00:00', 1452.00),
                   ('2012-06-15T00:00:00', 1875.00),
                   ('2012-07-23T00:00:00', 2125.00) ) dt (ExpenseDate, ExpenseAmount)
        CROSS APPLY (SELECT DATEADD(MONTH,
                        DATEDIFF(MONTH, @Base, ExpenseDate), @Base) ) ca (FirstOfMonth)
GROUP BY  ca.FirstOfMonth
), cteMonths AS
(
SELECT      DATEFROMPARTS(2012, M, 1) AS FirstOfMonth
FROM        ( VALUES (1), (2),  (3),  (4),
                     (5), (6),  (7),  (8),
                     (9), (10), (11), (12) ) Months (M)
)
SELECT CAST(FirstOfMonth AS DATE) AS FirstOfMonth,
       MonthlyExpenses
FROM   cteExpenses
UNION ALL
SELECT m.FirstOfMonth,
       0
FROM   cteMonths M
       LEFT JOIN cteExpenses e
         ON M.FirstOfMonth = e.FirstOfMonth
WHERE  e.FirstOfMonth IS NULL
ORDER  BY FirstOfMonth;
```

This query produces the following results:

```
FirstOfMonth     MonthlyExpenses
------------     ---------------
2012-01-01       2000.00
2012-02-01       0.00
2012-03-01       3760.00
2012-04-01       3102.00
2012-05-01       0.00
2012-06-01       1875.00
2012-07-01       2125.00
2012-08-01       0.00
2012-09-01       0.00
2012-10-01       0.00
2012-11-01       0.00
2012-12-01       0.00
```

How It Works

The cteExpenses common table expression builds a derived table of expense dates and amounts. The CROSS APPLY operator converts each date to the date at the beginning of the month. The expenses are then summed up and grouped by the beginning of the month date. If we run just this portion of the query, we get the following results:

```
FirstOfMonth               MonthlyExpenses
-----------------------    ---------------
2012-01-01 00:00:00.000    2000.00
2012-03-01 00:00:00.000    3760.00
2012-04-01 00:00:00.000    3102.00
2012-06-01 00:00:00.000    1875.00
2012-07-01 00:00:00.000    2125.00
```

As you can see, several months are missing. To include these missing months, the cteMonths common table expression is created, which uses the DATEFROMPARTS function to build the first day of the month for each month. Running just this portion of the query returns the following results:

```
FirstOfMonth
------------
2012-01-01
2012-02-01
2012-03-01
2012-04-01
2012-05-01
2012-06-01
2012-07-01
2012-08-01
```

```
2012-09-01
2012-10-01
2012-11-01
2012-12-01
```

Finally, the expenses are returned, and this result set is unioned to a second result set that returns the months left-joined to the expenses and is filtered to return only the months that do not exist in the expenses. The result is that all months are shown in the result set, with the months without data having a zero value.

In this recipe, a virtual calendar table was created that contains the first day of each month in the year. Frequently, calendar tables will contain days for every day in the year, with additional columns to hold other information such as the first day of the month, the day of the week for the date, and whether this is a weekday or a weekend date or a holiday. Using a prebuilt calendar table can greatly simplify many calculations that would need to be performed.

10-14. Finding Arbitrary Dates

Problem

You need to find the date of an arbitrary date, such as the third Thursday in November or the date for last Friday.

Solution

Use a calendar table with additional columns to query the desired dates.

```
CREATE TABLE dbo.Calendar (
  [Date] DATE CONSTRAINT PK_Calendar PRIMARY KEY CLUSTERED,
  FirstDayOfYear DATE,
  LastDayOfYear DATE,
  FirstDayOfMonth DATE,
  LastDayOfMonth DATE,
  FirstDayOfWeek DATE,
  LastDayOfWeek DATE,
  DayOfWeekName NVARCHAR(20),
  IsWeekDay BIT,
  IsWeekEnd BIT);
GO
DECLARE @Base  DATETIME = '1900-01-01T00:00:00',
        @Start DATETIME = '2000-01-01T00:00:00'
INSERT INTO dbo.Calendar
SELECT TOP 9497
       ca.Date,
       cy.FirstDayOfYear,
       cyl.LastDayOfYear,
       cm.FirstDayOfMonth,
       cml.LastDayOfMonth,
       cw.FirstDayOfWeek,
       cwl.LastDayOfWeek,
       cd.DayOfWeekName,
       cwd.IsWeekDay,
       CAST(cwd.IsWeekDay - 1 AS BIT) AS IsWeekEnd
```

```
FROM    (SELECT ROW_NUMBER() OVER (ORDER BY (SELECT 0))
         FROM sys.all_columns t1
         CROSS JOIN sys.all_columns t2) dt (RN)
CROSS APPLY (SELECT DATEADD(DAY, RN-1, @Start)) AS ca(Date)
CROSS APPLY (SELECT DATEADD(YEAR, DATEDIFF(YEAR, @Base, ca.Date), @Base)) AS cy(FirstDayOfYear)
CROSS APPLY (SELECT DATEADD(DAY, -1, DATEADD(YEAR, 1, cy.FirstDayOfYear))) AS cyl(LastDayOfYear)
CROSS APPLY (SELECT DATEADD(MONTH, DATEDIFF(MONTH, @Base, ca.Date), @Base)) AS
cm(FirstDayOfMonth)
CROSS APPLY (SELECT DATEADD(DAY, -1, DATEADD(MONTH, 1, cm.FirstDayOfMonth))) AS
cml(LastDayOfMonth)
CROSS APPLY (SELECT DATEADD(DAY,-(DATEPART(weekday ,ca.Date)-1),ca.Date)) AS cw(FirstDayOfWeek)
CROSS APPLY (SELECT DATEADD(DAY, 6, cw.FirstDayOfWeek)) AS cwl(LastDayOfWeek)
CROSS APPLY (SELECT DATENAME(weekday, ca.Date)) AS cd(DayOfWeekName)
CROSS APPLY (SELECT CASE WHEN cd.DayOfWeekName IN ('Monday', 'Tuesday', 'Wednesday',
                                                   'Thursday', 'Friday')
                         THEN 1
                         ELSE 0
                    END) AS cwd(IsWeekDay);
GO

WITH cte AS
(
SELECT  FirstDayOfMonth,
        Date,
        RN = ROW_NUMBER() OVER (PARTITION BY FirstDayOfMonth ORDER BY Date)
FROM    dbo.Calendar
WHERE   DayOfWeekName = 'Thursday'
)
SELECT Date
FROM   cte
WHERE  RN = 3
AND    FirstDayOfMonth = '2012-11-01T00:00:00';

SELECT  c1.Date
FROM    dbo.Calendar c1 -- prior week
        JOIN dbo.Calendar c2 -- current week
        ON c1.FirstDayOfWeek = DATEADD(DAY, -7, c2.FirstDayOfWeek)
WHERE   c1.DayOfWeekName = 'Friday'
AND     c2.Date = CAST(GETDATE() AS DATE);
```

This query returns the following result sets:

```
Date
----------
2012-11-15

Date
----------
2012-04-27
```

■ **Note** This recipe calls one or more functions that return a value based upon the current date and time. When you run this recipe on your system, you will get a different result that will be based upon the date and time as set on the computer running your instance of SQL Server.

How It Works

This recipe creates a calendar table with columns for extra information—the first and last days of the year, the month and week, the weekday name for the date, and whether this date is a weekday or weekend. This table is then populated for all the dates between January 1, 2000, and December 31, 2025.

The first date that is retrieved is the third Thursday in November. The query gets all of the Thursdays, along with the first day of the month. It then calculates a row number for that date in that month. Finally, the date for the third Thursday in November is returned.

The second date that is retrieved is the Friday of the previous week. The query starts off by performing a self-join to the calendar table. On the current week side of the join, the first day of the week for today's date is obtained and used to join to the previous week by subtracting seven days to get the first day of the previous week. It then returns the date for that week that has a weekday name of Friday.

As you can see, calendar tables can be easily adjusted to suit your needs. A column of `IsWorkingDay` could be added and populated, and then it would be easy to find the date five working days in the future. Holidays can be tracked, as can fiscal accounting periods, especially those that don't follow the norm of the calendar year.

Calendar tables are typically sized to hold several years worth of data. It takes less than 10,000 records to hold every date between January 1, 2000, and December 31, 2025. Because of its small size and static nature, this is one of those tables that benefits from being heavily indexed to provide covering indexes for all the queries you would run against it.

10-15. Querying for Intervals

Problem

You want to count the number of employees that were employed during each month.

Solution

Use a calendar table to get the months employees were active and aggregate the data.

```
WITH cte AS
(
SELECT  edh.BusinessEntityID,
        c.FirstDayOfMonth
FROM    AdventureWorks2012.HumanResources.EmployeeDepartmentHistory AS edh
        JOIN dbo.Calendar AS c
            ON c.Date BETWEEN edh.StartDate
                      AND     ISNULL(edh.EndDate, GETDATE())
GROUP BY edh.BusinessEntityID,
        c.FirstDayOfMonth
)
SELECT  FirstDayOfMonth,
        COUNT(*) AS EmployeeQty
FROM    cte
```

```
GROUP BY FirstDayOfMonth
ORDER BY FirstDayOfMonth;
```

This query returns the following (abridged) result set:

```
FirstDayOfMonth    EmployeeQty
---------------    -----------
2000-07-01         1
2000-08-01         1
2000-09-01         1
2000-10-01         1
2000-11-01         1
...
2007-03-01         287
2007-04-01         288
2007-05-01         288
2007-06-01         288
2007-07-01         290
2007-08-01         290
2007-09-01         290
```

How It Works

Using the 25-year calendar table created in Recipe 10-14, the beginning of the month and employee identifier are returned for each employee who is active between the start date and end date (or current date if null). The GROUP BY clause is utilized to eliminate duplicates created by each date within a month. The employees are then counted per month.

10-16. Working with Dates and Times Across National Boundaries

Problem

When exchanging data with a company in a different country, dates either are converted incorrectly or generate an error when attempting to import.

Solution

Use one of the ISO-8601 date formats to ensure that the date/time value is unambiguous.

```
SELECT 'sysdatetime' AS ConversionType, 126 AS Style,
       CONVERT(varchar(30), SYSDATETIME(), 126) AS [Value] UNION ALL
SELECT 'sysdatetime', 127,
       CONVERT(varchar(30), SYSDATETIME(), 127) UNION ALL
SELECT 'getdate', 126,
       CONVERT(varchar(30), GETDATE(), 126) UNION ALL
SELECT 'getdate', 127,
       CONVERT(varchar(30), GETDATE(), 127);
```

This code returns the following result set:

```
ConversionType   Style  Value
--------------   -----  ---------------------------
sysdatetime      126    2012-03-17T01:57:43.4321425
sysdatetime      127    2012-03-17T01:57:43.4321425
getdate          126    2012-03-17T01:57:43.430
getdate          127    2012-03-17T01:57:43.430
```

■ **Note** This recipe calls one or more functions that return a value based upon the current date and time. When you run this recipe on your system, you will get a different result that will be based upon the date and time as set on the computer running your instance of SQL Server.

How It Works

When working with dates across national boundaries, you frequently run into data conversion issues. For instance, take 02/04/2012: in the United States, this is February 4, 2012, while in the United Kingdom, this is April 2, 2012. In this example, the date is converted improperly. Another example is 12/25/2012: in the United States, this is December 25, 2012; in the United Kingdom, this would be attempted to be converted into the 12th day of the 25th month of 2012, and since there aren't 25 months, this would generate an error.

Any date with the month and day values both being less than or equal to 12 is ambiguous (unless the values are the same). Any date with a number greater than 12 may generate an error when attempting to convert it to a date data type.

To work with this date conversion issue, an international standard was created. This standard is ISO-8601: "Data elements and interchange formats - Information interchange - Representation of dates and times." There are two formats that are allowed to represent date with time:

```
YYYY-MM-DDThh:mm:ss[.nnnnnnn][{+|-}hh:mm]
YYYY-MM-DDThh:mm:ss[.nnnnnnn]Z (UTC, Coordinated Universal Time)
```

The following are examples of using these formats:

```
2012-07-28T16:45:33
2012-07-28T16:45:33.1234567+07:00
2012-07-28T16:45:33.1234567Z
```

To properly use the ISO-8601 format, the date and time portions must be specified, including the separators, meaning the *T*, the colons (:), the + or – , and the periods (.). The brackets indicate that the fractional seconds and time zone offset portions of the time are optional. The time is specified using the 24-hour clock format. The *T* is used to indicate the start of the time portion of the date-time value in the string. The *Z* indicates the time is in UTC time.

The date/time values that are specified in this format are unambiguous. The `SET DATEFORMAT` and `SET LANGUAGE` login default language settings do not affect the results.

When querying dates and times, the `CONVERT` function has two styles (126 and 127) that convert a date/time data type into the ISO-8601 formatted date with time values.

In this chapter, and throughout this book, examples with dates use the ISO-8601 standard.

CHAPTER 11

Working with Numbers

by Jonathan Gennick

SQL Server supports integer, decimal, and floating-point numbers. Working with numbers requires an understanding of the types available and what they are capable of. Implicit conversion rules sometimes lead to surprising results from seemingly simple-to-understand expressions. The recipes in this chapter show some of the more common operations as well as techniques for guarding against unexpected and unwanted results.

11-1. Representing Integers

Problem

You are writing T-SQL or creating a table, and you want to represent integer data in a binary format.

Solution

Choose one of the four integer data types provided in SQL Server. The following is a code block showing the four types and their range of valid values:

```
DECLARE @bip bigint, @bin bigint
DECLARE @ip int, @in int
DECLARE @sip smallint, @sin smallint
DECLARE @ti tinyint

SET @bip =  9223372036854775807 /* 2^63-1 */
SET @bin = -9223372036854775808 /* -2^63  */
SET @ip =            2147483647 /* 2^31-1 */
SET @in =           -2147483648 /* -2^31  */
SET @sip =                32767 /* 2^15-1 */
SET @sin =               -32768 /* -2^15  */
SET @ti =                   255 /* 2^8-1  */

SELECT 'bigint' AS type_name, @bip AS max_value, @bin AS min_value
UNION ALL
SELECT 'int', @ip, @in
UNION ALL
SELECT 'smallint', @sip, @sin
UNION ALL
SELECT 'tinyint', @ti, 0
ORDER BY max_value DESC
```

How It Works

SQL Server supports four integer data types. Each allocates a specific number of bytes for use in representing integer values. From largest to smallest, the types are as follows:

- bigint (eight bytes)
- int (four bytes)
- smallint (two bytes)
- tinyint (one byte)

The results from the solution example prove the range of values supported by each of the types:

```
type_name  max_value            min_value
---------  -------------------  --------------------
bigint     9223372036854775807  -9223372036854775808
int        2147483647           -2147483648
smallint   32767                -32768
tinyint    255                  0

(4 row(s) affected)
```

Attempts to store an out-of-range value result in an overflow error. For example, decrement the minimum value for smallint by 1, attempt to store that value, and you'll get the following results:

```
DECLARE @sin smallint
SET @sin =              -32769
Msg 220, Level 16, State 1, Line 2
Arithmetic overflow error for data type smallint, value = -32769.
```

tinyint is a single byte limited to positive values only. The other three types take negative values as well. SQL Server does not provide for unsigned versions of bigint, int, and smallint.

Choose from among the integer types based upon the range of values that you are working with. Don't forget to allow for future growth. If storing the national debt, for example, you might want to jump straight to the bigint data type. Any of the types may also be used in CREATE TABLE statements. You can create table columns based upon the four types, as well as T-SQL variables, as shown in the example.

■ **Note** The absolute value range in the negative direction is one greater than in the positive direction. That is because of the two's-complement notation used internally by the database engine. If you're curious, you can read more about two's-complement in the following Wikipedia article: http://en.wikipedia.org/wiki/Two%27s_complement.

SINGLE-BIT INTEGERS?

Integers decrease in size from eight bytes to one byte as you move from bigint to tinyint. But does SQL Server support anything smaller such as a single-bit integer? The answer is yes. Using the bit type, you can define a column or variable that can be set to 1, 0, or null. Here's an example:

```
DECLARE @SunnyDayFlag bit

SET @SunnyDayFlag = 1;
SET @SunnyDayFlag = 'true'

SELECT @SunnyDayFlag
```

The values `'true'` and `'false'` (case-insensitive) equate to 1 and 0, respectively. SQL Server coalesces `bit` variables into groups of eight or fewer, storing up to eight values in a single byte. While the official documentation lumps `bit` with the integer types, it is a type better suited for true/false flags than for numeric values you want to use in expressions.

11-2. Representing Decimal Amounts

Problem

You are working with decimal data such as monetary amounts for which precise, base-10 representation is critical. You want to create a variable or table column of an appropriate type.

Solution

Use the `decimal` data type. Specify the total number of digits needed. Also specify how many of those digits are to the right of the decimal point. Here's an example:

```
DECLARE @x0 decimal(7,0) = 1234567.
DECLARE @x1 decimal(7,1) = 123456.7
DECLARE @x2 decimal(7,2) = 12345.67
DECLARE @x3 decimal(7,3) = 1234.567
DECLARE @x4 decimal(7,4) = 123.4567
DECLARE @x5 decimal(7,5) = 12.34567
DECLARE @x6 decimal(7,6) = 1.234567
DECLARE @x7 decimal(7,7) = .1234567

SELECT @x0
SELECT @x1
SELECT @x2
SELECT @x3
SELECT @x4
SELECT @x5
SELECT @x6
SELECT @x7
```

The first parameter to `decimal` indicates the overall number of digits. The second parameter indicates how many of those digits are to the right of the decimal place.

How It Works

Choose the `decimal` type whenever accurate representation of decimal values is important. You'll be able to accurately represent values to the number of digits you specify, with none of the rounding or imprecision that often results from floating-point types and their use of base-2.

The two parameters to a decimal declaration are termed *precision* and *scale*. Precision refers to the overall number of digits. Scale refers to the location of the decimal point in respect to those digits. The output from the solution example—modified somewhat for readability—is as follows:

```
----------
1234567
123456.7
12345.67
1234.567
123.4567
12.34567
1.234567
0.1234567
```

The number of digits of precision is held constant at seven. The changing location of the decimal point indicates the effects of different values for scale.

Monetary values are a particularly good application of the `decimal` type. The following is an example declaration allowing for values into the hundreds of millions of pounds, including pence:

```
decimal(11,2)
```

This declaration gives nine digits to the left of the decimal point and two to the right. The range of valid values is thus as follows:

```
-999,999,999.99 to 999,999,999.99
```

The default precision and scale are 18 and 0. Therefore, a declaration of `decimal` is equivalent to `decimal(18,0)`. The maximum precision is 38, and the scale must be less than or equal to the precision.

11-3. Representing Monetary Amounts

Problem

You want to create a variable or a column for use in holding values representing money.

Solution #1

Choose the `decimal` type. Choose a suitable precision and scale. For example, to store rupees and paise to plus-or-minus 1 billion:

```
DECLARE @account_balance decimal(12,2)
```

Ten digits are to the left of the decimal, allowing you to reach into the single-digit billions. Having two digits to the right of the decimal enables you to store values to the pence.

Solution #2

Choose one of SQL Server's built-in monetary data types. Here's an example:

```
DECLARE @mp money, @mn money
DECLARE @smp smallmoney, @smn smallmoney
SET @mp = 922337203685477.5807
SET @mn = -922337203685477.5808
```

```
SET @smp = 214748.3647
SET @smn = -214748.3648
SELECT 'money' AS type_name, @mp AS max_value, @mn AS min_value
UNION ALL
SELECT 'smallmoney', @smp, @smn
```

How It Works

My preference leans toward Solution #1. Use the decimal type for money values. It is a standard, ISO SQL data type. You can specify however many digits to the right of the decimal point that you prefer. I often specify two digits to the right, because most money systems in use today resolve to the hundredth of their main unit. For example, there are 100 pence to the pound, 100 euro cents to the euro, 100 paise to the rupee, and so forth.

Your other option is to use one of SQL Server's built-in money types: money and smallmoney. These types both give four digits of precision to the right of the decimal place. Their ranges are as shown in the results from the Solution #2 example:

```
type_name  max_value             min_value
---------- --------------------  ---------------------
money      922337203685477.5807  -922337203685477.5808
smallmoney 214748.3647           -214748.3648
```

If you do use money or smallmoney, then take care to carefully consider whether and when to round values to two decimal places. Imagine you are storing a checking account balance. What would it mean to tell a customer that their balance is, say, 59 dollars and 20 and 2/10ths cents? On the other hand, you might be storing the price of gasoline, which in the United States is generally priced to the tenth of a cent.

■ **Note** The money types provoke a certain amount of discussion and debate. Aaron Bertrand has an interesting article in his blog on performance comparisons he made between money and decimal. You can find that article at http://sqlblog.com/blogs/aaron_bertrand/archive/2008/04/27/performance-storage-comparisons-money-vs-decimal.aspx.

11-4. Representing Floating-Point Values

Problem

You are performing scientific calculations and need the ability to represent floating-point values.

Solution

Choose one of the floating-point types supported by SQL Server. As a practical matter, you have the following choices:

```
DECLARE @x1 real /* same as float(24) */
DECLARE @x2 float /* same as float(53) */
DECLARE @x3 float(53)
DECLARE @x4 float(24)
```

How It Works

Table 11-1 gives the absolute-value ranges supported by the declarations in the solution. For example, the largest magnitude real is 3.40E+38. That value can, of course, be either positive or negative. The least magnitude value other than zero that you can represent is 1.18E-38. If you must represent a value of smaller magnitude, such as 1.18E-39, then you would need to look toward the float type.

All values in Table 11-1 can be either positive or negative. Storing zero is also always an option.

Table 11-1. *Floating-Point Value Ranges*

Declaration	Min Absolute Value	Max Absolute Value
real	1.18E-38	3.40E+38
float	2.23E-308	1.79E+308
float(53)	2.23E-308	1.79E+308
float(24)	1.18E-38	3.40E+38

You can specify float(n) using any n from 1 to 53. However, any value n from 1..24 is treated as 24. Likewise, any value n from 25..53 is treated as 53. A declaration of float(25) is thus the same as float(53).

Types real and float(24) are equivalent and require seven bytes of storage. Types float and float(53) are equivalent and require 15 bytes of storage.

11-5. Writing Mathematical Expressions

Problem

You are working with number values and want to write expressions to compute new values.

Solution

Write any expression you like, making use of SQL Server's supported operators and functions. For example, the expression in the following code block computes the new balance of a home loan after a payment of $500. The loan balance is $94,235.49. The interest rate is 6 percent. Twelve monthly payments are made per year.

```
DECLARE @cur_bal decimal(7,2) = 94235.49
DECLARE @new_bal decimal(7,2)

SET @new_bal = @cur_bal - (500.00 - ROUND(@cur_bal * 0.06 / 12.00, 2))
SELECT @new_bal
```

The results are as follows:

```
---------
94206.67
```

How It Works

You can write expressions of arbitrary length involving combinations of values, function calls, and operators. In doing so, you must be aware of and respect the rules of operator precedence. For example, multiplication occurs before addition, as is standard in mathematics.

Table 11-2 lists operators in order of their evaluation priority. The table lists all operators, including the nonmathematical ones.

Table 11-2. *Operator Precedence in SQL Server*

Priority Level	Operator	Description
1	~	Bitwise NOT
2	*, /, %	Multiply, divide, modulo
3	+, -	Positive sign, negative sign
3	+, -	Add, subtract
3	+	String concatenate
3	&, ^, |	Bitwise AND, Bitwise exclusive OR, Bitwise OR
4	=, <, <=, !<, >, >=, !>, <>, !=	Equals, less than, less than or equal, not less than, greater than, greater than or equal, not greater than, not equal, not equal
5	NOT	Logical NOT
6	AND	Logical AND
7	ALL, ANY, BETWEEN, IN, LIKE, OR, SOME	Logical OR and others
8	=	Assignment

Use parentheses to override the default priority. The solution example includes parentheses as follows to force the monthly interest amount to be subtracted from the $500 monthly payment, leaving the amount to be applied to the principal.

```
(500.00 - ROUND(@cur_bal * 0.06 / 12.00 ,2))
```

Omit the outer parentheses, and you'll get a very different result indeed.

■ **Tip** It's a reasonable practice to include parentheses for clarity, especially when using operators other than the fundamental four: +, -, *, and /. Not everyone has the precedence table memorized. You can make it easy on your successors and clarify your intentions by including parentheses in cases where misinterpretation is likely.

Another issue to contend with is data type precedence and the presence or absence of implicit conversions. Recipe 11-6, coming next, helps you guard against incorrect results from mixing data types within an expression.

11-6. Guarding Against Errors in Expressions with Mixed Data Types

Problem

You want to guard against trouble when writing an expression involving values from more than one data type.

Solution

Consider explicitly converting values between types to maintain full control over your expressions and their results. For example, invoke CAST and CONVERT as follows to change values from one type to another:

```
SELECT 6/100,
       CAST(6 AS DECIMAL(1,0)) / CAST(100 AS DECIMAL(3,0)),
       CAST(6.0/100.0 AS DECIMAL(3,2))

SELECT 6/100,
       CONVERT(DECIMAL(1,0), 6) / CONVERT(DECIMAL(3,0), 100),
       CONVERT(DECIMAL(3,2), 6.0/100.0)
```

The results from both these queries are as follows:

```
---          --------    -----
0            0.060000    0.06
```

Choose either CAST or CONVERT depending upon the importance you attach to complying with the ISO SQL standard. CAST is a standard function. CONVERT is specific to SQL Server. My opinion is to favor CAST unless you have some specific need for functionality offered by CONVERT.

How It Works

One of the most common implicit conversion errors in SQL Server is actually the result of implicit conversion *not* occurring in a specific case when a cursory glance would lead one to expect it to occur. That case involves division of numeric values written as integers, such as 6/100.

Recall the solution example from Recipe 11-5. Instead of writing the 6 percent interest rate as 0.06, write it as 6/100 inside parentheses. Make just that one change, and the resulting code looks as follows:

```
DECLARE @cur_bal decimal(7,2) = 94235.49
DECLARE @new_bal decimal(7,2)

SET @new_bal = @cur_bal - (500.00 - ROUND(@cur_bal * (6/100) / 12.00 ,2))
SELECT @new_bal
```

Execute this code, and the result changes from the correct result of 94206.67 as given in Recipe 11-5 to the incorrect result of 93735.49. Why the change? It's because 6 and 100 are written with no decimal points, so they are treated as integers. Integer division then ensues. The uninitiated expects 6/100 to evaluate to 0.06, but integer division leads to a result of zero. The interest rate evaluates to zero, and too much of the loan payment is applied to the principal.

■ **Caution** Keep in mind that numeric constants written without a decimal point are treated as integers. When writing an expression involving constants along with decimal values, include decimal points in your constants so they are treated also as decimals—unless, of course, you are certain you want them written as integers.

The solution in this case is to recognize that the expression requires decimal values and write either 0.06 or 6.0/100.0 instead. For example, the following version of the expression will yield the same correct results as in Recipe 11-5:

```
SET @new_bal = @cur_bal - (500.00 - ROUND(@cur_bal * (6.0/100.0) / 12.00 ,2))
```

What of the values 500.00 and 12.00? Can they be written as 500 and 12? It turns out that they can be written that way. The following expression yields correct results:

```
SET @new_bal = @cur_bal - (500 - ROUND(@cur_bal * (6.0/100.0) / 12 ,2))
```

You can get away in this case with 500 and 12, because SQL Server applies data type precedence. In the case of 500, the value being subtracted is a decimal value. Thus, the database engine implicitly converts 500 to a decimal. For much the same reason, the integer 12 is also promoted to decimal. That conversion makes sense in this particular case, but it may not always be what you want.

Table 11-3 lists data types by precedence. Anytime an operator works on values of two different types, the type lower on the scale is promoted to the type higher on the scale. If such a conversion is not what you want or if you just want to clearly specify the conversion to remove any doubt, invoke either the CAST or CONVERT function.

Table 11-3. *Data Type Precedence in SQL Server*

Precedence Level	Data Type	Precedence Level	Data Type
1	Any user-defined type	16	int
2	sql_variant	17	smallint
3	xml	18	tinyint
4	datetimeoffset	19	bit
5	datetime2	20	ntext
6	datetime	21	text
7	smalldatetime	22	image
8	date	23	timestamp
9	time	24	unique
10	float	25	nvarchar
11	real	26	nchar
12	decimal	27	varchar
13	money	28	char
14	smallmoney	29	varbinary
15	bigint	30	binary

The following is one last restatement of Recipe 11-5's solution. The original solution used ROUND to force the interest amount to two decimal places, but what was the resulting data type? Do you know? Perhaps it is better to be certain. The following code casts the result of the interest computation to the type decimal(7,2). The rounding still occurs, but this time as part of the casting operation.

```
DECLARE @cur_bal decimal(7,2) = 94235.49
DECLARE @new_bal decimal(7,2)

SET @new_bal = @cur_bal - (500.00 - CAST(@cur_bal * (6.0/100.0) / 12.00 AS decimal(7,2)))
SELECT @new_bal
```

The results are as follows:

```
--------
94206.67
```

Remember especially the tricky case of integer division in cases such as 6/100. That behavior is unintuitive and leads to many errors. Otherwise, the implicit conversions implied by the precedence in Table 11-3 tend to make sense and produce reasonable results. Whenever values from two types are involved in the same expression, the value of the type having the lower precedence is converted into an instance of the type having the higher precedence. Even so, I recommend explicit conversions in all but the obvious cases. If you aren't absolutely certain at a glance just what is occurring within an expression, then make the conversions explicit.

11-7. Rounding

Problem

You want to round a number value to a specific number of decimal places.

Solution

Invoke the ROUND function. Here's an example:

```
SELECT EndOfDayRate,
       ROUND(EndOfDayRate,0) AS EODR_Dollar,
       ROUND(EndOfDayRate,2) AS EODR_Cent
FROM Sales.CurrencyRate
```

The results are as follows:

```
EndOfDayRate  EODR_Dollar  EODR_Cent
------------  -----------  ---------
1.0002        1.00         1.00
1.55          2.00         1.55
1.9419        2.00         1.94
1.4683        1.00         1.47
8.2784        8.00         8.28
...
```

How It Works

Invoke ROUND to round a number to a specific number of decimal places, as specified by the second argument. The solution example shows rounding to the nearest integer (zero decimal places) and to the nearest hundredth (two decimal places).

■ **Note** Digit values of 5 and higher round upward. Rounding 0.5 to the nearest integer yields 1.0 as a result.

You can invoke ROUND with a negative argument to round to the left of the decimal place. The following is an example that rounds product inventories to the nearest 10 units and to the nearest 100 units:

```
SELECT ProductID, SUM(Quantity) AS Quantity,
       SUM(ROUND(Quantity,-1)) as Q10,
       SUM(ROUND(Quantity,-2)) as Q100
FROM Production.ProductInventory
GROUP BY ProductID
```

The results show the effects of rounding away from the decimal place:

```
ProductID   Quantity  Q10    Q100
---------   --------  ----   ----
1           1085      1080   1100
2           1109      1110   1100
3           1352      1350   1300
4           1322      1320   1300
...
```

ROUND usually returns a value. However, there is a case to beware of. It comes about because ROUND returns its result in the same data type as the input value. The following three statements illustrate the case in which ROUND will throw an error:

```
SELECT ROUND(500, -3)
SELECT ROUND(500.0, -4)
SELECT ROUND(500.0, -3)
```

The first and second statements will return 1000 and 0.0, respectively. But the third query will throw an error as follows:

```
Msg 8115, Level 16, State 2, Line 2
Arithmetic overflow error converting expression to data type numeric.
```

ROUND(500, -3) succeeds because the input value is an integer constant. (No decimal point means that 500 is considered as an integer.) The result is thus also an integer, and an integer is large enough to hold the value 1000.

ROUND(500.0, -4) returns zero. The input value indicates a type of decimal(4,1). The value rounds to zero because the value is being rounded too far to the left. Zero fits into the four-digit precision of the implied data type.

ROUND(500.0, -3) fails because the result is 1000. The value 1000 will not fit into the implied data type of decimal(4,1). You can get around the problem by casting your input value to a larger precision. Here's an example:

```
SELECT ROUND(CAST(500.0 as DECIMAL(5,1)), -3)
```

```
------
1000.0
```

This time, the input value is explicitly made to be decimal(5,1). The five digits of precision leave four to the left of the decimal place. Those four are enough to represent the value 1000.

11-8. Rounding Always Up or Down

Problem

You want to force a result to an integer value. You want to always round either up or down.

Solution

Invoke CEILING to always round up to the next integer value. Invoke FLOOR to always round down to the next lowest integer value. Here's an example:

```
SELECT CEILING(-1.23), FLOOR(-1.23), CEILING(1.23), FLOOR(1.23)
```

The results are as follows:

```
----    ----    ----    ----
-1      -2      2       1
```

How It Works

CEILING and FLOOR don't give quite the same flexibility as ROUND. You can't specify a number of decimal places. The functions simply round up or down to the nearest integer, period.

You can work around the *nearest integer* limitation using a bit of math. For example, to invoke CEILING to the nearest cent and to the nearest hundred, use this:

```
SELECT CEILING(123.0043*100.0)/100.0 AS toCent,
       CEILING(123.0043/100.0)*100.0 AS toHundred
```

```
toCent     toHundred
---------- ---------
123.010000 200.0
```

We don't trust this technique for binary floating-point values. However, it should work fine on decimal values so long as the extra math doesn't push those values beyond the bounds of precision and scale that decimal can support.

11-9. Discarding Decimal Places

Problem

You just want to "chop off" the digits past the decimal point. You don't care about rounding at all.

Solution

Invoke the ROUND function with a third parameter that is nonzero. Here's an example:

```
SELECT ROUND(123.99,0,1), ROUND(123.99,1,1), ROUND(123.99,-1,1)
```

```
------  ------  ------
123.00  123.90  120.00
```

How It Works

Some database brands (Oracle, for example) implement a TRUNCATE function to eliminate values past the decimal point. SQL Server accomplishes that task using the ROUND function. Make the third parameter anything but zero, and the function will truncate rather than round.

11-10. Testing Equality of Binary Floating-Point Values

Problem

You are testing two binary floating-point values for equality, but the imprecision inherent in floating-point representation is causing values that you consider equal to be rejected as not equal.

Solution

Decide on a difference threshold below which you will consider the two values to be equal. Then test the absolute value of the difference to see whether it is less than your threshold. For example, the following example assumes a threshold of 0.000001 (one one-millionth):

```
DECLARE @r1 real = 0.95
DECLARE @f1 float = 0.95
IF ABS(@r1-@f1) < 0.000001
   SELECT 'Equal'
ELSE
   SELECT 'Not Equal'
```

The difference is less than the threshold, so the values are considered as equal. The result is as follows:

```
-----
Equal
```

How It Works

Not all decimal values can be represented precisely in binary floating-point. In addition, different expressions that should in theory yield identical results sometimes differ by tiny amounts. The following is a query block to illustrate the problem:

```
DECLARE @r1 real = 0.95
DECLARE @f1 float = 0.95
SELECT @r1, @f1, @r1-@f1
```

Both values are the same but not really. The results are as follows:

```
----  ----   ----------------------
0.95  0.95   -1.19209289106692E-08
```

The fundamental problem is that the base-2 representation of 0.95 is a never-ending string of bits. The float type is larger, allowing for more bits, which is the reason for the nonzero difference. By applying the threshold method in the solution, you can pretend that the tiny difference does not exist.

■ **Caution** The solution in this recipe represents a conscious decision to disregard small differences in order to treat two values as being equal. Make that decision while keeping in mind the context of how the values are derived and of the problem being solved.

11-11. Treating Nulls as Zeros

Problem

You are writing expressions with numeric values that might be null. You want to treat nulls as zero.

Solution

Invoke the COALESCE function to supply a value of zero in the event of a null. For example, the following query returns the MaxQty column from Sales.SpecialOffer. That column is nullable. COALESCE is used to supply a zero as an alternate value.

```
SELECT SpecialOfferID, MaxQty, COALESCE(MaxQty, 0) AS MaxQtyAlt
FROM Sales.SpecialOffer
```

The results are as follows:

```
SpecialOfferID  MaxQty   MaxQtyAlt
--------------  -------  -----------
1               NULL     0
2               14       14
3               24       24
4               40       40
5               60       60
6               NULL     0
7               NULL     0
...
```

How It Works

COALESCE is an ISO standard function taking as input any number of values. It returns the first non-null value in the list. The solution example invokes COALESCE to return a zero in the event MaxQty is null.

SQL Server also implements an ISNULL function, which is propriety and takes only two arguments but otherwise is similar to COALESCE in that it returns the first non-null value in the list. You can implement the solution example using ISNULL as follows and get the same results:

```
SELECT SpecialOfferID, MaxQty, ISNULL(MaxQty, 0) AS MaxQtyAlt
FROM   Sales.SpecialOffer
```

It's generally good practice to avoid invoking COALESCE and ISNULL within a WHERE clause predicate. Applying functions to a column mentioned in a WHERE clause can inhibit the use of an index on the column. Here's an example of what we try to avoid:

```
SELECT SpecialOfferID
FROM   Sales.SpecialOffer
WHERE  COALESCE(MaxQty,0) = 0
```

In a case like this, we prefer to write an IS NULL predicate as follows:

```
SELECT SpecialOfferID
FROM   Sales.SpecialOffer
WHERE  MaxQty = 0 OR MaxQty IS NULL
```

We believe the IS NULL approach preserves the greatest amount of flexibility for the optimizer.

11-12. Generating a Row Set of Sequential Numbers

Problem

You need to generate a row set with an arbitrary number of rows. For example, you want to generate one row per day in the year so that you can join to another table that might be missing rows for some the days, so as to ultimately create a row set having one row per day.

Solution

Many row-generator queries are possible. The following is one solution I particularly like. It is a variation on a technique introduced to me by database expert Vladimir Przyjalkowski in 2004. It returns rows in power-of-ten increments controlled by the number of joins that you write in the outer query's FROM clause. This particular example returns 10,000 rows numbered from 0 to 9999.

```
WITH ones AS (
   SELECT *
   FROM (VALUES (0), (1), (2), (3), (4),
                (5), (6), (7), (8), (9)) AS numbers(x)
)
SELECT 1000*o1000.x + 100*o100.x + 10*o10.x + o1.x x
FROM ones o1, ones o10, ones o100, ones o1000
ORDER BY x
```

The results are as follows:

```
x
----
0
1
2
3
...
9997
9998
9999
```

If you like, you can restrict the number of rows returned by wrapping the main query inside of an enclosing query that restricts the results. Be sure to keep the WITH clause first. And specify an alias for the new, enclosing query. The following example specifies n as the alias:

```
WITH ones AS (
   SELECT *
   FROM (VALUES (0), (1), (2), (3), (4),
                (5), (6), (7), (8), (9)) AS numbers(x)
)
SELECT n.x FROM (
    SELECT 1000*o1000.x + 100*o100.x + 10*o10.x + o1.x x
    FROM ones o1, ones o10, ones o100, ones o1000
) n
WHERE n.x < 5000
ORDER BY x
```

This version returns 5,000 rows numbered from 0 through 4999.

How It Works

Row sets of sequential numbers are handy for *data densification*. Data densification refers to the filling in of missing rows, such as in time series data. Imagine, for example, that you want to generate a report showing how many employees were hired on each day of the year. A quick test of the data shows that hire dates are *sparse*—there are only a few days in a given year on which employees have been hired. Here's an example:

```
SELECT DISTINCT HireDate
FROM HumanResources.Employee
WHERE HireDate >= '2006-01-01'
  AND HireDate < '2007-01-01'
ORDER BY HireDate
```

The results indicate that hires occur sparsely throughout the year:

```
HireDate
----------
2006-05-18
2006-07-01
2006-11-01
```

Using the solution query, you can create a sequence table to use in densifying the data so as to return one row per day, regardless of number of hires. Begin by creating a 1,000-row table using a form of the solution query:

```
WITH ones AS (
    SELECT *
    FROM (VALUES (0), (1), (2), (3), (4),
                 (5), (6), (7), (8), (9)) AS numbers(x)
)
SELECT 100*o100.x + 10*o10.x + o1.x x
INTO SeqNum
FROM ones o1, ones o10, ones o100
```

Now it's possible to join against SeqNum and use that table as the basis for generating one row per day in the year. Here's an example:

```
SELECT DATEADD(day, x, '2006-01-01'), HireDate
FROM SeqNum LEFT OUTER JOIN HumanResources.Employee
     ON DATEADD(day, x, '2006-01-01') = HireDate
WHERE x < DATEDIFF (day, '2006-01-01', '2007-01-01')
ORDER BY x
```

The results are as follows. The HireDate column is non-null for days on which a hire was made.

```
                        HireDate
----------------------- ----------
2006-01-01 00:00:00.000 NULL
2006-01-02 00:00:00.000 NULL
...
2006-05-17 00:00:00.000 NULL
2006-05-18 00:00:00.000 2006-05-18
2006-05-19 00:00:00.000 NULL
...
2006-12-29 00:00:00.000 NULL
2006-12-30 00:00:00.000 NULL
2006-12-31 00:00:00.000 NULL
```

Add a simple GROUP BY operation to count the hires per date, and we're done! Here's the final query:

```
SELECT DATEADD(day, x, '2006-01-01'), COUNT(HireDate)
FROM SeqNum LEFT OUTER JOIN HumanResources.Employee
     ON DATEADD(day, x, '2006-01-01') = HireDate
WHERE x < DATEDIFF (day, '2006-01-01', '2007-01-01')
GROUP BY x
ORDER BY x
```

Results now show the number of hires per day. The following are results for the same days as in the previous output. This time, the count of hires is zero on all days having only null hire dates. The count is 1 on May 18, 2006, for the one person hired on that date.

```
----------------------- ----
2006-01-01 00:00:00.000 0
2006-01-02 00:00:00.000 0
...
2006-05-17 00:00:00.000 0
2006-05-18 00:00:00.000 1
2006-05-19 00:00:00.000 0
...
2006-12-29 00:00:00.000 0
2006-12-30 00:00:00.000 0
2006-12-31 00:00:00.000 0
```

You'll receive a warning message upon executing the final query. The message is nothing to worry about. It reads as follows:

```
Warning: Null value is eliminated by an aggregate or other SET operation.
```

This message simply indicates that the COUNT function was fed null values. And indeed that is the case. Null hire dates were fed into the COUNT function. Those nulls were ignored and not counted, which is precisely the behavior one wants in this case.

11-13. Generating Random Integers in a Row Set

Problem

You want each row returned by a query to include a random integer value. You further want to specify the range within which those random values will fall. For example, you want to generate a random number between 900 and 1,000 for each product.

Solution

Invoke the built-in RAND() function as shown in the following example:

```
DECLARE @rmin int, @rmax int;
SET @rmin = 900;
SET @rmax = 1000;
SELECT Name,
       CAST(RAND(CHECKSUM(NEWID())) * (@rmax-@rmin) AS INT) + @rmin
FROM Production.Product;
```

You'll get results as follows, except that your random numbers might be different from mine:

```
Name
----------------------  ----
Adjustable Race         939
All-Purpose Bike Stand  916
AWC Logo Cap            914
BB Ball Bearing         992
Bearing Ball            975
```

How It Works

RAND() returns a random float value between 0 exclusive and 1 exclusive. RAND() accepts a seed parameter, and any given seed will generate the same result. These are two characteristics you must keep in mind and compensate for as you use the function.

The following is the simplest possible invocation of RAND() in a query against Production.Product. The resulting "random" number is not very random at all. SQL Server treats the function as deterministic because of the lack of a parameter, invokes the function just one time, and applies the result of that invocation to all rows returned by the query.

```
SELECT Name, RAND()
FROM Production.Product;
```

```
Name
----------------------  -----------------
Adjustable Race         0.472241415009636
All-Purpose Bike Stand  0.472241415009636
```

```
AWC Logo Cap              0.472241415009636
BB Ball Bearing           0.472241415009636
Bearing Ball              0.472241415009636
```

What's needed is a seed value that changes for each row. A common and useful approach is to base the seed value on a call to NEWID(). NEWID() returns a value in a type not passable to RAND(). You can work around that problem by invoking CHECKSUM() on the NEWID() value to generate an integer value acceptable as a seed. Here's an example:

```
SELECT Name, RAND(CHECKSUM(NEWID()))
FROM Production.Product;
```

```
Name
----------------------    -----------------
Adjustable Race           0.943863936349248
All-Purpose Bike Stand    0.562297100626295
AWC Logo Cap              0.459806720686023
BB Ball Bearing           0.328415563433923
Bearing Ball              0.859439320073147
```

The NEWID() function generates a globally unique identifier. Because the result must be globally unique, no two invocations of NEWID() will return the same result. The function is therefore not deterministic, and the database engine thus invokes the RAND(CHECKSUM(NEWID())) expression anew for each row.

Now comes some math. It's necessary to shift the random values from their just-greater-than-zero to less-than-one range into the range, in this case, of 900 to 1000. Begin by multiplying the result from RAND() by the magnitude of the range. Do that by multiplying the random values by 100, which is the difference between the upper and lower bounds of the range. Here's an example:

```
DECLARE @rmin int, @rmax int;
SET @rmin = 900;
SET @rmax = 1000;
SELECT Name,
       RAND(CHECKSUM(NEWID())) * (@rmax-@rmin)
FROM Production.Product;
```

```
Name
----------------------    -----------------
Adjustable Race           12.5043506882683
All-Purpose Bike Stand    46.3611080374763
AWC Logo Cap              17.1908607269767
BB Ball Bearing           89.5318634996859
Bearing Ball              50.74511276104
...
```

Next is to shift the spread of values so that they appear in the desired range. Do that by adding the minimum value as shown in the following query and its output. The result is a set of random values beginning at just above 900 and going to just less than 1000.

```
DECLARE @rmin int, @rmax int;
SET @rmin = 900;
SET @rmax = 1000;
SELECT Name,
       RAND(CHECKSUM(NEWID())) * (@rmax-@rmin) + @rmin
FROM Production.Product;
```

```
Name
----------------------  ----------------
Adjustable Race         946.885865947398
All-Purpose Bike Stand  957.087533428096
AWC Logo Cap            924.321027483594
BB Ball Bearing         988.996724323006
Bearing Ball            943.797723186947
```

11-14. Reducing Space Used by Decimal Storage

Problem

You have very large tables with a great many decimal columns holding values notably smaller than their precisions allow. You want to reduce the amount of space to better reflect the actual values stored rather than the possible maximums.

> **Note** The solution described in this recipe is available only in the Enterprise Edition of SQL Server.

Solution

Enable vardecimal storage for your database. Do that by invoking `sp_db_vardecimal_storage_format` as follows:

```
EXEC sp_db_vardecimal_storage_format 'AdventureWorks2012', 'ON'
```

Then estimate the amount of space to be saved per table. For example, issue the following call to `sp_estimated_rowsize_reduction_for_vardecimal` to determine the average row length before and after vardecimal is enabled on the `Production.BillOfMaterials` table:

```
EXEC sys.sp_estimated_rowsize_reduction_for_vardecimal 'Production.BillOfMaterials'
```

Your results should be similar to the following:

```
avg_rowlen_fixed_format   avg_rowlen_vardecimal_format   row_count
----------------------    ----------------------------   ---------
57.00                     56.00                          2679
```

A one-byte-per-row savings is hardly worth pursuing. However, pursue it anyway by enabling vardecimal storage on the table:

```
sp_tableoption 'Production.BillOfMaterials', 'vardecimal storage format', 1
```

Be aware that converting to vardecimal is an offline operation. Be sure you can afford to take the table offline for the duration of the process.

How It Works

By switching on vardecimal storage for a table, you allow the engine to treat decimal values as variable length in much the same manner as variable-length strings, trading an increase in CPU time for a reduction in storage from not having to store unused bytes. You enable the use of the option at the database level. Then you can apply the option on a table-by-table basis.

While the vardecimal option sounds great on the surface, we recommend some caution. Make sure that the amount of disk space saved makes it really worth the trouble of enabling the option. Remember that there is a CPU trade-off. The example enables the option for a 2,679-row table and would save about one byte per row on average. Such a savings is fine for a book example but hardly worth pursing in real life. Go for a big win, or don't play at all.

■ **Note** You'll find a detailed and useful discussion of the vardecimal option at `http://msdn.microsoft.com/en-us/library/bb508963(v=SQL.90).aspx`.

You can generate a list of databases on your server showing for which ones vardecimal is enabled. Issue the following command to do that:

```
EXEC sp_db_vardecimal_storage_format
```

Your results should resemble the following. The `Database Name` values may be displayed extremely wide in Management Studio. You may need to scroll left and right to see the `Vardecimal State` values. I've elided much of the space between the columns in this output for the sake of readability.

```
Database Name            Vardecimal State
--------------------     ----------------
master                   OFF
tempdb                   OFF
model                    OFF
msdb                     OFF
ReportServer             ON
ReportServerTempDB       ON
AdventureWorks2008R2     ON
```

Similarly, you can issue the following query to generate a list of tables within a database for which the option is enabled. (Increase the VARCHAR size in the CAST if your table or schema names combine to be longer than 40 characters.)

```
SELECT CAST(ss.name + '.' + so.name AS VARCHAR(40)) AS 'Table Name',
       CASE objectproperty(so.object_id, N'TableHasVarDecimalStorageFormat')
            WHEN 1 then 'ON' ELSE 'OFF'
            END AS 'Vardecimal State'
FROM sys.objects so JOIN sys.schemas ss
     ON so.schema_id = ss.schema_id
WHERE so.type_desc = 'USER_TABLE'
ORDER BY ss.name, so.name
```

Your results should be similar to the following:

```
Table Name                   Vardecimal State
---------------------------  ----------------
dbo.AWBuildVersion           OFF
dbo.DatabaseLog              OFF
dbo.ErrorLog                 OFF
...
Production.BillOfMaterials   ON
...
```

To disable vardecimal storage on a table, invoke the `sp_tableoption` procedure with a third parameter of 0 rather than 1. Disable the option at the database level by first disabling it for all tables and then by executing `sp_db_vardecimal_storage_format` with a second parameter of `'OFF'`.

CHAPTER 12

Transactions, Locking, Blocking, and Deadlocking

By Jason Brimhall

In this chapter, I'll review recipes for handling transactions, lock monitoring, blocking, and deadlocking. I'll review the SQL Server table option that allows you to disable lock escalation or enable it for a partitioned table. I'll demonstrate the snapshot isolation level, as well as Dynamic Management Views (DMVs) that are used to monitor and troubleshoot blocking and locking.

Transaction Control

Transactions are an integral part of a relational database system, and they help define a single unit of work. This unit of work can include one or more Transact-SQL statements, which are either committed or rolled back as a group. This all-or-none functionality helps prevent partial updates or inconsistent data states. A partial update occurs when one part of an interrelated process is rolled back or cancelled without rolling back or reversing all of the other parts of the interrelated processes.

A transaction is bound by the four properties of the ACID test. ACID stands for Atomicity, Consistency, Isolation (or Independence), and Durability.

- *Atomicity* means that the transactions are an all-or-nothing entity—carrying out all the steps or none at all.
- *Consistency* ensures that the data is valid both before and after the transaction. Data integrity must be maintained (foreign key references, for example), and internal data structures need to be in a valid state.
- *Isolation* is a requirement that transactions not be dependent on other transactions that may be taking place concurrently (either at the same time or overlapping). One transaction can't see another transaction's data that is in an intermediate state but instead sees the data as it was either before the transaction began or after the transaction completes.
- *Durability* means that the transaction's effects are fixed after the transaction has committed, and any changes will be recoverable after system failures.

In this chapter, I'll demonstrate and review the SQL Server mechanisms and functionality that are used to ensure ACID test compliance, namely, locking and transactions.

There are three possible transaction types in SQL Server: autocommit, explicit, or implicit.

Autocommit is the default behavior for SQL Server, where each separate Transact-SQL statement you execute is automatically committed after it is finished. For example, it is possible for you to have two INSERT statements, with the first one failing and the second one succeeding; the second change is maintained because each INSERT is automatically contained in its own transaction. Although this mode frees the developer from having to worry about explicit transactions, depending on this mode for transactional activity can be a mistake. For example, if you have two transactions, one that credits an account and another that debits it, and the first transaction failed, you'll have a debit without the credit. This may make the bank happy but not necessarily the customer, who had his account debited. Autocommit is even a bit dangerous for ad hoc administrative changes; for example, if you accidentally delete all rows from a table, you don't have the option of rolling back the transaction after you've realized the mistake.

Implicit transactions occur when the SQL Server session automatically opens a new transaction when one of the following statements is first executed: ALTER TABLE, FETCH, REVOKE, CREATE, GRANT, SELECT, DELETE, INSERT, TRUNCATE TABLE, DROP, OPEN, and UPDATE.

A new transaction is automatically created (opened) once any of the aforementioned statements are executed and remains open until either a ROLLBACK or COMMIT statement is issued. The initiating command is included in the open transaction. Implicit mode is activated by executing the following command in your query session:

```
SET IMPLICIT_TRANSACTIONS ON;
```

To turn this off (back to explicit mode), execute the following:

```
SET IMPLICIT_TRANSACTIONS OFF;
```

Implicit mode can be *very* troublesome in a production environment, because application designers and end users could forget to commit transactions, leaving them open to block other connections (more on blocking later in the chapter).

Explicit transactions are those you define yourself. This is by far the recommended mode of operation when performing data modifications for your database application. This is because you explicitly control which modifications belong to a single transaction, as well as the actions that are performed if an error occurs. Modifications that must be grouped together are done using your own instruction.

Explicit transactions use the Transact-SQL commands and keywords described in Table 12-1.

Table 12-1. *Explicit Transaction Commands*

Command	Description
BEGIN TRANSACTION	Sets the starting point of an explicit transaction.
ROLLBACK TRANSACTION	Restores original data modified by a transaction and brings data back to the state it was in at the start of the transaction. Resources held by the transaction are freed.
COMMIT TRANSACTION	Ends the transaction if no errors were encountered and makes changes permanent. Resources held by the transaction are freed.
BEGIN DISTRIBUTED TRANSACTION	Allows you to define the beginning of a distributed transaction to be managed by Microsoft Distributed Transaction Coordinator (MSDTC). MSDTC must be running locally and remotely.
SAVE TRANSACTION	Issues a savepoint within a transaction, which allows you to define a location to which a transaction can return if part of the transaction is cancelled. A transaction must be rolled back or committed immediately after rolling back to a savepoint.
@@TRANCOUNT	Returns the number of active transactions for the connection. BEGIN TRANSACTION increments @@TRANCOUNT by 1, while ROLLBACK TRANSACTION and COMMIT TRANSACTION decrement @@TRANCOUNT by 1. ROLLBACK TRANSACTION to a savepoint has no impact.

12-1. Using Explicit Transactions

Problem

You are attempting to implement explicit transactions within your code and need to be able to commit the data changes only upon meeting certain criteria; otherwise, the data changes should not occur.

Solution

You can use explicit transactions to COMMIT or ROLLBACK a data modification depending on the return of an error in a batch of statements.

```
USE AdventureWorks2012;
GO
/* -- Before count */
SELECT BeforeCount = COUNT(*)
FROM HumanResources.Department;
/* -- Variable to hold the latest error integer value */
DECLARE @Error int;
BEGIN TRANSACTION
INSERT INTO HumanResources.Department (Name, GroupName)
    VALUES ('Accounts Payable', 'Accounting');
SET @Error = @@ERROR;
IF (@Error<> 0)
    GOTO Error_Handler;
INSERT INTO HumanResources.Department (Name, GroupName)
    VALUES ('Engineering', 'Research and Development');
SET @Error = @@ERROR;
IF (@Error <> 0)
    GOTO Error_Handler;
COMMIT TRANSACTION
Error_Handler:
IF @Error <> 0
BEGIN
ROLLBACK TRANSACTION;
END
/* -- After count */
SELECT AfterCount = COUNT(*)
FROM HumanResources.Department;
GO
```

This query returns the following:

```
BeforeCount 19
    (1 row(s) affected)

    (1 row(s) affected)
    Msg 2601, Level 14, State 1, Line 14
    Cannot insert duplicate key row in object 'HumanResources.Department'
    with unique index 'AK_Department_Name'.
```

```
The statement has been terminated.
AfterCount 19
    (1 row(s) affected)
```

How It Works

The first statement in this example validated the count of rows in the HumanResources.Department table, returning 19 rows.

```
-- Before count
SELECT BeforeCount = COUNT(*)
FROM HumanResources.Department;
```

A local variable was created to hold the value of the @@ERROR function (which captures the latest error state of a SQL statement).

```
-- Variable to hold the latest error integer value
DECLARE @Error int
```

Next, an explicit transaction was started.

```
BEGIN TRANSACTION
```

The next statement attempted an INSERT into the HumanResources.Department table. There was a unique key on the department name, but because the department name didn't already exist in the table, the insert succeeded.

```
INSERT INTO HumanResources.Department (Name, GroupName)
    VALUES ('Accounts Payable', 'Accounting');
```

Next was an error handler for the INSERT.

```
SET @Error = @@ERROR
IF (@Error <> 0) GOTO Error_Handler
```

This line of code evaluates the @@ERROR function. The @@ERROR system function returns the last error number value for the last-executed statement within the scope of the current connection. The IF statement says *if* an error occurs, the code should jump to the Error_Handler section of the code (using GOTO).

GOTO is a keyword that helps you control the flow of statement execution. The identifier after GOTO, Error_Handler, is a user-defined code section.

Next, another insert is attempted, this time for a department that already exists in the table. Because the table has a unique constraint on the Name column, this insert will fail:

```
INSERT INTO HumanResources.Department (Name, GroupName)
    VALUES ('Engineering', 'Research and Development');
```

The failure will cause the @@ERROR following this INSERT to be set to a nonzero value. The IF statement will then evaluate to TRUE, which will invoke the GOTO, thus skipping over the COMMIT TRAN to the Error_Handler section.

```
SET @Error = @@ERROR;
IF (@Error <> 0)
    GOTO Error_Handler;
COMMIT TRAN
```

Following the Error_Handler section is a ROLLBACK TRANSACTION.

```
Error_Handler:
IF @Error <> 0
BEGIN
ROLLBACK TRANSACTION;
END
```

Another count is performed after the rollback, and again, there are only 19 rows in the database. This is because both INSERTs were in the same transaction and one of the INSERTs failed. Since a transaction is all-or-nothing, no rows were inserted.

```
/* -- After count */
SELECT AfterCount = COUNT(*)
FROM HumanResources.Department;
```

The following are some thoughts and recommendations regarding how to handle transactions in your Transact-SQL code or through your application:

- Keep transaction time as short as possible for the business process at hand. Transactions that remain open can hold locks on resources for an extended period of time, which can block other users from performing work or reading data.
- Minimize resources locked by the transaction. For example, update only tables that are related to the transaction at hand. If the data modifications are logically dependent on each other, they belong in the same transaction. If not, the unrelated updates belong in their own transaction.
- Add only *relevant* Transact-SQL statements to a transaction. Don't add extra lookups or updates that are not germane to the specific transaction. Executing a SELECT statement within a transaction can create locks on the referenced tables, which can in turn block other users/sessions from performing work or reading data.
- Do not open new transactions that require user or external feedback within the transaction. Open transactions can hold locks on resources, and user feedback can take an indefinite amount of time to receive. Instead, gather user feedback *before* issuing an explicit transaction.

12-2. Displaying the Oldest Active Transaction

Problem

Your transaction log is growing, and a backup of the log is not alleviating the issue. You fear an uncommitted transaction may be the cause of the transaction log growth.

Solution

Use the DBCC OPENTRAN command to identify the oldest active transactions in a database. If a transaction remains open in the database, whether intentionally or not, this transaction can block other processes from performing activity against the modified data. Also, backups of the transaction log can only truncate the inactive portion of a transaction log, so open transactions can cause the log to grow (or reach the physical limit) until that transaction is committed or rolled back.

This example demonstrates using DBCC OPENTRAN to identify the oldest active transaction in the database:

```
USE AdventureWorks2012;
GO
BEGIN TRANSACTION
DELETE Production.ProductProductPhoto
WHERE ProductID = 317;

DBCC OPENTRAN('AdventureWorks2012');

ROLLBACK TRANSACTION;
GO
```

This query returns the following:

```
(1 row(s) affected)
Transaction information for database 'AdventureWorks2012'.

Oldest active transaction:
        SPID (server process ID):   54
        UID (user ID) : -1
        Name    : user_transaction
        LSN     :      (41:1021:39)
        Start time         : Sep 15 2008 10:45:53:780AM
        SID     : 0x010500000000000515000000a065cf7e784b9b5fe77c8770375a2900
DBCC execution completed. If DBCC printed error messages,
contact your system administrator.
```

How It Works

The recipe started by opening a new transaction and then deleting a specific row from the Production.ProductProductPhoto table. Next, the DBCC OPENTRAN was executed, with the database name in parentheses.

```
DBCC OPENTRAN('AdventureWorks2012');
```

These results showed information regarding the oldest active transaction, including the server process ID, user ID, and start time of the transaction. The key pieces of information from the results are the server process ID (SPID) and start time.

Once you have this information, you can validate the Transact-SQL being executed using DMVs, figure out how long the process has been running for, and, if necessary, shut down the process. DBCC OPENTRAN is useful for troubleshooting orphaned connections (connections still open in the database but disconnected from the application or client) and for identifying transactions missing a COMMIT or ROLLBACK.

This command also returns the oldest distributed and undistributed replicated transactions, if any exist within the database. If there are no active transactions, no session-level data will be returned.

12-3. Querying Transaction Information by Session

Problem

There is an active transaction that you want to investigate because of reported timeouts.

Solution

This recipe demonstrates how to find out more information about an active transaction by querying the sys.dm_tran_session_transactions DMV. To demonstrate, I'll describe a common scenario: your application is encountering a significant number of blocks with a high duration. You've been told that this application always opens an explicit transaction prior to each query.

To illustrate this scenario, I'll execute the following SQL (representing the application code causing the concurrency issue):

```
SET TRANSACTION ISOLATION LEVEL SERIALIZABLE;
GO
USE AdventureWorks2012;
GO
BEGIN TRAN
SELECT *
FROM HumanResources.Department;
INSERT INTO HumanResources.Department (Name, GroupName)
VALUES ('Test', 'QA');
```

In a new SQL Server Management Studio query window, I would like to identify all open transactions by querying the sys.dm_tran_session_transactions DMV:

```
SELECT session_id, transaction_id, is_user_transaction, is_local
FROM sys.dm_tran_session_transactions
WHERE is_user_transaction = 1;
GO
```

This results in the following (your actual session IDs and transaction IDs will vary):

```
session_id      transaction_id      is_user_transaction      is_local
51              145866              1                        1
```

Now that I have a session ID to work with (the session_id you receive may be different), I can dig into the details about the most recent query executed by querying sys.dm_exec_connections and sys.dm_exec_sql_text:

```
SELECT s.text
FROM sys.dm_exec_connections c
CROSS APPLY sys.dm_exec_sql_text(c.most_recent_sql_handle) s
WHERE c.most_recent_session_id = 51;--use the session_id returned by the previous query
GO
```

This returns the last statement executed. (I could have also used the sys.dm_exec_requests DMV for an ongoing and active session; however, nothing was currently executing for my example transaction, so no data would have been returned.)

```
text
SET TRANSACTION ISOLATION LEVEL SERIALIZABLE;
GO
USE AdventureWorks2012;
GO
BEGIN TRAN
SELECT *
FROM HumanResources.Department;
INSERT INTO HumanResources.Department (Name, GroupName)
VALUES ('Test', 'QA');
```

Since I also have the transaction ID from the first query against `sys.dm_tran_session_ transactions`, I can use `sys.dm_tran_active_transactions` to learn more about the transaction itself.

```
SELECT transaction_begin_time
,tran_type = CASE transaction_type
    WHEN 1 THEN 'Read/write transaction'
    WHEN 2 THEN 'Read-only transaction'
    WHEN 3 THEN 'System transaction'
    WHEN 4 THEN 'Distributed transaction'
    END
,tran_state = CASE transaction_state
    WHEN 0 THEN 'not been completely initialized yet'
    WHEN 1 THEN 'initialized but has not started'
    WHEN 2 THEN 'active'
    WHEN 3 THEN 'ended (read-only transaction)'
    WHEN 4 THEN 'commit initiated for distributed transaction'
    WHEN 5 THEN 'transaction prepared and waiting resolution'
    WHEN 6 THEN 'committed'
    WHEN 7 THEN 'being rolled back'
    WHEN 8 THEN 'been rolled back'
    END
FROM sys.dm_tran_active_transactions
WHERE transaction_id = 145866; -- change this value to the transaction_id returned in the first
--query of this recipe
GO
```

This returns information about the transaction start time, the type of transaction, and the state of the transaction:

transaction_begin_time	tran_type	tran_state
2012-04-07 10:03:26.520	Read/write transaction	active

How It Works

This recipe demonstrated how to use various DMVs to troubleshoot and investigate a long-running, active transaction. The columns you decide to use depend on the issue you are trying to troubleshoot. In this scenario, I used the following troubleshooting path:

- I queried `sys.dm_tran_session_transactions` in order to display a mapping between the session ID and the transaction ID (identifier of the individual transaction).
- I queried `sys.dm_exec_connections` and `sys.dm_exec_sql_text` in order to find the latest command executed by the session (referencing the `most_recent_sql_handle` column).
- Lastly, I queried `sys.dm_tran_active_transactions` in order to determine how long the transaction was opened, the type of transaction, and the state of the transaction.

Using this troubleshooting technique allows you to go back to the application and pinpoint query calls for abandoned transactions (opened but never committed) and transactions that are inappropriate because they run too long or are unnecessary from the perspective of the application. Before proceeding, you should now revisit the first query window and issue the following command to ensure the transaction is no longer running:

```
ROLLBACK TRANSACTION;
```

Locking

Locking is a normal and necessary part of a relational database system, ensuring the integrity of the data by not allowing concurrent updates to the same data or viewing of data that is in the middle of being updated. SQL Server manages locking dynamically; however, it is still important to understand how Transact-SQL queries impact locking in SQL Server. Before proceeding to the recipes, I'll briefly describe SQL Server locking fundamentals.

Locks help prevent concurrency problems from occurring. Concurrency problems (discussed in detail in the next section, "Transaction, Locking, and Concurrency") can happen when one user attempts to read data that another is modifying, modify data that another is reading, or modify data that another transaction is trying to modify.

Locks are placed against SQL Server resources. How a resource is locked is called its *lock mode.* Table 12-2 reviews the main lock modes that SQL Server has at its disposal.

Table 12-2. *SQL Server Lock Modes*

Name	Description
Shared lock	Shared locks are issued during read-only, nonmodifying queries. They allow data to be read but not updated by other processes while being held.
Intent lock	Intent locks effectively create a lock queue, designating the order of connections and their associated right to update or read resources. SQL Server uses intent locks to show future intention of acquiring locks on a specific resource.
Update lock	Update locks are acquired prior to modifying the data. When the row is modified, this lock is escalated to an exclusive lock. If not modified, it is downgraded to a shared lock. This lock type prevents deadlocks (discussed later in this chapter) if two connections hold a shared lock on a resource and attempt to convert to an exclusive lock but cannot because they are each waiting for the other transaction to release the shared lock.
Exclusive lock	This type of lock issues a lock on the resource that bars any kind of access (reads or writes). It is issued during `INSERT`, `UPDATE`, and `DELETE` statements.
Schema modification	This type of lock is issued when a DDL statement is executed.
Schema stability	This type of lock is issued when a query is being compiled. It keeps DDL operations from being performed on the table.
Bulk update	This type of lock is issued during a bulk-copy operation. Performance is increased for the bulk copy operation, but table concurrency is reduced.
Key-range	Key-range locks protect a range of rows (based on the index key)—for example, protecting rows in an `UPDATE` statement with a range of dates from 1/1/2012 to 12/31/2012. Protecting the range of data prevents row inserts into the date range that would be missed by the current data modification.

You can lock all manner of objects in SQL Server, from a single row in a database to a table to the database itself. Lockable resources vary in granularity, from small (at the row level) to large (the entire database). Small-grain locks allow for greater database concurrency, because users can execute queries against specified unlocked rows. Each lock placed by SQL Server requires memory, however, so thousands of individual row locks can also affect SQL Server performance. Larger-grained locks reduce concurrency but take up fewer resources. Table 12-3 details the resources SQL Server can apply locks to.

Table 12-3. SQL Server Lock Resources

Resource Name	Description
Allocation unit	A set of related pages grouped by data type, for example, data rows, index rows, and large object data rows.
Application	An application-specified resource.
Database	An entire database lock.
Extent	Allocation unit of eight contiguous 8KB data or index pages.
File	The database file.
HOBT	A heap (table without a clustered index) or B-tree.
Metadata	System metadata.
Key	Index row lock, helping prevent phantom reads. Also called a *key-range lock,* this lock type uses both a range and a row component. The range represents the range of index keys between two consecutive index keys. The row component represents the lock type on the index entry.
Object	A database object (for example a table, view, stored procedure, function).
Page	An 8KB data or index page.
RID	Row identifier, designating a single table row.
Table	A resource that locks entire table, data, and indexes.

Not all lock types are compatible with each other. For example, no other locks can be placed on a resource that has already been locked by an exclusive lock. The other transaction must wait or time out until the exclusive lock is released. A resource locked by an update lock can have a shared lock placed on it only by another transaction. A resource locked by a shared lock can have other shared or update locks placed on it.

Locks are allocated and escalated automatically by SQL Server. Escalation means that finer-grain locks (row or page locks) are converted into coarse-grain table locks. SQL Server will attempt to initialize escalation when a single Transact-SQL statement has more than 5,000 locks on a single table or index or if the number of locks on the SQL Server instance exceeds the available memory threshold. Locks take up system memory, so converting many locks into one larger lock can free up memory resources. The drawback to freeing up the memory resources, however, is reduced concurrency.

■ **Note** SQL Server has a table option that allows you to disable lock escalation or enable lock escalation at the partition (instead of table) scope. I'll demonstrate this in Recipe 12-5.

12-4. Viewing Lock Activity

Problem

You want to check the current locking activity in SQL Server.

Solution

This recipe shows you how to monitor locking activity in the database using the SQL Server `sys.dm_tran_locks` DMV. The example query being monitored by this DMV will use a table locking hint.

In the first part of this recipe, a new query editor window is opened, and the following command is executed:

```
USE AdventureWorks2012;
BEGIN TRAN
SELECT ProductID, ModifiedDate
FROM Production.ProductDocument WITH (TABLOCKX);
```

In a second query editor window, the following query is executed:

```
SELECT sessionid = request_session_id ,
ResType = resource_type ,
ResDBID = resource_database_id ,
ObjectName = OBJECT_NAME(resource_associated_entity_id, resource_database_id) ,
RMode = request_mode ,
RStatus = request_status
FROM sys.dm_tran_locks
WHERE resource_type IN ('DATABASE', 'OBJECT');
GO
```

■ **Tip** This recipe narrows down the result set to two SQL Server resource types of `DATABASE` and `OBJECT` for clarity. Typically, you'll monitor several types of resources. The resource type determines the meaning of the `resource_associated_entity_id` column, as I'll explain in the "How It Works" section.

The query returned information about the locking session identifier (server process ID, or `SPID`), the resource being locked, the database, the object, the resource mode, and the lock status.

```
sessionid    ResType     ResDBID    ObjectName         RMode    RStatus
53           DATABASE    8          NULL               S        GRANT
52           DATABASE    8          NULL               S        GRANT
52           OBJECT      8          ProductDocument    X        GRANT
```

How It Works

The example began by starting a new transaction and executing a query against the `Production.ProductDocument` table using a `TABLOCKX` locking hint (this hint places an exclusive lock on the table). To monitor what locks are open for the current SQL Server instance, the `sys.dm_tran_locks` DMV was queried. It returned a list of active locks in the `AdventureWorks2012` database. The exclusive lock on the `ProductDocument` table could be seen in the last row of the results.

The first three columns define the session lock, resource type, and database ID.

```
SELECT sessionid = request_session_id ,
ResType = resource_type ,
ResDBID = resource_database_id ,
```

The next column uses the OBJECT_NAME function. Notice that it uses two parameters (object ID and database ID) in order to specify which name to access.

```
ObjectName = OBJECT_NAME(resource_associated_entity_id, resource_database_id) ,
```

I also query the locking request mode and status.

```
RMode = request_mode ,
RStatus = request_status
```

Lastly, the FROM clause references the DMV, and the WHERE clause designates two resource types.

```
FROM sys.dm_tran_locks
WHERE resource_type IN ('DATABASE', 'OBJECT');
```

The resource_type column designates what the locked resource represents (for example, DATABASE, OBJECT, FILE, PAGE, KEY, RID, EXTENT, METADATA, APPLICATION, ALLOCATION_UNIT, or HOBT type). The resource_associated_entity_id depends on the resource type, determining whether the ID is an object ID, allocation unit ID, or HOBT ID:

- If the resource_associated_entity_id column contains an object ID (for a resource type of OBJECT)), you can translate the name using the sys.objects catalog view.
- If the resource_associated_entity_id column contains an allocation unit ID (for a resource type of ALLOCATION_UNIT), you can reference sys.allocation_units and reference the container_id. Container_id can then be joined to sys.partitions where you can then determine the object ID.
- If the resource_associated_entity_id column contains a HOBT ID (for a resource type of KEY, PAGE, ROW, or HOBT), you can directly reference sys.partitions and look up the associated object ID.
- For resource types such as DATABASE, EXTENT, APPLICATION, or METADATA, the resource_associated_entity_id column will be 0.

Use sys.dm_tran_locks to troubleshoot unexpected concurrency issues, such as a query session that may be holding locks longer than desired or issuing a lock resource granularity or lock mode that you hadn't expected (perhaps a table lock instead of a finer-grained row or page lock). Understanding what is happening at the locking level can help you troubleshoot query concurrency more effectively.

12-5. Controlling a Table's Lock Escalation Behavior

Problem

You want to alter how SQL Server behaves with regard to lock escalation.

Solution

Each lock that is created in SQL Server consumes memory resources. When the number of locks increases, memory decreases. If the percentage of memory being used for locks exceeds a certain threshold, SQL Server can convert fine-grained locks (page or row) into coarse-grained locks (table locks). This process is called *lock escalation*. Lock escalation reduces the overall number of locks being held on the SQL Server instance, reducing lock memory usage.

While finer-grained locks do consume more memory, they also can improve concurrency, because multiple queries can access unlocked rows. Introducing table locks may reduce memory consumption, but they also introduce blocking, because a single query holds an entire table. Depending on the application using the database, this behavior may not be desired, and you may want to exert more control over when SQL Server performs lock escalations.

SQL Server has the ability to control lock escalation at the table level using the `ALTER TABLE` command. You are now able to choose from the following three settings:

- `TABLE`, which is the default behavior used in SQL Server. When configured, lock escalation is enabled at the table level for both partitioned and nonpartitioned tables.
- `AUTO` enables lock escalation at the partition level (heap or B-tree) if the table is partitioned. If it is not partitioned, escalation will occur at the table level.
- `DISABLE` removes lock escalation at the table level. Note that you still may see table locks because of `TABLOCK` hints or for queries against heaps using a serializable isolation level.

This recipe demonstrates how to modify a table to use the `AUTO` and `DISABLE` settings.

```
USE AdventureWorks2012;
GO
ALTER TABLE Person.Address
    SET ( LOCK_ESCALATION = AUTO );

SELECT lock_escalation,lock_escalation_desc
FROM sys.tables WHERE name = 'Address';
GO
```

This query returns the following:

```
lock_escalation          lock_escalation_desc
2                        AUTO
```

Next, I'll disable escalation.

```
USE AdventureWorks2012;
GO
ALTER TABLE Person.Address
SET ( LOCK_ESCALATION = DISABLE);

SELECT lock_escalation,lock_escalation_desc
FROM sys.tables WHERE name = 'Address';
GO
```

This query returns the following:

```
lock_escalation          lock_escalation_desc
1                        DISABLE
```

How It Works

This recipe demonstrated enabling two SQL Server table options that control locking escalation. The command began with a standard ALTER TABLE designating the table name to modify.

```
ALTER TABLE Person.Address
```

The second line designated the SET command along with the LOCK_ESCALATION configuration to be used.

```
SET ( LOCK_ESCALATION = AUTO )
```

After changing the configuration, I was able to validate the option by querying the lock_escalation_desc column from the sys.tables catalog view.

Once the AUTO option is enabled, if the table is partitioned, lock escalation will occur at the partitioned level, which improves concurrency if there are multiple sessions acting against separate partitions.

Note For further information on partitioning, see Chapter 15.

If the table is not partitioned, table-level escalation will occur as usual. If you designate the DISABLE option, table-level lock escalation will not occur. This can help improve concurrency but could result in increased memory consumption if your requests are accessing a large number of rows or pages.

Transaction, Locking, and Concurrency

One of the ACID properties is *Isolation.* Transaction isolation refers to the extent to which changes made by one transaction can be seen by other transactions occurring in the database (in other words, under conditions of concurrent database access). At the highest possible degree of isolation, each transaction occurs as if it were the only transaction taking place at that time. No changes made by other transactions are visible to it. At the lowest level, anything done in one transaction, whether committed or not, is visible by another transaction.

The ANSI/ISO SQL standard defines four types of interactions between concurrent transactions.

- *Dirty reads:* These occur while a transaction is updating a row, and a second transaction reads the row before the first transaction is committed. If the original update rolls back, the uncommitted changes will be read by the second transaction, even though they are never committed to the database. This is the definition of a dirty read.
- *Nonrepeatable reads:* These occur when one transaction is updating data and a second is reading the same data while the update is in progress. The data retrieved before the update will not match data retrieved after the update.
- *Phantom reads:* These occur when a transaction issues two reads, and between the two reads, the underlying data is updated with data being inserted or deleted. This causes the results of each query to differ. Rows returned in one query that do not appear in the other are called *phantom rows.*
- *Lost updates:* This occurs when two transactions update a row's value and the transaction to last update the row "wins." Thus, the first update is lost.

SQL Server uses locking mechanisms to control the competing activity of simultaneous transactions. To avoid the concurrency issues such as dirty reads, nonrepeatable reads, and so on, it implements locking to control access to database resources and to impose a certain level of transaction isolation. Table 12-4 describes the available isolation levels in SQL Server.

Table 12-4. *SQL Server Isolation Levels*

Isolation Level	Description
READ COMMITTED (this is the default behavior of SQL Server)	While READ COMMITTED is used, uncommitted data modifications can't be read. Shared locks are used during a query, and data cannot be modified by other processes while the query is retrieving the data. Data inserts and modifications to the same table are allowed by other transactions, so long as the rows involved are not locked by the first transaction.
READ UNCOMMITTED	This is the least restrictive isolation level, issuing no locks on the data selected by the transaction. This provides the highest concurrency but the lowest amount of data integrity, because the data you read can be changed while you read it (as mentioned previously, these reads are known as *dirty reads*), or new data can be added or removed that would change your original query results. This option allows you to read data without blocking others but with the danger of reading data "in flux" that could be modified during the read itself (including reading data changes from a transaction that ends up getting rolled back). For relatively static and unchanging data, this isolation level can potentially improve performance by instructing SQL Server not to issue unnecessary locking on the accessed resources.
REPEATABLE READ	When enabled, dirty and nonrepeatable reads are not allowed. This is achieved by placing shared locks on all read resources. New rows that may fall into the range of data returned by your query can, however, still be inserted by other transactions.
SERIALIZABLE	When enabled, this is the most restrictive setting. Range locks are placed on the data based on the search criteria used to produce the result set. This ensures that actions such as insertion of new rows, modification of values, or deletion of existing rows that would have been returned within the original query and search criteria are not allowed.
SNAPSHOT	This isolation level allows you to read a transactionally consistent version of the data as it existed at the *beginning* of a transaction. Data reads do not block data modifications—however, the SNAPSHOT session will not detect changes being made.

Transactions and locking go hand in hand. Depending on your application design, your transactions can significantly impact database concurrency and performance. Concurrency refers to how many people can query and modify the database and database objects at the same time. For example, the READ UNCOMMITTED isolation level allows the greatest amount of concurrency since it issues no locks—with the drawback that you can encounter a host of data isolation anomalies (dirty reads, for example). The SERIALIZABLE mode, however, offers very little concurrency with other processes when querying a larger range of data.

12-6. Configuring a Session's Transaction Locking Behavior

Problem

You want to change the default transaction locking behavior for Transact-SQL statements used in a connection.

Solution

Use the SET TRANSACTION ISOLATION LEVEL command to set the default transaction locking behavior for Transact-SQL statements used in a connection. You can have only one isolation level set at a time, and the isolation level does not change unless explicitly set. SET TRANSACTION ISOLATION LEVEL allows you to change the locking behavior for a specific database connection. The syntax for this command is as follows:

```
SET TRANSACTION ISOLATION LEVEL { READ UNCOMMITTED | READ COMMITTED
REPEATABLE READ
SNAPSHOT | SERIALIZABLE }
```

In this first example, SERIALIZABLE isolation is used to query the contents of a table. In the *first query editor window*, the following code is executed:

```
USE AdventureWorks2012;
GO
SET TRANSACTION ISOLATION LEVEL SERIALIZABLE;
GO
BEGIN TRAN

SELECT  AddressTypeID, Name
FROM Person.AddressType
WHERE AddressTypeID BETWEEN 1 AND 6;
GO
```

This query returns the following results (while still leaving a transaction open for the query session):

```
AddressTypeID          Name
1                      Billing
2                      Home
3                      Main Office
4                      Primary
5                      Shipping
6                      Archive
```

In a *second query editor*, the following query is executed to view the kinds of locks generated by the SERIALIZABLE isolation level.

```
SELECT resource_associated_entity_id, resource_type,
request_mode, request_session_id
FROM sys.dm_tran_locks;
GO
```

This shows several key locks being held for request_session_id 52 (which is the other session's ID).

```
resource_associated_entity_id   resource_type   request_mode   request_session_id
0                               DATABASE        S              52
0                               DATABASE        S              53
72057594043039744               PAGE            IS             52
101575400                       OBJECT          IS             52
72057594043039744               KEY             RangeS-S       52
72057594043039744               KEY             RangeS-S       52
72057594043039744               KEY             RangeS-S       52
72057594043039744               KEY             RangeS-S       52
72057594043039744               KEY             RangeS-S       52
72057594043039744               KEY             RangeS-S       52
72057594043039744               KEY             RangeS-S       52
```

Back in the first query editor window, execute the following code to end the transaction and remove the locks.

```
COMMIT TRAN
```

In contrast, the same query is executed again in the first query editor window, this time using the READ UNCOMMITTED isolation level to read the range of rows.

```
USE AdventureWorks2012;
GO
SET TRANSACTION ISOLATION LEVEL READ UNCOMMITTED;
GO
BEGIN TRAN

SELECT  AddressTypeID, Name
FROM Person.AddressType
WHERE AddressTypeID BETWEEN 1 AND 6;
GO
```

In a second query editor, the following query is executed to view the kinds of locks generated by the READ UNCOMMITTED isolation level:

```
SELECT resource_associated_entity_id, resource_type,
request_mode, request_session_id
FROM sys.dm_tran_locks;
GO
```

This returns (abridged results) the following:

```
resource_associated_entity_id   resource_type   request_mode   request_session_id
0                               DATABASE        S              52
0                               DATABASE        S              53
```

Unlike SERIALIZABLE, the READ UNCOMMITTED isolation level creates no additional locks on the keys of the Person.AddressType table.

Returning to the first query editor with the READ UNCOMMITTED query, the transaction is ended for cleanup purposes.

```
COMMIT TRAN
```

I'll demonstrate the SNAPSHOT isolation level next. In the first query editor window, the following code is executed:

```
ALTER DATABASE AdventureWorks2012
SET ALLOW_SNAPSHOT_ISOLATION ON;
GO
USE AdventureWorks2012;
GO
SET TRANSACTION ISOLATION LEVEL SNAPSHOT;
GO
BEGIN TRAN
SELECT  CurrencyRateID,EndOfDayRate
FROM Sales.CurrencyRate
WHERE CurrencyRateID = 8317;
```

This query returns the following:

```
CurrencyRateID          EndOfDayRate
8317                    0.6862
```

In a second query editor window, the following query is executed:

```
USE AdventureWorks2012;
GO
UPDATE Sales.CurrencyRate
SET EndOfDayRate = 1.00
WHERE CurrencyRateID = 8317;
GO
```

Now back to the first query editor; the following query is reexecuted:

```
SELECT  CurrencyRateID,EndOfDayRate
FROM Sales.CurrencyRate
WHERE CurrencyRateID = 8317;
GO
```

This query returns the following:

```
CurrencyRateID          EndOfDayRate
8317                    0.6862
```

The same results are returned as before, even though the row was updated by the second query editor query. The SELECT was not blocked from reading the row, nor was the UPDATE blocked from making the modification.

Now return to the first query window to commit the transaction and reissue the query.

```
COMMIT TRAN
SELECT  CurrencyRateID,EndOfDayRate
FROM Sales.CurrencyRate
WHERE CurrencyRateID = 8317;
GO
```

This returns the updated value:

```
CurrencyRateID          EndOfDayRate
8317                    1.00
```

How It Works

In this recipe, I demonstrated how to change the locking isolation level of a query session by using SET TRANSACTION ISOLATION LEVEL. Executing this command isn't necessary if you want to use the default SQL Server isolation level, which is READ COMMITTED. Otherwise, once you set an isolation level, it remains in effect for the connection until explicitly changed again.

The first example in the recipe demonstrated using the SERIALIZABLE isolation level.

```
SET TRANSACTION ISOLATION LEVEL SERIALIZABLE GO
```

An explicit transaction was then started, and a query was executed against the Person.AddressType table for all rows that fell within a specific range of AddressTypeID values.

```
BEGIN TRAN
SELECT  AddressTypeID, Name
FROM Person.AddressType
WHERE AddressTypeID BETWEEN 1 AND 6;
```

In a separate connection, a query was then executed against the sys.dm_tran_locks DMV, which returned information about active locks being held for the SQL Server instance. In this case, we saw a number of key range locks, which served the purpose of prohibiting other connections from inserting, updating, or deleting data that would cause different results in the query's search condition (WHERE AddressTypeID BETWEEN 1 AND 6).

In the second example, the isolation level was set to READ UNCOMMITTED.

```
SET TRANSACTION ISOLATION LEVEL READ UNCOMMITTED;
GO
```

Querying sys.dm_tran_locks again, we saw that this time no row, key, or page locks were held at all on the table, allowing the potential for other transactions to modify the queried rows while the original transaction remained open. With this isolation level, the query performs dirty reads, meaning that the query could read data with in-progress modifications, whether or not the actual modification is committed or rolled back later.

In the third example from the recipe, the database setting ALLOW_SNAPSHOT_ISOLATION was enabled for the database.

```
ALTER DATABASE AdventureWorks2012
SET ALLOW_SNAPSHOT_ISOLATION ON;
GO
```

This option had to be ON in order to start a snapshot transaction. In the next line of code, the database context was changed, and SET TRANSACTION ISOLATION LEVEL was set to SNAPSHOT.

```
USE AdventureWorks2012;
GO
SET TRANSACTION ISOLATION LEVEL SNAPSHOT;
GO
```

A transaction was then opened, and a query against Sales.CurrencyRate was performed.

```
BEGIN TRAN
SELECT  CurrencyRateID,EndOfDayRate
FROM Sales.CurrencyRate
WHERE CurrencyRateID = 8317;
```

In the second query editor session, the same Sales.CurrencyRate row being selected in the first session query was modified.

```
USE AdventureWorks2012;
GO
UPDATE Sales.CurrencyRate
SET EndOfDayRate = 1.00
WHERE CurrencyRateID = 8317;
GO
```

Back at the first query editor session, although the EndOfDayRate was changed to 1.0 in the second session, executing the query again in the SNAPSHOT isolation level shows that the value of that column was still 0.6862. This new isolation level provided a consistent view of the data as of the beginning of the transaction. After committing the transaction, reissuing the query against Sales.CurrencyRate revealed the latest value.

What if you decide to UPDATE a row in the snapshot session that was updated in a separate session? Had the snapshot session attempted an UPDATE against CurrencyRateID 8317 instead of a SELECT, an error would have been raised, warning you that an update was made against the original row while in snapshot isolation mode.

```
Msg 3960, Level 16, State 1, Line 2
Cannot use snapshot isolation to access table 'Sales.CurrencyRate'
directly or indirectly in database 'AdventureWorks2012'.
Snapshot transaction aborted due to update conflict.
Retry transaction.
```

Blocking

Blocking occurs when one transaction in a database session is locking resources that one or more other session transactions wants to read or modify. Short-term blocking is usually OK and expected for busy applications. However, poorly designed applications can cause long-term blocking, unnecessarily keeping locks on resources and blocking other sessions from reading or updating them.

In SQL Server, a blocked process remains blocked indefinitely or until it times out (based on SET LOCK_TIMEOUT), the server goes down, the process is killed, the connection finishes its updates, or something happens to the original transaction to cause it to release its locks on the resource.

Here are some reasons why long-term blocking can happen:

- Excessive row locks on a table without an index can cause SQL Server to acquire a table lock, blocking out other transactions.
- Applications open a transaction and then request user feedback or interaction while the transaction stays open. This is usually when an end user is allowed to enter data in a GUI while a transaction remains open. While open, any resources referenced by the transaction may be held with locks.
- Transactions BEGIN and then look up data that could have been referenced prior to the transaction starting.

- Queries use locking hints inappropriately, for example, if the application uses only a few rows but uses a table lock hint instead.
- The application uses long-running transactions that update many rows or many tables within one transaction (chunking large updates into smaller update transactions can help improve concurrency).

12-7. Identifying and Resolving Blocking Issues

Problem

You need to identify any blocking processes, and associated TSQL being executed, within your database.

Solution

In this recipe, I'll demonstrate how to identify a blocking process, view the Transact-SQL being executed by the process, and then forcibly shut down the active session's connection (thus rolling back any open work not yet committed by the blocking session). First, however, let's go to a quick background on the commands used in this example.

This recipe demonstrates how to identify blocking processes with the SQL Server DMV `sys.dm_os_waiting_tasks`. This view is intended to be used instead of the `sp_who2` system stored procedure, which was used in previous versions of SQL Server.

After identifying the blocking process, this recipe will then use the `sys.dm_exec_sql_text` dynamic management function and `sys.dm_exec_connections` DMV used earlier in the chapter to identify the SQL text of the query that is being executed—and then, as a last resort, forcefully end the process.

To forcefully shut down a wayward active query session, the `KILL` command is used. `KILL` should be used only if other methods are not available, including waiting for the process to stop on its own or shutting down or canceling the operation via the calling application. The syntax for `KILL` is as follows:

```
KILL {spid | UOW} [WITH STATUSONLY]
```

Table 12-5 describes the arguments for this command.

Table 12-5. *`KILL` Command Arguments*

Argument	Description
`spid`	This indicates the session ID associated with the active database connection to be shut down.
`UOW`	This is the unit-of-work identifier for a distributed transaction, which is the unique identifier of a specific distributed transaction process.
`WITH STATUSONLY`	Some `KILL` statements take longer to roll back a transaction than others (depending on the scope of updates being performed by the session). To check the status of a rollback, you can use `WITH STATUSONLY` to get an estimate of rollback time.

Beginning the example, the following query is executed in the first query editor session in order to set up a blocking process:

```
USE AdventureWorks2012;
GO
BEGIN TRAN
UPDATE Production.ProductInventory
SET Quantity = 400
WHERE ProductID = 1 AND LocationID = 1;
```

Next, in a second query editor window, the following query is executed:

```
USE AdventureWorks2012;
GO
BEGIN TRAN
UPDATE Production.ProductInventory
SET Quantity = 406
WHERE ProductID = 1 AND LocationID = 1;
```

Now in a third query editor window, I'll execute the following query:

```
SELECT blocking_session_id, wait_duration_ms, session_id
FROM sys.dm_os_waiting_tasks
WHERE blocking_session_id IS NOT NULL;
GO
```

This query returns the following (your results will vary):

```
blocking_session_id        wait_duration_ms        session_id
53                         27371                   52
```

This query identified that session 53 is blocking session 52.

To see what session 53 is doing, I execute the following query in the same window as the previous query:

```
SELECT t.text
FROM sys.dm_exec_connections c
CROSS APPLY sys.dm_exec_sql_text (c.most_recent_sql_handle) t
WHERE c.session_id = 53;
GO
```

This query returns the following:

```
text
USE AdventureWorks2012;
GO
BEGIN TRAN
UPDATE Production.ProductInventory
SET Quantity = 400
WHERE ProductID = 1 AND LocationID = 1;
```

Next, to forcibly shut down the session, execute this query:

```
KILL 53;
```

This results in the following:

```
Command(s) completed successfully.
```

The second session's UPDATE is then allowed to proceed once the other session's connection is removed.

How It Works

The recipe demonstrated blocking by executing an UPDATE against the Production.ProductInventory table with a transaction that was opened but *not* committed. In a different session, a similar query was executed against the same table and the same row. Because the other connection's transaction never committed, the second connection must wait in line indefinitely before it has a chance to update the record.

In a third query editor window, the sys.dm_os_waiting_tasks DMV was queried, returning information on the session being blocked by another session.

When troubleshooting blocks, you'll want to see exactly what the blocking session_id is doing. To view this, the recipe used a query against sys.dm_exec_connections and sys.dm_exec_sql_text. The sys.dm_exec_connections DMV was used to retrieve the most_recent_sql_handle column for session_id 53. This is a pointer to the SQL text in memory and was used as an input parameter for the sys.dm_exec_sql_text dynamic management function. The text column is returned from sys.dm_exec_sql_text, displaying the SQL text of the blocking process.

■ **Note** Often blocks and you must work your way through each blocked process up to the original blocking process using the blocking_session_id and session_id columns.

KILL was then used to forcibly end the blocking process, but in a production scenario, you'll want to see whether the process is valid and, if so, whether it should be allowed to complete or whether it can be shut down or cancelled using the application (by the application end user, for example). Prior to stopping the process, be sure you are not stopping a long-running transaction that is critical to the business, like a payroll update, for example. If there is no way to stop the transaction (for example, the application that spawned it cannot commit the transaction), you can use the KILL command (followed by the SPID to terminate).

12-8. Configuring How Long a Statement Will Wait for a Lock to Be Released

Problem

You need to extend how long a transaction can wait if it is blocked by another transaction.

Solution

When a transaction or statement is being *blocked,* this means it is waiting for a lock on a resource to be released. This recipe demonstrates the SET LOCK_TIMEOUT option, which specifies how long the blocked statement should wait for a lock to be released before returning an error.

The syntax is as follows:

```
SET LOCK_TIMEOUT timeout_period
```

The timeout period is the number of milliseconds before a locking error will be returned. To set up this recipe's demonstration, I will execute the following batch:

```
USE AdventureWorks2012;
GO
BEGIN TRAN
UPDATE Production.ProductInventory
SET Quantity = 400
WHERE ProductID = 1 AND LocationID = 1;
```

In a second query window, this example demonstrates setting up a lock timeout period of one second (1,000 milliseconds).

```
USE AdventureWorks2012;
GO
SET LOCK_TIMEOUT 1000;
UPDATE Production.ProductInventory
SET Quantity = 406
WHERE ProductID = 1 AND LocationID = 1;
```

After one second (1,000 milliseconds), I receive the following error message:

```
Msg 1222, Level 16, State 51, Line 2
Lock request time out period exceeded.
The statement has been terminated.
```

How It Works

In this recipe, the lock timeout is set to 1000 milliseconds (1 second). This setting doesn't impact how long a resource can be *held* by a process, only how long it has to wait for another process to release access to the resource. Before proceeding, you should now revisit the first query window and issue the following command to ensure the transaction is no longer running:

```
ROLLBACK TRANSACTION;
```

Deadlocking

Deadlocking occurs when one user session (let's call it Session 1) has locks on a resource that another user session (let's call it Session 2) wants to modify and Session 2 has locks on resources that Session 1 needs to modify. Neither Session 1 nor Session 2 can continue until the other releases the locks, so SQL Server chooses one of the sessions in the deadlock as the *deadlock victim.*

■ **Note** A deadlock victim has its session killed, and transactions are rolled back.

Here are some reasons why deadlocks can happen:

- The application accesses tables in different order. For example, Session 1 updates `Customers` and then `Orders`, whereas Session 2 updates `Orders` and then `Customers`. This increases the chance of two processes deadlocking, rather than them accessing and updating a table in a serialized (in order) fashion.
- The application uses long-running transactions, updating many rows or many tables within one transaction. This increases the surface area of rows that can cause deadlock conflicts.
- In some situations, SQL Server issues several row locks, which it later decides must be escalated to a table lock. If these rows exist on the same data pages and two sessions are both trying to escalate the lock granularity on the same page, a deadlock can occur.

12-9. Identifying Deadlocks with a Trace Flag

Problem

You are experiencing a high volume of deadlocks within your database. You need to find out the causes of the deadlocks.

Solution

If you are having deadlock trouble in your SQL Server instance, this recipe demonstrates how to make sure deadlocks are logged to the SQL Server Management Studio SQL log appropriately using the `DBCC TRACEON`, `DBCC TRACEOFF`, and `DBCC TRACESTATUS` commands. These functions enable, disable, and check the status of trace flags.

■ **Tip** There are other methods in SQL Server for troubleshooting deadlocks, such as using SQL Profiler, but since this book is Transact-SQL focused, I don't cover them here.

Trace flags are used within SQL Server to enable or disable specific behaviors for the SQL Server instance. By default, SQL Server doesn't return significant logging when a deadlock event occurs. Using trace flag 1222, information about locked resources and types participating in a deadlock are returned in an XML format, helping you troubleshoot the event.

The `DBCC TRACEON` command enables trace flags. The syntax is as follows:

```
DBCC TRACEON ( trace# [ ,...n ][ ,-1 ] ) [ WITH NO_INFOMSGS ]
```

Table 12-6 describes the arguments for this command.

Table 12-6. *`DBCC TRACEON` Command Arguments*

Argument	Description
`trace#`	This specifies one or more trace flag numbers to enable.
`-1`	When -1 is designated, the specified trace flags are enabled globally.
`WITH NO_INFOMSGS`	When included in the command, `WITH NO_INFOMSGS` suppresses informational messages from the `DBCC` output.

The DBCC TRACESTATUS command is used to check on the status (enabled or disabled) for a specific flag or flags. The syntax is as follows:

```
DBCC TRACESTATUS ( [ [ trace# [,...n ]][,][ -1 ]]) [ WITH NO_INFOMSGS ]
```

Table 12-7 describes the arguments for this command.

Table 12-7. *DBCC TRACESTATUS Command Arguments*

Argument	Description
trace# [,...n]]	This specifies one or more trace flag numbers to check the status of.
-1	This shows globally enabled flags.
WITH NO_INFOMSGS	When included in the command, WITH NO_INFOMSGS suppresses informational messages from the DBCC output.

The DBCC TRACEOFF command disables trace flags. The syntax is as follows:

```
DBCC TRACEOFF ( trace# [ ,...n ] [ , -1 ] ) [ WITH NO_INFOMSGS ]
```

Table 12-8 describes the arguments for this command.

Table 12-8. *DBCC TRACEOFF Command Arguments*

Argument	Description
trace#	This indicates one or more trace flag numbers to disable.
-1	This disables the globally set flags.
WITH NO_INFOMSGS	When included in the command, WITH NO_INFOMSGS suppresses informational messages from the DBCC output.

To demonstrate this recipe, a deadlock will be simulated. In a new query editor window, the following query is executed:

```
USE AdventureWorks2012;
GO
SET NOCOUNT ON;
SET TRANSACTION ISOLATION LEVEL SERIALIZABLE;
WHILE 1 = 1
BEGIN
BEGIN TRAN
UPDATE Purchasing.Vendor
SET CreditRating = 1
WHERE BusinessEntityID = 1494;
UPDATE Purchasing.Vendor
SET CreditRating = 2
```

```
WHERE BusinessEntityID = 1492;
COMMIT TRAN
END
```

In a second query editor window, the following query is executed:

```
USE AdventureWorks2012;
GO
SET NOCOUNT ON;
SET TRANSACTION ISOLATION LEVEL SERIALIZABLE;
WHILE 1 = 1
BEGIN
BEGIN TRAN
UPDATE Purchasing.Vendor
SET CreditRating = 2
WHERE BusinessEntityID = 1492;
UPDATE Purchasing.Vendor
SET CreditRating = 1
WHERE BusinessEntityID = 1494;
COMMIT TRAN
END
```

After a few seconds, check each query editor window until the following error message appears on one of the query editors:

```
Msg 1205, Level 13, State 51, Line 9
Transaction (Process ID 52) was deadlocked on lock resources with another process and has been
chosen as the deadlock victim. Rerun the transaction.
```

Looking at the SQL log in SQL Server Management Studio, the deadlock event was not logged. I'll now open a third query editor window and execute the following command:

```
DBCC TRACEON (1222, -1)
GO
DBCC TRACESTATUS
```

DBCC TRACESTATUS shows the active traces running for both the local session and globally:

```
TraceFlag       Status  Global  Session
1222            110     1       1
```

To simulate another deadlock, I'll restart the "winning" connection query (the one that wasn't killed in the deadlock), and then the deadlock losing session, causing another deadlock after a few seconds.

After the deadlock has occurred, I stop the other executing query. Now the SQL log in SQL Server Management Studio contains a detailed error message from the deadlock event, including the database and object involved, the lock mode, and the Transact-SQL statements involved in the deadlock.

For example, when deadlocks occur, you'll want to make sure to find out the queries that are involved in the deadlock so you can troubleshoot them accordingly. The following excerpt from the log shows a deadlocked query:

```
05/08/2012 20:20:00,spidl6s,Unknown,
UPDATE [Purchasing].[Vendor] set [CreditRating] = @1
WHERE [BusinessEntityID] = @2
```

From this we can tell which query was involved in the deadlocking, which is often enough to get started with a solution. Other important information you can retrieve by using trace 1222 includes the login name of the deadlocked process, the client application used to submit the query, and the isolation level used for its connection (letting you know whether that connection is using an isolation level that doesn't allow for much concurrency).

```
... clientapp=Microsoft SQL Server Management Studio-Query hostname=LesRois hostpid=2388
loginname=LesRois\Administrator isolationlevel=serializable (4) xactid=1147351 currentdb=8
lockTimeout=4294967295 clientoption1=673187936 clientoption2=390200
```

After examining the SQL log, disable the trace flag in the query editor.

```
DBCC TRACEOFF (1222, -1)
GO
DBCC TRACESTATUS
```

Before proceeding, you should now revisit the first query window and issue the following command to ensure the transaction is no longer running:

```
ROLLBACK TRANSACTION;
```

How It Works

In this recipe, I simulated a deadlock using two separate queries that updated the same rows repeatedly: updating two rows in the opposite order. When a deadlock occurred, the error message was logged to the query editor window, but nothing was written to the SQL log.

To enable deadlock logging to the SQL log, the recipe enabled the trace flag 1222. Trace 1222 returns detailed deadlock information to the SQL log. The -1 flag indicated that trace flag 1222 should be enabled globally for all SQL Server connections. To turn on a trace flag, DBCC TRACEON was used, with the 1222 flag in parentheses.

```
DBCC TRACEON (1222, -1)
```

To verify that the flag was enabled, DBCC TRACESTATUS was executed.

```
DBCC TRACESTATUS
```

After encountering another deadlock, the deadlock information was logged in the SQL log. The flag was then disabled using DBCC TRACEOFF.

```
DBCC TRACEOFF (1222, -1)
```

12-10. Setting Deadlock Priority

Problem

While trying to resolve deadlock issues, you have determined that certain query sessions are less critical and want to increase the chance of those sessions to be chosen as the deadlock victim.

Solution

You can increase a query session's chance of being chosen as a deadlock victim by using the `SET DEADLOCK_PRIORITY` command. The syntax for this command is as follows:

```
SET DEADLOCK_PRIORITY { LOW | NORMAL | HIGH |<numeric-priority> }
```

Table 12-9 describes the arguments for this command.

Table 12-9. *SET DEADLOCK_PRIORITY Command Arguments*

Argument	Description
`LOW`	`LOW` makes the current connection the likely deadlock victim.
`NORMAL`	`NORMAL` lets SQL Server decide based on which connection seems least expensive to roll back.
`HIGH`	`HIGH` lessens the chances of the connection being chosen as the victim, unless the other connection is also `HIGH` or has a numeric priority greater than 5.
`<numeric-priority>`	The numeric priority allows you to use a range of values from -10 to 10, where -10 is the most likely deadlock victim, up to 10 being the least likely to be chosen as a victim. The higher number between two participants in a deadlock wins.

For example, had the first query from the previous recipe used the following deadlock priority command, it would almost certainly have been chosen as the victim (normally, the default deadlock victim is the connection SQL Server deems least expensive to cancel and roll back):

```
USE AdventureWorks2012;
GO
SET NOCOUNT ON;
SET TRANSACTION ISOLATION LEVEL SERIALIZABLE;
SET DEADLOCK_PRIORITY LOW;
WHILE 1 = 1
BEGIN
BEGIN TRAN
UPDATE Purchasing.Vendor
SET CreditRating = 1
WHERE BusinessEntityID = 2;
UPDATE Purchasing.Vendor
```

```
SET CreditRating = 2
WHERE BusinessEntityID = 1;
COMMIT TRAN
END
GO
```

How It Works

You can also set the deadlock priority to HIGH and NORMAL. HIGH means that unless the other session is of the same priority, it will not be chosen as the victim. NORMAL is the default behavior and will be chosen if the other session is HIGH, but not chosen if the other session is LOW. If both sessions have the same priority, the least expensive transaction to roll back will be chosen.

CHAPTER 13

Managing Tables

by Wayne Sheffield

Almost every database has one thing in common: they all use tables to store data. In this chapter, I'll present recipes that demonstrate table creation and manipulation. Tables are used to store data in the database, and they are the central unit upon which most SQL Server database objects depend. Tables are uniquely named within a database and schema and contain one or more columns. Each column has an associated data type that defines the kind of data that can be stored within it.

A table can have up to 1,024 columns (with the exception of sparse columns) but can't exceed a total of 8,060 actual used bytes per row. A data page size is 8KB, including the header, which stores information about the page. This byte limit is not applied to the large object data types—varchar(max), nvarchar(max), varbinary(max), text, image, xml—or any CLR data type based upon these formats, such as the geography or geometry data types.

Another exception to the 8,060-byte limit rule is SQL Server's *row overflow* functionality for regular varchar, nvarchar, varbinary, and sql_variant data types, or any CLR data type based upon these formats, such as the HierarchyId data type. If the lengths of these individual data types do not exceed 8,000 bytes but the combined width of more than one of these columns together in a table exceeds the 8,060-byte row limit, the column with the largest width will be dynamically moved to another 8KB page and replaced in the original table with a 24-byte pointer. Row overflow provides extra flexibility for managing large row sizes, but you should still limit your potential maximum variable data type length in your table definition when possible, because reliance on page overflow may decrease query performance, since more data pages need to be retrieved by a single query.

13-1. Creating a Table

Problem

You need to create a table to store data.

Solution

Use the `CREATE TABLE` statement to create a new table.

```
CREATE TABLE dbo.Person (
  PersonID INT IDENTITY CONSTRAINT PK_Person PRIMARY KEY CLUSTERED,
  BusinessEntityId INT NOT NULL
      CONSTRAINT FK_Person REFERENCES Person.BusinessEntity (BusinessEntityID),
  First_Name VARCHAR(50) NOT NULL);
```

How It Works

This recipe creates a relatively simple table of three columns. The first column (PersonID) has an integer data type, is automatically populated by having the IDENTITY property set, and has a clustered primary key constraint on it. Since PRIMARY KEY constraints do not allow columns to be nullable, this column is implicitly set to not allow NULL values.

The second column (BusinessEntityId) has an integer data type, and it is specified to not allow NULL values to be inserted into it. This column has a foreign key constraint on it referencing a second table; this foreign key constraint enforces that whatever value is in this column will have a corresponding value in the referenced table. The value in the referenced table must exist prior to adding the value in this table, and before a value can be deleted from the referenced table, there must be no corresponding values in this table.

The third column (First_Name) has a varchar(50) data type, and it is specified to not allow NULL values. The size of the name can be up to 50 characters in length.

Note that this format allows you to create constraints on a single column. If you need to build a constraint that encompasses multiple columns, you would need to use the following format for those columns:

```
CREATE TABLE dbo.Test (
  Column1 INT NOT NULL,
  Column2 INT NOT NULL,
  CONSTRAINT PK_Test PRIMARY KEY CLUSTERED (Column1, Column2));
```

■ **Note** To create a table variable, you need to use the DECLARE statement instead of the CREATE TABLE statement. See Recipe 13-23 for more details about using table variables.

13-2. Adding a Column

Problem

You need to add a new column to an existing table.

Solution

Use the ALTER TABLE statement to add new columns to a table.

```
ALTER TABLE dbo.Person
ADD Last_Name VARCHAR(50) NULL;
```

How It Works

The ALTER TABLE statement is used to make modifications to existing tables, including adding new columns. The first line of code specifies which table is to be modified, and the next line specifies to add a new column (Last_Name) with a varchar(50) data type. For all of the existing rows, the value of this column is NULL.

13-3. Adding a Column That Requires Data

Problem

You need to add a new column to an existing table, and you need to create it to have NOT NULL values.

Solution

Use the ALTER TABLE statement to add new columns to a table and simultaneously specify a *default constraint*.

```
ALTER TABLE dbo.Person
ADD IsActive BIT NOT NULL
CONSTRAINT DF__Person__IsActive DEFAULT (0);
```

How It Works

The ALTER TABLE statement is used to add the new column. The first line specifies the table to be modified, the second line specifies the column to be added with the NOT NULL specification, and the third line specifies a default constraint with a value of 0. SQL Server will add the column to the table with the NOT NULL attribute and will set the value of this column to 0 for all the existing rows in this table. Any new rows that do not specify a value for this column will also default to 0.

■ **Note** See Recipe 13-13 for how a *default constraint* works.

13-4. Changing a Column

Problem

You need to modify the data type or properties of an existing column in a table.

Solution

Use the ALTER TABLE statement to modify existing columns in a table.

```
ALTER TABLE dbo.Person
ALTER COLUMN Last_Name VARCHAR(75) NULL;
```

How It Works

The ALTER TABLE statement is used to make modifications to existing tables, including modifying existing columns. The first line of code specifies which table is to be modified, and the next line specifies to modify an existing column (Last_Name), followed by the column's new definition.

■ **Note** If the existing column is specified with the NOT NULL attribute, you must specify NOT NULL for the new column definition in order to retain the NOT NULL attribute on the column. Additionally, if the existing column already has data in it and the data is not able to be implicitly converted to the new data type, then the ALTER TABLE statement will fail.

13-5. Creating a Computed Column

Problem

You need to save a calculation used when querying a table.

Solution

Use the ALTER TABLE statement to add a computed column to an existing table or the CREATE TABLE statement to create a computed column as the table is created:

```
ALTER TABLE Production.TransactionHistory
ADD CostPerUnit AS (ActualCost/Quantity);

CREATE TABLE HumanResources.CompanyStatistic (
  CompanylD int NOT NULL,
  StockTicker char(4) NOT NULL,
  SharesOutstanding int NOT NULL,
  Shareholders int NOT NULL,
  AvgSharesPerShareholder AS (SharesOutstanding/Shareholders) PERSISTED);
```

How It Works

The ALTER TABLE statement is used to add a new computed column to an existing table.

In the first example, a new computed column (CostPerUnit) is added to a table. When querying this table, this column will be returned with the results of the calculation specified. The calculation results are not physically stored in the table.

If you were to run the following query:

```
SELECT TOP 1 CostPerUnit, Quantity, ActualCost
  FROM Production.TransactionHistory
 WHERE Quantity > 10
 ORDER BY ActualCost DESC;
```

you would get the following results:

```
CostPerUnit     Quantity        ActualCost
-----------     --------        ----------
132.0408        13              1716.5304
```

Computed columns can't be used within a DEFAULT or FOREIGN KEY constraint. A calculated column can't be explicitly updated or inserted into (since its value is always derived).

Computed columns can be used within indexes but must meet certain requirements, such as being deterministic (always returning the same result for a given set of inputs) and precise (not containing float values).

In the second example, a new table is created with a computed column. Since this calculated column is specified as PERSISTED, the calculation results are physically stored in the table (but the calculation is still performed by SQL Server). This means that any changes to the columns involved in the computation will result in the computed column being recalculated and updated. The stored data still can't be modified directly—the data is still computed. Storing the data does mean, however, that the column can be used to partition a table (see Chapter 15), or it can be used in an index with an imprecise (float-based) value—unlike its nonpersisted version.

13-6. Removing a Column

Problem

You need to remove a column from a table.

Solution

Use the ALTER TABLE statement to drop an existing column from a table.

```
ALTER TABLE dbo.Person
DROP COLUMN Last_Name;
```

How It Works

The first line of code specifies the table that is being modified. The second line of code specifies to drop the Last_Name column.

■ **Note** You can drop a column only if it isn't being used in a PRIMARY KEY, FOREIGN KEY, UNIQUE, or CHECK CONSTRAINT (these constraint types are all covered in this chapter). You also can't drop a column being used in an index or that has a DEFAULT value bound to it.

13-7. Removing a Table

Problem

You need to remove a table from the database.

Solution

Use the DROP TABLE statement to drop an existing table in the database.

```
DROP TABLE dbo.Person;
```

How It Works

The code specifies to remove the table definition and data for the specified table from the database.

■ **Note** The DROP TABLE statement will fail if any other table is referencing the table to be dropped through a foreign key constraint. If there are foreign key references, you must drop them first before dropping the primary key table.

13-8. Reporting on a Table's Definition

Problem

You need to see information about the metadata for a table.

Solution

Use the system stored procedure sp_help to report a table's metadata information.

```
EXECUTE sp_help 'Person.Person';
```

How It Works

The sp_help system stored procedure returns several different result sets with useful information regarding the specific object (in this example, it returns data about the table Person.Person). This system stored procedure can be used to gather information regarding other database object types as well. The results of this example include numerous columns and multiple result sets; therefore, the results are not being shown. Some of information in the results includes information about the columns in the table, what filegroup the table is located on, all indexes and the columns that are part of the index, information about all constraints, and whether this table is referenced by any foreign keys or views.

13-9. Reducing Storage Used by NULL Columns

Problem

You have a table with hundreds (or even thousands) of columns (for example, a table in a SharePoint site that stores data about uploaded documents, where different columns are used for data about different file types), and most of these columns are NULL. However, this table still consumes extremely large amounts of storage space. You need to reduce the storage needs of this table.

Solution

Specify the SPARSE column attribute for each of these nullable columns.

How It Works

Sparse columns are a storage optimization improvement that enables zero-byte storage of NULL values. Consequently, this allows a large number of sparse columns to be defined for a table (as of this writing, 30,000 sparse columns are allowed). This improvement is ideal for database designs and applications requiring a high number of infrequently populated columns or for tables having sets of columns related only with a subset of the data stored in the table.

To define a sparse column, you need add only the SPARSE storage attribute after the column definition within a CREATE or ALTER TABLE command, as the following query demonstrates:

```
CREATE TABLE dbo.WebsiteProduct (
    WebsiteProductID int NOT NULL PRIMARY KEY IDENTITY(1,1),
    ProductNM varchar(255) NOT NULL,
    PublisherNM varchar(255) SPARSE NULL,
    ArtistNM varchar(150) SPARSE NULL,
    ISBNNBR varchar(30) SPARSE NULL,
    DiscsNBR int SPARSE NULL,
    MusicLabelNM varchar(255) SPARSE NULL);
```

The previous table takes a somewhat denormalized approach to creating columns that apply only to specific product types. For example, the PublisherNM and ISBNNBR columns apply to a book product, whereas DiscsNBR, ArtistNM, and MusicLabelNM will more often apply to a music product. When a product row is stored, the sparse columns that do not apply to it will *not* incur a storage cost for each NULL value.

Let's now insert two new rows into the table, one representing a book and one a music album:

```
INSERT dbo.WebsiteProduct (ProductNM, PublisherNM, ISBNNBR)
  VALUES ('SQL Server 2012 Transact-SQL Recipes', 'Apress', '9781430242000');
INSERT dbo.WebsiteProduct (ProductNM, ArtistNM, DiscsNBR, MusicLabelNM)
  VALUES ('Etiquette', 'Casiotone for the Painfully Alone', 1, 'Tomlab');
```

Returning just the appropriate columns for book products is accomplished with the following query:

```
SELECT ProductNM, PublisherNM,ISBNNBR FROM dbo.WebsiteProduct WHERE ISBNNBR IS NOT NULL;
```

This query returns the following result set:

```
ProductNM                            PublisherNM  ISBNNBR
-----------------------------------  -----------  -------------
SQL Server 2012 Transact-SQL Recipes  Apress       9781430242000
```

If your table has a large number of columns and you want to return all the columns that have NOT NULL values, then you can utilize a COLUMN SET. A COLUMN SET allows you to logically group all sparse columns defined for the table. This column (with a data type of xml) allows for SELECTs and data modification and is defined by designating COLUMN_SET FOR ALL_SPARSE_COLUMNS after the column definitions. You can have only one COLUMN SET for a single table, and you also can't add one to a table that already has sparse columns defined in it. If you attempt to add a COLUMN SET to the dbo.WebsiteProduct table (which already has sparse columns) with the ALTER TABLE statement:

```
ALTER TABLE dbo.WebsiteProduct
ADD ProductAttributeCS XML COLUMN_SET FOR ALL_SPARSE_COLUMNS;
```

the following error is returned:

```
Msg 1734, Level 16, State 1, Line 1
Cannot create the sparse column set 'ProductAttributeCS' in the table 'WebsiteProduct' because
the table already contains one or more sparse columns. A sparse column set cannot be added to
a table if the table contains a sparse column.
```

Taking the previous table, this code will re-create it with a sparse column:

```
IF OBJECT_ID('dbo.WebsiteProduct', 'U') IS NOT NULL
   DROP TABLE dbo.WebsiteProduct;
CREATE TABLE dbo.WebsiteProduct (
    WebsiteProductID int NOT NULL PRIMARY KEY IDENTITY(1,1),
    ProductNM varchar(255) NOT NULL,
    PublisherNM varchar(255) SPARSE NULL,
    ArtistNM varchar(150) SPARSE NULL,
    ISBNNBR varchar(30) SPARSE NULL,
    DiscsNBR int SPARSE NULL,
    MusicLabelNM varchar(255) SPARSE NULL,
    ProductAttributeCS xml COLUMN_SET FOR ALL_SPARSE_COLUMNS);
```

After re-inserting the data by running the prior two INSERT statements, you can now query the table using this COLUMN SET (instead of the individual columns in the table), as demonstrated here:

```
SELECT ProductNM, ProductAttributeCS
  FROM dbo.WebsiteProduct
 WHERE ISBNNBR IS NOT NULL;
```

This query returns the following result set:

```
ProductNM                              ProductAttributeCS
------------------------------------   ---------------------------------
SQL Server 2012 Transact-SQL Recipes   <PublisherNM>Apress</PublisherNM>
                                       <ISBNNBR>9781430242000</ISBNNBR>
```

You can also execute INSERT and UPDATE statements against the COLUMN SET columns.

```
INSERT dbo.WebsiteProduct (ProductNM, ProductAttributeCS)
VALUES ('Roots & Echoes',
        '<ArtistNM>The Coral</ArtistNM>
         <DiscsNBR>1</DiscsNBR>
         <MusicLabelNM>Deltasonic</MusicLabelNM>');
```

■ **Caution** Any columns not specified will be set to NULL. If you use an UPDATE statement, data in existing columns will be set to NULL if the columns were not specified.

Once a column set is defined for a table, performing a SELECT * query no longer returns each individual sparse column, as the following query demonstrates (only nonsparse columns and then the column set):

```
SELECT * FROM dbo.WebsiteProduct;
```

This query returns the following result set:

```
WebsiteProductID  ProductNM                              ProductAttributeCS
----------------  -------------------------------------  --------------------------------------
1                 SQL Server 2012 Transact-SQL Recipes   <PublisherNM>Apress</PublisherNM>
                                                         <ISBNNBR>9781430242000</ISBNNBR>
2                 Etiquette                              <ArtistNM>Casiotone for the Painfully
                                                         Alone</ArtistNM>
                                                         <DiscsNBR>1</DiscsNBR>
                                                         <MusicLabelNM>Tomlab</MusicLabelNM>
3                 Roots & Echoes                         <ArtistNM>The Coral</ArtistNM>
                                                         <DiscsNBR>1</DiscsNBR>
                                                         <MusicLabelNM>Deltasonic</MusicLabelNM>
```

13-10. Adding a Constraint to a Table

Problem

You need to add one or more constraints (PRIMARY KEY, UNIQUE, or FOREIGN KEY) to a table in order to enforce referential integrity rules on the table or between tables.

Solution

Use the ALTER TABLE statement to add PRIMARY KEY, UNIQUE, or FOREIGN KEY constraints to enforce referential integrity rules on this table. The following statements create a table and then create PRIMARY KEY, UNIQUE, and FOREIGN KEY constraints on it:

```
CREATE TABLE dbo.Person (
  PersonID INT IDENTITY NOT NULL,
  BusinessEntityId INT NOT NULL,
  First_Name VARCHAR(50) NULL,
  Last_Name VARCHAR(50) NULL);

ALTER TABLE dbo.Person
  ADD CONSTRAINT PK_Person PRIMARY KEY CLUSTERED (PersonID),
      CONSTRAINT FK_Person FOREIGN KEY (BusinessEntityId)
          REFERENCES Person.BusinessEntity (BusinessEntityID),
      CONSTRAINT UK_Person_Name UNIQUE (First_Name, Last_Name);
```

How It Works

The ALTER TABLE statement allows you to modify an existing table, including adding constraints to it. You can also use the CREATE TABLE statement to create the table and add the constraints to it simultaneously:

```
IF OBJECT_ID('dbo.Person','U') IS NOT NULL
   DROP TABLE dbo.Person;
CREATE TABLE dbo.Person (
  PersonID INT IDENTITY NOT NULL,
  BusinessEntityId INT NOT NULL,
  First_Name VARCHAR(50) NULL,
  Last_Name VARCHAR(50) NULL,
  CONSTRAINT PK_Person PRIMARY KEY CLUSTERED (PersonID),
  CONSTRAINT FK_Person FOREIGN KEY (BusinessEntityId)
      REFERENCES Person.BusinessEntity (BusinessEntityID),
  CONSTRAINT UK_Person_Name UNIQUE (First_Name, Last_Name) );
```

Constraints place limitations on the data that can be entered into a column or columns. Constraints on a single column can be created as either a *table constraint* or a *column constraint*; constraints being created on more than one column must be created as a *table constraint*.

A *column constraint* is specified in the CREATE TABLE statement as part of the definition of the column. For a *column constraint*, the constraint applies to the single column. In comparison, a *table constraint* is specified in the CREATE TABLE statement after the comma separating the columns. Although not required, *table constraints* are generally placed after all column definitions. In the previous example, the constraints are created as *table constraints*. The same table, with *column constraints* for the single-column constraints, is shown here:

```
IF OBJECT_ID('dbo.Person','U') IS NOT NULL
   DROP TABLE dbo.Person;
CREATE TABLE dbo.Person (
  PersonID INT IDENTITY NOT NULL
      CONSTRAINT PK_Person PRIMARY KEY CLUSTERED (PersonID),
  BusinessEntityId INT NOT NULL
      CONSTRAINT FK_Person FOREIGN KEY (BusinessEntityId)
          REFERENCES Person.BusinessEntity (BusinessEntityID),
  First_Name VARCHAR(50) NULL,
  Last_Name VARCHAR(50) NULL,
  CONSTRAINT UK_Person_Name UNIQUE (First_Name, Last_Name) );
```

A *primary key* is a special type of constraint that identifies a single column or set of columns, which in turn uniquely identifies all rows in the table.

A primary key enforces *entity integrity,* meaning that rows are guaranteed to be unambiguous and unique. Best practices for database normalization dictate that every table has a primary key. A primary key provides a way to access the record and ensures that the key is unique. A primary key column can't contain NULL values.

Only one primary key is allowed for a table, and when a primary key is designated, an underlying table *index* is automatically created, defaulting to a clustered index (index types are reviewed in Chapter 18). You can also explicitly designate that a nonclustered index will be created when the primary key is created instead, if you have a better use for the single clustered index allowed for a table. An index created on the primary key counts against the 1,000 total indexes allowed for a table.

A *composite primary key* is the unique combination of *more* than one column in the table. To define a composite primary key, you must use a *table constraint* instead of a *column constraint.*

In the prior example, a PRIMARY KEY constraint is created on the PersonID column.

You can have only one primary key defined on a table. If you want to enforce uniqueness on other nonprimary key columns, you can use a UNIQUE constraint. A unique constraint, by definition, creates an alternate key. Unlike a PRIMARY KEY constraint, you can create multiple UNIQUE constraints for a single table, and you are also allowed to designate a UNIQUE constraint for columns that allow NULL values (although only one NULL value is allowed for a single-column key per table). Like primary keys, UNIQUE constraints enforce entity integrity by ensuring that rows can be uniquely identified.

The UNIQUE constraint creates an underlying table index when it is created. This index can be CLUSTERED or NONCLUSTERED (although you can't create the index as CLUSTERED if a clustered index already exists for the table).

As with PRIMARY KEY constraints, you can define a UNIQUE constraint when a table is created either on the column definition or at the table constraint level.

You can have only one NULL value for a single-column UNIQUE constraint. For a multiple-column UNIQUE constraint, you can have only a single NULL value in that column for the values of the remaining columns in the UNIQUE constraint. Consider the following code that inserts data into the previous table, which has a UNIQUE constraint defined on the nullable First_Name and Last_Name columns:

```
INSERT INTO dbo.Person (BusinessEntityId, First_Name) VALUES (1, 'MyName');
INSERT INTO dbo.Person (BusinessEntityId, First_Name) VALUES (1, 'MyName2');
INSERT INTO dbo.Person (BusinessEntityId) VALUES (1);
```

In the first two INSERT statements, NULL values are being inserted into the Last_Name column. You can have multiple NULL values in the Last_Name column as long as the First_Name column is different. Both of these statements are allowed once. Trying to run either of these a second time will generate an error:

```
Msg 2627, Level 14, State 1, Line 1
Violation of UNIQUE KEY constraint 'UK_Person_Name'. Cannot insert duplicate key in object
'dbo.Person'. The duplicate key value is (MyName2, <NULL>).
```

■ **Note** In SQL Server 2012, the constraint violation error messages have been enhanced to show the values that are causing the error. As such, you can tell that the previous error statement comes from the second INSERT statement.

In the third INSERT statement, NULL values are being inserted into both the First_Name and Last_Name columns. Again, this is allowed once. Subsequent attempts will generate the same error (except that the values being displayed will be different).

Foreign key constraints establish and enforce relationships between tables and help maintain referential integrity, which means that every value in the foreign key column(s) must exist in the corresponding column(s) for the referenced table. Foreign key constraints also help define domain integrity, in that they define the range of potential and allowed values for a specific column or columns. Domain integrity defines the validity of values in a column. Foreign key constraints can be defined only by referencing a table that has a constraint enforcing entity integrity, either a PRIMARY KEY or UNIQUE constraint.

Foreign key constraints can be created as a table constraint or, if the constraint is on a single column, as a column constraint. In the prior example, a FOREIGN KEY constraint is created between the BusinessEntityId column in the table being created, and the BusinessEntityId column in the Person.BusinessEntity table.

You can create multiple FOREIGN KEY constraints on a table. Creating a FOREIGN KEY constraint does not create any indexes on the table.

When there is a FOREIGN KEY constraint between tables, SQL Server restricts the ability to delete a row from the referenced table or update the column to a different value, unless the referencing table does not contain that value. Furthermore, SQL Server restricts the ability to insert a row into the referencing table unless there is a row with that value in the referenced table. Since SQL Server must check for this existence in the referencing table when updating or deleting records in the referenced table, it can be advantageous to create an index in the referencing table on the foreign key column(s) to support this lookup.

13-11. Creating a Recursive Foreign Key

Problem

You need to ensure that the values in a column exist in a different column in the same table. For example, an employee table might contain a column for employee_id and another column for manager_id. The data in manager_id column must exist in the employee_id column.

Solution

Create a recursive foreign key:

```
CREATE TABLE dbo.Employees (
    employee_id INT IDENTITY PRIMARY KEY CLUSTERED,
    manager_id INT NULL REFERENCES dbo.Employees (employee_id));
```

Note Some people will call a recursive foreign key a *self-referencing foreign key*. Use whichever you want; they mean the same thing.

How It Works

The table is created with two columns. The first column is employee_id, and it is an identity column, with a primary key created as a column constraint. The second column is manager_id. It is defined as nullable, and it has a foreign key that is referencing the employee_id column in the same table.

Tip When creating a FOREIGN KEY *column constraint*, the keywords FOREIGN KEY are optional.

Now let's insert some data by running the following statements and then query the results:

```
INSERT INTO dbo.Employees DEFAULT VALUES;
INSERT INTO dbo.Employees (manager_id) VALUES (1);
SELECT * FROM dbo.Employees;
```

This query returns the following results:

```
employee_id     manager_id
-----------     ----------
1               NULL
2               1
```

If we then run the following statement:

```
INSERT INTO dbo.Employees (manager_id) VALUES (10);
```

SQL Server will generate an error since there is no `employee_id` with a value of 10:

```
Msg 547, Level 16, State 0, Line 9
The INSERT statement conflicted with the FOREIGN KEY SAME TABLE constraint
"FK__Employees__manag__6EE06CCD". The conflict occurred in database
"AdventureWorks2008R2", table "dbo.Employees", column 'employee_id'.
```

13-12. Allowing Data Modifications to Foreign Keys Columns in the Referenced Table to Be Reflected in the Referencing Table

Problem

You need to change the value of a column on a table that is involved in a foreign key relationship as the referenced table, and there are rows in the referencing table using this value.

Solution

Create the foreign key with *cascading* changes.

How It Works

Foreign keys restrict the values that can be placed within the foreign key column or columns. If the associated primary key or unique value does not exist in the reference table, the `INSERT` or `UPDATE` to the table row fails. This restriction is bidirectional in that if an attempt is made to delete a primary key but one or more rows that reference that specific key exists in the foreign key table, an error will be returned. All referencing foreign key rows must be deleted prior to deleting the targeted primary key or unique value; otherwise, an error will be raised.

SQL Server provides an automatic mechanism for handling changes in the primary key/unique key column, called *cascading changes*. In previous examples, cascading options weren't used. You can allow cascading changes for deletions or updates using `ON DELETE` and `ON UPDATE`. The basic syntax for cascading options is as follows:

```
[ ON DELETE { NO ACTION | CASCADE | SET NULL | SET DEFAULT }    ]
[ ON UPDATE { NO ACTION | CASCADE | SET NULL | SET DEFAULT }    ]
[ NOT FOR REPLICATION ]
```

Table 13-1 details these arguments.

Table 13-1. *Cascading Change Arguments*

Argument	Description
NO ACTION	The default setting for a new foreign key is NO ACTION, meaning if an attempt to delete a row on the primary key/unique column occurs when there is a referencing value in a foreign key table, the attempt will raise an error and prevent the statement from executing.
CASCADE	For ON DELETE, if CASCADE is chosen, foreign key rows referencing the deleted primary key are also deleted. For ON UPDATE, foreign key rows referencing the updated primary key are also updated.
SET NULL	If the primary key row is deleted, the foreign key referencing row(s) can also be set to NULL (assuming NULL values are allowed for that foreign key column).
SET DEFAULT	If the primary key row is deleted, the foreign key referencing row(s) can also be set to a DEFAULT value. The new cascade SET DEFAULT option assumes the column has a default value set for a column. If not and the column is nullable, a NULL value is set.
NOT FOR REPLICATION	The NOT FOR REPLICATION option is used to prevent foreign key constraints from being enforced by SQL Server Replication Agent processes (allowing data to arrive via replication potentially out of order from the primary key data).

In this example, two parent tables are created and populated, and a third table is created using cascading options in the foreign key definitions to these parent tables. Data is then inserted into the third table. The data in the third table is selected. Finally, one of the rows in a parent table is deleted (causing a cascade delete), a row in the other parent table is modified (causing a cascade update to NULL), and the data in the third table is again selected.

```
IF OBJECT_ID('dbo.PersonPhone','U') IS NOT NULL DROP TABLE dbo.PersonPhone;
IF OBJECT_ID('dbo.PhoneNumberType','U') IS NOT NULL DROP TABLE dbo.PhoneNumberType;
IF OBJECT_ID('dbo.Person','U') IS NOT NULL DROP TABLE dbo.Person;

CREATE TABLE dbo.Person (
  BusinessEntityId INT PRIMARY KEY,
  FirstName VARCHAR(25),
  LastName  VARCHAR(25));

CREATE TABLE dbo.PhoneNumberType (
  PhoneNumberTypeId INT PRIMARY KEY,
  Name VARCHAR(25));

INSERT INTO dbo.PhoneNumberType
SELECT  PhoneNumberTypeId, Name
FROM    Person.PhoneNumberType;

INSERT INTO dbo.Person
SELECT BusinessEntityId, FirstName, LastName
FROM Person.Person
WHERE BusinessEntityID IN (1,2);

CREATE TABLE dbo.PersonPhone (
        [BusinessEntityID] [int] NOT NULL,
        [PhoneNumber] [dbo].[Phone] NOT NULL,
        [PhoneNumberTypeID] [int] NULL,
        [ModifiedDate] [datetime] NOT NULL,
```

```
    CONSTRAINT [UQ_PersonPhone_BusinessEntityID_PhoneNumber_PhoneNumberTypeID]
        UNIQUE CLUSTERED
            ([BusinessEntityID], [PhoneNumber], [PhoneNumberTypeID]),
    CONSTRAINT [FK_PersonPhone_Person_BusinessEntityID]
        FOREIGN KEY ([BusinessEntityID])
        REFERENCES [dbo].[Person] ([BusinessEntityID])
        ON DELETE CASCADE,
    CONSTRAINT [FK_PersonPhone_PhoneNumberType_PhoneNumberTypeID]
        FOREIGN KEY ([PhoneNumberTypeID])
        REFERENCES [dbo].[PhoneNumberType] ([PhoneNumberTypeID])
        ON UPDATE SET NULL
);

INSERT INTO dbo.PersonPhone (BusinessEntityId, PhoneNumber, PhoneNumberTypeId, ModifiedDate)
VALUES (1, '757-867-5309', 1, '2012-03-22T00:00:00'),
       (2, '804-867-5309', 2, '2012-03-22T00:00:00');

SELECT 'Initial Data', * FROM dbo.PersonPhone;

DELETE FROM dbo.Person
WHERE BusinessEntityID = 1;

UPDATE dbo.PhoneNumberType
   SET PhoneNumberTypeID = 4
 WHERE PhoneNumberTypeID = 2;

SELECT 'Final Data', * FROM dbo.PersonPhone;
```

This example produces the following results:

```
BusinessEntityID    PhoneNumber      PhoneNumberTypeID    ModifiedDate
----------------    -------------    -----------------    -------------------------
Initial Data 1      757-867-5309     1                    2012-03-22 00:00:00.000
Initial Data 2      804-867-5309     2                    2012-03-22 00:00:00.000

BusinessEntityID    PhoneNumber      PhoneNumberTypeID    ModifiedDate
----------------    ------------     -----------------    -------------------------
Final Data 2        804-867-5309     NULL                 2012-03-22 00:00:00.000
```

In this example, one of the foreign key constraints uses `ON DELETE CASCADE` in a `CREATE TABLE` definition.

```
CONSTRAINT [FK_PersonPhone_Person_BusinessEntityID]
    FOREIGN KEY([BusinessEntityID])
    REFERENCES [dbo].[Person] ([BusinessEntityID])
    ON DELETE CASCADE,
```

Using this cascade option, if a row is deleted in the `dbo.Person` table, any referencing `BusinessEntityID` in the `dbo.PersonPhone` table will also be deleted. This can be witnessed in the previous example, where the `dbo.Person` record for `BusinessEntityId` = 1 is deleted and the corresponding record in the `dbo.PhoneNumber` table is also deleted.

A second foreign key constraint is also defined in the `CREATE TABLE` using `ON UPDATE`:

```
    CONSTRAINT [FK_PersonPhone_PhoneNumberType_PhoneNumberTypeID]
      FOREIGN KEY([PhoneNumberTypeID])
      REFERENCES [dbo].[PhoneNumberType] ([PhoneNumberTypeID])
      ON UPDATE SET NULL
```

If an update is made to the primary key of the dbo.PhoneNumberType table, the PhoneNumberTypeID column in the referencing dbo.PhoneNumber table will be set to NULL. This can be witnessed in the previous example, where the dbo.PhoneNumberType record has the PhoneNumberTypeId value changed from 2 to 4 and the corresponding record in the dbo.PhoneNumber table has its PhoneNumberTypeId value changed to NULL.

13-13. Specifying Default Values for a Column

Problem

You need to ensure that if you don't specify a column when inserting data into the table, a default value is used to populate that column. For example, you have a column named InsertedDate that needs to contain the date/time whenever a record is added to the table.

Solution

Create a DEFAULT constraint:

```
IF OBJECT_ID('dbo.Employees', 'U') IS NOT NULL
   DROP TABLE dbo.Employees;
CREATE TABLE dbo.Employees (
    EmployeeId INT PRIMARY KEY CLUSTERED,
    First_Name VARCHAR(50) NOT NULL,
    Last_Name  VARCHAR(50) NOT NULL,
    InsertedDate DATETIME DEFAULT GETDATE());
```

How It Works

The table is created with a DEFAULT constraint that uses the GETDATE system function to return the current system date and time.

Default constraints are used only if the column is not specified in the INSERT statement. Here's an example:

```
INSERT INTO dbo.Employees (EmployeeId, First_Name, Last_Name)
VALUES (1, 'Wayne', 'Sheffield');
INSERT INTO dbo.Employees (EmployeeId, First_Name, Last_Name, InsertedDate)
VALUES (2, 'Jim', 'Smith', NULL);
SELECT * FROM dbo.Employees;
```

This query returns the following result set:

```
EmployeeId   First_Name  Last_Name  InsertedDate
----------   ----------  ---------  -----------------------
1            Wayne       Sheffield  2012-02-19 00:59:31.547
2            Jim         Smith      NULL
```

■ **Note** This recipe calls one or more functions that returns a value based upon the current date and time. When you run this recipe on your system, you will get a different result that will be based upon the date and time as set on the computer running your instance of SQL Server.

The first INSERT statement did not specify the InsertedDate column, so the default constraint was fired, and the current system date/time was inserted into the column. The second INSERT statement did specify the InsertedDate column, and a NULL value was specified. The NULL value is what was inserted into the column.

13-14. Validating Data as It Is Entered into a Column

Problem

You need to ensure that data entered into a column follows specific business rules. For example, the date in an EndingDate column must be after the date in the StartingDate column.

Solution

Create a CHECK constraint:

```
CREATE TABLE dbo.BooksRead (
  ISBN      VARCHAR(20),
  StartDate DATETIME NOT NULL,
  EndDate   DATETIME NULL,
  CONSTRAINT CK_BooksRead_EndDate CHECK (EndDate > StartDate));
```

How It Works

The CHECK constraint is created that ensures that the EndDate is greater than the StartDate. If a value is attempted to be entered into the EndDate column that is not greater than the StartDate, then the insert or update will fail.

```
INSERT INTO BooksRead (ISBN, StartDate, EndDate)
VALUES ('9781430242000', '2012-08-01T16:25:00', '2011-08-15T12:35:00 ');
```

Since the EndDate is in the previous year, this error will be generated:

```
Msg 547, Level 16, State 0, Line 7
The INSERT statement conflicted with the CHECK constraint "CK_BooksRead_EndDate". The conflict
occurred in database " AdventureWorks2012", table "dbo.BooksRead".
The statement has been terminated.
```

A CHECK constraint is used to define what format and values are allowed for a column. The syntax of the CHECK constraint is as follows:

```
CHECK ( logical_expression )
```

If the logical expression of the CHECK constraint evaluates to TRUE, and the row will be inserted or updated. If the CHECK constraint expression evaluates to FALSE, the row insert or update will fail.

In the previous example, the constraint is created as a table constraint. If the constraint references only the column it applies to, it can be created as a column constraint; otherwise, it must be created as a table constraint.

A CHECK constraint can perform any check that returns a logical value, including using a user-defined scalar function. It can perform pattern matching with the LIKE operator. For example, the following table has a check constraint on the phone number column to ensure that it follows the U.S. standard of XXX-YYY-ZZZZ where all positions are numbers except for the two dashes:

```
IF OBJECT_ID('dbo.Employees','U') IS NOT NULL
   DROP TABLE dbo.Employees;
CREATE TABLE dbo.Employees (
  EmployeeId INT IDENTITY,
  FirstName  VARCHAR(50),
  LastName   VARCHAR(50),
  PhoneNumber VARCHAR(12) CONSTRAINT CK_Employees_PhoneNumber
    CHECK (PhoneNumber LIKE '[0-9][0-9][0-9]-[0-9][0-9][0-9]-[0-9][0-9][0-9][0-9]'));
```

When inserting the following rows, the first insert is successful while the second insert fails:

```
INSERT INTO dbo.Employees (FirstName, LastName, PhoneNumber)
VALUES ('Wayne', 'Sheffield', '800-555-1212');

INSERT INTO dbo.Employees (FirstName, LastName, PhoneNumber)
VALUES ('Wayne', 'Sheffield', '555-1212');
```

```
Msg 547, Level 16, State 0, Line 12
The INSERT statement conflicted with the CHECK constraint " CK_Employees_PhoneNumber".
The conflict occurred in database "AdventureWorks2008R2", table "dbo.Employees", column
'PhoneNumber'.
The statement has been terminated.
```

13-15. Temporarily Turning Off a Constraint

...rily turn off a constraint on a table. For instance, you are performing a bulk-load process where ... verify that each row meets the constraint requirements.

...TABLE statement to disable a constraint:

```
...Employees
NOCHECK CONSTRAINT CK_Employees_PhoneNumber;
```

How It Works

The ALTER TABLE statement specifies to no longer check the specified foreign key or check constraint created on the specified table. In the previous example, the CK_Employees_PhoneNumber check constraint that was created on the dbo.Employees table in Recipe 13-14 is disabled. If we then rerun the second insert statement from that recipe, it succeeds.

You can alternatively disable all foreign key and check constraints by replacing the constraint name with ALL. Here's an example:

```
ALTER TABLE dbo.Employees
NOCHECK CONSTRAINT ALL;
```

You can turn the constraint back on to check future data changes by the following ALTER TABLE statement:

```
ALTER TABLE dbo.Employees
CHECK CONSTRAINT CK_Employees_PhoneNumber;
```

Note that this does not verify that the data currently existing in the table meets the constraint; it merely enables the constraint for future data changes.

To enable all disabled constraints and verify that all of the data in the table meets those constraint restrictions, you would use the following ALTER TABLE statement:

```
ALTER TABLE dbo.Employees
WITH CHECK CHECK CONSTRAINT ALL;
```

In this case, the record inserted from the second insert statement in Recipe 13-14 causes the check to fail. This record needs to be updated to pass the constraint, or it needs to be deleted.

■ **Caution** The query optimizer does not consider constraints that are defined WITH NOCHECK. Such constraints are ignored until they are reenabled by using ALTER TABLE <table> WITH CHECK CHECK CONSTRAINT ALL. This may cause performance degradation by not building optimal query execution plans.

13-16. Removing a Constraint

Problem

You need to remove a constraint from a table.

Solution

Utilize the ALTER TABLE statement to drop a constraint:

```
ALTER TABLE dbo.BooksRead
DROP CONSTRAINT CK_BooksRead_EndDate;
```

How It Works

The table_name designates the table you are dropping the constraint from, and the constraint_ name designates the name of the constraint to be dropped. In this example, the CK_BooksRead_EndDate check constraint is dropped from the dbo.BooksRead table that was created in Recipe 13-14. Any constraint (PRIMARY KEY, FOREIGN KEY, UNIQUE, DEFAULT, or CHECK) can be dropped.

13-17. Creating Auto-incrementing Columns

Problem

You need to create a column that automatically increments itself.

Solution

Utilize the IDENTITY property of a column:

```
IF OBJECT_ID('dbo.Employees','U') IS NOT NULL
   DROP TABLE dbo.Employees;
```

```
CREATE TABLE dbo.Employees (
    employee_id INT IDENTITY PRIMARY KEY CLUSTERED,
    manager_id INT NULL REFERENCES dbo.Employees (employee_id),
    First_Name VARCHAR(50) NULL,
    Last_Name  VARCHAR(50) NULL,
    CONSTRAINT UQ_Employees_Name UNIQUE (First_Name, Last_Name));
```

How It Works

The IDENTITY column property allows you to define an automatically incrementing numeric value for a single column in a table. An IDENTITY column is most often used for surrogate primary key columns, because they are more compact than non-numeric data type natural keys. When a new row is inserted into a table with an IDENTITY column property, the column is inserted with a unique incremented value. The data type for an IDENTITY column can be int, tinyint, smallint, bigint, decimal, or numeric (the decimal and numeric data types must have a scale of 0). Tables may have only one identity column defined, and the defined IDENTITY column can't have a DEFAULT or rule settings associated with it. The IDENTITY attribute must be specified when the column is created (either through the CREATE TABLE or ALTER TABLE statement); you cannot specify to change an existing column to have the IDENTITY attribute.

■ **Note** *Surrogate keys*, also called *artificial keys*, can be used as primary keys and have no inherent business/data meaning. Surrogate keys are independent of the data itself and are used to provide a single unique record locator in the table. A big advantage to surrogate primary keys is that they don't need to change. If you use business data to define your key (natural key), such as first name and last name, these values can change over time and change arbitrarily. Surrogate keys don't have to change, because their only meaning is within the context of the table itself.

The basic syntax for an IDENTITY property column is as follows:

```
[ IDENTITY [ ( seed ,increment ) ] [NOT FOR REPLICATION] ]
```

The IDENTITY property accepts two optional values: seed and increment. seed defines the starting number for the IDENTITY column, and increment defines the value added to the previous IDENTITY column value to get the value for the next row added to the table. The default for both seed and increment is 1. The NOT FOR REPLICATION option preserves the original values of the publisher IDENTITY column data when replicated to the subscriber, retaining any values referenced by foreign key constraints (preventing the break of relationships between tables that may use the IDENTITY column as a primary key and foreign key reference).

Using an IDENTITY column does not guarantee that there will not be gaps in the numbers. Identity values are never rolled back, even if the INSERT statement is in a transaction that subsequently is rolled back. Subsequent insert statements will skip those numbers. Here's an example:

```
INSERT INTO dbo.Employees (manager_id, First_Name, Last_Name)
       VALUES (NULL, 'Wayne', 'Sheffield')

BEGIN TRANSACTION
INSERT INTO dbo.Employees (manager_id, First_Name, Last_Name)
       VALUES (1, 'Jim', 'Smith');
ROLLBACK TRANSACTION;

INSERT INTO dbo.Employees (manager_id, First_Name, Last_Name)
       VALUES (1, 'Jane', 'Smith');

SELECT * FROM dbo.Employees;
```

This query produces the following result set:

```
employee_id  manager_id   First_Name  Last_Name
-----------  ----------   ----------  ---------
1            NULL         Wayne       Sheffield
3            1            Jane        Smith
```

In viewing these results, we can see that the rolled-back INSERT statement created a gap in the employee_id sequencing.

Using an IDENTITY column does not guarantee that the column will contain unique values. To guarantee this, the column needs to have a PRIMARY KEY or UNIQUE constraint on it.

When a table has an IDENTITY column, you can utilize IDENTITYCOL in a SELECT statement to return the IDENTITY column. If the SELECT statement contains more than one table in the FROM clause with an identity column, then IDENTITYCOL must be qualified with the table name or alias.

13-18. Obtaining the Identity Value Used

Problem

You need to know what the value is of the identity column for the row that you just inserted into a table.

Solution

Utilize the @@IDENTITY, SCOPE_IDENTITY, or IDENT_CURRENT system function:

```
SELECT @@IDENTITY, SCOPE_IDENTITY(), IDENT_CURRENT('dbo.Employees');
```

How It Works

The @@IDENTITY, SCOPE_IDENTIY, and IDENT_CURRENT system functions return the last identity value generated by the INSERT, SELECT INTO, or bulk copy statement. All three functions are similar in that they return the last value inserted into the IDENTITY column of a table.

@@IDENTITY returns the last identity value generated by any table in the current session. If the insert statement fires a trigger that inserts into another table with an identity column, the value returned by @@IDENTITY will be that of the table inserted into by the trigger.

SCOPE_IDENTITY returns the last identity value generated by any table in the current session and scope. In the previous scenario, SCOPE_IDENTITY returns the identity value returned by the first insert statement, not the insert into the second table from the trigger.

IDENT_CURRENT returns the last identity value generated for a table, in any session or scope.

13-19. Viewing or Changing the Seed Settings on an Identity Column

Problem

You need to see and/or change the seed value used on an IDENTITY column.

Solution

Utilize DBCC CHECKIDENT to view or change the IDENTITY column's seed value:

```
DBCC CHECKIDENT ('dbo.Employees');
```

How It Works

DBCC CHECKIDENT checks the current maximum value for the specified table. The syntax for this command is as follows:

```
DBCC CHECKIDENT
( 'table_name' [ , {NORESEED | { RESEED [ , new_reseed_value ] }}])
[ WITH NO_INFOMSGS ]
```

Table 13-2 details the arguments of this command.

***Table 13-2.** CHECKIDENT Arguments*

Argument	Description
table_name	This indicates the name of the table to check IDENTITY values for.
NORESEED | RESEED	NORESEED means that no action is taken other than to report the maximum identity value. RESEED specifies what the current IDENTITY value should be.
new_reseed_value	This specifies the new current IDENTITY value.
WITH NO_INFOMSGS	When included in the command, WITH NO_INFOMSGS suppresses informational messages from the DBCC output.

In this solution, the IDENTITY value is checked for the dbo.Employees table (from Recipe 13-17) and returns the following results:

```
Checking identity information: current identity value '3', current column value '3'.
DBCC execution completed. If DBCC printed error messages, contact your system administrator.
```

In Recipe 13-17, it was demonstrated how a gap can occur in an identity column. If there had been a failed insert of multiple records and new records had not been added since, we might want to reclaim those values for use. To accomplish that, we would use the RESEED option. The following code uses the example from Recipe 13-17, with the addition of resetting the IDENTITY column after the transaction was rolled back:

```
TRUNCATE TABLE dbo.Employees;
INSERT INTO dbo.Employees (manager_id, First_Name, Last_Name)
       VALUES (NULL, 'Wayne', 'Sheffield');

BEGIN TRANSACTION;
INSERT INTO dbo.Employees (manager_id, First_Name, Last_Name)
       VALUES (1, 'Jim', 'Smith');
ROLLBACK TRANSACTION;

DBCC CHECKIDENT ('dbo.Employees', RESEED, 1);
INSERT INTO dbo.Employees (manager_id, First_Name, Last_Name)
       VALUES (1, 'Jane', 'Smith');

SELECT * FROM dbo.Employees;

DBCC CHECKIDENT ('dbo.Employees');
```

■ **Tip** The TRUNCATE TABLE statement, in addition to deleting all of the data in that table, also resets the identity seed to the initial setting, which in this case is 0.

This code produces the following result set and messages:

```
Checking identity information: current identity value '2'.
DBCC execution completed. If DBCC printed error messages, contact your system administrator.

employee_id     manager_id     First_Name     Last_Name
-----------     ----------     ----------     ---------
1               NULL           Wayne          Sheffield
2               1              Jane           Smith

Checking identity information: current identity value '2'.
DBCC execution completed. If DBCC printed error messages, contact your system administrator.
```

You can see in the results that the gap is now omitted.

13-20. Inserting Values into an Identity Column

Problem

You have accidentally deleted some data from a table with an identity column, and you need to insert the missing data from a backup into the table. You need to keep the original identity column values.

Solution

Utilize the SET IDENTITY_INSERT ON statement to insert explicit values into an identity column.

```
SET IDENTITY_INSERT dbo.Employees ON;
INSERT INTO dbo.Employees (employee_id, manager_id, First_Name, Last_Name)
VALUES (5, 1, 'Joe', 'Smith');
SET IDENTITY_INSERT dbo.Employees OFF;
```

How It Works

The SET IDENTITY_INSERT ON statement toggles whether explicit values can be inserted into an identity column. You can have only one table at a time with the IDENTITY_INSERT property set to ON. To insert into an identity column, you must explicitly list the identity column in the list of columns being inserted into.

13-21. Automatically Inserting Unique Values

Problem

You have a database set up using merge replication to multiple subscribers at remote offices. Users at the remote offices insert data into their local database. You need to insert an automatically generated value that will be unique across all locations.

Solution

Utilize the UNIQUEIDENTIFIER data type, with a default constraint using the NEWID or NEWSEQUENTIALID system function.

```
CREATE TABLE HumanResources.BuildingAccess(
  BuildingEntryExitID uniqueidentifier ROWGUIDCOL
    CONSTRAINT DF_BuildingAccess_BuildingEntryExitID DEFAULT NEWID()
    CONSTRAINT UK_BuildingAccess_BuildingEntryExitID UNIQUE,
  EmployeeID int NOT NULL,
  AccessTime datetime NOT NULL,
  DoorID int NOT NULL);
```

How It Works

The UNIQUEIDENTIFIER data type is a 16-bit globally unique identifier (GUID) and is represented as a 32-character hexadecimal string. The total number of unique keys is 2^{128}. Since this number is so large, the chances of randomly generating the save value twice is negligible. (Microsoft claims that it will be unique for every database *networked* in the world.)

Just like an IDENTITY column, a column with the UNIQUEIDENTIFIER data type does not guarantee uniqueness; a PRIMARY KEY or UNIQUE constraint must be used to guarantee uniqueness of the values in the column. Keep in mind that the UNIQUEIDENTIFIER data type does not generate new GUID values; it simply stores the generated values. The UNIQUE constraint is necessary where you need to ensure that the same generated value cannot be inserted into the table twice.

The ROWGUIDCOL indicates that the column is a row GUID column. There can be just one column per table that is designated as a ROWGUIDCOL. Using ROWGUIDCOL allows one to use the $ROWGUID synonym for the column designated as the ROWGUIDCOL.

To automatically insert values into the UNIQUEIDENTIFIER data typed column, you need to use a default constraint with either the NEWID or NEWSEQUENTIALID system function. NEWID generates a random GUID; NEWSEQUENTIALID generates a GUID that is greater than any GUID previously generated by this function on this computer since Windows was started. Since NEWSEQUENTIALID generates an increasing value, its use can minimize page splits and fragmentation.

To show how this all works, the following statements insert one row into the previous table and then select that row:

```
INSERT HumanResources.BuildingAccess (EmployeeID, AccessTime, DoorID)
VALUES (32, GETDATE(), 2);

SELECT *
  FROM HumanResources.BuildingAccess;
SELECT $ROWGUID
  FROM HumanResources.BuildingAccess;
```

These queries return the following result sets:

```
BuildingEntryExitID                   EmployeeID   AccessTime                DoorID
------------------------------------  ----------   -----------------------   ------
06ADA180-DC37-4AAC-9AD5-8DE5FC0B9D73  32           2012-02-20 21:30:39.320   2

BuildingEntryExitID
z------------------------------------
06ADA180-DC37-4AAC-9AD5-8DE5FC0B9D73
```

■ **Note** Since this example utilizes a function that is virtually guaranteed to generate unique values each time it is called, you will see different GUID values when you run this query.

13-22. Using Unique Identifiers Across Multiple Tables

Problem

You need to have a unique identifier across multiple tables that is sequentially incremented.

Solution

Utilize a SEQUENCE.

```
CREATE SEQUENCE dbo.MySequence
    AS INTEGER
       START WITH 1
       INCREMENT BY 1;
GO
```

How It Works

A SEQUENCE generates numbers in sequential order. Unlike IDENTITY columns, they are not associated with tables. The complete syntax for a SEQUENCE object is as follows:

```
CREATE SEQUENCE [schema_name . ] sequence_name
    [ AS [ built_in_integer_type | user-defined_integer_type ] ]
    [ START WITH <constant> ]
    [ INCREMENT BY <constant> ]
    [ { MINVALUE [ <constant> ] } | { NO MINVALUE } ]
    [ { MAXVALUE [ <constant> ] } | { NO MAXVALUE } ]
    [ CYCLE | { NO CYCLE } ]
    [ { CACHE [ <constant> ] } | { NO CACHE } ]
    [ ; ]
```

Table 13-3 shows the arguments for the creation of a sequence object.

Table 13-3. *Sequence Creation Arguments*

Argument	Description
sequence_name	The unique name in the database for the sequence.
built_in_integer_type user-defined_integer_type	Sequences can be built upon any of the integer data types: tinyint, smallint, integer, bigint, or a user-defined data type that is based on one of these types. If the type is not specified, the sequence defaults to bigint.
START WITH <constant>	The first value returned by the sequence object. The default value is the minimum value for that data type for an ascending sequence or the maximum value for that data type for a descending sequence. It must lie between MINVALUE and MAXVALUE.

(continued)

Table 13-3. *continued*

Argument	Description
INCREMENT BY <constant>	The value used to increment (if positive) or decrement (if negative) the sequence object when the NEXT VALUE FOR function is called. INCREMENT BY cannot be zero; if not specified, it defaults to 1.
MINVALUE	Specifies the minimum value that the sequence object can be; if not specified, it defaults to the minimum value for the data type the sequence object is being built upon.
MAXVALUE	Specifies the maximum value that the sequence object can be; if not specified, it defaults to the maximum value for the data type the sequence object is being built upon.
CYCLE	Specifies whether the sequence restart at the minimum value when the maximum is exceeded (for descending sequences, restart at the maximum when the minimum is exceeded). Cycling restarts the sequencing from the minimum or maximum value, not the start value. The default is NO CYCLE.
CACHE	Increases the performance of sequence objects by caching the current value and the number of values left in the cache.

To retrieve the next sequence, you need to use the NEXT VALUE FOR system function. The following code utilizes the Test.MySequence sequence:

```
CREATE TABLE dbo.Table1 (
  Table1ID INTEGER NOT NULL,
  Table1Data VARCHAR(50));
CREATE TABLE dbo.Table2 (
  Table2ID INTEGER NOT NULL,
  Table2Data VARCHAR(50));

INSERT INTO dbo.Table1 (Table1ID, Table1Data)
VALUES (NEXT VALUE FOR dbo.MySequence, 'Ferrari'),
       (NEXT VALUE FOR dbo.MySequence, 'Lamborghini');

INSERT INTO dbo.Table2 (Table2ID, Table2Data)
VALUES (NEXT VALUE FOR dbo.MySequence, 'Apple'),
       (NEXT VALUE FOR dbo.MySequence, 'Orange');

SELECT * FROM dbo.Table1;
SELECT * FROM dbo.Table2;
```

These queries produce the following result sets:

```
Table1ID        Table1Data
--------        ----------
1               Ferrari
2               Lamborghini

Table2ID        Table2Data
--------        ----------
3               Apple
4               Orange
```

Like IDENTITY columns, SEQUENCE numbers are generated outside the scope of transactions; they are consumed whether the transaction is committed or rolled back. Sequences are useful over identity columns in the following scenarios:

- The application requires a number before the insert into the table is made.
- The application requires sharing a single series of numbers between multiple tables or multiple columns within a table.
- The application must restart the number series when a specified number is reached.
- The application requires the sequence values to be sorted by another field. To accomplish this, the NEXT VALUE FOR function can apply the OVER clause to the function call. (See Chapter 7 for more details of using the OVER clause.)
- The application requires that multiple numbers be assigned at the same time. For instance, you need to ensure that sequential numbers are used for the data being inserted. If other processes are also getting numbers, you could acquire numbers with a gap between some. This is accomplished by calling the sp_sequence_get_range stored procedure to retrieve several numbers from the sequence at once.
- You need to change the specification of the sequence, such as the increment value.

13-23. Using Temporary Storage

Problem

You need to temporarily store interim query results for further processing.

Solution #1

Utilize a temporary table.

```
CREATE TABLE #temp (
  Column1 INT,
  Column2 INT);
```

Solution #2

Utilize a table variable.

```
DECLARE @temp TABLE (
  Column1 INT,
  Column2 INT);
```

How It Works

Temporary storage can utilize either a temporary table or a table variable. Temporary tables come in two varieties: local (uses a single #) or global (uses two: ##). A global temporary table is visible to all sessions. A local temporary table is available to the current session, from the time the table is created to the time when all procedures are executed from that session after the table is created. A table variable is visible within the current batch only.

Temporary storage can be the target of any of the data manipulation language (DML) statements (INSERT, UPDATE, DELETE, SELECT, MERGE) that any permanent table can be the target of.

Temporary storage can be useful to do the following:

- Eliminate repeated use of a query or CTE
- Perform preaggregation or interim calculation storage
- Staging table/prevalidation table
- Data access to remote servers

Both temporary tables and table variables are stored in memory and are spilled to disk only when necessary. Table 13-4 shows the differences between temporary tables and table variables.

Table 13-4. *Temporary Table/Table Variable Differences*

Feature	Table Variables	Temporary Tables
Scope	Current batch only.	Current session, available to nested stored procedure called after creation. (Global temporary tables visible to all sessions.)
Usage	User-defined functions, stored procedures, triggers, batches.	Stored procedures, triggers, batches.
Creation	DECLARE statement only.	CREATE TABLE or SELECT INTO statement.
Table name	Maximum 128 characters.	Local: Maximum 116 characters. Global: Maximum 128 characters.
Column data types	Can use user-defined data types and XML collections defined in the current database.	Can use user-defined data types and XML collections defined in the tempdb database.
Collation	String columns inherit collation from the current database.	String columns inherit collation from the tempdb database for regular databases or from the current database if it is a contained database.
Indexes	Can only have indexes that are automatically created with PRIMARY KEY and UNIQUE constraints as part of the DECLARE statement.	Indexes can be created with PRIMARY KEY and UNIQUE constraints as part of the CREATE TABLE statement. Indexes can be added afterward with the CREATE INDEX statement.
Data insertion	INSERT statement only (including INSERT/EXEC).	INSERT statement (including INSERT/EXEC). SELECT INTO statement.
Constraints	PRIMARY KEY, UNIQUE, NULL, CHECK, and DEFAULT constraints are allowed, but they must be incorporated into the creation of the table variable in the DECLARE statement. FOREIGN KEY constraints are not allowed.	PRIMARY KEY, UNIQUE, NULL, CHECK, and DEFAULT constraints are allowed. They can be created as part of the CREATE TABLE statement, or they can be added with the ALTER TABLE statement. FOREIGN KEY constraints are not allowed.

(continued)

***Table 13-4.** continued*

Feature	Table Variables	Temporary Tables
Truncate table	Table variables cannot use the TRUNCATE TABLE statement.	Temporary tables can use the TRUNCATE TABLE statement.
Parallelism	Supported for SELECT statements only.	Supported for SELECT, INSERT, UPDATE, and DELETE statements.
SET IDENTITY_INSERT	Usage not supported.	Usage is supported.
Stored procedure recompilations	Not applicable.	Creating temporary tables and data inserts may cause stored procedure recompilations.
Destruction	Destroyed automatically at the end of the batch.	Destroyed explicitly with the DROP TABLE statement. Destroyed automatically when the session ends. For global temporary tables, they will not be dropped until no other session is running a statement that accesses the table.
Implicit transactions	Implicit transactions last only for the length of the update against the table variable. Table variables use fewer resources than temporary tables.	Implicit transactions last for the length of the transaction, which requires more resources than table variables.
Explicit transactions	Table variables are not affected by a ROLLBACK TRANSACTION statement.	Data is rolled back in temporary tables when a ROLLBACK TRANSACTION statement occurs.
Statistics	The query optimizer cannot create any statistics on table variable columns, so it treats all table variables has having one record when creating execution plans.	The query optimizer can create statistics on columns, so it can use the actual row count for generating execution plans.
Parameter to stored procedures	Table variables can be passed as a parameter to stored procedures (as a predefined user-defined table type).	Temporary tables cannot be passed to stored procedures. (They are still in scope to nested stored procedures.)
Explicitly named constraints	Explicitly named constraints are not allowed on table variables.	Explicitly name constraints are allowed on temporary tables except in contained databases. The schema that the table is in can have only one constraint with that name, so beware of multiuser issues.
Dynamic SQL	Must declare and populate table variables in the dynamic SQL to be executed.	Temporary tables can be created prior to being used in the dynamic SQL. Population of the temporary table can occur prior to or within the dynamic SQL.

Since statistics are not created on table variables, the performance of table variables can suffer when the result set becomes too large, when column data cardinality is critical to the query optimization process, and even when joined to other tables. When encountering performance issues, be sure to test all alternative solutions, and don't necessarily assume that either of these options is less desirable than other.

CHAPTER 14

Managing Views

by Wayne Sheffield

Views allow you to create a virtual representation of table data defined by a SELECT statement. The defining SELECT statement can join one or more tables and can include one or more columns. Once created, a view can be referenced in the FROM clause of a query.

Views can be used to simplify data access for query writers, obscuring the underlying complexity of the SELECT statement. Views are also useful for managing security and protecting sensitive data. If you want to restrict direct table access by the end user, you can grant permissions exclusively to views, rather than to the underlying tables. You can also use views to expose only those columns that you want the end user to see, including just the necessary columns in the view definition. Views can even allow direct data updates under specific circumstances that will be described later in this chapter. Views also provide a standard interface to the back-end data, which shouldn't need to change unless there are significant changes to the underlying table structures.

In addition to regular views, you can also create indexed views, which are views that actually have the index data persisted within the database (regular views do not actually store physical data). Also available are partitioned and distributed-partitioned views, which allow you to represent one logical table made up of multiple horizontally partitioned tables, each of which can be located on either the same or different SQL Server instances. Table 14-1 shows the three types of views used in SQL Server.

Table 14-1. *SQL Server View Types*

View Type	Description
Regular view	This view is defined by a Transact-SQL query. No data is actually stored in the database, only the view definition.
Indexed view	This view is first defined by a Transact-SQL query, and then, after certain requirements are met, a clustered index is created on it in order to materialize the index data similar to table data. Once a clustered index is created, multiple nonclustered indexes can be created on the indexed view as needed.
Partitioned view	This is a view that uses UNION ALL to combine multiple, smaller tables into a single, virtual table for performance or scalability purposes.
Distributed partitioned view	This is a partitioned view across two or more SQL Server instances.

In this chapter, I'll present recipes that create each of these types of views, and I'll also provide methods for reporting view metadata.

Regular Views

Views are a great way to filter data and columns before presenting them to end users. Views can be used to obscure numerous table joins and column selections and can also be used to implement security by allowing users authorization access only to the view, not to the actual underlying tables.

For all the usefulness of views, there are some performance shortcomings to be aware of. When considering views for your database, consider the following best practices:

- Performance-tune your views as you would performance-tune a SELECT query, because a regular view is essentially just a "stored" query. Poorly performing views can have a significant impact on server performance.
- Don't nest your views more than one level deep. Specifically, do not define a view that calls another view, and so on. This can lead to confusion when you attempt to tune inefficient queries and can degrade performance with each level of view nesting.
- When possible, use stored procedures instead of views. Stored procedures can offer a performance boost, because the execution plan can be reused. Stored procedures can also reduce network traffic, allow for more sophisticated business logic, and have fewer coding restrictions than a view (see Chapter 17 for more information).

When a view is created, its definition is stored in the database, but the actual data that the view returns is not stored separately from the underlying tables. When creating a view, you cannot use certain SELECT elements in a view definition, including INTO, OPTION, COMPUTE, COMPUTE BY, or references to table variables or temporary tables. You also cannot use ORDER BY, unless used in conjunction with the TOP keyword.

14-1. Creating a View

Problem

You have several processes that all need to run the same query. This query needs to return multiple columns from multiple tables for a specific product category. For example, you need to return product transaction history data for all bikes.

Solution

Create a view that uses just the necessary columns, joined to the proper tables, and filtered for *Bikes*. Here's an example:

```
CREATE VIEW dbo.v_Product_TransactionHistory
AS
SELECT  p.Name AS ProductName,
        p.ProductNumber,
        pc.Name AS ProductCategory,
        ps.Name AS ProductSubCategory,
        pm.Name AS ProductModel,
        th.TransactionID,
        th.ReferenceOrderID,
```

```
        th.ReferenceOrderLineID,
        th.TransactionDate,
        th.TransactionType,
        th.Quantity,
        th.ActualCost,
        th.Quantity * th.ActualCost AS ExtendedPrice
 FROM    Production.TransactionHistory th
        INNER JOIN Production.Product p
            ON th.ProductID = p.ProductID
        INNER JOIN Production.ProductModel pm
            ON pm.ProductModelID = p.ProductModelID
        INNER JOIN Production.ProductSubcategory ps
            ON ps.ProductSubcategoryID = p.ProductSubcategoryID
        INNER JOIN Production.ProductCategory pc
            ON pc.ProductCategoryID = ps.ProductCategoryID
WHERE   pc.Name = 'Bikes';
GO
```

How It Works

A view is created that retrieves multiple columns from multiple tables for the product category of Bikes. You can now query this data with this SELECT statement:

```
SELECT  ProductName,
        ProductNumber,
        ReferenceOrderID,
        ActualCost
FROM    dbo.v_Product_TransactionHistory
ORDER BY ProductName;
```

This returns the following (abridged) result set:

```
ProductName                ProductNumber    ReferenceOrderID    ActualCost
-----------------------    -------------    ----------------    ----------
Mountain-200 Black, 38     BK-M68B-38       53457               1652.3928
Mountain-200 Black, 38     BK-M68B-38       53463               1652.3928
...
Touring-3000 Yellow, 62    BK-T18Y-62       67117               0.00
Touring-3000 Yellow, 62    BK-T18Y-62       70594               742.35
```

In this case, the view benefits anyone needing to write a query to access this data, because the user doesn't need to specify the many table joins each time the query is written.

The view definition also used column aliases, using ProductName instead of just Name, making the column name unambiguous and reducing the possible confusion with other columns called Name. Qualifying what data is returned from the view in the WHERE clause also allows you to restrict the data that the query writer can see—in this case only letting the query writer reference products of a specific product category.

A view is also a good example of code reuse. Multiple processes can utilize this view for performing their actions. If at a later time it is decided that Bicycles should be included along with Bikes, all that is necessary is for the WHERE clause to be modified to include Bicycles, and all of the processes will now start returning bicycles as well as bikes.

14-2. Querying a View's Definition

Problem

You have a process that needs to know the definition of a view.

Solution

Utilize the sys.sql_modules system catalog view or the OBJECT_DEFINITION function. Here's an example:

```
SELECT  definition
FROM    sys.sql_modules AS sm
WHERE   object_id = OBJECT_ID('dbo.v_Product_TransactionHistory');

SELECT  OBJECT_DEFINITION(OBJECT_ID('dbo.v_Product_TransactionHistory'));
```

How It Works

Both of these queries return the following result set, which is the definition of the specified view:

```
CREATE VIEW dbo.v_Product_TransactionHistory
AS
SELECT  p.Name AS ProductName,
        p.ProductNumber,
        pc.Name AS ProductCategory,
        ps.Name AS ProductSubCategory,
        pm.Name AS ProductModel,
        th.TransactionID,
        th.ReferenceOrderID,
        th.ReferenceOrderLineID,
        th.TransactionDate,
        th.TransactionType,
        th.Quantity,
        th.ActualCost
FROM    Production.TransactionHistory th
        INNER JOIN Production.Product p
            ON th.ProductID = p.ProductID
        INNER JOIN Production.ProductModel pm
            ON pm.ProductModelID = p.ProductModelID
        INNER JOIN Production.ProductSubcategory ps
            ON ps.ProductSubcategoryID = p.ProductSubcategoryID
        INNER JOIN Production.ProductCategory pc
            ON pc.ProductCategoryID = ps.ProductCategoryID
WHERE   pc.Name = 'Bikes';
```

Both of these methods allow you to view the procedural code of all objects, including views, triggers, stored procedures, and functions. If the object is defined as encrypted or if the user does not have permission for this object, a NULL will be returned.

14-3. Obtaining a List of All Views in a Database

Problem

You need to know the names of all of the views in a database.

Solution

Query the `sys.views` or `sys.objects` system catalog view. Here's an example:

```
SELECT  OBJECT_SCHEMA_NAME(v.object_id) AS SchemaName,
        v.name
FROM    sys.views AS v ;

SELECT  OBJECT_SCHEMA_NAME(o.object_id) AS SchemaName,
        o.name
FROM    sys.objects AS o
WHERE   type = 'V' ;
```

How It Works

Both of these queries query a system catalog view to return the metadata for the name and schema for all views in the database. Each query returns the following result set:

```
SchemaName      name
--------------- -------------------------------
Person          vStateProvinceCountryRegion
Sales           vStoreWithDemographics
Sales           vStoreWithContacts
Sales           vStoreWithAddresses
Purchasing      vVendorWithContacts
Purchasing      vVendorWithAddresses
dbo             v_Product_TransactionHistory
Person          vAdditionalContactInfo
HumanResources  vEmployee
HumanResources  vEmployeeDepartment
HumanResources  vEmployeeDepartmentHistory
Sales           vIndividualCustomer
Sales           vPersonDemographics
HumanResources  vJobCandidate
HumanResources  vJobCandidateEmployment
HumanResources  vJobCandidateEducation
Production      vProductAndDescription
Production      vProductModelCatalogDescription
Production      vProductModelInstructions
Sales           vSalesPerson
Sales           vSalesPersonSalesByFiscalYears
```

14-4. Obtaining a List of All Columns in a View

Problem

You need to know the names of all the columns in a view.

Solution

Query the sys.columns system catalog view. Here's an example:

```
SELECT  name,
        column_id
FROM    sys.columns
WHERE   object_id = OBJECT_ID('dbo.v_Product_TransactionHistory');
```

How It Works

In this query, the metadata of the names and column positions for the view are returned in the following result set:

```
name                  column_id
--------------------  ---------
ProductName           1
ProductNumber         2
ProductCategory       3
ProductSubCategory    4
ProductModel          5
TransactionID         6
ReferenceOrderID      7
ReferenceOrderLineID  8
TransactionDate       9
TransactionType       10
Quantity              11
ActualCost            12
ExtendedPrice         13
```

■ **Tip** Views can reference other views or tables within the view definition. These referenced objects are object dependencies (the view depends on them to return data). If you would like to query object dependencies for views, use the sys.sql_expression_dependencies catalog view, which is covered in Chapter 30.

14-5. Refreshing the Definition of a View

Problem

You have modified the structure of one of the tables used in a view, and now the view is returning incorrect results.

Solution

Refresh the definition of the view by utilizing the `sp_refreshview` or `sys.sp_refreshsqlmodule` system stored procedure. Here's an example:

```
EXECUTE dbo.sp_refreshview N'dbo.v_Product_TransactionHistory';
EXECUTE sys.sp_refreshsqlmodule @name = N'dbo.v_Product_TransactionHistory';
```

How It Works

When table objects referenced by a view are changed, the view's metadata can become outdated. For instance, if you change the width of a column in a table, this change may not be reflected in the view until the metadata has been refreshed. You can refresh the view's metadata with either the `dbo.sp_refreshview` or `sys.sp_refreshsqlmodule` system stored procedure.

14-6. Modifying a View

Problem

You need to make a change to the definition of a view.

Solution

Utilize the `ALTER VIEW` statement to change the definition of a view.

How It Works

The `ALTER VIEW` statement allows you to change the definition of a view by specifying a new definition. This is performed by first removing the existing definition from the system catalogs (including any indexes if it is an indexed view) and then adding the new definition. For example, to change the view created in Recipe 14-1 to include Bicycles, the following script would be executed:

```
ALTER VIEW dbo.v_Product_TransactionHistory
AS
SELECT  p.Name AS ProductName,
        p.ProductNumber,
        pc.Name AS ProductCategory,
        ps.Name AS ProductSubCategory,
        pm.Name AS ProductModel,
        th.TransactionID,
        th.ReferenceOrderID,
        th.ReferenceOrderLineID,
        th.TransactionDate,
        th.TransactionType,
        th.Quantity,
        th.ActualCost,
        th.Quantity * th.ActualCost AS ExtendedPrice
FROM    Production.TransactionHistory th
        INNER JOIN Production.Product p
            ON th.ProductID = p.ProductID
```

```
        INNER JOIN Production.ProductModel pm
            ON pm.ProductModelID = p.ProductModelID
        INNER JOIN Production.ProductSubcategory ps
            ON ps.ProductSubcategoryID = p.ProductSubcategoryID
        INNER JOIN Production.ProductCategory pc
            ON pc.ProductCategoryID = ps.ProductCategoryID
WHERE   pc.Name IN ('Bikes', 'Bicycles');
GO
```

This query returns the following (abridged) result set:

```
ProductName                 ProductNumber    ReferenceOrderID    ActualCost
-----------------------     -------------    ----------------    ----------
Mountain-200 Black, 38      BK-M68B-38       53457               1652.3928
Mountain-200 Black, 38      BK-M68B-38       53463               1652.3928
...
Touring-3000 Yellow, 62     BK-T18Y-62       67117               0.00
Touring-3000 Yellow, 62     BK-T18Y-62       70594               742.35
```

Since there are no entries (yet) in the Production.ProductCategory table with a name of Bicycle, the same number of rows is returned.

14-7. Modifying Data Through a View

Problem

You need to make data modifications to a table, but you have access to the table only through a view.

Solution

Provided that you are modifying columns from one base table, you can issue INSERT, UPDATE, DELETE, and MERGE statements against a view.

How It Works

INSERT, UPDATE, DELETE, and MERGE statements can be issued against a view, with the following provisions:

- Any modifications must reference columns from only one base table.
- The columns being modified in the view must directly reference the underlying data in the table. The columns cannot be derived in any way, such as through the following:
  - An aggregate function
  - computed column
- The columns being modified are not affected by GROUP BY, HAVING, or DISTINCT clauses.
- TOP is not used anywhere in the select statement of the view together with the WITH CHECK OPTION clause.

Generally, the database engine must be able to unambiguously trace modifications from the view definition to one base table.

In the view created in Recipe 14-1, the query references multiple tables and has a calculated column. To examine the results for ReferenceOrderId = 53463, the following query is issued:

```
SELECT  ProductName,
        ProductNumber,
        ReferenceOrderID,
        Quantity,
        ActualCost,
        ExtendedPrice
FROM    dbo.v_Product_TransactionHistory
WHERE   ReferenceOrderID = 53463
ORDER BY ProductName;
```

This query returns the following result set:

```
ProductName             ProductNumber  ReferenceOrderID  Quantity  ActualCost  ExtendedPrice
----------------------  -------------  ----------------  --------  ----------  -------------
Mountain-200 Black, 38  BK-M68B-38     53463             1         1652.3928   1652.3928
```

It is decided to update the quantity of this record to 3, so the following query is issued:

```
UPDATE  dbo.v_Product_TransactionHistory
SET     Quantity = 3
WHERE   ReferenceOrderID = 53463;
```

Running the previous query now returns the following result set:

```
ProductName             ProductNumber  ReferenceOrderID  Quantity  ActualCost  ExtendedPrice
----------------------  -------------  ----------------  --------  ----------  -------------
Mountain-200 Black, 38  BK-M68B-38     53463             3         1652.3928   4957.1784
```

What this example demonstrates is that even though the view is created against multiple tables, as long as the update is against just one of the tables, the data exposed by the view can be updated. Now, if it wasn't realized that the ExtendedPrice column is a calculated column and the UPDATE statement tries to update that column also with this query:

```
UPDATE  dbo.v_Product_TransactionHistory
SET     Quantity = 3,
        ExtendedPrice = 4957.1784
WHERE   ReferenceOrderID = 53463;
```

then the following error is generated:

```
Msg 4406, Level 16, State 1, Line 12

Update or insert of view or function 'dbo.v_Product_TransactionHistory' failed because it
contains a derived or constant field.
```

14-8. Encrypting a View

Problem

You have a SQL Server-based commercial application, and you need to hide the definition of the view.

Solution

Encrypt the view with the `WITH ENCRYPTION` clause of the view definition.

How It Works

The `WITH ENCRYPTION` clause in the `CREATE VIEW` and `ALTER VIEW` statements allow you to encrypt the Transact-SQL code of the view. Once encrypted, you can no longer view the definition in the `sys.sql_modules` catalog view or the `OBJECT_DEFINITION` system function.

Software vendors that use SQL Server as the back-end database management system often encrypt the Transact-SQL code in order to prevent tampering or reverse-engineering from clients or competitors. If you use encryption, be sure to save the original, unencrypted definition so that you can make modifications to it in the future.

The following example creates an encrypted view:

```
CREATE VIEW dbo.v_Product_TopTenListPrice
WITH ENCRYPTION
AS
SELECT TOP 10
        p.Name,
        p.ProductNumber,
        p.ListPrice
FROM    Production.Product p
ORDER BY p.ListPrice DESC;
GO
```

When the following queries are run to view the definition (as shown in Recipe 14-2):

```
SELECT  definition
FROM    sys.sql_modules AS sm
WHERE   object_id = OBJECT_ID('dbo.v_Product_TopTenListPrice');
SELECT  OBJECT_DEFINITION(OBJECT_ID('dbo.v_Product_TopTenListPrice')) AS definition;
```

the following results are returned:

```
definition
---------
NULL

definition
---------
NULL
```

Note Encrypting a view (or any other code in SQL Server such as a stored procedure) is performed with an encryption method that is easily broken. In fact, there are third-party products that will decrypt the "encrypted" code. You should not rely upon this encryption to keep others from viewing the code.

14-9. Indexing a View

Problem

You need to optimize the performance of a view that is defined against multiple tables, all of which have infrequent data modifications.

Solution

Create an index on the view.

How It Works

Indexed views allow you to materialize the results of the view as a physical object, similar to a regular table and associated indexes. This allows the SQL Server query optimizer to retrieve results from a single physical area instead of having to process the view definition query each time it is called.

To create an indexed view, you are required to use the `WITH SCHEMABINDING` option, which binds the view to the schema of the underlying tables. This prevents any changes in the base table that would impact the view definition. The `WITH SCHEMABINDING` option also adds additional requirements to the view's `SELECT` definition. Object references in a schema-bound view must include the two-part `schema.object` naming convention, and all referenced objects have to be located in the same database.

In the following example, a view is created using the `SCHEMABINDING` option:

```
CREATE VIEW dbo.v_Product_Sales_By_LineTotal
WITH SCHEMABINDING
AS
SELECT  p.ProductID,
        p.Name AS ProductName,
        SUM(LineTotal) AS LineTotalByProduct,
        COUNT_BIG(*) AS LineItems
FROM    Sales.SalesOrderDetail s
        INNER JOIN Production.Product p
            ON s.ProductID = p.ProductID
GROUP BY p.ProductID,
        p.Name;
GO
```

Before creating an index, we'll demonstrate querying the regular view, returning the query I/O cost statistics using the `SET STATISTICS IO` command:

```
SET STATISTICS IO ON;
GO

SELECT TOP 5
```

```
        ProductName,
        LineTotalByProduct
FROM    dbo.v_Product_Sales_By_LineTotal
ORDER BY LineTotalByProduct DESC ;
GO
```

This query produces the following result set:

```
ProductName                LineTotalByProduct
-----------------------    ------------------
Mountain-200 Black, 38     4400592.800400
Mountain-200 Black, 42     4009494.761841
Mountain-200 Silver, 38    3693678.025272
Mountain-200 Silver, 42    3438478.860423
Mountain-200 Silver, 46    3434256.941928
```

This query also returns the following I/O information reporting the various activities against the tables involved in the query that was run (if you are following along with the recipe, keep in mind that unless your system is identical in every way to mine, then you will probably have different statistic values returned from the following statistics):

```
Table 'Product'. Scan count 0, logical reads 10, physical reads 0, read-ahead reads 0, lob
logical reads 0, lob physical reads 0, lob read-ahead reads 0.
Table 'Worktable'. Scan count 0, logical reads 0, physical reads 0, read-ahead reads 0, lob
logical reads 0, lob physical reads 0, lob read-ahead reads 0.
Table 'SalesOrderDetail'. Scan count 1, logical reads 1240, physical reads 0, read-ahead reads
0, lob logical reads 0, lob physical reads 0, lob read-ahead reads 0.
```

Now we can add the clustered and nonclustered indexes to this view:

```
CREATE UNIQUE CLUSTERED INDEX UCI_v_Product_Sales_By_LineTotal
ON dbo.v_Product_Sales_By_LineTotal (ProductID);
GO
CREATE NONCLUSTERED INDEX NI_v_Product_Sales_By_LineTotal
ON dbo.v_Product_Sales_By_LineTotal (ProductName);
GO
```

When the previous query is now run, the same results are returned. However, the statistics have changed:

```
Table 'v_Product_Sales_By_LineTotal'. Scan count 1, logical reads 5, physical reads 0, read-
ahead reads 0, lob logical reads 0, lob physical reads 0, lob read-ahead reads 0.
```

Let's step through the process. First, a view is created that utilizes the `WITH SCHEMABINDING` clause.

```
CREATE VIEW dbo.v_Product_Sales_By_LineTotal
WITH SCHEMABINDING
AS
```

The rest of the view is a regular `SELECT` statement that sums the `LineTotal` column and counts the number of records for the `ProductID` and `Name` grouping.

```
SELECT  p.ProductID,
        p.Name AS ProductName,
        SUM(LineTotal) AS LineTotalByProduct,
        COUNT_BIG(*) AS LineItems
FROM    Sales.SalesOrderDetail s
        INNER JOIN Production.Product p
            ON s.ProductID = p.ProductID
GROUP BY p.ProductID,
        p.Name;
```

Notice that the query referenced the COUNT_BIG aggregate function. COUNT_BIG is required in order for SQL Server to maintain the number of rows in each group within the indexed view. Once the view is successfully created with SCHEMABINDING, a unique clustered index can then be created on it.

```
CREATE UNIQUE CLUSTERED INDEX UCI_v_Product_Sales_By_LineTotal
ON dbo.v_Product_Sales_By_LineTotal (ProductID);
GO
```

To index a view, you must first create a unique clustered index on it. This process materializes the view, making it have a physical existence instead of its normal virtual existence. Once this index has been built, the view data is stored in much the same way as a clustered index for a table is stored. After a clustered index is created, you can also create additional nonclustered indexes, as you would for a regular table. In the example, a nonclustered index is created on the ProductName column of the indexed view.

```
CREATE NONCLUSTERED INDEX NI_v_Product_Sales_By_LineTotal
ON dbo.v_Product_Sales_By_LineTotal (ProductName);
GO
```

Once a view is indexed, view indexes can then be used by SQL Server Enterprise Edition whenever the view or underlying tables are referenced in a query. The SET STATISTICS IO command was used to demonstrate how SQL Server performs the data page retrieval both before and after the view was indexed.

Indexed views can provide performance benefits for relatively static data. Frequently updated base tables, on the other hand, are not an ideal choice for being referenced in an indexed view, because the updates will also cause frequent updates to the view's indexes, potentially reducing the benefit of any query performance gained. This is a trade-off between data modification speed and query speed.

Also, although indexed views can be created using any edition of SQL Server, they will be automatically considered during the query execution if you are using Enterprise Edition. To make sure SQL Server uses it in other editions, you need to use the view hint NOEXPAND, which is reviewed in the next recipe.

14-10. Creating a Partitioned View

Problem

You have a table that has an extremely large row count and is causing performance issues. Only the current month's data is actively changing. You want to reduce the size of this table in order to improve the performance of DML operations; yet you still want to keep all of the rows in the table for your queries and to keep the same object name in your queries.

Solution

Split the table into multiple tables, and create a partitioned view with the same name as the original table name.

How It Works

Partitioned views allow you to create a single logical representation (view) of two or more horizontally partitioned tables that are located on the same SQL Server instance.

To set up a partitioned view, a large table is split into smaller tables based on a range of values defined in a CHECK constraint. This CHECK constraint ensures that each smaller table holds unique data that cannot be stored in the other tables. The partitioned view is then created using a UNION ALL to join each smaller table into a single result set.

The performance benefit is realized when a query is executed against the partitioned view. If the view is partitioned by a date range, for example, and a query is used to return rows that are stored only in a single table of the partition, SQL Server is smart enough to search only that one partition instead of all tables in the partitioned view.

To demonstrate partitioned views, let's work with the fictional company MegaCorp. They want to track all of the hits to their web site. Anticipating a large amount of traffic, a WebHits table is created for each month in the TSQLRecipe_A database.

```
IF DB_ID('TSQLRecipe_A') IS NULL
   CREATE DATABASE TSQLRecipe_A;
GO
USE TSQLRecipe_A;
GO
CREATE TABLE dbo.WebHits_201201
        (
         HitDt DATETIME
             NOT NULL
             CONSTRAINT PK__WebHits_201201 PRIMARY KEY
             CONSTRAINT CK__WebHits_201201__HitDt
             CHECK (HitDt >= '2012-01-01'
                    AND HitDt < '2012-02-01'),
         WebSite VARCHAR(20) NOT NULL
        );
GO
CREATE TABLE dbo.WebHits_201202
        (
         HitDt DATETIME
             NOT NULL
             CONSTRAINT PK__WebHits_201202 PRIMARY KEY
             CONSTRAINT CK__WebHits_201202__HitDt
             CHECK (HitDt >= '2012-02-01'
                    AND HitDt < '2012-03-01'),
         WebSite VARCHAR(20) NOT NULL
        );
GO
CREATE TABLE dbo.WebHits_201203
        (
         HitDt DATETIME
             NOT NULL
             CONSTRAINT PK__WebHits_201203 PRIMARY KEY
             CONSTRAINT CK__WebHits_201203__HitDt
             CHECK (HitDt >= '2012-03-01'
                    AND HitDt < '2012-04-01'),
         WebSite VARCHAR(20) NOT NULL
        );
GO
```

Now that the tables are set up, it is time to create the partitioned view. There are three areas that have specific requirements that need to be met in order to create a partitioned view:

1. The SELECT list
    - All columns in the affected tables need to be selected in the column list of the view.
    - The columns in the same ordinal position need to be of the same type, including the collation.
    - At least one of these columns must appear in the select list in the same ordinal position. This column (in each table) must be defined to have a check constraint such that any specified value for that column can satisfy at most only one of the constraints from the involved tables. This column is known as the *partitioning column*, and it may have a different name in each of the tables. The constraints need to be enabled and trusted.
    - The same column cannot be used multiple times in the select list.
2. The partitioning column
    - The partitioning column is part of the PRIMARY KEY constraint for the table.
    - It cannot be a computed, identity, default, or timestamp column.
    - There can be only one check constraint on the partitioning column.
3. The underlying tables
    - The same table cannot appear more than once in the set of tables in the view.
    - The underlying tables cannot have indexes on computed columns.
    - The underlying tables need to have their PRIMARY KEY constraints on the same number of columns.
    - All underlying tables need to have the same ANSI padding setting.

Notice the check constraints on the HitDt columns. These check constraints create the partitioning column necessary for the view.

For the partitioned view to be able to update data in the underlying tables, the following conditions must be met:

- INSERT statements must supply values for all the columns in the view, even if the underlying tables have a default constraint or they allow null values. If the column does have a default definition, the INSERT statement cannot use the DEFAULT keyword for this column.
- The value being inserted into the partitioning column should satisfy at least one of the underlying constraints.
- UPDATE statements cannot specify the DEFAULT keyword as a value in the SET clause.
- Columns in the view that are identity columns in any underlying table cannot be modified by either the INSERT or UPDATE statement.
- If any underlying table contains a TIMESTAMP column, the data cannot be modified by using an UPDATE or INSERT statement.

- None of the underlying tables can contain a trigger or an `ON UPDATE CASCADE/SET NULL/SET DEFAULT`or `ON DELETE CASCADE/SET NULL/SET DEFAULT` constraint.
- `INSERT`, `UPDATE`, and `DELETE` actions are not allowed if there is a self-join with the same view or any of the underlying tables in the statement.
- Bulk importing data from the bcp utility or the `BULK INSERT` and `INSERT ... SELECT * FROM OPENROWSET(BULK...)` statements is not supported.

Considering all of the previous requirements, the following view is created:

```
CREATE VIEW dbo.WebHits
AS
SELECT  HitDt,
        WebSite
FROM    dbo.WebHits_201201
UNION ALL
SELECT  HitDt,
        WebSite
FROM    dbo.WebHits_201202
UNION ALL
SELECT  HitDt,
        WebSite
FROM    dbo.WebHits_201203;
GO
```

Next, some records are inserted into the view. If everything works correctly, they will be inserted into their underlying tables.

```
INSERT  INTO dbo.WebHits
        (HitDt,
         WebSite)
VALUES  ('2012-01-15T13:22:18.456',
         'MegaCorp');
INSERT  INTO dbo.WebHits
        (HitDt,
         WebSite)
VALUES  ('2012-02-15T13:22:18.456',
         'MegaCorp');
INSERT  INTO dbo.WebHits
        (HitDt,
         WebSite)
VALUES  ('2012-03-15T13:22:18.456',
         'MegaCorp');
GO
```

To check whether the records are in the proper tables, run the following queries:

```
SELECT  *
FROM    dbo.WebHits_201201;
```

This query returns the following result set:

```
HitDt                      WebSite
-----------------------    --------------------
2012-01-15 13:22:18.457    MegaCorp
```

```
SELECT  *
FROM    dbo.WebHits_201202;
```

This query returns the following result set:

```
HitDt                      WebSite
-----------------------    --------------------
2012-02-15 13:22:18.457    MegaCorp
```

```
SELECT  *
FROM    dbo.WebHits_201203;
```

This query returns the following result set:

```
HitDt                      WebSite
-----------------------    --------------------
2012-03-15 13:22:18.457    MegaCorp
```

Now that you can see the data is going into the proper tables, let's look at how SQL Server retrieves data.

```
SET STATISTICS IO ON;
GO
SELECT  *
FROM    dbo.WebHits
WHERE   HitDt >= '2012-02-01'
        AND HitDt < '2012-03-01';
```

This query returns the following result set:

```
HitDt                      WebSite
-----------------------    --------------------
2012-02-15 13:22:18.457    MegaCorp

Table 'WebHits_201202'. Scan count 1, logical reads 2, physical reads 0, read-ahead reads 0,
lob logical reads 0, lob physical reads 0, lob read-ahead reads 0.
```

If SELECT statements that are referencing the view specify a search condition, the query optimizer uses the check constraints to determine which underlying tables contain the data, and the execution plan is built referencing only those tables. In the previous query, even though the query is being run against the view, the check constrains on the underlying tables tell SQL Server that for the date range being selected, only the WebHits_201202 table will need to be accessed to retrieve data. When the execution plan is built and executed, this is exactly what happens.

There are several benefits to utilizing partitioned views. These include the following:

- Allowing easier archiving of data, without extra transaction log activity. (You don't need to move records from one table to another to archive or even to just delete the records. Moving records would require transaction log entries for the table both being deleted from and being inserted into, potentially growing the transaction log to an undesired size.)
- Assuming that data is modified only on the current month's underlying table, only the indexes on that table will need maintenance activities. Since the size of the indexes will be much smaller, the time required for the index maintenance will be shorter.
- Queries can run against a smaller number of records.

■ **Note** It is recommended that if all of the underlying tables are on the same SQL Server instance, a partitioned table be used instead. However, this is an Enterprise Edition and greater feature; if you are using a lesser edition, using a partitioned view may be the only choice available to you.

14-11. Creating a Distributed Partitioned View

Problem

You need to spread the workload of a table across multiple servers.

Solution

Create a table on each instance of SQL Server, and create a distributed partitioned view on each server to access the data from all of the servers.

How It Works

Distributed partitioned views allow you to create a single logical representation (view) of two or more horizontally partitioned tables that are located on multiple SQL Server instances. Distributed partitioned views have a few more conditions to them than partitioned views; however, the only difference between them is whether all of the underlying tables are on the same SQL Server instance. The additional conditions for distributed partitioned views are as follows:

- distributed transaction will be initiated in order to guarantee atomicity across all instances affected by the update.
- `SET XACT_ABORT ON` should be run in order for `INSERT`, `UPDATE`, and `DELETE` statements to work.
- Any smallmoney and smalldatetime columns in remote tables will be mapped as money and datetime. Therefore, the corresponding columns in the same ordinal position in the select list in the local tables must be money or datetime data types.
- Linked servers utilized in the partitioned view cannot be a loopback linked server (the linked server points to the same instance of SQL Server).

In a distributed partitioned view, each server has a view that references its local table(s), and the remote tables are referenced in a four-part naming schema (`Server.Database.Schema.Table`) utilizing a linked server.

CHAPTER 15

Managing Large Tables and Databases

By Wayne Sheffield

Very large tables (where you have row counts in the tens of millions) have special needs. All data manipulations and maintenance operations need special considerations. This chapter will deal with features in SQL Server that can help; specifically, I'll cover how partitioning a table can ease data movements and how the use of filegroups and data compression can help you improve performance by distributing data I/O across multiple drives and having a smaller amount of data to store on disk.

Table partitioning provides you with a built-in method of horizontally partitioning data within a table or index while still maintaining a single logical object. *Horizontal partitioning* involves keeping the same number of columns in each partition but reducing the number of rows. Partitioning can ease management of very large tables or indexes; data can be loaded into a partitioned table in seconds instead of minutes or hours; query performance can be improved; and you can perform maintenance operations quicker, allowing for smaller maintenance windows. You can also improve performance by enabling lock escalation to lock at the partition level before locking at the table level. The recipes in this chapter will demonstrate how to use Transact-SQL commands to create, modify, and manage partitions and to partition database objects.

This chapter will also cover *filegroup* placement. Database data files belong to filegroups. Every database has a primary filegroup, and you can add filegroups as needed. Adding new filegroups to a database is often used for *very large databases* (VLDBs), because they can ease backup administration and potentially improve performance by distributing data over multiple arrays. *Data compression* is used to put more data in a given amount of space, reducing disk I/O at the cost of increased CPU usage in performing the compression and decompression to work with the data.

Note Files and filegroups are covered in detail in Chapter 25.

The recipes in this chapter will be utilizing your company's database, `MegaCorpData`. The database and additional files will be created on your C: drive, in a folder named `Apress`. The database is created from the following script:

```
USE master;
GO

IF db_id('MegaCorpData') IS NOT NULL DROP DATABASE MegaCorpData;
GO
```

```
CREATE DATABASE MegaCorpData
ON PRIMARY
(NAME = 'MegaCorpData',
 FILENAME = 'C:\Apress\MegaCorpData.MDF',
 SIZE = 3MB,
 MAXSIZE = UNLIMITED,
 FILEGROWTH = 1MB)
LOG ON
(NAME = 'MegaCorpData_Log',
 FILENAME = 'C:\Apress\MegaCorpData.LDF',
 SIZE = 3MB,
 MAXSIZE = UNLIMITED,
 FILEGROWTH = 1MB);
GO
```

■ **Note** Table partitioning is a Developer or Enterprise edition (or higher) feature.

15-1. Partitioning a Table

Problem

You are adding a table (`dbo.WebSiteHits`) to your company's database (`MegaCorpData`) to track each hit to your company's web site. This table is expected to grow very large, very quickly. Because of its potential size, you are concerned that queries will not perform very well and that database backups may take longer than what your maintenance window allows for.

Solution

Partition the table into multiple filegroups, with each filegroup having files on a different disk.

How It Works

The first step is to create multiple filegroups.

```
ALTER DATABASE MegaCorpData ADD FILEGROUP hitfg1;
ALTER DATABASE MegaCorpData ADD FILEGROUP hitfg2;
ALTER DATABASE MegaCorpData ADD FILEGROUP hitfg3;
ALTER DATABASE MegaCorpData ADD FILEGROUP hitfg4;
```

The next step is to add files to each filegroup.

```
ALTER DATABASE MegaCorpData
ADD FILE (NAME = mchitfg1,
         FILENAME = 'C:\Apress\mc_hitfg1.ndf',
         SIZE = 1MB)
TO FILEGROUP hitfg1;
ALTER DATABASE MegaCorpData
ADD FILE (NAME = mchitfg2,
         FILENAME = 'C:\Apress\mc_hitfg2.ndf',
         SIZE = 1MB)
TO FILEGROUP hitfg2;
ALTER DATABASE MegaCorpData
ADD FILE (NAME = mchitfg3,
         FILENAME = 'C:\Apress\mc_hitfg3.ndf',
         SIZE = 1MB)
TO FILEGROUP hitfg3;
ALTER DATABASE MegaCorpData
ADD FILE (NAME = mchitfg4,
         FILENAME = 'C:\Apress\mc_hitfg4.ndf',
         SIZE = 1MB)
TO FILEGROUP hitfg4;
```

Now that we have filegroups with files ready to receive data, we need to create a partition function, which determines how the table will have its data horizontally partitioned by mapping columns to partitions based upon the value of a specified column.

```
USE MegaCorpData;
GO
CREATE PARTITION FUNCTION HitsDateRange (datetime)
AS RANGE LEFT FOR VALUES ('2006-01-01T00:00:00', '2007-01-01T00:00:00', '2008-01-01T00:00:00');
```

The partition function specifies the name of the function, the data type, whether the range of boundaries is bound to the left or right (in this example, left was used), and the values that define the data in each boundary. You can not specify a data type of text, ntext, image, xml, timestamp, varchar(max), varbinary(max), nvarchar(max), alias data types, or CLR-defined data types. The number of values that you choose amounts to a total of $n+1$ partitions. You can have up to 15,000 partitions, so you can specify up to 14,999 boundaries. If the values are not specified in order, the database engine sorts the values, creates the function, and returns a warning that the values were not provided in order. If there are any duplicate values, the database engine returns an error. The first partition contains values less than the lowest specified value, and the last partition contains values higher than the highest specified value. `RANGE LEFT` is used to specify that the upper boundary of each partition is the value specified; `RANGE RIGHT` is used to specify that the upper boundary of each partition is less than the specified value. In this case, we are specifying the first day of each year, creating yearly partitions. If you wanted to partition the data by month, you would just include values for the first of each month. Tables 15-1 and 15-2 show how the partition boundaries for the previous values are set for the specified dates.

Once a partition function is created, it can be used in one or more partition schemes. A partition scheme maps the partitions defined in a partition function to actual filegroups.

Table 15-1. *RANGE LEFT Boundaries*

Partition #	Values
1	<= '2006-01-01'
2	> '2006-01-01' and <= '2007-01-01'
3	> '2007-01-01' and <= '2008-01-01'
4	> '2008-01-01'

Table 15-2. *RANGE RIGHT Boundaries*

Partition #	Values
1	< '2006-01-01'
2	> = '2006-01-01' and <'2007-01-01'
3	> = '2007-01-01' and <'2008-01-01'
4	> = '2008-01-01'

```
CREATE PARTITION SCHEME HitDateRangeScheme
AS PARTITION HitsDateRange
TO (hitfg1, hitfg2, hitfg3, hitfg4);
```

In this statement, you assign a name to the partition scheme, what partition function that the scheme is bound to, and which filegroups are assigned to each partition.

Now that all of the preliminary work is done, the new partitioned table can be built.

```
CREATE TABLE dbo.WebSiteHits (
    WebSiteHitID BIGINT NOT NULL IDENTITY(1, 1),
    WebSitePage VARCHAR(255) NOT NULL,
    HitDate DATETIME NOT NULL,
    CONSTRAINT PK_WebSiteHits PRIMARY KEY CLUSTERED (WebSiteHitId, HitDate)
)
ON [HitDateRangeScheme] (HitDate);
```

There are a couple of items to note about this `CREATE TABLE` statement. The first is the `ON` clause; it specifies the partition scheme to put the table on. The second item is the `PRIMARY KEY` constraint definition; while the primary key is unique with just the identity column (unless you deliberately add duplicate values to that column), the partitioning column has been added to it. This is because all unique indexes, including those that are automatically built from `PRIMARY KEY` and `UNIQUE` constraints, need to have the partitioning column included in the index key.

15-2. Locating Data in a Partition

Problem

You want to ensure that data is being stored in the expected partitions.

Solution

Utilize the $PARTITION function to return the partition that a row is stored in.

```
INSERT  dbo.WebSiteHits (WebSitePage, HitDate)
VALUES  ('Home Page', '2007-10-22T00:00:00'),
        ('Home Page', '2006-10-02T00:00:00'),
        ('Sales Page', '2008-05-09T00:00:00'),
        ('Sales Page', '2000-03-04T00:00:00');

SELECT  WebSitePage,
        HitDate,
        $PARTITION.HitsDateRange (HitDate) AS [Partition]
FROM    dbo.WebSiteHits;
```

This query returns the following result set:

```
WebSitePage HitDate                  Partition
----------- -----------------------  ---------
Sales Page  2000-03-04 00:00:00.000  1
Home Page   2006-10-02 00:00:00.000  2
Home Page   2007-10-22 00:00:00.000  3
Sales Page  2008-05-09 00:00:00.000  4
```

How It Works

This example starts by inserting four rows into the table. Based on the dates inserted, each row should be in a separate partition. Next, a query is run to select the data from the table, and the query utilizes the $PARTITION function to return which partition the data is in. The syntax of the $PARTITION function is as follows:

```
$PARTITION.partition_function_name(expression)
```

where partition_function_name is the name of the partition function used to partition the table, and expression is the name of the partitioning column.

The $PARTITION function evaluates each HitDate and determines which partition it is stored in based on the partition function. This allows you to see how your data is stored and how it is distributed across the different partitions. If one partition has an uneven distribution, you can explore creating new partitions or removing existing partitions, both of which are demonstrated in the upcoming recipes.

15-3. Adding a Partition

Problem

You're into the last year that your partition scheme covers, so you need to add partitions.

Solution

Utilize the ALTER PARTITION SCHEME and ALTER PARTITION FUNCTION statements to extend the partition onto a new or existing filegroup and to create the new partition.

```
ALTER PARTITION SCHEME HitDateRangeScheme NEXT USED [PRIMARY];
GO

ALTER PARTITION FUNCTION HitsDateRange () SPLIT RANGE ('2009-01-01T00:00:00');
GO
```

How It Works

This example starts by using the ALTER PARTITION SCHEME statement to designate the next partition filegroup to use. The syntax for ALTER PARTITION SCHEME is as follows:

```
ALTER PARTITION SCHEME partition_scheme_name NEXT USED [ filegroup_name ]
```

where partition_scheme_name is the name of the partition scheme to modify. NEXT USED [filegroup_name] queues the specified filegroup to be used next by the next new partition created with an ALTER PARTITION FUNCTION statement.

In a given partition scheme, you can have only one filegroup that is designated NEXT USED. The filegroup does not need to be empty to be used.

In this example, we are specifying that the PRIMARY filegroup will be the filegroup that the next partition is placed on.

Next the example uses the ALTER PARTITION FUNCTION statement to create (split) the new partition by splitting the partition boundaries. The syntax for ALTER PARTITION FUNCTION is as follows:

```
ALTER PARTITION FUNCTION partition_function_name() {
SPLIT RANGE ( boundary_value ) | MERGE RANGE ( boundary_value ) }
```

where partition_function_name is the name of the partition function to add or remove a partition from SPLIT RANGE is used to create a new partition by defining a new boundary value; MERGE RANGE is used to remove an existing partition at the specified boundary and to move any existing records to another partition.

The existing partition is split, using the original boundary type of LEFT or RIGHT. You can split only one partition at a time. After this split, the partition layout now looks like Table 15-3.

Table 15-3. *New RANGE LEFT Boundaries*

Partition #	Values
1	<= '2006-01-01'
2	> '2006-01-01' and <= '2007-01-01'
3	> '2007-01-01' and <= '2008-01-01'
4	> '2008-01-01' and <= '2009-01-01'
5	> '2009-01-01'

After the new partition is created, when a new row is added that qualifies to go to the new partition, it will be stored in that partition.

```
INSERT  dbo.WebSiteHits
        (WebSitePage, HitDate)
VALUES  ('Sales Page', '2009-03-04T00:00:00');

SELECT  WebSitePage,
        HitDate,
        $PARTITION.HitsDateRange (HitDate) AS [Partition]
FROM    dbo.WebSiteHits;
```

This query returns the following result set:

```
WebSitePage HitDate                 Partition
----------- ----------------------- ---------
Sales Page  2000-03-04 00:00:00.000 1
Home Page   2006-10-02 00:00:00.000 2
Home Page   2007-10-22 00:00:00.000 3
Sales Page  2008-05-09 00:00:00.000 4
Sales Page  2009-03-04 00:00:00.000 5
```

15-4. Removing a Partition

Problem

You need to remove a partition and move the data in that partition into another partition.

Solution

Utilize the `ALTER PARTITION FUNCTION` statement to remove a partition and merge the data in that partition into another partition.

```
ALTER PARTITION FUNCTION HitsDateRange () MERGE RANGE ('2007-01-01T00:00:00');
GO
```

```
SELECT  WebSitePage,
        HitDate,
        $PARTITION.HitsDateRange(HitDate) Partition
FROM    dbo.WebSiteHits;
```

This query returns the following result set:

```
WebSitePage HitDate                 Partition
----------- ----------------------- ---------
Sales Page  2000-03-04 00:00:00.000 1
Home Page   2007-10-22 00:00:00.000 2
Home Page   2006-10-02 00:00:00.000 2
Sales Page  2008-05-09 00:00:00.000 3
Sales Page  2009-03-04 00:00:00.000 4
```

How It Works

The previous recipe showed the syntax for the `ALTER PARTITION FUNCTION` statement, including a description of the `MERGE RANGE` functionality that is used to remove an existing partition. Removing a partition merges the specified partition with the preceding partition, with the rows being moved into the new partition.

In this example, the partition with the boundary `'2007-01-01'` is removed. When the table is queried, you can see that the row in the year 2007 has been moved from the third partition to the second partition.

Table 15-4 shows the new partition layout.

Table 15-4. *New RANGE LEFT Boundaries*

Partition #	Values
1	<= '2006-01-01'
2	> '2006-01-01' and <= '2008-01-01'
3	> '2008-01-01' and <= '2009-01-01'
4	> '2009-01-01'

15-5. Determining Whether a Table Is Partitioned

Problem

You need to determine whether a table is partitioned.

Solution

Query the `sys.partitions` system view to determine the partitions on an object.

```
SELECT  p.partition_id,
        p.object_id,
        p.partition_number
FROM    sys.partitions AS p
WHERE   p.partition_id IS NOT NULL
        AND p.object_id = OBJECT_ID('dbo.WebSiteHits');
```

This query returns the following result set:

```
partition_id        object_id   partition_number
-----------------   ---------   ----------------
72057594039042048   245575913   1
72057594039173120   245575913   2
72057594039238656   245575913   4
72057594039304192   245575913   3
```

■ **Note** The `partition_id` and `object_id` values will be different on your system.

How It Works

The system view `sys.partitions` contains a row for each partition of a table and most types of indexes. (All tables contain at least one partition, whether they are specifically partitioned or not.)

15-6. Determining the Boundary Values for a Partitioned Table

Problem

You want to determine what the existing boundaries are for a partition function.

Solution

Query the system views to obtain this information.

```
SELECT  t.name AS TableName,
        i.name AS IndexName,
        p.partition_number AS [Part#],
        f.type_desc,
        CASE WHEN f.boundary_value_on_right = 1 THEN 'RIGHT' ELSE 'LEFT' END AS BoundaryType,
        r.boundary_id,
        r.value AS BoundaryValue
FROM    sys.tables AS t
        JOIN sys.indexes AS i
            ON t.object_id = i.object_id
        JOIN sys.partitions AS p
            ON i.object_id = p.object_id
               AND i.index_id = p.index_id
        JOIN sys.partition_schemes AS s
            ON i.data_space_id = s.data_space_id
        JOIN sys.partition_functions AS f
            ON s.function_id = f.function_id
        LEFT JOIN sys.partition_range_values AS r
            ON f.function_id = r.function_id
               AND r.boundary_id = p.partition_number
```

```
WHERE   t.object_id = OBJECT_ID('dbo.WebSiteHits')
        AND i.type<= 1
ORDER BY p.partition_number;
```

This query returns the following result set:

```
TableName   IndexName      Part# type_desc BoundaryType boundary_id BoundaryValue
----------- -------------- ----- --------- ------------ ----------- -----------------------
WebSiteHits PK_WebSiteHits 1     RANGE     LEFT         1           2006-01-01 00:00:00.000
WebSiteHits PK_WebSiteHits 2     RANGE     LEFT         2           2008-01-01 00:00:00.000
WebSiteHits PK_WebSiteHits 3     RANGE     LEFT         3           2009-01-01 00:00:00.000
WebSiteHits PK_WebSiteHits 4     RANGE     LEFT         NULL        NULL
```

How It Works

The sys.partition_range_values system view contains the information about boundary values for a partition function. Join to the other system views to return more information such as the table, index, partition number, and type of boundary.

15-7. Determining the Partitioning Column for a Partitioned Table

Problem

You need to determine what the partitioning column is on a partitioned table.

Solution

Query the system views to obtain the partitioning column for a table.

```
SELECT  t.object_id AS Object_ID,
        t.name AS TableName,
        ic.column_id AS PartitioningColumnID,
        c.name AS PartitioningColumnName
FROM    sys.tables AS t
        JOIN sys.indexes AS i
            ON t.object_id = i.object_id
        JOIN sys.partition_schemes AS ps
            ON ps.data_space_id = i.data_space_id
        JOIN sys.index_columns AS ic
            ON ic.object_id = i.object_id
               AND ic.index_id = i.index_id
               AND ic.partition_ordinal > 0
        JOIN sys.columns AS c
            ON t.object_id = c.object_id
               AND ic.column_id = c.column_id
```

```
WHERE   t.object_id = OBJECT_ID('dbo.WebSiteHits')
        AND i.type <= 1;
```

This query returns the following result set:

```
Object_ID   TableName   PartitioningColumnID PartitioningColumnName
---------   ----------- -------------------- ----------------------
773577794   WebSiteHits 3                    HitDate
```

How It Works

The system views sys.partition_schemes and sys.index_columns can be joined together and, with other system views, can be used to determine which column is the partitioning column.

15-8. Moving a Partition to a Different Partitioned Table

Problem

You want to move the older data in your partitioned table to a history table.

Solution

Utilize the ALTER TABLE statement to move partitions between tables.

```
CREATE TABLE dbo.WebSiteHitsHistory
        (
         WebSiteHitID BIGINT NOT NULL IDENTITY,
         WebSitePage VARCHAR(255) NOT NULL,
         HitDate DATETIME NOT NULL,
         CONSTRAINT PK_WebSiteHitsHistory PRIMARY KEY (WebSiteHitID, HitDate)
        )
ON      [HitDateRangeScheme](HitDate);
GO

ALTER TABLE dbo.WebSiteHits SWITCH PARTITION 1 TO dbo.WebSiteHitsHistory PARTITION 1;
GO

SELECT  WebSitePage,
        HitDate,
        $PARTITION.HitsDateRange(HitDate) Partition
FROM    dbo.WebSiteHits;
SELECT  WebSitePage,
        HitDate,
        $PARTITION.HitsDateRange(HitDate) Partition
FROM    dbo.WebSiteHitsHistory;
```

These queries return the following result sets:

```
WebSitePage HitDate                 Partition
----------- ----------------------- ---------
Home Page   2007-10-22 00:00:00.000 2
Home Page   2006-10-02 00:00:00.000 2
Sales Page  2008-05-09 00:00:00.000 3
Sales Page  2009-03-04 00:00:00.000 4

WebSitePage HitDate                 Partition
----------- ----------------------- ---------
Sales Page  2000-03-04 00:00:00.000 1
```

How It Works

With SQL Server's partitioning functionality, you can transfer partitions between different tables with a minimum of effort or overhead. Partitions are transferred between tables with the `ALTER TABLE ... SWITCH` statement. Transfers can take place in three ways: switching a partition from one partitioned table to another partitioned table (both tables need to be partitioned on the same column), transferring an entire table from a nonpartitioned table to a partitioned table, or moving a partition from a partitioned table to a nonpartitioned table. The basic syntax of the `ALTER TABLE` statement to switch partitions is as follows:

```
ALTER TABLE [ schema_name. ] tablename
SWITCH [ PARTITION source_partition_number_expression ]
TO [ schema_name. ] target_table
[ PARTITION target_partition_number_expression ]
```

Table 15-5 details the arguments of this command.

Table 15-5. *`ALTER TABLE ... SWITCH` Arguments*

Argument	Description
`[ schema_name. ] tablename`	The source table to move the partition from
`source_partition_number_expression`	The partition number being relocated
`[ schema_name. ] target_table`	The target table to receive the partition
`partition.target_partition_number_expression`	The destination partition number

This example starts by creating a history table (`WebSiteHitsHistory`). Next, the `ALTER TABLE` statement is used to move partition 1 from the `WebSiteHits` table to partition 1 of the `WebSiteHitsHistory` table. Finally, both tables are queried to show the data that is in each table and which partition it is in.

Moving partitions between tables is much faster than performing a manual row operation (`INSERT ... SELECT`, for example) because you aren't actually moving physical data. Instead, you are only changing the metadata regarding which table the partition is currently associated with. Also, keep in mind that the target partition of any existing table needs to be empty for the destination partition. If it is a nonpartitioned table, the table must be empty.

15-9. Moving Data from a Nonpartitioned Table to a Partition in a Partitioned Table

Problem

You have just found the long-lost spreadsheet that the original web site designer saved the web hits into. You have loaded this data into a table, and you want to add it to your `WebSiteHits` table.

Solution

Utilize the `ALTER TABLE` statement to move the data from the nonpartitioned to an empty partition in the partitioned table.

```
IF OBJECT_ID('dbo.WebSiteHitsImport','U') IS NOT NULL DROP TABLE dbo.WebSiteHitsImport;
GO
CREATE TABLE dbo.WebSiteHitsImport
       (
        WebSiteHitID BIGINT NOT NULL IDENTITY,
        WebSitePage VARCHAR(255) NOT NULL,
        HitDate DATETIME NOT NULL,
        CONSTRAINT PK_WebSiteHitsImport PRIMARY KEY (WebSiteHitID, HitDate),
        CONSTRAINT CK_WebSiteHitsImport CHECK (HitDate <= '2006-01-01T00:00:00')
       )
ON hitfg1;
GO
INSERT INTO dbo.WebSiteHitsImport (WebSitePage, HitDate)
VALUES ('Sales Page', '2005-06-01T00:00:00'),
       ('Main Page', '2005-06-01T00:00:00');
GO

-- partition 1 is empty - move data to this partition
ALTER TABLE dbo.WebSiteHitsImport SWITCH TO dbo.WebSiteHits PARTITION 1;
GO

-- see the data
SELECT  WebSiteHitId,
        WebSitePage,
        HitDate,
        $PARTITION.HitsDateRange(HitDate) Partition
FROM    dbo.WebSiteHits;
SELECT  WebSiteHitId,
        WebSitePage,
        HitDate,
        $PARTITION.HitsDateRange(HitDate) Partition
FROM    dbo.WebSiteHitsImport;
```

These queries return the following result sets:

```
WebSiteHitId        WebSitePage     HitDate                     Partition
------------        -----------     -----------------------     ---------
1                   Sales Page      2005-06-01 00:00:00.000     1
2                   Main Page       2005-06-01 00:00:00.000     1
1                   Home Page       2007-10-22 00:00:00.000     2
2                   Home Page       2006-10-02 00:00:00.000     2
3                   Sales Page      2008-05-09 00:00:00.000     3
5                   Sales Page      2009-03-04 00:00:00.000     4

WebSiteHitId        WebSitePage     HitDate                     Partition
------------        -----------     -------                     ---------
```

How It Works

In this example, we first create a new, nonpartitioned table that the imported data will be loaded into and insert some records into that table. Next, the `ALTER TABLE` statement is utilized to move the data from the new, nonpartitioned into an empty partition in the partitioned table. Finally, `SELECT` statements are run against the two tables to show where the data is at on those tables. Since the source table is not partitioned, the partition number on the source table is not specified in the `ALTER TABLE` statement.

To move the data from one table to the partitioned table, the table being moved must be on the same filegroup as the partition that the data is to be moved into for the partitioned table. Additionally, the table being moved must have the same structure (columns, indexes, constraints) as the partitioned table, and it must have an additional check constraint that enforces that the data in the partitioned column has the same allowable values as that partition on the partitioned table. Finally, the partition on the partitioned table that the data is being moved to must be empty. Since this is a metadata operation (assigning the existing data pages from one table to another), it makes sense that the data must exist on the same filegroup as the partition and that the partition is empty; otherwise, data would need to be moved through `INSERT ... SELECT` statements.

■ **Caution** In this example, both tables have an identity column. If you look at the returned results, there are duplicate values for this identity column. Since the unique constraints include the partitioning column in addition to the identity column value, these values are valid even though duplicated identity column values are not normally seen.

15-10. Moving a Partition from a Partitioned Table to a Nonpartitioned Table

Problem

You want to move all of the data in a partition of a partitioned table to a nonpartitioned table.

Solution

Utilize the ALTER TABLE statement to move the data from a partition of a partitioned table to a nonpartitioned table.

```
ALTER TABLE dbo.WebSiteHits SWITCH PARTITION 1 TO dbo.WebSiteHitsImport;
GO

-- see the data
SELECT  WebSiteHitId,
        WebSitePage,
        HitDate,
        $PARTITION.HitsDateRange(HitDate) Partition
FROM    dbo.WebSiteHits;
SELECT  WebSiteHitId,
        WebSitePage,
        HitDate,
        $PARTITION.HitsDateRange(HitDate) Partition
FROM    dbo.WebSiteHitsImport;
```

These queries return the following result sets:

```
WebSiteHitId WebSitePage HitDate                 Partition
------------ ----------- ----------------------- ---------
1            Home Page   2007-10-22 00:00:00.000 2
2            Home Page   2006-10-02 00:00:00.000 2
3            Sales Page  2008-05-09 00:00:00.000 3
5            Sales Page  2009-03-04 00:00:00.000 4
WebSiteHitId WebSitePage HitDate                 Partition
------------ ----------- ----------------------- ---------
1            Sales Page  2005-06-01 00:00:00.000 1
2            Main Page   2005-06-01 00:00:00.000 1
```

How It Works

In this example, the ALTER TABLE statement is utilized to move the data from a partition of the partitioned table to an empty, nonpartitioned table. Next, SELECT statements are run against the two tables to show where the data is at on those tables. Since the destination table is not partitioned, the partition number on the destination table is not specified in the ALTER TABLE statement.

To move the data from one partition of a partitioned table to the nonpartitioned table, the nonpartitioned table must be on the same filegroup as the partition that the data is to be removed from for the partitioned table, and the nonpartitioned table must be empty. Additionally, the nonpartitioned table must have the same structure (columns, indexes, constraints) as the partitioned table. In the prior recipe, the nonpartitioned column required an additional check constraint; this additional check constraint is not necessary when moving data into a nonpartitioned table. However, if you plan on moving the data back into the partitioned table, it is a good idea to add it when you create the table to ensure that data does not get inserted into this table, which would violate the partition.

15-11. Reducing Table Locks on Partitioned Tables

Problem

Your partition table is incurring an excessive number of table locks, and you want to reduce them as much as you can.

Solution

Change the lock escalation of the table to lock at the partition level instead of at the table level.

```
ALTER TABLE dbo.WebSiteHits SET (LOCK_ESCALATION = AUTO);
```

How It Works

Locks on a table normally go from row to table. If a query is performing all of its activity in one partition of a partitioned table, it can be beneficial to change this behavior on the partitioned table to escalate from row to the partition. This is performed utilizing the `ALTER TABLE` statement, as shown earlier.

■ **Caution** If queries that are locking different partitions need to expand their locks to other partitions, it is possible that this could increase the potential for deadlocks.

■ **Note** See Chapter 12 for more information about lock escalation.

15-12. Removing Partition Functions and Schemes

Problem

You are no longer using a partition function or scheme, and you want to remove them from the database.

Solution

Utilize the `DROP PARTITION SCHEME` and `DROP PARTITION FUNCTION` statements to drop the partition scheme and function.

```
DROP TABLE dbo.WebSiteHits;
DROP TABLE dbo.WebSiteHitsHistory;
DROP PARTITION SCHEME HitDateRangeScheme;
DROP PARTITION FUNCTION HitsDateRange;
GO
```

How It Works

Dropping a partition scheme and function requires that they are no longer being bound to a table. In this example, we removed their usage by dropping the test tables that were utilizing the partition function and schema. If you don't want to lose this data, you should copy this data to another table. If your goal is to simply have all of the data in one partition, you can merge all of the partitions while keeping the partition scheme and function. (A partitioned table with a single partition is functionally equivalent to a nonpartitioned table.)

If you had originally created the table without any clustered indexes, you can use the `CREATE INDEX DROP EXISTING` option to rebuild the index without the partition scheme reference.

To remove the partition scheme, you utilize the `DROP PARTITION SCHEME` statement, specifying the name of the partition scheme to drop. To remove the partition function, you utilize the `DROP PARTITION FUNCTION` statement, specifying the name of the partition function to drop.

15-13. Easing VLDB Manageability (with Filegroups)

Problem

You have a very large database with some very large tables. You want to minimize the performance impact of these tables on the rest of the database.

Solution

Place the large tables on specific filegroups that are placed on different disks than the rest of the database.

How It Works

Filegroups are often used for very large databases because they can ease backup administration and potentially improve performance by distributing data over disk LUNs or arrays. When creating a table, you can specify that it be created on a specific filegroup. For example, if you have a table that you know will become very large, you can designate that it be created on a specific filegroup.

The basic syntax for designating a table's filegroup is as follows:

```
CREATE TABLE ...
[ ON {filegroup | "default" }] [ { TEXTIMAGE_ON { filegroup | "default" } ]
```

Table 15-6 details the arguments of this command.

Table 15-6. *Arguments for Creating a Table on a Filegroup*

Argument	Description
`filegroup`	This specifies the name of the filegroup on which the table will be created.
`"DEFAULT"`	This sets the table to be created on the default filegroup defined for the database.
`TEXTIMAGE_ON { filegroup | "DEFAULT" }`	This option stores in a separate filegroup the data from text, ntext, image, xml, varchar(max), nvarchar(max), and varbinary(max) data types.

Recipe 15-1 demonstrated how to create additional filegroups in a database, and Recipe 15-9 demonstrated how to create a table on a specific filegroup.

15-14. Compressing Table Data

Problem

You want to reduce the amount of disk space required for storing data in a table.

Solution

Utilize row or page data compression.

How It Works

Two forms of compression are available in SQL Server for tables, indexes, and filegroups: row-level and page-level compression.

Row compression applies variable-length storage to numeric data types (for example, int, bigint, and decimal) and fixed-length types such as money and datetime. Row compression also applies variable-length format to fixed-character strings and doesn't store trailing blank characters, NULL, and 0 values.

Page compression includes row compression and also adds prefix and dictionary compression. Prefix compression involves the storage of column prefix values that are stored multiple times in a column across rows and replaces the redundant prefixes with references to the single value. Dictionary compression occurs after prefix compression and involves finding repeated data values anywhere on the data page (not just prefixes) and then replacing the redundancies with a pointer to the single value.

To enable compression on a new table being created, utilize the DATA_COMPRESSION option in the CREATE TABLE statement, and select either NONE, ROW, or PAGE.

```
CREATE TABLE dbo.DataCompressionTest
       (
        JobPostinglD INT NOT NULL IDENTITY PRIMARY KEY CLUSTERED,
        CandidatelD INT NOT NULL,
        JobDESC CHAR(2000) NOT NULL
       )
WITH (DATA_COMPRESSION = ROW);
GO
```

The following example creates a table and inserts 100,000 rows into this table of a random integer in one column and a string consisting of 50 a characters. (The GO command, followed by a number, repeats that batch the specified number of times.)

```
CREATE TABLE dbo.ArchiveJobPosting
       (
        JobPostinglD INT NOT NULL IDENTITY PRIMARY KEY CLUSTERED,
        CandidatelD INT NOT NULL,
        JobDESC CHAR(2000) NOT NULL
       );
GO
```

```
INSERT  dbo.ArchiveJobPosting
        (CandidateID,
         JobDESC)
VALUES (CAST(RAND() * 10 AS INT),
        REPLICATE('a', 50))
GO 100000
```

The sp_estimate_data_compression_savings system stored procedure estimates the amount of disk savings if enabling row- or page-level compression. The stored procedure takes five arguments: the schema name of the table to be compressed, object name, index ID, partition number, and data compression method (NONE, ROW, or PAGE). The following example checks to see how much space can be saved by using row compression:

```
EXECUTE sp_estimate_data_compression_savings @schema_name = 'dbo', @object_name =
'ArchiveJobPosting', @index_id = NULL, @partition_number = NULL, @data_compression = 'ROW';
```

This returns the following information (results pivoted for readability):

```
object_name                                        ArchiveJobPosting
schema_name                                        dbo
index_id                                           1
partition_number                                   1
size_with_current_compression_setting(KB)          200752
size_with_requested_compression_setting(KB)        6712
sample_size_with_current_compression_setting(KB)   39240
sample_size_with_requested_compression_setting(KB) 1312
```

■ **Note** You may receive different results on your system.

As you can see from the stored procedure results, adding row compression would save more than 194,000KB with the current data set. The sample size data is based on the stored procedure loading sample data into a cloned table in tempdb and validating the compression ratio accordingly.

The following example tests to see whether there are benefits to using page-level compression:

```
EXECUTE sp_estimate_data_compression_savings @schema_name = 'dbo', @object_name =
'ArchiveJobPosting', @index_id = NULL, @partition_number = NULL, @data_compression = 'PAGE';
```

This returns the following:

```
object_name                                        ArchiveJobPosting
schema_name                                        dbo
index_id                                           1
partition_number                                   1
size_with_current_compression_setting(KB)          200752
size_with_requested_compression_setting(KB)        1368
sample_size_with_current_compression_setting(KB)   39776
sample_size_with_requested_compression_setting(KB) 272
```

Note You may receive different results on your system.

Sure enough, the page-level compression shows additional benefits beyond just row-level compression. To turn page-level compression on for the table, execute the following statement:

```
ALTER TABLE dbo.ArchiveJobPosting REBUILD WITH (DATA_COMPRESSION = PAGE);
```

Data compression can also be configured at the partition level. In the next set of commands, a new partitioning function and scheme are created and applied to a new table. The table will use varying compression levels based on the partition.

```
CREATE PARTITION FUNCTION pfn_ArchivePart(int)
AS RANGE LEFT FOR VALUES (50000, 100000, 150000);
GO
CREATE PARTITION SCHEME psc_ArchivePart
AS PARTITION pfn_ArchivePart
TO (hitfg1, hitfg2, hitfg3, hitfg4);
GO
CREATE TABLE dbo.ArchiveJobPosting_V2
        (
         JobPostingID INT NOT NULL IDENTITY PRIMARY KEY CLUSTERED,
         CandidateID INT NOT NULL,
         JobDesc CHAR(2000) NOT NULL
        )
ON      psc_ArchivePart(JobPostingID)
WITH (
    DATA_COMPRESSION = PAGE ON PARTITIONS (1 TO 3),
    DATA_COMPRESSION = ROW ON PARTITIONS (4));
GO
```

The partitions to apply a data compression type to can be specified as a single partition number, a range of partitions with the starting and ending partitions separated by the TO keyword, or a comma-delimited list of partition numbers and ranges. All of these partition options can be used at the same time.

If you want to change the compression level for any of the partitions, utilize the ALTER TABLE statement. This example changes partition 4 from row to page compression:

```
ALTER TABLE dbo.ArchiveJobPosting_V2
REBUILD PARTITION = 4
WITH (DATA_COMPRESSION = PAGE);
GO
```

15-15. Rebuilding a Heap

Problem

You have a heap (a table without a clustered index) that has become severely fragmented, and you want to reduce both the fragmentation and the number of forwarded records in the table.

Solution

Utilize the REBUILD option of the ALTER TABLE statement to rebuild a heap.

```
CREATE TABLE dbo.HeapTest
(
        HeapTest VARCHAR(1000)
);
GO
INSERT INTO dbo.HeapTest (HeapTest)
VALUES ('Test');
GO 10000
SELECT  index_type_desc,
        fragment_count,
        page_count,
        forwarded_record_count
FROM    sys.dm_db_index_physical_stats(DB_ID(), DEFAULT, DEFAULT, DEFAULT, 'DETAILED')
WHERE   object_id = OBJECT_ID('HeapTest');
GO
UPDATE dbo.HeapTest
SET HeapTest = REPLICATE('Test',250);
GO
SELECT  index_type_desc,
        fragment_count,
        page_count,
        forwarded_record_count
FROM    sys.dm_db_index_physical_stats(DB_ID(), DEFAULT, DEFAULT, DEFAULT, 'DETAILED')
WHERE   object_id = OBJECT_ID('HeapTest');
GO
ALTER TABLE dbo.HeapTest REBUILD;
GO
SELECT  index_type_desc,
        fragment_count,
        page_count,
        forwarded_record_count
FROM    sys.dm_db_index_physical_stats(DB_ID(), DEFAULT, DEFAULT, DEFAULT, 'DETAILED')
WHERE   object_id = OBJECT_ID('HeapTest');
GO
```

These queries return the following result sets:

```
index_type_desc    fragment_count    page_count    forwarded_record_count
---------------    --------------    ----------    ----------------------
HEAP               5                 23            0
index_type_desc    fragment_count    page_count    forwarded_record_count
---------------    --------------    ----------    ----------------------
HEAP               5                 1442          9934
index_type_desc    fragment_count    page_count    forwarded_record_count
---------------    --------------    ----------    ----------------------
HEAP               3                 1431          0
```

■ **Note** The `fragment_count` value will differ on your system and will even change if you run this recipe multiple times.

How It Works

In this example, a table is created with a single `VARCHAR(1000)` column and 10,000 rows are added to this table with the value `Test`. An `UPDATE` statement is then run, which expands the data in this column to be `Test` repeated 250 times, for a total length of 1,000, which completely fills up the column. When the data is initially populated with the `INSERT` statement, the data pages are filled with as many rows as can fit. When the `UPDATE` statement is run, most of these rows have to move to other pages because fewer rows can fit onto a page. When rows are moved on a heap, a forwarding record is left in the place of the original row, causing an even further increased need for data pages.

During this process, the physical index statistics are being computed. From the results, it is obvious that the `UPDATE` statement causes a massive growth in the number of pages required to hold the data and in the number of forwarded records. After the table is rebuilt, the table now uses fewer pages, and the table no longer has any forwarded records.

CHAPTER 16

Managing Indexes

by Jason Brimhall

Indexes assist with query processing by speeding up access to the data stored in tables and views. Indexes allow for ordered access to data based on an ordering of data rows. These rows are ordered based upon the values stored in certain columns. These columns comprise the index key columns, and their values (for any given row) are a row's index key.

This chapter contains recipes for creating, altering, and dropping different types of indexes. I demonstrate how indexes can be created, including the syntax for index options, support for partition schemes, the `INCLUDE` command, page and row lock disabling, index disabling, and the ability to perform online operations.

For the exercises performed in this chapter, you may wish to back up the `AdventureWorks2012` database beforehand so that you can restore it to its original state after going through the recipes.

Note For coverage of index maintenance, reindexing, and rebuilding (`ALTER INDEX`), see Chapter 23. Indexed views are covered in Chapter 14. For coverage of index performance troubleshooting and fragmentation, see Chapter 23.

Index Overview

An index is a database object that, when created, can provide faster access paths to data and can facilitate faster query execution. Indexes are used to provide SQL Server with a more efficient method of accessing the data. Instead of always searching every data page in a table, an index facilitates retrieving specific rows without having to read a table's entire content.

By default, rows in a regular unindexed table aren't stored in any particular order. A table in an orderless state is called a *heap*. To retrieve rows from a heap based on a matching set of search conditions, SQL Server would have to read through all the rows in the table. Even if only one row matched the search criteria and that row just happened to be the first row the SQL Server database engine read, SQL Server would still need to evaluate every single table row because there is no other way for it to know if other matching rows exist. Such a scan for information is known as a *full-table scan*. For a large table, that might mean reading hundreds, thousands, millions, or even billions of rows just to retrieve a single row. However, if SQL Server knows that there is an index on a column (or columns) of a table, then it may be able to use that index to search for matching records more efficiently.

In SQL Server, a table is contained in one or more *partitions*. A partition is a unit of organization that allows you to separate allocation of data horizontally within a table and/or index while still maintaining a single logical object. When a table is created, by default, all of its data is contained within a single partition. A partition contains heaps or, when indexes are created, *B-tree structures*.

When an index is created, its index key data is stored in a B-tree structure. A B-tree structure starts with a root node, which is the beginning of the index. This *root node* has index data that contains a range of index key values that point to the next level of index nodes, called the *intermediate leaf level* The bottom level of the node is called the *leaf level.* The leaf level differs based on whether the actual index type is *clustered* or *nonclustered.* If it is a clustered index, the leaf level is the actual data page. If it's a nonclustered index, the leaf level contains pointers to the heap or clustered index data pages.

A clustered index determines how the actual table data is physically stored. You can designate only one clustered index. This index type stores the data according to the designated index key column or columns. Figure 16-1 demonstrates the B-tree structure of the clustered index. Notice that the leaf level consists of the actual data pages.

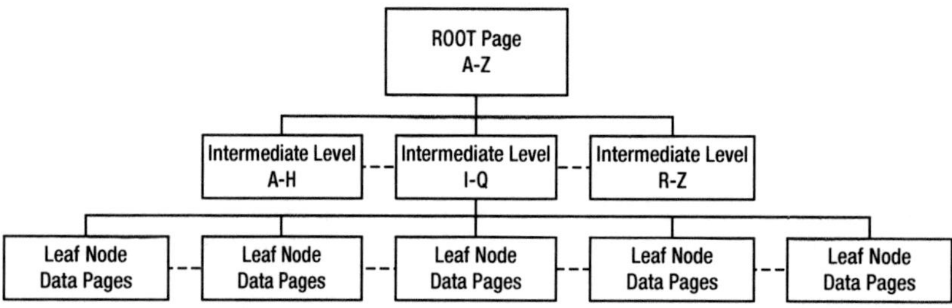

Figure 16-1. *B-tree structure of a clustered index*

Clustered index selection is a critical choice, because you can have only one clustered index for a single table. In general, good candidates for clustered indexes include columns that are queried often in range queries because the data is then physically organized in a particular order. Range queries use the BETWEEN keyword and the greater-than (>) and less-than (<) operators. Other columns to consider are those used to order large result sets, those used in aggregate functions, and those that contain entirely unique values. Frequently updated columns and non-unique columns are usually not a good choice for a clustered index key, because the clustered index key is contained in the leaf level of all dependent nonclustered indexes, causing excessive reordering and modifications. For this same reason, you should also avoid creating a clustered index with too many or very wide (many bytes) index keys.

Nonclustered indexes store index pages separately from the physical data, with pointers to the physical data located in the index pages and nodes. Nonclustered index columns are stored in the order of the index key column values. You can have up to 999 nonclustered indexes on a table or indexed view. For nonclustered indexes, the leaf node level is the index key coupled to a row locator that points to either the row of a heap or the clustered index row key, as shown in Figure 16-2.

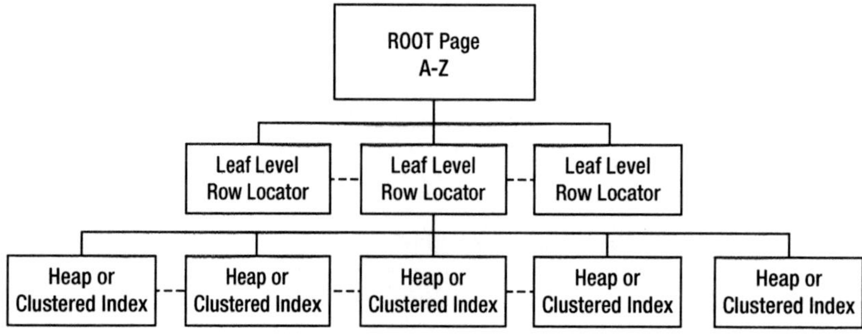

Figure 16-2. *B-tree structure of a nonclustered index*

When selecting columns to be used for nonclustered indexes, look for those columns that are frequently referenced in WHERE, JOIN, and ORDER BY clauses. Search for highly selective columns that would return smaller result sets (less than 20 percent of all rows in a table). *Selectivity* refers to how many rows exist for each unique index key value. If a column has poor selectivity, for example, containing only zeros or ones, it is unlikely that SQL Server will take advantage of that query when creating the query execution plan, because of its poor selectivity.

An index, either clustered or nonclustered, is based on one or more key values. The index key refers to columns used to define the index itself. SQL Server also has a feature that allows the addition of non-key columns to the leaf level of the index by using the new INCLUDE clause demonstrated later in the chapter. This feature allows more of your query's selected columns to be returned or "covered" by a single nonclustered index, thus reducing total I/O, because SQL Server doesn't have to access the clustered leaf level data pages at all.

You can use up to 16 key columns in a single index, so long as you don't exceed 900 bytes of all index key columns combined. You can't use large object data types within the index key, including varchar(max), nvarchar(max), varbinary(max), xml, ntext, text, and the image data types.

A clustered or nonclustered index can be specified as either unique or non-unique. Choosing a unique index ensures that the data values inserted into the key column or columns are unique. For unique indexes using multiple keys (called a *composite index*), the combination of the key values has to be unique for every row in the table.

As noted earlier, indexes can be massively beneficial in terms of your query performance, but there are also costs associated with them. You should only add indexes based on expected query activity, and you should continually monitor whether indexes are still being used over time. If not, they should be removed. Too many indexes on a table can cause performance overhead whenever data modifications are performed in the table, because SQL Server must maintain the index changes alongside the data changes. Ongoing maintenance activities such as index rebuilding and reorganizations will also be prolonged with excessive indexing.

These next few recipes demonstrate how to create, modify, disable, view, and drop indexes.

■ **Note** See Chapter 23 to learn how to view which indexes are being used for a query. This chapter also covers how to view index fragmentation and identify whether an index is being used over time. To learn how to rebuild or reorganize indexes, see Chapter 23.

16-1. Creating a Table Index

Problem

You have a table that has been created without any indexes. You need to create indexes on this table.

Solution

Here I show you how to create two types of indexes, one clustered and the other nonclustered. An index is created by using the CREATE INDEX command. This chapter reviews the many facets of this command; however, the basic syntax used in this solution is as follows:

```
CREATE [ UNIQUE ] [ CLUSTERED | NONCLUSTERED ] INDEX index_name
ON {
[ database_name. [ schema_name ] . | schema_name. ] table_or_view_name} ( column [ ASC | DESC ]
[ ,...n ] )
```

The arguments of this command are described in Table 16-1.

Table 16-1. CREATE INDEX Command Arguments

Argument	Description
[UNIQUE]	You can have only one primary key on each table. However, if you wish to enforce uniqueness in other non-key columns, you can designate that the index be created with the UNIQUE constraint. You can create multiple UNIQUE indexes for a single table and can include columns that contain NULL values (although only one NULL value is allowed per column combo).
[CLUSTERED | NONCLUSTERED]	This specifies the index type, either CLUSTERED or NONCLUSTERED. You can have only one CLUSTERED index but up to 999 NONCLUSTERED indexes.
index_name	This defines the name of the new index.
[database_name. [schema_name].	This indicates the table or view to be indexed.
| schema_name.] table_or_view_name}Column	This specifies the column or columns to be used as part of the index key.
[ASC | DESC]	This defines the specific column order of indexing, either ASC for ascending order or DESC for descending order.

To help demonstrate the creation of indexes for this example, I create a new table in the AdventureWorks2012 database and intentionally exclude a PRIMARY KEY in the table definition:

```
USE AdventureWorks2012;
GO
If Not Exists (Select 1 from sys.objects where name = 'TerminationReason' and SCHEMA_
NAME(schema_id) = 'HumanResources')
BEGIN
CREATE TABLE HumanResources.TerminationReason(
  TerminationReasonID smallint IDENTITY(1,1) NOT NULL,
  TerminationReason varchar(50) NOT NULL,
  DepartmentID smallint NOT NULL,
  CONSTRAINT FK_TerminationReason_DepartmentID FOREIGN KEY (DepartmentID)
REFERENCES HumanResources.Department(DepartmentID)
      );
END
```

Before I demonstrate how to use CREATE INDEX, it is important to remember that when a primary key is created on a column using CREATE TABLE or ALTER TABLE, that primary key also creates an index. Instead of defining this up front, in this example, I create a CLUSTERED index on TerminationReasonID using ALTER TABLE with ADD CONSTRAINT:

```
USE AdventureWorks2012;
GO
ALTER TABLE HumanResources.TerminationReason
ADD CONSTRAINT PK_TerminationReason PRIMARY KEY CLUSTERED (TerminationReasonID);
```

Next, I create a nonclustered index on the Departments column.

```
USE AdventureWorks2012;
GO
CREATE NONCLUSTERED INDEX NCI_TerminationReason_DepartmentID ON HumanResources.TerminationReason
(DepartmentID);
```

How It Works

In this exercise, the TerminationReason table was created without a primary key defined, meaning that, initially, the table was a heap. The primary key was then added afterward using ALTER TABLE. The word CLUSTERED follows the PRIMARY KEY statement, thus designating a clustered index with the new constraint.

```
ALTER TABLE HumanResources.TerminationReason
ADD CONSTRAINT PK_TerminationReason PRIMARY KEY CLUSTERED (TerminationReasonID)
```

Had the TerminationReasonID column not been chosen as the primary key, you could have still defined a clustered index on it by using CREATE INDEX.

```
USE AdventureWorks2012;
GO
CREATE CLUSTERED INDEX CI_TerminationReason_TerminationReasonID ON
HumanResources.TerminationReason (TerminationReasonID);
```

Had a nonclustered index already existed for the table, the creation of the new clustered index would have caused the nonclustered index to be rebuilt in order to swap the nonclustered leaf level row identifier with the clustered key.

The nonclustered index in the example was created as follows:

```
USE AdventureWorks2012;
GO
CREATE NONCLUSTERED INDEX NCI_TerminationReason_DepartmentID ON HumanResources.TerminationReason
(DepartmentID);
```

The only difference in syntax between the two index types is the use of CLUSTERED or NONCLUSTERED between the keywords CREATE and INDEX.

16-2. Enforcing Uniqueness on Non-key Columns

Problem

You need to enforce uniqueness on a non-key column in a table.

Solution

Using the table created in the previous recipe (HumanResources.TerminationReason), execute the following script to create a unique index:

```
USE AdventureWorks2012;
GO
CREATE UNIQUE NONCLUSTERED INDEX UNI_TerminationReason ON HumanResources.TerminationReason
(TerminationReason);
```

Now, I insert two new rows into the table with success.

```
USE AdventureWorks2012;
GO
INSERT INTO HumanResources.TerminationReason (DepartmentID, TerminationReason)
  VALUES (1, 'Bad Engineering Skills')
  ,(2, 'Breaks Expensive Tools');
```

If I attempt to insert a row with a duplicate TerminationReason value, an error will be raised:

```
USE AdventureWorks2012;
GO
INSERT INTO HumanResources.TerminationReason (DepartmentID, TerminationReason)
  VALUES (2, 'Bad Engineering Skills');
```

This query returns the following (results pivoted for formatting):

```
Msg 2601, Level 14, State 1, Line 9
Cannot insert duplicate key row in object 'HumanResources.TerminationReason'
with unique index 'UNI_TerminationReason'.
The duplicate key value is (Bad Engineering Skills).
The statement has been terminated.
```

Selecting the current rows from the table shows that only the first two rows were inserted.

```
USE AdventureWorks2012;
GO
SELECT TerminationReasonID, TerminationReason, DepartmentID
  FROM HumanResources.TerminationReason;
```

This query returns the following (results pivoted for formatting):

```
TerminationReasonID  TerminationReason       DepartmentID
-------------------  ----------------------  ------------
1                    Bad Engineering Skills  1
2                    Breaks Expensive Tools  2
```

How It Works

A unique index was created on the TerminationReason column, which means that each row must have a unique value. You can choose multiple unique constraints for a single table. NULL values are permitted in a unique index and may not be duplicated, much like non-NULL values. Like a primary key, unique indexes enforce entity integrity by ensuring that rows can be uniquely identified.

16-3. Creating an Index on Multiple Columns

Problem

You need to create a composite index to support queries that utilize multiple columns in a search predicate or result set.

Solution

In previous recipes, I've shown you how to create an index on a single column; however, many times you will want more than one column to be used in a single index. Use composite indexes when two or more columns are often searched within the same query or are often used in conjunction with one another.

In this example, I have determined that TerminationReason and DepartmentID will often be used in the same WHERE clause of a SELECT query. With that in mind, I create the following multi-column NONCLUSTERED INDEX:

```
USE AdventureWorks2012;
GO
CREATE NONCLUSTERED INDEX NI_TerminationReason_TerminationReason_DepartmentID
  ON HumanResources.TerminationReason(TerminationReason, DepartmentID);
```

How It Works

Choosing which columns to index is a bit of an art. You'll want to add indexes to columns that you know will be commonly queried; however, you must always keep a column's selectivity in mind. If a column has poor selectivity (containing a few unique values across thousands of rows), for example, it is unlikely that SQL Server will take advantage of that index when creating the query execution plan.

One general rule of thumb when creating a composite index is to put the most selective columns at the beginning, followed by the other, less-selective columns. In this recipe's example, the TerminationReason was chosen as the first column, followed by DepartmentID. Both are guaranteed to be totally unique in the table and are, therefore, equally selective.

■ **Tip** Use the Database Tuning Advisor to help make index suggestions for you based on a query or batch of queries. See Chapter 23 for more information on index usage and performance.

16-4. Defining Index Column Sort Direction

Problem

You need to create an index to support the sort order expected by the application and business requirements.

Solution

The default sort for an indexed column is ascending order. You can explicitly set the ordering using ASC or DESC in the column definition of CREATE INDEX:

```
( column [ ASC | DESC ] [ ,...n ] )
```

In this example, I add a new column to a table and then index the column using a descending order:

```
USE AdventureWorks2012;
GO
ALTER TABLE HumanResources.TerminationReason
ADD ViolationSeverityLevel smallint;
GO
CREATE NONCLUSTERED INDEX NI_TerminationReason_ViolationSeverityLevel
  ON HumanResources.TerminationReason (ViolationSeverityLevel DESC);
```

How It Works

In this recipe's example, a new column, ViolationSeverityLevel, was added to the TerminationReason table:

```
USE AdventureWorks2012;
GO
ALTER TABLE HumanResources.TerminationReason
ADD ViolationSeverityLevel smallint;
GO
```

Query authors may want to most commonly sort on this value, showing ViolationSeverityLevel from highest to lowest. Matching index order to how you think users will use ORDER BY in the query can improve query performance, because SQL Server isn't then required to re-sort the data when the query is processed. The index is created with the DESC instruction after the column name:

```
(ViolationSeverityLevel DESC)
```

If you have multiple key columns in your index, each can have its own sort order.

16-5. Viewing Index Metadata

Problem

You have created indexes in your database. Now you need some mechanism for tracking where they have been created and what the names, types, and columns are that define them.

Solution

Use the sp_helpindex system stored procedure to view the index names, descriptions, and keys for indexes on a specific table. This system stored procedure only takes a single argument, the name of the table whose indexes you want to view.

This example demonstrates viewing all indexes on the Employee table:

```
USE AdventureWorks2012;
GO
EXEC sp_helpindex 'HumanResources.Employee';
```

This returns the following sample results:

index_name	index_description	index_keys
AK_Employee_LoginID	nonclustered, unique located on PRIMARY	LoginID
AK_Employee_NationalIDNumber	nonclustered, unique located on PRIMARY	NationalIDNumber
AK_Employee_rowguid	nonclustered, unique located on PRIMARY	rowguid
IX_Employee_OrganizationLevel_ OrganizationNode	nonclustered located on PRIMARY	OrganizationLevel, OrganizationNode
IX_Employee_OrganizationNode	nonclustered located on PRIMARY	OrganizationNode

For more in-depth analysis of indexes, you can use the sys.indexes system catalog view. For example, the following query shows index options (which are discussed later in the chapter) for the HumanResources.Employee table:

```
USE AdventureWorks2012;
GO
SELECT index_name = SUBSTRING(name, 1,30) ,
   allow_row_locks,
   allow_page_locks,
   is_disabled,
   fill_factor,
   has_filter
  FROM  sys.indexes
  WHERE object_id = OBJECT_ID('HumanResources.Employee');
```

This returns the following sample results:

index_name	allow_row_locks	allow_page_locks	is_disabled	fill_factor	has_filter
PK_Employee_ BusinessEntityID	1	1	0	0	0
IX_Employee_ OrganizationNode	1	1	0	0	0
IX_Employee_ OrganizationLevel_	1	1	0	0	0
AK_Employee_LoginID	1	1	0	0	0
AK_Employee_ NationalIDNumber	1	1	0	0	0

How It Works

You can use the system stored procedure sp_helpindex call to list the indexes on a specific table. The output also returns a description of the indexes, including the type and filegroup location. The key columns defined for the index are also listed.

The sys.indexes system catalog view can also be used to find out more about the configured settings of a specific index.

■ **Tip** For related index keys and included columns, use the sys.index_columns catalog view.

Several of the options shown in this system catalog view haven't been covered yet, but Table 16-2 discusses some of them that I've discussed.

Table 16-2. *A Subset of the sys.indexes System Catalog Columns*

Column	Description
object_id	This is the object identifier of the table or view to which the index belongs. You can use the OBJECT_NAME function to show the table or view name, or you can use OBJECT_ID to convert a table or view name into its database object identifier.
name	This indicates the index name.
index_id	When index_id is 0, the index is a heap. When index_id is 1, the index is a clustered index. When index_id is greater than 1, it is a nonclustered index.

(continued)

Table 16-2. *(continued)*

Column	Description
type	This specifies the index type, which can be 0 for heap, 1 for clustered index, 2 for nonclustered, 3 for an XML index, 4 for spatial, 5 for clustered columnstore index, and 6 for nonclustered columnstore index.
type_desc	This defines the index type description.
is_unique	When is_unique is 1, the index is a unique index.
is_primary_key	When is_primary_key is 1, the index is the result of a primary key constraint.
is_unique_constraint	When is_unique_constraint is 1, the index is the result of a unique constraint.

16-6. Disabling an Index

Problem

You have had a disk error and would like to defer creation of an index affected by the disk error.

Solution

Disable the index. Consider disabling an index as an index troubleshooting technique or if a disk error has occurred and you would like to defer the index's re-creation.

■ **Caution** If you disable a clustered index, keep in mind that the table index data will no longer be accessible. This is because the leaf level of a clustered index is the actual table data itself. Also, reenabling the index means either re-creating or rebuilding it (see the "How It Works" section for more information).

An index is disabled by using the ALTER INDEX command. The syntax is as follows:

```
ALTER INDEX index_name ON
table_or_view_name DISABLE
```

The command takes two arguments: the name of the index and the name of the table or view on which the index is created. In this example, I disable the UNI_TerminationReason index on the TerminationReason table:

```
USE AdventureWorks2012;
GO
ALTER INDEX UNI_TerminationReason
  ON HumanResources.TerminationReason DISABLE
```

How It Works

This recipe demonstrated how to disable an index. If an index is disabled, the index definition remains in the system tables, although the user can no longer use the index. For nonclustered indexes on a table, the index data is actually removed from the database. For a clustered index on a table, the data remains on disk, but because the index is disabled, you can't query it. For a clustered or nonclustered index on the view, the index data is removed from the database.

To reenable the index, you can use either the `CREATE INDEX` with `DROP_EXISTING` command (see later in this chapter) or `ALTER INDEX REBUILD` (described in Chapter 23). Rebuilding a disabled nonclustered index reuses the existing space used by the original index.

16-7. Dropping Indexes

Problem

You have determined that an index is no longer used and needs to be removed from the database.

Solution

Drop the index. When you drop an index, it is physically removed from the database. If this is a clustered index, the table's data remains in an unordered (heap) form. You can remove an index entirely from a database by using the `DROP INDEX` command. The basic syntax is as follows:

```
DROP INDEX <table_or_view_name>.<index_name> [ ,...n ]
```

In this example, I demonstrate dropping a single index from a table:

```
USE AdventureWorks2012;
GO
DROP INDEX HumanResources.TerminationReason.UNI_TerminationReason;
```

How It Works

You can drop one or more indexes for a table using the `DROP ... INDEX` command. Dropping an index frees the space taken up by the index and removes the index definition from the database. You can't use `DROP INDEX` to remove indexes that result from the creation of a `PRIMARY KEY` or `UNIQUE CONSTRAINT`. If you drop a clustered index that has nonclustered indexes on it, those nonclustered indexes will also be rebuilt in order to swap the clustered index key for a row identifier of the heap.

16-8. Changing an Existing Index

Problem

You need to alter an existing index to add or remove columns or to reorganize the column order.

Solution

Change the column definition of an existing index by using `CREATE INDEX ... DROP_EXISTING`. This option also has the advantage of dropping and re-creating an index within a single command (instead of using both `DROP INDEX` and `CREATE INDEX`). Also, using `DROP_EXISTING` on a clustered index will not cause existing nonclustered indexes to be automatically rebuilt, unless the index column definition has changed.

Here I show you how to drop and re-create an index within a single execution, as well as change the key column definition of an existing index. The `ALTER INDEX` can be used to change index options, rebuild and reorganize indexes (reviewed in Chapter 23), and disable an index, but it is not used to add, delete, or rearrange columns in the index.

The following example demonstrates just rebuilding an existing nonclustered index (no change in the column definition):

```
USE AdventureWorks2012;
GO
CREATE NONCLUSTERED INDEX NI_TerminationReason_TerminationReason_DepartmentID
  ON HumanResources.TerminationReason(TerminationReason, DepartmentID)
WITH (DROP_EXISTING = ON);
GO
```

Next, a new column is added to the existing nonclustered index.

```
USE AdventureWorks2012;
GO
CREATE NONCLUSTERED INDEX NI_TerminationReason_TerminationReason_DepartmentID
  ON HumanResources.TerminationReason(TerminationReason, ViolationSeverityLevel, DepartmentID
DESC)
WITH (DROP_EXISTING = ON);
GO
```

How It Works

In the first example, `CREATE INDEX` didn't change anything about the existing index definition but instead just rebuilt it by using the `DROP_EXISTING` clause. Rebuilding an index can help defragment the data, something that is discussed in more detail in Chapter 23.

In the second statement, a new column was added to the existing index and placed right before the `DepartmentID` column. The index was re-created with the new index key column. You cannot use `DROP_EXISTING` to change the name of the index. For that, use `DROP INDEX` and `CREATE INDEX` with the new index name.

Controlling Index Build Performance and Concurrency

So far in this chapter, I've reviewed how an index is defined, but note that you can also determine under what circumstances an index is built. For example, when creating an index in SQL Server, to improve the performance, you can designate that a parallel plan of execution is used, instantiating multiple processors to help complete a time-consuming build. In addition to this, you could also direct SQL Server to create the index in `tempdb`, instead of causing file growth operations in the index's home database. If you are using Enterprise Edition, you can also allow concurrent user query access to the underlying table during the index creation by using the `ONLINE` option.

The next three recipes demonstrate methods for improving the performance of the index build, as well as improving user concurrency during the operation.

16-9. Sorting in Tempdb

Problem

You need to mitigate the length of time to create indexes as well as minimize potential for file growth operations in the user database.

Solution

If index creation times are taking too long for what you expect, you can try to use the index option SORT_IN_TEMPDB to improve index build performance (for larger tables). This option pushes the intermediate index build results to the tempdb database instead of using the user database where the index is housed.

In this recipe, I show you how to push index creation processing to the tempdb system database. The tempdb system database is used to manage user connections, temporary tables, temporary stored procedures, or temporary work tables needed to process queries on the SQL Server instance. Depending on the database activity on your SQL Server instance, you can sometimes reap performance benefits by isolating the tempdb database on its own disk array, separate from other databases.

The syntax for this option, which can be used in both CREATE INDEX and ALTER INDEX, is as follows:

```
WITH (SORT_IN_TEMPDB = { ON | OFF })
```

The default for this option is OFF. In this example, I create a new nonclustered index with the SORT_IN_TEMPDB option enabled.

```
USE AdventureWorks2012;
GO
CREATE NONCLUSTERED INDEX NI_Address_PostalCode
  ON Person.Address (PostalCode)
  WITH (SORT_IN_TEMPDB = ON);
```

How It Works

The SORT_IN_TEMPDB option enables the use of the tempdb database for intermediate index results. This option may decrease the amount of time it takes to create the index for a large table, but with the trade-off that the tempdb system database will need additional space to participate in this operation.

16-10. Controlling Index Creation Parallelism

Problem

You need to limit the number of processors that index creation can utilize.

Solution

If using SQL Server Enterprise Edition with a multiprocessor server, you can control/limit the number of processors potentially used in an index creation operation by using the MAXDOP index option. *Parallelism,* which in this context is the use of two or more processors to fulfill a single query statement, can potentially improve the performance of the index creation operation.

The syntax for this option, which can be used in both CREATE INDEX and ALTER INDEX, is as follows:

```
MAXDOP = max_degree_of_parallelism
```

The default value for this option is 0, which means that SQL Server can choose any or all of the available processors for the operation. A MAXDOP value of 1 disables parallelism on the index creation.

■ **Tip** Limiting parallelism for index creation may improve concurrency for user activity running during the build but may also increase the time it takes for the index to be created.

This example demonstrates how to control the number of processors used in parallel plan execution (parallelism) during an index creation:

```
USE AdventureWorks2012;
GO
CREATE NONCLUSTERED INDEX NI_Address_AddressLine1
  ON Person.Address (AddressLine1)
  WITH (MAXDOP = 4);
```

How It Works

In this recipe, the index creation was limited to four processors.

```
WITH (MAXDOP = 4)
```

Just because you set MAXDOP doesn't guarantee that SQL Server will actually use the number of processors that you designate. It only ensures that SQL Server will not exceed the MAXDOP threshold.

16-11. User Table Access During Index Creation

Problem

Users must have continued access throughout the creation of indexes.

Solution

In this recipe, I show you how to allow query activity to continue to access the index even while an index creation process is executing. If you are using SQL Server Enterprise Edition, you can allow concurrent user query access to the underlying table during index creation by using the new ONLINE option, which is demonstrated in this next recipe.

```
USE AdventureWorks2012;
GO
CREATE NONCLUSTERED INDEX NCI_ProductVendor_MinOrderQty
  ON Purchasing.ProductVendor(MinOrderQty)
  WITH (ONLINE = ON); -- Online option is an Enterprise Edition feature
```

How It Works

With the ONLINE option in the WITH clause of the index creation, long-term table locks are not held during index creation. This can provide better concurrency on larger indexes that contain frequently accessed data. When the ONLINE option is set ON, only intent share locks are held on the source table for the duration of the index creation, instead of the default behavior of a longer-term table lock held for the duration of the index creation.

Index Options

The next three recipes cover options that affect performance, each in its own different way. For example, the INCLUDE keyword allows you to add non-key columns to a nonclustered index. This allows you to create a covering index that can be used to return data to the user without having to access the clustered index data.

The second recipe discusses how the PAD_INDEX and FILLFACTOR options determine how to set the initial percentage of rows to fill the index leaf level pages and intermediate levels of an index. The recipe discusses how the fill factor affects the performance of not only queries but also insert, update, and delete operations.

The third recipe covers how to disable certain locking types for a specific index. As discussed in the recipe, using these options allows you to control both concurrency and resource usage when queries access the index.

16-12. Using an Index INCLUDE

Problem

You need to provide a covering index for a query that requires the use of several non-key columns.

Solution

One solution to this problem is the INCLUDE keyword, which allows you to add up to 1,023 non-key columns to the nonclustered index, helping you improve query performance by creating a covered index. These non-key columns are not stored at each level of the index but instead are found only in the leaf level of the nonclustered index.

A *covering query* is a query whose referenced columns are found entirely within a nonclustered index. This scenario often results in better query performance, because SQL Server does not have to retrieve the actual data from the clustered index or heap: it only needs to read the data stored in the nonclustered index. The drawback, however, is that you can only include up to 16 columns or up to 900 bytes for an index key.

The syntax for using INCLUDE with CREATE NONCLUSTERED INDEX is as follows:

```
CREATE NONCLUSTERED INDEX index_name
ON table_or_view_name ( column [ ASC | DESC ] [ ,...n ] ) INCLUDE ( column [,...n ] )
```

The first column list is for key index columns, and the column list after INCLUDE is for non-key columns. In this example, I create a new large object data type column to the TerminationReason table. I drop the existing index on DepartmentID and re-create it with the new non-key value in the index.

```
USE AdventureWorks2012;
GO
ALTER TABLE HumanResources.TerminationReason
  ADD LegalDescription varchar(max);
Go
DROP INDEX HumanResources.TerminationReason.NI_TerminationReason_TerminationReason_DepartmentID;
Go
CREATE NONCLUSTERED INDEX NI_TerminationReason_TerminationReason_DepartmentID
  ON HumanResources.TerminationReason (TerminationReason, DepartmentID)
  INCLUDE (LegalDescription);
```

How It Works

This recipe demonstrated a technique for enhancing the usefulness of a nonclustered index. The example started with creating a new varchar(max) data type column. Because of its data type (large object, LOB), it cannot be used as a key value in the index; however, using it within the INCLUDE keyword will allow you to reference the new large object data types. The existing index on the TerminationReason table was then dropped and re-created using INCLUDE with the new non-key column.

You can use INCLUDE only with a nonclustered index (where it comes in handy for covering queries), and you still can't include the deprecated image, ntext, and text data types. Also, if the index size increases too significantly because of the additional non-key values, you may lose some of the query benefits that a covering index can give you, so be sure to test comparatively before and after performance.

16-13. Using PADINDEX and FILLFACTOR

Problem

You need to create an index that will help minimize page splits due to insert operations.

Solution

Set the initial percentage of rows to fill the index leaf level pages and intermediate levels of an index. The fill factor percentage of an index refers to how full the leaf level of the index pages should be when the index is first created. The default fill factor, if not explicitly set, is 0, which equates to filling the pages as full as possible (SQL Server does leave some space available, enough for a single index row). Leaving some space available, however, allows new rows to be inserted without resorting to page splits. A page split occurs when a new row is added to a full index page. To make room, half the rows are moved from the existing full page to a new page. Numerous page splits can slow down INSERT operations. On the other hand, however, fully packed data pages allow for faster read activity, because the database engine can retrieve more rows from fewer data pages.

The PAD_INDEX option, used only in conjunction with FILLFACTOR, specifies that the specified percentage of free space be left open on the intermediate level pages of an index. These options are set in the WITH clause of the CREATE INDEX and ALTER INDEX commands. The syntax is as follows:

```
WITH (PADINDEX = { ON | OFF } FILLFACTOR = fillfactor)
```

In this example, an index is dropped and re-created with a 50 percent fill factor and PADINDEX enabled:

```
USE AdventureWorks2012;
GO
DROP INDEX HumanResources.TerminationReason.NI_TerminationReason_TerminationReason_DepartmentID;
GO
CREATE NONCLUSTERED INDEX NI_TerminationReason_TerminationReason_DepartmentID
  ON HumanResources.TerminationReason (TerminationReason ASC, DepartmentID ASC)
  WITH (PAD_INDEX=ON, FILLFACTOR=50);
GO
```

How It Works

In this recipe, the fill factor was configured to 50 percent, leaving 50 percent of the index pages free for new rows. PADINDEX was also enabled, so the intermediate index pages will also be left half free. Both options are used in the WITH clause of the CREATE INDEX syntax.

```
WITH (PAD_INDEX=ON, FILLFACTOR=50)
```

Using FILLFACTOR can be a balancing act between reads and writes. For example, a 100 percent fill factor can improve reads but slow down write activity, causing frequent page splitting because the database engine must continually shift row locations in order to make space in the data pages. Having too low of a fill factor can benefit row inserts, but it can also slow down read operations, because more data pages must be accessed in order to retrieve all required rows. If you're looking for a general rule of thumb, use a 100 percent (default) fill factor for tables with almost no data modification activity, 80 to 90 percent for low activity, and 70 to 80 percent for moderate to high activity on the index key. When setting this value, test your performance extensively before and after the change to ensure it will work as desired.

16-14. Disabling Page and/or Row Index Locking

Problem

You need to eliminate resource locking during index creation while also troubleshooting performance issues.

Solution

Change the lock resource types that can be locked for a specific index. In Chapter 12, I discussed various lock types and resources within SQL Server. Specifically, various resources can be locked by SQL Server from small (row and key locks) to medium (page locks, extents) to large (table, database). Multiple, smaller-grained locks help with query concurrency, assuming there are a significant number of queries simultaneously requesting data from the same table and associated indexes. Numerous locks take up memory, however, and can lower performance for the SQL Server instance as a whole. The trade-off is larger-grained locks, which increase memory resource availability but also reduce query concurrency.

You can create an index that restricts certain locking types when it is queried. Specifically, you can designate whether page or row locks are allowed.

In general, you should allow SQL Server to automatically decide which locking type is best; however, there may be a situation where you want to temporarily restrict certain resource locking types for troubleshooting or a severe performance issue. The syntax for configuring these options for both `CREATE INDEX` and `ALTER INDEX` is as follows:

```
WITH ( ALLOW_ROW_LOCKS = { ON | OFF } ALLOW_PAGE_LOCKS = { ON | OFF })
```

This recipe shows you how to disable the database engine's ability to place row or page locks on an index, forcing it to use table locking instead:

```
USE AdventureWorks2012;
GO
-- Disable page locks. Table and row locks can still be used.
CREATE INDEX NI_EmployeePayHistory_Rate
  ON HumanResources.EmployeePayHistory (Rate)
  WITH (ALLOW_PAGE_LOCKS=OFF);
-- Disable page and row locks. Only table locks can be used.
ALTER INDEX NI_TerminationReason_TerminationReason_DepartmentID
  ON HumanResources.TerminationReason
  SET (ALLOW_PAGE_LOCKS=OFF,ALLOW_ROW_LOCKS=OFF );
-- Allow page and row locks.
ALTER INDEX NI_TerminationReason_TerminationReason_DepartmentID
  ON HumanResources.TerminationReason
  SET (ALLOW_PAGE_LOCKS=ON,ALLOW_ROW_LOCKS=ON );
```

How It Works

This recipe demonstrated three variations. The first query created a new index on the table, configured so that the database engine couldn't issue page locks against the index:

```
WITH (ALLOW_PAGE_LOCKS=OFF)
```

In the next statement, both page and row locks were turned `OFF` (the default for an index is for both to be set to `ON`):

```
ALTER INDEX NI_TerminationReason_TerminationReason_DepartmentID
ON HumanResources.TerminationReason
SET (ALLOW_PAGE_LOCKS=OFF,ALLOW_ROW_LOCKS=OFF );
```

In the last statement, page and row locking is reenabled:

```
SET (ALLOW_PAGE_LOCKS=ON,ALLOW_ROW_LOCKS=ON )
```

Removing locking options should only be done if you have a good reason to do so; for example, you may have activity that causes too many row locks, which can eat up memory resources. Instead of row locks, you may want to have SQL Server use larger-grained page or table locks instead.

Managing Very Large Indexes

This next set of recipes for this chapter cover methods for managing very large indexes; however, the features demonstrated here can be applied to smaller and medium-sized indexes as well. For example, you can designate that an index be created on a separate filegroup. Doing so can provide benefits from both the manageability and performance sides, because you can then perform separate backups by filegroup, as well as improve I/O performance of a query if the filegroup has files that exist on a separate array.

As was reviewed in Chapter 15, also in addition to table partitioning you can implement index partitioning. Partitioning allows you to break down the index data set into smaller subsets of data. As discussed in the recipe, if large indexes are separated onto separate partitions, this can positively impact the performance of a query (particularly for very large indexes).

SQL Server provides us with the filtered index feature and the ability to compress data at the page and row level. The filtered index feature allows you to create an index and associated statistics for a subset of values. If incoming queries hit only a small percentage of values within a column, for example, you can create a filtered index that will target only those common values, thus reducing the overall index size compared to a full-table index, and also improving the accuracy of the underlying statistics.

As for the compression feature, available in the Enterprise and Developer Editions, you can designate row or page compression for an index or specified partitions. I demonstrated this feature for CREATE TABLE and ALTER TABLE in Chapter 15. In this chapter, I continue this discussion with how to enable compression using CREATE INDEX and ALTER INDEX.

16-15. Creating an Index on a Filegroup

Problem

You have been required to create indexes in a filegroup other than the filegroup containing the tables and data.

Solution

Create an index on a specific filegroup. If not explicitly designated, an index is created on the same filegroup as the underlying table. This is accomplished using the ON clause of the CREATE INDEX command.

```
ON filegroup_name  | default
```

This option can take an explicit filegroup name or the database default filegroup. (For more information on filegroups, see Chapter 15.)

This example demonstrates how to explicitly define in which filegroup an index is stored. First, I create a new filegroup on the AdventureWorks2012 database.

```
Use master;
GO
ALTER DATABASE AdventureWorks2012
  ADD FILEGROUP FG2;
```

Next, I add a new file to the database and the newly created filegroup in a folder on the root of C called Apress.

```
Use AdventureWorks2012;
GO
ALTER DATABASE AdventureWorks2012
  ADD FILE
--Please ensure the Apress directory exists or change the path in the FILENAME statement
  ( NAME = AW2,FILENAME = 'c:\Apress\aw2.ndf',SIZE = 1MB )
  TO FILEGROUP FG2;
```

Lastly, I create a new index, designating that it be stored on the newly created filegroup.

```
Use AdventureWorks2012;
GO
CREATE INDEX NI_ProductPhoto_ThumnailPhotoFileName
  ON Production.ProductPhoto (ThumbnailPhotoFileName)
  ON [FG2];
```

How It Works

The first part of the recipe creates a new filegroup in the AdventureWorks2012 database called FG2 using the ALTER DATABASE command. After that, a new database data file is created on the new filegroup. Lastly, a new index is created on the FG2 filegroup. The ON clause designated the filegroup name for the index in square brackets.

```
ON [FG2]
```

Filegroups can be used to help manage very large databases, both by allowing separate backups by filegroup and by improving I/O performance if the filegroup has files that exist on a separate array.

16-16. Implementing Index Partitioning

Problem

You have a partitioned table that is being queried. The indexes on this table are touching each partition and performing less than optimally. You need to optimize the index performance.

Solution

Apply partitioning to a nonclustered index. In Chapter 15, I demonstrated table partitioning. Partitioning can provide manageability, scalability, and performance benefits for large tables. This is because partitioning allows you to break down the data set into smaller subsets of data. Depending on the index key(s), an index on a table can also be quite large. Applying the partitioning concept to indexes, if large indexes are separated onto separate partitions, this can positively affect the performance of a query. Queries that target data from just one partition will benefit because SQL Server will only target the selected partition instead of accessing all partitions for the index.

This recipe demonstrates index partitioning using the HitDateRangeScheme partition scheme that was created in Chapter 15 on the Sales.WebSiteHits table:

```
Use AdventureWorks2012;
GO
CREATE NONCLUSTERED INDEX NI_WebSiteHits_WebSitePage
  ON Sales.WebSiteHits (WebSitePage)
  ON [HitDateRangeScheme] (HitDate);
```

How It Works

The partition scheme is applied using the ON clause.

```
ON [HitDateRangeScheme] (HitDate)
```

Notice that although the HitDate column wasn't a nonclustered index key, it was included in the partition scheme, matching that of the table. When the index and table use the same partition scheme, they are said to be *aligned*.

You can choose to use a different partitioning scheme for the index than the table; however, that scheme must use the same data type argument, number of partitions, and boundary values. Unaligned indexes can be used to take advantage of co-located joins, meaning if you have two columns from two tables that are frequently joined that also use the same partition function, same data type, number of partitions, and boundaries, you can potentially improve query join performance. However, the common approach will most probably be to use aligned partition schemes between the index and table, for administration and performance reasons.

16-17. Indexing a Subset of Rows

Problem

You have a query that is performing subpar. The query searches on a column for a range of values that comprise less than 10 percent of the total rows in the table. You need to optimize this index.

Solution

Add a filtered index to support this query. SQL Server 2008 introduced the ability to create filtered nonclustered indexes in support of queries that require only a small percentage of table rows. The CREATE INDEX command includes a filter predicate that can be used to reduce index size by indexing only rows that meet certain conditions. That reduced index size saves on disk space and potentially improves the performance of queries that now need only read a fraction of the index entries that they would otherwise have to process.

The filter predicate allows for several comparison operators to be used, including IS, IS NOT, =, <>, >, <, and more. In this recipe, I demonstrate how to add filtered indexes to one of the larger tables in the AdventureWorks2012 database, Sales.SalesOrderDetail. To set up this example, let's assume that I have the following common query against the UnitPrice column:

```
Use AdventureWorks2012;
GO
SELECT SalesOrderID
  FROM Sales.SalesOrderDetail
  WHERE UnitPrice BETWEEN 150.00 AND 175.00;
```

Let's also assume that the person executing this query is the only one who typically uses the UnitPrice column in the search predicate. When she does query it, she is concerned only with values between $150 and $175. Creating a full index on this column may be considered to be wasteful. If this query is executed often, and a full clustered index scan is performed against the base table each time, this may cause performance issues.

I have just described an ideal scenario for a filtered index on the UnitPrice column. You can create that filtered index as follows:

```
Use AdventureWorks2012;
GO
CREATE NONCLUSTERED INDEX NCI_UnitPrice_SalesOrderDetail
  ON Sales.SalesOrderDetail(UnitPrice)
  WHERE UnitPrice >= 150.00 AND UnitPrice <= 175.00;
```

Queries that search against UnitPrice and that also search in the defined filter predicate range will likely use the filtered index instead of performing a full-index scan or using full-table index alternatives.

In another example, let's assume it is common to query products with two distinct IDs. In this case, I am also querying anything with an order quantity greater than 10. However, this is not my desired filtering scenario, just filtering on the product ID:

```
Use AdventureWorks2012;
GO
SELECT SalesOrderDetailID
  FROM Sales.SalesOrderDetail
  WHERE ProductID IN (776, 777)
  AND OrderQty > 10;
```

This query performs a clustered index scan. I can improve the performance of the query by adding a filtered index, which will result in an index seek against that nonclustered index instead of the clustered index scan. Here's how to create that filtered index:

```
Use AdventureWorks2012;
GO
CREATE NONCLUSTERED INDEX NCI_ProductID_SalesOrderDetail
  ON Sales.SalesOrderDetail(ProductID,OrderQty)
  WHERE ProductID IN (776, 777);
```

The result will be less I/O, because the query can operate against the much smaller, filtered index.

How It Works

This recipe demonstrates how to use the filtered index feature to create a fine-tuned index that requires less storage than the full-table index alternative. Filtered indexes require that you understand the nature of incoming queries against the tables in your database. If you have a high percentage of queries that consistently query a small percentage of data in a set of tables, filtered indexes will allow you to improve I/O performance while also minimizing on-disk storage.

The CREATE INDEX statement isn't modified much from its original format. To implement the filter, I used a WHERE clause after the ON clause (if using an INCLUDE, the WHERE should appear after it):

```
Use AdventureWorks2012;
GO
CREATE NONCLUSTERED INDEX NCI_UnitPrice_SalesOrderDetail
  ON Sales.SalesOrderDetail(UnitPrice)
  WHERE UnitPrice >= 150.00 AND UnitPrice <= 175.00;
```

The filter predicate allows for simple logic using operators such as IN, IS, IS NOT, =, <>, >, >=, !>, <, <=, and !<. You should also be aware that filtered indexes have filtered statistics created along with them. These statistics use the same filter predicate and can result in more accurate results because the sampling is against a smaller row set.

16-18. Reducing Index Size

Problem

You have discovered that your indexes are significantly large. You need to reduce the size of these indexes without altering the definition of the index.

Solution

Implement compression on the indexes in question. As was covered in Chapter 15, the SQL Server 2012 Enterprise and Developer editions provide options for page and row-level compression of tables, indexes, and the associated partitions. That chapter demonstrated how to enable compression using the DATA_COMPRESSION clause in conjunction with the CREATE TABLE and ALTER TABLE commands. It also covered how you compress clustered indexes and heaps. For nonclustered indexes, you use CREATE INDEX and ALTER INDEX to implement compression. The syntax remains the same, designating the DATA_ COMPRESSION option along with a value of NONE, ROW, or PAGE. The following example demonstrates adding a nonclustered index with PAGE-level compression (based on the example table ArchiveJobPosting created in Recipe 15-14):

```
Use AdventureWorks2012;
GO
CREATE NONCLUSTERED INDEX NCI_SalesOrderDetail_CarrierTrackingNumber
  ON Sales.SalesOrderDetail (CarrierTrackingNumber)
  WITH (DATA_COMPRESSION = PAGE);
```

I can modify the compression level after the fact by using ALTER INDEX. In this example, I use ALTER INDEX to change the compression level to row-level compression:

```
Use AdventureWorks2012;
GO
ALTER INDEX NCI_SalesOrderDetail_CarrierTrackingNumber
ON Sales.SalesOrderDetail
REBUILD
WITH (DATA_COMPRESSION = ROW);
```

How It Works

This recipe demonstrated enabling row and page compression for a nonclustered index. The process for adding compression is almost identical to that of adding compression for the clustered index or heap, using the DATA_COMPRESSION index option. When creating a new index, the WITH clause follows the index key definition. When modifying an existing index, the WITH clause follows the REBUILD keyword.

CHAPTER 17

Stored Procedures

by Jonathan Gennick

A *stored procedure* groups one or more Transact-SQL statements into a logical unit, stored as an object in a SQL Server database. After the stored procedure is created, its T-SQL definition is accessible from the `sys.sqlmodule` catalog view.

When a stored procedure is executed for the first time, SQL Server creates an execution plan and stores it in the plan cache. SQL Server can then reuse the plan on subsequent executions of this stored procedure. Plan reuse allows stored procedures to provide fast and reliable performance compared to noncompiled and unprepared ad hoc query equivalents.

17-1. Selling the Benefits

Problem

You are having trouble selling other developers on the prospect of using stored procedures.

Solution

Recite some of the benefits, which include the following:

Stored procedures help centralize your Transact-SQL code in the data tier. Web sites or applications that embed ad hoc SQL are notoriously difficult to modify in a production environment. When ad hoc SQL is embedded in an application, you may spend too much time trying to find and debug the embedded SQL. Once you've found the bug, chances are you'll need to recompile the program executable, causing unnecessary application outages or application distribution nightmares. If you centralize your Transact-SQL code in stored procedures, you'll have a centralized place to look for SQL code or SQL batches. If you document and standardize the code properly, your stored procedures will improve overall supportability of the application.

Stored procedures can reduce network traffic for larger ad hoc queries. Programming your application to execute a stored procedure, rather than push across a 500-line SQL call, can have a positive impact on your network and application performance, particularly if the call is repeated thousands of times a minute.

Stored procedures encourage code reusability. For example, if your web application uses a drop-down menu containing a list of cities and this drop-down is used in multiple web pages, you can call the stored procedure from each web page rather than embed the same SQL in multiple places.

Stored procedures allow you to obscure the method of data retrieval. If you change the underlying tables from which the source data is pulled, stored procedures (similar to views) can obscure this change from the application. This allows you to make changes without forcing a code change at the application tier. You can swap in new tables for the old, and as long as the same columns and data types are sent back to the application, the application is none the wiser.

Stored procedures can do more than views. They can take advantage of control-of-flow techniques, temporary tables, table variables, and much more.

Stored procedures have a stabilizing influence on query response time. If you've worked extensively with ad hoc queries, you may have noticed that sometimes the amount of time it takes to return results from a query can vary wildly. This may be because of external factors, such as concurrent activity against the table (locking) or resource issues (memory, CPU). On the other hand, an ad hoc query may be performing erratically because SQL Server periodically chooses less efficient execution plans. With stored procedures, you gain more reliable query-plan caching and hence reuse. Notice that I use the word *reliable* here, rather than *faster*. Ad hoc queries can sometimes perform better than their stored procedure counterparts, but it all depends on the circumstances in which the execution plan was cached and how you have tested, tuned, and then implemented the code within.

How It Works

There are many good reasons to use stored procedures, and very few bad ones. Usually, reasons against using stored procedures come from application developers who are more comfortable writing ad hoc SQL within the application tier and may not be trained in the use of stored procedures. In companies with a separate application and database administration staff, stored procedures also imply a loss of control over the Transact-SQL code from the application developer to the database administration staff. Assuming your database administration team is competent and willing to assist with a move to stored procedures in a timely fashion, the benefits of using them should far outweigh any loss of control.

If none of the reasons in the solution convinces your colleagues that stored procedures are largely beneficial, then also review the security benefits. Direct table access (or worse, sysadmin access) to the SQL Server instance and its database poses a security risk. For example, if someone gets hold of the inline code, he'll be able to glean information about the underlying schema of your database and direct his hacking attempts accordingly. Keeping all SQL within stored procedures keeps only the stored procedure reference in the application instead of each individual column and table name.

Another security benefit to stored procedures is that you can grant database users and/or database roles access to them specifically instead of having to grant direct access to tables. The stored procedures can act as a control layer, allowing you to choose which columns and rows can and cannot be modified by the stored procedure (and hence also by the caller).

17-2. Creating a Stored Procedure

Problem

You want to create a simple stored procedure. For example, you want to return the results from a `SELECT` statement.

Solution

Issue a CREATE PROCEDURE statement. The first parameters are the schema and new procedure name. Next is the Transact-SQL body of your stored procedure. The body contains SQL statements implementing one or more tasks that you want to accomplish. The following example demonstrates creating a stored procedure that queries the database and returns a list of customers having known names (that is, who have corresponding entries in Person.Person):

```
CREATE PROCEDURE dbo.ListCustomerNames
AS
       SELECT   CustomerID,
                LastName,
                FirstName
       FROM     Sales.Customer sc
                INNER JOIN Person.Person pp
                    ON sc.CustomerID = pp.BusinessEntityID
       ORDER BY LastName,
                FirstName;
```

Next, the new stored procedure is executed using the EXEC command, which is shorthand for EXECUTE.

```
EXEC dbo.ListCustomerNames;
```

This returns the following results:

```
CustomerID   LastName        FirstName
----------   -------------   -------------
       285   Abbas           Syed
       293   Abel            Catherine
       295   Abercrombie     Kim
        38   Abercrombie     Kim
       211   Abolrous        Hazem
          ...
```

How It Works

This recipe demonstrates creating a stored procedure that queries the contents of two tables, returning a result set. This stored procedure works like a view, but it will have a cached query plan when executed for the first time, which will also make its execution time consistent in consecutive executions.

The example started off by creating a stored procedure called ListCustomerNames.

```
CREATE PROCEDURE dbo.ListCustomerNames
AS
```

The procedure is created in the dbo schema. The letters dbo stand for "database owner." The dbo schema is one that is always present in a database, and it can be a convenient repository for stored procedures.

> ■ **Tip** Regardless of target schema, it is good practice to specify that schema explicitly when creating a stored procedure. By doing so, you ensure there is no mistake as to where the procedure is created.

The Transact-SQL query definition then follows the AS keyword:

```
SELECT    CustomerID,
          LastName,
          FirstName
FROM      Sales.Customer sc
          INNER JOIN Person.Person pp
              ON sc.CustomerID = pp.BusinessEntityID
ORDER BY LastName,
          FirstName;
```

After the procedure is created, it is executed using the EXEC command:

```
EXEC dbo.ListCustomerNames;
```

During the stored procedure creation process, SQL Server checks that the SQL syntax is correct, but it doesn't check for the existence of referenced tables. This means you can reference a table name incorrectly, and the incorrect name will not cause an error until runtime. That process of checking names at runtime is called *deferred name resolution.* It is actually helpful in that it allows you to create or reference objects that don't exist yet. It also means that you can drop, alter, or modify the objects referenced in the stored procedure without invalidating the procedure.

■ **Tip** Avoid problems from deferred name resolution by testing queries ad hoc whenever conveniently possible. That way, you can be sure your syntax is correct and that names resolve properly before creating the procedure.

17-3. Generalizing a Stored Procedure

Problem

You want to pass values to a stored procedure to affect its behavior or the results it returns. For example, you want to pass an account number and get the customer's name in return. You also want to specify whether the name is returned in all-uppercase letters.

Solution

Parameterize the stored procedure. Define one or more parameters between the procedure name and the AS keyword when creating the procedure. Enclose your parameter list within parentheses. Preface each parameter name with an @ character.

For example, the following procedure returns the customer name associated with the account number passed as the first parameter. Use the second parameter to control whether the name is forced to uppercase.

```
CREATE PROCEDURE dbo.LookupByAccount
(@AccountNumber VARCHAR(10),
 @UpperFlag CHAR(1))
AS
       SELECT    CASE UPPER(@UpperFlag)
                   WHEN 'U' THEN UPPER(FirstName)
                   ELSE FirstName
                 END AS FirstName,
                 CASE UPPER(@UpperFlag)
```

```
                WHEN 'U' THEN UPPER(LastName)
                ELSE LastName
              END AS LastName
    FROM      Person.Person
    WHERE     BusinessEntityID IN (SELECT CustomerID
                                   FROM   Sales.Customer
                                   WHERE  AccountNumber = @AccountNumber) ;
```

Invoke this procedure as follows:

```
EXEC LookupByAccount 'AW00000019', 'u';
```

The results from this invocation should be as follows:

```
FirstName  LastName
---------  --------
MARY       DEMPSEY
```

You can pass the second parameter in either uppercase or lowercase. Pass any letter but 'U' or 'u' to leave the name in mixed case while it is stored in the database. Here's an example:

```
EXEC LookupByAccount 'AW00000019', 'U';
EXEC LookupByAccount 'AW00000019', 'x';
```

```
FirstName       LastName
---------       ----------
MARY            DEMPSEY
...
FirstName       LastName
---------       ----------
Mary            Dempsey
```

How It Works

The earlier Recipe 17-2 demonstrates a nonparameterized stored procedure, meaning that no external parameters are passed to it. The ability to pass parameters is part of why stored procedures are one of the most important database object types in SQL Server. Using parameters, you can pass information into the body of a procedure in order to control how the procedure operates and to pass values that cause queries to return needed results.

The solution example shows a procedure having two input parameters. The first parameter is an account number. The second is a flag controlling whether the results are forced to uppercase. The procedure queries the database to find out the name of the person behind the number.

Developers executing the procedure given in the recipe solution do not need to worry about how the underlying query is written; they can simply accept that they provide an account number and get back a name. You are able to change the implementation when needed without affecting the interface and thus without having to change any of the code invoking the procedure.

You're able to make parameters optional by giving default values. Recipe 17-4 shows how. You're also able to return values through so-called *output parameters*, and Recipe 17-6 shows how to do that.

17-4. Making Parameters Optional

Problem

You want to make certain parameters optional. For example, you are tired of having to always pass an 'x' to the LookupByAccount procedure. You want your names back in mixed case but without ruining it for those who pass a 'U' to force uppercase.

Solution

Re-create the procedure and make the @UpperFlag parameter optional. First, drop the version of the procedure currently in place from Recipe 17-3.

```
DROP PROCEDURE dbo.LookupByAccount;
```

Then, create a new version of the procedure having a default value specified for @UpperFlag. Do that by appending = 'x' following the parameter's data type. Here's an example:

```
CREATE PROCEDURE dbo.LookupByAccount
(@AccountNumber VARCHAR(10),
 @UpperFlag CHAR(1) = 'x')
AS
       SELECT   CASE UPPER(@UpperFlag)
                  WHEN 'U' THEN UPPER(FirstName)
                  ELSE FirstName
                END AS FirstName,
                CASE UPPER(@UpperFlag)
                  WHEN 'U' THEN UPPER(LastName)
                  ELSE LastName
                END AS LastName
       FROM     Person.Person
       WHERE    BusinessEntityID IN (SELECT CustomerID
                                     FROM   Sales.Customer
                                     WHERE  AccountNumber = @AccountNumber) ;
```

Now, you can invoke the procedure without needing to specify that pesky flag.

```
EXEC LookupByAccount 'AW00000019';
```

```
FirstName  LastName
---------  -----------
Mary       Dempsey
```

But others who want their results forced to uppercase are still free to do that.

```
EXEC LookupByAccount 'AW00000019', 'U';
```

```
FirstName      LastName
---------      -----------
MARY           DEMPSEY
```

The default value takes effect whenever the parameter is not specified but can be overridden when needed.

How It Works

The solution example makes a parameter optional by specifying a default value as follows:

```
@UpperFlag VARCHAR(1) = 'x'
```

It's now possible to invoke the procedure by passing only an account number. The default value takes effect in that case, and the person's name is returned unchanged, without being forced to uppercase.

It's common to specify default parameters at the end of the parameter list. Doing so makes it easier to invoke a procedure in an ad hoc manner from SQL Management Studio. Also, many are used to this convention. However, you can define optional parameters earlier in the list, and the next recipe shows how.

17-5. Making Early Parameters Optional

Problem

The parameter you want to make optional precedes one that is mandatory. You are thus unable to skip that parameter even though you've specified a default value for it.

Solution

Invoke your procedure using named notation rather than positional notation. In doing so, you can name the parameter that you do want to pass, and it won't matter where in the list that parameter occurs.

For example, begin with the following version of the procedure from Recipe 17-4. In this version, the UpperFlag parameter comes first.

```
CREATE PROCEDURE dbo.LookupByAccount2
(@UpperFlag CHAR(1) = 'x',
@AccountNumber VARCHAR(10))
AS
       SELECT   CASE UPPER(@UpperFlag)
                  WHEN 'U' THEN UPPER(FirstName)
                  ELSE FirstName
                END AS FirstName,
                CASE UPPER(@UpperFlag)
                  WHEN 'U' THEN UPPER(LastName)
                  ELSE LastName
                END AS LastName
       FROM     Person.Person
       WHERE    BusinessEntityID IN (SELECT CustomerID
                                     FROM   Sales.Customer
                                     WHERE  AccountNumber = @AccountNumber) ;
```

Using named notation, you can pass just the account number as follows:

```
EXEC LookupByAccount2 @AccountNumber = 'AW00000019';
```

You can use the DEFAULT keyword to make it explicit that you are accepting a default parameter value for @UpperFlag.

```
EXEC LookupByAccount2 @AccountNumber = 'AW00000019', @UpperFlag = DEFAULT;
```

Using named notation, you can specify the parameter values in any order.

How It Works

It's common to pass parameters using positional notation. Named notation takes some extra typing but in return can be a bit more self-documenting. That's because each procedure invocation names all the parameters, helping you remember later what the associated parameter values represent.

Using named notation also allows you to specify parameters in any order. That ability allows you to skip parameters having default values, no matter where those parameters occur in the list. Don't try to mix the two notations. SQL Server requires that you choose one or the other. Specify all parameters by name or all by position. Don't try to mix the two approaches.

17-6. Returning Output

Problem

You are writing a stored procedure. You want to return values to the code calling the procedure.

Solution

Specify some parameters as OUTPUT parameters. The following example creates a stored procedure that returns the list of departments for a specific group. In addition to returning the list of departments, an OUTPUT parameter is defined to return the number of departments found for the specific group.

```
CREATE PROCEDURE dbo.EL_Department
       @GroupName NVARCHAR(50),
       @DeptCount INT OUTPUT
AS
       SELECT   Name
       FROM     HumanResources.Department
       WHERE    GroupName = @GroupName
       ORDER BY Name;
       SELECT   @DeptCount = @@ROWCOUNT;
```

Now you can define a local variable to hold the output and invoke the procedure. Here's an example:

```
DECLARE @DeptCount INT;
EXEC dbo.SEL_Department 'Executive General and Administration',
    @DeptCount OUTPUT;
PRINT @DeptCount;
```

The query in the procedure generates the row set. The PRINT command displays the row count value passed back through the @DeptCount variable. The query in this example returns the following five rows:

```
Name
--------------------------
Executive
Facilities and Maintenance
Finance
Human Resources
Information Services
```

Next, the stored procedure uses the PRINT statement to return the count of rows. If you're executing the query ad hoc using Management Studio, you will see the value 5 on the Messages tab if you are viewing results as a grid and at the bottom of the Results tab if you are viewing results as text. Here's an example:

```
5
```

How It Works

The solution begins by creating a stored procedure with a defined parameter called @DeptCount, followed by the data type and OUTPUT keyword:

```
@DeptCount INT OUTPUT
```

The stored procedure executes the query and then stores the row count in the parameter.

```
SELECT @DeptCount = @@ROWCOUNT
```

The invoking code creates the following variable to pass as the output parameter:

```
DECLARE @DeptCount INT
```

The EXEC statement must also specify that a parameter is an output parameter. Do that by following the passed value with the OUTPUT keyword, as in the following:

```
EXEC dbo.SEL_Department 'Executive General and Administration',
    @DeptCount OUTPUT;
```

You can use OUTPUT parameters as an alternative or additional method for returning information back to the caller of the stored procedure. If you're using OUTPUT only to communicate information back to the calling application, it's usually just as easy to create a second result set containing the information you need. This is because .NET applications, for example, can easily consume the multiple result sets that are returned from a stored procedure. The technique of using OUTPUT parameters versus using an additional result set to return information is often just a matter of preference.

17-7. Modifying a Stored Procedure

Problem

You have an existing stored procedure and want to change its behavior.

Solution

Redefine the procedure using the ALTER PROCEDURE command. You can change everything but the original stored procedure name. The syntax is almost identical to CREATE PROCEDURE.

The following example modifies the stored procedure created in the previous recipe in order to return the number of departments returned by the query as a separate result set instead of via an OUTPUT parameter.

```
ALTER PROCEDURE dbo.SEL_Department
      @GroupName NVARCHAR(50)
AS
      SELECT    Name
      FROM      HumanResources.Department
```

```
WHERE     GroupName = @GroupName
ORDER BY  Name;
SELECT    @@ROWCOUNT AS DepartmentCount;
```

You may now execute the stored procedure as follows, and two result sets are returned:

```
EXEC dbo.SEL_Department 'Research and Development';
```

```
Name
------------------------
Engineering
Research and Development
Tool Design
DepartmentCount
---------------
              3
```

How It Works

ALTER PROCEDURE is used to modify the definition of an existing stored procedure, in this case both removing a parameter and adding a second result set. You can change everything but the procedure name. Using ALTER PROCEDURE also preserves any existing permissions on the stored procedure. If you drop and re-create the procedure, you'll need to re-grant permissions. Using ALTER PROCEDURE avoids the need for that tedium.

17-8. Removing a Stored Procedure

Problem

You are no longer using a stored procedure and want to remove it from your database.

Solution

Drop the stored procedure from the database using the DROP PROCEDURE command. Here's an example:

```
DROP PROCEDURE dbo.SEL_Department;
```

How It Works

Once a stored procedure is dropped, its definition is removed from the database's system tables. Any cached query execution plans are also removed for that stored procedure. Code references to the stored procedure by other procedures or triggers will fail upon execution once the stored procedure has been dropped.

17-9. Automatically Run a Stored Procedure at Start-Up

Problem

You want to execute some code every time a particular instance is started. For example, you might want to document start-up times or clear out work tables on each restart.

Solution

Invoke the sp_procoption system stored procedure to designate a procedure that you write to execute automatically upon instance start-up. In the example to follow, a stored procedure is set to execute automatically whenever SQL Server is started. First, set the database context to the master database (which is the only place that start-up stored procedures can be placed).

```
USE master;
```

Next, create a start-up logging table. Do this because the procedure this recipe creates as an example writes to this table. Here is the creation statement:

```
CREATE TABLE dbo.SQLStartupLog
       (
        SQLStartupLogID INT IDENTITY(1, 1)
                            NOT NULL
                            PRIMARY KEY,
        StartupDateTime DATETIME NOT NULL
       );
```

Then create a stored procedure to insert a value into the new table.

```
CREATE PROCEDURE dbo.INS_TrackSQLStartups
AS
       INSERT   dbo.SQLStartupLog
                (StartupDateTime)
       VALUES   (GETDATE());
```

Finally, invoke sp_procoption to set this new procedure to execute when the SQL Server service restarts.

```
EXEC sp_procoption @ProcName = 'INS_TrackSQLStartups',
    @OptionName = 'startup', @OptionValue = 'true';
```

From now on, starting the instance triggers execution of the stored procedure, which in turn inserts a row into the table to log the start-up event.

How It Works

This recipe creates a new table in the master database to track SQL Server start-ups. A stored procedure is also created in the master database to insert a row into the table with the current date and time of execution.

■ **Caution** We are not espousing the creation of objects in the system databases, because it isn't generally a good idea to create them there. However, if you must use auto-execution functionality as discussed in this recipe, you have no choice but to create your objects in the system database.

The stored procedure *must* be created in the master database; otherwise, you'll see the following error message when trying to use sp_procoption:

```
Msg 15398, Level 11, State 1, Procedure sp_procoption, Line 73 Only objects in the master
database owned by dbo can have the startup setting changed.
```

To disable the stored procedure, execute the following command:

```
EXEC sp_procoption @ProcName = 'INS_TrackSQLStartups',
```

```
@OptionName = 'startup', @OptionValue = 'false'
```

Setting @OptionValue to false disables the start-up procedure.

■ **Note** If you're going to test further recipes in this chapter, be sure to execute USE AdventureWorks2012 to change your database back to the example database generally being used in this chapter.

17-10. Viewing a Stored Procedure's Definition

Problem

You want to view the definition for a stored procedure so that you can ascertain exactly how that procedure operates.

Solution

From an ad hoc session, it's often easiest to execute sp_helptext. Here's an example:

```
EXEC sp_helptext 'LookupByAccount';
```

Your results will be in the form of a CREATE PROCEDURE statement:

```
Text
---------------------------------------------------------------------------
CREATE PROCEDURE dbo.LookupByAccount
(@AccountNumber VARCHAR(10),
 @UpperFlag VARCHAR(1) = 'x')
AS
       SELECT   CASE UPPER(@UpperFlag)
                  WHEN 'U' THEN UPPER(FirstName)
                  ELSE FirstName
                END AS FirstName,
                CASE UPPER(@UpperFlag)
                  WHEN 'U' THEN UPPER(LastName)
                  ELSE LastName
                END AS LastName
       FROM     Person.Person
       WHERE    BusinessEntityID IN (SELECT CustomerID
                                     FROM   Sales.Customer
                                     WHERE  AccountNumber = @AccountNumber) ;
```

From code, you may prefer to query sys.sql_modules and related catalog views. Doing so allows access to a great wealth of information from code, information that you can use in writing helpful utilities to manage objects in your database. For example, execute the following query to retrieve the definition for the stored procedure created in Recipe 17-3:

```
SELECT  definition
FROM    sys.sql_modules m
        INNER JOIN sys.objects o
```

```
        ON m.object_id = o.object_id
WHERE   o.type = 'P'
        AND o.name = 'LookupByAccount';
```

Your results will be the following output showing the definition in the form of a CREATE PROCEDURE statement. (If outputting as text, be sure to set the maximum number of characters displayed in each column to something higher than the default of just 256.)

```
definition
----------------------------------------------------------------------------
CREATE PROCEDURE dbo.LookupByAccount
(@AccountNumber VARCHAR(10),
 @UpperFlag CHAR(1) = 'x')
AS
       SELECT   CASE UPPER(@UpperFlag)
                  WHEN 'U' THEN UPPER(FirstName)
                  ELSE FirstName
                END AS FirstName,
                CASE UPPER(@UpperFlag)
                  WHEN 'U' THEN UPPER(LastName)
                  ELSE LastName
                END AS LastName
       FROM     Person.Person
       WHERE    BusinessEntityID IN (SELECT CustomerID
                                     FROM   Sales.Customer
                                     WHERE  AccountNumber = @AccountNumber ) ;
```

You can save these results and execute them to re-create the procedure at some future time or on another database server.

How It Works

Invoke sp_helptext whenever you want to see the definition for a stored procedure or other user-defined object. You'll get the result back in the form of a single text value.

Query the view sys.sql_modules to retrieve the definitions of stored procedures, triggers, views, and other SQL-defined objects. Join sys.sql_modules to sys.objects to gain access to object names and types. For example, the solution query specifically requested o.type = 'P'. That is the type code used to indicate stored procedures.

The two system views expose several other columns giving useful information or that you can use to restrict query results to only procedures and other objects of interest. It's worth reviewing the view definitions (by visiting the SQL Server Books Online manual set) to become familiar with the values available.

17-11. Documenting Stored Procedures

Problem

You are writing a stored procedure and want to leave some notes for the next person (perhaps it will be yourself!) who must maintain that procedure.

Solution

Define a format for stored procedure headers that includes room for commentary and for a history of change over time. The following is an example of a standard stored procedure header:

```
CREATE PROCEDURE dbo.IMP_DWP_FactOrder AS
-- Purpose: Populates the data warehouse, Called by Job
-- Maintenance Log
-- Update By   Update Date
Description
-- Joe Sack     8/15/2008    Created
-- Joe Sack     8/16/2008    A new column was added to
--the base table, so it was added here as well.
... Transact-SQL code here
```

For brevity, the stored procedure examples in this chapter have not included extensive comments or headers. However, in your production database, you should at the very least define headers for each stored procedure created in a production database.

How It Works

This recipe is more of a best practice rather than a review of a command or function. It is important to comment your stored procedure code very well so that future support staff, authors, and editors will understand the business rules and intents behind your Transact-SQL code. Although some code may seem self-evident at the time of authoring, the original logic may not seem so clear a few months after it was written. Business logic is often transient and difficult to understand over time, so including a written description of that logic in the body of the code can save hours of troubleshooting and investigation.

■ **Caution** One drawback of making your code self-documenting is that other developers who edit your code may not include documentation of their own changes. You may end up being blamed for code you didn't write, just because you were the last person to log a change. This is where your company should strongly consider a source control system to track all check-in and check-out activities, as well as be able to compare changes between procedure versions.

No doubt you'll see other procedure headers out in the field with much more information. Don't demand too much documentation. Include enough to bring clarity, but not so much that you introduce redundancy. For example, if you include the stored procedure name in the header, in addition to the actual `CREATE PROCEDURE` statement, you'll soon start seeing code in which the header name doesn't match the stored procedure name. Why not just document the information that isn't already included in the stored procedure definition? That is the approach we recommend.

17-12. Determining the Current Nesting Level

Problem

You are developing a stored procedure that invokes itself or a set of procedures that invoke each other. You want to detect programaticallyhow deeply nested you are in the call stack.

Solution

Execute a query to retrieve the @@NESTLEVEL value. This value begins at zero and is incremented by one for each procedure call. The following are two CREATE PROCEDURE statements to set up the solution example:

```
-- First procedure
CREATE PROCEDURE dbo.QuickAndDirty
AS
SELECT @@NESTLEVEL;
GO
-- Second procedure
CREATE PROCEDURE dbo.Call_QuickAndDirty
AS
SELECT @@NESTLEVEL
EXEC dbo.QuickAndDirty;
GO
```

After creating these two stored procedures, execute the following set of statements to demonstrate the operation of @@NESTLEVEL:

```
SELECT @@NESTLEVEL;
EXEC dbo.Call_QuickAndDirty;
```

Your results should be as follows:

```
-----------
          0
...
-----------
          1
...
-----------
          2
```

How It Works

@@NESTLEVEL returns the current nesting level for the stored procedure context. A stored procedure nesting level indicates how many times a stored procedure has called another stored procedure. SQL Server allows stored procedures to make up to a maximum of 32 nested (incomplete) calls.

The solution example begins by creating two stored procedures. One of those procedures invokes the other. The final query and procedure execution show that @@NESTLEVEL begins at zero. It is incremented and reported as 1 by the Call_QuickAndDirty procedure when that procedure is invoked by the EXEC statement. Then @@NESTLEVEL is incremented one more time when the first-invoked stored procedure executes QuickAndDirty.

17-13. Encrypting a Stored Procedure

Problem

You want to encrypt a stored procedure to prevent others from querying the system catalog views to view your code.

Solution

Create the procedure using the WITH ENCRYPTION option. Specify the option after the name of the new stored procedure, as the next example demonstrates:

```
CREATE PROCEDURE dbo.SEL_EmployeePayHistory
       WITH ENCRYPTION
AS
       SELECT   BusinessEntityID,
                RateChangeDate,
                Rate,
                PayFrequency,
                ModifiedDate
       FROM     HumanResources.EmployeePayHistory;
```

Once you've created WITH ENCRYPTION, you'll be unable to view the procedure's text definition. You can try to query for the definition:

```
EXEC sp_helptext SEL_EmployeePayHistory;
```

but you will receive only the following message:

```
The text for object 'SEL_EmployeePayHistory' is encrypted.
```

Even querying the system catalog directly won't be of help. For example, you can try this:

```
SELECT  definition
FROM    sys.sql_modules m
        INNER JOIN sys.objects o
            ON m.object_id = o.object_id
WHERE   o.type = 'P'
        AND o.name = 'SEL_EmployeePayHistory';
```

and you will be rewarded with only an empty result:

```
definition
----------
NULL
```

The procedure's definition is encrypted, and there is nothing you can do to retrieve the definition. So, be sure to keep a copy outside the database.

How It Works

Stored procedure definitions can have their contents encrypted in the database, removing the ability to read a procedure's definition later. Software vendors who use SQL Server in their back end often encrypt stored procedures in order to prevent tampering or reverse engineering from clients or competitors. If you use encryption, be sure to save the original T-SQL definition, because it can't easily be decoded later (legally and reliably, anyhow). Also perform your encryption only prior to a push to production.

■ **Caution** Be sure to save your source code, because the encrypted text cannot be decrypted easily.

17-14. Specifying a Security Context

Problem

You want to specify the source for the rights and privileges under which a stored procedure executes. For example, you might want a caller to be able to execute a procedure but not also to have the privileges needed to execute the SELECT statements that the procedure executes internally.

Solution

Create or alter the procedure and specify the EXECUTE AS clause to define the security context under which a stored procedure is executed, regardless of the caller. The options for EXECUTE AS in a stored procedure are as follows:

```
EXECUTE AS { CALLER | SELF | OWNER | 'user_name' }
```

The default behavior for EXECUTE AS is the CALLER option, which means that the permissions of the executing user are used (and if the user doesn't have proper access, that execution will fail). If the SELF option is used, the execution context of the stored procedure will be that of the user who created or last altered the stored procedure. When the OWNER option is designated, the owner of the stored procedure's schema is used. The user_name option is an explicit reference to a database user under whose security context the stored procedure will be executed.

The following example creates a version of SEL_Department that is owned by HumanResources. The clause EXECUTE AS OWNER specifies that invocations of the procedure will run under the rights and privileges granted to the schema owner.

```
CREATE PROCEDURE HumanResources.SEL_Department
      @GroupName NVARCHAR(50)
WITH EXECUTE AS OWNER
AS
      SELECT    Name
      FROM      HumanResources.Department
      WHERE     GroupName = @GroupName
      ORDER BY  Name;
      SELECT    @@ROWCOUNT AS DepartmentCount;
```

How It Works

SQL Server implements a concept termed *ownership chaining* that comes into play when a stored procedure is created and used to perform an INSERT, UPDATE, DELETE, or SELECT against another database object. If the schema of the stored procedure object is the same as the schema of the object referenced within, SQL Server checks only that the stored procedure caller has EXECUTE permissions to the stored procedure.

Ownership chaining applies only to the INSERT, UPDATE, DELETE, or SELECT commands. This is why stored procedures are excellent for securing the database, because you can grant a user access to execute a stored procedure without giving the user access to the underlying tables.

An issue arises, however, when you are looking to execute commands that are not INSERT, UPDATE, DELETE, or SELECT. In those situations, even if a caller has EXECUTE permissions to a stored procedure that, for example, truncates a table using the TRUNCATE TABLE command, she must still have permissions to use the TRUNCATE TABLE command in the first place. You may not want to grant such broad permission.

Using EXECUTE AS, you can create the procedure to run as the schema owner or as a user that you specify. You need not grant permission for TRUNCATE TABLE to all users who might invoke the procedure but only to the user you specify in the security context.

The same "gotcha" goes for dynamic SQL within a stored procedure. SQL Server will ensure that the caller has both EXECUTE permission and the appropriate permissions in order to perform the task the dynamic SQL is attempting to perform, even if that dynamic SQL is performing an INSERT, UPDATE, DELETE, or SELECT. Specifying a security context lets you avoid granting those privileges broadly to all users who might need to invoke the procedure.

17-15. Avoiding Cached Query Plans

Problem

Your procedure produces wildly different query results based on the application calling it because of varying selectivity of qualified columns, so much so that the retained execution plan causes performance issues when varying input parameters are used.

Solution

Force a recompilation upon each invocation of the procedure. Do that by including the WITH RECOMPILE clause when creating (or altering) the procedure. Here's an example:

```
ALTER PROCEDURE dbo.LookupByAccount2
      (
       @UpperFlag VARCHAR(1) = 'x',
       @AccountNumber VARCHAR(10)
      )
      WITH RECOMPILE
AS
      SELECT    CASE UPPER(@UpperFlag)
                  WHEN 'U' THEN UPPER(FirstName)
                  ELSE FirstName
                END AS FirstName,
                CASE UPPER(@UpperFlag)
                  WHEN 'U' THEN UPPER(LastName)
                  ELSE LastName
                END AS LastName
      FROM      Person.Person
      WHERE     BusinessEntityID IN (SELECT CustomerID
                                     FROM   Sales.Customer
                                     WHERE  AccountNumber = @AccountNumber);
```

Now whenever this procedure is called, a new execution plan will be created by SQL Server.

How It Works

Recompilations occur automatically when underlying table or other object changes occur to objects that are referenced within a stored procedure. They can also occur with changes to indexes used by the plan or after a large number of updates to table keys referenced by the stored procedure. The goal of an automatic recompilation is to make sure the SQL Server execution plan is using the most current information and not using out-of-date assumptions about the schema and data.

SQL Server is able to perform statement-level recompiles within a stored procedure, instead of recompiling the entire stored procedure. Because recompiles cause extra overhead in generating new plans, statement-level recompiles help decrease this overhead by correcting only what needs to be corrected.

After every recompile, SQL Server caches the execution plan for use until the next time a change to an underlying object triggers another recompile. Cached query plans are a good thing but sometimes can cause inefficient plans to be chosen. Parameter sniffing, for example, is the process of deferring the generation of an execution plan until the first invocation of a query or procedure, at which time parameter values are examined and a plan is chosen based upon those values passed that very first time. The problem sometimes arises that a plan good for one set of values is actually terrible with another set. The problem can sometimes be bad enough that it is best to recompile at each execution. That is what the solution example accomplishes.

The solution example specifies `WITH RECOMPILE` to ensure that a query plan is not cached for the procedure during creation or execution. It is rare to need the option, because generally the cached plan chosen by SQL Server will suffice. Use the option if you want to take advantage of a stored procedure's other benefits such as security and modularization but don't want SQL Server to store an inefficient plan (such as from a "parameter sniff") based on wildly varying result sets.

17-16. Flushing the Procedure Cache

Problem

You want to remove all cached query plans from the plan cache. For example, you might want to test procedure performance against a so-called *cold cache*, reproducing the cache as though SQL Server had just been restarted.

■ **Caution** Think very carefully before unleashing this recipe in a production environment because you could be knocking out several cached query plans that are perfectly fine.

Solution

Execute the `DBCC FREEPROCCACHE` command to clear existing cached plans. If you like, you can query the number of cached query plans first. Here's an example:

```
SELECT  COUNT(*) 'CachedPlansBefore'
FROM    sys.dm_exec_cached_plans;
```

```
CachedPlansBefore
-----------------
               20
```

This example shows 20 cached plans. Your results may vary, depending upon the number of procedures you have executed. Clear the cached plans by executing `DBCC FREEPROCCACHE` as follows, and retrieve the number of cached plans again. Here's an example:

```
DBCC FREEPROCCACHE;
SELECT  COUNT(*) 'CachedPlansAfter'
FROM    sys.dm_exec_cached_plans;
```

You should see output similar to the following:

```
DBCC execution completed. If DBCC printed error messages, contact your system administrator.

CachedPlansAfter
----------------
               0
```

How It Works

DBCC FREEPROCCACHE clears the procedure cache. The count of cached plans both before and after will vary based on the activity on your SQL Server instance. The query against sys.dm_exec_cached_plans shows one way to retrieve the count of plans currently in the cache. Background processes and jobs that may be running before and after the clearing of the cache can affect the results, and you may not necessarily see a zero for the number of cached plans after you've cleared the cache.

CHAPTER 18

User-Defined Functions and Types

by Jason Brimhall

In this chapter, I'll present recipes for user-defined functions and types. User-defined *functions* (UDFs) allow you to encapsulate both logic and subroutines into a single function that can then be used within your Transact-SQL queries and programmatic objects. User-defined *types* (UDTs) allow you to create an alias type based on an underlying system data type, enforcing a specific data type, length, and nullability.

In this chapter, I'll also cover the SQL Server user-defined table type, which can be used as a user-defined table parameter for passing table result sets within your T-SQL code.

UDF Basics

Transact-SQL user-defined functions fall into three categories: *scalar, inline table-valued* and *multi-statement table-valued.*

A scalar user-defined function is used to return a single value based on zero or more parameters. For example, you could create a scalar UDF that accepts a `CountryID` as a parameter and returns the `CountryNM`.

Caution If you use a scalar user-defined function in the `SELECT` clause, the function will be executed for each row in the `FROM` clause, potentially resulting in poor performance, depending on the design of your function.

An inline table-valued UDF returns a table data type based on a single `SELECT` statement that is used to define the returned rows and columns. Unlike a stored procedure, an inline UDF can be referenced in the `FROM` clause of a query, as well as be joined to other tables. Unlike a view, an inline UDF can accept parameters.

A multi-statement table-valued UDF also returns a tabular result set and is referenced in the `FROM` clause. Unlike inline table-valued UDFs, they aren't constrained to use a single `SELECT` statement within the function definition and instead allow multiple Transact-SQL statements in the body of the UDF definition in order to define a single, final result set to be returned.

UDFs can also be used in places where a stored procedure can't, like in the `FROM` and `SELECT` clauses of a query. UDFs also encourage code reusability. For example, if you create a scalar UDF that returns the `CountryNM` based on a `CountryID` and the same function is needed across several different stored procedures, rather than repeat the 20 lines of code needed to perform the lookup, you can call the UDF function instead.

In the next few recipes, I'll demonstrate how to create, drop, modify, and view metadata for each of these UDF types.

18-1. Creating Scalar Functions

Problem

You need to create a function to check or alter the values in the parameters passed into the function (such as you might do when checking for SQL Injection).

Solution

Create a scalar user-defined function. A scalar user-defined function accepts zero or more parameters and returns a single value. Scalar UDFs are often used for converting or translating a current value to a new value or performing other sophisticated lookups based on specific parameters. Scalar functions can be used within search, column, and join expressions.

The simplified syntax for a scalar UDF is as follows:

```
CREATE FUNCTION [ schema_name. ] function_name
( [ { @parameter_name [ AS ] [ type_schema_name. ] parameter_data_type [ = default ]
[ READONLY ] } [ ,...n ] ] ) RETURNS return_data_type
[ WITH <function_option> [ ,...n ] ]
[ AS ]
BEGIN
function_body RETURN scalar_expression END
```

■ **Note** The full syntax for `CREATE FUNCTION` can be found in SQL Server Books Online.

Table 18-1 briefly describes each argument's intended use.

Table 18-1. *Scalar UDF Arguments*

Argument	Description
`[ schema_name. ] function_name`	This argument defines the optional schema name and required function name of the new scalar UDF.
`@parameter_name`	This is the name of the parameter to pass to the UDF, and it must be prefixed with an `@` sign.
`[ type_schema_name. ] scalar_parameter_data_type`	This is the parameter data type and its associated (optional) schema.
`[ ,...n ]`	Although not an actual argument, this syntax element indicates that one or more parameters can be defined (up to 1,024).
`return_data_type`	This specifies the data type the user-defined function will return.
`function_body`	This function body contains one or more of the Transact-SQL statements that are used to produce and evaluate a scalar value.
`scalar_expression`	This is the actual value that will be returned by the scalar function (notice that it is defined after the function body).

This example creates a scalar UDF that accepts a varchar(max) data type parameter. It returns a bit value (1 or 0) based on whether the passed parameter contains suspicious values (as defined by the function). So, if the input parameter contains a call to a command such as `DELETE` or `SHUTDOWN`, the flag is set to 1:

```
Use AdventureWorks2012;
GO

Create Function dbo.udf_CheckForSQLInjection (@TSQLString varchar(max))
Returns bit

AS

BEGIN

DECLARE @IsSuspect bit;

-- UDF assumes string will be left padded with a single space
SET @TSQLString = ' ' + @TSQLString;

IF    (PATINDEX('% xp_%' , @TSQLString ) <> 0 OR
   PATINDEX('% sp_%' , @TSQLString ) <> 0   OR
   PATINDEX('% DROP %' , @TSQLString ) <> 0  OR
   PATINDEX('% GO %' , @TSQLString ) <> 0 OR
   PATINDEX('% INSERT %' , @TSQLString ) <> 0 OR
   PATINDEX('% UPDATE %' , @TSQLString ) <> 0 OR
   PATINDEX('% DBCC %' , @TSQLString ) <> 0  OR
   PATINDEX('% SHUTDOWN %' , @TSQLString )<> 0 OR
   PATINDEX('% ALTER %' , @TSQLString )<> 0  OR
   PATINDEX('% CREATE %' , @TSQLString ) <> 0 OR
   PATINDEX('%;%' , @TSQLString )<> 0 OR
   PATINDEX('% EXECUTE %' , @TSQLString )<> 0 OR
   PATINDEX('% BREAK %' , @TSQLString )<> 0  OR
   PATINDEX('% BEGIN %' , @TSQLString )<> 0  OR
   PATINDEX('% CHECKPOINT %' , @TSQLString )<> 0 OR
   PATINDEX('% BREAK %' , @TSQLString )<> 0  OR
   PATINDEX('% COMMIT %' , @TSQLString )<> 0  OR
   PATINDEX('% TRANSACTION %' , @TSQLString )<> 0 OR
   PATINDEX('% CURSOR %' , @TSQLString )<> 0  OR
   PATINDEX('% GRANT %' , @TSQLString )<> 0  OR
   PATINDEX('% DENY %' , @TSQLString )<> 0   OR
   PATINDEX('% ESCAPE %' , @TSQLString )<> 0  OR
   PATINDEX('% WHILE %' , @TSQLString )<> 0  OR
   PATINDEX('% OPENDATASOURCE %' , @TSQLString )<> 0 OR
   PATINDEX('% OPENQUERY %' , @TSQLString )<> 0 OR
   PATINDEX('% OPENROWSET %' , @TSQLString )<> 0   OR
   PATINDEX('% EXEC %' , @TSQLString )<> 0)

BEGIN
   SELECT @IsSuspect =   1;
END
ELSE
BEGIN
   SELECT @IsSuspect =   0;
END
   RETURN (@IsSuspect);
END

GO
```

Next, you should test the function by evaluating three different string input values. The first contains a SELECT statement.

```
Use AdventureWorks2012;
GO
SELECT dbo.udf_CheckForSQLInjection ('SELECT * FROM HumanResources.Department');
```

This query returns the following:

```
0
```

The next string contains the SHUTDOWN command.

```
Use AdventureWorks2012;
GO
SELECT dbo.udf_CheckForSQLInjection (';SHUTDOWN');
```

This query returns the following:

```
1
```

The last string tested contains the DROP command.

```
Use AdventureWorks2012;
GO
SELECT dbo.udf_CheckForSQLInjection ('DROP HumanResources.Department');
```

This query returns the following:

```
1
```

In the next example, I create a user-defined function that can be used to set a string to the proper case:

```
Use AdventureWorks2012;
GO
CREATE FUNCTION dbo.udf_ProperCase(@UnCased varchar(max))
RETURNS varchar(max)
AS
BEGIN
SET @UnCased = LOWER(@UnCased)
DECLARE @C int
SET @C = ASCII('a')
WHILE @C <= ASCII('z') BEGIN
SET @UnCased = REPLACE( @UnCased, ' ' + CHAR(@C), ' ' + CHAR(@C-32)) SET @C = @C + 1
END
SET @UnCased = CHAR(ASCII(LEFT(@UnCased, 1))-32) + RIGHT(@UnCased, LEN(@UnCased)-1)

RETURN @UnCased END
GO
```

Once the user-defined function is created, the string to modify (to proper case) can be used as the function parameter.

```
SELECT dbo.udf_ProperCase(DocumentSummary)
FROM Production.Document
WHERE FileName = 'Installing Replacement Pedals.doc'
```

This query returns the following:

```
Detailed Instructions For Replacing Pedals With Adventure Works Cycles Replacement Pedals.
Instructions Are Applicable To All Adventure Works Cycles Bicycle Models And Replacement
Pedals. Use Only Adventure Works Cycles Parts When Replacing Worn Or Broken Components.
```

How It Works

This recipe demonstrated a scalar UDF, which in this case accepted one parameter and returned a single value. Some of the areas where you can use a scalar function in your Transact-SQL code include the following:

- A column expression in a SELECT or GROUP BY clause
- A search condition for a JOIN in a FROM clause
- A search condition of a WHERE or HAVING clause

The recipe began by defining the UDF name and parameter:

```
CREATE FUNCTION dbo.udf_CheckForSQLInjection (@TSQLString varchar(max))
```

The @TSQLString parameter held the varchar(max) string to be evaluated. In the next line of code, the scalar_return_data_type was defined as bit. This means that the single value returned by the function will be the bit data type.

```
RETURNS BIT AS
```

The BEGIN marked the start of the function_body, where the logic to return the bit value was formulated.

```
BEGIN
```

A local variable was created to hold the bit value. Ultimately, this is the parameter that will be passed as the function's output:

```
DECLARE @IsSuspect bit
```

Next, the string passed to the UDF has a space concatenated to the front of it.

```
-- UDF assumes string will be left padded with a single space SET @TSQLString = ' ' +
@TSQLString
```

The @TSQLString was padded with an extra space in order to make the search of suspicious words or patterns easier to do. For example, if the suspicious word is at the beginning of the @TSQLString and you were searching for the word *drop*, you would have to use PATINDEX to search for both '%DROP %' and '% DROP %'. Of course, searching '%DROP %' could give you false positives, such as the word *gumdrop*, so you should prevent this confusion by padding the beginning of the string with a space.

In the IF statement, @TSQLString is evaluated using PATINDEX. For each evaluation, if a match is found, the condition will evaluate to TRUE.

```
IF  (PATINDEX('% xp_%' , @TSQLString ) <> 0 OR PATINDEX('% sp_%' , @TSQLString ) <> 0 OR
PATINDEX('% DROP %' , @TSQLString ) <> 0 OR PATINDEX('% GO %' , @TSQLString ) <> 0 OR
PATINDEX('% BREAK %' , @TSQLString )<> 0 OR
```

If any of the conditions evaluates to TRUE, the @IsSuspect bit flag will be set to 1.

```
BEGIN
   SELECT @IsSuspect =   1;
END
ELSE
BEGIN
   SELECT @IsSuspect =   0;
END
```

The RETURN keyword is used to pass the scalar value of the @IsSuspect variable back to the caller.

```
RETURN (@IsSuspect)
```

The END keyword is then used to close the UDF, and GO is used to end the batch.

```
END
GO
```

The new scalar UDF created in this recipe was then used to check three different string values. The first string, SELECT * FROM HumanResources.Department, comes up clean, but the second and third strings, SHUTDOWN and DROP HumanResources.Department, both return a bit value of 1 because they match the suspicious word searches in the function's IF clause.

SQL Server doesn't provide a built-in proper case function, so in my second example, I demonstrate creating a user-defined function that performs this action. The first line of the CREATE FUNCTION definition defines the name and parameter expected—in this case, a varchar(max) data type parameter.

```
CREATE FUNCTION dbo.udf_ProperCase(@UnCased varchar(max))
```

The RETURNS keyword defined what data type would be returned by the function after the logic has been applied.

```
RETURNS varchar(max)
AS
BEGIN
```

Next, the variable passed to the function was first modified to lowercase using the LOWER function.

```
SET @UnCased = LOWER(@UnCased)
```

A new integer local variable, @C, was set to the ASCII value of the letter *a*.

```
DECLARE @C int
SET @C = ASCII('a')
```

A WHILE loop was initiated to go through every letter in the alphabet and, for each, search for a space preceding that letter and then replace each occurrence of a letter preceded by a space with the uppercase version of the character.

```
WHILE @C <= ASCII('z') BEGIN
SET @UnCased = REPLACE( @UnCased, ' ' + CHAR(@C), ' ' + CHAR(@C-32)) SET @C = @C + 1
END
```

The conversion to uppercase is performed by subtracting 32 from the ASCII integer value of the lowercase character. For example, the ASCII value for a lowercase *a* is 97, while the uppercase *A* is 65.

```
SET @UnCased = CHAR(ASCII(LEFT(@UnCased, 1))-32) + RIGHT(@UnCased, LEN(@UnCased)-1)
```

The final proper case string value of @UnCased is then returned from the function.

```
RETURN @UnCased END GO
```

Next, I used the new scalar UDF in the SELECT clause of a query to convert the DocumentSummary text to the proper case:

```
SELECT dbo.udf_ProperCase(DocumentSummary)
```

18-2. Creating Inline Functions

Problem

You need to create a reusable query that can return data in a table form and potentially be joined to tables in queries found throughout views and stored procedures in your database.

Solution

Create an inline user-defined function. An inline UDF returns a `table` data type. In the UDF definition, you do not explicitly define the returned table but use a single `SELECT` statement for defining the returned rows and columns instead. An inline UDF uses one or more parameters and returns data using a single `SELECT` statement. Inline UDFs are very similar to views, in that they are referenced in the `FROM` clause. However, unlike views, UDFs can accept parameters that can then be used in the function's `SELECT` statement. The basic syntax is as follows:

```
CREATE FUNCTION [ schema_name. ] function_name
( [ { @parameter_name [ AS ] [ type_schema_name. ] scalar_parameter_data_type [ = default ]
} [ ,...n ] ]
) RETURNS TABLE [ AS ] RETURN [ ( ] select_stmt [ ) ]
```

■ **Note** The full syntax for `CREATE FUNCTION` can be found in SQL Server Books Online.

Table 18-2 details the arguments of this command.

Table 18-2. *Inline UDF Arguments*

Argument	Description
`[ schema_name. ] function_name`	This defines the optional schema name and required function name of the new inline UDF.
`@parameter_name`	This is the name of the parameter to pass to the UDF. It must be prefixed with an @ sign.
`[ type_schema_name. ] scalar_parameter_data_type`	This is the `@parameter_name` data type and the optional `scalar_parameter_data_type` owning schema (used if you are employing a user-defined type).
`[ ,...n ]`	Although not an actual argument, this syntax element indicates that one or more parameters can be defined (up to 1,024).
`select_stmt`	This is the single `SELECT` statement that will be returned by the inline UDF.

The following example demonstrates creating an inline table UDF that accepts an integer parameter and returns the associated addresses of a business entity:

```
Use AdventureWorks2012;
GO
CREATE FUNCTION dbo.udf_ReturnAddress
(@BusinessEntityID int)
RETURNS TABLE
AS RETURN (
SELECT t.Name AddressTypeNM, a.AddressLine1, a.City,
```

```
a.StateProvinceID, a.PostalCode
FROM Person.Address a
INNER JOIN Person.BusinessEntityAddress e
ON a.AddressID = e.AddressID
INNER JOIN Person.AddressType t
ON e.AddressTypeID = t.AddressTypeID
WHERE e.BusinessEntityID = @BusinessEntityID )
;
GO
```

Next, the new function is tested in a query, referenced in the FROM clause for business entity 332:

```
Use AdventureWorks2012;
GO
SELECT AddressTypeNM, AddressLine1, City, PostalCode
FROM dbo.udf_ReturnAddress(332);
GO
```

This query returns the following:

```
AddressTypeNM   AddressLine1           City       PostalCode
-------------   --------------------   --------   ----------
Shipping        26910 Indela Road      Montreal   H1Y 2H5
Main Office     25981 College Street   Montreal   H1Y 2H5
```

How It Works

In this recipe, I created an inline table UDF to retrieve the addresses of a business entity based on the @BusinessEntityID value passed. The UDF started off just like a scalar UDF, but the RETURNS command used a TABLE data type (which is what distinguishes it from a scalar UDF):

```
CREATE FUNCTION dbo.udf_ReturnAddress
(@BusinessEntityID int)
RETURNS TABLE
AS
```

After the AS keyword, the RETURN statement was issued with a single SELECT statement in parentheses:

```
RETURN (
SELECT t.Name AddressTypeNM, a.AddressLine1, a.City,
a.StateProvinceID, a.PostalCode
FROM Person.Address a
INNER JOIN Person.BusinessEntityAddress e
ON a.AddressID = e.AddressID
INNER JOIN Person.AddressType t
ON e.AddressTypeID = t.AddressTypeID
WHERE e.BusinessEntityID = @BusinessEntityID )
;
GO
```

After it was created, the new inline UDF was then used in the FROM clause of a SELECT query. The @BusinessEntityID value of 332 was passed into the function in parentheses:

```
SELECT AddressTypeNM, AddressLine1, City, PostalCode
FROM dbo.udf_ReturnAddress(332);
GO
```

This function then returns a result set, just like when you are querying a view or a table. Also, just like a view or stored procedure, the query you create to define this function must be tuned as you would a regular SELECT statement. Using an inline UDF offers no inherent performance benefits over using a view or stored procedure.

18-3. Creating Multi-Statement User-Defined Functions

Problem

You need to create a function that can accept multiple parameters and that will be able to execute multiple SELECT statements.

Solution

Create a multi-statement table user-defined function. Multi-statement table UDFs are referenced in the FROM clause just like inline UDFs, but unlike inline UDFs, they are not constrained to use a single SELECT statement within the function definition. Instead, multi-statement UDFs can use multiple Transact-SQL statements in the body of the UDF definition in order to define that a single, final result set be returned. The basic syntax of a multi-statement table UDF is as follows:

```
CREATE FUNCTION [ schema_name. ] function_name
( [ { @parameter_name [ AS ] [ type_schema_name. ] parameter_data_type [ = default ] [READONLY]
} [ ,...n ] ] )
RETURNS @return_variable TABLE <table_type_definition> [ WITH <function_option> [ ,...n ] ] [ AS ]
 BEGIN
function_body RETURN END
```

Table 18-3 describes the arguments of this command.

Table 18-3. Multi-Statement UDF Arguments

Argument	Description
[schema_name.] function_name	This specifies the optional schema name and required function name of the new inline UDF.
@parameter_name	This is the name of the parameter to pass to the UDF. It must be prefixed with an @ sign.
[type_schema_name.] scalar_parameter_data_type	This is the data type of the @parameter_name and the scalar_parameter_data_type optional owning schema (used if you are using a user-defined type).
[,...n]	Although not an actual argument, this syntax element indicates that one or more parameters can be defined (up to 1,024).
@return_variable	This is the user-defined name of the table variable that will hold the results to be returned by the UDF.
< table_type_definition >	This argument contains one or more column definitions for the table variable. Each column definition contains the name and data type and can optionally define a PRIMARY KEY, UNIQUE, NULL, or CHECK constraint.
function_body	The function body contains one or more Transact-SQL statements that are used to populate and modify the table variable that will be returned by the UDF.

Notice the RETURNS keyword, which defines a *table variable* definition. Also notice the RETURN keyword at the end of the function, which doesn't have any parameter or query after it, because it is assumed that the defined table variable will be returned.

In this example, a multi-statement UDF will be created that accepts two parameters: one to hold a string and the other to define how that string will be delimited. The string is then broken apart into a result set based on the defined delimiter:

```
-- Creates a UDF that returns a string array as a table result set
Use AdventureWorks2012;
GO
CREATE FUNCTION dbo.udf_ParseArray
( @StringArray varchar(max), @Delimiter char(1) ) RETURNS @StringArrayTable TABLE (Val
varchar(50))
AS
BEGIN
DECLARE @Delimiter_position int
IF RIGHT(@StringArray,1) != @Delimiter
SET @StringArray = @StringArray + @Delimiter
WHILE CHARINDEX(@Delimiter, @StringArray) <> 0
BEGIN
SELECT @Delimiter_position = CHARINDEX(@Delimiter, @StringArray)
INSERT INTO @StringArrayTable (Val)
   VALUES (LEFT(@StringArray, @Delimiter_position - 1));
SELECT @StringArray = STUFF(@StringArray, 1, @Delimiter_position, '') ;
END

RETURN
END
GO
```

Now it will be used to break apart a comma-delimited array of values.

```
SELECT Val
FROM dbo.udf_ParseArray('A,B,C,D,E,F,G', ',');
GO
```

This returns the following results:

```
Val
---
A
B
C
D
E
F
G
```

How It Works

The multi-statement table UDF in this recipe was created using two parameters, the first to hold a string and the second to define the character that delimits the string:

```
CREATE FUNCTION dbo.udf_ParseArray
( @StringArray varchar(max), @Delimiter char(1) )
```

Next, a table variable was defined after the RETURNS token. The @StringArrayTable was used to hold the values of the string array after being shredded into the individual values:

```
RETURNS @StringArrayTable TABLE (Val varchar(50))
```

The function body started after AS and BEGIN.

```
AS
BEGIN
```

A local variable was created to hold the delimiter position in the string.

```
DECLARE @Delimiter_position int
```

If the last character of the string array wasn't the delimiter value, then the delimiter value was concatenated to the end of the string array.

```
IF RIGHT(@StringArray,1) != @Delimiter
SET @StringArray = @StringArray + @Delimiter
```

A WHILE loop was created, looping until there were no remaining delimiters in the string array.

```
WHILE CHARINDEX(@Delimiter, @StringArray) <> 0
BEGIN
```

Within the loop, the position of the delimiter was identified using CHARINDEX.

```
SELECT @Delimiter_position = CHARINDEX(@Delimiter, @StringArray)
```

The LEFT function was used with the delimiter position to extract the individual-delimited string part into the table variable:

```
INSERT INTO @StringArrayTable (Val)
   VALUES (LEFT(@StringArray, @Delimiter_position - 1));
```

The inserted chunk was then removed from the string array using the STUFF function.

```
SELECT @StringArray = STUFF(@StringArray, 1, @Delimiter_position, '') ;
```

STUFF is used to delete a chunk of characters and insert another character string in its place. This first parameter of the STUFF function is the character expression, which in this example is the string array. The second parameter is the starting position of the deleted and inserted text, and in this case I am removing text from the string starting at the first position and stopping at the first delimiter. The third parameter is the length of the characters to be deleted, which for this example is the delimiter-position variable value. The last argument is the string to be inserted, which in this case was a blank string represented by two single quotes. The net effect is that the first comma-separated entry was replaced by an empty string—the same result as if the first entry had been deleted.

This process of inserting values continued until there were no longer delimiters in the string array. After this, the WHILE loop ended, and RETURN was called to return the table variable result set.

```
END RETURN END GO
```

The new UDF was then referenced in the FROM clause. The first parameter of the UDF was a comma-delimited list of letters. The second parameter was the delimiting parameter (a comma):

```
-- Now use it to break apart a comma-delimited array
SELECT Val
FROM dbo.udf_ParseArray('A,B,C,D,E,F,G', ',');
GO
```

The list was then broken into a result set, with each individual letter as its own row. As you can see, multi-statement table UDFs allow for much more sophisticated programmability than an inline table-valued UDF, which can use only a single SELECT statement.

18-4. Modifying User-Defined Functions

Problem

You have determined that a user-defined function is not producing the desired results. You need to modify this function.

Solution

A function can be modified by using the ALTER FUNCTION command, as I demonstrate in this next recipe:

```
Use AdventureWorks2012;
GO
ALTER FUNCTION dbo.udf_ParseArray ( @StringArray varchar(max),
@Delimiter char(1),
@MinRowSelect int,
@MaxRowSelect int)
RETURNS @StringArrayTable TABLE (RowNum int IDENTITY(1,1), Val varchar(50))
AS
BEGIN

DECLARE @Delimiter_position int
IF RIGHT(@StringArray,1) != @Delimiter
   SET @StringArray = @StringArray + @Delimiter;
WHILE CHARINDEX(@Delimiter, @StringArray) <> 0
BEGIN
SELECT @Delimiter_position = CHARINDEX(@Delimiter, @StringArray);

INSERT INTO @StringArrayTable (Val)
   VALUES (LEFT(@StringArray, @Delimiter_position - 1));

SELECT @StringArray = STUFF(@StringArray, 1, @Delimiter_position, '');
END
DELETE @StringArrayTable
   WHERE RowNum < @MinRowSelect OR RowNum > @MaxRowSelect;
RETURN
END
GO

Now use it to break apart a comma delimited array
Use AdventureWorks2012;
GO
SELECT RowNum,Val
FROM dbo.udf_ParseArray('A,B,C,D,E,F,G', ',',3,5);
GO
```

This query returns the following:

```
RowNum  Val
------  ---
3       C
4       D
5       E
```

How It Works

ALTER FUNCTION allows you to modify an existing UDF by using syntax that is almost identical to that of CREATE FUNCTION, with some limitations:

- You can't change the name of the function using ALTER FUNCTION. What you're doing is replacing the code of an *existing* function—therefore, the function needs to exist first.
- You can't convert a scalar UDF to a table UDF (either inline or multi-statement), and you cannot convert a table UDF to a scalar UDF.

In this recipe, the udf_ParseArray from the previous recipe was modified to add two new parameters, @MinRowSelect and @MaxRowSelect.

```
ALTER FUNCTION dbo.udf_ParseArray ( @StringArray varchar(max),
@Delimiter char(1) ,
@MinRowSelect int,
@MaxRowSelect int)
```

The @StringArrayTable table variable also had a new column added to it called RowNum, which was given the IDENTITY property (meaning that it will increment an integer value for each row in the result set).

```
RETURNS @StringArrayTable TABLE (RowNum int IDENTITY(1,1), Val varchar(50))
```

The other modification came after the WHILE loop was finished. Any RowNum values less than the minimum or maximum values were deleted from the @StringArrayTable table array.

```
DELETE @StringArrayTable
   WHERE RowNum < @MinRowSelect OR RowNum > @MaxRowSelect;
```

After altering the function, the function was called using the two new parameters to define the row range to view (in this case, rows 3 through 5).

```
Use AdventureWorks2012;
GO
SELECT RowNum,Val
FROM dbo.udf_ParseArray('A,B,C,D,E,F,G', ',',3,5);
GO
```

This returned the third, fourth, and fifth characters from the string array passed to the UDF.

18-5. Viewing UDF Metadata

Problem

You want to view a list and the definitions of all user-defined functions in your database.

Solution

Query the catalog view sys.sql_modules. You can use the sys.sql_modules catalog view to view information regarding all user-defined functions within a database. In this recipe, I will demonstrate how to view the name and the definition of each function.

```
Use AdventureWorks2012;
GO
SELECT name, o.type_desc
   ,(Select definition as [processing-instruction(definition)]
      FROM sys.sql_modules
      Where object_id = s.object_id
      FOR XML PATH(''), TYPE
   )
FROM sys.sql_modules s
INNER JOIN sys.objects o
   ON s.object_id = o.object_id
WHERE o.type IN ('IF', -- Inline Table UDF
   'TF', -- Multistatement Table UDF
   'FN') -- Scalar UDF
;
```

How It Works

The sys.sql_modules and sys.objects system views are used to return the UDF name, type description, and SQL definition in a query result set.

```
FROM sys.sql_modules s
INNER JOIN sys.objects o
   ON s.object_id = o.object_id
```

The SQL definition is maintained in sys.sql_modules. In this example, I have shown how to return the result in a clickable format, which will render the function formatted as it is stored in the database (and for readability). This is done through the FOR XML PATH command using the processing-instruction directive.

```
   ,(Select definition as [processing-instruction(definition)]
      FROM sys.sql_modules
      Where object_id = s.object_id
      FOR XML PATH(''), TYPE
   )
```

Because sys.sql_modules contains rows for other object types, sys.objects must also be qualified to return only UDF rows.

```
WHERE o.type IN ('IF', -- Inline Table UDF
   'TF', -- Multistatement Table UDF
   'FN') -- Scalar UDF
;
```

Benefitting from UDFs

User-defined functions are useful for both the performance enhancements they provide because of their cached execution plans and their ability to encapsulate reusable code. In this next section, I'll discuss some of the benefits of UDFs. For example, scalar functions in particular can be used to help make code more readable and allow you to apply lookup rules consistently across an application rather than repeating the same code multiple times throughout different stored procedures or views.

Table-valued functions are also useful for allowing you to apply parameters to results, for example, using a parameter to define row-level security for a data set (demonstrated later in the chapter).

■ **Caution** When designing user-defined functions, consider the multiplier effect. For example, if you create a scalar user-defined function that performs a lookup against a million-row table in order to return a single value and if a single lookup with proper indexing takes 30 seconds, chances are you are going to see a significant performance hit if you use this UDF to return values based on each row of another large table. If scalar user-defined functions reference other tables, make sure that the query you use to access the table information performs well and doesn't return a result set that is too large.

The next few recipes will demonstrate some of the more common and beneficial ways in which user-defined functions are used in the field.

18-6. Maintaining Reusable Code

Problem

You have discovered that a code segment has been duplicated numerous times throughout your database. You want to reduce the amount of code bloat in the database.

Solution

Create an appropriate UDF. For instance, scalar UDFs allow you to reduce code bloat by encapsulating logic within a single function, rather than repeating the logic multiple times wherever it happens to be needed.

The following scalar, user-defined function is used to determine the kind of personal computer that an employee will receive. There are several lines of code that evaluate different input parameters, including the employee's title, hire date, and salaried status. Rather than include this logic in multiple areas across your database application, you can encapsulate the logic in a single function.

```
Use AdventureWorks2012;
GO
CREATE FUNCTION dbo.udf_GET_AssignedEquipment (@Title nvarchar(50), @HireDate datetime,
@SalariedFlag bit)
RETURNS nvarchar(50)
AS
BEGIN
DECLARE @EquipmentType nvarchar(50)
IF @Title LIKE 'Chief%' OR
   @Title LIKE 'Vice%' OR
   @Title = 'Database Administrator'
BEGIN
   SET @EquipmentType = 'PC Build A' ;
END
IF @EquipmentType IS NULL AND @SalariedFlag = 1
BEGIN
```

```
   SET @EquipmentType = 'PC Build B' ;
END
IF @EquipmentType IS NULL AND @HireDate < '1/1/2002'
BEGIN
   SET @EquipmentType = 'PC Build C' ;
END
IF @EquipmentType IS NULL
BEGIN
   SET @EquipmentType = 'PC Build D' ;
END
RETURN @EquipmentType ;
END
GO
```

Once you've created it, you can use this scalar function in many areas of your Transact-SQL code without having to recode the logic within. In the following example, the new scalar function is used in the SELECT, GROUP BY, and ORDER BY clauses of a query:

```
Use AdventureWorks2012;
GO
SELECT PC_Build = dbo.udf_GET_AssignedEquipment(JobTitle, HireDate, SalariedFlag)
   , Employee_Count = COUNT(*)
FROM HumanResources.Employee
GROUP BY dbo.udf_GET_AssignedEquipment(JobTitle, HireDate, SalariedFlag)
ORDER BY dbo.udf_GET_AssignedEquipment(JobTitle, HireDate, SalariedFlag);
```

This query returns the following:

```
PC_Build        Employee_Count
----------      --------------
PC Build A      7
PC Build B      45
PC Build C      2
PC Build D      236
```

This second query uses the scalar function in both the SELECT and WHERE clauses, too:

```
Use AdventureWorks2012;
GO
SELECT JobTitle,BusinessEntityID
   ,PC_Build = dbo.udf_GET_AssignedEquipment(JobTitle, HireDate, SalariedFlag)
FROM HumanResources.Employee
WHERE dbo.udf_GET_AssignedEquipment(JobTitle, HireDate, SalariedFlag)
   IN ('PC Build A', 'PC Build B');
```

This returns the following (abridged) results:

```
JobTitle                        BusinessEntityID   PC_Build
-----------------------------   ----------------   ----------
Chief Executive Officer         1                  PC Build A
Vice President of Engineering   2                  PC Build A
Engineering Manager             3                  PC Build B
Design Engineer                 5                  PC Build B
Design Engineer                 6                  PC Build B
...
```

How It Works

Scalar, user-defined functions can help you encapsulate business logic so that it isn't repeated across your code, providing a centralized location for you to make a single modification to a single function when necessary. This also provides consistency so that you and other database developers are consistently using and writing the same logic in the same way. One other benefit is code readability, particularly with large queries that perform multiple lookups or evaluations.

18-7. Cross-Referencing Natural Key Values

A *surrogate key* is an artificial primary key, as opposed to a *natural key*, which represents a unique descriptor of data (for example, a Social Security number is an example of a natural key, but an `IDENTITY` property column is a surrogate key). `IDENTITY` values are often used as surrogate primary keys but are also referenced as foreign keys.

In my own OLTP and star schema database designs, I assign each table a surrogate key by default, unless there is a significant reason not to do so. Doing this helps you abstract your own unique key from any external legacy natural keys. If you are using, for example, an `EmployeeNumber` that comes from the HR system as your primary key instead, you could run into trouble later if that HR system decides to change its data type (forcing you to change the primary key, any foreign key references, and composite primary keys). Surrogate keys help protect you from changes like this because they are under your control and so they make good primary keys. You can keep your natural keys' unique constraints without worrying about external changes impacting your primary or foreign keys.

When importing data from legacy systems into production tables, you'll often still need to reference the natural key in order to determine which rows get inserted, updated, or deleted. This isn't very tricky if you're just dealing with a single column (for example, `EmployeeID`, `CreditCardNumber`, `SSN`, `UPC`). However, if the natural key is made up of multiple columns, the cross-referencing to the production tables may not be quite so easy.

Problem

You are using natural keys and surrogate keys within your database. You need to verify that a natural key exists prior to performing certain actions.

Solution

You can create a scalar, user-defined function that can be used to perform natural key lookups.

The following demonstrates a scalar, user-defined function that can be used to simplify natural key lookups, by checking for their existence prior to performing an action. To set up the example, I'll create a few objects and execute a few commands.

First, I'll create a new table that uses its own surrogate keys, along with three columns that make up the composite natural key (these three columns form the unique value that was received from the legacy system).

```
Use AdventureWorks2012;
GO
CREATE TABLE dbo.DimProductSalesperson
(DimProductSalespersonID int IDENTITY(1,1) NOT NULL PRIMARY KEY,
ProductCD char(10) NOT NULL,
CompanyNBR int NOT NULL,
SalespersonNBR int NOT NULL );
GO
```

■ **Caution** This recipe doesn't add indexes to the tables (beyond the default clustered index that is created on `dbo.DimProductSalesperson`); however, in a real-life scenario, you'll want to add indexes for key columns used for join operations or qualified in the `WHERE` clause of a query.

Next, I'll create a staging table that holds rows from the external legacy data file. For example, this table could be populated from an external text file that is dumped out of the legacy system. This table doesn't have a primary key, because it is just used to hold data prior to being moved to the `dbo.DimProductSalesperson` table.

```
Use AdventureWorks2012;
GO
CREATE TABLE dbo.Staging_PRODSLSP ( ProductCD char(10) NOT NULL,
CompanyNBR int NOT NULL,
SalespersonNBR int NOT NULL );
GO
```

Next, I'll insert two rows into the staging table.

```
Use AdventureWorks2012;
GO
INSERT dbo.Staging_PRODSLSP (ProductCD, CompanyNBR, SalespersonNBR)
   VALUES ('2391A23904', 1, 24);
INSERT dbo.Staging_PRODSLSP (ProductCD, CompanyNBR, SalespersonNBR)
   VALUES ('X129483203', 1, 34);
GO
```

Now, these two rows can be inserted into the `DimProductSalesperson` table using the following query, which *doesn't* use a scalar UDF.

```
Use AdventureWorks2012;
GO
INSERT Into dbo.DimProductSalesperson (ProductCD, CompanyNBR, SalespersonNBR)
   SELECT s.ProductCD, s.CompanyNBR, s.SalespersonNBR
      FROM  dbo.Staging_PRODSLSP s
      LEFT  OUTER JOIN dbo.DimProductSalesperson d
         ON  s.ProductCD = d.ProductCD
         AND s.CompanyNBR = d.CompanyNBR
         AND s.SalespersonNBR = d.SalespersonNBR
   WHERE  d.DimProductSalespersonID IS NULL;
GO
```

Because each column forms the natural key, I must `LEFT` join each column from the inserted table against the staging table and then check to see whether the row does not already exist in the destination table using `IS NULL`.

An alternative to this, allowing you to reduce the code in each INSERT/UPDATE/DELETE, is to create a scalar UDF like the following:

```
Use AdventureWorks2012;
GO
CREATE FUNCTION dbo.udf_GET_Check_NK_DimProductSalesperson (@ProductCD char(10), @CompanyNBR
int, @SalespersonNBR int )
RETURNS bit
AS
BEGIN
DECLARE @Exists bit
IF EXISTS (SELECT DimProductSalespersonID
       FROM dbo.DimProductSalesperson
       WHERE @ProductCD = @ProductCD
       AND @CompanyNBR = @CompanyNBR
       AND @SalespersonNBR = @SalespersonNBR)
BEGIN
   SET @Exists = 1;
END
ELSE
BEGIN
   SET @Exists = 0;
END
RETURN @Exists
END
GO
```

The UDF certainly looks like more code up front, but you'll obtain the benefit later during the data import process. For example, now you can rewrite the INSERT operation demonstrated earlier, as follows:

```
Use AdventureWorks2012;
GO
INSERT INTO dbo.DimProductSalesperson(ProductCD, CompanyNBR, SalespersonNBR)
   SELECT ProductCD, CompanyNBR, SalespersonNBR
      FROM dbo.Staging_PRODSLSP
      WHERE dbo.udf_GET_Check_NK_DimProductSalesperson
         (ProductCD, CompanyNBR, SalespersonNBR) = 0;
GO
```

How It Works

In this recipe, I demonstrated how to create a scalar UDF that returned a bit value based on three parameters. If the three values already existed for a row in the production table, a 1 was returned; otherwise, a 0 was returned. Using this function simplifies the INSERT/UPDATE/DELETE code that you must write in situations where a natural key spans multiple columns.

Walking through the UDF code, the first lines defined the UDF name and parameters. Each of these parameters is for the composite natural key in the staging and production tables.

```
CREATE FUNCTION dbo.udf_GET_Check_NK_DimProductSalesperson (@ProductCD char(10), @CompanyNBR
int, @SalespersonNBR int )
```

Next, a bit data type was defined to be returned by the function.

```
RETURNS bit
AS
BEGIN
```

A local variable was created to hold the bit value.

```
DECLARE @IfExists bit
```

An IF was used to check for the existence of a row matching all three parameters for the natural composite key. If there is a match, the local variable is set to 1. If not, it is set to 0.

```
IF EXISTS (SELECT DimProductSalespersonID
        FROM dbo.DimProductSalesperson
        WHERE @ProductCD = @ProductCD
        AND @CompanyNBR = @CompanyNBR
        AND @SalespersonNBR = @SalespersonNBR)
BEGIN
   SET @Exists = 1;
END
ELSE
BEGIN
   SET @Exists = 0;
END
```

The local variable was then passed back to the caller.

```
RETURN @IfExists END
GO
```

The function was then used in the WHERE clause, extracting from the staging table those rows that returned a 0 from the scalar UDF and therefore do not exist in the DimProductSalesperson table.

```
WHERE dbo.udf_GET_Check_NK_DimProductSalesperson (ProductCD, CompanyNBR, SalespersonNBR) = 0
```

18-8. Replacing a View with a Function

Problem

You have a view in your database that you need to parameterize.

Solution

Create a multi-statement UDF to replace the view. Multi-statement UDFs allow you to return data in the same way you would from a view, only with the ability to manipulate data like a stored procedure.

In this example, a multi-statement UDF is created to apply row-based security based on the caller of the function. Only rows for the specified salesperson will be returned. In addition to this, the second parameter is a bit flag that controls whether rows from the SalesPersonQuotaHistory table will be returned in the results.

```
Use AdventureWorks2012;
GO
CREATE FUNCTION dbo.udf_SEL_SalesQuota ( @BusinessEntityID int, @ShowHistory bit )
RETURNS @SalesQuota TABLE (BusinessEntityID int, QuotaDate datetime, SalesQuota money)
AS
BEGIN
```

```
INSERT Into @SalesQuota(BusinessEntityID, QuotaDate, SalesQuota)
   SELECT BusinessEntityID, ModifiedDate, SalesQuota
   FROM Sales.SalesPerson
   WHERE BusinessEntityID = @BusinessEntityID;
IF @ShowHistory = 1
BEGIN
INSERT Into @SalesQuota(BusinessEntityID, QuotaDate, SalesQuota)
   SELECT BusinessEntityID, QuotaDate, SalesQuota
   FROM Sales.SalesPersonQuotaHistory
   WHERE BusinessEntityID = @BusinessEntityID;
END
RETURN
END
GO
```

After the UDF is created, the following query is executed to show sales quota data for a specific salesperson from the Salesperson table:

```
Use AdventureWorks2012;
GO

SELECT BusinessEntityID, QuotaDate, SalesQuota
   FROM dbo.udf_SEL_SalesQuota (275,0);
```

This query returns the following:

```
BusinessEntityID        QuotaDate                   SalesQuota
----------------        -----------------------     ----------
275                     2001-06-24 00:00:00.000     300000.00
```

Next, the second parameter is switched from a 0 to a 1 in order to display additional rows for Salespersons 275 from the SalesPersonQuotaHistory table.

```
Use AdventureWorks2012;
GO

SELECT BusinessEntityID, QuotaDate, SalesQuota
   FROM dbo.udf_SEL_SalesQuota (275,1);
```

This returns the following (abridged) results:

```
BusinessEntityID        QuotaDate                   SalesQuota
----------------        -----------------------     ----------
275                     2001-06-24 00:00:00.000     300000.00
275                     2001-07-01 00:00:00.000     367000.00
275                     2001-10-01 00:00:00.000     556000.00
275                     2002-01-01 00:00:00.000     502000.00
275                     2002-04-01 00:00:00.000     550000.00
275                     2002-07-01 00:00:00.000     1429000.00
275                     2002-10-01 00:00:00.000     1324000.00
...
```

How It Works

This recipe demonstrated a multi-statement table-valued UDF to return sales quota data based on the BusinessEntityID value that was passed. It also included a second bit flag that controlled whether history was also returned.

Walking through the function, you'll notice that the first few lines defined the input parameters (something that a view doesn't allow).

```
CREATE FUNCTION dbo.udf_SEL_SalesQuota ( @BusinessEntityID int, @ShowHistory bit )
```

After this, the table columns that are to be returned by the function were defined.

```
RETURNS @SalesQuota TABLE (BusinessEntityID int, QuotaDate datetime, SalesQuota money)
```

The function body included two separate batch statements, the first being an INSERT into the table variable of rows for the specific salesperson.

```
AS
BEGIN
INSERT Into @SalesQuota(BusinessEntityID, QuotaDate, SalesQuota)
   SELECT BusinessEntityID, ModifiedDate, SalesQuota
   FROM Sales.SalesPerson
   WHERE BusinessEntityID = @BusinessEntityID;
```

Next, an IF statement (another construct not allowed in views) evaluated the bit parameter. If equal to 1, quota history will also be inserted into the table variable:

```
IF @ShowHistory = 1
BEGIN
INSERT Into @SalesQuota(BusinessEntityID, QuotaDate, SalesQuota)
   SELECT BusinessEntityID, QuotaDate, SalesQuota
   FROM Sales.SalesPersonQuotaHistory
   WHERE BusinessEntityID = @BusinessEntityID;
END
```

Lastly, the RETURN keyword signaled the end of the function (and, unlike a scalar function, no local variable is designated after it).

```
RETURN END
GO
```

Although the UDF contained Transact-SQL not allowed in a view, it was still able to be referenced in the FROM clause.

```
Use AdventureWorks2012;
GO

SELECT BusinessEntityID, QuotaDate, SalesQuota
   FROM dbo.udf_SEL_SalesQuota (275,0);
```

The results could be returned in a view using a UNION statement, but with that you wouldn't be able to have the control logic to either show or not show history in a single view.

In this recipe, I demonstrated a method to create your own parameter-based result sets. This can be used to implement row-based security. Row-level security is not built natively into the SQL Server security model. You can use functions to return only the rows that are allowed to be viewed by designating input parameters that are used to filter the data.

18-9. Dropping a Function

Problem

You no longer need a user-defined function in your database. You have confirmed that it is not used anywhere else, and you need to remove it from the database.

Solution

You can use DROP FUNCTION to remove a function. I demonstrate how to drop a user-defined function. The syntax, like other DROP commands, is very straightforward.

```
DROP FUNCTION { [ schema_name. ] function_name } [ ,...n ]
```

Table 18-4 details the arguments of this command.

Table 18-4. *DROP FUNCTION Arguments*

Argument	Description
[schema_name.] function_name	This defines the optional schema name and required function name of the user-defined function.
[,...n]	Although not an actual argument, this syntax element indicates that one or more user-defined functions can be dropped in a single statement.

This recipe demonstrates how to drop the dbo.udf_ParseArray function created in an earlier recipe.

```
Use AdventureWorks2012;
GO
DROP FUNCTION dbo.udf_ParseArray;
```

How It Works

Although there are three different types of user-defined functions (scalar, inline, and multi-statement), you need only drop them using the single DROP FUNCTION command. You can also drop more than one UDF in a single statement, for example.

```
Use AdventureWorks2012;
GO
DROP FUNCTION dbo.udf_ParseArray, dbo.udf_ReturnAddress,
dbo.udf_CheckForSQLInjection;
```

UDT Basics

User-defined types are useful for defining a consistent data type that is named after a known business or application-centric attribute, such as PIN, PhoneNBR, or EmailAddress. Once a user-defined type is created in the database, it can be used within columns, parameters, and variable definitions, providing a consistent underlying data type. The next two recipes will show you how to create and drop user-defined types. Note that unlike some other database objects, there isn't a way to modify an existing type using an ALTER command.

18-10. Creating and Using User-Defined Types

Problem

You have a frequently used account number field throughout the database. You want to try to enforce a consistent definition for this field while providing convenience to the database developers.

Solution

Create a user-defined type (also called an *alias data type),* which is a specific configuration of a data type that is given a user-specified name, data type, length, and nullability. You can use all base data types except the new `xml` data type.

■ **Caution** One drawback when using user-defined data types is their inability to be changed without cascading effects, as you'll see in the last recipe of this chapter.

The basic syntax for creating a user-defined type is as follows:

```
CREATE TYPE [ schema_name. ] type_name {
FROM base_type
[ (precision [ ,scale ] ) ]
[ NULL | NOT NULL ] }
```

Table 18-5 details the arguments of these commands.
In this recipe, I'll create a new type based on a 14-character string.

Table 18-5. *CREATE TYPE Arguments*

Argument	Description
`[ schema_name. ] type_name`	This specifies the optional schema name and required type name of the new user-defined type.
`base_type`	This is the base data type used to define the new user-defined type. You are allowed to use all base system data types except the `xml` data type.
`(precision [ ,scale ] )`	If using a numeric base type, `precision` is the maximum number of digits that can be stored both left and right of the decimal point. `Scale` is the maximum number of digits to be stored right of the decimal point.
`NULL | NOT NULL`	This defines whether your new user-defined type allows `NULL` values.

```
Use AdventureWorks2012;
GO
/*
-- In this example, we assume the company's Account number will
-- be used in multiple tables, and that it will always have a fixed
-- 14 character length and will never allow NULL values
*/

CREATE TYPE dbo.AccountNBR FROM char(14) NOT NULL;
GO
```

Next, I'll use the new type in the column definition of two tables.

```
Use AdventureWorks2012;
GO
-- The new data type is now used in two different tables
CREATE TABLE dbo.InventoryAccount
(InventoryAccountID int NOT NULL,
InventoryID int NOT NULL,
InventoryAccountNBR AccountNBR);
GO
CREATE TABLE dbo.CustomerAccount
(CustomerAccountID int NOT NULL,
CustomerID int NOT NULL,
CustomerAccountNBR AccountNBR);
GO
```

This type can also be used in the definition of a local variable or input parameter. For example, the following stored procedure uses the new data type to define the input parameter for a stored procedure:

```
Use AdventureWorks2012;
GO
CREATE PROCEDURE dbo.usp_SEL_CustomerAccount
@CustomerAccountNBR AccountNBR

AS
SELECT CustomerAccountID, CustomerID, CustomerAccountNBR
FROM dbo.CustomerAccount
WHERE CustomerAccountNBR = CustomerAccountNBR;
GO
```

Next, a local variable is created using the new data type and is passed to the stored procedure.

```
Use AdventureWorks2012;
GO
DECLARE @CustomerAccountNBR AccountNBR
SET @CustomerAccountNBR = '1294839482';
EXECUTE dbo.usp_SEL_CustomerAccount @CustomerAccountNBR;
GO
```

To view the underlying base type of the user-defined type, you can use the sp_help system stored procedure.

```
Use AdventureWorks2012;
GO
EXECUTE sp_help 'dbo.AccountNBR';
GO
```

This returns the following results (only a few columns are displayed for presentation purposes):

```
Type_name      Storage_type    Length    Nullable
----------     ------------    ------    --------
AccountNbr     char            14        no
```

How It Works

In this recipe, a new user-defined type called dbo.AccountNBR was created with a char(14) data type and NOT NULL. Once the user-defined type was created, it was then used in the column definition of two different tables.

```
CREATE TABLE dbo.InventoryAccount
(InventoryAccountID int NOT NULL,
InventoryID int NOT NULL,
InventoryAccountNBR AccountNBR);
GO
CREATE TABLE dbo.CustomerAccount
(CustomerAccountID int NOT NULL,
CustomerID int NOT NULL,
CustomerAccountNBR AccountNBR);
GO
```

Because NOT NULL was already inherent in the data type, it wasn't necessary to explicitly define it in the column definition.

After creating the tables, a stored procedure was created that used the new data type in the input parameter definition. The procedure was then called using a local variable that also used the new type.

Although Transact-SQL types may be an excellent convenience for some developers, creating your application's data dictionary and abiding by the data types may suit the same purpose. For example, if an AccountNBR is always 14 characters, as a DBA/developer, you can communicate and check to make sure that new objects are using a consistent name and data type.

18-11. Identifying Dependencies on User-Defined Types

Problem

You want to list all of the columns and parameters that have a dependency on a user-defined data type within your database.

Solution

Query the sys.types catalog view. Before showing you how to remove a user-defined data type, you'll need to know how to identify all database objects that depend on that type. As you'll see later, removing a UDT doesn't automatically cascade changes to the dependent table.

This example shows you how to identify which database objects are using the specified user-defined type. This first query in the recipe displays all columns that use the AccountNBR user-defined type.

```
Use AdventureWorks2012;
GO
SELECT Table_Name = OBJECT_NAME(c.object_id) , Column_name = c.name
FROM sys.columns c
   INNER JOIN sys.types t
      ON c.user_type_id = t.user_type_id
WHERE t.name = 'AccountNBR';
```

This query returns the following:

```
Table_Name          Column_Name
----------------    -------------------
InventoryAccount    InventoryAccountNBR
CustomerAccount     CustomerAccountNBR
```

This next query shows any procedures or functions that have parameters defined using the AccountNBR user-defined type.

```
Use AdventureWorks2012;
GO
/*
-- Now see what parameters reference the AccountNBR data type
*/
SELECT ProcFunc_Name = OBJECT_NAME(p.object_id) , Parameter_Name = p.name
FROM sys.parameters p
   INNER JOIN sys.types t
      ON c.user_type_id = t.user_type_id
WHERE t.name = 'AccountNBR';
```

This query returns the following:

```
ProcFunc_Name              Parameter_Name
-----------------------    -------------------
usp_SEL_CustomerAccount    @CustomerAccountNBR
```

How It Works

To report which table columns use the user-defined type, the system catalog views `sys.columns` and `sys.types` are used.

```
FROM sys.columns c
   INNER JOIN sys.types t
      ON c.user_type_id = t.user_type_id
```

The `sys.columns` view contains a row for each column defined for a table-valued function, table, and view in the database. The `sys.types` view contains a row for each user and system data type.

To identify which function or procedure parameters reference the user-defined type, the system catalog views `sys.parameters` and `sys.types` are used.

```
FROM sys.parameters p
   INNER JOIN sys.types t
      ON p.user_type_id = t.user_type_id
```

The `sys.parameters` view contains a row for each database object that can accept a parameter, including stored procedures, for example.

Identifying which objects reference a user-defined type is necessary if you plan on dropping the user-defined type, as the next recipe demonstrates.

18-12. Passing Table-Valued Parameters

Problem

You have an application that calls a stored procedure repetitively to insert singleton records. You would like to alter this process to reduce the number of calls to this stored procedure.

Solution

Table-valued parameters can be used to pass rowsets to stored procedures and user-defined functions. This functionality allows you to encapsulate multi-rowset capabilities within stored procedures and functions without having to make multiple row-by-row calls to data modification procedures or create multiple input parameters that inelegantly translate to multiple rows.

For example, the following stored procedure has several input parameters that are used to insert rows into the Department table:

```
Use AdventureWorks2012;
GO
CREATE PROCEDURE dbo.usp_INS_Department_Oldstyle
@Name_1 nvarchar(50),
@GroupName_1 nvarchar(50),
@Name_2 nvarchar(50),
@GroupName_2 nvarchar(50),
@Name_3 nvarchar(50),
@GroupName_3 nvarchar(50),
@Name_4 nvarchar(50),
@GroupName_4 nvarchar(50),
@Name_5 nvarchar(50),
@GroupName_5 nvarchar(50)

AS
INSERT INTO HumanResources.Department(Name, GroupName)
   VALUES (@Name_1, @GroupName_1)
INSERT INTO HumanResources.Department(Name, GroupName)
   VALUES (@Name_2, @GroupName_2);
INSERT INTO HumanResources.Department(Name, GroupName)
   VALUES (@Name_3, @GroupName_3);
INSERT INTO HumanResources.Department (Name, GroupName)
   VALUES (@Name_4, @GroupName_4);
INSERT INTO HumanResources.Department (Name, GroupName)
   VALUES (@Name_5, @GroupName_5);
GO
```

This previous example procedure has several limitations. First, it assumes that each call will contain five rows. If you have ten rows, you must call the procedure twice. If you have three rows, you need to modify the procedure to test for NULL values in the parameters and skip inserts accordingly. If NULL values are allowed in the underlying table, you would also need a method to indicate when a NULL should be stored and when a NULL represents a value not to be stored.

A more common technique is to create a singleton insert procedure.

```
Use AdventureWorks2012;
GO
CREATE PROCEDURE dbo.usp_INS_Department_Oldstyle_V2
@Name nvarchar(50),
@GroupName nvarchar(50)
AS
INSERT INTO HumanResources.Department (Name, GroupName)
   VALUES (@Name, @GroupName);
GO
```

If you have five rows to be inserted, you would call this procedure five times. This may be acceptable in many circumstances. However, if you will always be inserting multiple rows in a single batch, SQL Server provides a better alternative. Instead of performing singleton calls, you can pass the values to be inserted into a single parameter that represents a table of values. Such a parameter is called a *table-valued parameter.*

To use a table-valued parameter, the first step is to define a user-defined table data type, as I demonstrate here:

```
Use AdventureWorks2012;
GO
CREATE TYPE Department_TT AS TABLE (Name nvarchar(50), GroupName nvarchar(50));
GO
```

Once the new table type is created in the database, I can now reference it in module definitions and within the code.

```
Use AdventureWorks2012;
GO
CREATE PROCEDURE dbo.usp_INS_Department_NewStyle
   @DepartmentTable as Department_TT
READONLY
AS

INSERT INTO HumanResources.Department (Name, GroupName)
   SELECT Name, GroupName
      FROM @DepartmentTable;
GO
```

Let's assume that an external process is used to populate a list of values, which I will then pass to the procedure. In your own applications, the data source that you pass in can be generated from a populated staging table, directly from an application rowset, or from a constructed rowset, as demonstrated next:

```
Use AdventureWorks2012;
GO
/*
-- I can declare our new type for use within a T-SQL batch
-- Insert multiple rows into this table-type variable
*/

DECLARE @StagingDepartmentTable as Department_TT
INSERT INTO @StagingDepartmentTable(Name, GroupName)
   VALUES ('Archivists', 'Accounting');
INSERT INTO @StagingDepartmentTable(Name, GroupName)
   VALUES ('Public Media', 'Legal');
INSERT @StagingDepartmentTable(Name, GroupName)
   VALUES ('Internal Admin', 'Office Administration');
/*
-- Pass this table-type variable to the procedure in a single call
*/
EXECUTE dbo.usp_INS_Department_NewStyle @StagingDepartmentTable;
GO
```

How It Works

To pass result sets to modules, I must first define a user-defined table type within the database. I used the CREATE TYPE command and defined it AS TABLE:

```
CREATE TYPE Department_TT AS TABLE
```

Next, I defined the two columns that made up the table, just as one would for a regular table.

```
(Name nvarchar(50), GroupName nvarchar(50)) GO
```

I could have also defined the table type with PRIMARY KEY, UNIQUE, and CHECK constraints. I can also designate nullability as well as define whether the column was computed.

Next, I created a new procedure that uses the newly created table type. In the input parameter argument list, I created an input parameter with a type of Department_TT.

```
CREATE PROCEDURE dbo.usp_INS_Department_NewStyle
   @DepartmentTable as Department_TT
READONLY
AS
```

Notice the READONLY keyword after the data type designation. This is a requirement for stored procedure and user-defined function input parameters, because you are not allowed to modify the table-valued result set in this version of SQL Server.

The next block of code handled the INSERT to the table, using the input parameter as the data source of the multiple rows.

```
INSERT INTO HumanResources.Department (Name, GroupName)
   SELECT Name, GroupName
      FROM @DepartmentTable;
GO
```

After that, I demonstrated declaring a local variable that would contain multiple rows that will be passed to the procedure. The DECLARE statement defines the variable name, followed by the name of the table user-defined type defined earlier in the recipe.

```
DECLARE @StagingDepartmentTable as Department_TT
```

Once declared, I inserted multiple rows into this table and then passed it as a parameter to the stored procedure call.

```
INSERT INTO @StagingDepartmentTable(Name, GroupName)
   VALUES ('Archivists', 'Accounting');
INSERT INTO @StagingDepartmentTable(Name, GroupName)
   VALUES ('Public Media', 'Legal');
INSERT @StagingDepartmentTable(Name, GroupName)
   VALUES ('Internal Admin', 'Office Administration');
EXECUTE dbo.usp_INS_Department_NewStyle @StagingDepartmentTable;
GO
```

The benefits of this new functionality come into play when you consider procedures that handle business processes. For example, if you have a web site that handles product orders, you can now pass result sets to a single procedure that includes the general header information, along with multiple rows representing the products that were ordered. This application process can be constructed as a single call versus having to issue several calls for each unique product line item ordered. For extremely busy systems, using table-valued parameters allows you to reduce the chatter between the application and the database server, resulting in increased network bandwidth and more efficient batching of transactions on the SQL Server side.

18-13. Dropping User-Defined Types

Problem

You suspect there are unused user-defined types within your database. You would like to remove these types from the database.

Solution

To remove a user-defined type (also called an *alias* data type) from the database, use the DROP TYPE command. As with most DROP commands, the syntax for removing a user-defined type is very straightforward.

```
DROP TYPE [ schema_name. ] type_name
```

The DROP TYPE command uses the schema and type name, as this recipe will demonstrate. First, however, any references to the user-defined type need to be removed beforehand. In this example, the AccountNBR type is changed to the base equivalent for two tables and a stored procedure.

```
Use AdventureWorks2012;
GO
ALTER TABLE dbo.InventoryAccount
ALTER COLUMN InventoryAccountNBR char(14);
GO
ALTER TABLE dbo.CustomerAccount
ALTER COLUMN CustomerAccountNBR char(14);
GO

ALTER PROCEDURE dbo.usp_SEL_CustomerAccount
@CustomerAccountNBR char(14)

AS

SELECT CustomerAccountID, CustomerID, CustomerAccountNBR
FROM dbo.CustomerAccount
WHERE CustomerAccountNBR = @CustomerAccountNBR;
GO
```

With the referencing objects now converted, it is OK to go ahead and drop the type.

```
Use AdventureWorks2012;
GO
DROP TYPE dbo.AccountNBR;
```

How It Works

To remove a type, you must first change or remove any references to the type in a database table. If you are going to change the definition of a UDT, you need to remove *all* references to that UDT everywhere in *all* database objects that use that UDT. That means changing tables, views, stored procedures, and so on, first, before dropping the type. This can be very cumbersome if your database objects depend very heavily on them. Also, if any schema-bound stored procedures, functions, or triggers use the data type as parameters or variables, these references must be changed or removed. In this recipe, ALTER TABLE...ALTER COLUMN was used to change the data type to the system data type.

```
ALTER TABLE dbo.InventoryAccount
ALTER COLUMN InventoryAccountNBR char(14)
```

A stored procedure parameter was also modified using ALTER PROCEDURE:

```
ALTER PROCEDURE usp_SEL_CustomerAccount (@CustomerAccountNBR char(14))
```

CHAPTER 19

Triggers

by Andy Roberts

This chapter presents recipes for creating and using Data Manipulation Language (DML) and Data Definition Language (DDL) triggers. *DML triggers* respond to INSERT, UPDATE, and DELETE operations against tables and views. *DDL triggers* respond to server and database events such as CREATE TABLE and DROP TABLE statements.

Triggers, when used properly, can provide a convenient automatic response to specific actions. They are appropriate for situations where you must create a business-level response to an action. However, they should not be used in place of constraints such as primary key, foreign key, and check and unique constraints because constraints will outperform triggers and are better suited to these operations.

Remember that the code inside a trigger executes in response to an action. A user may be attempting to update a table, and the trigger code executes, in many cases, unknown to the user who executed the update. If trigger code is not optimized properly, the triggers may have a severe impact on system performance. Use DML triggers sparingly, and take care to ensure that they are optimized and bug-free.

DDL triggers open a realm of new functionality for monitoring and auditing server activity that cannot be easily replaced by other database object types.

This chapter will cover the following topics:

- How to create an AFTER DML trigger
- How to create an INSTEAD OF DML trigger
- How to create a DDL trigger
- How to modify or drop an existing trigger
- How to enable or disable triggers
- How to limit trigger nesting, set the firing order, and control recursion
- How to view trigger metadata
- How to use triggers to respond to logon events

First, however, I'll start with a background discussion of DML triggers.

19-1. Creating an AFTER DML Trigger

Problem

You want to track the inserts and deletes from your production inventory table. A number of applications access this table, and you cannot dictate that these applications use a common set of stored procedures to access the table.

Solution

DML triggers respond to `INSERT`, `UPDATE`, or `DELETE` operations against a table or a view. When a data modification event occurs, the trigger performs a set of actions defined by that trigger. Similar to stored procedures, triggers are defined as a batch of Transact-SQL statements.

A DML trigger may be declared specifically as `FOR UPDATE`, `FOR INSERT`, `FOR DELETE`, or any combination of the three. `UPDATE` triggers respond to data modified in one or more columns within the table, `INSERT` triggers respond to new data being added to a table, and `DELETE` triggers respond to data being deleted from a table. There are two types of DML triggers: `AFTER` and `INSTEAD OF`.

`AFTER` triggers are allowed only for tables, and they execute *after* the data modification has been completed against the table. `INSTEAD OF` triggers execute *instead of* the original data modification and can be created for both tables and views.

DML triggers perform actions in response to data modifications. For example, a trigger could populate an audit table based on an operation performed. Or perhaps a trigger could be used to decrement the value of an inventory quantity in response to a sales transaction. Though the ability to trigger actions automatically is a powerful feature, there are a few things to keep in mind when deciding whether to use a trigger for a specific set of application or business logic.

- Triggers are often forgotten about and therefore become a hidden problem. When troubleshooting performance or logical issues, DBAs and developers often forget that triggers are executing in the background. Make sure that the use of triggers is "visible" in data and application documentation.
- If all data modifications flow through a stored procedure, a set of stored procedures, or even a common data access layer, then perform all activities within the stored procedure layer or data access layer rather than using a trigger. For example, if an inventory quantity should be updated after inserting a sales record, why not put this logic in the stored procedure instead?
- Always keep performance in mind: write triggers that execute quickly. Long-running triggers can significantly impact data modification operations. Take particular care in putting triggers onto tables that are subject to either a high rate of data modification or data modifications that affect large numbers of rows.
- Nonlogged updates do not cause a DML trigger to fire (for example, `WRITETEXT`, `TRUNCATE TABLE`, and bulk insert operations).
- Constraints usually run faster than a DML trigger, so if business requirements can be modeled using constraints, then use constraints instead of triggers.
- `AFTER` triggers run *after* the data modification has occurred, so they cannot be used to alter data modification to prevent constraint violations.
- Don't allow result sets from a `SELECT` statement to be returned within your trigger. Most applications cannot consume results from a trigger, and embedded queries may hurt the trigger's performance.

■ **Caution** The ability to return results from triggers is deprecated in SQL Server 2012 and will be removed in a future version of SQL Server. To disable this feature today, use the SQL Server configuration option `disable results from triggers`.

As long as you keep these general guidelines in mind and use them properly, triggers are an excellent means of enforcing business rules in your database.

■ **Caution** Some of the triggers demonstrated in the chapter may interfere with existing triggers on the SQL instance and database. If you are following along with the code, be sure to test this functionality only on a development SQL Server environment.

An AFTER DML trigger can track the changes to the ProductionInventory table. This recipe creates an AFTER DML trigger that executes when INSERT and DELETE statements are executed against the table.

An AFTER DML trigger executes after an INSERT, UPDATE, and/or DELETE modification has been completed successfully against a table. The specific syntax for an AFTER DML trigger is as follows:

```
CREATE TRIGGER [schema_name.]trigger_name
ON table
[WITH <dml_trigger_option> [...,n]]
AFTER
{[INSERT][,] [UPDATE] [,][DELETE]}
[NOT FOR REPLICATION]
AS {sql_statement[...n]}
```

Table 19-1 details the arguments of this command.

Table 19-1. *CREATE TRIGGER Arguments*

Argument	Description
[schema_name .] trigger_name	Defines the optional schema owner and required user-defined name of the new trigger.
Table	Defines the table name that the trigger applies to.
<dml_trigger_option> [...,n]	Allows specification of ENCRYPTION and/or the EXECUTE AS clause. ENCRYPTION encrypts the Transact-SQL definition of the trigger, making it unreadable within the system tables. EXECUTE AS allows the developer to define a security context under which the trigger executes.
[INSERT][,][UPDATE][,] [DELETE]	Defines which DML event or events the trigger reacts to including INSERT, UPDATE, and DELETE. A single trigger can react to one or more of these actions against the table.
NOT FOR REPLICATION	In some cases, the table on which the trigger is defined is updated through the SQL Server replication processes. In many cases, the published database has already accounted for any business logic that would normally be executed in the trigger. The NOT FOR REPLICATION option instructs SQL Server not to execute the trigger when the data modification is made as part of a replication process.
sql_statement[...n]	Allows one or more Transact-SQL statements that are used to carry out actions such as performing validations against the DML changes or performing other table DML actions.

Before proceeding to the recipe, it is important to note that SQL Server creates two "virtual" tables that are available specifically for triggers, called the *inserted* and *deleted* tables. These two tables capture the before and after pictures of the modified rows. Table 19-2 shows the tables that each DML operation impacts.

Table 19-2. Inserted and Deleted Virtual Tables

DML Operation	Inserted Table Holds...	Deleted Table Holds...
INSERT	Rows to be inserted	Empty
UPDATE	New (proposed) version of rows modified by the update	Existing (pre-update) version of rows modified by the update
DELETE	Empty	Rows to be deleted

The inserted and deleted tables can be used within your trigger to access the versions of data before and after the data modifications. These tables store data for both single and multirow updates. Triggers should be coded with both types of updates (single and multirow) in mind. For example, a DELETE statement may impact either a single row or multiple, say 50, rows—the trigger must handle both cases appropriately.

This recipe demonstrates how to use a trigger to track row inserts or deletes from the Production.ProductInventory table.

```
-- Create a table to Track all Inserts and Deletes
CREATE TABLE Production.ProductInventoryAudit
    (
    ProductID INT NOT NULL,
    LocationID SMALLINT NOT NULL,
    Shelf NVARCHAR(10) NOT NULL,
    Bin TINYINT NOT NULL,
    Quantity SMALLINT NOT NULL,
    rowguid UNIQUEIDENTIFIER NOT NULL,
    ModifiedDate DATETIME NOT NULL,
    InsertOrDelete CHAR(1) NOT NULL
    );
GO
-- Create trigger to populate Production.ProductInventoryAudit table
CREATE TRIGGER Production.trg_id_ProductInventoryAudit ON Production.ProductInventory
     AFTER INSERT, DELETE
AS
BEGIN
     SET NOCOUNT ON;
-- Inserted rows
    INSERT  Production.ProductInventoryAudit
            (ProductID,
            LocationID,
            Shelf,
            Bin,
            Quantity,
            rowguid,
            ModifiedDate,
            InsertOrDelete)
           SELECT DISTINCT
                   i.ProductID,
                   i.LocationID,
                   i.Shelf,
                   i.Bin,
                   i.Quantity,
```

```
                i.rowguid,
                GETDATE(),
                'I'
        FROM  inserted i
        UNION ALL
        SELECT d.ProductID,
                d.LocationID,
                d.Shelf,
                d.Bin,
                d.Quantity,
                d.rowguid,
                GETDATE(),
                'D'
        FROM   deleted d;

END
GO

-- Insert a new row
INSERT Production.ProductInventory
        (ProductID,
        LocationID,
        Shelf,
        Bin,
        Quantity)
VALUES (316,
        6,
        'A',
        4,
        22);

-- Delete a row
DELETE Production.ProductInventory
WHERE  ProductID = 316
       AND LocationID = 6;

-- Check the audit table
SELECT ProductID,
       LocationID,
       InsertOrDelete
FROM   Production.ProductInventoryAudit;
```

This returns the following:

```
ProductID  LocationID  InsertOrDelete
---------  ----------  --------------
316        6           I
316        6           D
```

How It Works

This recipe starts by creating a new table for tracking rows inserted to or deleted from the Production.ProductInventory table. The new table's schema matches the original table but has added a new column named InsertOrUpdate to indicate whether the change was because of an INSERT or DELETE operation.

```
CREATE TABLE Production.ProductInventoryAudit
       (
        ProductID INT NOT NULL,
        LocationID SMALLINT NOT NULL,
        Shelf NVARCHAR(10) NOT NULL,
        Bin TINYINT NOT NULL,
        Quantity SMALLINT NOT NULL,
        rowguid UNIQUEIDENTIFIER NOT NULL,
        ModifiedDate DATETIME NOT NULL,
        InsertOrDelete CHAR(1) NOT NULL
       );
GO
```

Next, an AFTER DML trigger is created using CREATE TRIGGER. The schema and name of the new trigger are designated in the first line of the statement.

```
CREATE TRIGGER Production.trg_id_ProductInventoryAudit
```

The table (which when updated will cause the trigger to fire) is designated in the ON clause.

```
ON Production.ProductInventory
```

Two types of DML activity will be monitored: inserts and deletes.

```
AFTER INSERT, DELETE
```

The body of the trigger begins after the AS keyword.

```
AS
BEGIN
```

The SET NOCOUNT is set ON in order to suppress the "rows affected" messages from being returned to the calling application whenever the trigger is fired.

```
    SET NOCOUNT ON;
```

The trigger contains one INSERT statement of the form INSERT INTO ... SELECT where the SELECT statement is a UNION of two selects. The first SELECT in the UNION returns the rows from the INSERTED table, and the second SELECT in the union returns rows from the DELETED table.

First, set up the INSERT statement and specify the table into which the statement inserts rows as well as the columns that should be specified for each row that is inserted.

```
      INSERT  Production.ProductInventoryAudit
              (ProductID,
               LocationID,
               Shelf,
               Bin,
               Quantity,
               rowguid,
               ModifiedDate,
               InsertOrDelete)
```

Next, select rows from the INSERTED table (this is a list of rows that are inserted into the ProductInventory table) and specify the columns that will be mapped to the INSERT clause.

```
            SELECT i.ProductID,
                   i.LocationID,
                   i.Shelf,
                   i.Bin,
                   i.Quantity,
                   i.rowguid,
                   GETDATE(),
                   'I'
            FROM   inserted i
```

The second select returns rows from the DELETED table and concatenates the results with a UNION ALL. The DELETED table contains a list of rows that are deleted from the ProductInventory table.

```
            UNION ALL
            SELECT d.ProductID,
                   d.LocationID,
                   d.Shelf,
                   d.Bin,
                   d.Quantity,
                   d.rowguid,
                   GETDATE(),
                   'D'
            FROM   deleted d;
    END
GO
```

After creating the trigger, in order to test it, a new row is inserted into and then deleted from Production.ProductInventory.

```
INSERT Production.ProductInventory
       (ProductID,
        LocationID,
        Shelf,
        Bin,
        Quantity)
VALUES (316,
        6,
        'A',
        4,
        22);

-- Delete a row
DELETE Production.ProductInventory
WHERE  ProductID = 316
       AND LocationID = 6;
```

A query executed against the audit table shows two rows tracking the insert and delete activities against the Production.ProductInventory table.

```
SELECT ProductID,
       LocationID,
       InsertOrDelete
FROM   Production.ProductInventoryAudit;
```

19-2. Creating an INSTEAD OF DML Trigger

Problem

You have a table that contains a list of departments for your human resources group. An application needs to insert new departments; however, new departments should be routed to a separate table that holds these departments "pending approval" by a separate application function. You want to create a view that concatenates the "approved" and "pending approval" departments and allow the application to insert into this view such that any new departments are added to the "pending approval" table.

Solution

An INSTEAD OF DML trigger allows data to be updated in a view that would otherwise not be updateable. The code inside the INSTEAD OF DML trigger executes *instead of* the original data modification statement. They are allowed on both tables and views and are often used to handle data modifications to views that do not allow for data modifications (see Chapter 14 for a review of what rules a view must follow in order to be updateable). INSTEAD OF DML triggers use the following syntax:

```
CREATE TRIGGER [ schema_name . ]trigger_name ON { table | view }
[ WITH <dml_trigger_option> [...,n ] ] INSTEAD OF

{ [ INSERT ] [ , ] [ UPDATE ] [ , ] [ DELETE ] }
[ NOT FOR REPLICATION ]
AS { sql_statement [...n ] }
```

Table 19-3 details the arguments of this command.

Table 19-3. *INSTEAD OF Trigger Arguments*

Argument	Description
[schema_name .]trigger_ name	Defines the optional schema owner and required user-defined name of the new trigger.
table | view	Defines the table name that the trigger applies to.
<dml_trigger_option> [...,n]	Allows specification of ENCRYPTION and/or the EXECUTE AS clause. ENCRYPTION encrypts the Transact-SQL definition of the trigger, making it unreadable within the system tables. EXECUTE AS allows the developer to define a security context under which the trigger executes.
[INSERT] [,] [UPDATE] [,] [DELETE]	Defines which DML event or events the trigger reacts to including INSERT, UPDATE, and DELETE. A single trigger can react to one or more of these actions against the table.
NOT FOR REPLICATION	In some cases, the table on which the trigger is defined is updated through SQL Server replication processes. In many cases, the published database has already accounted for any business logic that would normally be executed in the trigger. The NOT FOR REPLICATION option instructs SQL Server not to execute the trigger when the data modification is made as part of a replication process.
sql_statement [...n]	Allows one or more Transact-SQL statements that are used to carry out actions such as performing validations against the DML changes or performing other table DML actions.

This recipe creates a new table that holds "pending approval" rows for the HumanResources.Department table. These are new departments that require manager approval before being added to the actual table. A view is created to display all "approved" and "pending approval" departments from the two tables, and an INSTEAD OF trigger is created for inserts on the view. This INSTEAD OF trigger allows the developer to define an action to take *instead of* the INSERT statement. In this case, the trigger will insert the data into one of the base tables of the view. HumanResources.Department.

```
-- Create Department "Approval" table
CREATE TABLE HumanResources.DepartmentApproval
       (
        Name NVARCHAR(50) NOT NULL
                          UNIQUE,
        GroupName NVARCHAR(50) NOT NULL,
        ModifiedDate DATETIME NOT NULL
                              DEFAULT GETDATE()
       ) ;
GO
-- Create view to see both approved and pending approval departments
CREATE VIEW HumanResources.vw_Department
AS
       SELECT  Name,
               GroupName,
               ModifiedDate,
               'Approved' Status
       FROM    HumanResources.Department
       UNION
       SELECT  Name,
               GroupName,
               ModifiedDate,
               'Pending Approval' Status
       FROM   HumanResources.DepartmentApproval ;
GO

-- Create an INSTEAD OF trigger on the new view
CREATE TRIGGER HumanResources.trg_vw_Department ON HumanResources.vw_Department
       INSTEAD OF INSERT
AS
       SET NOCOUNT ON
       INSERT  HumanResources.DepartmentApproval
               (Name,
               GroupName)
               SELECT i.Name,
                      i.GroupName
               FROM   inserted i
               WHERE  i.Name NOT IN (
                      SELECT Name
                      FROM  HumanResources.DepartmentApproval) ;
GO

-- Insert into the new view, even though view is a UNION
-- of two different tables
INSERT HumanResources.vw_Department
       (Name,
        GroupName)
```

```
VALUES ('Print Production',
        'Manufacturing') ;

-- Check the view's contents
SELECT Status,
       Name
FROM   HumanResources.vw_Department
WHERE  GroupName = 'Manufacturing' ;
```

This returns the following result set:

```
Status              Name
----------------    -------------------
Approved            Production
Approved            Production Control
Pending Approval    Print Production
```

How It Works

The recipe begins by creating a separate table to hold "pending approval" department rows.

```
CREATE TABLE HumanResources.DepartmentApproval
       (
       Name NVARCHAR(50) NOT NULL
                         UNIQUE,
       GroupName NVARCHAR(50) NOT NULL,
       ModifiedDate DATETIME NOT NULL
                            DEFAULT GETDATE()
       ) ;
GO
```

Next, a view is created to display both "approved" and "pending approval" departments.

```
CREATE VIEW HumanResources.vw_Department
AS
       SELECT  Name,
               GroupName,
               ModifiedDate,
               'Approved' Status
       FROM    HumanResources.Department
       UNION
       SELECT  Name,
               GroupName,
               ModifiedDate,
               'Pending Approval' Status
       FROM    HumanResources.DepartmentApproval ;
GO
```

The UNION in the CREATE VIEW prevents this view from being updateable. INSTEAD OF triggers allow data modifications against nonupdateable views.

A trigger is created to react to INSERTs against the view and insert the specified data into the approval table as long as the department name does not already exist in the HumanResources.DepartmentApproval table.

```
CREATE TRIGGER HumanResources.trg_vw_Department ON HumanResources.vw_Department
       INSTEAD OF INSERT
AS
       SET NOCOUNT ON;
       INSERT HumanResources.DepartmentApproval
              (Name,
               GroupName)
              SELECT i.Name,
                     i.GroupName
              FROM   inserted i
              WHERE  i.Name NOT IN (
                     SELECT  Name
                     FROM    HumanResources.DepartmentApproval) ;
GO
```

A new INSERT is tested against the view to see whether it is inserted in the approval table.

```
INSERT HumanResources.vw_Department
       (Name,
        GroupName)
VALUES ('Print Production',
        'Manufacturing') ;
```

Query the view to show that the row is inserted and displays a "pending approval" status.

```
SELECT Status,
       Name
FROM   HumanResources.vw_Department
WHERE  GroupName = 'Manufacturing';
```

19-3. Handling Transactions in Triggers

Problem

You have been viewing the ProductInventory changes that are tracked in your ProductInventoryAudit table. You notice that some applications are violating business rules, and this breaks other applications that are using the ProductInventory table. You want to prevent these changes and roll back the transaction that violates the business rules.

Solution

When a trigger is fired, SQL Server always creates a transaction around it. This allows any changes made by the firing trigger, or the caller, to roll back to the previous state. In this example, the trg_uid_ProductlnventoryAudit trigger has been rewritten to fail if certain Shelf or Quantity values are encountered. If they are, ROLLBACK is used to cancel the trigger and undo any changes.

Note These examples work with the objects created in Recipe 19-1 and assume that the Production.ProductInventoryAudit table and Production.trg_uid_ProductInventoryAudit trigger have been created.

```
ALTER TRIGGER Production.trg_id_ProductInventoryAudit ON Production.ProductInventory
       AFTER INSERT, DELETE
AS
       SET NOCOUNT ON ;
       IF EXISTS ( SELECT  Shelf
                   FROM    inserted
                   WHERE   Shelf = 'A' )
          BEGIN
                 PRINT 'Shelf ''A'' is closed for new inventory.' ;
                 ROLLBACK ;
          END
-- Inserted rows
        INSERT  Production.ProductInventoryAudit
                (ProductID,
                LocationID,
                Shelf,
                Bin,
                Quantity,
                rowguid,
                ModifiedDate,
                InsertOrDelete)
                SELECT DISTINCT
                       i.ProductID,
                       i.LocationID,
                       i.Shelf,
                       i.Bin,
                       i.Quantity,
                       i.rowguid,
                       GETDATE(),
                       'I'
                FROM   inserted i ;
-- Deleted rows
        INSERT  Production.ProductInventoryAudit
                (ProductID,
                LocationID,
                Shelf,
                Bin,
                Quantity,
                rowguid,
                ModifiedDate,
                InsertOrDelete)
                SELECT d.ProductID,
                       d.LocationID,
                       d.Shelf,
                       d.Bin,
                       d.Quantity,
                       d.rowguid,
                       GETDATE(),
                       'D'
                FROM   deleted d ;
```

```
        IF EXISTS ( SELECT  Quantity
                    FROM    deleted
                    WHERE   Quantity > 0 )
           BEGIN
                PRINT 'You cannot remove positive quantity rows!' ;
                ROLLBACK ;
           END
GO
```

Now, attempt an insert of a row using Shelf A:

```
INSERT Production.ProductInventory
       (ProductID,
       LocationID,
       Shelf,
       Bin,
       Quantity)
VALUES (316,
       6,
       'A',
       4,
       22) ;
```

Because this is not allowed based on the trigger logic, the trigger neither inserts a row into the ProductInventoryAudit table nor allows the INSERT into the ProductInventory table. The following is returned as a result of the INSERT statement:

```
Shelf 'A' is closed for new inventory.

Msg 3609, Level 16, State 1, Line 2

The transaction ended in the trigger. The batch has been aborted.
```

In the previous example, the INSERT that caused the trigger to fire didn't use an explicit transaction; however, the operation was still rolled back. This next example demonstrates two deletions: one that is allowed (according to the rules of the trigger) and another that is not allowed. Both inserts are embedded in an explicit transaction.

```
BEGIN TRANSACTION ;
-- Deleting a row with a zero quantity
DELETE Production.ProductInventory
WHERE  ProductID = 853
       AND LocationID = 7 ;
-- Deleting a row with a non-zero quantity
DELETE Production.ProductInventory
WHERE  ProductID = 999
       AND LocationID = 60 ;
COMMIT TRANSACTION ;
```

This returns the following:

```
(1 row(s) affected)

You cannot remove positive quantity rows!

Msg 3609, Level 16, State 1, Line 9

The transaction ended in the trigger. The batch has been aborted.
```

Because the trigger issued a rollback, the outer transaction is also rolled back. Even though the first row was a valid deletion because they were in the same calling transaction, neither row was deleted.

```
SELECT ProductID,
       LocationID
FROM   Production.ProductInventory
WHERE  (ProductID = 853
        AND LocationID = 7)
      OR (ProductID = 999
          AND LocationID = 60) ;
```

This returns the following:

ProductID	LocationID
853	7
999	60

How It Works

This recipe demonstrates the interaction between triggers and transactions. If a trigger issues a ROLLBACK, any data modifications performed by the trigger or the statements in the calling transaction are undone. The Transact-SQL query or batch that invoked the trigger is canceled and rolled back. If you use explicit transactions within a trigger, SQL Server will treat it as a nested transaction. As discussed in Chapter 12, a ROLLBACK rolls back all transactions, no matter how many levels deep they may be nested.

19-4. Linking Trigger Execution to Modified Columns

Problem

You have a table, and you want to restrict updates to one column in the table.

Solution

When a trigger is fired, you can determine which columns have been modified by using the UPDATE function.

UPDATE, not to be confused with the DML command, returns a TRUE value if an INSERT or DML UPDATE has occurred against a column. For example, the following DML UPDATE trigger checks to see whether a specific column has been modified and, if so, returns an error and rolls back the modification.

```
CREATE TRIGGER HumanResources.trg_U_Department ON HumanResources.Department
       AFTER UPDATE
AS
```

```
        IF UPDATE(GroupName)
           BEGIN
                  PRINT 'Updates to GroupName require DBA involvement.' ;
                  ROLLBACK ;
           END
GO
```

An attempt is made to update a GroupName value in the following query:

```
UPDATE HumanResources.Department
SET    GroupName = 'Research and Development'
WHERE  DepartmentID = 10 ;
```

This returns the warning message and error telling us that the batch has been aborted (no updates made).

```
Updates to GroupName require DBA involvement.

Msg 3609, Level 16, State 1, Line 1

The transaction ended in the trigger. The batch has been aborted.
```

How It Works

When trigger logic is aimed at more granular, column-based changes, use the UPDATE function and conditional processing to ensure that code is executed only against specific columns. Embedding the logic in conditional processing can help reduce the overhead each time the trigger fires.

19-5. Viewing DML Trigger Metadata

Problem

You have a number of DML triggers defined in your database, and you want to list the triggers in the database and the objects on which they are defined.

Solution

This recipe demonstrates how to view information about the triggers in the current database.

The first example queries the sys.triggers catalog view and returns the name of the view or table, the trigger name, whether the trigger is an INSTEAD OF trigger, and whether the trigger is disabled.

```
-- Show the DML triggers in the current database
SELECT OBJECT_NAME(parent_id) Table_or_ViewNM,
       name TriggerNM,
       is_instead_of_trigger,
       is_disabled
FROM   sys.triggers
WHERE  parent_class_desc = 'OBJECT_OR_COLUMN'
ORDER BY OBJECT_NAME(parent_id),
       Name ;
```

This returns the following results (your results may vary slightly depending on what triggers you have defined):

```
Table_or_ViewNM      TriggerNM                        is_instead_of_trigger  is_disabled
-------------------  -------------------------------  ---------------------  -----------
Department           trg_U_Department                 0                      0
Employee             dEmployee                        1                      0
Person               iuPerson                         0                      0
ProductInventory     trg_uid_ProductInventoryAudit    0                      0
PurchaseOrderDetail  iPurchaseOrderDetail             0                      0
PurchaseOrderDetail  uPurchaseOrderDetail             0                      0
PurchaseOrderHeader  uPurchaseOrderHeader             0                      0
SalesOrderDetail     iduSalesOrderDetail              0                      0
SalesOrderHeader     uSalesOrderHeader                0                      0
Vendor               dVendor                          1                      0
vw_Department        trg_vw_Department                1                      0
WorkOrder            iWorkOrder                       0                      0
WorkOrder            uWorkOrder                       0                      0
```

To display a specific trigger's Transact-SQL definition, you can query the sys.sql_modules system catalog view.

```
-- Displays the trigger SQL definition --(if the trigger is not encrypted)
SELECT o.name,
       m.definition
FROM   sys.sql_modules m
       INNER JOIN sys.objects o
           ON m.object_id = o.object_id
WHERE  o.type = 'TR'
       AND o.name = 'trg_id_ProductInventoryAudit'
```

How It Works

The first query in this recipe queries the sys.triggers catalog view to show all the DML triggers in the current database. There are DDL triggers in the sys.triggers catalog view as well. To prevent DDL from being displayed in the results, the query filters on parent_class_desc "OBJECT_OR_COLUMN". DDL triggers have a different parent class, as we will discuss in Recipe 19-8.

The second query shows the actual Transact-SQL trigger name and definition of each trigger in the database. If the trigger is encrypted (similar to an encrypted view or stored procedure, for example), the trigger definition will be displayed as NULL.

19-6. Creating a DDL Trigger

Problem

You are testing index changes in a system and want to log any index changes so that you can correlate the index change with performance data that you are capturing on the server.

Solution

DDL triggers respond to server or database events rather than table data modifications. For example, a DDL trigger could write to an audit table whenever a database user issues a `CREATE TABLE` or `DROP TABLE` statement. Or, at the server level, a DDL trigger could respond to the creation of a new login and prevent that login from being created or log the activity.

■ **Tip** System stored procedures that perform DDL operations will fire DDL triggers. For example, `sp_create_plan_guide` and `sp_control_plan_guide` will fire the `CREATE_PLAN_GUIDE` event and execute any triggers defined on that event type.

DDL triggers may be defined as database or server triggers. Database DDL triggers are stored as objects within the database that they were created, and server DDL triggers are stored in the master database. The syntax for a DDL trigger is as follows:

```
CREATE TRIGGER trigger_name
ON { ALL SERVER | DATABASE }
[ WITH <ddl_trigger_option> [...,n ] ]
FOR { event_type | event_group } [ ,...n ]
AS { sql_statement [...n ]}
```

Table 19-4 details the arguments of this command.

Table 19-4. *CREATE TRIGGER (DDL) Arguments*

Argument	Description
`trigger_name`	This argument is the user-defined name of the new DDL trigger (notice that a DDL trigger does not have an owning schema, since it isn't related to an actual database table or view).
`ALL SERVER | DATABASE`	This argument designates whether the DDL trigger will respond to server-scoped (`ALL SERVER`) or `DATABASE`-scoped events.
`<ddl_trigger_option> [...,n ]`	This argument allows you to specify the `ENCRYPTION` and/or the `EXECUTE AS` clause. `ENCRYPTION` will encrypt the Transact-SQL definition of the trigger. `EXECUTE AS` allows you to define the security context under which the trigger will be executed.
`{ event_type | event_group } [ ,...n ]`	The `event_type` indicates a DDL event that the trigger subscribes to, for example `CREATE_TABLE`, `ALTER_TABLE`, and `DROP_INDEX`. An `event_group` is a logical grouping of `event_type` events. A single DDL trigger can subscribe to one or more event types or groups. For example, the `DDL_PARTITION_FUNCTION_EVENTS` group is comprised of the following events: `CREATE_PARTITION_FUNCTION`, `ALTER_PARTITION_FUNCTION`, and `DROP_PARTITION_FUNCTION`. You can find the complete list of trigger event types in the SQL Server Books Online topic "DDL Events" (`http://msdn.microsoft.com/en-us/library/bb522542.aspx`) and a complete list of trigger event groups in the SQL Server Books Online topic "DDL Event Groups" (`http://msdn.microsoft.com/en-us/library/bb510452.aspx`).
`sql_statement [...n ]`	This argument defines one or more Transact-SQL statements that can be used to carry out actions in response to the DDL database or server event.

This recipe demonstrates how to create an audit table that can contain information on any CREATE INDEX, ALTER INDEX, or DROP INDEX statements in the AdventureWorks2012 database.

First, create an audit table to hold the results.

```
CREATE TABLE dbo.DDLAudit
            (
            EventData XML NOT NULL,
            AttemptDate DATETIME NOT NULL
                        DEFAULT GETDATE(),
            DBUser CHAR(50) NOT NULL
            ) ;
GO
```

Next, create a database DDL trigger to track index operations and insert the event data to the audit table.

```
CREATE TRIGGER db_trg_INDEXChanges ON DATABASE
       FOR CREATE_INDEX, ALTER_INDEX, DROP_INDEX
AS
       SET NOCOUNT ON ;
       INSERT  dbo.DDLAudit
               (EventData, DBUser)
       VALUES  (EVENTDATA(), USER) ;
GO
```

Next, attempt an index creation in the database.

```
CREATE NONCLUSTERED INDEX ni_DDLAudit_DBUser ON
dbo.DDLAudit(DBUser) ;
GO
```

Next, I'll query the ChangeAttempt audit table to see whether the new index creation event was captured by the trigger.

```
SELECT EventData
FROM   dbo.DDLAudit
```

This returns the actual event information, stored in XML format (see Chapter 24 for more information on XML in SQL Server).

```
EventData
------------------------------------------------------------
<EVENT_INSTANCE>
        <EventType>CREATE_INDEX</EventType>
        <PostTime>2012-05-01T02:55:39.170</PostTime>
        <SPID>52</SPID>
        <ServerName>ANDYROB2012WIN7\RTM</ServerName>
        <LoginName>NORTHAMERICA\andyrob</LoginName>
        <UserName>dbo</UserName>
        <DatabaseName>AdventureWorks2012</DatabaseName>
        <SchemaName>dbo</SchemaName>
        <ObjectName>ni_ChangeAttempt_DBUser</ObjectName>
        <ObjectType>INDEX</ObjectType>
        <TargetObjectName>ChangeAttempt</TargetObjectName>
        <TargetObjectType>TABLE</TargetObjectType>
        <TSQLCommand>
```

```
            <SetOptions ANSI_NULLS="ON"
                  ANSI_NULL_DEFAULT="ON"
                  ANSI_PADDING="ON"
                  QUOTED_IDENTIFIER="ON"
                  ENCRYPTED="FALSE" />
            <CommandText>
CREATE NONCLUSTERED INDEX ni_ChangeAttempt_DBUser ON dbo.ChangeAttempt(DBUser)
        </CommandText>
      </TSQLCommand>
</EVENT_INSTANCE>
```

How It Works

The recipe begins by creating a table that could contain audit information on index modifications. The EventData column uses SQL Server's xml data type, which is populated by the new EVENTDATA function (described later in this recipe).

```
CREATE TABLE dbo.DDLAudit
          (
          EventData XML NOT NULL,
          AttemptDate DATETIME NOT NULL
                      DEFAULT GETDATE(),
          DBUser CHAR(50) NOT NULL
          ) ;
GO
```

The DDL trigger is created to subscribe to CREATE INDEX, ALTER INDEX, or DROP INDEX statements.

```
CREATE TRIGGER db_trg_INDEXChanges ON DATABASE
    FOR CREATE_INDEX, ALTER_INDEX, DROP_INDEX
AS
```

The SET NOCOUNT statement is used in the trigger to suppress the number of row-affected messages from SQL Server (otherwise, every time you make an index modification, you'll see a "1 row affected" message).

```
    SET NOCOUNT ON ;
```

A row is inserted to the audit table containing the event data and user who performed the statement that fired the event.

```
    INSERT  dbo.ChangeAttempt
            (EventData, DBUser)
    VALUES  (EVENTDATA(), USER) ;
GO
```

The EVENTDATA function returns server and data event information in XML format. The XML data returned from the EVENTDATA function includes useful information such as the event statement text, the login name that attempted the statement, the target object name, and the time the event occurred. For more information about the EVENTDATA function, please refer to SQL Server Books Online (http://msdn.microsoft.com/en-us/library/ms187909.aspx).

19-7. Creating a Logon Trigger

Problem

You want to restrict the times at which certain users log into your database server. If an attempt is made to log in during incorrect hours, you want to log that attempt to an audit table.

Solution

Logon triggers fire synchronously in response to a logon event to the SQL Server instance. You can use logon triggers to create reactions to specific logon events or simply to track information about a logon event.

Caution Be very careful about how you design your logon trigger. Test it in a development environment first before deploying to production. If you are using a logon trigger to restrict entry to the SQL Server instance, be careful that you do not restrict all access!

This recipe demonstrates how to create a logon trigger that restricts a login from accessing SQL Server during certain time periods. The example will also log any invalid logon attempts to a table.

First, create the new login.

```
CREATE LOGIN nightworker WITH PASSWORD = 'pass@word1' ;
GO
```

Note This example assumes that your SQL Server instance is set to Mixed Mode authentication.

Next, create an audit database and a table to track the logon attempts.

```
CREATE DATABASE ExampleAuditDB ;
GO
USE ExampleAuditDB ;
GO
CREATE TABLE dbo.RestrictedLogonAttempt
       (
       LoginNM SYSNAME NOT NULL,
       AttemptDT DATETIME NOT NULL
       ) ;
GO
```

Create the logon trigger to restrict the new login from logging into the server from 7 a.m. to 6 p.m.:

Note You may need to adjust the times used in this example based on what time you are testing the trigger.

```
USE master ;
GO
```

```
CREATE TRIGGER trg_logon_attempt ON ALL SERVER
 WITH EXECUTE AS 'sa'
       FOR LOGON
AS
       BEGIN
             IF ORIGINAL_LOGIN() = 'nightworker'
                AND DATEPART(hh, GETDATE()) BETWEEN 7 AND 18
                BEGIN
                      ROLLBACK ;
                      INSERT  ExampleAuditDB.dbo.RestrictedLogonAttempt
                              (LoginNM, AttemptDT)
                      VALUES  (ORIGINAL_LOGIN(), GETDATE()) ;
                END
       END
GO
```

Now attempt to log on as the `nightworker` login with the password `pass@word1` during the specified time range. The login attempt should yield the following error message:

```
Logon failed for login 'nightworker' due to trigger execution.
```

After the attempt, query the audit table to see whether the logon was tracked.

```
SELECT LoginNM,
       AttemptDT
FROM   ExampleAuditDB.dbo.RestrictedLogonAttempt
```

This returns the following (results will vary based on when you execute this recipe):

```
LoginNM                AttemptDT
-----------            -----------------------
nightworker            2012-05-01 03:20:19.577
```

How It Works

Logon triggers allow you to restrict and track logon activity after authentication to the SQL Server instance before an actual session is generated. If you want to apply custom business rules to logons above and beyond what is offered within the SQL Server feature set, you can implement them using the logon trigger.

This recipe creates a test login, a new auditing database, and an auditing table to track attempts. The logon trigger is created in the master database. Stepping through the code, note that `ALL SERVER` is used to set the scope of the trigger execution; this is a server DDL trigger as opposed to a database DDL trigger.

```
CREATE TRIGGER trg_logon_attempt ON ALL SERVER
```

The `EXECUTE AS` clause is used to define the permissions under which the trigger will execute. The recipe could have used a lower privileged login—any login with permission to write to the login table would suffice.

```
WITH EXECUTE AS 'sa'
```

`FOR LOGON` designates the event that this trigger subscribes to.

```
    FOR LOGON
AS
```

The body of the trigger logic then started at the BEGIN keyword.

```
BEGIN
```

The original security context of the logon attempt was then evaluated. In this case, the trigger is interested in enforcing logic only if the login is for nightworker.

```
        IF ORIGINAL_LOGIN() = 'nightworker'
```

Included in this logic is an evaluation of the hour of the day. If the current time is between 7 a.m. and 6 p.m., two actions will be performed.

```
           AND DATEPART(hh, GETDATE()) BETWEEN 7 AND 18
           BEGIN
```

The first action is to roll back the logon attempt.

```
               ROLLBACK ;
```

The second action is to track the attempt to the audit table.

```
               INSERT  ExampleAuditDB.dbo.RestrictedLogonAttempt
                       (LoginNM, AttemptDT)
               VALUES  (ORIGINAL_LOGIN(), GETDATE()) ;
           END
    END
GO
```

Again, it is worthwhile to remind you that how you code the logic of a logon trigger is very important. Improper logging can cause unexpected results. Also, if your logon trigger isn't performing the actions you expect, be sure to check your latest SQL log for clues. Logon trigger attempts that are rolled back also get written to the SQL log. If something was miscoded in the trigger, for example, if I hadn't designated the proper fully qualified table name for RestrictedLogonAttempt, the SQL log would have shown the error message "Invalid object name 'dbo.RestrictedLogon-Attempt'.

■ **Note** Don't forget about disabling this recipe's trigger when you are finished testing it. To disable it, execute DISABLE TRIGGER trg_logon_attempt ON ALL SERVER in the master database.

19-8. Viewing DDL Trigger Metadata

Problem

You want to list the server and database DDL triggers defined on your server.

Solution

This recipe demonstrates the retrieval of DDL trigger metadata.

The first example queries the sys.triggers catalog view, returning the associated *database-scoped* trigger name and trigger enabled/disabled status.

```
-- Show the DML triggers in the current database
SELECT name TriggerNM,
       is_disabled
FROM   sys.triggers
WHERE  parent_class_desc = 'DATABASE'
ORDER BY OBJECT_NAME(parent_id),
       Name ;
```

This returns the following results:

```
TriggerNM                    is_disabled
ddlDatabaseTriggerLog        1
```

This next example queries the sys.server_triggers and sys.server_trigger_events system catalog views to retrieve a list of server-scoped DDL triggers. This returns the name of the DDL trigger, the type of trigger (Transact-SQL or CLR), the disabled state of the trigger, and the events the trigger subscribed to.

```
SELECT name,
       s.type_desc SQL_or_CLR,
       is_disabled,
       e.type_desc FiringEvents
FROM   sys.server_triggers s
       INNER JOIN sys.server_trigger_events e
            ON s.object_id = e.object_id ;
```

This returns data based on the previous server-level trigger created earlier.

```
name                SQL_or_CLR    is_disabled FiringEvents
------------------- ------------- ----------- --------------
trg_logon_attempt   SQL_TRIGGER   1           LOGON
```

To display *database-scoped* DDL trigger Transact-SQL definitions, you can query the sys.sql_modules system catalog view.

```
SELECT t.name,
       m.Definition
FROM   sys.triggers AS t
       INNER JOIN sys.sql_modules m
           ON t.object_id = m.object_id
WHERE  t.parent_class_desc = 'DATABASE' ;
```

To display *server-scoped* DDL triggers, you can query the sys.server_sql_modules and sys.server_triggers system catalog views.

```
SELECT t.name,
       m.definition
FROM   sys.server_sql_modules m
       INNER JOIN sys.server_triggers t
            ON m.object_id = t.object_id ;
```

How It Works

The first query in this recipe returns a list of database-scoped triggers using the sys.triggers system catalog view. To display only DDL database-scoped triggers, the query filters the parent_class_desc value to DATABASE.

The second query returns a list of server-scoped triggers and their associated triggering events. These triggers are accessed through the `sys.server_triggers` and `sys.server_trigger_events` system catalog views.

The third query returns the Transact-SQL definitions of database-scoped triggers through the `sys.triggers` and `sys.sql_modules` catalog views. In the final query, the `sys.server_sql_modules` and `sys.server_triggers` system catalog views are joined to return a server-scoped trigger's Transact-SQL definitions.

19-9. Modifying a Trigger

Problem

You have an existing trigger and need to modify the trigger definition.

Solution

To modify an existing DDL or DML trigger, use the `ALTER TRIGGER` command. `ALTER TRIGGER` takes the same arguments as the associated DML or DDL `CREATE TRIGGER` syntax.

This example will modify the login trigger that was created in Recipe 19-7. The login trigger should no longer restrict users from logging in but instead allow the login and write the login only to the audit table.

■ **Note** If you have cleaned up the objects that were created in Recipe 19-7, you will need to re-create these objects for this recipe.

The following statement modifies the login trigger. Note the rollback has been commented out.

```
USE master ;
GO
ALTER TRIGGER trg_logon_attempt ON ALL SERVER
 WITH EXECUTE AS 'sa'
       FOR LOGON
AS
       BEGIN
             IF ORIGINAL_LOGIN() = 'nightworker'
                AND DATEPART(hh, GETDATE()) BETWEEN 7 AND 18
                BEGIN
                    --ROLLBACK ;
                    INSERT  ExampleAuditDB.dbo.RestrictedLogonAttempt
                            (LoginNM, AttemptDT)
                    VALUES  (ORIGINAL_LOGIN(), GETDATE()) ;
                END
       END
GO
```

An attempt to log in to the server with the login `nightworker` and password `pass@word1` should now be allowed, and you should see the login attempt recorded in the audit table.

```
SELECT LoginNM,
       AttemptDT
FROM   ExampleAuditDB.dbo.RestrictedLogonAttempt ;
```

The preceding select statement returns the following:

```
LoginNM          AttemptDT
---------------- -----------------------
nightworker      2012-05-01 012:20:19.577
nightworker      2012-05-02 14:20:33.577
```

How It Works

ALTER TRIGGER allows you to modify existing DDL or DML triggers. The arguments for ALTER TRIGGER are the same as for CREATE TRIGGER.

19-10. Enabling and Disabling a Trigger

Problem

You have a trigger defined on a table that you would like to disable temporarily but still keep the definition in the database so that you can reenable the trigger easily.

Solution

Sometimes triggers must be disabled if they are causing problems that you need to troubleshoot or if you need to import or recover data that shouldn't fire the trigger. In this recipe, I demonstrate how to disable a trigger from firing using the DISABLE TRIGGER command, as well as how to reenable a trigger using ENABLE TRIGGER.

The syntax for DISABLE TRIGGER is as follows:

```
DISABLE TRIGGER [ schema . ] trigger_name ON { object_name | DATABASE | SERVER }
```

The syntax for enabling a trigger is as follows:

```
ENABLE TRIGGER [ schema_name . ] trigger_name ON { object_name | DATABASE | SERVER }
```

Table 19-5 details the arguments of this command.

Table 19-5. *ENABLE and DISABLE Trigger Arguments*

Argument	Description
[schema_name .]trigger_name	The optional schema owner and required user-defined name of the trigger you want to disable.
object_name | DATABASE | SERVER	object_name is the table or view that the trigger was bound to (if it's a DML trigger). Use DATABASE if the trigger was a DDL database-scoped trigger and SERVER if the trigger was a DDL server-scoped trigger.

This example starts by creating a trigger (which is enabled by default) that prints a message that an INSERT has been performed against the HumanResources.Department table.

■ **Note** The previous few examples use the master database. The next few examples are back in the AdventureWorks2012 database.

```
CREATE TRIGGER HumanResources.trg_Department ON HumanResources.Department
       AFTER INSERT
AS
       PRINT 'The trg_Department trigger was fired' ;
GO
```

■ **Note** At the beginning of this chapter, I mentioned that you should not return result sets from triggers. The PRINT statement is a way to return informational information to a calling application without a result set. Be careful with the use of PRINT statements because some client APIs interpret PRINT as error messages. The purposes of debugging execution within SQL Server Management Studio or the SQLCMD application PRINT can be very helpful. For further information on PRINT, see SQL Server Books Online (http://msdn.microsoft.com/en-US/library/ms190715(v=sql.90).aspx).

Disable the trigger using the DISABLE TRIGGER command.

```
DISABLE TRIGGER HumanResources.trg_Department
ON HumanResources.Department;
```

Because the trigger was disabled, no printed message will be returned when the following INSERT is executed.

```
INSERT HumanResources.Department
       (Name,
        GroupName)
VALUES ('Construction',
        'Building Services') ;
```

This returns the following:

```
(1 row(s) affected)
```

Next, the trigger is enabled using the ENABLE TRIGGER command.

```
ENABLE TRIGGER HumanResources.trg_Department ON HumanResources.Department ;
```

Now when another INSERT is attempted, the trigger will fire, returning a message to the connection.

```
INSERT HumanResources.Department
       (Name, GroupName)
VALUES ('Cleaning', 'Building Services') ;
```

This returns the following:

```
The trg_Department trigger was fired
(1 row(s) affected)
```

How It Works

This recipe starts by creating a new trigger that prints a statement whenever a new row is inserted into the HumanResources.Department table.

After creating the trigger, the DISABLE TRIGGER command is used to keep it from firing (although the trigger's definition still stays in the database).

```
DISABLE TRIGGER HumanResources.trg_Department
ON HumanResources.Department
```

An insert is performed that does not fire the trigger. The ENABLE TRIGGER command is then executed, and then another insert is attempted; this time, the INSERT fires the trigger.

19-11. Nesting Triggers

Problem

Your trigger inserts data into another table with triggers defined. You want to control whether the data modifications performed in a trigger will cause additional triggers to fire.

Solution

Trigger nesting occurs when a trigger is fired, that trigger performs some DML, and that DML in turn fires another trigger. Depending on a given database schema and a group's coding standards, this may or may not be a desirable behavior.

The SQL Server instance may be configured to allow or disallow trigger nesting. Disabling the nested triggers option prevents any AFTER trigger from causing the firing of another trigger.

This example demonstrates how to disable or enable this behavior:

```
USE master ;
GO
-- Disable nesting
EXEC sp_configure 'nested triggers', 0 ;
RECONFIGURE WITH OVERRIDE ;
GO
-- Enable nesting
EXEC sp_configure 'nested triggers', 1 ;
RECONFIGURE WITH OVERRIDE ;
GO
```

This returns the following:

```
Configuration option 'nested triggers' changed from 1 to 0. Run the RECONFIGURE statement to
install.

Configuration option 'nested triggers' changed from 0 to 1. Run the RECONFIGURE statement to
install.
```

How It Works

This recipe uses the `sp_configure` system stored procedure to change the nested trigger behavior at the server level. To disable nesting altogether, `sp_configure` is executed for the `nested trigger` server option, followed by the parameter 0, which disables nesting.

```
EXEC sp_configure 'nested triggers', 0
RECONFIGURE WITH OVERRIDE
GO
```

Because server options contain both a current configuration versus an actual runtime configuration value, the `RECONFIGURE WITH OVERRIDE` command was used to update the runtime value so that it takes effect right away.

To enable nesting again, this server option is set back to 1 in the second batch of the recipe.

■ **Note** There is a limit of 32 levels to trigger nesting. The function `TRIGGER_NESTLEVEL` will tell how many levels into trigger nesting you are. See SQL Server Books Online for more information on the `TRIGGER_NESTLEVEL` function (`http://msdn.microsoft.com/en-us/library/ms182737.aspx`).

19-12. Controlling Recursion

Problem

You have a table in which a data modification causes a trigger to execute and update the table on which that trigger is defined.

Solution

A specific case of trigger nesting is trigger recursion. Trigger nesting is considered to be recursive if the action performed when a trigger fires causes the *same* trigger to fire again. This may happen directly; for instance, a trigger is defined on a table, and that trigger executes DML back to the table on which it is defined. Or, it may be indirect; for example, a trigger updates another table, and a trigger on that other table updates the original table.

Recursion may be allowed or disallowed by configuring the `RECURSIVE_TRIGGERS` database option. If recursion is allowed, `AFTER` triggers are still limited by the 32-level nesting limit to prevent an infinite loop.

This example demonstrates enabling and disabling this option.

```
-- Allow recursion
ALTER DATABASE AdventureWorks2012
SET RECURSIVE_TRIGGERS ON ;
```

```
-- View the db setting
SELECT is_recursive_triggers_on
FROM   sys.databases
WHERE  name = 'AdventureWorks2012' ;

-- Prevents recursion
ALTER DATABASE AdventureWorks2012
SET RECURSIVE_TRIGGERS OFF ;

-- View the db setting
SELECT is_recursive_triggers_on
FROM   sys.databases
WHERE  name = 'AdventureWorks2012' ;
```

This returns the following:

```
is_recursive_triggers_on 1

is_recursive_triggers_on 0
```

How It Works

`ALTER DATABASE` is used to configure database-level options including whether triggers are allowed to fire recursively within the database. The option was enabled by setting `RECURSIVE_TRIGGERS ON`.

```
ALTER DATABASE AdventureWorks2012
SET RECURSIVE_TRIGGERS ON ;
```

The option is then queried by using the `sys.databases` system catalog view that shows the current database option in the `is_recursive_triggers_on` column (1 for on, 0 for off).

```
SELECT is_recursive_triggers_on
FROM   sys.databases
WHERE  name = 'AdventureWorks2012' ;
```

The recipe then disables trigger recursion by setting the option `OFF` and confirms this by selecting from the `sys.databases` view.

19-13. Specifying the Firing Order

Problem

Over time you have accumulated multiple triggers on the same table. You are concerned that the order that the triggers execute is nondeterministic, and you are seeing inconsistent results from simple insert, update, and delete activity.

Solution

In general, triggers that react to the same event (or events) should be consolidated by placing all their business logic into just one trigger. This improves the manageability and supportability of the triggers. Also, this issue of determining and specifying trigger order is avoidable if the trigger logic is consolidated.

That said, conditions arise where multiple triggers may fire in response to the same DML or DDL action, and often the order in which they are fired is important. The system stored procedure sp_settriggerorder allows you to specify trigger order.

The syntax for sp_settriggerorder is as follows:

```
sp_settriggerorder [ (@triggername = ] '[ triggerschema.]triggername' , [ (@order = ] 'value' ,
[ (@stmttype = ] 'statement_type' [ , [ (@namespace = ] { 'DATABASE' | 'SERVER' | NULL } ]
```

Table 19-6 details the arguments of this command.

Table 19-6. *sp_settriggerorder Arguments*

Argument	Description
'[triggerschema.]triggername'	This defines the optional schema owner and required user-defined name of the trigger to be ordered.
[@order =] 'value'	This can be either First, None, or Last. Any triggers in between these will be fired in a random order after the first and last firings.
[@stmttype =] 'statement_type'	This designates the type of trigger to be ordered, for example, INSERT, UPDATE, DELETE, CREATE_INDEX, ALTER_INDEX, and so forth.
[@namespace =] { 'DATABASE' | 'SERVER' | NULL}	This designates whether this is a DDL trigger and, if so, whether it is database- or server-scoped.

This recipe creates a test table and adds three DML INSERT triggers to it. sp_settriggerorder will then be used to define the execution order of the triggers.

```
CREATE TABLE dbo.TestTriggerOrder (TestID INT NOT NULL) ;
GO

CREATE TRIGGER dbo.trg_i_TestTriggerOrder ON dbo.TestTriggerOrder
       AFTER INSERT
AS
       PRINT 'I will be fired first.' ;
GO

CREATE TRIGGER dbo.trg_i_TestTriggerOrder2 ON dbo.TestTriggerOrder
       AFTER INSERT
AS
       PRINT 'I will be fired last.' ;
GO

CREATE TRIGGER dbo.trg_i_TestTriggerOrder3 ON dbo.TestTriggerOrder
       AFTER INSERT
AS
       PRINT 'I will be somewhere in the middle.' ;
GO

EXEC sp_settriggerorder 'trg_i_TestTriggerOrder', 'First', 'INSERT' ;
EXEC sp_settriggerorder 'trg_i_TestTriggerOrder2', 'Last', 'INSERT' ;
```

```
INSERT dbo.TestTriggerOrder
       (TestID)
VALUES (1) ;
```

This returns the following:

```
I will be fired first.

I will be somewhere in the middle.

I will be fired last.
```

How It Works

This recipe starts by creating a single column test table, and three DML INSERT triggers are added to it. Using sp_settriggerorder, the first and last triggers to fire are defined.

```
EXEC sp_settriggerorder 'trg_i_TestTriggerOrder', 'First', 'INSERT' ;
EXEC sp_settriggerorder 'trg_i_TestTriggerOrder2', 'Last', 'INSERT' ;
```

An INSERT is then executed against the table, and the trigger messages are returned in the expected order.

To reiterate this point, use a single trigger on a table when you can. If you must create multiple triggers of the same type and your trigger contains ROLLBACK functionality if an error occurs, be sure to set the trigger that has the most likely chance of failing as the first trigger to execute. This way, only the first-fired trigger needs to be executed, preventing the other triggers from having to fire and roll back transactions unnecessarily.

19-14. Dropping a Trigger

Problem

You are deploying a new version of your database schema, and DML is now executed through stored procedures. You have consolidated the business logic that was enforced by your triggers into these stored procedures; it is now time to drop the triggers.

Solution

The syntax for dropping a trigger differs by trigger type (DML or DDL). The syntax for dropping a DML trigger is as follows:

```
DROP TRIGGER schema_name.trigger_name [ ,...n ]
```

Table 19-7 details the argument of this command.

***Table 19-7.** DROP TRIGGER Argument (DML)*

Argument	Description
schema_name.trigger_name	The owning schema name of the trigger and the DML trigger name to be removed from the database

The syntax for dropping a DDL trigger is as follows:

```
DROP TRIGGER trigger_name [ ,...n ]
ON { DATABASE | ALL SERVER }
```

Table 19-8 details the arguments of this command.

Table 19-8. *DROP TRIGGER Arguments (DDL)*

Argument	Description
trigger_name	Defines the DDL trigger name to be removed from the database (for a database-level DDL trigger) or SQL Server instance (for a server-scoped trigger)
DATABASE | ALL SERVER	Defines whether you are removing a DATABASE-scoped DDL trigger or a server-scoped trigger (ALL SERVER)

In the case of both DDL and DML syntax statements, the [,... n] syntax block indicates that more than one trigger can be dropped at the same time.

The following example demonstrates dropping a DML and a DDL trigger.

■ **Note** The triggers dropped in this recipe were created in previous recipes in this chapter.

```
-- Switch context back to the AdventureWorks2012 database
USE AdventureWorks2012 ;
GO
-- Drop a DML trigger
DROP TRIGGER dbo.trg_i_TestTriggerOrder ;
-- Drop multiple DML triggers
DROP TRIGGER dbo.trg_i_TestTriggerOrder2, dbo.trg_i_TestTriggerOrder3 ;
-- Drop a DDL trigger
DROP TRIGGER db_trg_INDEXChanges
ON DATABASE ;
```

How It Works

In this recipe, DML and DDL triggers were explicitly dropped using the DROP TRIGGER command. You will also drop all DML triggers when you drop the table or view that they are bound to. You can also remove multiple triggers in the same DROP command if each of the triggers were created using the same ON clause.

CHAPTER 20

Error Handling

by David Dye

In this chapter you'll learn several methods of error handling in T-SQL including structured error handling.

20-1. Handling batch errors

Problem

You have a script containing numerous Data Definition Language(DDL) and Data Manipulation Language(DML) statements that completely fail to run. You need to insure that if part of the script fails due to an error the remaining script will complete, if there are no errors.

Solution

A single script can contain multiple statements and if run as a single batch the entire script will fail. When using SSMS or SQLCMD batches can be separated with the GO command, but used in an application using an OLEDB or ODBC API an error will be returned. The below script contains both DDL and DML statements and when executed as a whole will fail within SSMS.

```
USE master;

IF EXISTS(SELECT * FROM sys.databases WHERE name='Errors')
BEGIN
DROP DATABASE Errors;
CREATE DATABASE Errors;
END;
ELSE CREATE DATABASE Errors;

USE Errors;

CREATE TABLE Works(
number  INT);
```

```
INSERT Works
VALUES(1),
        ('A'),
        (3);

SELECT *
FROM Works;
```

The script returns immediately with an error indicating that the Errors database does not exist .

```
Msg 911, Level 16, State 1, Line 11
Database 'Errors' does not exist. Make sure that the name is entered correctly.
```

Reviewing the initial DDL statement shows the use of and IF statement that will create the Errors databse if it does not exist so this may seem a bit confusing. The fact is that SQL Server evaluates the entire script as a single batch and returns the error since the USE statement references a database that does not exist.

This type of error can be easily overcome by separating each statement with a batch directive. The below code demonstrates how to use the GO key word to insure that each statement is executed and evaluated separately.

```
USE master;

IF EXISTS(SELECT * FROM sys.databases WHERE name='Errors')
BEGIN
DROP DATABASE Errors;
CREATE DATABASE Errors;
END;
ELSE CREATE DATABASE Errors;
GO

USE Errors;

CREATE TABLE Works(
number  INT);
GO

INSERT Works
VALUES(1),
        ('A'),
        (3);
GO

INSERT Works
VALUES(1),
        (2),
        (3);
GO
SELECT *
FROM Works;
GO
```

An error message is still returned showing a data type mismatch trying to insert the character "A" into the Errors table, however all other statements complete as is shown with the results of the select statement:

```
Msg 245, Level 16, State 1, Line 2
Conversion failed when converting the varchar value 'A' to data type int.

number
------
1
2
3
```

How It Works

The GO statement is a Microsoft proprietary batch directive. SQL Server can accept multiple T-SQL statements for execution as a batch. The statements in the batch are parsed, bound, and compiled into a single execution. If any of the batch fails to parse or bind then the query fails. By using the GO directive to separate statements insures that one batch containing an error will not cause the other statements to fail.

The GO directive is one of the only statements that must be on their own line of code. For example the following statement would fail:

```
SELECT *
FROM Works; GO
```

```
A fatal scripting error occurred.
Incorrect syntax was encountered while parsing GO.
```

■ **Tip** A semicolon, ";" is not a batch directive, but rather an ANSI standard. The semicolon is a statement terminator and is currently not required for most statements in T-SQL, but it will be required in future versions.

http://msdn.microsoft.com/en-us/library/ms177563.aspx

20-2. What are the error numbers and messages within SQL?

Problem

You need to view the error numbers and messages that are contained within an instance of SQL.

Solution

SQL contains a catalog view that can be used to query he error messages contained within an instance of SQL. The view contains all messages for a number of languages so it is best to filter the query based on the language_id. The below query will return all United States English messages:

```
SELECT message_id,
          severity,
          text
FROM sys.messages
WHERE language_id=1033;
GO
```

This example returns the following abridged results::

```
message_id,  severity,          text
101,         15,                Query not allowed in Waitfor.
102,         15,                Incorrect syntax near '%.*ls'.
103,         15,                The %S_MSG that starts with '%.*ls' is too long. Maximum
                                length is %d.
```

How It Works

The catalog view maintains a list of all system and user error and information messages. The view contains the messageid, language id, error severity, if the error is written to the application log and the message text. The error severity column from the sys.messages catalog viewcan be very insightful in finding user and system errors. The severity level of system and user defined messages are displayed below in Table 20-1

Table 20-1. *Severity level of system and user defined messages*

Severity level	Description
0–9	Informational messages status only and are not logged.
10	Informational messages status information. Not logged
11–16	Error can be corrected by the user. Not logged
17–19	Software errors that cannot be corrected by the user. Errors will be logged
20–24	System problem and are fatal errors. Errors can affect all processes accessing data in the same database. Errors will be logged.

Based on the severity level, targeting and debugging a query or process can be made easier as it can be ascertained if the error is user or system based.

20-3. How can I implement structured error handling in my queries?

Problem

You are required to write T-SQL statements that have structured error handling so that the application will not incur a runtime error.

Solution

SQL Server 2005 introduced structured error handling using a `BEGIN TRY...BEGIN CATCH` block. SQL 2012 enhanced structured error handling by adding FINALLY to structured error handling. Structured error handling can be easily implemented within a query by placing the query within the `BEGIN TRY` block immediately followed by the `BEGIN CATCH` block:

```
BEGIN TRY
 SELECT 1/0  --This will raise a divide by zero error if not handled
END TRY
BEGIN CATCH
END CATCH;
GO
```

The outcome is that no error or results are returned:

```
(0 row(s) affected)
```

How It Works

A query error is handled withint the try and catch block insuring that rather than an error being returned only an empty result set is returned. There are several functions that can be called wihtin the scope of a catch block that can be used to return error information. These functions can be returned with a select statement so rather than returning an error a result set can be returned with the information as demonstrated in the below code:

```
BEGIN TRY
  SELECT 1/0 --This will raise a divide by zero error if not handled
END TRY
BEGIN CATCH
  SELECT ERROR_LINE() AS 'Line',
               ERROR_MESSAGE() AS 'Message',
               ERROR_NUMBER() AS 'Number',
               ERROR_PROCEDURE() AS 'Procedure',
               ERROR_SEVERITY() AS 'Severity',
               ERROR_STATE() AS 'State'
END CATCH;
```

The results are displayed below showing that an error is not encountered, but the details are returned as a result set:

```
Line,     Message,                  Number,     Procedure,     Severity,    State
-----     ---------                 -------     ---------      -------      -----
2,        Divide by zero            8134        NULL            16,         1
           error encountered.
```

The ERROR_LINE() retunrs the approximate line number in which the error occurred. The ERROR_MESSAGE() function retunrs the text message of the error that is caught in the CATCH block. The ERROR_NUMBER() function returns the error number that caused the error. The ERROR_PROCEDURE() will return the name of the stored procedure or trigger that raised the error. ERROR_SEVERITY() returns the severity irrespective of how many times it is run, or where it is caught within the scope of the CATCH block. The ERROR_STATE() returns the state number of the error message that caused the CATCH block to be run and will return NULL if called outside the scope of a CATCH block.

T-SQL structured error handling is very useful, but it does have it's limitations. Unfortunately not all error can be captured within a try catch block. For example compilation errors will not be caught. This is easily demonstrated by placing syntactically incorrect statements within a try catch block as demonstrated here:

```
BEGIN TRY
  SELECT
END TRY
BEGIN CATCH
END CATCH;
GO
```

```
Msg 102, Level 15, State 1, Line 2
Incorrect syntax near 'SELECT'.
```

Since SELECT was misspelled the query could not be compiled. Binding errors will also not be caught within a try catch block as is demonstrated here:

```
 BEGIN TRY
  SELECT NoSuchTable
END TRY
BEGIN CATCH
END CATCH;
GO
```

```
Msg 207, Level 16, State 1, Line 3
Invalid column name 'NoSuchTable'.
```

Error messages with a severity of 20 or higher will not be caught within try catch as well as statements that span batches or recompilation errors. Errors, or messages, with a severity of 10 or less will not be caught within the catch block as these are informational messages. The below code demonstrates using RAISERROR to throw an informational message within a try catch block.

```
BEGIN TRY
  RAISERROR('Information ONLY', 10, 1)
END TRY
```

```
BEGIN CATCH
END CATCH;
GO
```

The messages tab of SSMS returns the messagae as shown below:

```
Information ONLY
```

20-4. How can I use structured error handling, but still return an error?

Problem

You are required to write T-SQL statements that have structured error handling, but will also need to return the system or user defined error to insure that the execution fails returning the sppropriate error message.

Solution

SQL 2012 introduced the THROW statement, which can be included in a try and catch block. The below code demonstrates how using THROW in the catch block will still return a divide by zero error.

```
BEGIN TRY
   SELECT 1/0
END TRY
BEGIN CATCH
    PRINT 'In catch block.';
    THROW;
END CATCH;
```

```
(0 row(s) affected)
In catch block.
Msg 8134, Level 16, State 1, Line 2
Divide by zero error encountered.
```

How It Works

The try and catch block works as outlined in the solution above with the only difference being the `THROW` statement is contained in the catch block. The result is that the message "In catch block" is printed in the messages tab followed by the resulting error being raised by the `THROW` statement.

The severity of any error passed in the throw statement is set to 16, which will cause the batch to fail. In this example the throw is being used without any parameters, which can only be done within a catch block, so all error information is from the error that is being handled from within the try catch block.

A custom error can be thrown based on the error that is raised. The below code demonstrates how to throw an error based upon the error unber that is returned:

```
BEGIN TRY
   SELECT 1/0
END TRY
BEGIN CATCH
        IF (SELECT @@ERROR)=8134
        BEGIN;
        THROW 51000, 'Divide by zero error occurred', 10;
          END
          ELSE
        THROW 52000, 'Unknown error occurred', 10;
END CATCH;
```

```
(0 row(s) affected)
Msg 51000, Level 16, State 10, Line 7
Divide by zero error occurred
```

20-5. Nested error handling

Problem

There may be times when you will be required to use structured error handling, but you will need to insure that errors are handled in either the try or catch block .

Solution

Try and catch blocks can be nested either within the TRY or the CATCH blocks. The below example displays nesting inside the TRY block.

```
BEGIN TRY
  SELECT 1/0 --This will raise a divide by zero error if not handled
        BEGIN TRY
                PRINT 'Inner Try'
        END TRY
        BEGIN CATCH
                PRINT CONVERT(CHAR(5), ERROR_NUMBER())+'Inner Catch'
        END CATCH
END TRY
BEGIN CATCH
  PRINT CONVERT(CHAR(5), ERROR_NUMBER())+'Outer Catch'
END CATCH;
GO
```

```
(0 row(s) affected)
8134 Outer Catch
```

How It Works

The outer try block begins and raises a divide by zero error. Immediately after the intial outer try raises and error it bypasses both the inner try and catch block and goes immediately to the outer catch block to handle the divide by zero error. The outer catch block prints the error number and the message "Outer Catch".

To better understand the how this works examine the code below that reverses the code between the outer and inner try causing the error to be raised within the outer try.

```
BEGIN TRY
  PRINT 'Outer Try'
        BEGIN TRY
                SELECT 1/0 --This will raise a divide by zero error if not handled
        END TRY
    BEGIN CATCH
                PRINT CONVERT(CHAR(5), ERROR_NUMBER())+'Inner Catch'
        END CATCH
END TRY
BEGIN CATCH
  PRINT CONVERT(CHAR(5), ERROR_NUMBER())+'Outer Catch'
END CATCH;
GO
```

The results show that the outer try executed without error then going to the inner try code. Once an error was raised in the inner try the inner catch block handles the error.

```
Outer Try
(0 row(s) affected)
8134 Inner Catch
```

The above demonstrates the order in which a nested try catch will occur when nested in the try block:

1. Outer TRY block
2. Outer CATCH block if an error occurs
3. Inner TRY block
4. Outer CATCH if an error occurs

A more complex nested try catch demonstrates how the code can dynamically handle errors based on the error number:

```
BEGIN TRY
  PRINT 'Outer Try'
        BEGIN TRY
                PRINT ERROR_NUMBER()+' Inner try'
        END TRY
    BEGIN CATCH
                IF ERROR_NUMBER()=8134
                   PRINT CONVERT(CHAR(5), ERROR_NUMBER()) + 'nner Catch Divide by zero'
                ELSE
                   BEGIN;
```

```
   PRINT CONVERT(CHAR(6), ERROR_NUMBER())+' '+ERROR_MESSAGE() +
              CONVERT(CHAR(2), ERROR_SEVERITY()) + ' ' +
              CONVERT(CHAR(2), ERROR_STATE())+'INITIAL Catch';
                END
END CATCH
END TRY
        BEGIN CATCH
                IF ERROR_NUMBER()=8134
                   PRINT CONVERT(CHAR(5), ERROR_NUMBER())+'Outer Catch Divide by zero'
                ELSE
                   BEGIN;
   PRINT CONVERT(CHAR(6), ERROR_NUMBER())+' '+ERROR_MESSAGE() +
              CONVERT(CHAR(2), ERROR_SEVERITY()) + ' ' +
              CONVERT(CHAR(2), ERROR_STATE())+'OUTER Catch';
                 THROW
                END
        END CATCH
```

The results show that the outer try executed without error then going to the inner try code. Once an error was raised in the inner try the inner catch block handles the error.

```
Outer Try
245    Conversion failed when converting the varchar value ' Inner try' to data type int.161
INITIAL Catch
```

The above results are drastically changed by adding a THROW in the first catch block as shown in this code:

```
        BEGIN TRY
  PRINT 'Outer Try'
        BEGIN TRY
                PRINT ERROR_NUMBER()+' Inner try'
        END TRY
    BEGIN CATCH
                IF ERROR_NUMBER()=8134
                   PRINT CONVERT(CHAR(5), ERROR_NUMBER())+'Inner Catch Divide by zero'
                ELSE
                   BEGIN;
   PRINT CONVERT(CHAR(6), ERROR_NUMBER())+' '+ERROR_MESSAGE() +
              CONVERT(CHAR(2), ERROR_SEVERITY())+' ' +
              CONVERT(CHAR(2), ERROR_STATE())+'INITIAL Catch';
                 THROW --This THROW is added in the initial CATCH
                END
END CATCH
END TRY
        BEGIN CATCH
                IF ERROR_NUMBER()=8134
                   PRINT CONVERT(CHAR(5), ERROR_NUMBER())+'Outer Catch Divide by zero'
                ELSE
                   BEGIN;
```

```
    PRINT CONVERT(CHAR(6), ERROR_NUMBER())+' '+ERROR_MESSAGE() +
               CONVERT(CHAR(2), ERROR_SEVERITY())+' '  +
               CONVERT(CHAR(2), ERROR_STATE())+'OUTER Catch';
                  THROW
                 END
END CATCH
```

The results now show that the outer try executed without error and proceeded to the inner try code. Once an error was raised in the inner try the inner catch block handles the error and prints out in the messages tab the concantanated string of the error number, message, severity and state as well as where the error is handled. The execution goes immediately to the outer catch block where the error string is printed out once again and then the conversion error is raised.

```
Outer Try
245    Conversion failed when converting the varchar value ' Inner try' to data type int.16
1 INITIAL Catch
245    Conversion failed when converting the varchar value ' Inner try' to data type int.16
1 OUTER Catch
Msg 245, Level 16, State 1, Line 5
Conversion failed when converting the varchar value ' Inner try' to data type int.
```

The confusing part of the execution is why both catch blocks are entered and why the error is raised. The reason is the THROW statement in the inner and outer catch block. Once the error is encountered the inner catch handles the error, but then rethrows the error. Since the error has been rethrown once leaving the inner catch block the code goes immediately to the outer catch again raising the error message that was rethrown. The outer catch handles the error with the PRINT statement and finally rethrows the error.

20-6. Throwing an error

Problem

Certain instances require that a user defined error should be thrown.

Solution #1: Use RAISERROR to throw an error

Throwing an error within a block of code is as simple as using the RAISERROR statement.

```
RAISERROR ('User defined error', -- Message text.
              16, -- Severity.
              1 -- State.
              );
```

The above example throws a user defined eror with the message "User defined error" with a severity of 16 and state of 1:

```
Msg 50000, Level 16, State 1, Line 1
User defined error
```

How It Works

User defined errors must have an error number that is equal to or greater than 50000 so if a number isn't defined in the raise error statement the default error number will be 50000.

A more practical example can be given by using RAISERROR in a DELETE trigger on a table that does not allow the deletion of records. Using RAISERROR can stop the transaction from occurring by raising a user defined error that specifies that deletions are not permitted.

The below code creates a table in the tempdb called Creditor and then creates an after delete trigger that raises an error. The result is that any attempt to delete a record will return an error with a message explaining that deletions are not permitted.

```
USE tempdb;

CREATE TABLE Creditor(
CreditorID              INT IDENTITY PRIMARY KEY,
CreditorName    VARCHAR(50)
);
GO

INSERT Creditor
VALUES('You Owe Me'),
        ('You Owe Me More');
GO

SELECT *
FROM Creditor;
GO
```

Executing the above query shows that the table is created and populated with two rows.

```
CreditorID,       CreditorName,
-----------       ---------------
1                 You Owe Me
2                 You Owe Me More
```

```
CREATE TRIGGER Deny_Delete
ON Creditor
FOR DELETE
AS
RAISERROR('Deletions are not permitted',
                16,
                1)
ROLBACK TRAN;
GO

DELETE Creditor
WHERE CreditorID=1;
GO
```

Once the trigger is created and a deletion is attempted the transaction fails with two errors. The first error is the error thrown using RAISERROR and the second is thrown from the ROLLBACK command that is within the trigger.

```
Msg 50000, Level 16, State 1, Procedure Deny_Delete, Line 6
Deletions are not permitted
Msg 3609, Level 16, State 1, Line 1
The transaction ended in the trigger. The batch has been aborted.
```

```
SELECT *
FROM Creditor;
GO
```

The results of selecting all the records from the Creditor table shows that both rows are still in the table :

```
CreditorID,          CreditorName,
-----------          ---------------
1,                   You Owe Me
2,                   You Owe Me More
```

Solution #2: Use THROW to throw an error.

SQL 2012 introduced the THROW statement that can also be used to throw an error. The below example demonstrates unsing the THROW statement:

```
THROW 50000, 'User defined error', 1;
```

The results of the above statement throws the following error:

```
Msg 50000, Level 16, State 1, Line 1
User defined error
```

How It Works

The throw statement is very similar to raise error, but each has their own nuissances and usefulness. The most notable difference is how both are handled within a try catch block. The solution above, 20-5, demonstrates how THROW can be used without any parameters in a try and catch block to rethrow the original error. Raise error requires that the associated error parameters be passed. By rewriting the statement from above using RAISERROR in place of THROW will return an error as demonstrated below:

```
BEGIN TRY
  PRINT 'Outer Try'
        BEGIN TRY
                PRINT ERROR_NUMBER()+' Inner try'
        END TRY
```

```
BEGIN TRY
  PRINT 'Outer Try'
        BEGIN TRY
                PRINT ERROR_NUMBER()+' Inner try'
        END TRY
    BEGIN CATCH
                IF ERROR_NUMBER()=8134
                   PRINT CONVERT(CHAR(5), ERROR_NUMBER())+'Inner Catch Divide by zero'
                ELSE
                   BEGIN;
   PRINT CONVERT(CHAR(6), ERROR_NUMBER())+' '+ERROR_MESSAGE() +
              CONVERT(CHAR(2), ERROR_SEVERITY())+' ' +
              CONVERT(CHAR(2), ERROR_STATE())+'INITIAL Catch';
                 RAISERROR --This THROW is added in the initial CATCH
                END
END CATCH
END TRY
        BEGIN CATCH
                IF ERROR_NUMBER()=8134
                   PRINT CONVERT(CHAR(5), ERROR_NUMBER())+'Outer Catch Divide by zero'
                ELSE
                   BEGIN;
   PRINT CONVERT(CHAR(6), ERROR_NUMBER())+' '+ERROR_MESSAGE() +
              CONVERT(CHAR(2), ERROR_SEVERITY())+' '  +
              CONVERT(CHAR(2), ERROR_STATE())+'OUTER Catch';
                 RAISERROR
                END
        END CATCH
```

```
Msg 156, Level 15, State 1, Line 15
Incorrect syntax near the keyword 'END'.
Msg 156, Level 15, State 1, Line 27
Incorrect syntax near the keyword 'END'
```

Although raise error can be used in place of throw in such a case it requires substantially more code and the end result still provides a different error number.

```
BEGIN TRY
  PRINT 'Outer Try'
        BEGIN TRY
                PRINT ERROR_NUMBER()+' Inner try'
        END TRY
    BEGIN CATCH
        DECLARE @error_message AS VARCHAR(500)=ERROR_MESSAGE()
        DECLARE @error_severity AS INT=ERROR_SEVERITY()
        DECLARE @error_state AS INT=ERROR_STATE()
                IF ERROR_NUMBER()=8134
                   PRINT CONVERT(CHAR(5), ERROR_NUMBER())+'Inner Catch Divide by zero'
                ELSE
                   BEGIN;
```

```
   PRINT CONVERT(CHAR(6), ERROR_NUMBER())+' '+ERROR_MESSAGE() +
            CONVERT(CHAR(2), ERROR_SEVERITY())+' ' +
            CONVERT(CHAR(2), ERROR_STATE())+'INITIAL Catch';

               RAISERROR (@error_message,
                           @error_severity,
                           @error_state);
              END
END CATCH
END TRY
     BEGIN CATCH
     IF ERROR_NUMBER()=8134
               PRINT CONVERT(CHAR(5), ERROR_NUMBER())+'Outer Catch Divide by zero'
              ELSE
               BEGIN;
   PRINT CONVERT(CHAR(6), ERROR_NUMBER())+' '+ERROR_MESSAGE() +
            CONVERT(CHAR(2), ERROR_SEVERITY())+' ' +
            CONVERT(CHAR(2), ERROR_STATE())+'OUTER Catch';
               RAISERROR(@error_message,
                           @error_severity,
                           @error_state);
              END
     END CATCH
```

The results appear almost identical to the query above using throw except for the error number:

```
Outer Try
245    Conversion failed when converting the varchar value ' Inner try' to data type int.16
1 INITIAL Catch
50000  Conversion failed when converting the varchar value ' Inner try' to data type int.16
1 OUTER Catch
Msg 50000, Level 16, State 1, Line 33
Conversion failed when converting the varchar value ' Inner try' to data type int.
```

20-7. Creating a user defined error

Problem

A user defined error message needs to be created to be used from RAISERROR.

Solution: Use sp_addmessage to create user defined error message.

Messages can be added to an instance of SQL using the system stored procedure sp_addmessage. User defined messages are added to an instance and can be viewed from the sys.messages system catalog view and called from either throw or the raise error command. The below query creates a user defined message:

```
USE master
GO
EXEC sp_addmessage 50001, 16,
   N'This is a user defined error that can be corrected by the user';
GO
```

This message will then be made available within an instance of SQL and can be viewed within the sys.messages catalog view:

```
SELECT message_id,
        text
FROM sys.messages
WHERE message_id = 50001;
GO
```

```
message_id,                      text
-----------                      ------------------------------------------------------------
50001,                           This is a user defined error that can be corrected by the user
```

Once the message is created in the instance of SQL it can be called from the raise error statement as demonstrated below.

```
RAISERROR (50001,
                 16,
                 1);
GO
```

```
Msg 50001, Level 16, State 1, Line 1
This is a user defined error that can be corrected by the user
```

How It Works

The system stored procedure adds the user defined message to the master database where it can be called by using the raise error command. The error number must be 50000 or greater, but the message, severity, and whether the message is logged to the application log can be specified when adding the message to the master database.

The below example adds a message of severity 16, user caused, to the master database, but will be logged to the application log:

```
USE master
GO
sp_addmessage @msgnum = 50002 ,
                        @severity = 16 ,
                        @msgtext = 'User error that IS logged',
                        @with_log = 'TRUE';
GO

RAISERROR (50001,
                  16,
                  1);
GO
```

```
Msg 50002, Level 16, State 1, Line 1
User error that IS logged
```

Despite the severity of this error being set to 16, user defined, the error will still be logged to the Windows application log as the "with_log" parameter was set to true. This can be verified by viewing the application log as displayed in Figure 20-1:

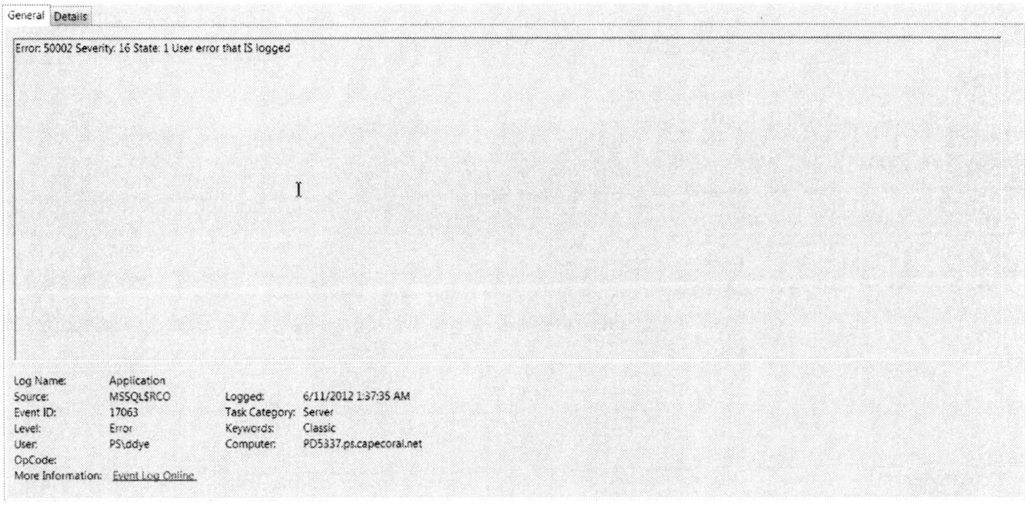

Figure 20-1. *Whenever raised the message is recorded in the application log*

Anytime the alert is called it will still be recorded in the application log, which provides a great deal of functionality in administration as it can be used to fire off events from SQL alerts. This demonstrates how user defined errors can be created and leveraged for both development and administrative purposes.

20-7. Removing a user defined error

Problem

A user defined error has been created and needs to be removed.

Solution: Use sp_dropmessage to remove the user defined error message

Messages can be removed from an instance of SQL using the system stored procedure sp_dropmessage. Once dropped the message will be removed from the master database and no longer be available withinthe instance. The below query first verifies that error messageid 50001 exists by querying the sys.messages catalog view and then drops the message using sp_dropmessage:

```
USE master
GO

SELECT message_id,
       text
```

```
FROM sys.messages
WHERE message_id = 50001;
GO

EXEC sp_dropmessage 50001;
GO

SELECT message_id,
        text
FROM sys.messages
WHERE message_id = 50001;
GO
```

```
message_id,                      text
-----------                      ----------------------------------------------------------------
50001,                           This is a user defined error that can be corrected by the user
message_id,                      text
-----------                      ------
```

How It Works

The system stored procedure drops the user defined message from the master database removing it from the entire instance of SQL Server. Any future attempts to call the error with either RAISERROR or THROW will result in an error indicating that the message does not exist.

```
RAISERROR(50001,
                16,
                1);
GO
```

```
Msg 18054, Level 16, State 1, Line 1
Error 50001, severity 16, state 1 was raised, but no message with that error number was
found in sys.messages. If error is larger than 50000, make sure the user-defined message is
added using sp_addmessage.
```

CHAPTER 21

Query Performance Tuning

By Jason Brimhall

SQL Server query performance tuning and optimization requires a multilayered approach. The following are a few key factors that impact SQL Server query performance:

- *Database design*: Probably one of the most important factors influencing both query performance and data integrity, design decisions impact both read and modification performance. Standard designs include OLTP-normalized databases, which focus on data integrity, removal of redundancy, and the establishment of relationships between multiple entities. This is a design most appropriate for quick transaction processing. You'll usually see more tables in a normalized OLTP design, which means more table joins in your queries. Data warehouse designs, on the other hand, often use a more denormalized star or snowflake design. These designs use a central fact table, which is joined to two or more description dimension tables. For snowflake designs, the dimension tables can also have related tables associated to it. The focus of this design is on query speed, not on fast updates to transactions.
- *Configurations*: This category includes databases, the SQL instance, and operating system configurations. Poor choices in configurations (such as enabling automatic shrinking and automatic closing of a database) can lead to performance issues for a busy application.
- *Hardware*: I once spent a day trying to get a three-second query down to one second. No matter which indexes I tried to add or query modifications I made, I couldn't get its duration lowered. This was because there were simply too many rows required in the result set. The limiting factor was I/O. A few months later, I migrated the database to the higher-powered production server. After that, the query executed consistently in less than one second. This underscores the fact that well-chosen hardware *does* matter. Your choice of processor architecture, available memory, and disk subsystem can have a significant impact on query performance.
- *Network throughput*: The time it takes to obtain query results can be impacted by a slow or unstable network connection. This doesn't mean you should be quick to blame the network engineers whenever a query executes slowly, but do keep this potential cause on your list of areas to investigate.

In this chapter, I'll demonstrate the T-SQL commands and techniques you can use to help evaluate and troubleshoot your query performance. I will follow that up in Chapter 23 when I discuss the related topics of fragmented indexes, out-of-date statistics, and the usage of indexes in the database.

■ **Note** Since this is a T-SQL book, I don't review the graphical interface tools that also assist with performance tuning such as SQL Server Profiler, graphical execution plans, System Monitor, and the Database Engine Tuning Advisor. These are all extremely useful tools—so I still encourage you to use them as part of your overall performance-tuning strategy in addition to the T-SQL commands and techniques you'll learn about in this chapter.

In this chapter, I'll demonstrate how to do the following:

- Control workloads and associated CPU and memory resources using Resource Governor
- Create statistics on a subset of data using the new filtered statistics improvement
- Display query statistics aggregated across near-identical queries (queries that are identical with the exception of nonparameterized literal values) or queries with identical query execution plans
- Create plan guides based on *existing* query plans in the query plan cache using the `sp_create_plan_guide_from_handle` system stored procedure

I will also demonstrate some changes in SQL Server 2012 relevant to the `sys.dm_exec_query_stats` DMV.

This chapter will also review a few miscellaneous query performance topics, including how to use `sp_executesql` as an alternative to dynamic SQL, how to apply query hints to a query without changing the query itself, and how to force a query to use a specific query execution plan.

Query Performance Tips

Before I start discussing the commands and tools you can use to evaluate query performance, I will first briefly review a few basic query performance-tuning guidelines. Query performance is a vast topic, and in many of the chapters I've tried to include small tips along with the various content areas. Since this is a chapter that discusses query performance independently of specific objects, the following list details a few query performance best practices to be aware of when constructing SQL Server queries (note that indexing tips are reviewed later in Chapter 23):

- In your `SELECT` query, return only the columns you need. Having fewer columns in your query translates to less I/O and network bandwidth.
- Along with fewer columns, you should also be thinking about fewer rows. Use a `WHERE` clause to help reduce the rows returned by your query. Don't let the application return 20,000 rows when you need to display only the first 10.
- Keep the `FROM` clause under control. Each table you `JOIN` to in a single query can add overhead. I can't give you an exact number to watch out for, because it depends on your database's design, size, and columns used to join a query. However, over the years, I've seen enormous queries that are functionally correct but take far too long to execute. Although it is convenient to use a single query to perform a complex operation, don't underestimate the power of smaller queries. If I have a very large query in a stored procedure that is taking too long to execute, I'll usually try breaking that query down into smaller intermediate result sets. This usually results in a significantly faster generation of the final desired result set.
- Use `ORDER BY` only if you *need* ordered results. Sorting operations of larger result sets can incur additional overhead. If it isn't necessary for your query, remove it.

- Avoid implicit data type conversions in your `JOIN`, `FROM`, `WHERE`, and `HAVING` clauses. Implicit data type conversions happen when the underlying data types in your predicates don't match and are automatically converted by SQL Server. One example is a Java application sending Unicode text to a non-Unicode column. For applications processing hundreds of transactions per second, these implicit conversions can really add up.
- Don't use `DISTINCT` or `UNION` (instead of `UNION ALL`) if the unique rows aren't necessary.
- Beware of testing in a vacuum. When developing your database on a test SQL Server instance, it is very important that you populate the tables with a representative data set. This means you should populate the table with the estimated number of rows you would actually see in production, as well as a representative set of values. Don't use dummy data in your development database and then expect the query to execute with similar performance in production. SQL Server performance is highly dependent on indexes and statistics, and SQL Server will make decisions based on the actual values contained within a table. If your test data isn't representative of "real-life" data, you'll be in for a surprise when queries in production don't perform as you saw them perform on the test database.
- When choosing between cursors and set-based approaches, always favor the latter. If you must use cursors, be sure to close and deallocate them as soon as possible.
- Query hints can sometimes be necessary in more complex database-driven applications; however, they often outlast their usefulness once the underlying data volume or distribution changes. Avoid overriding SQL Server's decision process by using hints sparingly.
- Avoid nesting views. I've often seen views created that reference other views, which in turn reference objects that are already referenced in the calling view! This overlap and redundancy can often result in nonoptimal query plans because of the resulting query complexity.
- I pushed this point hard in Chapter 19, and I think it is worth repeating here: stored procedures often yield excellent performance gains over regular ad hoc query calls. Stored procedures also promote query execution stability (reusing existing query execution plans). If you have a query that executes with unpredictable durations, consider encapsulating the query in a stored procedure.

When reading about SQL Server performance tuning (like you are now), be careful about saying "never" and "always." Instead, get comfortable with the answer "it depends." When it comes to query tuning, results may vary. Keep your options open and feel free to experiment (in a test environment, of course). Ask questions, and don't accept conventional wisdom at face value.

Capturing and Evaluating Query Performance

In this next set of recipes, I'll demonstrate how to capture and evaluate query performance and activity. I'll also demonstrate several other Transact-SQL commands, which can be used to return detailed information about the query execution plan.

21-1. Capturing Executing Queries

Problem

You need to find the currently executing queries in your database while incurring minimal performance impact.

Solution

Use sys.dm_exec_requests. In addition to capturing queries in SQL Server Profiler, you can also capture the SQL for currently executing queries by querying the sys.dm_exec_requests dynamic management view (DMV), as this recipe demonstrates:

```
USE AdventureWorks2012;
GO

SELECT r.session_id, r.status, r.start_time, r.command, s.text
FROM sys.dm_exec_requests r
CROSS APPLY sys.dm_exec_sql_text(r.sql_handle) s
WHERE r.status = 'running';
```

This captures any queries that are currently being executed, even the current query used to capture those queries:

```
session_id    status    start_time      command    text
----------    -------   -----------     -------    -----------------
55            running   2012-04-05      SELECT     SELECT r.session_id,
                        13:53:52.670               r.status, r.start_
                                                   time, r.command,
                                                   s.text FROM sys.
                                                   dm_exec_requests r
                                                   CROSS APPLY sys.
                                                   dm_exec_sql_text(r.
                                                   sql_handl e) s WHERE
                                                   r.status = 'running'
```

How It Works

The sys.dm_exec_requests DMV returns information about all requests executing on a SQL Server instance.

The first line of the query selected the session ID, status of the query, start time, command type (for example, SELECT, INSERT, UPDATE, DELETE), and actual SQL text:

```
SELECT r.session_id, r.status, r.start_time, r.command, s.text
```

In the FROM clause, the sys.dm_exec_requests DMV was cross-applied against the sys.dm_exec_sql_text dynamic management function. This function takes the sql_handle from the sys.dm_exec_requests DMV and returns the associated SQL text.

```
FROM sys.dm_exec_requests r
CROSS APPLY sys.dm_exec_sql_text(r.sql_handle) s
```

The WHERE clause then designates that currently running processes be returned.

```
WHERE r.status = 'running'
```

21-2. Viewing Estimated Query Execution Plans

Problem

You are troubleshooting a query, and you need to see how SQL Server is executing that query.

Solution

Use the following Transact-SQL commands: `SET SHOWPLAN_ALL`, `SET SHOWPLAN_TEXT`, and `SET SHOWPLAN_XML`.

Knowing how SQL Server executes a query can help you determine how best to fix a poorly performing query. Details you can identify by viewing a query's execution plan (graphical or command-based) include the following:

- Highest-cost queries within a batch and highest-cost operators within a query
- Index or table scans (accessing all the pages in a heap or index) versus using seeks (accessing only selected rows)
- Missing statistics or other warnings
- Costly sort or calculation activities
- Lookup operations where a nonclustered index is used to access a row but then needs to access the clustered index to retrieve columns not covered by the nonclustered index
- High row counts being passed from operator to operator
- Discrepancies between the estimated and actual row counts
- Implicit data type conversions (identified in an XML plan where the `Implicit` attribute of the `Convert` element is equal to 1)

In SQL Server, three commands can be used to view detailed information about a query execution plan for a SQL statement or batch: `SET SHOWPLAN_ALL`, `SET SHOWPLAN_TEXT`, and `SET SHOWPLAN_XML`. The output of these commands helps you understand how SQL Server plans to process and execute your query, identifying information such as table join types used and the indexes accessed. For example, using the output from these commands, you can see whether SQL Server is using a specific index in a query and, if so, whether it is retrieving the data using an index seek (a nonclustered index is used to retrieve selected rows for the operation) or index scan (all index rows are retrieved for the operation).

When enabled, the `SET SHOWPLAN_ALL`, `SET SHOWPLAN_TEXT`, and `SET SHOWPLAN_XML` commands provide you with the plan information without executing the query, allowing you to adjust the query or indexes on the referenced tables before actually executing it.

Each of these commands returns information in a different way. `SET SHOWPLAN_ALL` returns the estimated query plan in a tabular format, with multiple columns and rows. The output includes information such as the estimated I/O or CPU of each operation, estimated rows involved in the operation, operation cost (relative to itself and variations of the query), and the physical and logical operators used.

■ **Note** Logical operators describe the conceptual operation SQL Server must perform in the query execution. Physical operators are the actual implementation of that logical operation. For example, a logical operation in a query, `INNER JOIN`, could be translated into the physical operation of a nested loop in the actual query execution.

The SET SHOWPLAN_TEXT command returns the data in a single column, with multiple rows for each operation. You can also return a query execution plan in XML format using the SET SHOWPLAN_XML command.

The syntax for each of these commands is very similar. Each command is enabled when set to ON and disabled when set to OFF:

```
SET SHOWPLAN_ALL { ON | OFF }
SET SHOWPLAN_TEXT { ON | OFF}
SET SHOWPLAN_XML { ON | OFF }
```

This recipe's example demonstrates returning the estimated query execution plan of a query in the AdventureWorks2012 database using SET SHOWPLAN_TEXT and then SET SHOWPLAN_XML.

```
USE AdventureWorks2012;
GO
SET SHOWPLAN_TEXT ON;
GO
SELECT p.Name, p.ProductNumber, r.ReviewerName
FROM Production.Product p
INNER JOIN Production.ProductReview r
ON p.ProductID=r.ProductID
WHERE r.Rating>2;
GO
SET SHOWPLAN_TEXT OFF;
GO
```

This returns the following estimated query execution plan output:

```
StmtText
SELECT p.Name, p.ProductNumber, r.ReviewerName
FROM Production.Product p
INNER JOIN Production.ProductReview r
ON p.ProductID=r.ProductID
WHERE r.Rating>2;

(1 row(s) affected)

StmtText
  |--Nested Loops(Inner Join, OUTER REFERENCES:([r].[ProductID]))
       |--Clustered Index
Scan(OBJECT:([AdventureWorks2012].[Production].[ProductReview].
[PK_ProductReview_ProductReviewID] AS [r]), WHERE:([AdventureWorks2012].[Production].
[ProductReview].[Rating] as [r].[Rating]>(2)))
       |--Clustered Index
Seek(OBJECT:([AdventureWorks2012].[Production].[Product].[PK_Product_ProductID] AS [p]),
SEEK:([p].[ProductID]=[AdventureWorks2012].[Production].[ProductReview].[ProductID] as [r].
[ProductID]) ORDERED FORWARD)

(3 row(s) affected)
```

The next example returns estimated query plan results in XML format:

```
USE AdventureWorks2012;
GO
SET SHOWPLAN_XML ON;
```

```
GO
SELECT p.Name, p.ProductNumber, r.ReviewerName
FROM Production.Product p
INNER JOIN Production.ProductReview r
ON p.ProductID=r.ProductID
WHERE r.Rating>2;
GO
SET SHOWPLAN_XML OFF;
GO
```

This returns the following (this is an abridged snippet, because the actual output is more than a page long):

```
<ShowPlanXML xmlns="http://schemas.microsoft.com/sqlserver/2004/07/showplan" Version="1.2"
Build="11.0.1750.32">
    <BatchSequence>
      <Batch>
        <Statements>
...
                <RelOp NodeId="0" PhysicalOp="Nested Loops" LogicalOp="Inner Join"
EstimateRows="2.625" EstimateIO="0" EstimateCPU="1.254e-005" AvgRowSize="105"
EstimatedTotalSubtreeCost="0.00996521" Parallel="0" EstimateRebinds="0" EstimateRewinds="0"
EstimatedExecutionMode="Row">
                <OutputList>
          <ColumnReference Database="[AdventureWorks2012]" Schema="[Production]"
Table="[Product]" Alias="[p]" Column="Name" />
                  <ColumnReference Database="[AdventureWorks2012]" Schema="[Production]"
Table="[Product]" Alias="[p]" Column="ProductNumber" />
                  <ColumnReference Database="[AdventureWorks2012]" Schema="[Production]"
Table="[ProductReview]" Alias="[r]" Column="ReviewerName" />
               </OutputList>
...
```

How It Works

You can use SHOWPLAN_ALL, SHOWPLAN_TEXT, or SHOWPLAN_XML to tune your Transact-SQL queries and batches. These commands show you the estimated execution plan without actually executing the query. You can use the information returned in the command output to take action toward improving the query performance (for example, adding indexes to columns being used in search or join conditions). Looking at the output, you can determine whether SQL Server is using the expected indexes and, if so, whether SQL Server is using an index seek, index scan, or table scan operation. In this recipe, the SET SHOWPLAN for both TEXT and XML was set to ON and then followed by GO.

```
SET SHOWPLAN_TEXT ON;
GO
```

A query referencing Production.Product and Production.ProductReview was then evaluated. The two tables were joined using an INNER join on the ProductID column, and only those products with a product rating of 2 or higher would be returned:

```
SELECT p.Name, p.ProductNumber, r.ReviewerName
FROM Production.Product p
INNER DOIN Production.ProductReview r
ON p.ProductID=r.ProductID
WHERE r.Rating>2;
```

The SHOWPLAN was set OFF at the end of the query, so as not to keep executing SHOWPLAN for subsequent queries for that connection.

Looking at snippets from the output, you can see that a nested loop join (physical operation) was used to perform the INNER JOIN (logical operation).

```
--Nested Loops(Inner Join, OUTER REFERENCES:([r].[ProductID]))
```

You can also see from this output that a clustered index scan was performed using the PK_ProductReview_ProductReviewID primary key clustered index to retrieve data from the ProductReview table.

```
|--Clustered Index Scan (OBJECT:([AdventureWorks2012].[Production].[ProductReview].
[PK_ProductReview_ProductReviewID] AS [r]),
```

A clustered index *seek*, however, was used to retrieve data from the Product table.

```
|--Clustered Index Seek(OBJECT:([AdventureWorks2012].[Production].[Product]. [PK_Product_
ProductID] AS [p]),
```

The SET SHOWPLAN_XML command returned the estimated query plan in an XML document format, displaying similar data as SHOWPLAN_TEXT. The XML data is formatted using attributes and elements.

For example, the attributes of the RelOp element show a physical operation of nested loops and a logical operation of Inner Join—along with other statistics such as estimated rows impacted by the operation.

```
<RelOp NodeId="0" PhysicalOp="Nested Loops" LogicalOp="Inner Join"
EstimateRows="2.625" EstimateIO="0" EstimateCPU="1.254e-005" AvgRowSize="105"
EstimatedTotalSubtreeCost="0.00996521" Parallel="0" EstimateRebinds="0" EstimateRewinds="0"
EstimatedExecutionMode="Row">
```

The XML document follows a specific schema definition format that defines the returned XML elements, attributes, and data types. This schema can be viewed at the following URL:
http://schemas.microsoft.com/sqlserver/2004/07/showplan/showplanxml.xsd.

21-3. Viewing Execution Runtime Information

Problem

You want to evaluate various execution statistics for a query that you are attempting to tune for better performance.

Solution

SQL Server provides four commands that are used to return query and batch execution statistics and information: SET STATISTICS IO, SET STATISTICS TIME, SET STATISTICS PROFILE, and SET STATISTICS XML.

Unlike the SHOWPLAN commands, STATISTICS commands return information for queries that have actually executed in SQL Server. The SET STATISTICS IO command is used to return disk activity (hence I/O) generated by the executed statement. The SET STATISTICS TIME command returns the number of milliseconds taken to parse, compile, and execute each statement executed in the batch.

SET STATISTICS PROFILE and SET STATISTICS XML are the equivalents of SET SHOWPLAN_ALL and SET SHOWPLAN_XML, only the actual (*not* estimated) execution plan information is returned along with the actual results of the query.

The syntax of each of these commands is similar, with ON enabling the statistics and OFF disabling them.

```
SET STATISTICS IO  { ON | OFF }
SET STATISTICS TIME { ON | OFF }
```

```
SET STATISTICS PROFILE { ON | OFF }
SET STATISTICS XML { ON | OFF }
```

In the first example, STATISTICS IO is enabled prior to executing a query that totals the amount due by territory from the Sales.SalesOrderHeader and Sales.SalesTerritory tables.

```
USE AdventureWorks2012;
GO
SET STATISTICS IO ON;
GO
SELECT t.Name TerritoryNM,
SUM(TotalDue) TotalDue
FROM Sales.SalesOrderHeader h
INNER JOIN Sales.SalesTerritory t
ON h.TerritoryID=t.TerritoryID
WHERE OrderDate BETWEEN '1/1/2008' AND '12/31/2008'
GROUP BY t.Name
ORDER BY t.Name
SET STATISTICS IO OFF;
GO
```

This returns the following (abridged) results:

```
TerritoryNM          TotalDue
--------------       ------------
Australia            3674099.2456
Canada               3437016.3271
...
Southwest            5810706.5024
United Kingdom       2776218.1086
```

```
Table 'Worktable'. Scan count 1, logical reads 39, physical reads 0, read-ahead
reads 0, lob logical reads 0, lob physical reads 0, lob read-ahead reads 0.

Table 'SalesOrderHeader'. Scan count 1, logical reads 686, physical reads 0, read-ahead
reads 0, lob logical reads 0, lob physical reads 0, lob read-ahead reads 0.

Table 'SalesTerritory'. Scan count 1, logical reads 2, physical reads 0, read-ahead
reads 0, lob logical reads 0, lob physical reads 0, lob read-ahead reads 0.
```

Substituting SET STATISTICS IO with SET STATISTICS TIME would have returned the following (abridged) results for that same query:

```
TerritoryNM          TotalDue
-----------          ------------
Australia            3674099.2456
...
Southeast            1330567.5918
Southwest            5810706.5024
United Kingdom       2776218.1086
```

```
SQL Server parse and compile time:
CPU time=20 ms, elapsed time=21 ms.

(10 row(s) affected)

SQL Server Execution Times:
CPU time=30 ms, elapsed time=24 ms.
```

How It Works

The SET STATISTICS commands return information about the actual execution of a query or batch of queries. In this recipe, SET STATISTICS IO returned information about logical, physical, and large object read events for tables referenced in the query. For a query that is having performance issues (based on your business requirements and definition of *issues*), you can use SET STATISTICS IO to see where the I/O hot spots are occurring. For example, in this recipe's result set, you can see that SalesOrderHeader had the highest number of logical reads.

```
...
Table 'SalesOrderHeader'. Scan count 1, logical reads 686, physical reads 0,
read-ahead reads 0, lob logical reads 0, lob physical reads 0, lob read-ahead
  reads 0.
...
```

Pay attention to high physical (reads from disk) or logical read values (reads from the data cache), even if the physical read is zero and the logical read is a high value. Also look for worktables (which were also seen in this recipe).

```
Table 'Worktable'. Scan count 1, logical reads 39, physical reads 0, read-ahead reads 0, lob
logical reads 0, lob physical reads 0, lob read-ahead reads 0.
```

Worktables are usually seen in conjunction with GROUP BY, ORDER BY, hash joins, and UNION operations in the query. Worktables are created in tempdb for the duration of the query and are removed automatically when SQL Server has finished the operation.

In the second example in this recipe, SET STATISTICS TIME was used to show the parse and compile time of the query (shown before the actual query results) and then the actual execution time (displayed after the query results). This command is useful for measuring the amount of time a query takes to execute from end to end, allowing you to see whether precompiling is taking longer than you realized or whether the slowdown occurs during the actual query execution.

The two other STATISTICS commands, SET STATISTICS PROFILE and SET STATISTICS XML, return information similar to SET SHOWPLAN_ALL and SET SHOWPLAN_XML, only the results are based on the *actual,* rather than the estimated, execution plan.

21-4. Viewing Statistics for Cached Plans

Problem

You need to determine the number of reads or writes that occur when a query is executed.

Solution

Query the `sys.dm_exec_query_stats` DMV to view performance statistics for cached query plans.

■ **Tip** SQL Server 2008 introduced various improvements for managed collection and analysis of performance statistics. For example, the Data Collector uses stored procedures, SQL Server Integration Services, and SQL Server Agent jobs to collect data and load it into the Management Data Warehouse (MDW). These features are available in SQL Server 2012.

In this example, a simple query that returns all rows from the `Sales.Salesperson` table is executed against the `AdventureWorks2012` database. Prior to executing it, you'll clear the procedure cache so that you can identify the query more easily in this demonstration (remember that you should clear out the procedure cache only on test SQL Server instances).

```
DBCC FREEPROCCACHE;
GO
USE AdventureWorks2012;
GO
SELECT BusinessEntityID, TerritoryID, SalesQuota
FROM Sales.SalesPerson;
```

Now, I'll query the `sys.dm_exec_query_stats` DMV, which contains statistical information regarding queries cached on the SQL Server instance. This view contains a `sql_handle`, which I'll use as an input to the `sys.dm_exec_sql_text` dynamic management function. This function is used to return the text of a Transact-SQL statement:

```
USE AdventureWorks2012;
GO
SELECT  t.text,
st.total_logical_reads,
st.total_physical_reads,
st.total_elapsed_time/1000000 Total_Time_Secs,
st.total_logical_writes
FROM sys.dm_exec_query_stats st
CROSS APPLY sys.dm_exec_sql_text(st.sql_handle) t;
```

This returns the following abridged results:

text	total_logical_reads	total_physical_reads	Total_Time_Secs	total_logical_writes
SELECT BusinessEntityID ...	2	8	0	0

How It Works

This recipe demonstrated clearing the procedure cache and then executing a query that took a few seconds to finish executing. After that, the sys.dm_exec_query_stats DMV was queried to return statistics about the cached execution plan.

The SELECT clause retrieved information on the Transact-SQL text of the query, number of logical and physical reads, total time elapsed in seconds, and logical writes (if any).

```
SELECT  t.text,
st.total_logical_reads, st.total_physical_reads,
st.total_elapsed_time/1000000 Total_Time_Secs, st.total_logical_writes
```

The total elapsed time column was in microseconds, so it was divided by 1000000 in order to return the number of full seconds.

In the FROM clause, the sys.dm_exec_query_stats DMV was cross-applied against the sys.dm_exec_sql_text dynamic management function in order to retrieve the SQL text of the cached query.

```
FROM sys.dm_exec_query_stats st
CROSS APPLY sys.dm_exec_sql_text(st.sql_handle) t
```

This information is useful for identifying read-intensive and/or write-intensive queries, helping you determine which queries should be optimized. Keep in mind that this recipe's query can retrieve information only on queries still in the cache. This query returned the totals, but the sys.dm_ exec_query_stats also includes columns that track the minimum, maximum, and last measurements for reads and writes. Also note that sys.dm_exec_query_stats has other useful columns that can measure CPU time (total_worker_time, last_worker_time, min_worker_time, and max_worker_time) and .NET CLR object execution time (total_clr_time, last_clr_time, min_clr_time, max_clr_time).

21-5. Viewing Record Counts for Cached Plans

Problem

A query suddenly started taking twice as long to complete as it did in prior executions. You suspect that the decrease in performance is related to the number of records being returned. You need to find out whether there has been a variance in the number of records returned by this query.

Solution

Query the sys.dm_exec_query_stats DMV to view performance statistics for cached query plans.

In this example, we will reuse the query from the previous example to query Sales.SalesPerson.

```
USE AdventureWorks2012;
GO
SELECT BusinessEntityID, TerritoryID, SalesQuota
FROM Sales.SalesPerson;
```

Now, I'll query the sys.dm_exec_query_stats DMV, which contains four new columns introduced in SQL Server 2012. This DMV contains statistical information regarding queries cached on the SQL Server instance. This view contains a sql_handle, which I'll use as an input to the sys.dm_exec_sql_text dynamic management function. This function is used to return the text of a Transact-SQL statement:

```
USE AdventureWorks2012;
GO
SELECT  t.text,
```

```
st.total_rows,
st.last_rows,
st.min_rows,
st.max_rows
FROM sys.dm_exec_query_stats st
CROSS APPLY sys.dm_exec_sql_text(st.sql_handle) t;
```

This returns the following abridged results:

```
text                        total_rows     last_rows     min_rows     max_rows
SELECT BusinessEntityID...  17             17            17           17
```

How It Works

The sys.dm_exec_query_stats DMV was queried to return statistics about the cached execution plan.

The SELECT clause retrieved information on the Transact-SQL text of the query, minimum and maximum number of rows returned by the query, total rows returned by the query, and number of rows returned by the query on its last execution.

```
SELECT  t.text,
st.total_rows,
st.last_rows,
st.min_rows,
st.max_rows
FROM sys.dm_exec_query_stats st
```

Like the last query, we cross-applied to the sys.dm_exec_sql_text dynamic management function using sql_handle from sys.dm_exec_query_stats.

This information is useful in determining variances in the number of rows returned by a query. If the number of records to be returned has suddenly grown, the query to return those records may also increase in duration. Querying sys.dm_exec_query_stats, you can determine whether the query in question is returning a different number of records. Remember, though, this query will return values only for queries that are presently in the cache.

21-6. Viewing Aggregated Performance Statistics Based on Query or Plan Patterns

Problem

You have an application that utilizes ad hoc queries. You need to aggregate performance statistics for the similar ad hoc queries.

Solution

Query the sys.dm_exec_query_stats DMV. The previous recipe demonstrated viewing query statistics using the sys.dm_exec_query_stats DMV. Statistics in this DMV are displayed as long as the query plan remains in the cache. For applications that use stored procedures or prepared plans, sys.dm_exec_query_stats can give an accurate picture of overall aggregated statistics and resource utilization. However, if the application sends unprepared query text and does not properly parameterize literal values, individual statistic rows will be generated for each variation of an almost identical query, making the statistics difficult to correlate and aggregate.

For example, assume that the application sends the following three individual SELECT statements:

```
USE AdventureWorks2012;
GO
SELECT BusinessEntityID
FROM Purchasing.vVendorWithContacts
WHERE EmailAddress = 'cheryl1@adventure-works.com';
SELECT BusinessEntityID
FROM Purchasing.vVendorWithContacts
WHERE EmailAddress = 'stuart2@adventure-works.com';
SELECT BusinessEntityID
FROM Purchasing.vVendorWithContacts
WHERE EmailAddress = 'suzanne0@adventure-works.com';
```

After executing each query, I execute the following query:

```
USE AdventureWorks2012;
GO
SELECT  t.text,
st.total_logical_reads
FROM sys.dm_exec_query_stats st
CROSS APPLY sys.dm_exec_sql_text(st.sql_handle) t
WHERE t.text LIKE '%Purchasing.vVendorWithContacts%';
```

This query returns the following:

```
Text                                               total_logical_reads
-----------------------------------------------    -------------------

SELECT BusinessEntityID
FROM Purchasing.vVendorWithContacts
WHERE EmailAddress = 'stuart2@adventure-works.com'      12
SELECT BusinessEntityID
FROM Purchasing.vVendorWithContacts
WHERE EmailAddress = 'cheryl1@adventure-works.com'      12
SELECT BusinessEntityID
FROM Purchasing.vVendorWithContacts
WHERE EmailAddress = 'suzanne0@adventure-works.com'     12
```

Notice that a statistics row was created for each query, even though each query against Purchasing.vVendorWithContacts was identical with the exception of the EmailAddress literal value. This is an issue you'll see for applications that do not prepare the query text.

To address this issue, there are two columns in the sys.dm_exec_ query_stats DMV: query_hash and query_plan_hash. Both of these columns contain a binary hash value. The query_hash binary value is the same for those queries that are identical with the exception of literal values (in this example, differing e-mail addresses). The generated query_plan_hash binary value is the same for those queries that use identical query plans. These two columns add the ability to aggregate overall statistics across identical queries or query execution plans. Here's an example:

```
USE AdventureWorks2012;
GO
SELECT st.query_hash,
COUNT(t.text) query_count,
```

```
SUM(st.total_logical_reads) total_logical_reads
FROM sys.dm_exec_query_stats st
CROSS APPLY sys.dm_exec_sql_text(st.sql_handle) t
WHERE text LIKE '%Purchasing.vVendorWithContacts%'
GROUP BY st.query_hash;
```

This query returns the following:

```
query_ hash          query_count     total_logical_reads
------------------   -----------     -------------------

0x5C4B94191341266A   3               36
```

How It Works

I started the recipe by executing three queries that were identical with the exception of the literal values defined for the EmailAddress column in the WHERE clause. After that, I demonstrated querying the sys.dm_exec_query_stats DMV to view the logical read statistics for each query. Three separate rows were generated for each query against Purchasing.vVendorWithContacts, instead of showing an aggregated single row. This can be problematic if you are trying to capture the TOP X number of high-resource-usage queries because your result may not reflect the numerous variations of the same query that exists in the query plan cache.

To address this problem, I demonstrated using the query_hash column introduced to the sys.dm_exec_query_stats DMV back in SQL Server 2008.

Walking through the query, the SELECT clause of the query referenced this new query_hash column and produced a COUNT of the distinct queries using different literal values and a SUM of the logical reads across these queries.

```
SELECT st.query_hash,
COUNT(t.text) query_count, SUM(st.total_logical_reads) total_logical_reads
```

The FROM clause referenced the sys.dm_exec_query_stats DMV and used CROSS APPLY to access the query text based on the sql_handle.

```
FROM sys.dm_exec_query_stats st
CROSS APPLY sys.dm_exec_sql_text(st.sqljandle) t
```

I narrowed down the result set to those queries referencing the Purchasing.vVendorWithContacts view.

```
WHERE text LIKE '%Purchasing.vVendorWithContacts%'
```

Lastly, since I was aggregating the statistics by the query_hash, I used a GROUP BY clause with the query_hash column.

```
GROUP BY st.query_hash
```

The query_hash value of 0x5C4B94191341266A was identical across all three queries, allowing me to aggregate each of the individual rows into a single row and properly summing up the statistic columns I was interested in. Aggregating by the query_hash or query_plan_hash improves visibility to specific query or plan patterns and their associated resource costs.

21-7. Identifying the Top Bottleneck

Problem

Have you ever been approached by a customer or co-worker who reports that "SQL Server is running slow"? When you ask for more details, that person may not be able to properly articulate the performance issue or may attribute the issue to some random change or event without having any real evidence to back it up.

Solution

In this situation, your number-one tool for identifying and narrowing down the field of possible explanations is the `sys.dm_os_wait_stats` DMV. This DMV provides a running total of all waits encountered by executing threads in the SQL Server instance. Each time SQL Server is restarted or if you manually clear the statistics, the data is reset to zero and accumulates over the uptime of the SQL Server instance.

SQL Server categorizes these waits across several different types. Some of these types only indicate quiet periods on the instance where threads lay in waiting, whereas other wait types indicate external or internal contention on specific resources.

■ **Tip** The technique described here is part of the Waits and Queues methodology. An in-depth discussion of this methodology can be found under the Technical White Papers section of `http://technet.microsoft.com/en-us/sqlserver/bb671430`.

The following recipe shows the top two wait types that have accumulated for the SQL Server instance since it was last cleared or since the instance started:

```
USE AdventureWorks2012;
GO
SELECT  TOP 2
wait_type, wait_time_ms FROM sys.dm_os_wait_stats WHERE wait_type NOT IN
('LAZYWRITER_SLEEP', 'SQLTRACE_BUFFER_FLUSH', 'REQUEST_FOR_DEADLOCK_SEARCH', 'LOGMGR_QUEUE',
'CHECKPOINT_QUEUE', 'CLR_AUTO_EVENT','WAITFOR', 'BROKER_TASK_STOP', 'SLEEP_TASK', 'BROKER_TO_
FLUSH')
ORDER BY wait_time_ms DESC;
```

This returns the following (your results will vary based on your SQL Server activity):

```
wait_type          wait_time_ms
LCK_M_U            31989
LCK_M_S            12133
```

In this case, the top two waits for the SQL Server instance are related to requests waiting to acquire update and shared locks. You can interpret these wait types by looking them up in SQL Server Books Online or in the Waits and Queues white papers published by Microsoft. In this recipe's case, the top two wait types are often associated with long-running blocks. This is then the indication that if an application is having performance issues, you would be wise to start looking at additional evidence of long-running blocks using more granular tools (DMVs, SQL Profiler). The key purpose of looking at `sys.dm_os_wait_stats` is that you troubleshoot the predominant issue, not just the root cause of an unrelated issue or something that isn't a lower-priority issue.

If you want to clear the currently accumulated wait type statistics, you can then run the following query:

```
DBCC SQLPERF ('sys.dm_os_wait_stats', CLEAR);
```

Clearing the wait type statistics allows you to provide a delta later of accumulated wait statistics based on a defined period of time.

How It Works

This recipe demonstrated using the sys.dm_os_wait_stats DMV to help determine what the predominant wait stats were for the SQL Server instance.

The SELECT clause chose the wait type and wait time (in milliseconds) columns.

```
SELECT  TOP 2
wait_type, wait_time_ms FROM sys.dm_os_wait_stats
```

Since not all wait types are necessarily indicators of real issues, the WHERE clause was used to filter out nonexternal or nonresource waits (although this isn't a definitive list of those wait types you would need to filter out).

```
WHERE wait_type NOT IN
('LAZYWRITER_SLEEP', 'SQLTRACE_BUFFER_FLUSH', 'REQUEST_FOR_DEADLOCK_SEARCH', 'LOGMGR_QUEUE',
'CHECKPOINT_QUEUE', 'CLR_AUTO_EVENT','WAITFOR', 'BROKER_TASK_STOP', 'SLEEP_TASK', 'BROKER_TO_
FLUSH')
ORDER BY wait_time_ms DESC;
```

The DMV's data is grouped at the instance level, not at the database level, so it is a good first step in your performance troubleshooting mission. It is *not* your end-all be-all solution but rather a very useful tool for helping point you in the right direction when troubleshooting a poorly defined performance issue. This DMV also comes in handy for establishing trends over time. If a new wait type arises, this may be a leading indicator of a new performance issue.

21-8. Identifying I/O Contention by Database and File

Problem

Assume for a moment that you queried sys.dm_os_wait_stats and found that most of your waits are attributed to I/O. Since the wait stats are scoped at the SQL Server instance level, you now need to identify which databases are experiencing the highest amount of I/O contention.

Solution

One method you can use to determine which databases have the highest number of read, write, and I/O stall behavior is the sys.dm_io_virtual_file_stats DMV (this DMV shows data equivalent to the fn_virtualfilestats function).

This recipe demonstrates viewing database I/O statistics, ordered by I/O stalls. I/O stalls are measured in milliseconds and represent the total time users had to wait for read or write I/O operations to complete on a file since the instance was last restarted or the database created.

```
USE master;
GO
SELECT DB_NAME(ifs.database_id) DatabaseNM,
ifs.file_id FileID,
mf.type_desc FileType,
```

```
io_stall IOStallsMs,
size_on_disk_bytes FileBytes,
num_of_bytes_written BytesWritten,
num_of_bytes_read BytesRead
FROM sys.dm_io_virtual_file_stats(NULL, NULL) ifs
    Inner Join sys.master_files mf
        On ifs.database_id=mf.database_id
        And ifs.file_id=mf.file_id
ORDER BY io_stall DESC;
```

This query returns (your results will vary):

```
DatabaseNM            FileID  FileType   IOStallsMs   FileBytes   BytesWritten
--------------------  ------- --------   ----------   ---------   ------------

AdventureWorks2012    1       ROWS       179475       209453056   25501696
msdb                  1       ROWS       90742        14417920    1048576
AdventureWorks2008R2  1       ROWS       83948        209453056   3104768
master                1       ROWS       62727        4194304     2785280
tempdb                1       ROWS       37860        8388608     10854400
model                 1       ROWS       19647        3211264     720896
AdventureWorks2012    2       LOG        5190         12648448    18268160
tempdb                2       LOG        1245         1310720     5873664
AdventureWorks2012    3       ROWS       626          1048576     139264
msdb                  2       LOG        266          786432      561152
model                 2       LOG        234          786432      512000
master                2       LOG        224          786432      1028096
AdventureWorks2008R2  2       LOG        194          2097152     729088
```

How It Works

This recipe demonstrated using the sys.dm_io_virtual_file_stats DMV to return statistics about each database and file on the SQL Server instance. This DMV takes two input parameters: the first is the database ID, and the second is the file ID. Designating NULL for the database ID shows results for all databases. Designating NULL for the file ID results in showing all files for the database.

In this recipe, I designated that all databases and associated files be returned.

```
FROM sys.dm_io_virtual_file_stats(NULL, NULL)
```

I also ordered the I/O stalls in descending order to see the files with the most I/O delay activity first.

```
ORDER BY io_stall DESC
```

These results identified that the highest number of stalls were seen on file ID 1 for the AdventureWorks2012 database, which in this example is one of the data files. If you have identified that I/O is the predominant performance issue, using sys.dm_io_virtual_file_stats is an efficient method for narrowing down which databases and files should be the focus of your troubleshooting efforts.

Miscellaneous Techniques

The next several recipes detail techniques that don't cleanly fall under any of the previous sections in this chapter. These recipes will demonstrate how to do the following:

- Employ an alternative to dynamic SQL and stored procedures using the `sp_executesql` system stored procedure
- Force a query to use a specified query plan
- Apply query hints to an existing query without having to actually modify the application's SQL code using plan guides
- Create a plan guide based on a pointer to the cached plan
- Check the validity of a plan guide (in case reference objects have rendered the plan invalid)
- Force parameterization of a nonparameterized query
- Use the Resource Governor feature to limit query resource consumption (for both CPU and memory)

I'll start this section by describing an alternative to using dynamic SQL.

21-9. Parameterizing Ad Hoc Queries

Problem

You have an application that performs queries using Dynamic SQL and ad hoc queries. You are required to provide a means to prevent SQL injection for use by this application.

Solution

If stored procedures are not an option for your application, an alternative, the `sp_executesql` system stored procedure, addresses the dynamic SQL performance issue by allowing you to create and use a reusable query execution plan where the only items that change are the query parameters. Parameters are also type safe, meaning you cannot use them to hold unintended data types. This is a worthy solution when given a choice between ad hoc statements and stored procedures.

Using the `EXECUTE` command, you can execute the contents of a character string within a batch, procedure, or function. You can also abbreviate `EXECUTE` to `EXEC`.

For example, the following statement performs a `SELECT` from the `Sales.Currency` table:

```
EXEC ('SELECT CurrencyCode FROM Sales.Currency')
```

Although this technique allows you to dynamically formulate strings that can then be executed, this technique comes with some major hazards. The first and most important hazard is the risk of SQL injection. SQL injection occurs when harmful code is inserted into an existing SQL string prior to being executed on the SQL Server instance. Allowing user input into variables that are concatenated to a SQL string and then executed can cause all sorts of damage to your database (not to mention the potential privacy issues). The malicious code, if executed under a context with sufficient permissions, can drop tables, read sensitive data, or even shut down the SQL Server process.

The second issue with character string execution techniques is in their performance. Although performance of dynamically generated SQL may sometimes be fast, the query performance can also be unreliable. Unlike stored procedures, dynamically generated and regular ad hoc SQL batches and statements will cause SQL Server to generate a new execution plan each time they are run.

Caution sp_executesql addresses some performance issues but does not entirely address the SQL injection issue. Beware of allowing user-passed parameters that are concatenated into a SQL string! Stick with the parameter functionality described next.

The syntax for sp_executesql is as follows:

```
sp_executesql [ @stmt = ] stmt
[
        {,  [@params=] N'@parameter_name data_type [ OUT | OUTPUT ][,...n]' }
        {, [ @param1 = ] 'value1' [ ,...n ] }
]
 sp_executesql [ (@stmt = ] stmt [
{, [|@params=] N'@parameter_name data_type [ OUT | OUTPUT ][,...n]' } {, [ (@param1 = ] 'value1'
[ ,...n ] } ]
```

Table 21-1 describes the arguments of this command.

Table 21-1. sp_executesql Arguments

Argument	Description
stmt	The string to be executed.
@parameter_name data_type [[OUTPUT][,...n]	One or more parameters that are embedded in the string statement. OUTPUT is used similarly to a stored procedure OUTPUT parameter.
'value1' [,...n]	The actual values passed to the parameters.

In this example, the Production.TransactionHistoryArchive table is queried based on a specific ProductID, TransactionType, and minimum Quantity values.

```
USE AdventureWorks2012;
GO
EXECUTE sp_executesql N'SELECT TransactionID, ProductID, TransactionType, Quantity FROM
Production.TransactionHistoryArchive WHERE   ProductID=@ProductID AND
TransactionType=@TransactionType AND Quantity>@Quantity', N'@ProductID int, @TransactionType
char(1), @Quantity int', @ProductID =813, @TransactionType='S', @Quantity=5
;
```

This returns the following results (your results will vary):

```
TransactionID   ProductID   TransactionType   Quantity
-------------   ---------   ---------------   --------
28345           813         S                 7
31177           813         S                 9
35796           813         S                 6
36112           813         S                 7
40765           813         S                 6
47843           813         S                 7
69114           813         S                 6
73432           813         S                 6
```

How It Works

The sp_executesql allows you to execute a dynamically generated Unicode string. This system procedure allows parameters, which in turn allow SQL Server to reuse the query execution plan generated by its execution.

Notice in the recipe that the first parameter was preceded with the N' Unicode prefix, because sp_executesql requires a Unicode statement string. The first parameter also included the SELECT query itself, including the parameters embedded in the WHERE clause.

```
USE AdventureWorks2012;
GO
EXECUTE sp_executesql N'SELECT TransactionID, ProductID, TransactionType, Quantity FROM
Production.TransactionHistoryArchive WHERE   ProductID=@ProductID AND
TransactionType=@TransactionType AND Quantity>@Quantity',
```

The second argument further defined the data type of each parameter that was embedded in the first parameter's SQL statement. Each parameter is separated by a comma.

```
N'@ProductID int,
@TransactionType char(1),
@Quantity int',
```

The last argument assigned each embedded parameter a value, which was put into the query dynamically during execution.

```
@ProductID =813,
@TransactionType='S',
@Quantity=5
```

The query returned eight rows based on the three parameters provided. If the query is executed again, only with different parameter values, it is likely that the original query execution plan will be used by SQL Server (instead of creating a new execution plan).

21-10. Forcing Use of a Query Plan

Problem

You suspect that a less optimal query plan is being used for a poorly performing query. You want to test the query using different query plans.

Solution

The USE PLAN command allows you to force the query optimizer to use an existing, specific query plan for a SELECT query. You can use this functionality to override SQL Server's choice, in those rare circumstances when SQL Server chooses a less efficient query plan over one that is more efficient. Like plan guides (covered later), this option should be used only by an experienced SQL Server professional, because SQL Server's query optimizer usually makes good decisions when deciding whether to reuse or create new query execution plans. The syntax for USE PLAN is as follows:

```
USE PLAN N'xml_plan'
```

The xml_plan parameter is the XML data type representation of the stored query execution plan. The specific XML query plan can be derived using several methods, including SET SHOWPLAN_XML, SET STATISTICS XML, the sys.dm_exec_query_plan DMV, sys.dm_exec_text_query_plan, and via SQL Server Profiler's Showplan XML events.

In this example, SET STATISTICS XML is used to extract the XML-formatted query plan for use in the USE PLAN command.

```
SET STATISTICS XML ON
SELECT TOP 10 Rate
FROM HumanResources.EmployeePayHistory
ORDER BY Rate DESC
SET STATISTICS XML OFF
```

The XMLDocument results returned from SET STATISTICS XML are then copied to the next query. Note that all the single quotes (') in the XML document have to be escaped with an additional single quote (except for the quotes used for USE PLAN).

```
USE AdventureWorks2012;
GO
SELECT TOP 10 Rate
FROM HumanResources.EmployeePayHistory
ORDER BY Rate DESC
OPTION (USE PLAN
'<ShowPlanXML xmlns="http://schemas.microsoft.com/sqlserver/2004/07/showplan" Version="1.2"
Build="11.0.1750.32">
  <BatchSequence>
    <Batch>
      <Statements>
        <StmtSimple StatementText="SELECT TOP 10 Rate&#xD;&#xA;FROM
HumanResources.EmployeePayHistory&#xD;&#xA;ORDER BY Rate DESC;&#xD;" StatementId="1"
StatementCompId="2" StatementType="SELECT" RetrievedFromCache="true"
StatementSubTreeCost="0.019825" StatementEstRows="10" StatementOptmLevel="TRIVIAL"
QueryHash="0x2B741030C68225F9" QueryPlanHash="0x705E7CF258D9C17E">
          <StatementSetOptions QUOTED_IDENTIFIER="true" ARITHABORT="true"
CONCAT_NULL_YIELDS_NULL="true" ANSI_NULLS="true" ANSI_PADDING="true" ANSI_WARNINGS="true"
NUMERIC_ROUNDABORT="false" />
          <QueryPlan DegreeOfParallelism="1" MemoryGrant="1024" CachedPlanSize="16"
CompileTime="1" CompileCPU="1" CompileMemory="96">
            <MemoryGrantInfo SerialRequiredMemory="16" SerialDesiredMemory="24"
RequiredMemory="16" DesiredMemory="24" RequestedMemory="1024" GrantWaitTime="0"
GrantedMemory="1024" MaxUsedMemory="16" />
            <OptimizerHardwareDependentProperties EstimatedAvailableMemoryGrant="104190"
EstimatedPagesCached="52095" EstimatedAvailableDegreeOfParallelism="4" />
            <RelOp NodeId="0" PhysicalOp="Sort" LogicalOp="TopN Sort"
EstimateRows="10" EstimateIO="0.0112613" EstimateCPU="0.00419345" AvgRowSize="15"
EstimatedTotalSubtreeCost="0.019825" Parallel="0" EstimateRebinds="0" EstimateRewinds="0"
EstimatedExecutionMode="Row">
              <OutputList>
                <ColumnReference Database="[AdventureWorks2012]" Schema="[HumanResources]"
Table="[EmployeePayHistory]" Column="Rate" />
              </OutputList>
              <MemoryFractions Input="1" Output="1" />
              <RunTimeInformation>
                <RunTimeCountersPerThread Thread="0" ActualRows="10" ActualRebinds="1"
```

```
ActualRewinds="0" ActualEndOfScans="1" ActualExecutions="1" />
              </RunTimeInformation>
              <TopSort Distinct="0" Rows="10">
                <OrderBy>
                  <OrderByColumn Ascending="0">
                    <ColumnReference Database="[AdventureWorks2012]" Schema="[HumanResources]"
Table="[EmployeePayHistory]" Column="Rate" />
                  </OrderByColumn>
                </OrderBy>
                <RelOp NodeId="1" PhysicalOp="Clustered Index Scan" LogicalOp="Clustered Index
Scan" EstimateRows="316" EstimateIO="0.00386574" EstimateCPU="0.0005046" AvgRowSize="15"
EstimatedTotalSubtreeCost="0.00437034" TableCardinality="316" Parallel="0" EstimateRebinds="0"
EstimateRewinds="0" EstimatedExecutionMode="Row">
                  <OutputList>
                    <ColumnReference Database="[AdventureWorks2012]" Schema="[HumanResources]"
Table="[EmployeePayHistory]" Column="Rate" />
                  </OutputList>
                  <RunTimeInformation>
                    <RunTimeCountersPerThread Thread="0" ActualRows="316" ActualEndOfScans="1"
ActualExecutions="1" />
                  </RunTimeInformation>
                  <IndexScan Ordered="0" ForcedIndex="0" ForceScan="0" NoExpandHint="0">
                    <DefinedValues>
                      <DefinedValue>
                        <ColumnReference Database="[AdventureWorks2012]"
Schema="[HumanResources]" Table="[EmployeePayHistory]" Column="Rate" />
                      </DefinedValue>
                    </DefinedValues>
                    <Object Database="[AdventureWorks2012]" Schema="[HumanResources]"
Table="[EmployeePayHistory]" Index="[PK_EmployeePayHistory_BusinessEntityID_RateChangeDate]"
IndexKind="Clustered" />
                  </IndexScan>
                </RelOp>
              </TopSort>
            </RelOp>
          </QueryPlan>
        </StmtSimple>
      </Statements>
    </Batch>
  </BatchSequence>
</ShowPlanXML>');
```

How It Works

USE PLAN allows you to capture the XML format of a query's execution plan and then force the query to use it on subsequent executions. In this recipe, I used SET STATISTICS XML ON to capture the query's XML execution plan definition. That definition was then copied into the OPTION clause. The USE PLAN hint requires a Unicode format, so the XML document text was prefixed with an N'.

Both USE PLAN and plan guides should be used only as a *last resort*—after you have thoroughly explored other possibilities such as query design, indexing, database design, index fragmentation, and out-of-date statistics. USE PLAN may have short-term effectiveness, but as data changes, so too will the needs of the query execution plan. In the end, the odds are that, over time, SQL Server will be better able to dynamically decide on the correct SQL plan than you. Nevertheless, Microsoft provided this option for those advanced troubleshooting cases when SQL Server doesn't choose a query execution plan that's good enough.

21-11. Applying Hints Without Modifying a SQL Statement

Problem

You are experiencing performance issues in a database in which you are not permitted to make changes to the code.

Solution

As was discussed at the beginning of the chapter, troubleshooting poor query performance involves reviewing many areas such as database design, indexing, and query construction. You can make modifications to your code, but what if the problem is with code that you *cannot* change?

If you are encountering issues with a database and/or queries that are not your own to change (in shrink-wrapped software, for example), then your options become more limited. Usually in the case of third-party software, you are restricted to adding new indexes or archiving data from large tables. Making changes to the vendor's actual database objects or queries is usually off-limits.

SQL Server provides a solution to this common issue using plan guides. Plan guides allow you to apply hints to a query without having to change the actual query text sent from the application.

■ **Tip** In SQL Server 2012, you can designate both query and table hints within plan guides.

Plan guides can be applied to specific queries embedded within database objects (stored procedures, functions, triggers) or specific stand-alone SQL statements.
A plan guide is created using the sp_create_plan_guide system stored procedure.

```
sp_create_plan_guide [ @name = ] N'plan_guide_name'
    , [  @stmt = ] N'statement_text'
    , [  @type = ] N' { OBJECT | SQL | TEMPLATE }'
    , [  @module_or_batch = ]
        {
        N'[ schema_name.]object_name'
        |  N'batch_text'
        |  NULL
        }
    , [  @params = ] { N'@parameter_name data_type [,...n ]' | NULL }
    , [  @hints = ] { N'OPTION ( query_hint [,...n ] ) ' | N'XML_showplan' | NULL }
```

Table 21-2 describes the arguments of this command.

Table 21-2. *sp_create_plan_guide Arguments*

Argument	Description
plan_guide_name	This defines the name of the new plan guide.
statement_text	This specifies the SQL text identified for optimization.
OBJECT | SQL | TEMPLATE	When OBJECT is selected, the plan guide will apply to the statement text found within a specific stored procedure, function, or DML trigger. When SQL is selected, the plan guide will apply to statement text found in a stand-alone statement or batch. The TEMPLATE option is used to either enable or disable parameterization for a SQL statement. Note that the PARAMETERIZATION option, when set to FORCED, increases the chance that a query will become parameterized, allowing it to form a reusable query execution plan. SIMPLE parameterization, however, affects a smaller number of queries (at SQL Server's discretion). The TEMPLATE option is used to override a database's SIMPLE or FORCED parameterization option. If a database is using SIMPLE parameterization, you can force a specific query statement to be parameterized. If a database is using FORCED parameterization, you can force a specific query statement to *not* be parameterized.
N'[schema_name.]object_name' | N'batch_text' | NULL	This specifies either the name of the object the SQL text will be in, the batch text, or NULL, when TEMPLATE is selected.
N'@parameter_name data_type [,...n]' | NULL N'OPTION (query_hint [,...n])' | N'XML_showplan' | NULL	This defines the name of the parameters to be used for either SQL or TEMPLATE type plan guides. This defines the hint or hints to be applied to the statement, the XML query plan to be applied, or NULL, used to indicate that the OPTION clause will not be employed for a query.

■ **Note** In SQL Server 2012, the @hints argument accepts XML Showplan output as direct input.

To remove or disable a plan guide, use the sp_control_plan_guide system stored procedure.

```
sp_control_plan_guide [ @operation = ] N'<control_option>'
    [ , [ @name = ] N'plan_guide_name' ]

<control_option>::=
{
        DROP
      | DROP ALL
      | DISABLE
      | DISABLE ALL
      | ENABLE
      | ENABLE ALL
}
```

Table 21-3 describes the arguments of this command.

Table 21-3. *sp_control_plan_guide Arguments*

Argument	Description
DROP	The DROP operation removes the plan guide from the database.
DROP ALL	DROP ALL drops all plan guides from the database.
DISABLE	DISABLE disables the plan guide but doesn't remove it from the database.
DISABLE ALL	DISABLE ALL disables all plan guides in the database.
ENABLE	ENABLE enables a disabled plan guide.
ENABLE ALL	ENABLE ALL does so for all disabled plan guides in the database.
plan_guide_name	plan_guide_name defines the name of the plan guide to perform the operation on.

In this recipe's example, I'll create a plan guide in order to change the table join type method for a stand-alone query. In this scenario, assume the third-party software package is sending a query that is causing a LOOP join. In this scenario, I want the query to use a MERGE join instead.

■ **Caution** SQL Server should almost always be left to make its own decisions regarding how a query is processed. Only under special circumstances and administered by an experienced SQL Server professional should plan guides be created in your SQL Server environment.

In this example, the following query is executed using sp_executesql:

```
USE AdventureWorks2012;
GO
EXEC sp_executesql
N'SELECT v.Name ,a.City
FROM Purchasing.Vendor v
INNER JOIN [Person].BusinessEntityAddress bea
ON bea.BusinessEntityID=v.BusinessEntityID
INNER JOIN Person.Address a
ON a.AddressID=bea.AddressID';
```

Looking at a snippet of this query's execution plan using SET STATISTICS XML ON shows that the Vendor and BusinessEntityAddress tables are joined together through the use of a nested loop operator.

```
<RelOp NodeId="0" PhysicalOp="Nested Loops" LogicalOp="Inner Join"
EstimateRows="105.447" EstimateIO="0" EstimateCPU="0.000440767" AvgRowSize="93"
EstimatedTotalSubtreeCost="0.322517" Parallel="0" EstimateRebinds="0" EstimateRewinds="0">
```

If, for example, I want SQL Server to use a different join method, but without having to change the actual query sent by the application, I can enforce this change by creating a plan guide. The following plan guide is created to apply a join hint onto the query being sent from the application:

```
USE AdventureWorks2012;
GO
EXEC sp_create_plan_guide
@name=N'Vendor_Query_Loop_to_Merge',
@stmt=N'SELECT v.Name ,a.City FROM Purchasing.Vendor v INNER JOIN
[Person].BusinessEntityAddress bea
ON bea.BusinessEntityID=v.BusinessEntityID INNER JOIN Person.Address a
ON a.AddressID=bea.AddressID',
@type=N'SQL', @module_or_batch=NULL, @params=NULL, @hints=N'OPTION (MERGE JOIN)';
```

■ **Tip** Since SQL Server 2008, you can also designate *table* hints in the plan guide `@hints` parameter.

I can confirm that the plan guide was created (as well as confirm the settings) by querying the `sys.plan_guides` catalog view.

```
USE AdventureWorks2012;
GO
SELECT name, is_disabled, scope_type_desc, hints
FROM sys.plan_guides;
```

This query returns the following:

```
name                          is_disabled    scope_type_desc       hints
Vendor_Query_Loop_to_Merge    0              SQL                   OPTION (MERGE JOIN)
```

After creating the plan guide, I execute the query again using sp_executesql. Looking at the XML execution plan, I now see that the nested loop joins have changed into merge join operators instead—all without changing the actual query being sent from the application to SQL Server.

```
<RelOp NodeId="0" PhysicalOp="Merge Join" LogicalOp="Inner Join" EstimateRows="105.447"
EstimateIO="0" EstimateCPU="0.0470214" AvgRowSize="93" EstimatedTotalSubtreeCost="0.491476"
Parallel="0" EstimateRebinds="0" EstimateRewinds="0">
```

In fact, all joins in the query were converted from loops to a merge join, which may not be a desired effect of designating the hint for a multijoin statement! If it is decided that this merge join is no longer more effective than a nested loop join, you can drop the plan guide using the `sp_control_plan_guide` system stored procedure.

```
USE AdventureWorks2012;
GO
EXEC sp_control_plan_guide N'DROP', N'Vendor_Query_Loop_to_Merge';
```

How It Works

Plan guides allow you to add query hints to a query being sent from an application without having to change the application itself. In this example, a particular SQL statement was performing nested loop joins. Without changing the actual query itself, SQL Server "sees" the plan guide and matches the incoming query to the query in the plan guide. When matched, the hints in the plan guide are applied to the incoming query.

The `sp_create_plan_guide` stored procedure allows you to create plans for stand-alone SQL statements, SQL statements within objects (procedures, functions, DML triggers), and SQL statements that are either being parameterized or not, because of the database's `PARAMETERIZATION` setting.

In this recipe, the first parameter sent to `sp_create_plan_guide` was the name of the new plan guide.

```
USE AdventureWorks2012;
GO
EXEC sp_create_plan_guide
@name = N'Vendor_Query_Loop_to_Merge',
```

The second parameter was the SQL statement to apply the plan guide to (whitespace characters, comments, and semicolons will be ignored).

```
@stmt = N'SELECT v.Name ,a.City FROM Purchasing.Vendor v
INNER JOIN [Person].BusinessEntityAddress bea
ON bea.BusinessEntityID = v.BusinessEntityID
INNER JOIN Person.Address a
ON a.AddressID = bea.AddressID',
```

The third parameter was the type of plan guide, which in this case was stand-alone SQL.

```
@type = N'SQL',
```

For the fourth parameter, since it was not for a stored procedure, function, or trigger, the `@module_or_batch` parameter was `NULL`.

```
@module_or_batch = NULL,
```

The `@params` parameter was also sent `NULL` since this was not a `TEMPLATE` plan guide.

```
@params = NULL,
```

The last parameter contained the actual hint to apply to the incoming query—in this case forcing all joins in the query to use a `MERGE` operation.

```
@hints = N'OPTION (MERGE JOIN)'
```

Finally, the `sp_control_plan_guide` system stored procedure was used to drop the plan guide from the database, designating the operation of `DROP` in the first parameter and the plan guide name in the second parameter.

21-12. Creating Plan Guides from Cache

Problem

You are planning the migration of a database to a new server. You want to ensure that a particular query continues to perform the same on the new server as the current server.

Solution

In SQL Server (since SQL Server 2008), you have the ability to create plan guides based on existing query plans in a query plan cache using the `sp_create_plan_guide_from_handle` system stored procedure. Consider using this functionality under the following circumstances:

- You need a query plan (or plans) to remain stable after an upgrade or database migration.
- You have a specific query that uses a "bad" plan, and you want it to use a known "good" plan.
- Your application has mission-critical queries that have service-level agreements regarding specific response times, and you want to keep that time stable.
- You need to reproduce the exact query execution plan on another SQL Server instance (test, QA, for example).
- You have a query that needs to execute predictably but not necessarily perform as optimally as it always could.

■ Caution You should almost always let SQL Server compile and recompile plans as needed instead of relying on plan guides. SQL Server can adapt to any new changes in the data distribution and objects referenced in the query by recompiling an existing plan when appropriate.

The syntax for the `sp_create_plan_guide_from_handle` system stored procedure is as follows:

```
sp_create_plan_guide_from_handle [ @name = ] N'plan_guide_name' , [ @plan_handle = ] plan_handle
, [ [ @statement_start_offset = ] { statement_start_offset | NULL } ]
```

Table 21-4 describes the arguments of this command.

Table 21-4. *sp_create_plan_guide_from_handle Arguments*

Argument	Description
plan_guide_name	This defines the name of the new plan guide.
plan_handle	This designates the plan handle from the sys.dm_exec_query_stats DMV.
statement_start_offset | NULL	The statement start offset designates the starting position within the query batch. If NULL, the query plan for each statement in the batch will have a plan guide created for it.

This functionality allows you to preserve desired query plans for future reuse on the SQL Server instance. In this recipe, I'll demonstrate creating a plan guide from the cache for the following query (which I will execute first in order to get a plan created in cache).

```
USE AdventureWorks2012;
GO
SELECT
p.Title,
p.FirstName,
```

```
p.MiddleName,
p.LastName
FROM HumanResources.Employee e
INNER JOIN Person.Person p
ON p.BusinessEntityID=e.BusinessEntityID
WHERE Title='Ms.';
GO
```

After executing the query, I can retrieve the plan handle pointing to the query plan in the cache by executing the following query:

```
USE AdventureWorks2012;
GO
SELECT plan_handle
FROM sys.dm_exec_query_stats qs
CROSS APPLY sys.dm_exec_sql_text(plan_handle) t
WHERE t.text LIKE 'SELECT%p.Title%'
AND t.text LIKE '%Ms%';
```

This query returns the following (your results will vary):

```
Plan_handle
0x06000600AEC426269009DAFC020000000100000000000000000000000000000000000000000000000000000
```

Next, I will create a plan guide based on the plan handle (returned in the previous query) using the `sp_create_plan_guide_from_handle` system stored procedure.

```
EXEC sp_create_plan_guide_from_handle 'PlanGuide_EmployeeContact',
@plan_handle=
0x06000600AEC426269009DAFC020000000100000000000000000000000000000000000000000000000000000,
@statement_start_offset=NULL;
```

Querying the `sys.plan_handles` system catalog view, I can confirm that the plan guide was created properly (results not displayed, because of the query plan and text display issues on the printed page).

```
USE AdventureWorks2012;
GO
SELECT name, query_text, hints
FROM sys.plan_guides;
```

The `hints` column from `sys.plan_guides` actually contains the query execution plan in XML format.

■ **Tip** You can confirm whether your plan guide is being successfully used by tracking the SQL Server Profiler events "Plan Guide Successful" and "Plan Guide Unsuccessful."

How It Works

This recipe demonstrated how to preserve an existing cached plan as a plan guide. This is the execution plan that will be used for the query matching the query text of the plan guide. Even after a SQL Server instance restart or flushing of the procedure cache, the associated plan guide query plan will still be used.

I started off the recipe by executing the SELECT query so that a query plan would be cached on the SQL Server instance. After doing that, I can search for the plan handle of the cached plan by querying sys.dm_exec_query_stats. I also used CROSS APPLY with sys.dm_exec_sql_text so that I could search for text that contained the start and end of my query.

Once I had the plan handle, I executed the sp_create_plan_guide_from_handle system stored procedure. The first parameter was the name of the plan guide.

```
EXEC sp_create_plan_guide_from_handle 'PlanGuide_EmployeeContact',
```

The second parameter contains the plan handle (note that I could have placed the plan handle in a local variable and then fed it to the stored procedure in a single batch with the sys.dm_exec_query_stats query).

Lastly, I designated the statement start offset as NULL. This is because the cached plan contained only a single statement. If this were a multistatement batch, I could have used this parameter to designate the statement start offset number.

```
@statement_start_offset = NULL
```

Once the plan guide is created, any matching SQL that is executed will use the query execution plan designated in the plan guide (look at the hints column of the sys.plan_guides system catalog view to confirm). This allows you to keep a plan stable across several scenarios—for example, after a database migration to a new SQL Server instance, service pack upgrade, or version upgrade. Highly volatile query execution plans (recompiled often with varying execution plan performance impacts) can benefit from the "freezing" of the most efficient or best-performing plan for the associated query.

21-13. Checking the Validity of a Plan Guide

Problem

You want to confirm that existing plan guides are still valid after having made significant object changes in the database.

Solution

Use the system function sys.fn_validate_plan_guide, which allows you to check the validity of existing plan guides. SQL Server typically does a great job of compiling and recompiling query execution plans based on changes to objects referenced within a query. Plan guides, on the other hand, are not automatically modified based on changing circumstances.

The sys.fn_validate_plan_guide is a table-valued function that takes a single argument, the plan_guide_id. In this recipe, I demonstrate validating all plan guides within the database context I am interested in (for example, AdventureWorks2012).

```
USE AdventureWorks2012;
GO
SELECT pg.plan_guide_id, pg.name, v.msgnum,
v.severity, v.state, v.message
FROM sys.plan_guides pg
CROSS APPLY sys.fn_validate_plan_guide(pg.plan_guide_id) v;
```

If this query returns no rows, this means there are no errors with existing plan guides. If rows are generated, you will need to re-create a valid plan guide based on the changed circumstances.

How It Works

This recipe demonstrated how to check the validity of each plan guide in a specific database. The SELECT statement referenced the plan guide ID and name, along with the message number, severity, state, and message if errors exist.

```
SELECT pg.plan_guide_id, pg.name, v.msgnum, v.severity, v.state, v.message
```

The FROM clause included sys.plan_guides, which returns all plan guides for the database context.

```
FROM sys.plan_guides pg
```

Since this is a table-valued function expecting an input argument, I used CROSS APPLY against sys.fn_validate_plan_guide and used the plan guide from sys.plan_guides as input.

```
CROSS APPLY sys.fn_validate_plan_guide(pg.plan_guide_id) v
```

This query returns rows for any plan guides invalidated by changes because of underlying object changes.

21-14. Parameterizing a Nonparameterized Query Using Plan Guides

Problem

You have been monitoring the server health and have noticed that there is a very large query cache filled with nearly identical queries.

Solution

When I am evaluating the overall performance of a SQL Server instance, I like to take a look at the sys.dm_exec_cached_plans DMV to see what kind of plans are cached on the SQL Server instance. In particular, I'm interested in the objtype column, seeing whether the applications using the SQL Server instance are using mostly prepared statements, stored procedures, or ad hoc queries.

For applications that make heavy use of ad hoc queries, I'll often see a very large query cache filled with nearly identical queries. For example, the following query shows the object type and associated query text:

```
USE AdventureWorks2012;
GO
SELECT cp.objtype, st.text
FROM sys.dm_exec_cached_plans cp
CROSS APPLY sys.dm_exec_sql_text(cp.plan_handle) st
WHERE st.text LIKE 'SELECT BusinessEntityID%';
GO
```

In my database, I see three rows returned.

```
objtype         text
-------         ----
Adhoc           SELECT BusinessEntityID
                FROMHumanResources.Employee
                WHERE NationalIDNumber=509647174
Adhoc           SELECT BusinessEntityID
                FROM HumanResources.Employee
                WHERE NationalIDNumber=245797967
```

Adhoc	SELECT BusinessEntityID FROM HumanResources.Employee WHERE NationalIDNumber = 295847284

Notice that each row is almost identical—except that the NationalIDNumber value is different. Ideally, this form of query should be encapsulated in a stored procedure or called using sp_executesql in order to prevent identical plans in the cache and encourage plan reuse.

If you cannot control the form in which queries are called by the execution, one option you have is to use a plan guide to force parameterization of the query, which I will demonstrate in this recipe.

In Recipe 21-11, I introduced the sp_create_ plan_guide system stored procedure. The TEMPLATE option in that procedure is used to override a database's SIMPLE or FORCED parameterization option. If a database is using SIMPLE parameterization, you can force a specific query statement to be parameterized. If a database is using FORCED parameterization, you can force a specific query statement to not be parameterized.

The sp_get_query_template system stored procedure makes deploying template plan guides a little easier by taking a query and outputting the parameterized form of it for use by sp_create_ plan_guide. The syntax for this procedure is as follows:

```
sp_get_query_template
[ @querytext = ] N'query_text' , @templatetext OUTPUT , @parameters OUTPUT
```

Table 21-5 describes the arguments of this command.

***Table 21-5.** sp_get_query_template Arguments*

Argument	Description
querytext	The query you want to parameterize
templatetext	The output parameter containing the parameterized form of the query
parameters	The output parameter containing the list of parameter names and data types

In this recipe, I'll start by populating the template SQL and parameters using sp_get_query_ template and then sending these values to sp_create_plan_guide (I'll walk through the code step-by-step in the "How It Works" section).

```
DECLARE @sql  nvarchar(max) DECLARE @parms nvarchar(max)
EXEC sp_get_query_template
N'SELECT BusinessEntityID FROM HumanResources.Employee WHERE NationallDNumber=295847284',
@sql OUTPUT,
@parms OUTPUT;

EXEC sp_create_plan_guide N'PG_Employee_Contact_Ouery', @sql,
N'TEMPLATE', NULL, @parms, N'OPTION(PARAMETERIZATION FORCED)';
```

After the plan guide is created, I can execute three different versions of the same query (three different values for NationallDNumber—each executed separately and not part of the same batch).

```
USE AdventureWorks2012;
GO
SELECT BusinessEntityID
        FROM HumanResources.Employee
        WHERE NationalIDNumber = 509647174;
```

```
GO
SELECT BusinessEntityID
        FROM HumanResources.Employee
        WHERE NationalIDNumber = 245797967;
GO
SELECT BusinessEntityID
        FROM HumanResources.Employee
        WHERE NationalIDNumber = 295847284;
GO
```

After executing these queries, I will now check the cache to see whether there is a prepared plan for this query.

```
USE AdventureWorks2012;
GO
SELECT usecounts,objtype,text
FROM sys.dm_exec_cached_plans cp
CROSS APPLY sys.dm_exec_sql_text(cp.plan_handle) st
WHERE st.text LIKE '%SELECT BusinessEntityID%' AND objtype = 'Prepared';
```

This returns the number of times the prepared plan has been used (three times since the plan guide was created), the object type, and the parameterized SQL text.

```
usecounts       objtype         text
---------       --------        -----------------------------------------------------------
3               Prepared        (@0 int)Select BusinessEntityID from HumanResources.Employee

                                WHERE NationalIDNumber = @0
```

How It Works

In this recipe, I demonstrated how to force parameterization for a single query. Near-identical queries such as the one I demonstrated can unnecessarily expand the cache, consuming memory and creating excessive compilation operations. By reducing compilation and encouraging the use of prepared plans, you can improve performance of the query itself and reduce resource consumption on the SQL Server instance.

Walking through the code, I started off by declaring two local variables that would be used to hold the template SQL and associated parameters.

```
DECLARE @sql  nvarchar(max)
DECLARE @parms nvarchar(max)
```

I then executed a call against the `sp_get_query_template` system stored procedure.

```
EXEC sp_get_query_template
```

The first parameter of this procedure expects the SQL to be converted to template format.

```
N'SELECT BusinessEntityID
FROM HumanResources.Employee
WHERE NationalIDNumber = 295847284',
```

The second parameter is used for the output parameter that will contain the template SQL.

```
@sql OUTPUT,
```

The third parameter is used for the output parameter that will contain the parameters used in association with the template SQL.

```
@parms OUTPUT
```

Next, I called `sp_create_plan_guide` to create a plan guide: `EXEC sp_create_plan_guide`.
The first parameter of this procedure took the name of the new plan guide.

```
N'PG_Employee_Contact_Query',
```

The second parameter took the value of the template SQL.

```
@sql,
```

The third parameter designated that this would be a `TEMPLATE` plan guide.

```
N'TEMPLATE',
```

The `@module_or_batch` parameter was given a `NULL` value, which is the required value for `TEMPLATE` plan guides.

```
NULL,
```

The next parameter contained the definition of all parameters associated with the template SQL.

```
@parms,
```

The last parameter designated the hints to attach to the query. In this case, I asked that the query use forced parameterization.

```
N'OPTION(PARAMETERIZATION FORCED)'
```

Once the plan guide was created, I executed the query in three different forms, each with a different `NationalIDNumber` literal value. I then checked `sys.dm_exec_cached_plans` to see whether there was a new row for a prepared plan. I confirmed that the `usecounts` column had a value of `3` (one for each query execution I had just performed), which helped me confirm that the newly parameterized prepared plan was being reused.

21-15. Limiting Competing Query Resource Consumption

Problem

You have various processes that regularly compete for CPU resources. You need to implement a solution that will limit the resource consumption of some of these processes.

Solution

Utilize the Resource Governor to constrain resource consumption for workloads. Resource Governor allows you to define resource pools that constrain the minimum and maximum CPU task scheduling bandwidth and memory reserved.

■ **Tip** CPU task scheduling is limited only when there is CPU contention across all available schedulers.

SQL Server provides two resource pools out of the box: *default* and *internal*. The internal resource pool, which cannot be modified, uses unrestricted resources for SQL Server ongoing process activity. The default resource pool is used for connections and requests prior to Resource Governor being configured and by default has no limitations on resources (although you can change this later).

You can create your own resource pools using the `CREATE RESOURCE POOL` command. The syntax for this command is as follows:

```
CREATE RESOURCE POOL pool_name [ WITH
( [ MIN_CPU_PERCENT=value ] [ [ , ] MAX_CPU_PERCENT=value ]
[ [ , ] CAP_CPU_PERCENT=value ]
[ [ , ] AFFINITY {SCHEDULER=AUTO | (Scheduler_range_spec) | NUMANODE=(NUMA_node_range_spec)} ]
[ , ] MIN_MEMORY_PERCENT=value ] [ [ , ] MAX_MEMORY_PERCENT=value ] )]
```

Table 21-6 describes the arguments of this command.

Table 21-6. *CREATE RESOURCE POOL Arguments*

Argument	Description
Pool_name	This defines the name of the resource pool.
MIN_CPU_PERCENT=value	When there is query contention, this defines a minimum guaranteed average CPU task scheduling percentage from 0 to 100.
MAX_CPU_PERCENT=value	When there is query contention, this defines the maximum CPU task scheduling percentage for all query requests in the resource pool.
CAP_CPU_PERCENT=value	Hard cap for CPU task scheduling percentage that all requests in the resource pool will receive. This is a new option in SQL Server 2012.
AFFINITY {SCHEDULER=AUTO | (Scheduler_range_spec) | NUMANODE=(NUMA_node_range_spec)}	New to SQL Server 2012, this option allows you to specify schedulers for each resource pool.
MIN_MEMORY_PERCENT=value	This specifies the minimum percent of reserved memory for the resource pool.
MAX_MEMORY_PERCENT=value	This specifies the maximum percent of server memory that can be used for query requests in the pool.

Once you create one or more resource pools, you can then associate them with workload groups. One or more workload groups can be bound to a single resource pool. Workload groups allow you to define the importance of requests within the pool, maximum memory grant percentage, maximum CPU time in seconds, maximum memory grant time out, maximum degree of parallelism, and maximum number of concurrently executing requests. You can create resource pools using the `CREATE WORKLOAD GROUP` command. The syntax for this command is as follows:

```
CREATE WORKLOAD GROUP group_name
[ WITH
        ( [ IMPORTANCE={ LOW | MEDIUM | HIGH } ]
        [ [ , ]     REQUEST_MAX_MEMORY_GRANT_PERCENT=value ]
        [ [ , ] REQUEST_MAX_CPU_TIME_SEC=value ]
        [ [ , ]     REQUEST_MEMORY_GRANT_TIMEOUT_SEC=value ]
        [ [ , ] MAX_DOP=value ]
        [ [ , ] GROUP_MAX_REQUESTS=value ] )]
[ USING { pool_name | "default" } ]
```

Table 21-7 describes the arguments of this command.

Table 21-7. *`CREATE WORKLOAD GROUP` Arguments*

Argument	Description
`group_name`	Defines the name of the workload group.
`IMPORTANCE={LOW | MEDIUM | HIGH}`	Defines the importance of requests within the workload group. If two workloads share the same resource pool, the importance of each workload can determine which requests have a higher priority.
`REQUEST_MAX_MEMORY_GRANT_PERCENT=value`	Caps maximum memory a request can use from the resource pool.
`REQUEST_MAX_CPU_TIME_SEC=value`	Caps maximum CPU time (seconds) a single request can use from the resource pool.
`REQUEST_MEMORY_GRANT_TIMEOUT_SEC=value`	Caps maximum seconds a request will wait for memory before failing.
`MAX_DOP=value`	Defines maximum degree of parallelism allowed for requests in the workload group.
`GROUP_MAX_REQUESTS=value`	Caps concurrently executing requests in the workload group.
`USING { pool_name | "default" }`	Designates which pool the workload group will be bound to.

■ **Note** Multiple workload *groups* can be associated with a single resource *pool*, but a workload group cannot be associated with multiple resource pools.

Just as there are the internal and default resource pools, there are also the internal and default workload groups. The default workload group is used for any requests that are not covered by the classifier user-defined function (a function that determines which workload group's incoming connections are assigned to, demonstrated later in this recipe).

After creating user-defined workload groups and their binding to resource pools, you can then create a single classifier user-defined function that will help determine which workload group an incoming SQL Server connection and request belongs to.

For example, if you have a SQL login named Sue, you can assign that login in the classifier function to belong to a specific workload group that is associated with a specific resource pool.

The classifier user-defined function is created in the master database and returns the workload group name that the incoming SQL Server connection will use. To activate the classifier for incoming connections, the `ALTER RESOURCE GOVERNOR` command is used, which I'll demonstrate later in this recipe.

Beginning the recipe, let's assume I have a SQL Server instance that is used by an application with two general types of activity. The first type of activity relates to the application. The application uses ongoing automated processes with specific connection qualities and must run reliably. The second type of activity comes from ad hoc query users. These are users who require periodic information about transactional activity, but getting that information must never hamper the performance of the main application. Granted, the best practice would be to separate this activity onto two SQL Server instances; however, if this isn't possible, I can use Resource Governor to constrain resources instead.

I'll start by creating two separate user-defined resource pools for the SQL Server instance. The first pool will be used for the high-priority application. I will make sure that this pool reserves at least 25% of CPU and memory during times of query contention.

```
USE master;
GO
CREATE RESOURCE POOL priority_app_queries WITH ( MIN_CPU_PERCENT = 25,
MAX_CPU_PERCENT = 75,
MIN_MEMORY_PERCENT = 25,
MAX_MEMORY_PERCENT = 75);
GO
```

Next, I will create a second resource pool that will be reserved for ad hoc queries. I will cap the maximum CPU and memory of these pools at 25% during times of high query contention in order to preserve resources for the previously created resource pool.

```
USE master;
GO
CREATE RESOURCE POOL ad_hoc_queries WITH ( MIN_CPU_PERCENT = 5,
MAX_CPU_PERCENT = 25,
MIN_MEMORY_PERCENT = 5,
MAX_MEMORY_PERCENT = 25);
GO
```

I can change the values of the resource pools using the `ALTER RESOURCE POOL` command. For example, I am now going to change the minimum memory for the ad hoc query pool to 10% and maximum memory to 50%.

```
USE master;
GO
ALTER RESOURCE POOL ad_hoc_queries WITH ( MIN_MEMORY_PERCENT = 10, MAX_MEMORY_PERCENT = 50);
GO
```

Once I have created the pools, I can now confirm the settings using the `sys.resource_ governor_ resource_pools` catalog view.

```
USE master;
GO
SELECT pool_id,name,min_cpu_percent,max_cpu_percent,
min_memory_percent,max_memory_percent
FROM sys.resource_governor_resource_pools;
GO
```

This query returns the following:

```
pool_id         name            min_cpu_        max_cpu_        min_memory_     max_memory_
                percent         percent         percent         percent
-------         --------------  --------        --------        -----------     -----------
1               internal        0               100             0               100
2               default         0               100             0               100
258             ad_hoc_queries  5               25              10              50
259             priority_app    25              75              25              75
                _queries
```

Now that I have created the resource pools, I can bind workload groups to them. In this case, I will start by creating a workload group for my highest-priority application connections. I will set this workload group to a high importance and be generous with the maximum memory grant percentage and other arguments.

```
USE master;
GO
CREATE WORKLOAD GROUP application_alpha WITH
( IMPORTANCE = HIGH,
REQUEST_MAX_MEMORY_GRANT_PERCENT = 75,
REQUEST_MAX_CPU_TIME_SEC = 75,
REQUEST_MEMORY_GRANT_TIMEOUT_SEC = 120,
MAX_DOP = 8,
GROUP_MAX_REQUESTS = 8 ) USING priority_app_queries;
GO
```

Next, I will create another workload group that will share the same resource pool as `application_alpha`, but with a lower importance and less generous resource consumption capabilities.

```
USE master;
GO
CREATE WORKLOAD GROUP application_beta WITH
( IMPORTANCE = LOW,
REQUEST_MAX_MEMORY_GRANT_PERCENT = 50,
REQUEST_MAX_CPU_TIME_SEC = 50,
REQUEST_MEMORY_GRANT_TIMEOUT_SEC = 360,
MAX_DOP = 1,
GROUP_MAX_REQUESTS = 4 ) USING priority_app_queries;
GO
```

I can modify the various limits of the workload group by using `ALTER WORKLOAD GROUP`. Here's an example:

```
USE master;
GO
ALTER WORKLOAD GROUP application_beta WITH ( IMPORTANCE = MEDIUM);
GO
```

The prior two workload groups will share the same resource pool. I will now create one more workload group that will bind to the ad hoc resource pool I created earlier. This workload group will be able to use the maximum memory available to the ad hoc pool.

```
USE master;
GO
CREATE WORKLOAD GROUP adhoc_users WITH
( IMPORTANCE = LOW,
REQUEST_MAX_MEMORY_GRANT_PERCENT = 100,
REQUEST_MAX_CPU_TIME_SEC = 120,
REQUEST_MEMORY_GRANT_TIMEOUT_SEC = 360,
MAX_DOP = 1,
GROUP_MAX_REQUESTS = 5 ) USING ad_hoc_queries;
GO
```

Once finished, I can confirm the configurations of the workload groups by querying the `sys.resource_governor_workload_groups` catalog view.

```
USE master;
GO
```

```
SELECT name,
Importance impt,
request_max_memory_grant_percent max_m_g,
request_max_cpu_time_sec max_cpu_sec,
request_memory_grant_timeout_sec m_g_to,
max_dop,
group_max_requests max_req,
pool_id
FROM sys.resource_governor_workload_groups;
```

This query returns the following:

```
name              impt    max_m_g   max_cpu_sec  m_g_to  max_dop  max_req   pool_id
----------------- ------  -------   -----------  ------  -------  -------   -------
internal          Medium  25        0            0       0        0         1
default           Medium  25        0            0       0        0         2
application_alpha High    75        75           120     8        8         256
application_beta  Medium  50        50           360     1        4         256
adhoc_users       Low     100       120          360     1        5         257
```

Now I am ready to create the classifier function. This function will be called for each new connection. The logic of this function will return the workload group where all connection requests will be sent. The classifier function can use several different connection-related functions for use in the logic, including HOST_NAME, APP_NAME, SUSER_NAME, SUSER_SNAME, IS_SRVROLEMEMBER, and IS_MEMBER.

■ **Caution** Make sure this function is tuned properly and executes quickly.

I create the following function that looks at the SQL Server login name and connection host name in order to determine which workload group the new connection should be assigned to.

```
USE master;
GO
CREATE FUNCTION dbo.RECIPES_classifier()
RETURNS sysname
WITH SCHEMABINDING
AS
BEGIN
DECLARE @resource_group_name sysname;
IF SUSER_SNAME() IN ('AppLoginl', 'AppLogin2')
SET @resource_group_name = 'application_alpha';
IF SUSER_SNAME() IN ('AppLogin3', 'AppLogin4')
SET @resource_group_name = 'application_beta';
IF HOST_NAME() IN ('Workstationl234', 'Workstation4235')
SET @resource_group_name = 'adhoc_users';
-- If the resource group is still unassigned, use default
IF @resource_group_name IS NULL
SET @resource_group_name = 'default';
RETURN @resource_group_name;
END
GO
```

Now that I've created the classifier function, I can activate it using ALTER RESOURCE GOVERNOR and the CLASSIFIER_FUNCTION argument.

```
USE master;
GO
-- Assign the classifier function
ALTER RESOURCE GOVERNOR
WITH (CLASSIFIER_FUNCTION=dbo.RECIPES_classifier);
GO
```

To enable the configuration, I must also execute ALTER RESOURCE GOVERNOR with the RECONFIGURE option.

```
USE master;
GO
ALTER RESOURCE GOVERNOR RECONFIGURE;
GO
```

I'll validate the settings using the sys.resource_governor_configuration catalog view.

```
USE master;
GO
SELECT OBJECT_NAME(classifier_function_id,DB_ID('master')) Fn_Name,
is_enabled
FROM sys.resource_governor_configuration;
```

This query returns the following:

```
Fn_Name                is_enabled
-------                ----------
RECIPES_classifier     1
```

Now incoming activity for new connections will be routed to the appropriate workload groups and will use resources from their associated resource pools.

■ **Tip** You can monitor the incoming request statistics for resource pools and workload groups using the sys.dm_resource_governor_resource_pools and sys.dm_resource_governor_workload_groups DMVs.

To disable the settings, I can execute the ALTER RESOURCE GOVERNOR with the DISABLE argument:

```
USE master;
GO
ALTER RESOURCE GOVERNOR DISABLE;
GO
```

I can remove the user-defined workload groups and resource pools by executing DROP WORKLOAD GROUP and DROP RESOURCE POOL.

```
USE master;
GO
```

```
DROP WORKLOAD GROUP application_alpha;
DROP WORKLOAD GROUP application_beta;
DROP WORKLOAD GROUP adhoc_users;
DROP RESOURCE POOL ad_hoc_queries;
DROP RESOURCE POOL priority_app_queries;
```

I can also drop the classifier function once it is no longer being used.

```
USE master;
GO
ALTER RESOURCE GOVERNOR
WITH (CLASSIFIER_FUNCTION=NULL);
DROP FUNCTION dbo.RECIPES_classifier;
GO
```

How It Works

This recipe demonstrated how to use Resource Governor to allocate memory and CPU resources into separate user-defined resource pools. Once the resource pools were defined, I created workload groups, which in turn had associated limits within the confines of their assigned user-defined resource pool. I then created a classifier user-defined function, which was used to assign workload groups to incoming connection requests. This allowed me to confine lower-priority requests to fewer resources than higher priority requests.

This functionality allows you to maintain significant control over SQL Server instances that have varying workload requirements and limited system resources. Even on systems with generous system resources, you can use Resource Governor to protect higher-priority workloads from being negatively impacted by lower-priority requests.

CHAPTER 22

Hints

By Jonathan Gennick

SQL Server's query optimization process is responsible for producing a query execution plan when a SELECT query is executed. Typically SQL Server will choose an efficient plan over an inefficient one. When this doesn't happen, you will want to examine the query execution plan, table statistics, supporting indexes, and other factors that are discussed in more detail in Chapters 21 and 23. Ultimately, after researching the query's performance, you may decide to override the decision-making process of the SQL Server query optimizer by using *hints.*

Caution You should almost always let SQL Server's query optimization process formulate the query execution plan without the aid of hints. Even if a hint works for the short term, keep in mind that in the future there may be more efficient query plans that could be used as the contents of the database change, but they won't be, because you have overridden the optimizer with the specified hint. Also, the validity or effectiveness of a hint may change when new service packs or editions of SQL Server are released.

22-1. Forcing a Join's Execution Approach

Problem

You are joining two tables. The optimizer has made a poor choice on the approach to take in executing the join. You want to override the optimizer and exert control over the mechanism used to perform the join.

Solution

Apply one of the join hints from Table 22-1 in the section "How It Works." For example, the following is a query with no hints that will trigger a nested-loops join operation:

```
SELECT  p.Name,
        r.ReviewerName,
        r.Rating
FROM    Production.Product p
        INNER JOIN Production.ProductReview r
            ON r.ProductID = p.ProductID;
```

Figure 22-1 shows the relevant part of the execution plan. You can see that the optimizer has chosen a nested loops join.

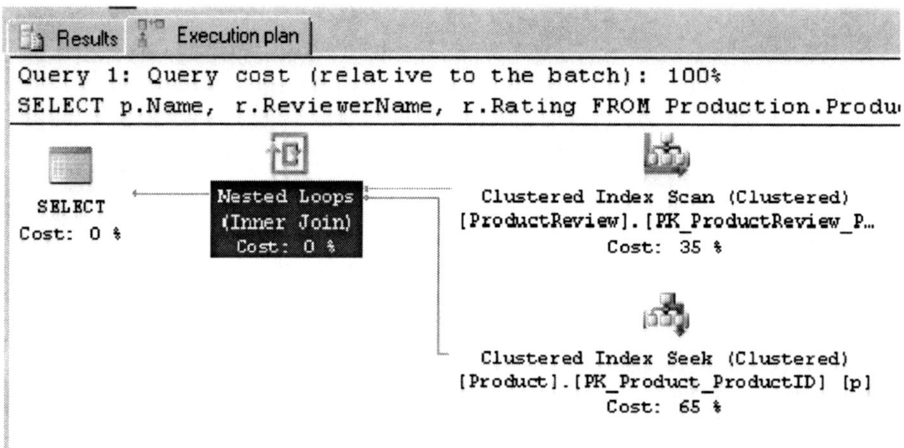

Figure 22-1. *A nested loops join*

You can force one of the other join types by placing the relevant hint from Table 22-1 between the words `INNER` and `JOIN`. The following example uses `INNER HASH JOIN` to force a hash join:

```
SELECT  p.Name,
        r.ReviewerName,
        r.Rating
FROM    Production.Product p
        INNER HASH JOIN Production.ProductReview r
            ON r.ProductID = p.ProductID;
```

Figure 22-2 shows the new execution plan, this time with a hash join operation.

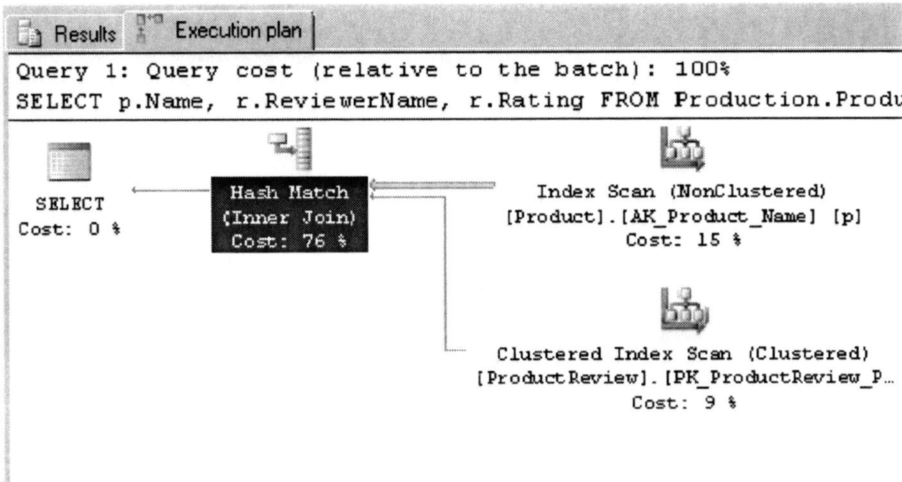

Figure 22-2. *A hash join operation*

How It Works

Table 22-1 shows the join hints at your disposal. The table also provides some general guidance on the situations in which each join method is optimally used. Generally the optimizer will make a reasonable choice. You should think about overriding the optimizer only when you have good reason and no other alternative.

Table 22-1. *Join Hints*

Hint Name	Description
LOOP	Loop joins operate best when one table is small and the other is large, with indexes on the joined columns.
HASH	Hash joins are optimal for large unsorted tables.
MERGE	Merge joins are optimal for medium or large tables that are sorted on the joined column.

The first solution query generates an execution plan showing a nested loops join. The second solution query shows the HASH hint from Table 22-1 being used to force a hash join.

Be careful and thoughtful in applying hints. Don't get carried away. Once you apply a hint, you freeze that hint's aspect of the execution plan until such time as you later change the hint or remove it. Future improvements to the optimizer and future join methods won't ever get applied, because your hint forces the one approach you've chosen.

22-2. Forcing a Statement Recompile

Problem

Normally SQL Server saves the execution plan from a query so as to reuse that plan the next time the query is executed, perhaps with a differing set of values. Your data is skewed, and plans for one set of values may work poorly for others. You want the optimizer to generate a new plan for each execution.

Solution

Submit your query using the RECOMPILE query hint. Typically you will want to use this RECOMPILE query hint within a stored procedure—so that you can control which statements automatically recompile—instead of having to recompile the entire stored procedure. Here's an example:

```
DECLARE @CarrierTrackingNumber nvarchar(25) = '5CE9-4D75-8F';

SELECT  SalesOrderID,
        ProductID,
        UnitPrice,
        OrderQty
FROM    Sales.SalesOrderDetail
WHERE   CarrierTrackingNumber = @CarrierTrackingNumber
ORDER BY SalesOrderID,
        ProductID
OPTION (RECOMPILE);
```

This returns the following:

```
SalesOrderID        ProductID        UnitPrice        OrderQty
------------        ---------        ---------        --------
       47964              760        469.794                 1
       47964              789        1466.01                 1
       47964              819        149.031                 4
       47964              843        15.00                   1
       47964              844        11.994                  6
```

How It Works

This example uses the RECOMPILE query hint to recompile the query, forcing SQL Server to discard the plan generated for the query after it executes. With the RECOMPILE query hint, a new plan will be generated the next time the same or a similar query is executed. The hint goes in the OPTION clause at the end of the query.

```
OPTION (RECOMPILE)
```

You may decide you want to take this recipe's approach when faced with a query for which query plans are volatile, in which differing search condition values for the same plan cause extreme fluctuations in the number of rows returned. In such a scenario, using a compiled query plan may hurt, not help, query performance. The benefit of a cached and reusable query execution plan (the avoided cost of compilation) may occasionally be outweighed by the actual performance of the query as it is executed using the saved plan.

■ **Note** It bears repeating that SQL Server should be relied upon most of the time to make the correct decisions when processing a query. Query hints can provide you with more control for those exceptions when you need to override SQL Server's choices.

22-3. Executing a Query Without Locking

Problem

You want to execute a query without being blocked and without blocking others. You are willing to risk seeing uncommitted changes from other transactions.

Solution #1: The NOLOCK Hint

Apply the NOLOCK table hint, as in the following example:

```
SELECT  DocumentNode,
        Title
FROM    Production.Document WITH (NOLOCK)
WHERE   Status = 1;
```

Solution #2: The Isolation Level

Another approach here is to execute a SET TRANSACTION statement to specify an isolation level having the same effect as the NOLOCK hint. Here's an example:

```
SET TRANSACTION ISOLATION LEVEL READ UNCOMMITTED;
SELECT  DocumentNode,
        Title
FROM    Production.Document
WHERE   Status = 1;
```

How It Works

The crux of this example is the WITH clause, which specifies the NOLOCK table hint in parentheses.

```
WITH (NOLOCK)
```

The example in Solution #1 returns the DocumentID and Title from the Production.Document table where the Status column is equal to 1. The NOLOCK table hint prevents the query from placing shared locks on the Production.Document table. You can then read without being blocked or blocking others (although you are now subject to reading uncommitted and possibly inconsistent data).

The example in Solution #2 accomplishes the same thing by setting the transaction isolation level in a separate statement. Doing that avoids the need for a hint in the query. The command affects all subsequent transactions in the session.

Your transaction isolation level options are as follows:

READ UNCOMMITTED*:* You can read uncommitted changes from other transactions.

READ COMMITTED*:* You see only committed changes from other transactions.

REPEATABLE READ*:* You are not able to read data that has been modified, but not yet committed, by other transactions.

SNAPSHOT*:* You see all data as it existed at the precise moment the transaction began.

SERIALIZABLE*:* Transactions are guaranteed to be serializable, meaning they can be played back in sequence. You won't be able to read uncommitted data from other transactions. Other transactions will not be able to modify data that you have read, nor will other transactions be allowed to insert new rows that have key values falling into any of the ranges selected by your transaction.

READ COMMITTED is the default level. If you aren't reasonably familiar with what the various levels mean, take the time to read the Books Online section on "Transaction Statements." The URL for the 2012 version of that section is http://msdn.microsoft.com/en-us/library/ms174377.aspx.

22-4. Forcing an Index Seek

Problem

You are executing a query that you know is best executed via an index seek operation, yet the optimizer persists in choosing to scan the index. You've done your due diligence by updating statistics. You are still getting the scan operation.

Solution

Specify the FORCESEEK hint, which is available from SQL Server 2008 onward. Here's an example:

```
SELECT DISTINCT
        TransactionID,
        TransactionDate
FROM    Production.TransactionHistory WITH (FORCESEEK)
WHERE   ReferenceOrderID BETWEEN 1000 AND 100000;
```

You also have the option to designate which index should be used. Here's an example:

```
SELECT DISTINCT
        TransactionID,
        TransactionDate
FROM    Production.TransactionHistory WITH (FORCESEEK,
        INDEX (IX_TransactionHistory_ReferenceOrderID_ReferenceOrderLineID))
WHERE   ReferenceOrderID BETWEEN 1000 AND 100000;
```

Your query will now seek directly to the index keys needed to resolve the query.

■ **Caution** This example is for illustrative purposes only. The forced seek in this query is nonoptimal.

How It Works

Bad query plans happen for several reasons. For example, if your table data is highly volatile and your statistics are no longer accurate, a bad plan can be produced. Another example would be a query with a poorly constructed WHERE clause that doesn't provide sufficient or useful information to the query optimization process.

If the intent of your query is to perform a singleton lookup against a specific value and instead you see that the query scans the entire index before retrieving your single row, the I/O costs of the scan can be significant (particularly for very large tables). You may then consider using the new FORCESEEK table hint. FORCESEEK can be used in the FROM clause of a SELECT, UPDATE, or DELETE.

The solution example invokes the hint by placing the WITH keyword into the query, followed by the hint name in parentheses:

```
FROM Production.TransactionHistory WITH (FORCESEEK)
```

Using the hint overrides the query's original clustered index scan access path.

You further narrow down the instructions by designating the INDEX hint as well, forcing the seek to occur against the specific index you name. Here's an example:

```
FROM Production.TransactionHistory WITH (FORCESEEK,
     INDEX (IX_TransactionHistory_ReferenceOrderID_ReferenceOrderLineID))
```

The INDEX hint is followed by the name of the index within parentheses. You can also specify the index number.

22-5. Forcing an Index Scan

Problem

The optimizer underestimates the number of rows to be returned from a table and chooses to execute a seek operation against an index on the table. You know from your knowledge of the data that an index scan is the better choice.

Solution

Specify the FORCESCAN hint, which is available from SQL Server 2008 R2 SP1 onward. Here's an example:

```
SELECT DISTINCT
        TransactionID,
        TransactionDate
FROM    Production.TransactionHistory WITH (FORCESCAN)
WHERE   ReferenceOrderID BETWEEN 1000 AND 100000;
```

If you like, you can specify the index to scan.

```
SELECT DISTINCT
        TransactionID,
        TransactionDate
FROM    Production.TransactionHistory WITH (FORCESCAN,
        INDEX (PK_TransactionHistory_TransactionID))
WHERE   ReferenceOrderID BETWEEN 1000 AND 100000;
```

Your query will now scan the specified index to resolve the query.

How It Works

The FORCESCAN hint is the complement of FORCESEEK described in Recipe 22-4. The hint applies to SELECT, INSERT, and UPDATE statements. With it, you can specify that you want an index seek operation to take place when executing a query.

22-6. Optimizing for First Rows

Problem

You want the optimizer to favor execution plans that will return some number of rows very quickly. For example, you are writing a query for an interactive application and would like to display the first screen full of results as soon as possible.

Solution

Place the FAST n hint into the OPTION clause at the end of your query. Specify the number of rows that you would like to be returned quickly. Here's an example:

```
SELECT  ProductID, TransactionID, ReferenceOrderID
FROM    Production.TransactionHistory
ORDER BY ProductID
OPTION (FAST 20);
```

How It Works

Specify FAST n to alert the optimizer to your need for n rows to come back very quickly. In theory, the optimizer then favors execution plans yielding quick initial results at the expense of plans that might be more efficient overall.

An example of a typical trade-off would be for the optimizer to choose a nested loops join over a hash join or some other operation. Figure 22-3 shows the execution plan for the solution query when that query is executed without the hint. Figure 22-4 shows the plan with the hint included. You can see the nested loops operation in the second figure.

In the case of the solution query, the hint FAST 20 causes the optimizer to drive the query from an index on the ProductID column. By doing so, the query engine is able to begin immediately returning the rows in sorted order, because the query engine can simply read the index in order. The trade-off, which you can see when you compare the two plans as shown in Figures 22-3 and 22-4, is that each access of the one index is accompanied by a key lookup into the table to return the other two column values. Figure 22-4's plan is probably more costly, but it does begin to return rows immediately. Figure 22-3's plan might be more efficient, but no rows can be returned until the table has been scanned and the sort operation has been completed.

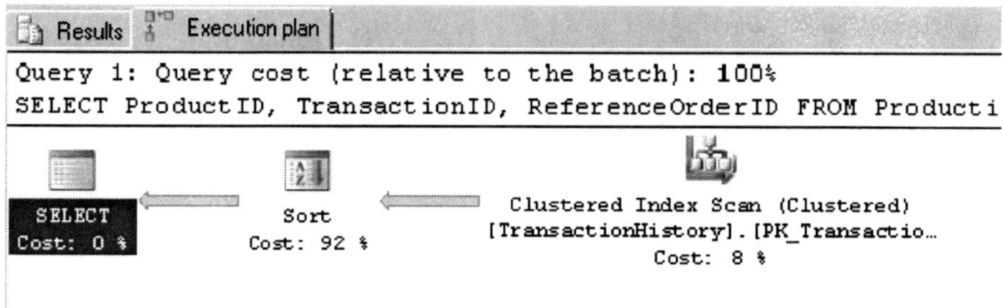

***Figure 22-3.** Query plan optimized for overall execution*

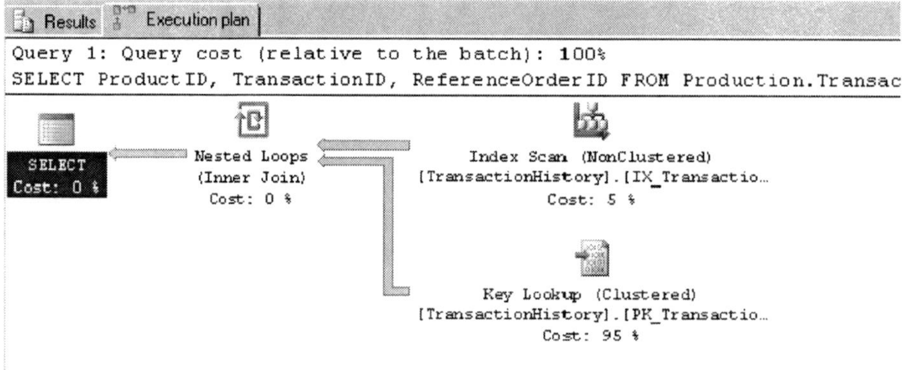

***Figure 22-4.** Query plan with FAST 20 in effect*

FAST n is no guarantee that you'll get n rows any faster than before. Results depend upon available indexes and join types and upon the various possibilities that the programmers writing the optimizer happened to think about ahead of time. Check your query's execution plan before and after adding the hint to see whether doing so made a difference.

■ **Caution** There used to be a FASTFIRSTROW hint. It is no longer supported in SQL Server 2012. Specify FAST 1 instead.

22-7. Specifying Join Order

Problem

You are joining two or more tables. You want to force the order in which the tables are accessed while executing the join.

Solution

List the tables in the FROM clause in the order in which you want them to be accessed. Then specify FORCE ORDER in an OPTION clause at the end of the query. Here's an example:

```
SELECT  PP.FirstName, PP.LastName, PA.City
FROM    Person.Person PP
        INNER JOIN Person.BusinessEntityAddress PBA
            ON PP.BusinessEntityID = PBA.BusinessEntityID
        INNER JOIN Person.Address PA
            ON PBA.AddressID = PA.AddressID
OPTION (FORCE ORDER)
```

The join order will now be Person to BusinessEntityID and then will come the join to Address.

How It Works

Specifying FORCE ORDER causes tables to be joined in the order listed in the FROM cause. Figures 22-5 and 22-6 show the effect of the hint on the solution query. Without the hint (Figure 22-5), the first two tables to be joined are Address and BusinessEntityAddress. With the hint (Figure 22-6), the first two tables are Person and BusinessEntityAddress, matching the order specified in the FROM clause.

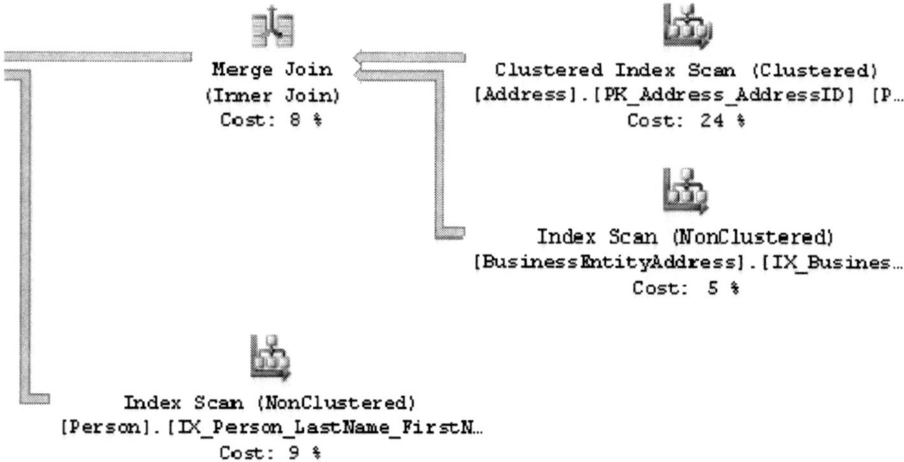

Figure 22-5. *Execution plan without the FORCE ORDER hint*

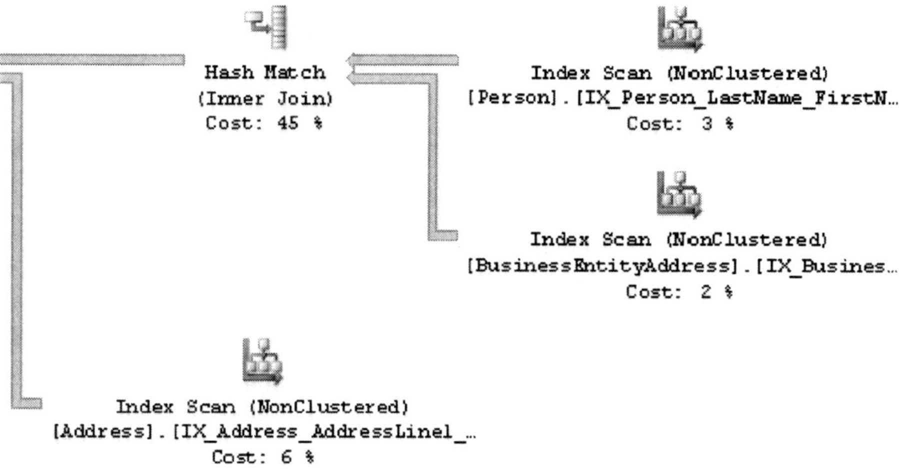

Figure 22-6. *Forced execution from the solution query*

22-8. Forcing Use of a Specific Index

Problem

You aren't happy with the optimizer's index choice. You want to force the use of a specific index in connection with a given table.

Solution

Specify the `INDEX` hint at the table level. For example, the following is another rendition of the query first shown in Recipe 22-6. This time, the table reference is followed by a `WITH` clause containing an `INDEX` hint.

```
SELECT  ProductID, TransactionID, ReferenceOrderID
FROM    Production.TransactionHistory
        WITH (INDEX (IX_TransactionHistory_ProductID))
ORDER BY ProductID
```

The INDEX hint in this query forces the use of the named index: IX_TransactionHistory_ProductID.

How It Works

Figures 22-7 and 22-8 show an execution plan without and with the INDEX hint. You can see in Figure 22-8 that the hint forces the use of the index on the ProductID column.

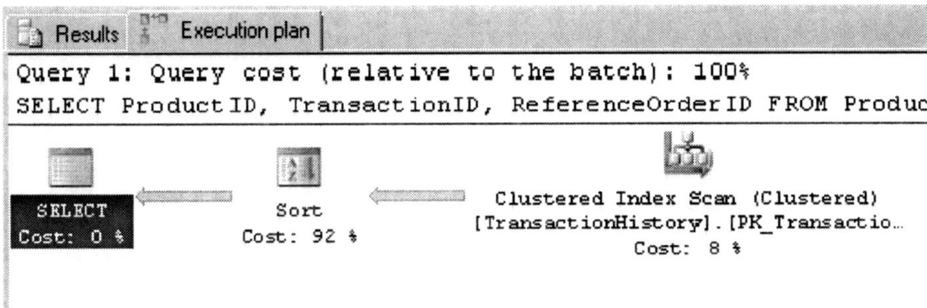

Figure 22-7. Unhinted execution plan

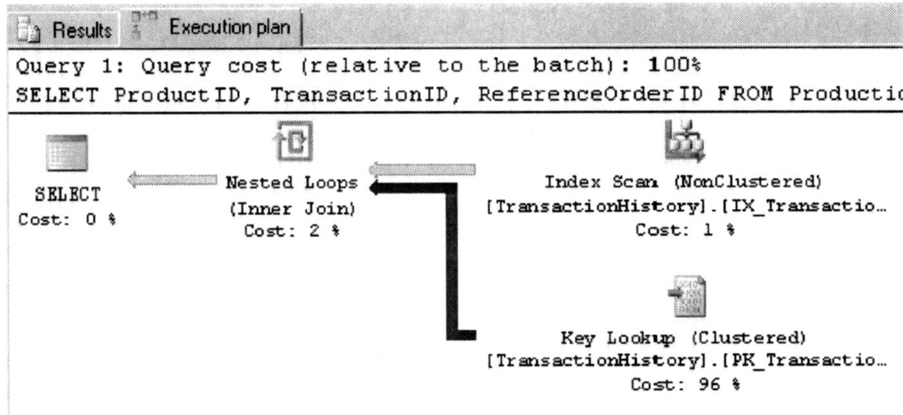

Figure 22-8. Execution plan forcing use of an index

Think twice before forcing the use of an index as shown in this recipe. Whenever you lock in an index choice with a hint, that choice remains locked in no matter what optimizer improvements are made. It remains locked in even if the data changes to favor use of some other index. Before hinting an index, consider whether the statistics are up-to-date and whether you can do something to trigger the use of the index without having to hard-code that usage in the form of a table hint.

22-9. Optimizing for Specific Parameter Values

Problem

You want to avoid trouble from parameter sniffing by instructing the optimizer on which value to consider when parsing a query that has bind variables.

Solution

Specify the OPTIMIZE FOR hint. Here's an example:

```
DECLARE @TTYPE NCHAR(1);
SET @TTYPE = 'P';

SELECT  *
FROM    Production.TransactionHistory TH
WHERE   TH.TransactionType = @TTYPE
OPTION (OPTIMIZE FOR (@TTYPE = 'S'));
```

How It Works

The solution example specifies the hint OPTIMIZE FOR (@TTYPE = 'S'). The optimizer will take the value 'S' into account when building a query plan. Hinting like this can sometimes be helpful in cases in which data is badly skewed, especially when the risk is high that the first execution of a given query will be done using a value resulting in a plan that will work poorly for subsequent values passed in subsequent executions.

If you execute the solution query and choose to view the actual execution plan in XML form, you'll find the following:

```
<ColumnReference Column="@TTYPE"
   ParameterCompiledValue="N'S'"
   ParameterRuntimeValue="N'P'" />
```

Here you can see that the compiled query took into account the value S. But the query as actually executed used the value P. The plan actually executed is the one compiled for the S, just as the hint specified.

■ **Tip** You may specify OPTIMIZE FOR UNKNOWN to essentially inhibit parameter sniffing altogether. In doing so, you cause the optimizer to rely upon table and index statistics alone, without regard to the initial value that is ultimately passed to the query.

CHAPTER 23

Index Tuning and Statistics

By Jason Brimhall

As discussed in Chapter 21, SQL Server query performance tuning and optimization requires a multilayered approach. This chapter focuses on the index and statistics tuning aspects of that approach. The following are a few key factors that impact SQL Server query performance:

- *Appropriate indexing:* Your table indexes should be based on your high-priority or frequently executed queries. If a query is executing thousands of times a day and is completing in two seconds but could be running in less than one second with the proper index, adding this index could reduce the I/O pressure on your SQL Server instance significantly. You should create indexes as needed and remove indexes that aren't being used (this chapter shows you how to do this). As with most changes, there is a trade-off. Each index on your table adds overhead to data modification operations and can even slow down `SELECT` queries if SQL Server decides to use the less efficient index. When you're initially designing your database, it is better for you to keep the number of indexes at a minimum (having at least a clustered index and nonclustered indexes for your foreign keys). Add indexes once you have a better idea about the actual queries that will be executed against the database. Indexing requirements are organic, particularly on volatile, frequently updated databases, so your approach to adding and removing indexes should be flexible and iterative.
- *Index fragmentation:* As data modifications are made over time, your indexes will become fragmented. As fragmentation increases, index data will become spread out over more data pages. The more data pages your query needs to retrieve, the higher the I/O and memory requirements and the slower the query.
- *Up-to-date statistics:* The `AUTO_CREATE_STATISTICS` database option enables SQL Server to automatically generate statistical information regarding the distribution of values in a column. The `AUTO_UPDATE_STATISTICS` database option enables SQL Server to automatically update statistical information regarding the distribution of values in a column. If you disable these options, statistics can get out-of-date. Since SQL Server depends on statistics to decide how to best execute the query, SQL Server may choose a less-than-optimal plan if it is basing its execution decisions on stale statistics.

In this chapter, I'll demonstrate the T-SQL commands and techniques you can use to help address fragmented indexes and out-of-date statistics and evaluate the usage of indexes in the database.

■ **Note** Since this is a book about T-SQL, I don't review the graphical interface tools that also assist with performance tuning such as SQL Server Profiler, graphical execution plans, System Monitor, and the Database Engine Tuning Advisor. These are all extremely useful tools—so I still encourage you to use them as part of your overall performance-tuning strategy in addition to the T-SQL commands and techniques you'll learn about in this chapter.

Index Tuning

This first batch of recipes demonstrates techniques for managing indexes. Specifically, I'll be covering how to do the following:

- Identify index fragmentation, so you can figure out which indexes should be rebuilt or reorganized
- Display index usage, so you can determine which indexes *aren't being* used by SQL Server

Before getting into the recipes, I'll take a moment to discuss some general indexing best practices. When considering these best practices, always remember that, like query tuning, there are few hard and fast "always" or "never" rules. Index usage by SQL Server depends on a number of factors, including, but not limited to, the query construction, referenced tables in the query, referenced columns, number of rows in the table, data distribution, and uniqueness of the index column(s) data. The following are some basic guidelines to keep in mind when building your index strategy:

- Add indexes based on your high-priority and high-execution count queries. Determine ahead of time what acceptable query execution durations might be based on your business requirements.
- Don't add too many indexes at the same time. Instead, add an index and test the query to see that the new index is used. If it is not used, remove it. If it is used, test to make sure there are no negative side effects to other queries. Remember that each additional index adds overhead to data modifications to the base table.
- Unless you have a very good reason not to do so, always add a clustered index to each table. A table without a clustered index is a heap, meaning that the data is stored in no particular order. Clustered indexes are ordered according to the clustered key, and its data pages are reordered during an index rebuild or reorganization. Heaps, however, are not rebuilt during an index rebuild or reorganization process and therefore can grow out of control, taking up many more data pages than necessary.
- Monitor query performance over time and index usage over time. As your data and application activity changes, so too will the performance and effectiveness of your indexes.
- Fragmented indexes can slow down query performance, since more I/O operations are required in order to return results for a query. Keep index fragmentation to a minimum by rebuilding and/or reorganizing your indexes on a scheduled or as-needed basis.
- Select clustered index keys that are rarely modified, highly unique, and narrow in data type width. Width is particularly important because each nonclustered index also contains within it the clustered index key. Clustered indexes are useful when applied to columns used in range queries. This includes queries that use the operators `BETWEEN`, `>`, `>=`, `<`, and `<=`. Clustered index keys also help reduce execution time for queries that return large result sets or depend heavily on `ORDER BY` and `GROUP BY` clauses. With all these factors in mind, remember that you can have only a single clustered index for your table, so choose carefully.

- Nonclustered indexes are ideal for small or one-row result sets. Again, columns should be chosen based on their use in a query, specifically in the `JOIN` or `WHERE` clause. Nonclustered indexes should be made on columns containing highly unique data. As discussed in Chapter 16, don't forget to consider using covering queries and the `INCLUDE` functionality for nonkey columns.
- Use a 100 percent fill factor for those indexes that are located within read-only filegroups or databases. This reduces I/O and can improve query performance because fewer data pages are required to fulfill a query's result set.
- Try to anticipate which indexes will be needed based on the queries you perform—but also don't be afraid to make frequent use of the Database Engine Tuning Advisor tool. Using the Database Engine Tuning Advisor, SQL Server can evaluate your query or batch of queries and suggest index changes for you to review.

The next recipe will now demonstrate how to display index fragmentation.

Index Maintenance

Fragmentation is the natural by-product of data modifications to a table. When data is updated in the database, the logical order of indexes (based on the index key) gets out of sync with the actual physical order of the data pages. As data pages become further and further out of order, more I/O operations are required in order to return results requested by a query. Rebuilding or reorganizing an index allows you to defragment the index by synchronizing the logical index order and reordering the physical data pages to match the logical index order. In the next two recipes, I'll demonstrate two methods you can use to defragment your indexes.

■ **Tip** It is important that you rebuild only the indexes that require it. The rebuild process is resource intensive.

23-1. Displaying Index Fragmentation

Problem

You suspect that you have indexes that are heavily fragmented. You need to run a query to confirm the fragmentation levels of the indexes in your database.

Solution

Query the `sys.dm_db_index_physical_stats` dynamic management function.

Fragmentation is the natural by-product of data modifications to a table. When data is updated in the database, the logical order of indexes (based on the index key) gets out of sync with the actual physical order of the data pages. As data pages become further and further out of order, more I/O operations are required in order to return results requested by a query. Rebuilding or reorganizing an index allows you to defragment the index by synchronizing the logical index order, reordering the physical data pages to match the logical index order.

■ **Note** See Chapter 16 for a review of index management and later in this chapter for a review of index defragmentation and reorganization.

The sys.dm_db_index_physical_stats dynamic management function returns information that allows you to determine the fragmentation level of an index. The syntax for sys.dm_db_index_physical_stats is as follows:

```
sys.dm_db_index_physical_stats (
{       database_id | NULL }
,       { object_id | NULL }
,       { index_id | NULL | 0 }
,       { partition_number | NULL }
,       { mode | NULL | DEFAULT }
)
```

Table 23-1 describes the arguments of this command.

Table 23-1. *sys.dm_db_index_physical_stats Arguments*

Argument	Description
database_id | NULL	This defines the database ID of the indexes to evaluate. If NULL, all databases for the SQL Server instance are returned.
object_id | NULL	This specifies the object ID of the table and views (*indexed* views) to evaluate. If NULL, all tables are returned.
index_id | NULL | 0	This gives the specific index ID of the index to evaluate. If NULL, all indexes are returned for the table(s).
partition_number | NULL	This defines the specific partition number of the partition to evaluate. If NULL, all partitions are returned based on the defined database/table/indexes selected.
LIMITED | SAMPLED | DETAILED | NULL | DEFAULT	These modes impact how the fragmentation data is collected. The LIMITED mode scans all pages for a heap and the pages above the leaf level. SAMPLED collects data based on a 1 percent sampling of pages in the heap or index. The DETAILED mode scans all pages (heap or index). DETAILED is the slowest, but most accurate, option. Designating NULL or DEFAULT is the equivalent of the LIMITED mode.

In this example, the sys.dm_db_index_physical_stats dynamic management function is queried for all objects in the AdventureWorks2012 database with an average fragmentation percent greater than 30.

```
USE AdventureWorks2012;
GO
SELECT OBJECT_NAME(object_id) ObjectName,
index_id,
index_type_desc,
avg_fragmentation_in_percent
FROM sys.dm_db_index_physical_stats (DB_ID('AdventureWorks2012'),NULL, NULL, NULL, 'LIMITED')
WHERE avg_fragmentation_in_percent>30
ORDER BY OBJECT_NAME(object_id);
```

This returns the following (abridged) results:

```
ObjectName              index_id    index_type_desc       avg_fragmentation_in_percent
---------------------   --------    ------------------    ----------------------------
BillOfMaterials         2           NONCLUSTERED INDEX    33.3333333333333
BusinessEntityContact   1           CLUSTERED INDEX       50
BusinessEntityContact   2           NONCLUSTERED INDEX    50
BusinessEntityContact   3           NONCLUSTERED INDEX    50
BusinessEntityContact   4           NONCLUSTERED INDEX    50
CountryRegion           1           CLUSTERED INDEX       50
DatabaseLog             0           HEAP                  32.6732673267327
...
```

This second example returns fragmentation for a specific database, table, and index.

```
USE AdventureWorks2012;
GO
SELECT OBJECT_NAME(f.object_id) ObjectName,
        i.name IndexName,
        f.index_type_desc,
        f.avg_fragmentation_in_percent
FROM sys.dm_db_index_physical_stats
        (DB_ID('AdventureWorks2012'), OBJECT_ID('Production.ProductDescription'), 2, NULL,
'LIMITED')  f
INNER JOIN sys.indexes i
        ON i.object_id=f.object_id
        AND i.index_id=f.index_id;
```

This query returns the following:

```
ObjectName           IndexName               index_type_desc       avg_fragmentationin_
                                                                   percent
------------------   ---------------------   ------------------    ---------------------
ProductDescription   AK_ProductDescription_  NONCLUSTERED INDEX    66.6666666666667
                     rowguid
```

How It Works

The first example started by changing the database context to the AdventureWorks2012 database.

```
USE AdventureWorks2012;
GO
```

Since the OBJECT_NAME function is database-context sensitive, changing the database context ensures that you are viewing the proper object name.

Next, the SELECT clause displayed the object name, index ID, description, and average fragmentation percent.

```
SELECT OBJECT_NAME(object_id) ObjectName, index_id, index_type_desc,
avg_fragmentation_in_percent
```

The index_type_desc column tells you if the index is a heap, clustered index, nonclustered index, primary XML index, spatial index, or secondary XML index.

Next, the FROM clause referenced the sys.dm_db_index_physical_stats dynamic management function. The parameters, which were put in parentheses, included the database name and NULL for all other parameters except the scan mode.

```
FROM sys.dm_db_index_physical_stats (DB_ID('AdventureWorks2012'),NULL, NULL, NULL, 'LIMITED')
```

Since sys.dm_db_index_physical_stats is table-valued function, the WHERE clause was used to qualify that only rows with a fragmentation percentage greater than 30 percent be returned in the results.

```
WHERE avg_fragmentation_in_percent>30
```

The query returned several rows for objects in the AdventureWorks2012 database with a fragmentation level greater than 30 percent. The avg_fragmentation_in_percent column shows logical fragmentation of nonclustered or clustered indexes, returning the percentage of disordered pages at the leaf level of the index. For heaps, avg_fragmentation_in_percent shows extent-level fragmentation. Regarding extents, recall that SQL Server reads and writes data at the page level. Pages are stored in blocks called *extents,* which consist of eight contiguous 8KB pages. Using the avg_fragmentation_in_percent, you can determine whether the specific indexes need to be rebuilt or reorganized using ALTER INDEX.

In the second example, fragmentation was displayed for a specific database, table, and index. The SELECT clause included a reference to the index name (instead of index number).

```
SELECT OBJECT_NAME(f.object_id) ObjectName, i.name IndexName, f.index_type_desc,
f.avg_fragmentation_in_percent
```

The FROM clause included the specific table name, which was converted to an ID using the OBJECT_ID function. The third parameter included the index number of the index to be evaluated for fragmentation.

```
FROM sys.dm_db_index_physical_stats
(DB_ID('AdeventureWorks2012'),
OBJECT_ID('Production.ProductDescription'),
2,
NULL,
'LIMITED') f
```

The sys.indexes system catalog view was joined to the sys.dm_db_index_physical_stats function based on the object_id and index_id.

```
INNER JOIN sys.indexes i ON i.object_id=f.object_id AND i.index_id=f.index_id;
```

The query returned the fragmentation results just for that specific index.

23-2. Rebuilding Indexes

Problem

After analyzing fragmentation levels of your indexes, you have determined that many indexes need to be rebuilt.

Solution

Rebuild the indexes using ALTER INDEX.

Rebuilding an index serves many purposes, the most popular being the removal of fragmentation that occurs as data modifications are made to a table over time. As fragmentation increases, query performance can slow. Rebuilding an index removes fragmentation of the index rows and frees up physical disk space.

Large indexes that are quite fragmented can reduce query speed. The frequency of how often you rebuild your indexes depends on your database size, how much data modification occurs, how much activity occurs against your tables, and whether your queries typically perform ordered scans or singleton lookups.

The syntax for ALTER INDEX to rebuild an index is as follows:

```
ALTER INDEX { index_name | ALL }
        ON <object>
        {       REBUILD
        [ [ WITH ( <rebuild_index_option> [ ,...n ] ) ]
        | [ PARTITION = partition_number
[ WITH ( <single_partition_rebuild_index_option>
        [ ,...n ] )
        ]
        ]
        ]
        }
```

Table 23-2 describes the arguments of this command.

***Table 23-2.** ALTER INDEX... REBUILD Arguments*

Argument	Description
index_name | ALL	This defines the name of the index to rebuild. If ALL is chosen, all indexes for the specified table or view will be rebuilt.
<object>	This specifies the name of the table or view that the index is built on.
<rebuild_index_option>	One or more index options can be applied during a rebuild, including FILLFACTOR, PAD_INDEX, SORT_IN_TEMPDB, IGNORE_DUP_KEY, STATISTICS_NORECOMPUTE, ONLINE, ALLOW_ROW_LOCKS, ALLOW_PAGE_LOCKS, DATA_COMPRESSION, and MAXDOP.
partition_number	If using a partitioned index, partition_number designates that only one partition of the index is rebuilt.
<single_partition_rebuild_index_option>	If designating a partition rebuild, you are limited to using the following index options in the WITH clause: SORT_IN_TEMPDB, DATA_COMPRESSION, and MAXDOP.

This recipe demonstrates ALTER INDEX REBUILD, which drops and re-creates an existing index. It demonstrates a few variations for rebuilding an index in the AdventureWorks2012 database.

```
-- Rebuild a specific index
USE AdventureWorks2012;
GO
ALTER INDEX PK_ShipMethod_ShipMethodID ON Purchasing.ShipMethod REBUILD;

-- Rebuild all indexes on a specific table
USE AdventureWorks2012;
GO
ALTER INDEX ALL
ON Purchasing.PurchaseOrderHeader REBUILD;

-- Rebuild an index, while keeping it available -- for queries (requires Enterprise Edition)
USE AdventureWorks2012;
GO
ALTER INDEX PK_ProductReview_ProductReviewID
ON Production.ProductReview REBUILD WITH (ONLINE=ON);
```

```
-- Rebuild an index, using a new fill factor and -- sorting in tempdb
USE AdventureWorks2012;
GO
ALTER INDEX PK_TransactionHistory_TransactionID
ON Production.TransactionHistory REBUILD WITH (FILLFACTOR=75, SORT_IN_TEMPDB=ON);

-- Rebuild an index with page-level data compression enabled
USE AdventureWorks2012;
GO
ALTER INDEX PK_ShipMethod_ShipMethodID
ON Purchasing.ShipMethod REBUILD WITH (DATA_COMPRESSION=PAGE);
```

How It Works

In this recipe, the first ALTER INDEX was used to rebuild the primary key index on the Purchasing.ShipMethod table (rebuilding a clustered index does not cause the rebuild of any nonclustered indexes for the table).

```
ALTER INDEX PK_ShipMethod_ShipMethodID ON Purchasing.ShipMethod REBUILD
```

In the second example, the ALL keyword was used, which means that any indexes, whether nonclustered or clustered (remember, only one clustered index exists on a table), will be rebuilt.

```
ALTER INDEX ALL
ON Purchasing.PurchaseOrderHeader REBUILD
```

The third example in the recipe rebuilt an index *online*, which means that user queries can continue to access the data of the PK_ProductReview_ProductReviewID index while it's being rebuilt.

```
WITH (ONLINE=ON)
```

The ONLINE option requires SQL Server Enterprise Edition, and it can't be used with XML indexes, disabled indexes, or partitioned indexes. Also, indexes using large object data types or indexes made on temporary tables can't take advantage of this option.

In the fourth example, two index options were modified for an index—the fill factor and a directive to sort the temporary index results in tempdb.

```
WITH (FILLFACTOR=75, SORT_IN_TEMPDB=ON)
```

In the previous example, an uncompressed index was rebuilt using page-level data compression.

```
WITH (DATA_COMPRESSION=PAGE)
```

■ **Tip** You can validate whether an index/partition is compressed by looking at the data_compression_desc column in sys.partitions.

23-3. Defragmenting Indexes

Problem

In addition to the many indexes that need to be rebuilt, you have determined that several need to be defragmented.

Solution

Use ALTER INDEX REORGANIZE to reduce fragmentation in the leaf level of an index (clustered and nonclustered), causing the physical order of the database pages to match the logical order. During this reorganization process, the indexes are also compacted based on the fill factor, resulting in freed space and a smaller index. ALTER TABLE REORGANIZE is automatically an online operation, meaning that you can continue to query the target data during the reorganization process. The syntax is as follows:

```
ALTER INDEX { indexname | ALL } ON<object>{ REORGANIZE
[ PARTITION=partition_number ]
[ WITH ( LOB_COMPACTION={ ON | OFF } ) ] }
```

Table 23-3 describes the arguments of this command.

Table 23-3. *ALTER INDEX... REORGANIZE Arguments*

Argument	Description
index_name | ALL	This defines the name of the index that you want to rebuild. If ALL is chosen, all indexes for the table or view will be rebuilt.
<object>	This specifies the name of the table or view that you want to build the index on.
partition_number	If using a partitioned index, the partition_number designates that partition to reorganize.
LOB_COMPACTION = { ON | OFF }	When this argument is enabled, large object data types (varchar(max), navarchar(max), varbinary(max), xml, text, ntext, and image data) are compacted.

This recipe demonstrates how to defragment a single index, as well as all indexes on a single table.

```
-- Reorganize a specific index
USE AdventureWorks2012;
GO
ALTER INDEX PK_TransactionHistory_TransactionID
ON Production.TransactionHistory
REORGANIZE;
-- Reorganize all indexes for a table
-- Compact large object data types
USE AdventureWorks2012;
GO
ALTER INDEX ALL
ON HumanResources.JobCandidate
REORGANIZE
WITH (LOB_COMPACTION=ON);
```

How It Works

In the first example of this recipe, the primary key index of the Production.TransactionHistory table was reorganized (defragmented). The syntax was very similar to rebuilding an index, only instead of REBUILD, the REORGANIZE keyword was used.

In the second example, all indexes (using the ALL keyword) were defragmented for the HumanResources.Jobcandidate table. Using the WITH clause, large object data type columns were also compacted.

Use ALTER INDEX REORGANIZE if you cannot afford to take the index offline during an index rebuild (and if you cannot use the ONLINE option in ALTER INDEX REBUILD because you aren't running SQL Server Enterprise Edition). Reorganization is always an online operation, meaning that an ALTER INDEX REORGANIZE operation doesn't block database traffic for significant periods of time, although it may be a slower process than a REBUILD.

23-4. Rebuilding a Heap

Problem

You have a table in the database that does not have a clustered index and is a heap. You have noticed that this table is nearly 90 percent fragmented, and you want to defragment that table.

Solution

Since SQL Server 2008, you can rebuild a heap (a table without a clustered index) using the ALTER TABLE command. In previous versions, rebuilding a heap required adding and removing a temporary clustered index or performing a data migration or table re-creation.

In this example, I will create a heap table (using SELECT INTO) and then rebuild it.

```
USE AdventureWorks2012;
GO
-- Create an unindexed table based on another table
SELECT ShiftID, Name, StartTime, EndTime, ModifiedDate
INTO dbo.Heap_Shift FROM HumanResources.Shift;
```

I can validate whether the new table is a heap by querying the sys.indexes system catalog view.

```
USE AdventureWorks2012;
GO
SELECT type_desc FROM sys.indexes
WHERE object_id=OBJECT_ID('Heap_Shift');
```

This query returns the following:

```
type_desc

HEAP
```

If I want to rebuild the heap, I can issue the following ALTER TABLE command.

```
USE AdventureWorks2012;
GO
ALTER TABLE dbo.Heap_Shift REBUILD;
```

How It Works

In this recipe, I created a heap table and then rebuilt it using ALTER TABLE...REBUILD. Using ALTER TABLE...REBUILD, you can rebuild a table, even if it does not have a clustered index (heap). If the table is partitioned, this command also rebuilds all partitions on that table and rebuilds the clustered index if one exists.

23-5. Displaying Index Usage

Problem

You are concerned you may have some indexes in the database that are more costly than the benefit they provide or that are no longer being used. You want to find which indexes fit these criteria.

Solution

You can query the sys.dm_db_index_usage_stats dynamic management view (DMV).

Creating useful indexes in your database is a balancing act between read and write performance. Indexes can slow down data modifications while at the same time speed up SELECT queries. You must balance the cost/benefit of index overhead with read activity versus data modification activity. Every additional index added to a table may improve query performance at the expense of data modification speed. On top of this, index effectiveness changes as the data changes, so an index that was useful a few weeks ago may not be useful today. If you are going to have indexes on a table, they should be put to good use on high-priority queries.

To identify disused indexes, you can query the sys.dm_db_index_usage_stats DMV. This view returns statistics on the number of index seeks, scans, updates, or lookups since the SQL Server instance was last restarted. It also returns the last dates the index was referenced.

In this example, the sys.dm_db_index_usage_stats DMV is queried to see whether the indexes on the Sales.Customer table are being used. Prior to referencing sys.dm_db_index_usage_stats, two queries will be executed against the Sales.Customer table: one query returning all rows and columns and the second returning the AccountNumber column for a specific TerritoryID.

```
USE AdventureWorks2012;
GO
SELECT *
FROM Sales.Customer;
```

```
USE AdventureWorks2012;
GO
SELECT AccountNumber
FROM Sales.Customer
WHERE TerritoryID=4;
```

After executing the queries, the sys.dm_db_index_usage_stats DMV is queried.

```
USE AdventureWorks2012;
GO
SELECT i.name IndexName, user_seeks, user_scans, last_user_seek, last_user_scan
FROM sys.dm_db_index_usage_stats s
INNER JOIN sys.indexes i
ON s.object_id=i.object_id
AND s.index_id=i.index_id
WHERE database_id=DB_ID('AdventureWorks2012')
AND s.object_id=OBJECT_ID('Sales.Customer');
```

This query returns the following:

```
IndexName                user_seeks  user_scans  last_user_seek           last_user_scan
-----------------------  ----------  ----------- -----------------------  -----------------------
IX_Customer_TerritoryID  1           0           2012-03-15 17:13:35.487  NULL
PK_Customer_CustomerID   0           1           NULL                     2012-03-15 17:13:34.237
```

How It Works

The sys.dm_db_index_usage_stats DMV allows you to see what indexes are being used in your SQL Server instance. The statistics are valid since the last SQL Server restart.

In this recipe, two queries were executed against the Sales.Customer table. After executing the queries, the sys.dm_db_index_usage_stats DMV was queried.

The SELECT clause displayed the name of the index, the number of user seeks and user scans, and the dates of the last user seeks and user scans.

```
SELECT i.name IndexName, user_seeks, user_scans, last_user_seek, last_user_scan
```

The FROM clause joined the sys.dm_db_index_usage_stats DMV to the sys.indexes system catalog view (so the index name could be displayed in the results) on object_id and index_id.

```
FROM sys.dm_db_index_usage_stats s INNER JOIN sys.indexes i ON
s.object_id=i.object_id AND
s.index_id=i.index_id
```

The WHERE clause qualified that only indexes for the AdventureWorks2012 database be displayed and, of those indexes, only those for the Sales.Customer table. The DB_ID function was used to get the database system ID, and the OBJECT_ID function was used to get the table's object ID.

```
WHERE database_id = DB_ID('AdventureWorks2012')
AND s.object_id = OBJECT_ID('Sales.Customer');
```

The query returned two rows, showing that the PK_Customer_CustomerID clustered index of the Sales.Customer table had indeed been scanned recently (most likely by the first SELECT * query) and the IX_Customer_TerritoryID nonclustered index had been used in the second query (which qualified TerritoryID = 4).

Indexes assist with query performance but also add disk space and data modification overhead. Using the sys.dm_db_index_usage_stats DMV, you can monitor whether indexes are actually being used and, if not, replace them with more effective indexes.

Statistics

The AUTO_CREATE_STATISTICS database option enables SQL Server to automatically generate statistical information regarding the distribution of values in a column. The AUTO_UPDATE_STATISTICS database option automatically updates existing statistics on your table or indexed view. Unless you have a *very* good reason for doing so, these options should never be disabled in your database, because they are critical for good query performance.

Statistics are critical for efficient query processing and performance, allowing SQL Server to choose the correct physical operations when generating an execution plan. Table and indexed view statistics, which can be created manually or generated automatically by SQL Server, collect information that is used by SQL Server to generate efficient query execution plans.

The next few recipes will demonstrate how to work directly with statistics. When reading these recipes, remember to let SQL Server manage the automatic creation and update of statistics in your databases whenever possible. Save most of these commands for special troubleshooting circumstances or when you've made significant data changes (for example, executing sp_updatestats right after a large data load).

23-6. Manually Creating Statistics

Problem

You have noticed that a high-use query is performing poorly. After some investigation, you have noted that AUTO_CREATE_STATISTICS and AUTO_UPDATE_STATISTICS are enabled. You are certain that new statistics are needed.

Solution

Use the CREATE STATISTICS command and create new statistics.

SQL Server will usually generate the statistics it needs based on query activity. However, if you still want to explicitly create statistics on a column or columns, you can use the CREATE STATISTICS command.

The syntax is as follows:

```
CREATE STATISTICS statistics_name ON { table | view } ( column [ ,...n ] )
[ WHERE <filter_predicate> ]
[ WITH
[ [ FULLSCAN
| SAMPLE number { PERCENT | ROWS } STATS_STREAM = stats_stream ] [ , ] ]

[ NORECOMPUTE ] ]
```

Table 23-4 describes the arguments of this command.

Table 23-4. *CREATE STATISTICS Arguments*

Argument	Description
statistics_name	This defines the name of the new statistics.
table | view	This specifies the table or indexed view from which the statistics are based.
column [,...n]	This specifies one or more columns used for generating statistics.
WHERE <filter_predicate>	Expression for filtering a subset of rows on the statistics object.
FULLSCAN| SAMPLE number { PERCENT | ROWS }	FULLSCAN, when specified, reads all rows when generating the statistics. SAMPLE reads either a defined number of rows or a defined percentage of rows.
STATS_STREAM = stats_stream	This is reserved for Microsoft's internal use.
NORECOMPUTE	This option designates that once the statistics are created, they should not be updated—even when data changes occur afterward. This option should rarely, if ever, be used. Fresh statistics allow SQL Server to generate good query plans.

In this example, new statistics are created on the Sales.Customer AccountNumber column.

```
USE AdventureWorks2012;
GO
CREATE STATISTICS Stats_Customer_AccountNumber
ON Sales.Customer (AccountNumber) WITH FULLSCAN;
```

How It Works

This recipe demonstrated manually creating statistics on the Sales.Customer table. The first line of code designated the statistics name.

```
CREATE STATISTICS Stats_Customer_AccountNumber
```

The second line of code designated the table to create statistics on, followed by the column name used to generate the statistics.

```
ON Sales.Customer (AccountNumber)
```

The last line of code designated that all rows in the table would be read in order to generate the statistics.

```
WITH FULLSCAN
```

Using the FULLSCAN option will typically take longer to generate but provide a higher-quality sampling. The default behavior in SQL Server is to use SAMPLE with an automatically determined sample size.

23-7. Creating Statistics on a Subset of Rows

Problem

You have a very large table that is frequently queried. Most of the queries performed are against a range of data that comprises less than 20 percent of the records in the table. You have determined that the indexes are appropriate, but you may be missing a statistic. You want to improve the performance of these queries.

Solution

Create filtered statistics.

In Chapter 16, in Recipe 16-17, I demonstrated the ability to create filtered, nonclustered indexes that cover a small percentage of rows. Doing this reduced the index size and improved the performance of queries that needed to read only a fraction of the index entries that they would otherwise have to process. Creating the filtered index also creates associated statistics.

These statistics use the same filter predicate and can result in more accurate results because the sampling is against a smaller row set.

You can also explicitly create filtered statistics using the CREATE STATISTICS command. Similar to creating a filtered index, filtered statistics also support filter predicates for several comparison operators to be used, including IS, IS NOT, =, <>, >, <, and more.

The following query demonstrates creating filtered statistics on a range of values for the UnitPrice column in the Sales.SalesOrderDetail table:

```
USE AdventureWorks2012;
GO
CREATE STATISTICS Stats_SalesOrderDetail_UnitPrice_Filtered ON Sales.SalesOrderDetail
(UnitPrice)
WHERE UnitPrice>= 1000.00 AND UnitPrice<= 1500.00
WITH FULLSCAN;
```

How It Works

This recipe demonstrated creating filtered statistics. Similar to filtered indexes, I just added a WHERE clause within the definition of the CREATE STATISTICS call and defined a range of allowed values for the UnitPrice column. Creating statistics on a column creates a histogram with up to 200 interval values designating how many rows are at each interval value, as well as how many rows are smaller than the current key but less than the previous key. The query optimization process depends on highly accurate statistics. Filtered statistics allow you to specify the key range of values your application focuses on, resulting in even more accurate statistics for that subset of data.

23-8. Updating Statistics

Problem

You have created some statistics on a table in your database and now want to update them immediately.

Solution

You can use the UPDATE STATISTICS command.

The syntax is as follows:

```
UPDATE STATISTICS table | view
        [
        {
        {  index | statistics_name }
        |  (  {  index |statistics_name } [ ,...n ] )
        }
        ]
        [       WITH
        [
        [  FULLSCAN ]
        |  SAMPLE number { PERCENT | ROWS }
        |  RESAMPLE
        ]
        [  ,  ]  [  ALL | COLUMNS | INDEX ]
        [  [  ,  ]  NORECOMPUTE ]
        ]
```

Table 23-5 shows the arguments of this command.

Table 23-5. *UPDATE STATISTICS Arguments*

Argument	Description
`table | view`	This defines the table name or indexed view for which to update statistics.
`{ index | statistics_name}|`	This specifies the name of the index or named statistics to update.
`FULLSCAN| SAMPLE number { PERCENT | ROWS } |RESAMPLE`	FULLSCAN, when specified, reads all rows when generating the statistics. SAMPLE reads either a defined number of rows or a percentage. RESAMPLE updates statistics based on the original sampling method.
`[ ALL | COLUMNS | INDEX ]`	When ALL is designated, all existing statistics are updated. When COLUMN is designated, only column statistics are updated. When INDEX is designated, only index statistics are updated.
`NORECOMPUTE`	This option designates that once the statistics are created, they should not be updated—even when data changes occur. Again, this option should rarely, if ever, be used. Fresh statistics allow SQL Server to generate good query plans.

This example updates all the statistics for the `Sales.Customer` table, populating statistics based on the latest data.

```
USE AdventureWorks2012;
GO
UPDATE STATISTICS Sales.Customer
WITH FULLSCAN;
```

How It Works

This example updated all the statistics for the `Sales.Customer` table, refreshing them with the latest data. The first line of code designated the table name containing the statistics to be updated.

```
UPDATE STATISTICS Sales.Customer
```

The last line of code designated that all rows in the table would be read in order to update the statistics.

```
WITH FULLSCAN
```

23-9. Generating Statistics Across All Tables

Problem

You are benchmarking new queries and do not want to wait for the query optimizer to create new single-column statistics.

Solution

Execute `sp_createstats` to create single-column statistics.

You can automatically generate statistics across all tables in a database for those columns that don't already have statistics associated with them, by using the system stored procedure sp_createstats. The syntax is as follows:

```
sp_createstats [ [ @indexonly = ] 'indexonly' ] [ , [ @fullscan = ] 'fullscan' ] [ , [
@norecompute = ] 'norecompute' ]
```

Table 23-6 describes the arguments of this command.

Table 23-6. *sp_createstats Arguments*

Argument	Description
indexonly	When indexonly is designated, only columns used in indexes will be considered for statistics creation.
fullscan	When fullscan is designated, all rows will be evaluated for the generated statistics. If not designated, the default behavior is to extract statistics via sampling.
norecompute	The norecompute option designates that once the statistics are created, they should not be updated, even when data changes occur. Like with CREATE STATISTICS and UPDATE STATISTICS, this option should rarely, if ever, be used. Fresh statistics allow SQL Server to generate good query plans.

This example demonstrates creating new statistics on columns in the database that don't already have statistics created for them.

```
USE AdventureWorks2012;
GO
EXECUTE sp_createstats;
GO
```

This returns the following (abridged) result set:

```
Table 'AdventureWorks2012.Production.ProductProductPhoto':
Creating statistics for the following columns:
        Primary
        ModifiedDate
Table 'AdventureWorks2012.Sales.StoreContact':
Creating statistics for the following columns:
        ModifiedDate
Table 'AdventureWorks2012.Person.Address':
Creating statistics for the following columns:
        AddressLine2
        City
        PostalCode
        ModifiedDate
...
```

How It Works

This example created single-column statistics for the tables within the AdventureWorks2012 database, refreshing them with the latest data.

23-10. Updating Statistics Across All Tables

Problem

You want to update statistics across all tables in the current database.

Solution

You can execute the stored procedure sp_updatestats.

If you want to update all statistics in the current database, you can use the system stored procedure sp_updatestats. This stored procedure updates statistics only when necessary (when data changes have occurred). Statistics on unchanged data will not be updated.

The next example automatically updates all statistics in the current database.

```
USE AdventureWorks2012;
GO
EXECUTE sp_updatestats;
GO
```

This returns the following (abridged) results. Notice the informational message of "update is not necessary." The results you see may differ based on the state of your table statistics.

```
Updating [Production].[ProductProductPhoto]
[PK_ProductProductPhoto_ProductID_ProductPhotoID], update is not necessary...
[AK_ProductProductPhoto_ProductID_ProductPhotoID], update is not necessary...
[_WA_Sys_00000002_01142BA1], update is not necessary...
[Primary], update is not necessary...
[ModifiedDate], update is not necessary...
0 index(es)/statistic(s) have been updated, 5 did not require update.
...
```

How It Works

This example updated statistics for the tables within the AdventureWorks2012 database, updating only the statistics where data modifications had impacted the reliability of the statistics.

23-11. Viewing Statistics Details

Problem

You want to see detailed information about column statistics.

Solution

To view detailed information about column statistics, you can use the DBCC SHOW STATISTICS command.

The syntax is as follows:

```
DBCC SHOW_STATISTICS ( 'tablename' | 'viewname' , target )
[ WITH [ NO_INFOMSGS ]
< STAT_HEADER | DENSITY_VECTOR | HISTOGRAM>[ , n ] ]
```

Table 23-7 shows the arguments of this command.

Table 23-7. *DBCC SHOW_STATISTICS Arguments*

Argument	Description
'table_name' | 'view_name'	This defines the table or indexed view to evaluate.
target	This specifies the name of the index or named statistics to evaluate.
NO_INFOMSGS	When designated, NO_INFOMSGS suppresses informational messages.
STAT_HEADER | DENSITY_VECTOR | HISTOGRAM [, n]	Specifying STAT_HEADER, DENSITY_VECTOR, or HISTOGRAM designates which result sets will be returned by the command (you can display one or more). Not designating any of these means that all three result sets will be returned.

This example demonstrates how to view the statistics information on the Sales.Customer Stats_Customer_CustomerType statistics.

```
USE AdventureWorks2012;
GO
DBCC SHOW_STATISTICS ('Sales.Customer' , Stats_Customer_AccountNumber);
```

This returns the following result sets:

Name	Updated	Rows	Rows Sampled	Steps	Density	Average key length	String Index	Filter Expression	Unfiltered Rows
Stats_Customer_AccountNumber	Apr 10 2012 12:49PM	19820	19820	152	1	10	YES	NULL	19820

All density	Average Length	Columns
5.045409E-05	10	AccountNumber

RANGE_HI_KEY	RANGE_ROWS	EQ_ROWS	DISTINCT_RANGE_ROWS	AVG_RANGE_ROWS
AW00000001	0	1	0	1
...				
AW00027042	127	1	127	1
AW00027298	255	1	255	1
AW00027426	127	1	127	1
...				
AW00030118	0	1	0	1

How It Works

This recipe demonstrated how to get more specific information about column statistics. In the results of this recipe's example, the `All density` column points to the selectivity of a column. *Selectivity* refers to the percentage of rows that will be returned given a specific column's value. Columns with a low density and high selectivity often make for useful indexes (useful to the query optimization process).

In this recipe's example, the `All density` value was 5.045409E-05 (float), which equates to a decimal value of 0.00005045409. This is the result of dividing 1 by the number of rows, in this case 19,820.

If you had a column with a high density of similar values and low selectivity (one value is likely to return many rows), you can make an educated assumption that an index on this particular column is unlikely to be very useful to SQL Server in generating a query execution plan.

23-12. Removing Statistics

Problem

You have finished a cycle in your benchmarking and want to remove statistics that were created during that cycle.

Solution

To remove statistics, use the `DROP STATISTICS` command. The syntax is as follows:

```
DROP STATISTICS table.statistics_name | view.statistics_name [ ,... n ]
```

This command allows you to drop one or more statistics, prefixed with the table or indexed view name.

In this example, the `Sales.Customer_Stats_Customer_AccountNumber` statistics are dropped from the database.

```
USE AdventureWorks2012;
GO
DROP STATISTICS Sales.Customer.Stats_Customer_AccountNumber;
```

How It Works

This recipe dropped user-created statistics using `DROP STATISTICS`. The statistics were dropped using the three-part name of `schema.table.statistics_name`.

CHAPTER 24

XML

By Wayne Sheffield

In SQL Server 2000, if you wanted to store XML data within the database, you had to store it in a character or binary format. This wasn't too troublesome if you just used SQL Server for XML document storage, but attempts to query or modify the stored document within SQL Server were not so straightforward. Introduced in SQL Server 2005, the SQL Server native xml data type helps address this issue.

Relational database designers may be concerned about this data type, and rightly so. The normalized database provides performance and data integrity benefits that put into question why we would need to store XML documents in the first place. Having an xml data type allows you to have your relational data stored alongside your unstructured data. By providing this data type, Microsoft isn't suggesting that you run your high-speed applications based on XML documents. Rather, you may find XML document storage is useful when data must be "somewhat" structured. For example, let's say your company's web site offers an online contract. This contract is available over the Web for your customer to fill out and then submit. The submitted data is stored in an xml data type. You might choose to store the submitted data in an XML document because your legal department is always changing the document's fields. Also, since this document is submitted only a few times a day, throughput is not an issue. Another good reason to use native xml data type is for "state" storage. For example, if your .NET applications use XML configuration files, you can store them in a SQL Server database in order to maintain a history of changes and as a backup/recovery option.

Caution The elements in an XML document and the XQuery methods are case sensitive, regardless of the case sensitivity of the SQL Server instance.

24-1. Creating an XML Column

Problem

You want to store an XML document in your database.

Solution

Store the document in a column with the xml data type.

```
CREATE TABLE dbo.Book
        (
         BookID INT IDENTITY PRIMARY KEY,
         ISBNNBR CHAR(13) NOT NULL,
         BookNM VARCHAR(250) NOT NULL,
```

```
        AuthorID INT NOT NULL,
        ChapterDesc XML NULL
       );
GO
```

How It Works

Native xml data types can be used as a data type for columns in a table. Data stored in the xml data type can contain an XML document or XML fragments. An *XML fragment* is an XML instance without a single top-level element for the contents to nest in. Creating an XML data type column is as easy as just using it in the table definition, as shown earlier.

The xml data type can also be used as a parameter to a procedure.

```
CREATE PROCEDURE dbo.usp_INS_Book
       @ISBNNBR CHAR(13),
       @BookNM VARCHAR(250),
       @AuthorID INT,
       @ChapterDesc XML
AS
INSERT  dbo.Book
        (ISBNNBR,
         BookNM,
         AuthorID,
         ChapterDesc)
VALUES  (@ISBNNBR,
         @BookNM,
         @AuthorID,
         @ChapterDesc);
GO
```

And it can be used as a variable in a batch.

```
DECLARE @Book XML;
SET @Book =
'
<Book name="SQL Server 2012 T-SQL Recipes">
<Chapters>
<Chapter id="1">Getting Started with SELECT</Chapter>
<Chapter id="2">Elementary Programming</Chapter>
<Chapter id="3">Nulls and Other Pitfalls</Chapter>
<Chapter id="4">Combining Data from Multiple Tables</Chapter>
</Chapters>
</Book>
';
```

In the previous example, the variable is declared and then populated with XML data. The next recipe will show you how to use the XML data in the variable.

24-2. Inserting XML Data

Problem

You want to insert XML data into an XML column in a table.

Solution

Utilize the INSERT statement to insert XML data into a column of the xml data type.

```
INSERT  dbo.Book
        (ISBNNBR,
         BookNM,
         AuthorID,
         ChapterDesc)
VALUES  ('9781430242000',
         'SQL Server 2012 T-SQL Recipes',
         55,
'<Book name="SQL Server 2012 T-SQL Recipes">
<Chapters>
<Chapter id="1">Getting Started with SELECT</Chapter>
<Chapter id="2">Elementary Programming</Chapter>
<Chapter id="3">Nulls and Other Pitfalls</Chapter>
<Chapter id="4">Combining Data from Multiple Tables</Chapter>
</Chapters>
</Book>');
```

How It Works

In this example, data is inserted directly into the table with the INSERT statement. The XML data is passed as a string, which is implicitly converted to the xml data type.

XML data can also be saved into a variable, and the variable can then be used in the INSERT statement.

```
DECLARE @Book XML;
SET @Book =
CAST('<Book name="SQL Server 2012 Fast Answers">
<Chapters>
<Chapter id="1">Installation, Upgrades... </Chapter>
<Chapter id="2">Configuring SQL Server </Chapter>
<Chapter id="3">Creating and Configuring Databases </Chapter>
<Chapter id="4">SQL Server Agent and SQL Logs </Chapter>
</Chapters>
</Book>' as XML);

INSERT  dbo.Book
        (ISBNNBR,
         BookNM,
         AuthorID,
         ChapterDesc)
VALUES  ('1590591615',
         'SQL Server 2012 Fast Answers',
         55,
         @Book);
```

In this example, the XML data is first explicitly converted to the xml data type with the CAST function and stored in a variable of the xml data type. The variable is then used in the SELECT statement to insert the data into the table.

In either example, when the string XML data is being converted to the xml data type (in the first example when being inserted into the column and in the second when being converted with the CAST function), the XML data is checked to ensure that it is well formed. means that it follows the general rules of an XML document. For example, the following code is not well formed (it is missing the closing </Book> tag):

```
DECLARE @Book XML;
SET @Book =
CAST('<Book name="SOL Server 2000 Fast Answers">
<Chapters>
<Chapter id="1">Installation, Upgrades... </Chapter>
<Chapter id="2">Configuring SQL Server </Chapter>
<Chapter id="3">Creating and Configuring Databases </Chapter>
<Chapter id="4">SQL Server Agent and SQL Logs </Chapter>
</Chapters>
' as XML);
```

When executing this code, the following error is generated:

```
Msg 9400, Level 16, State 1, Line 2
XML parsing: line 8, character 0, unexpected end of input
```

The XML column in this example is untyped. When an XML column is untyped, it means that the contents inserted into the column are not validated against an XML schema. An XML schema is used to define the allowed elements and attributes for an XML document and is discussed in the next recipe.

24-3. Validating XML Data

Problem

You want to ensure that all the elements and attributes of XML data are verified to be in accordance with an agreed upon standard.

Solution

Utilize an XML schema collection to validate that the elements, attributes, data types, and allowed values are followed in an XML document.

```
CREATE XML SCHEMA COLLECTION BookStoreCollection
AS
N'<xsd:schema  targetNamespace="http://PROD/BookStore"
               xmlns:xsd="http://www.w3.org/2001/XMLSchema"
               xmlns:sqltypes="http://schemas.microsoft.com/sqlserver/2004/sqltypes"
               elementFormDefault="qualified">
    <xsd:import  namespace="http://schemas.microsoft.com/sqlserver/2004/sqltypes"/>
    <xsd:element  name="Book">
        <xsd:complexType>
            <xsd:sequence>
                <xsd:element  name="BookName"  minOccurs="0">
                    <xsd:simpleType>
                        <xsd:restriction        base="sqltypes:varchar">
```

```
                        <xsd:maxLength  value="50"    />
                    </xsd:restriction>
                </xsd:simpleType>
            </xsd:element>
            <xsd:element  name="ChapterID"  type="sqltypes:int" minOccurs="0"    />
            <xsd:element  name="ChapterNM"  minOccurs="0">
                <xsd:simpleType>
                    <xsd:restriction        base="sqltypes:varchar">
                        <xsd:maxLength  value="50"    />
                    </xsd:restriction>
                </xsd:simpleType>
            </xsd:element>
        </xsd:sequence>
    </xsd:complexType>
  </xsd:element>
</xsd:schema>';
GO
```

How It Works

This example builds an XML schema (which is also referred to as an XML schema definition, or XSD). An XML schema defines the elements, attributes, data types, and allowed values for the XML document.

■ **Tip** For a review of XML schema fundamentals, visit the World Wide Web Consortium (W3C) standards site at `www.w3.org/TR/XMLschema-0/`.

The syntax for the `CREATE XML SCHEMA COLLECTION` statement is as follows:

```
CREATE XML SCHEMA COLLECTION [ <relational_schema>. ]sql_identifier AS Expression
```

Table 24-1 describes the arguments.

Table 24-1. *`CREATE XML SCHEMA COLLECTION` Arguments*

Argument	Description
`relational_schema`	Identifies the relational schema name. If it's not specified, the default relational schema is assumed.
`sql_identifier`	The SQL identifier for the XML schema collection.
`Expression`	A string constant or scalar variable of the varchar, varbinary, nvarchar, or xml type.

You can now create a variable that requires that the XML document adheres to this definition.

```
DECLARE @Book XML (DOCUMENT BookStoreCollection);
SET @Book =
CAST('
<Book xmlns="http://PROD/BookStore">
    <BookName>"SQL Server 2012 Fast Answers"</BookName>
```

```
    <ChapterID>1</ChapterID>
    <ChapterNM>Installation, Upgrades...</ChapterNM>
</Book>' as XML);
GO
```

Note that the <Book> tag specifies the xmlns for the default namespace of the XML schema collection. Using the keyword DOCUMENT or CONTENT with the schema collection reference lets you determine whether the allowed XML will allow only a full XML document (DOCUMENT) or XML fragments (CONTENT).

If you attempt to set this variable to XML data that does not adhere to the XML schema, an error is generated.

```
DECLARE @Book XML (DOCUMENT BookStoreCollection);
SET @Book =
CAST('
<Book xmlns="http://PROD/BookStore">
    <BookName>"SQL Server 2012 Fast Answers"</BookName>
    <ChapterID>1</ChapterID>
    <ChapterNM>Installation, Upgrades...</ChapterNM>
    <ChapterID>2</ChapterID>
    <ChapterNM>Configuring SQL Server</ChapterNM>
</Book>' as XML);
GO
```

This XML data has extra ChapterID and ChapterNM tags. Executing this code generates the following error:

```
Msg 6923, Level 16, State 1, Line 2
XML Validation: Unexpected element(s): {http://PROD/BookStore}ChapterID. Location:
/*:Book[1]/*:ChapterID[2]
```

You can also build a table with a column of the xml data type that is required to adhere to this XML schema.

```
CREATE TABLE dbo.BookInfoExport
       (
        BookID INT IDENTITY PRIMARY KEY,
        ISBNNBR CHAR(10) NOT NULL,
        BookNM VARCHAR(250) NOT NULL,
        AuthorID INT NOT NULL,
        ChapterDesc XML(BookStoreCollection) NULL
       );
```

To add additional XML schemas to an existing XML schema collection, you can use the ALTER XML SCHEMA COLLECTION statement. The syntax is as follows:

```
ALTER XML SCHEMA COLLECTION [ relational_schema. ]sql_identifier ADD 'Schema Component'
```

To remove the entire XML schema collection from the database, use the DROP XML SCHEMA COLLECTION statement. The syntax is as follows:

```
DROP XML SCHEMA COLLECTION [ relational_schema. ]sql_identifier
```

The only argument for dropping an existing XML schema collection is the name of the collection. Prior to dropping an XML schema collection, it cannot be used in any table definitions.

24-4. Verifying the Existence of XML Schema Collections

Problem

You need to determine what XML schema collections exist on a database.

Solution

Use the system catalog views `XML_schema_collections` and `XML_schema_namespaces` to retrieve information about existing XML schema collections.

```
SELECT   name
FROM     sys.XML_schema_collections
ORDER BY create_date;
```

This query returns the following result set:

```
name
-------------------
sys
BookStoreCollection
```

How It Works

The system catalog views `XML_schema_collections` and `XML_schema_namespaces` contain information about existing XML schema collections, and they can be queried to return this information. In the previous example, all of the XML schema collections for this database are returned by querying the `XML_schema_collections` system catalog view. The namespaces used by XML schema collections can be returned with the following query:

```
SELECT   n.name
FROM     sys.XML_schema_namespaces n
         INNER JOIN sys.XML_schema_collections c
             ON c.XML_collection_id = n.XML_collection_id
WHERE    c.name = 'BookStoreCollection';
```

This query returns the following result set:

```
name
---------------------
http://PROD/BookStore
```

24-5. Retrieving XML Data

Problem

You need to extract data from the XML document.

Solution

To extract data from an XML document, you would utilize one of the various XQuery methods.

```
CREATE  TABLE dbo.BookInvoice
        (
        BookInvoiceID INT IDENTITY PRIMARY  KEY,
        BookInvoiceXML XML NOT  NULL
        )
GO

INSERT  dbo.BookInvoice (BookInvoiceXML)
VALUES
('<BookInvoice  invoicenumber="1"  customerid="22"     orderdate="2008-07-01Z">
<OrderItems>
<Item  id="22"  qty="1"  name="SQL Fun in the Sun"/>
<Item  id="24"  qty="1"  name="T-SQL Crossword Puzzles"/>
</OrderItems>
</BookInvoice>'),

('<BookInvoice  invoicenumber="1"  customerid="40"  orderdate="2008-07-11Z">
<OrderItems>
<Item  id="11"  qty="1"  name="MCITP Cliff Notes"/>
</OrderItems>
</BookInvoice>'),

('<BookInvoice  invoicenumber="1"  customerid="9"  orderdate="2008-07-22Z">
<OrderItems>
<Item  id="11"  qty="1"  name=" MCITP Cliff Notes"/>
<Item  id="24"  qty="1"  name="T-SQL Crossword Puzzles"/>
</OrderItems>
</BookInvoice>');

SELECT  BookInvoiceID
FROM    dbo.BookInvoice
WHERE   BookInvoiceXML.exist('/BookInvoice/OrderItems/Item[@id=11]')=1;
```

This query returns the following result set:

```
BookInvoiceID
-------------
2
3
```

How It Works

The xml data type column can be queried and the data can be modified using XQuery methods. *XQuery* is a query language that is used to search XML documents. These XQuery methods described in Table 24-2 are integrated into SQL Server and can be used in regular Transact-SQL queries. (Data modifications using XQuery are demonstrated in the next recipe.)

Table 24-2. XQuery Methods

Method	Description
exist	Returns 1 for an XQuery expression when it evaluates to TRUE; otherwise, returns 0 for FALSE
modify	Performs updates against XML data (demonstrated after this recipe)
nodes	Shreds XML data to relational data, identifying nodes-to-row mapping
query	Returns XML results based on an XQuery expression
value	Returns a scalar SQL data type value based on an XQuery expression

■ **Tip** For an in-depth review of XQuery fundamentals, visit the World Wide Web Consortium (W3C) standards site at www.w3.org/TR/xquery/. XQuery supports iteration syntax using the `for`, `let`, `where`, `order by`, and `return` clauses (acronym FLWOR). In SQL Server 2005, `let` was not supported. SQL Server now supports `let`, starting from SQL Server 2008.

The XQuery methods are implemented as a method of the xml column. Thus, they are called in the format `(XML Column).(XQuery method)`. Additionally, as pointed out at the beginning of the chapter, these methods are case sensitive and must be used in lowercase, regardless of the case sensitivity of your SQL Server instance.

In the previous example, the `exist` method is used to find all rows from the table for purchases of the item with an ID of 11. The next example demonstrates the `nodes` method, which shreds a document into a relational rowset. A local variable is used to populate a single XML document from the `BookInvoice` table, which is then referenced using the `nodes` method. This query retrieves a document and lists the ID element of each `BookInvoice/OrderItems/Item` node.

```
DECLARE @BookInvoiceXML XML;
SELECT  @BookInvoiceXML = BookInvoiceXML
FROM    dbo.BookInvoice
WHERE   BookInvoiceID = 2;

SELECT  BookID.value('@id', 'integer') BookID
FROM    @BookInvoiceXML.nodes('/BookInvoice/OrderItems/Item') AS BookTable (BookID);
```

This query returns the following result set:

```
BookID
-----------
11
```

The next example demonstrates the `query` method, which is used to return the two-item elements from a specific XML document:

```
DECLARE @BookInvoiceXML XML;
SELECT  @BookInvoiceXML = BookInvoiceXML
FROM    dbo.BookInvoice
WHERE   BookInvoiceID = 3;
SELECT  @BookInvoiceXML.query('/BookInvoice/OrderItems');
```

This query returns the following result set:

```
<OrderItems><Item id="11" qty="1" name="MCITP Cliff Notes" /><Item id="24" qty="1"
name="T-SQL Crossword Puzzles" /></OrderItems>
```

The previous example of this recipe demonstrates the value method, which is used to find the distinct book names from the first and second items within the BookInvoiceXML xml column.

```
SELECT DISTINCT
        BookInvoiceXML.value('(/BookInvoice/OrderItems/Item/@name)[1]',
                             'varchar(30)') AS BookTitles
FROM    dbo.BookInvoice
UNION
SELECT DISTINCT
        BookInvoiceXML.value('(/BookInvoice/OrderItems/Item/@name)[2]',
                             'varchar(30)')
FROM    dbo.BookInvoice;
```

This query returns the following result set:

```
BookTitles
-----------------------
NULL
MCDBA Cliff Notes
SQL Fun in the Sun
T-SQL Crossword Puzzles
```

24-6. Modifying XML Data

Problem

You want to modify data stored in a column with the xml data type.

Solution

Utilize the XQuery modify method to update xml data.

```
SELECT BookInvoiceXML
FROM dbo.BookInvoice
WHERE BookInvoiceID=2;

UPDATE dbo.BookInvoice
SET BookInvoiceXML.modify
('insert<Item id="920" qty="1" name="SQL Server 2012 Transact-SOL Recipes"/>
into (/BookInvoice/OrderItems)[1]')
WHERE BookInvoiceID=2;

SELECT BookInvoiceXML
FROM dbo.BookInvoice
WHERE BookInvoiceID=2;
```

These queries return the following result sets:

```
BookInvoiceXML
--------------------------------------------------------------------------------------
<BookInvoice invoicenumber="1" customerid="40" orderdate="2008-07-11Z"><OrderItems><Item
id="11" qty="1" name="MCDBA Cliff Notes" /></OrderItems></BookInvoice>
BookInvoiceXML
--------------------------------------------------------------------------------------
<BookInvoice invoicenumber="1" customerid="40" orderdate="2008-07-11Z"><OrderItems><Item
id="11" qty="1" name="MCDBA Cliff Notes" /><Item id="920" qty="1" name="SQL Server 2012
Transact-SOL Recipes" /></OrderItems></BookInvoice>
```

How It Works

xml data type columns can be modified using the modify method in conjunction with the UPDATE statement, allowing you to insert, update, or delete an XML node in the xml data type column. In this example, the XQuery modify function is used to call an insert command to add a new item element into the existing XML document. The insert command inside the XQuery modify method is known as the XML DML operator; other XML DML operators are delete (which removes a node from the XML) and replace (which updates XML data).

24-7. Indexing XML Data

Problem

You want to improve the performance of queries that are selecting data from xml data-typed columns.

Solution

Add an XML index on the xml column.

```
CREATE PRIMARY XML INDEX idx_XML_Primary_Book_ChapterDESC
ON dbo.Book(ChapterDesc);
```

How It Works

XML columns can store up to 2 GB per column, per row. Because of this potentially large amount of data, querying against the XML column can cause poor query performance. You can improve the performance of queries against XML data type columns by using XML indexes. When you create the primary XML index, the XML data is persisted to a special internal table in tabular form, which allows for more efficient querying. To create an XML index, the table must first already have a clustered index defined on the primary key of the table.

XML columns can have only primary XML index defined and then up to secondary indexes (of different types described in a bit). The CREATE INDEX command is used to define XML indexes. The abridged syntax is as follows:

```
CREATE [ PRIMARY ] XML INDEX index_name ON<object>( xml_column_name ) [ USING XML INDEX
xml_index_name
[ FOR { VALUE | PATH | PROPERTY } ] ] [ WITH ( <xml_index_option>[ ,... n ] ) ][ ; ]
```

Creating an index for an XML column uses several of the same arguments as a regular table index (see Chapter 17 for more information). Table 24-3 describes the XML-specific arguments of this command.

Table 24-3. *CREATE XML INDEX Arguments*

Argument	Description
Object	This specifies the name of the table the index is being added to.
XML_column_name	This defines the name of the XML data type column.
XML_index_name	This is the unique name of the XML index.
VALUE | PATH | PROPERTY	These are arguments for secondary indexes only and relate to XQuery optimization. A VALUE secondary index is used for indexing based on imprecise paths. A PATH secondary index is used for indexing via a path and value. A PROPERTY secondary index is used for indexing based on querying node values based on a path.

In the first example shown earlier, a primary XML index is created on an xml data type column. Now that a primary XML index has been created, secondary XML indexes can be created. The following example creates a secondary value XML index:

```
CREATE XML INDEX idx_XML_Value_Book_ChapterDESC ON dbo.Book(ChapterDESC)
USING XML INDEX idx_XML_Primary_Book_ChapterDESC FOR VALUE;
```

XML indexes may look a little odd at first because you are adding secondary indexes to the same xml data type column. Adding the different types of secondary indexes helps benefit performance, based on the different types of XQuery queries you plan to execute. All in all, you can have up to four indexes on a single xml data type column: one primary and three secondary. A primary XML index must be created prior to being able to create secondary indexes. A secondary PATH index is used to enhance performance for queries that specify a path and value from the xml column using XQuery. A secondary PROPERTY index is used to enhance the performance of queries that retrieve specific node values by specifying a path using XQuery. The secondary VALUE index is used to enhance the performance of queries that retrieve data using an imprecise path (for example, for an XPath expression that employs //, which can be used to find nodes in a document no matter where they exist).

24-8. Formatting Relational Data as XML

Problem

You need to convert relational data stored in your database as an XML document.

Solution

Utilize the FOR XML clause of a SELECT statement to return an XML document from the tables and columns being selected.

```
SELECT  ShiftID,
        Name
FROM    AdventureWorks2012.HumanResources.[Shift]
FOR     XML RAW('Shift'),
            ROOT('Shifts'),
            TYPE;
```

This query returns the following result set:

```
<Shifts>
    <Shift ShiftID="1" Name="Day" />
    <Shift ShiftID="2" Name="Evening" />
    <Shift ShiftID="3" Name="Night" />
</Shifts>
```

How It Works

The FOR XML clause is included at the end of a SELECT query in order to return data in an XML format. FOR XML extends a SELECT statement by returning the relational query results in an XML format. FOR XML operates in four different modes: RAW, AUTO, EXPLICIT, and PATH. The AUTO and RAW modes allow for a quick and semi-automated formatting of the results, whereas EXPLICIT and PATH provide more control over the hierarchy of data and the assignment of elements versus attributes. FOR XML PATH, on the other hand, is an easier alternative to EXPLICIT mode for those developers who are more familiar with the XPath language.

In RAW mode, a single-row element is generated for each row in the result set, with each column in the result converted to an attribute within the element.

In this example, FOR XML RAW is used to return the results of the HumanResources.Shift table in an XML format. The TYPE option is used to return the results in the XML data type, and ROOT is used to define a top-level element where the results will be nested. The FOR XML AUTO mode creates XML elements in the results of a SELECT statement and also automatically nests the data, based on the columns in the SELECT clause. AUTO shares the same options as RAW.

In this example, Employee, Shift, and Department information is queried from the AdventureWorks2012 database, with XML AUTO automatically arranging the hierarchy of the results.

```
SELECT TOP 3
        BusinessEntityID,
        Shift.Name,
        Department.Name
FROM    AdventureWorks2012.HumanResources.EmployeeDepartmentHistory Employee
        INNER JOIN AdventureWorks2012.HumanResources.Shift Shift
            ON Employee.ShiftID = Shift.ShiftID
        INNER JOIN AdventureWorks2012.HumanResources.Department Department
            ON Employee.DepartmentID = Department.DepartmentID
ORDER BY BusinessEntityID
FOR     XML AUTO,
            TYPE;
```

This query returns the following result set:

```
<Employee BusinessEntityID="1">
    <Shift Name="Day">
       <Department Name="Executive" />
    </Shift>
</Employee>
<Employee BusinessEntityID="2">
    <Shift Name="Day">
       <Department Name="Engineering" />
    </Shift>
</Employee>
```

```
<Employee BusinessEntityID="3">
    <Shift Name="Day">
       <Department Name="Engineering" />
    </Shift>
</Employee>
```

Notice that the second INNER JOIN caused the values from the Department table to be children of the Shift table's values. The Shift element was then included as a child of the Employee element. Rearranging the order of the columns in the SELECT clause, however, impacts how the hierarchy is returned. Here's an example:

```
SELECT TOP 3
        Shift.Name,
        Department.Name,
        BusinessEntityID
FROM    AdventureWorks2012.HumanResources.EmployeeDepartmentHistory Employee
        INNER JOIN AdventureWorks2012.HumanResources.Shift Shift
            ON Employee.ShiftID=Shift.ShiftID
        INNER JOIN AdventureWorks2012.HumanResources.Department Department
            ON Employee.DepartmentID=Department.DepartmentID
ORDER BY Shift.Name,
        Department.Name,
        BusinessEntityID
FOR     XML AUTO,
            TYPE;
```

This query returns the following result set:

```
<Shift Name="Day">
   <Department Name="Document Control">
       <Employee BusinessEntityID="217" />
       <Employee BusinessEntityID="219" />
       <Employee BusinessEntityID="220" />
   </Department>
</Shift>
```

This time, the top of the hierarchy is Shift, with a child element of Department and where Employees are child elements of the Department elements.

The FOR XML EXPLICIT mode allows you more control over the XML results, letting you define whether columns are assigned to elements or attributes. The EXPLICIT parameters have the same use and meaning as for RAW and AUTO; however, EXPLICIT also makes use of , which are used to define the resulting elements and attributes. For example, the following query displays the VendorID and CreditRating columns as attributes and displays the VendorName column as an element. The column is defined after the column alias using an element name, tag number, attribute, and directive.

```
SELECT TOP 3
        1 AS Tag,
        NULL AS Parent,
        BusinessEntityID AS [Vendor!1!VendorID],
        Name AS [Vendor!1!VendorName!ELEMENT],
        CreditRating AS [Vendor!1!CreditRating]
FROM    AdventureWorks2012.Purchasing.Vendor
```

```
ORDER BY CreditRating
FOR     XML EXPLICIT,
            TYPE;
```

This query returns the following result set:

```
<Vendor VendorID="1496" CreditRating="1">
    <VendorName>Advanced Bicycles</VendorName>
</Vendor>
<Vendor VendorID="1492" CreditRating="1">
    <VendorName>Australia Bike Retailer</VendorName>
</Vendor>
<Vendor VendorID="1500" CreditRating="1">
    <VendorName>Morgan Bike Accessories</VendorName>
</Vendor>
```

The Tag column in the SELECT clause is required in EXPLICIT mode in order to produce the XML document output. Each tag number represents a constructed element. The Parent column alias is also required, providing the hierarchical information about any parent elements. The Parent column references the tag of the parent element. If the Parent column is NULL, this indicates that the element has no parent and is top-level.

The TYPE directive in the FOR XML clause of the previous query was used to return the results as a true SQL Server native xml data type, allowing you to store the results in XML or query it using XQuery.

Next, the FOR XML PATH option defines column names and aliases as XPath expressions. XPath is a language used for searching data within an XML document.

■ **Tip** For information on XPath, visit the World Wide Web Consortium (W3C) standards site at www.w3.org/TR/xpath.

FOR XML PATH uses some of the same arguments and keywords as other FOR XML variations. Where it differs, however, is in the SELECT clause, where XPath syntax is used to define elements, subelements, attributes, and data values. Here's an example:

```
SELECT  Name AS "@Territory",
        CountryRegionCode AS "@Region",
        SalesYTD
FROM    AdventureWorks2012.Sales.SalesTerritory
WHERE   SalesYTD>6000000
ORDER BY SalesYTD DESC
FOR     XML PATH('TerritorySales'),
            ROOT('CompanySales'),
            TYPE;
```

This query returns the following result set:

```
<CompanySales>
    <TerritorySales Territory="Southwest" Region="US">
        <SalesYTD>10510853.8739</SalesYTD>
    </TerritorySales>
    <TerritorySales Territory="Northwest" Region="US">
        <SalesYTD>7887186.7882</SalesYTD>
    </TerritorySales>
```

```
    <TerritorySales Territory="Canada" Region="CA">
        <SalesYTD>6771829.1376</SalesYTD>
    </TerritorySales>
</CompanySales>
```

This query returned results with a root element of CompanySales and a subelement of TerritorySales. The TerritorySales element was then attributed based on the territory and region code (both prefaced with @ in the SELECT clause). The SalesYTD, which was unmarked with XPath directives, became a subelement to TerritorySales. Using a column alias starting with @ and not containing a / is an example of an *XPath-like name*.

In this next example, the query explicitly specifies the hierarchy of the elements:

```
SELECT   Name AS "Territory",
         CountryRegionCode AS "Territory/Region",
         SalesYTD AS "Territory/Region/YTDSales"
FROM     AdventureWorks2012.Sales.SalesTerritory
WHERE    SalesYTD > 6000000
ORDER BY SalesYTD DESC
FOR      XML PATH('TerritorySales'),
             ROOT('CompanySales'),
             TYPE;
```

This query returns the following result set:

```
<CompanySales>
    <TerritorySales>
        <Territory>Southwest
            <Region>US
                <YTDSales>10510853.8739</YTDSales>
            </Region>
        </Territory>
    </TerritorySales>
    <TerritorySales>
        <Territory>Northwest
            <Region>US
                <YTDSales>7887186.7882</YTDSales>
            </Region>
        </Territory>
    </TerritorySales>
    <TerritorySales>
        <Territory>Canada
            <Region>CA
                <YTDSales>6771829.1376</YTDSales>
            </Region>
        </Territory>
    </TerritorySales>
</CompanySales>
```

The query specifies the CountryRegionCode to have an element name of Region as a subelement to the Territory element and specifies the SalesYTD to have an element name of YTDSales as a subelement to the Region element.

24-9. Formatting XML Data as Relational

Problem

You need to return parts of an XML document as relational data.

Solution

Utilize the OPENXML function to parse a document and return the selected parts as a rowset.

```
DECLARE @XMLdoc XML,
        @iDoc   INTEGER;
SET  @XMLdoc  =
'<Book  name="SQL Server 2000 Fast Answers">
    <Chapters>
        <Chapter  id="1"  name="Installation, Upgrades"/>
        <Chapter  id="2"  name="Configuring SQL Server"/>
        <Chapter  id="3"  name="Creating and Configuring Databases"/>
        <Chapter  id="4"  name="SQL Server Agent and SQL Logs"/>
    </Chapters>
</Book>';

EXECUTE sp_XML_preparedocument @iDoc OUTPUT, @XMLdoc;

SELECT Chapter, ChapterNm
FROM OPENXML(@iDoc, '/Book/Chapters/Chapter', 0)
WITH (Chapter INT '@id', ChapterNm VARCHAR(50) '@name');

EXECUTE sp_xml_removedocument @idoc;
```

This query returns the following result set:

```
Chapter     ChapterNm
-------     ---------------------------------
1           Installation, Upgrades
2           Configuring SQL Server
3           Creating and Configuring Databases
4           SQL Server Agent and SQL Logs
```

How It Works

OPENXML converts XML format to a relational form. To perform this conversion, the sp_XML_preparedocument system stored procedure is used to create an internal pointer to the XML document, which is then used with OPENXML in order to return the rowset data.

The syntax for the sp_XML_preparedocument system stored procedure is as follows:

```
sp_xml_preparedocument
hdoc
OUTPUT
[ , xmltext ]
[ , xpath_namespaces ]
```

Table 24-4 describes the arguments for this command.

Table 24-4. sp_XML_preparedocument Arguments

Argument	Description
hdoc	The handle to the newly created document.
xmltext	The original XML document. The MSXML parser parses this XML document. xmltext is a text parameter: char, nchar, varchar, nvarchar, text, ntext, or xml. The default value is NULL, in which case an internal representation of an empty XML document is created.
xpath_namespaces	Specifies the namespace declarations that are used in row and column XPath expressions in OPENXML. xpath_namespaces is a text parameter: char, nchar, varchar, nvarchar, text, ntext, or xml.

The syntax for the OPENXML command is as follows:

```
OPENXML(idoc ,rowpattern, flags)
[WITH (SchemaDeclaration | TableName)]
```

Table 24-5 shows the arguments for this command.

Table 24-5. OPENXML Arguments

Argument	Description
idoc	This is the internal representation of the XML document as represented by the sp_XML_preparedocument system stored procedure.
rowpattern	This defines the XPath pattern used to return nodes from the XML document.
flags	When the flag 0 is used, results default to attribute-centric mappings. When flag 1 is used, attribute-centric mapping are used. If combined with XML_ELEMENTS, then attribute-centric mapping is applied first and then element-centric mapping for columns that are not processed. Flag 2 uses element-centric mapping. If combined with XML_ATTRIBUTES, then attribute-centric mapping is applied first and then element-centric mapping for columns that are not processed. Flag 8 specifies that consumed data should not be copied to the overflow property @mp:xmltext. This flag can be combined with XML_ATTRIBUTES or XML_ELEMENTS, and when specified then they are combined with a logical OR.
SchemaDeclaration | TableName	SchemaDeclaration defines the output of the column name (rowset name), column type (valid data type), column pattern (optional XPath pattern), and optional metadata properties (about the XML nodes). If Tablename is used instead, a table must already exist for holding the rowset data.

In this example, the XML document is stored in an XML data typed variable. The document is then passed to the `sp_XML_preparedocument` system stored procedure, and the document handle is returned.

Next, a `SELECT` statement calls the `OPENXML` function, passing the XML document handle returned from the `sp_XML_preparedocument` system stored procedure for the first parameter and the XPath expression of the node to be queried in the second parameter. For the `flags` parameter, a 0 is passed in, specifying to use attribute-centric mappings. The `WITH` clause defines the actual result output. Two columns are defined: the chapter and the chapter name (`Chapter` and `ChapterNm`). For the column definitions, the column name, the data type, and the attribute from the XML document that will be used for this column are specified.

Finally, the `sp_xml_removedocument` system stored procedure is called, which removes the internal representation of the XML document specified by the document handle and invalidates the document handle.

■ **Note** A parsed XML document is stored in the internal cache of SQL Server, and it uses one-eighth of the total memory available for SQL Server. `sp_xml_removedocument` should be run to free up the memory used by this parsed XML document.

CHAPTER 25

Files, Filegroups, and Integrity

by Wayne Sheffield

Every database has a minimum of two files associated with it: the data file and the log file. However, sometimes you may want to add more files (of either type) to the database, increase their size, move them to a different drive, or perform other file-level activities. And once you have all the files on your databases placed and sized appropriately, you will need to perform regular maintenance activities on them to ensure that their integrity does not become compromised. This chapter will show you how to perform these activities.

This chapter assumes that you have three disk drives (N, O, and P) with a directory named Apress on each and that you perform each recipe in order. These drives will each need 250MB free space to perform the recipes. The following database is created utilizing these drives and directories:

```
CREATE DATABASE BookStoreArchive
ON PRIMARY
(NAME = 'BookStoreArchive',
 FILENAME = 'N:\Apress\BookStoreArchive.MDF',
 SIZE = 3MB,
 MAXSIZE = UNLIMITED,
 FILEGROWTH = 10MB)
LOG ON
(NAME = 'BookStoreArchive_log',
 FILENAME = 'P:\Apress\BookStoreArchive_log.LDF',
 SIZE = 512KB,
 MAXSIZE = UNLIMITED,
 FILEGROWTH = 512KB);
```

Tip I created these drives on my system by using Disk Management to create three VHD drives and assigned the new drives to the appropriate drive letter.

25-1. Adding a Data File or a Log File

Problem

You need to add a data file and transaction log file to your database.

Solution

Utilize the ALTER DATABASE statement to add new files to a database.

```
ALTER DATABASE BookStoreArchive
ADD FILE
( NAME = 'BookStoreArchive2',
FILENAME = 'O:\Apress\BookStoreArchive2.NDF' ,
SIZE = 1MB ,
MAXSIZE = 10MB,
FILEGROWTH = 1MB )
TO FILEGROUP [PRIMARY];

ALTER DATABASE BookStoreArchive
ADD LOG FILE
( NAME = 'BookStoreArchive2Log',
FILENAME = 'P:\Apress\BookStoreArchive2_log.LDF' ,
SIZE = 1MB ,
MAXSIZE = 5MB,
FILEGROWTH = 1MB );
GO
```

How It Works

Once a database is created, assuming you have available disk space, you can add data files or transaction log files to it as needed. This allows you to expand to new drives if the current physical drive/array is close to filling up or if you are looking to improve performance by spreading I/O across multiple drives. It usually makes sense to add additional data and log files to a database only if you plan on putting these files on a separate drive/array. Putting multiple files on the same drive/array doesn't improve performance and may benefit you only if you plan on performing separate file or filegroup backups for a very large database.

Adding files doesn't require you to bring the database offline. The syntax for ALTER DATABASE for adding a data or transaction log file is as follows:

```
ALTER DATABASE database_name {ADD FILE <filespec> [ , ... n ]
[ TO FILEGROUP { filegroup_name | DEFAULT } ] ADD LOG FILE <filespec> [ , ... n ] }
```

Table 25-1 describes the syntax arguments.

Table 25-1. *ALTER DATABASE...ADD FILE Arguments*

Argument	Description
database_name	Defines the name of the existing database.
<filespec> [, ... n]	Designates one or more explicitly defined data files to add to the database.
filegroup_name | DEFAULT	Designates the logical name of the filegroup. If followed by the DEFAULT keyword, this filegroup will be the default filegroup of the database (meaning all objects will by default be created there).
[LOG ON { <filespec> [, ... n] }]	Designates one or more explicitly defined transaction log files for the database.

In this recipe, a new data and transaction log file are added to the BookStoreArchive database. To add the data file, the ALTER DATABASE statement is used with the ADD FILE argument, followed by the file specification.

```
ALTER DATABASE BookStoreArchive ADD FILE
```

The filegroup where the new file is added is specified using the TO FILEGROUP clause, followed by the filegroup name in brackets.

```
TO FILEGROUP [PRIMARY]
```

In the second query in the recipe, a new transaction log file is added using the ALTER DATABASE statement and the ADD LOG FILE argument.

```
ALTER DATABASE BookStoreArchive ADD LOG FILE
```

Neither file addition requires the database to be offline.

25-2. Removing a Data File or a Log File

Problem

You need to remove a data or transaction log file from a database.

Solution

Utilize the ALTER DATABASE statement to remove data or transaction log files from a database.

```
ALTER DATABASE BookStoreArchive REMOVE FILE BookStoreArchive2;
```

Running this command produces the following message:

```
The file 'BookStoreArchive2' has been removed.
```

How It Works

The ALTER DATABASE statement removes the specified logical file name from the database. You might want to do this if you are relocating a database from one drive to another by creating a new file on the one drive and then dropping the old file.

The syntax for dropping a file is as follows:

```
ALTER DATABASE database_name
REMOVE FILE logical_file_name
```

where database_name is the name of an existing database, and logical_file_name is the name of the logical file to be removed from the database.

The logical file being removed must be empty (no data and no active transactions), and it cannot be the primary data or primary transaction log file. You can use DBCC SHRINKFILE with the EMPTYFILE parameter to empty a file and move any data within it to another file.

25-3. Relocating a Data File or a Log File

Problem

You need to move a data or transaction log file from one physical location to another, for example, from one drive to another.

Solution

Utilize the ALTER DATABASE statement to move data or transaction log files belonging to a database.

```
ALTER DATABASE BookStoreArchive
MODIFY FILE
(NAME = 'BookStoreArchive', FILENAME = 'O:\Apress\BookStoreArchive.mdf')
GO
```

Upon executing this statement, the following message is returned:

```
The file "BookStoreArchive" has been modified in the system catalog. The new path will be used
the next time the database is started.
```

How It Works

The ALTER DATABASE statement updates the specified logical file name to a new file name. As the returned message indicates, this new path will be used when the database is next started. This can occur by stopping/starting the SQL Server instance or by taking the database offline and then back online. After the SQL Server instance has been shut down or the database has been taken offline, you will have to move this file to its new location before starting up the SQL Server instance or bringing the database back online. The database can be taken offline, and brought back online, with the following commands:

```
USE master;
GO
ALTER DATABASE BookStoreArchive SET RESTRICTED_USER WITH ROLLBACK IMMEDIATE;
GO
ALTER DATABASE BookStoreArchive SET OFFLINE;
GO
-- Move BookStoreArchive.mdf file from N:\Apress\ to O:\Apress now.
-- On my Windows 7 PC, I had to use Administrator access to move the file.
-- On other operating systems, you may have to modify file/folder permissions
-- to prevent an access denied error.



USE master;
GO
ALTER DATABASE BookStoreArchive SET ONLINE;
GO
ALTER DATABASE BookStoreArchive SET MULTI_USER WITH ROLLBACK IMMEDIATE;
GO
```

The ALTER DATABASE BookStoreArchive SET RESTRICTED_USER WITH ROLLBACK IMMEDIATE; statement sets the database to where only users that are members of the db_owner database role, or the db_creator or sysadmin server roles, can connect to the database. Any statements currently being run by other connections are canceled and rolled back. The database is then taken offline.

After the database file has been physically moved to its new location, the database is brought back online, and then the database is opened back up to all users.

25-4. Changing a File's Logical Name

Problem

You need to change the logical name of a file in a database.

Solution

Utilize the ALTER DATABASE statement to rename the logical name of a file belonging to a database.

```
SELECT name
FROM   sys.database_files;

ALTER DATABASE BookStoreArchive
MODIFY FILE
(NAME = 'BookStoreArchive',
NEWNAME = 'BookStoreArchive_Data');

SELECT name
FROM   sys.database_files;
```

This statement returns the following message and result set:

```
name
---------------------------------------------------
BookStoreArchive
BookStoreArchive_log
BookStoreArchive2Log

The file name 'BookStoreArchive_Data' has been set.
name
---------------------------------------------------
BookStoreArchive_Data
BookStoreArchive_log
BookStoreArchive2Log
```

How It Works

The ALTER DATABASE statement allows you to change the logical name of a file belonging to the database without taking the database offline. The logical name of a database doesn't affect the functionality of the database itself, allowing you to change the name for consistency and naming convention purposes. For example, if you restore a database from a backup using a new database name, you may want the logical name to match the new database name.

The syntax of the ALTER DATABASE statement to change the logical name is as follows:

```
ALTER DATABASE database_name
MODIFY FILE
(NAME = logical_file_name, NEWNAME = new_logical_name);
```

where database_name is the name of an existing database, logical_file_name is the logical name of the file to be renamed, and new_logical_name is the new logical file name.

25-5. Increasing the Size of a Database File

Problem

You have a scheduled downtime for your database. During this downtime, you want to increase its size to prevent autogrowth operations until your next scheduled downtime.

Solution

Utilize the ALTER DATABASE statement to increase the size of a file belonging to a database.

```
SELECT name, size FROM BookStoreArchive.sys.database_files;

ALTER DATABASE BookStoreArchive
MODIFY FILE
(NAME = 'BookStoreArchive_Data',
 SIZE = 5MB);

SELECT name, size FROM BookStoreArchive.sys.database_files;
```

This statement returns the following result sets:

```
name                   size
---------------------- ----
BookStoreArchive_Data  384
BookStoreArchive_log   64
BookStoreArchive2Log   128

name                   size
---------------------- ----
BookStoreArchive_Data  640
BookStoreArchive_log   64
BookStoreArchive2Log   128
```

How It Works

The MODIFY FILE clause of the ALTER DATABASE statement allows you to increase the size of a file. In the previous example, the size of the BookStoreArchive_Data file is changed from 3MB to 5MB. If you specify the same file size, or lower, you will receive this error message:

```
Msg 5039, Level 16, State 1, Line 1
MODIFY FILE failed. Specified size is less than or equal to current size.
```

> ■ **Note** The size column of the `sys.databases_files` system view reports the quantity of 8KB pages.

The syntax of the ALTER DATABASE statement to increase a file size is as follows:

```
ALTER DATABASE database_name
MODIFY FILE
(
NAME = logical_file_name
[ , SIZE = size [ KB | MB | GB | TB ] ]
[ , MAXSIZE = { max_size [ KB | MB | GB | TB ]
UNLIMITED } ]
[ , FILEGROWTH = growth_increment [ KB | MB | % ] ]
)
```

Table 25-2 shows the arguments of this syntax.

Table 25-2. *ALTER DATABASE...MODIFY FILE Arguments*

Argument	Description
`database_name`	The name of the existing database.
`logical_file_name`	The logical file name to change size or growth options for.
`size [ KB | MB | GB | TB ]`	The new size (must be larger than the existing size) of the file based on the sizing attribute of choice (kilobytes, megabytes, gigabytes, terabytes).
`{ max_size [ KB | MB | GB | TB ] | UNLIMITED } ]`	The new maximum allowable size of the file based on the chosen sizing attributes. If UNLIMITED is chosen, the file can grow to the available space of the physical drive.
`growth_increment [ KB | MB | % ] ]`	The new amount that the file size increases when space is required. You can designate either the number of kilobytes or megabytes or the percentage of existing file size to grow. If you select 0, file growth will not occur.

25-6. Adding a Filegroup

Problem

You want to add a new filegroup to your database.

Solution

Utilize the ALTER DATABASE statement to add a filegroup to a database.

```
ALTER DATABASE BookStoreArchive
ADD FILEGROUP FG2;
GO
```

How It Works

The ALTER DATABASE is utilized to add a filegroup to a database. The syntax is as follows:

```
ALTER DATABASE database_name
ADD FILEGROUP filegroup_name
```

where database_name is the name of an existing database, and filegroup_name is the name of the new filegroup being added.

You might want to add a new filegroup for a multitude of reasons. Some of these include the following:

- Putting read-only tables into a read-only filegroup.
- Moving data that must be restored first into a separate file group in order to bring your application back up faster in the event of a disaster. Filegroups can be backed up and restored individually. This may enable your core business functions to get back online faster while the restoration of other filegroups proceeds.
- Relocating the database for disk maintenance.

25-7. Adding a File to a Filegroup

Problem

You want to add a new file to a filegroup.

Solution

Utilize the ALTER DATABASE statement to add a new file to a specified filegroup.

```
ALTER DATABASE BookStoreArchive
ADD FILE
( NAME = 'BW2',
FILENAME = 'N:\Apress\FG2_BookStoreArchive.NDF' ,
SIZE = 1MB ,
MAXSIZE = 50MB,
FILEGROWTH = 5MB )
TO FILEGROUP [FG2];
```

How It Works

Just like in Recipe 25-1, this adds a new file to the database. The difference is the specification of the filegroup that the file should be added to. Without this specification, the file would be added to the default filegroup.

25-8. Setting the Default Filegroup

Problem

You want to change which filegroup will have new tables added to the files in a filegroup.

Solution

Utilize the `ALTER DATABASE` statement to make a filegroup the default filegroup for a database.

```
ALTER DATABASE BookStoreArchive
MODIFY FILEGROUP FG2 DEFAULT;
GO
```

This query returns the following message:

```
The filegroup property 'DEFAULT' has been set.
```

How It Works

The `ALTER DATABASE` statement is used to set the default filegroup for a database. The default filegroup is the filegroup to which new objects will be built in if a filegroup is not specified. Only one filegroup can be the default filegroup at any point in time. The syntax for this statement is as follows:

```
ALTER DATABASE database_name
MODIFY FILEGROUP filegroup_name DEFAULT
```

where `database_name` is the name of an existing database, and `filegroup_name` is the name of an existing filegroup within the specified database.

25-9. Adding Data to a Specific Filegroup

Problem

You want to add a new table to a specific filegroup.

Solution

In the `CREATE TABLE` statement, specify the filegroup that the table is to be added to.

```
CREATE TABLE dbo.Test
       (
         TestID INT IDENTITY,
         Column1 INT,
         Column2 INT,
         Column3 INT
       )
ON     [FG2];
```

How It Works

The ON clause specifies the partition scheme or filegroup that the table will be built in.

■ **Note** If the CREATE TABLE statement also specifies the creation of a clustered index on a different partition or filegroup, the specification of the clustered index has precedence.

25-10. Moving Data to a Different Filegroup

Problem

You need to remove a table from one filegroup and place it on a different filegroup.

Solution #1

If the table does not have a clustered index, add a clustered index or constraint to the table, specifying the new filegroup.

```
ALTER TABLE dbo.Test
 ADD CONSTRAINT PK_Test PRIMARY KEY CLUSTERED (TestId)
 ON [PRIMARY];
```

Solution #2

If the table does have a clustered index that is enforcing a constraint, drop and re-create the clustered constraint, specifying the new filegroup.

```
CREATE TABLE dbo.Test2
       (
         TestID INT IDENTITY
                    CONSTRAINT PK__Test2 PRIMARY KEY CLUSTERED,
         Column1 INT,
         Column2 INT,
         Column3 INT
       )
ON     [FG2];
GO

ALTER TABLE dbo.Test2
DROP CONSTRAINT PK__Test2;

ALTER TABLE dbo.Test2
ADD CONSTRAINT PK__Test2 PRIMARY KEY CLUSTERED (TestId)
ON [PRIMARY];
```

Solution #3

If the table has a clustered index that is not enforcing a constraint, rebuild the index with the DROP EXISTING clause and specify the file group that it should be moved to.

```
CREATE TABLE dbo.Test3
       (
         TestID INT IDENTITY,
         Column1 INT,
         Column2 INT,
         Column3 INT
       )
ON     [FG2];
GO

CREATE CLUSTERED INDEX IX_Test3 ON dbo.Test3 (TestId)
ON [FG2];
GO

CREATE CLUSTERED INDEX IX_Test3 ON dbo.Test3 (TestId)
WITH (DROP_EXISTING = ON)
ON [PRIMARY];
GO
```

How It Works

Since a clustered index contains, at the leaf level, all the data for the table, moving the clustered index to a different filegroup moves the table to the new filegroup. In the same manner, adding a clustered index to a table without one will move the data from the table into the clustered index to the filegroup as specified by the index. If the clustered index is enforcing a constraint, the constraint will need to be dropped and re-created to move the table; you can rebuild an index on a constraint only if everything about the new index is identical to the current index and the filegroup that the index is on is being changed. If this is the only method available to you, you should do this during a maintenance period so that you can ensure that data won't be entered that would violate the constraint.

In the first solution, the dbo.Test table does not have a clustered index, so one is created on it with the ALTER TABLE statement, specifying the filegroup to put the index on. Creating the clustered index on a different filegroup moves the table to the other filegroup.

In the second solution, a new table is created on filegroup FG2 with a clustered index on a primary key constraint. To move this table, the constraint is first dropped with the ALTER TABLE statement, creating a table without any clustered index. The clustered primary key constraint is then re-created on the desired filegroup, moving the table to that filegroup.

In the third solution, a table and a clustered index are created on FG2. Since the clustered index is not enforcing a constraint, this table can be moved to the new filegroup by utilizing the CREATE INDEX statement and by specifying the DROP_EXISTING = ON clause and the filegroup to put the index on.

■ **Tip** For more information on utilizing the ALTER TABLE statement, see Chapter 15. For more information on utilizing indexes and the CREATE INDEX statement, see Chapter 18.

25-11. Removing a Filegroup

Problem

You want to remove an empty filegroup from your database.

Solution

Utilize the ALTER DATABASE statement to remove filegroups from a database.

```
ALTER DATABASE BookStoreArchive
MODIFY FILEGROUP [PRIMARY] DEFAULT;
GO

ALTER DATABASE BookStoreArchive
REMOVE FILE BW2;
GO

ALTER DATABASE BookStoreArchive
REMOVE FILEGROUP FG2;
GO
```

These statements return the following messages:

```
The filegroup property 'DEFAULT' has been set.
The file 'BW2' has been removed.
The filegroup 'FG2' has been removed.
```

How It Works

To remove a filegroup, it cannot contain any files within it. Furthermore, you cannot remove the last file from the default filegroup. Therefore, the first ALTER DATABASE statement is necessary to change the default filegroup back to the PRIMARY filegroup. Since the filegroup name PRIMARY is a keyword, it must be enclosed in brackets. The second ALTER DATABASE statement removes the empty file from the filegroup (see Recipe 25-2). The third ALTER DATABASE statement removes the filegroup. The syntax is as follows:

```
ALTER DATABASE database_name
REMOVE FILEGROUP filegroup_name
```

where database_name is the name of the existing database, and filegroup_name is the name of the existing and empty filegroup to be removed.

25-12. Making a Database or a Filegroup Read-Only

Problem #1

You have historical data in your database that cannot have any modifications made to it. However, the data needs to be available for querying.

Problem #2

You entire database contains historical data, and it cannot have any modifications made to it. However, the data needs to be available for querying.

Solution #1

Move the historical data to a separate filegroup, and then set the filegroup to be read-only.

```
ALTER DATABASE BookStoreArchive SET RESTRICTED_USER WITH ROLLBACK IMMEDIATE;
GO

ALTER DATABASE BookStoreArchive
ADD FILEGROUP FG3;
GO

ALTER DATABASE BookStoreArchive
ADD FILE
( NAME = 'ArchiveData',
FILENAME = 'N:\Apress\BookStoreArchiveData.NDF' ,
SIZE = 1MB ,
MAXSIZE = 10MB,
FILEGROWTH = 1MB )
TO FILEGROUP [FG3];
GO
-- move historical tables to this filegroup

ALTER DATABASE BookStoreArchive
MODIFY FILEGROUP FG3 READ_ONLY;
GO

ALTER DATABASE BookStoreArchive SET MULTI_USER;
GO
```

Solution #2

Since the entire database consists of the historical data, you can set the entire database to READ_ONLY with this statement:

```
ALTER DATABASE BookStoreArchive SET READ_ONLY;
GO
```

How It Works

In Solution #1, a new filegroup is created on this database, and a file is added to this filegroup. You would then move the archived data into this filegroup. Finally, you set the filegroup to READ_ONLY. In changing the status of the filegroup, you cannot have other users in the database, so the database is first set to only allow restricted users in before these actions, and once all work has been finished, it is opened back up to all users. The filegroup can be set back to a read-write status by executing this statement (after setting it to restricted users again).

```
ALTER DATABASE BookStoreArchive
MODIFY FILEGROUP FG3 READ_ONLY;
```

In Solution #2, the entire database is set to a READ_ONLY status. You can set it back to a read-write status with this statement:

```
ALTER DATABASE BookStoreArchive SET READ_WRITE;
```

25-13. Viewing Database Space Usage

Problem

You need to know how much space is being used by the objects in the database.

Solution #1

Utilize the sp_spaceused stored procedure to obtain information about space usage within the database and transaction log.

```
EXECUTE sp_spaceused;
```

Executing the sp_spaceused stored procedure without any parameters returns the following result set:

```
database_name     database_size      unallocated space
----------------- ------------------ ------------------
BookStoreArchive  7.50 MB            3.88 MB

reserved           data               index_size         unused
------------------ ------------------ ------------------ ------
2168 KB            824 KB             1128 KB            216 KB
```

Solution #2

Utilize the sp_spaceused stored procedure to obtain information about space usage for a specific object within a database.

```
EXECUTE sp_spaceused 'dbo.test';
```

Executing the sp_spaceused stored procedure with an object name returns the following result set:

```
name      rows   reserved           data               index_size         unused
--------- ------ ------------------ ------------------ ------------------ ------
Test      0      0 KB               0 KB               0 KB               0 KB
```

Solution #3

Utilize DBCC_SQLPERF to obtain space used information about all transaction logs on your SQL Server instance.

```
DBCC SQLPERF(LOGSPACE);
```

Executing this returns the following result set (results will contain a row for each database on your SQL Server instance that this command is being run on):

```
Database Name       Log Size (MB)  Log Space Used (%)  Status
------------------  -------------  ------------------  ------
master              0.9921875      45.52165            0
tempdb              0.4921875      85.71429            0
model               0.4921875      91.76588            0
msdb                0.7421875      48.02632            0
AdventureWorks2012  12.05469       14.25794            0
BookStoreArchive    1.484375       38.94737            0

DBCC execution completed. If DBCC printed error messages, contact your system administrator.
```

How It Works

The sp_spaceused system stored procedure returns information about the specified object, including the number of rows in the object, how much space the data and indexes are using, and unused space. If an object isn't specified, the information returned is about the database: the size, unallocated space, data space, index space, and unused space. The syntax for this procedure is as follows:

```
sp_spaceused [[ (@objname = ] 'objname' ]
[,[ (@updateusage = ] 'updateusage' ]
```

Table 25-3 describes the parameters of this procedure.

***Table 25-3.** sp_spaceused Parameters*

Parameter	Description
'objname'	This parameter defines the optional object name (table, for example) to view space usage. If not designated, the entire database's space usage information is returned.
'updateusage'	This parameter is used with a specific object and accepts either true or false. If true, DBCC UPDATEUSAGE is used to update space usage information in the system tables.

In Solution #3, DBCC SQLPERF is used to obtain transaction log space usage statistics for all databases. (It can also be used to reset wait and latch statistics.) The syntax for DBCC SOLPERF is as follows:

```
DBCC SQLPERF
(
     [ LOGSPACE ]
     |
     [ "sys.dm_os_latch_stats" , CLEAR ]
     |
     [ "sys.dm_os_wait_stats" , CLEAR ]
)
   [WITH NO_INFOMSGS ]
```

Table 25-4 briefly describes this DBCC command's arguments.

Table 25-4. *DBCC SQLPERF Arguments*

Parameter	Description
LOGSPACE	Returns the current size of the transaction log and the percentage of log space used for each database. You can use this information to monitor the amount of space used in a transaction log.
"sys.dm_os_latch_stats", CLEAR	Resets the last statistics. For more information, see sys.dm_os_latch_stats.
"sys.dm_os_wait_stats", CLEAR	Resets the wait statistics. For more information, see sys.dm_os_wait_stats.
WITH NO_INFOMSGS	When included in the command, WITH NO_INFOMSGS suppresses informational messages from the DBCC output that have severity levels from 0 through 10.

25-14. Shrinking the Database or a Database File

Problem

You need to shrink one database file or the entire database.

Solution #1

Utilize DBCC SHRINKDATABASE to shrink an entire database. We will first expand some of the files in the database, and then we will use DBCC SHRINKDATABASE to shrink all of the files in the database (we will use sp_spaceused to show the information before and after executing DBCC SHRINKDATABASE).

```
ALTER DATABASE BookStoreArchive
MODIFY FILE (NAME = 'BookStoreArchive_log', SIZE = 100MB);

ALTER DATABASE BookStoreArchive
MODIFY FILE (NAME = 'BookStoreArchive_Data', SIZE = 200MB);
GO

USE BookStoreArchive;
GO
```

```
EXECUTE sp_spaceused;
GO

DBCC SHRINKDATABASE ('BookStoreArchive', 10);
GO

EXECUTE sp_spaceused;
GO
```

These statements produce the following results sets and messages:

```
database_name    database_size      unallocated space
---------------- ------------------ -----------------
BookStoreArchive 302.00 MB          198.88 MB

reserved     data         index_size     unused
--------     ------       ----------     ------
2168 KB      824 KB       1128 KB        216 KB

DbId  FileId      CurrentSize MinimumSize UsedPages   EstimatedPages
---- ----------- ----------- ----------- ----------- --------------
10    1           384         384         272         272
10    2           1656        64          1656        64
10    4           128         128         128         128

DBCC execution completed. If DBCC printed error messages, contact your system administrator.

database_name    database_size      unallocated space
---------------- ------------------ -----------------
BookStoreArchive 17.94 MB           1.88 MB

reserved     data         index_size     unused
--------     ------       ----------     -------
2168 KB      824 KB       1128 KB        216 KB
```

Solution #2

Utilize DBCC SHRINKFILE to shrink one file in the database. Here we will expand one file in the database and then use DBCC SHRINKFILE to shrink that file. Again, we will use sp_spaceused to view the database space information before and after shrinking the file.

```
ALTER DATABASE BookStoreArchive
MODIFY FILE (NAME = 'BookStoreArchive_Log', SIZE = 200MB);
GO

USE BookStoreArchive;
GO

EXECUTE sp_spaceused;
GO
```

```
DBCC SHRINKFILE ('BookStoreArchive_Log', 2);
GO

EXECUTE sp_spaceused;
GO
```

These statements produce the following result sets and messages:

```
database_name    database_size      unallocated space
---------------- ------------------ ------------------
BookStoreArchive 204.19 MB          1.07 MB

reserved      data         index_size     unused
--------      ------       ----------     -------
2168 KB       824 KB       1128 KB        216 KB

DbId   FileId      CurrentSize MinimumSize UsedPages   EstimatedPages
------ ----------- ----------- ----------- ----------- --------------
10     2           1656        64          1656        64

DBCC execution completed. If DBCC printed error messages, contact your system administrator.

database_name    database_size      unallocated space
---------------- ------------------ ------------------
BookStoreArchive 17.13 MB           1.07 MB

reserved      data         index_size     unused
--------      ------       ----------     -------
2168 KB       824 KB       1128 KB        216 KB
```

How It Works

DBCC SHRINKDATABASE shrinks the data and log files in your database. In the first example, data and log files are both increased to a larger size. After that, the DBCC SHRINKDATABASE command is used to reduce it down to a target free-space size of 10 percent.

```
DBCC SHRINKDATABASE (BookStoreArchive, 10)
```

After execution, the command returns a result set showing the current size (in 8KB pages), minimum size (in 8KB pages), currently used 8KB pages, and estimated 8KB pages that SQL Server could shrink the file down to.

The syntax for DBCC SHRINKDATABASE is as follows:

```
DBCC SHRINKDATABASE
( 'database_name' | database_id | 0
[ ,target_percent ]
[ , { NOTRUNCATE | TRUNCATEONLY } ] ) [ WITH NO_INFOMSGS ]
```

Table 25-5 describes the arguments for this command.

Table 25-5. *DBCC SHRINKDATABASE Arguments*

Argument	Description
`'database_name' | database_id | 0`	You can designate a specific database name to shrink the system database ID or, if 0 is specified, the current database your query session is connected to.
`target_percent`	The target percentage designates the free space remaining in the database file after the shrinking event.
`NOTRUNCATE | TRUNCATEONLY`	NOTRUNCATE performs the data movements needed to create free space but retains the freed space in the file without releasing it to the operating system. If NOTRUNCATE is not designated, the free file space is released to the operating system. TRUNCATEONLY frees up space without relocating data within the files. If not designated, data pages are reallocated within the files to free up space, which can lead to extensive I/O.
`WITH NO_INFOMSGS`	This argument prevents informational messages from being returned from the DBCC command.

In the second solution, one of the log files is increased to a larger size. This time, the DBCC SHRINKFILE command is used to shrink that individual file down to a specified size (in megabytes).

```
DBCC SHRINKFILE ('BookStoreArchive_Log', 2);
```

The syntax for DBCC SHRINKFILE is as follows:

```
DBCC SHRINKFILE (
{ ' file_name ' | file_id }
{ [ , EMPTYFILE]
| [ [ , target_size ] [ , { NOTRUNCATE | TRUNCATEONLY } ] ]
} ) [ WITH NO_INFOMSGS ]
```

Table 25-6 describes the arguments for this command.

Table 25-6. *DBCC SHRINKFILE Arguments*

Argument	Description
' file_name ' | file_id	This option defines the specific logical file name or file ID to shrink.
EMPTYFILE	This argument moves all data off the file so that it can be dropped using ALTER DATABASE and REMOVE FILE.
target_size	This option specifies the free space to be left in the database file (in megabytes). Leaving this blank instructs SQL Server to free up space to the default file size.
NOTRUNCATE | TRUNCATEONLY	NOTRUNCATE relocates allocated pages from within the file to the front of the file but does not free the space to the operating system. Target size is ignored when used with NOTRUNCATE. TRUNCATEONLY causes unused space in the file to be released to the operating system but does so only with free space found at the end of the file. No pages are rearranged or relocated. Target size is also ignored with the TRUNCATEONLY option. Use this option if you must free up space on the database file with minimal impact on database performance (rearranging pages on an actively utilized production database can cause performance issues, such as slow query response time).
WITH NO_INFOMSGS	This argument prevents informational messages from being returned from the DBCC command.

This command shrinks the physical file by removing inactive virtual log files. The transaction log for any database is managed as a set of *virtual log files (VLFs)*. VLFs are created when the transaction log is created or undergoes expansion, and the quantity and size of the new VLFs are based upon the size of the growth of the transaction log file, with a minimum size of 256KB.

Within the transaction log is the "active" logical portion of the log. This is the area of the transaction log containing active transactions. This active portion does not usually match the physical bounds of the file but will instead "round-robin" from VLF to VLF. Once a VLF no longer contains active transactions, it can be marked as reusable through a BACKUP LOG operation or automated system truncation, which makes the VLFs available for new log records.

It needs to be pointed out that when SQL Server talks about truncating the transaction log, the transaction log is not actually truncated; the process will mark zero or more VLFs as reusable. This is an example of misused verbiage in SQL Server documentation.

DBCC SHRINKFILE or DBCC SHRINKDATABASE will make its best effort to remove inactive VLFs from the end of the physical file. SQL Server will also attempt to add "dummy" rows to push the active logical log toward the beginning of the physical file—so sometimes issuing a BACKUP LOG after the first execution of the DBCC SHRINKFILE command and then issuing the DBCC SHRINKFILE command again will allow you to free up the originally requested space.

Database files, when autogrowth is enabled, can expand because of index rebuilds or data modification activity. You may have extra space in the database because of those data modifications and index rebuilds. If you don't need to free up the unused space, you should allow the database to keep it reserved. However, if you do need the unused space and want to free it up, use DBCC SHRINKDATABASE or DBCC SHRINKFILE.

■ **Caution** Keep in mind that shrinking databases and database files is a relatively expensive operation, introduces fragmentation, and should be performed only when absolutely necessary.

25.15. Checking Consistency of Allocation Structures

Problem

You want to test a database's disk space allocation structures for consistency.

Solution

Utilize DBCC CHECKALLOC to check page usage and allocation within the database.

```
DBCC CHECKALLOC ('BookStoreArchive');
```

This statement produces the following messages. (Since this actually produces more than 500 lines of output, this result set as shown is greatly abridged.)

```
DBCC results for 'BookStoreArchive'.
***************************************************************
Table sys.sysrscols        Object ID 3.
Index ID 1, partition ID 196608, alloc unit ID 196608 (type In-row data). FirstIAM (1:157). Root
(1:158). Dpages 12.
Index ID 1, partition ID 196608, alloc unit ID 196608 (type In-row data). 14 pages used in 1
dedicated extents.
Total number of extents is 1.
***************************************************************
Table sys.sysrowsets        Object ID 5.
Index ID 1, partition ID 327680, alloc unit ID 327680 (type In-row data). FirstIAM (1:131). Root
(1:270). Dpages 1.
Index ID 1, partition ID 327680, alloc unit ID 327680 (type In-row data). 4 pages used in 0
dedicated extents.
Total number of extents is 0.
***************************************************************
...
File 3. The number of extents = 1, used pages = 6, and reserved pages = 8.
            File 3 (number of mixed extents = 0, mixed pages = 0).
  Object ID 99, index ID 0, partition ID 0, alloc unit ID 6488064 (type Unknown), index extents
1, pages 6, mixed extent pages 0.
The total number of extents = 36, used pages = 257, and reserved pages = 288 in this database.
    (number of mixed extents = 21, mixed pages = 168) in this database.
CHECKALLOC found 0 allocation errors and 0 consistency errors in database 'BookStoreArchive'.
DBCC execution completed. If DBCC printed error messages, contact your system administrator.
```

How It Works

DBCC CHECKALLOC checks page usage and allocation in the database and will report on any errors that are found (this command is automatically included in the execution of DBCC CHECKDB, so if you are already running CHECKDB periodically, there is no need to also run CHECKALLOC). The syntax is as follows:

```
DBCC CHECKALLOC (
[ 'database_name' | database_id | 0 ] [ , NOINDEX
{ REPAIR_ALLOW_DATA_LOSS | REPAIR_FAST |  REPAIR_REBUILD } ] )
[ WITH { [ ALL_ERRORMSGS ]
[ , NO_INFOMSGS ]
[ , TABLOCK ]
[ , ESTIMATEONLY ]
}
]
```

Table 25-7 describes the arguments of this command.

Table 25-7. *DBCC CHECKALLOC Arguments*

Argument	Description
'database_name' | database_id | 0	This defines the database name or database ID that you want to check for errors. When 0 is selected, the current database is used.
NOINDEX	When NOINDEX used, nonclustered indexes are not included in the checks. This is a backward-compatible option that has no effect on DBCC CHECKALLOC.
REPAIR_ALLOW_DATA_LOSS | REPAIR_FAST | REPAIR_REBUILD	REPAIR_ALLOW_DATA_LOSS attempts a repair of the table or indexed view, with the risk of losing data in the process. REPAIR_FAST and REPAIR_REBUILD are maintained for backward compatibility only.
ALL_ERRORMSGS	When ALL_ERRORMSGS is chosen, every error found will be displayed. If this option isn't designated, a maximum of 200 error messages can be displayed.
NO_INFOMSGS	NO_INFOMSGS represses all informational messages from the DBCC output.
TABLOCK	When TABLOCK is selected, an exclusive table lock is placed on the table instead of using an internal database snapshot, thus potentially decreasing query concurrency in the database.
ESTIMATEONLY	This provides the estimated space needed by the tempdb database to execute the command.

■ **Caution** This DBCC command has several REPAIR options. Microsoft recommends that you solve data integrity issues by restoring the database from the last good backup rather than resorting to a REPAIR option. If restoring from backup is not an option, the REPAIR option should be used only as a last resort. Depending on the REPAIR option selected, data loss can and will occur, and the problem may still not be resolved.

The output includes information about pages used and extents for each index. The key piece of information is in the next-to-last line, where you can see the reporting of the number of allocation and consistency errors encountered in the database being checked.

When DBCC CHECKALLOC is executed, an internal database snapshot is created to maintain transactional consistency during the operation. If for some reason a database snapshot can't be created or if TABLOCK is specified, an exclusive database lock is acquired during the execution of the command (thus potentially hurting database query concurrency). Unless you have a good reason not to, you should allow SQL Server to issue an internal database snapshot so that concurrency in your database is not impacted.

25-16. Checking Allocation and Structural Integrity

Problem

You want to check the integrity of all objects in a database.

Solution

Use DBCC CHECKDB to check the allocation and structural integrity of all objects in the database.

```
ALTER DATABASE BookStoreArchive SET RESTRICTED_USER WITH ROLLBACK IMMEDIATE;
ALTER DATABASE BookStoreArchive MODIFY FILEGROUP FG3 READ_WRITE;
ALTER DATABASE BookStoreArchive SET MULTI_USER;

DBCC CHECKDB ('BookStoreArchive');
```

Executing this command produces the following messages (as in the previous recipe, this output can be quite large, so only abridged results are being displayed):

```
DBCC results for 'BookStoreArchive'.
Service Broker Msg 9675, State 1: Message Types analyzed: 14.
Service Broker Msg 9676, State 1: Service Contracts analyzed: 6.
...
DBCC results for 'sys.sysrscols'.
There are 883 rows in 12 pages for object "sys.sysrscols".
DBCC results for 'sys.sysrowsets'.
There are 127 rows in 2 pages for object "sys.sysrowsets".
...
DBCC results for 'Test'.
There are 0 rows in 0 pages for object "Test".
...
DBCC results for 'sys.queue_messages_1977058079'.
There are 0 rows in 0 pages for object "sys.queue_messages_1977058079".
DBCC results for 'sys.queue_messages_2009058193'.
There are 0 rows in 0 pages for object "sys.queue_messages_2009058193".
DBCC results for 'sys.queue_messages_2041058307'.
There are 0 rows in 0 pages for object "sys.queue_messages_2041058307".
DBCC results for 'sys.filestream_tombstone_2073058421'.
There are 0 rows in 0 pages for object "sys.filestream_tombstone_2073058421".
DBCC results for 'sys.syscommittab'.
There are 0 rows in 0 pages for object "sys.syscommittab".
DBCC results for 'sys.filetable_updates_2105058535'.
There are 0 rows in 0 pages for object "sys.filetable_updates_2105058535".
CHECKDB found 0 allocation errors and 0 consistency errors in database 'BookStoreArchive'.
DBCC execution completed. If DBCC printed error messages, contact your system administrator.
```

How It Works

The DBCC CHECKDB command checks the integrity of objects in a database. Running DBCC CHECKDB periodically against your databases is a good maintenance practice. Weekly execution is usually sufficient; however, the optimal frequency depends on the activity and size of the database in question. If possible, DBCC CHECKDB should be executed during periods of light or no database activity. Executing DBCC CHECKDB in this manner will allow DBCC CHECKDB to finish faster and keep other processes from being slowed down by its overhead.

When executing DBCC CHECKDB, an internal database snapshot is created to maintain transactional consistency during the operation when this command is executed. If for some reason a database snapshot cannot be created (or the TABLOCK option is specified), shared table locks are held for table checks and exclusive database locks for allocation checks. (One of the reasons a snapshot cannot be created is if there are read-only filegroups; for this reason, the example first changes the FG3 filegroup to be read-write.)

As part of its execution, DBCC CHECKDB executes other DBCC commands that are discussed elsewhere in this chapter, including DBCC CHECKTABLE, DBCC CHECKALLOC, and DBCC CHECKCATALOG. In addition to this, CHECKDB verifies the integrity of Service Broker data indexed views and FILESTREAM link consistency for table and file system directories.

The syntax for DBCC CHECKDB is as follows:

```
DBCC CHECKDB
(
       'database_name' | database_id | 0
       [ , NOINDEX
       | { REPAIR_ALLOW_DATA_LOSS
       | REPAIR_FAST
       | REPAIR_REBUILD
       } ]
)
       [ WITH {
       [ ALL_ERRORMSGS  ]
       [ , [EXTENDED_LOGICAL_CHECKS] ]
       [ , [ NO_INFOMSGS ] ]
       [ , [ TABLOCK ]  ]
       [ , [ ESTIMATEONLY ] ]
       [ , { PHYSICAL_ONLY | DATA_PURITY } ]
       }
       ]
```

Table 25-8 describes the arguments of this command.

Table 25-8. *DBCC CHECKDB Arguments*

Argument	Description
'database_name' | database_id | 0	This defines the database name or database ID that you want to check for errors. When 0 is selected, the current database is used.
NOINDEX	Nonclustered indexes are not included in the integrity checks when this option is selected.
REPAIR_ALLOW_DATA_LOSS | REPAIR_FAST | REPAIR_REBUILD	REPAIR_ALLOW_DATA_LOSS attempts a repair of the table or indexed view, with the risk of losing data in the process. REPAIR_FAST is maintained for backward compatibility only, and REPAIR_REBUILD performs fixes without risk of data loss.
ALL_ERRORMSGS	When ALL_ERRORMSGS is chosen, every error found will be displayed (instead of just the default 200 error message limit). If you should happen to run CHECKDB and receive more than 200 error messages, you should rerun it with this option so that you can ascertain the full extent of errors in the database.
EXTENDED_LOGICAL_CHECKS	When EXTENDED_LOGICAL_CHECKS is chosen, it enables logical consistency checks on spatial and XML indexes, as well as indexed views. This option can impact performance significantly and should be used sparingly.
NO_INFOMSGS	NO_INFOMSGS represses all informational messages from the DBCC output.
TABLOCK	When TABLOCK is selected, an exclusive database lock is used instead of an internal database snapshot. Using this option decreases concurrency with other queries being executed against objects in the database.
ESTIMATEONLY	This argument provides the estimated space needed by the tempdb database to execute the command.
PHYSICAL_ONLY | DATA_PURITY	The PHYSICAL_ONLY argument limits the integrity checks to physical issues only, skipping logical checks. If DATA_PURITY is selected, this is for use on upgraded databases (pre-SQL Server 2005 databases); this instructs DBCC CHECKDB to detect column values that do not conform to the data type (for example, if an integer value has a bigint-sized value stored in it). Once all bad values in the upgraded database are cleaned up, SQL Server maintains the column-value integrity moving forward.

■ **Caution** This DBCC command has several REPAIR options. Microsoft recommends that you solve data integrity issues by restoring the database from the last good backup rather than resorting to a REPAIR option. If restoring from backup is not an option, the REPAIR option should be used only as a last resort. Depending on the REPAIR option selected, data loss can and will occur, and the problem may still not be resolved.

Despite all of these syntax options, the common form of executing this command is also most likely the simplest. The example for this recipe executes DBCC CHECKDB against the BookStoreArchive database. For thorough integrity and data checking of your database, the default is often suitable.

```
DBCC CHECKDB('BookStoreArchive');
```

As with the previous recipe, it is the next-to-last line of output that is the most important, where CHECKDB reports on the number of allocation and consistency errors found.

25-17. Checking Integrity of Tables in a Filegroup

Problem

You want to perform CHECKDB on a database, but you want to limit it to running against a specific filegroup.

Solution

Utilize DBCC CHECKFILEGROUP to perform CHECKDB operations against a specific filegroup.

```
USE BookStoreArchive;
GO
DBCC CHECKFILEGROUP ('PRIMARY');
GO
```

This returns the following abridged results:

```
DBCC results for 'BookStoreArchive'.
DBCC results for 'sys.sysrscols'.
There are 883 rows in 12 pages for object "sys.sysrscols".
DBCC results for 'sys.sysrowsets'.
There are 127 rows in 2 pages for object "sys.sysrowsets".
...
DBCC results for 'sys.syscommittab'.
There are 0 rows in 0 pages for object "sys.syscommittab".
DBCC results for 'sys.filetable_updates_2105058535'.
There are 0 rows in 0 pages for object "sys.filetable_updates_2105058535".
CHECKFILEGROUP found 0 allocation errors and 0 consistency errors in database
'BookStoreArchive'.
DBCC execution completed. If DBCC printed error messages, contact your system administrator.
```

How It Works

The DBCC CHECKFILEGROUP command is very similar to DBCC CHECKDB, limiting its integrity and allocation checking to objects within a single filegroup. For very large databases (VLDBs), performing a DBCC CHECKDB operation may be time prohibitive. If you use user-defined filegroups in your database, you can employ DBCC CHECKFILEGROUP to perform your weekly (or periodic) checks instead—spreading out filegroup checks across different days.

When this command is executed, an internal database snapshot is created to maintain transactional consistency during the operation. If for some reason a database snapshot can't be created (or the TABLOCK option is specified), shared table locks are created by the command for table checks, as well as an exclusive database lock for the allocation checks.

Again, if errors are found by DBCC CHECKFILEGROUP, Microsoft recommends that you solve any discovered issues by restoring from the last good database backup. Unlike other DBCC commands in this chapter, DBCC

CHECKFILEGROUP doesn't have repair options, so you would need to utilize DBCC CHECKDB to resolve them (although repair options are no longer recommended by Microsoft anyway).

The syntax is as follows:

```
DBCC CHECKFILEGROUP
(
[  { 'filegroup' | filegroup_id | 0 } ]
[  , NOINDEX ]
)
      [ WITH
      {
      [ ALL_ERRORMSGS | NO_INFOMSGS ]
      [ , [ TABLOCK ] ]
      [ , [ ESTIMATEONLY ] ]
      }
      ]
```

Table 25-9 describes the arguments of this command.

Table 25-9. DBCC CHECKFILEGROUP Arguments

Argument	Description
'filegroup' | filegroup_id | 0	This defines the filegroup name or filegroup ID that you want to check. If 0 is designated, the primary filegroup is used.
NOINDEX	When NOINDEX is designated, nonclustered indexes are not included in the integrity checks.
ALL_ERRORMSGS	When ALL_ERRORMSGS is chosen, all errors are displayed in the output, instead of the default 200 message limit.
NO_INFOMSGS	NO_INFOMSGS represses all informational messages from the DBCC output.
TABLOCK	When TABLOCK is selected, an exclusive database lock is used instead of using an internal database snapshot (using this option decreases concurrency with other database queries but speeds up the DBCC command execution).
ESTIMATEONLY	ESTIMATEONLY provides the estimated space needed by the tempdb database to execute the command.

As with the previous recipes, it is the next-to-last line of output that is the most important, where the number of allocation and consistency errors are reported.

25-18. Checking Integrity of Specific Tables and Indexed Views

Problem

You want to check for integrity issues with a specific table or indexed view.

Solution

Utilize DBCC CHECKTABLE to check a specific table or indexed view for integrity issues. (This solution utilizes the AdventureWorks2012 database.)

```
DBCC CHECKTABLE ('Production.Product');
```

Executing this command produces the following messages:

```
DBCC results for 'Production.Product'.
There are 504 rows in 13 pages for object "Production.Product".
DBCC execution completed. If DBCC printed error messages, contact your system administrator.
```

```
DBCC CHECKTABLE ('Sales.SalesOrderDetail') WITH ESTIMATEONLY;
```

Executing this command produces the following messages:

```
Estimated TEMPDB space (in KB) needed for CHECKTABLE on database AdventureWorks2012 = 1154.
DBCC execution completed. If DBCC printed error messages, contact your system administrator.
```

```
SELECT index_id
FROM sys.indexes
WHERE object_id = OBJECT_ID('Sales.SalesOrderDetail')
AND name = 'IX_SalesOrderDetail_ProductID';

DBCC CHECKTABLE ('Sales.SalesOrderDetail', 3) WITH PHYSICAL_ONLY;
```

Executing this command produces the following result set and messages:

```
index_id
--------
3

DBCC execution completed. If DBCC printed error messages, contact your system administrator.
```

How It Works

To identify issues in a specific table or indexed view, you can use the DBCC CHECKTABLE command. (If you want to run it for all tables and indexed views in the database, use DBCC CHECKDB instead, which performs DBCC CHECKTABLE for each table in your database.)

When DBCC CHECKTABLE is executed, an internal database snapshot is created to maintain transactional consistency during the operation. If for some reason a database snapshot can't be created, a shared table lock is applied to the target table or indexed view instead (thus potentially hurting database query concurrency against the target objects). DBCC CHECKTABLE checks for errors regarding data page linkages, pointers, verification that rows in a partition are actually in the correct partition, and more.

The syntax is as follows:

```
DBCC CHECKTABLE
(
    table_name | view_name
    [ , { NOINDEX | index_id }
     |, { REPAIR_ALLOW_DATA_LOSS | REPAIR_FAST | REPAIR_REBUILD }
    ]
)
    [ WITH
        { ALL_ERRORMSGS ]
          [ , EXTENDED_LOGICAL_CHECKS ]
          [ , NO_INFOMSGS ]
          [ , TABLOCK ]
          [ , ESTIMATEONLY ]
          [ , { PHYSICAL_ONLY | DATA_PURITY } ]
        }
  ]
```

Table 25-10 describes the arguments of this command.

Table 25-10. *DBCC CHECKTABLE Arguments*

Argument	Description
'table_name' | 'view_name'	This defines the table or indexed view you want to check.
NOINDEX	This keyword instructs the command not to check nonclustered indexes.
index_id	This specifies the specific ID of the index to be checked (if you are checking a specific index).
REPAIR_ALLOW_DATA_LOSS | REPAIR_FAST | REPAIR_REBUILD	REPAIR_ALLOW_DATA_LOSS attempts a repair of the table or indexed view, with the risk of losing data in the process. REPAIR_FAST is no longer used and is kept for backward compatibility only. REPAIR_REBUILD does repairs and index rebuilds without any risk of data loss.
ALL_ERRORMSGS	When ALL_ERRORMSGS is chosen, every error found during the command execution will be displayed.
EXTENDED_LOGICAL_CHECKS	When EXTENDED_LOGICAL_CHECKS is designated, it enables logical consistency checks on spatial and XML indexes, as well as indexed views. This option can impact performance significantly and should be used sparingly.
NO_INFOMSGS	NO_INFOMSGS represses all informational messages from the DBCC output.
TABLOCK	When TABLOCK is selected, a shared table lock is placed on the table instead of using an internal database snapshot. Using this option decreases concurrency with other database queries accessing the table or indexed view.
ESTIMATEONLY	ESTIMATEONLY provides the estimated space needed by the tempdb database to execute the command (but doesn't actually execute the integrity checking).
PHYSICAL_ONLY	PHYSICAL_ONLY limits the integrity checks to physical issues only, skipping logical checks.
DATA_PURITY	This argument is used on upgraded databases (pre–SQL Server 2005 databases); this instructs DBCC CHECKTABLE to detect column values that do not conform to the data type (for example, if an integer value has a bigint-sized value stored in it). Once all bad values in the upgraded database are cleaned up, SQL Server maintains the column-value integrity moving forward.

■ **Caution** This DBCC command has several REPAIR options. Microsoft recommends that you solve data integrity issues by restoring the database from the last good backup rather than resorting to a REPAIR option. If restoring from backup is not an option, the REPAIR option should be used only as a last resort. Depending on the REPAIR option selected, data loss can and will occur, and the problem may still not be resolved.

In the first example, the integrity of the AdventureWorks2012.Production.Product table is examined for integrity issues.

In the second example, an estimate of tempdb space required for a check on the AdventureWorks2012.Sales.SalesOrderDetail table is returned. This allows you to know ahead of time if a specific CHECKTABLE operation requires more space than you have available.

The third example examines a specific index for physical errors only (not logical errors). To specify an index, you must pass in the index_id, so we first have to query the sys.indexes system view to obtain this value.

25-19. Checking Constraint Integrity

Problem

You want to check a specific table or constraint for any violations in CHECK or FOREIGN KEY constraints.

Solution

Utilize DBCC CHECKCONSTRAINTS to validate that CHECK or FOREIGN KEY constraints in a table are valid. (This solution utilizes the AdventureWorks2012 database.)

```
ALTER TABLE Production.WorkOrder NOCHECK CONSTRAINT CK_WorkOrder_EndDate;
GO
-- Set an EndDate to earlier than a StartDate
UPDATE Production.WorkOrder
SET EndDate = '2001-01-01T00:00:00'
WHERE WorkOrderID = 1;
GO
ALTER TABLE Production.WorkOrder CHECK CONSTRAINT CK_WorkOrder_EndDate;
GO
DBCC CHECKCONSTRAINTS ('Production.WorkOrder');
GO
```

This code produces the following messages:

```
Table                      Constraint                Where
-------------------------  ------------------------  -------------------------------------------
[Production].[WorkOrder]  [CK_WorkOrder_EndDate]  [StartDate] = '2005-07-04 00:00:00.000'
                                                      AND [EndDate] = '2001-01-01 00:00:00.000'

DBCC execution completed. If DBCC printed error messages, contact your system administrator.
```

How It Works

DBCC CHECKCONSTRAINTS alerts you to any CHECK or foreign key constraint violations found in a specific table or constraint. This command allows you to return the violating data so that you can correct the constraint violation accordingly (although this command does not catch constraints that have been disabled using NOCHECK). The syntax is as follows:

```
DBCC CHECKCONSTRAINTS
[( 'table_name' | table_id | 'constraint_name'
constraint_id )]
[ WITH
{ ALL_CONSTRAINTS | ALL_ERRORMSGS } [ , NO_INFOMSGS ] ]
```

Table 25-11 describes the arguments of this command.

Table 25-11. *DBCC CHECKCONSTRAINTS Arguments*

Argument	Description
'table_name' | table_id | 'constraint_name' | constraint_id	This defines the table name, table ID, constraint name, or constraint ID that you want to validate. If a specific object isn't designated, all the objects in the database will be evaluated.
ALL_CONSTRAINTS | ALL_ERRORMSGS	When ALL_CONSTRAINTS is selected, all constraints (enabled or disabled) are checked. When ALL_ERRORMSGS is selected, all rows that violate constraints are returned in the result set (instead of the default maximum of 200 rows).
NO_INFOMSGS	NO_INFOMSGS represses all informational messages from the DBCC output.

In this recipe, the check constraint named CK_WorkOrder on the Production.WorkOrder table is disabled, using the ALTER TABLE...NOCHECK CONSTRAINT command.

```
ALTER TABLE Production.WorkOrder NOCHECK CONSTRAINT CK_WorkOrder_EndDate;
```

This disabled constraint restricts values in the EndDate column from being less than the date in the StartDate column. After disabling the constraint, a row is updated to violate this check constraint's rule.

```
UPDATE Production.WorkOrder SET EndDate = '2001-01-01T00:00:00' WHERE WorkOrderID = 1;
```

The constraint is then reenabled.

```
ALTER TABLE Production.WorkOrder CHECK CONSTRAINT CK_WorkOrder_EndDate;
```

The DBCC CHECKCONSTRAINTS command is then executed against the table.

```
DBCC CHECKCONSTRAINTS('Production.WorkOrder');
```

When the command is run, it returns the data that failed the validation. Now that we know that the table has invalid data in the table, the data can be corrected and validated.

```
UPDATE Production.WorkOrder
SET EndDate = '2005-07-14T00:00:00'
WHERE WorkOrderID = 1;
GO

DBCC CHECKCONSTRAINTS ('Production.WorkOrder');
GO
```

This code returns the following message:

```
DBCC execution completed. If DBCC printed error messages, contact your system administrator.
```

■ **Note** Unlike several other database integrity DBCC commands, DBCC CHECKCONSTRAINTS is *not* run within DBCC CHECKDB, so you must execute it as a stand-alone process if you need to identify data constraint violations in the database.

25-20. Checking System Table Consistency

Problem

You want to check for consistency in and between system tables in your database.

Solution

Execute DBCC CHECKCATALOG against the database to verify consistency in and between system tables.

```
DBCC CHECKCATALOG ('BookStoreArchive');
```

Assuming no errors are found, the following message is returned:

```
DBCC execution completed. If DBCC printed error messages, contact your system administrator.
```

How It Works

DBCC CHECKCATALOG checks for consistency in and between system tables. The syntax is as follows:

```
DBCC CHECKCATALOG
[ ( 'database_name' | database_id | 0)] [ WITH NO_INFOMSGS ]
```

Table 25-12 describes the arguments of this command.

Table 25-12. DBCC CHECKCATALOG Arguments

Argument	Description
'database_name' | database_id | 0	This defines the database name or database ID to be checked for errors. When 0 is selected, the current database is used.
NO_INFOMSGS	NO_INFOMSGS suppresses all informational messages from the DBCC output.

In this recipe, the system catalog data is checked in the BookStoreArchive database. If any errors are identified, they will be returned in the command output. DBCC CHECKCATALOG doesn't have repair options, so if any errors are found, then a restore from the last good database backup may be your only repair option.

When DBCC CHECKCATALOG is executed, an internal database snapshot is created to maintain transactional consistency during the operation. If for some reason a database snapshot cannot be created, an exclusive database lock is acquired during the execution of the command (thus potentially hurting database query concurrency).

■ **Note** CHECKCATALOG is already executed automatically within a DBCC CHECKDB command, so a separate execution is not necessary unless you want to investigate only system table consistency issues.

CHAPTER 26

Backup

By David Dye

In this chapter, you'll find recipes covering several methods of backing up a database using T-SQL. This chapter is in no way meant to be a comprehensive source for database backups but rather provides greater insight into the problems or limitations you may encounter. This chapter will outline the different types of backup methods using T-SQL as well as how to query the msdb database to find information about backup information.

26-1. Backing Up a Database

Problem

You want to do a full backup of the AdventureWorks2012 database to your C:\Apress\ folder using T-SQL.

Solution

Execute a BACKUP DATABASE statement. Specify TO DISK, and provide the path and desired file name. There are several options that can be used with the BACKUP DATABASE statement that will be covered in the following recipes.

The following example demonstrates using the BACKUP DATABASE statement, specifying the file location where the backup will be stored:

```
BACKUP DATABASE AdventureWorks2012
TO DISK = 'C:\Apress\Adventureworks2012.bak';
GO
```

```
Processed 25568 pages for database 'AdventureWorks2012', file 'AdventureWorks2012_Data' on file 1.
Processed 2 pages for database 'AdventureWorks2012', file 'AdventureWorks2012_Log' on file 1.
BACKUP DATABASE successfully processed 25570 pages in 8.186 seconds (24.403 MB/sec).
```

Tip Make sure that the Apress folder exists on the C: drive or change the path in the previous query.

This command will make a full backup of all data and log files of the AdventureWorks2012 database, including the FILESTREAM file.

How It Works

The BACKUP DATABASE command, absent all options, will make a full backup of all data and log files of the specified database to the path or device declared in the statement. The process involves copying the data files as well as the active portion of any log files.

This process is rather straightforward, but the resulting backup can be a bit confusing. Consider a database that has a single 50GB data file and a 10MB log file. The resultant backup should be just more than 50GB, but this is not always the case.

During the backup process, SQL Server does not back up empty data pages, meaning that the backup will contain only partially or fully used data pages within the data files. Comparing the backups may lead some to believe that proprietary compression is involved in the backup process, but really only "used" space is copied to the backup media.

I hate to jump ahead, but I need to answer the most common question that arises when describing the backup process: "When I restore the database, will it be the exact size of the backup?" The data files sizes are contained in the backup media, and that file size is what is used to reserve the space to write the data pages to. In this example, this would mean that another 50GB data file would be created in the restored path, and the data pages would then be written to the data file.

26-2. Compressing a Backup

Problem

As a database grows, disk space can be a fleeting commodity, and the space needed to store a full backup can be prohibitive. So you want to compress your backup files to free up disk space.

Solution

Backing up the database using the WITH COMPRESSION clause will compress the associated backup. The following example demonstrates creating a full backup of the AdventureWorks2012 database using compression:

```
BACKUP DATABASE AdventureWorks2012
TO DISK = 'C:\Apress\AdventureWorks2012compress.bak'
WITH COMPRESSION;
GO
```

```
Processed 25568 pages for database 'AdventureWorks2012', file 'AdventureWorks2012_Data' on file 1.
Processed 2 pages for database 'AdventureWorks2012', file 'AdventureWorks2012_Log' on file 1.
BACKUP DATABASE successfully processed 25570 pages in 5.145 seconds (38.825 MB/sec).
```

How It Works

The solution command will create a full backup to the `C:\Apress\` folder with the file name `AdventureWorks2012.bak` that utilizes compression to reduce the size of the backup file. There are several notable benefits of using compression in your backup sets, the first being reducing the space that is being taken by backups. Another notable advantage of backup compression is reduced disk I/O. This seems only reasonable: because there is less to write to disk, there is noticeable reduced disk I/O.

The specific compression ratio is dependent on the data that is compressed, which is based on several factors including the following:

- The type of data
- The consistency of the data among rows on a page
- Whether the data is encrypted
- Whether the database is compressed

This makes it difficult to ascertain the specific compression ratio and the resulting backup size without first comparing a compressed file to an uncompressed backup file. Since the exact compressed size is mostly unknown until completion, the database engine uses a preallocation algorithm to reserve space for the backup file. The algorithm reserves a predefined percentage of the size of the database for the backup. During the backup process, if more space is required, then the database engine will grow the file as needed. Upon completing the backup, the database engine will shrink the file size of the backup as needed.

The following script illustrates the noticeable difference, as a ratio, between a compressed and uncompressed backup file of the `AdventureWorks2012` database.

```
--Compressed Full Backup
BACKUP DATABASE AdventureWorks2012
TO DISK = 'C:\Apress\AdventureWorks2012.bak'
WITH COMPRESSION;
GO

--Uncompressed Full Backup
BACKUP DATABASE AdventureWorks2012
TO DISK = 'C:\Apress\UnAdventureWorks2012.bak';
GO

--Retrieve the compression ratio
SELECT TOP 2 backup_size,compressed_backup_size,
        backup_size/compressed_backup_size  AS ratio
FROM msdb..backupset
ORDER BY backup_start_date DESC;
GO
```

Results may vary:

```
----------    ------------
209797120      209797120       1.000000000000000000
209797120      52287373        4.012385934936911058
```

This shows that the compressed backup had a compression ratio of just over 4 to 1, while the uncompressed was obviously 1 to 1. This in turn means the compressed backup was just less than 24 percent of the size of the uncompressed. This substantially reduced file size can also be evaluated by comparing the physical file size within Windows Explorer, as shown in Figure 26-1.

Name	Size	Type
UnAdventureWorks2012.bak	204,890 KB	BAK File
AdventureWorks2012.bak	51,063 KB	BAK File

***Figure 26-1.** Comparison of compressed and uncompressed backup*

So as not to paint a one-sided picture, it is important to note that there are some considerations regarding backup compression. One of the most limiting constraints for utilizing backup compression is that it is an Enterprise and Developer edition feature. This means that any edition less than Enterprise is stuck with uncompressed backups.

After discussing the performance benefits in both backup size and disk I/O, I may have convinced you to begin changing all your maintenance plans and scripts to utilize `WITH COMPRESSION`, but all good things come with a cost. The reduced file size and disk I/O are replaced with increased CPU usage during the backup process, which can prove to be significant. The increase in CPU can be mitigated by using Resource Governor, another Enterprise edition feature, but it does need to be weighed against server resources and priorities.

Compressed backups also cannot coexist with uncompressed backups on the same media set, which means that full, differential, and transaction log compressed backups must be stored in separate media sets than ones that are uncompressed.

26-3. Ensuring That a Backup Can Be Restored

Problem

Backing up a database is straightforward, but you want to make sure that the backup is not corrupt and can be successfully restored.

Solution

There are several ways to ensure that a backup can be successfully restored, the first of which is to utilize the `WITH CHECKSUM` option in the backup command.

```
BACKUP DATABASE AdventureWorks2012
TO  DISK = 'C:\Apress\AdventureWorks2012check.bak'
WITH CHECKSUM
```

This can be partnered with the command `RESTORE VERIFYONLY` to ensure not only that a backup is not corrupted but that it can be restored.

```
RESTORE VERIFYONLY
FROM  DISK = 'C:\Apress\AdventureWorks2012.bak'
WITH CHECKSUM;
```

Results may vary:

```
Processed 25568 pages for database 'AdventureWorks2012', file 'AdventureWorks2012_Data' on file 2.

Processed 2 pages for database 'AdventureWorks2012', file 'AdventureWorks2012_Log' on file 2.

BACKUP DATABASE successfully processed 25570 pages in 13.932 seconds (14.338 MB/sec).
The backup set on file 1 is valid.
```

How It Works

Using the `WITH CHECKSUM` option in a backup will verify each page checksum, if it is present on the page. Regardless of whether page checksums are available, the backup will generate a separate checksum for the backup streams. The backup checksums are stored in the backup media and not the database pages, which means they can be used in restore operations to validate that the backup is not corrupt.

Using the `WITH CHECKSUM` option in a backup command allows you to control the behavior of what will happen if an error occurs. The default behavior if a page checksum does not verify that the backup will stop reporting an error. This can be changed by adding `CONTINUE_AFTER_ERROR`.

```
BACKUP DATABASE AdventureWorks2012
TO  DISK = 'C:\Apress\AdventureWorks2012.bak'
WITH CHECKSUM, CONTINUE_AFTER_ERROR
```

Using `WITH CHECKSUM` to ensure a backup's integrity is a good start, but it does not validate the ability to restore the backup. The `RESTORE VERIFYONLY` command, when used in tandem `WITH CHECKSUM`, will validate the backup checksum values, that the backup set is complete, some header fields of the database pages, and that there is sufficient space in the restore path.

Using `WITH CHECKSUM` alongside `RESTORE VERIFYONLY` helps validate a backup's integrity, but it is not fool-proof. Database backups are stored in a format called Microsoft Tape Format (MTF), which includes MTF blocks that contain the backup metadata while the backed-up data is stored outside of the MTF blocks. `RESTORE VERIFYONLY` performs simple checks on the MTF blocks and not the actual data blocks, which means the blocks could be consistent while the backup files could be corrupted. In such a case, `RESTORE VERIFYONLY` would show that the backup set could be restored, but issuing a restore would result in failure.

The moral of this solution is that you can try to ensure backup integrity, but the only sure way to test backup integrity is to restore backups and run `DBCC CHECKDB` on the restored database.

26-4. Understanding Why the Transaction Log Continues to Grow

Problem

A database transaction log has grown larger than the data files and continues to grow larger by the day. You want to know why.

Solution

The solution to this is easy enough for databases that are set to the full or bulk logged recovery model. Back up the transaction log!

```
BACKUP LOG AdventureWorks2012
TO DISK = 'C:\Apress\AdventureWorks2012.trn';
```

How It Works

As a moderator on MSDN forums, I see this issue posted at least once a week, and the solution exemplifies the saying "An ounce of prevention is better than a pound of the cure." Databases that are set to a bulk logged or full recovery model have the possibility of being restored to a point in time because the transaction log can be backed up. A database that is set to the simple recovery model can never be restored to a point in time because the transaction log is truncated upon a checkpoint.

So you fully understand this concept, I'll cover each of the recovery models beginning with the simple model. Because transactions occur in a database, SQL Server will first check to see whether the affected data pages are in memory, and if they're not, then the page(s) will be read into memory. Subsequent requests for affected pages are presented from memory because these reflect the most up-to-date information. All transactions are then written to the transaction log. Occasionally, based upon the recovery interval, SQL will run a checkpoint in which all "dirty" pages and log file information will be written to the data file.

Databases that use the simple recovery model will then truncate the inactive portion of the log, thereby preventing the ability to back up the transaction log but reducing and possibly eliminating the pesky problem of runaway log file size.

The following script creates a database, `Logging`, that uses the simple recovery model and creates a single table, `FillErUp`:

```
--Create the Logging database
CREATE DATABASE Logging;
GO

ALTER DATABASE Logging
SET RECOVERY SIMPLE;
GO

USE Logging;

CREATE TABLE FillErUp(
RowInfo CHAR(150)
);
GO
```

Monitoring the log file size and the reason why a log file is waiting to reclaim space can be done through the `sys.database_files` and `sys.databases` catalog views. The following queries show the initial log and data file sizes as well as the `log_reuse_wait_desc` description; keep in mind that the size column represents the size in 8KB data pages.

```
SELECT type_desc,
       size
FROM sys.database_files
WHERE type_desc = 'LOG';
GO
SELECT name,
```

```
        log_reuse_wait_desc
FROM sys.databases
WHERE database_id = DB_ID('Logging');
GO
```

Execute this query, and the results should be similar to the following:

```
type_desc  size
---------  ----
LOG        98

name,      log_reuse_ wait_desc
-------    --------------------
Logging    NOTHING
```

The log_reuse_wait_desc option is of particular importance in this solution because it provides the reason that the log file is not being truncated. Since the database has just been created and no transactions have been posted to it, there is nothing preventing the log from being truncated.

The following query uses a loop to post 100,000 rows to the FillErUp table and again queries the log file size and the log_reuse_wait_desc:

```
DECLARE @count INT = 10000
WHILE @count > 0
BEGIN
   INSERT FillErUp
   SELECT 'This is row # ' + CONVERT(CHAR(4), @count)
   SET @count - = 1
END;
GO

CHECKPOINT;
GO

SELECT type_desc AS filetype,
         size AS size
FROM sys.database_files
WHERE type_desc = 'LOG';
GO

SELECT name AS name,
         log_reuse_wait_desc AS reuse_desc
FROM sys.databases
WHERE database_id = DB_ID('Logging');
GO
```

The results of the query show that the log file size is the same and that the log_reuse_wait_desc description is still nothing.

```
filetype  size
-------   ----
LOG       98

name       log_reuse_ wait_desc
------     --------------------
Logging    NOTHING
```

Since the database recovery model is set to simple recovery, the log file can be truncated after a checkpoint is issued so the log file size remains the same size. Keep in mind that just because a database is set to the simple recovery model does not mean that the log file will not grow. Upon issuing a checkpoint, the nonactive portion of the log will be truncated, but the active portion cannot be truncated. The following example uses a BEGIN TRAN to display the effects of a long-running transaction and log file growth and also uses DBCC SQLPERF to display some statistics on the log file after the transaction runs:

```
BEGIN TRAN

DECLARE @count INT = 10000
WHILE @count > 0
BEGIN
   INSERT FillErUp
   SELECT 'This is row # ' + CONVERT(CHAR(4), @count)
   SET @count - = 1
END;
GO

SELECT type_desc AS filetype,
         size AS size
FROM sys.database_files
WHERE type_desc = 'LOG';
GO

SELECT name AS name,
         log_reuse_wait_desc AS reuse_desc
FROM sys.databases
WHERE database_id = DB_ID('Logging');
GO

DBCC SQLPERF(LOGSPACE);
GO
```

The results of the query show that the log file has grown, and it cannot be truncated because of an open transaction. A portion of the DBCC SQLPERF results are included to show the size and percent of used log space.

```
filetype     size
---------    ----
LOG          728

name         log_reuse_ wait_desc
------       --------------------
Logging      ACTIVE TRANSACTION
```

```
Database Name  Log Size (MB)       Log Space Used (%)
-------------  -------------       ------------------
Logging        5.679688            98.62448
```

The results show that the log file size has grown and that the log space is more than 98 percent used. Issuing a `COMMIT TRAN` and a manual `CHEKPOINT` will close the transaction, but you will also notice that the log file remains the same size.

```
COMMIT TRAN;
GO
CHECKPOINT;
GO

SELECT type_desc AS filetype,
       size AS size
FROM sys.database_files
WHERE type_desc = 'LOG';
GO
SELECT name AS name,
           log_reuse_wait_desc AS reuse_desc
FROM sys.databases
WHERE database_id = DB_ID('Logging');
GO

DBCC SQLPERF(LOGSPACE);
GO
```

```
filetype  size
-------   ----
LOG       728

name      log_reuse_ wait_desc
-------   --------------------
Logging   NOTHING

Database Name  Log Size (MB)   Log Space Used (%)
-------------  -------------   ------------------
Logging        5.679688        16.72971
```

It is obvious from the query results that the transaction has been closed, but the log file size is the same size when the transaction remained unopened. The difference between the results is the percentage of log space that is used. The log space used before the commit and checkpoint is more than 98 percent, while afterward, the used space falls to just more than 16 percent.

■ **Tip** There are ways in which to regain disk space from bloated log files, but the focus of this solution is to highlight maintenance. Any steps taken to shrink the log file is always user beware.

Because log size can become complex while a database is set to the simple recovery model, full and bulk logged add many more considerations that must be taken into account. Unlike the simple recovery model, both the full and bulk logged recovery models require transaction log backups to be taken before a transaction log will be truncated.

To demonstrate, the following query will drop and re-create the `Logging` database and, again, use a loop to create a number of transactions. The log file size and log reuse wait description are queried immediately after the creation of the database.

```
USE master;
GO

--Create the Logging database
IF EXISTS (SELECT * FROM sys.databases WHERE name = 'Logging')
BEGIN
DROP DATABASE Logging;
CREATE DATABASE Logging;
END
GO

ALTER DATABASE Logging
SET RECOVERY FULL;
GO

USE Logging;

CREATE TABLE FillErUp(
RowInfo CHAR(150)
);
GO

--Size is 98
SELECT type_desc,
           size
FROM sys.database_files
WHERE type_desc = 'LOG';
GO

SELECT name,
           log_reuse_wait_desc
FROM sys.databases
WHERE database_id = DB_ID('Logging');
GO

DECLARE @count INT = 10000
WHILE @count > 0
```

```
BEGIN
   INSERT FillErUp
   SELECT 'This is row # ' + CONVERT(CHAR(4), @count)
   SET @count - = 1
END;
GO

CHECKPOINT;
GO

SELECT type_desc,
           size AS size
FROM sys.database_files
WHERE type_desc = 'LOG';
GO

SELECT name AS name,
           log_reuse_wait_desc
FROM sys.databases
WHERE database_id = DB_ID('Logging');
GO
```

```
type_desc  size
---------  -------
LOG        98

name      log_reuse_ wait_desc
-------   --------------------
Logging   NOTHING

type_desc size
--------- -------
LOG       98

name      log_reuse_ wait_desc
-------   --------------------
Logging   NOTHING
```

The results are obviously not what were expected, but this is for good reason. The database was created and then altered to the full recovery model. After a number of transactions, the log file remains the same size. Based on the definition of the full recovery model, the log should have grown. The log file will continue to be truncated upon a checkpoint until a full backup is taken. This is by design because the transaction log backup requires a full backup be taken first, and until a transaction log backup is taken, the log file will grow.

After taking a full backup of the database and again running the `INSERT` loop, the results are much different.

```
BACKUP DATABASE Logging
TO DISK =  'C:\Apress\Logging.bak';
GO

DECLARE @count INT = 10000
WHILE @count > 0
BEGIN
```

```
   INSERT FillErUp
   SELECT 'This is row # ' + CONVERT(CHAR(4), @count)
   SET @count - = 1
END;
GO

CHECKPOINT;
GO

SELECT type_desc,
       size AS size
FROM sys.database_files
WHERE type_desc = 'LOG';
GO

SELECT name,
       log_reuse_wait_desc
FROM sys.databases
WHERE database_id = DB_ID('Logging');
GO
```

```
type_desc  size
---------  -------
LOG        1432


name      log_reuse_ wait_desc
-------   --------------------
Logging   LOG_BACKUP
```

The end result is that the log file continued to grow, and the log reuse wait description reflects that a transaction log backup is required. The size of the transaction log can be maintained by scheduled transaction log backups. The following script re-creates the Logging database and uses the INSERT loop to fill the log but includes a transaction log backup after each transaction to demonstrate the effect it has on log growth.

```
USE master;
GO

--Create the Logging database
IF EXISTS (SELECT * FROM sys.databases WHERE name = 'Logging')
BEGIN
DROP DATABASE Logging;
CREATE DATABASE Logging;
END
GO

ALTER DATABASE Logging
SET RECOVERY FULL;
GO
```

```
USE Logging;

CREATE TABLE FillErUp(
RowInfo CHAR(150)
);
GO

USE Logging;
GO

SELECT type_desc,
          size AS size
FROM sys.database_files
WHERE type_desc = 'LOG';
GO

SELECT name,
          log_reuse_wait_desc
FROM sys.databases
WHERE database_id = DB_ID('Logging');
GO

BACKUP DATABASE Logging
TO DISK =  'C:\Apress\Logging.bak';
GO

DECLARE @count INT = 100
WHILE @count > 0
BEGIN
   INSERT FillErUp
   SELECT 'This is row # ' + CONVERT(CHAR(4), @count)
   BACKUP LOG Logging
   TO DISK =  'C:\Apress\Logging.trn'
   SET @count - = 1
END;
GO

SELECT type_desc AS filetype,
          size AS size
FROM sys.database_files
WHERE type_desc = 'LOG';
GO

SELECT name,
          log_reuse_wait_desc
FROM sys.databases
WHERE database_id = DB_ID('Logging');
GO
```

```
type_desc  size
---------  ----
LOG         98

name      log_reuse_ wait_desc
-------   --------------------
Logging   NOTHING

type_desc  size
---------  ----
LOG         98

name      log_reuse_ wait_desc
-------   --------------------
Logging   NOTHING
```

The results show that the size of the log file before and after the loop remains the same, as does the log reuse wait description. This example obviously does not simulate real-life situations in scope or scheduling but does demonstrate that transaction log backups provide a proactive means of maintaining manageable log size files for full or bulk logged recovery models.

A database using the bulk logged recovery model still uses the log file to record transactions, but bulk transactions are minimally logged, causing less growth in the log. Unlike the full recovery model, bulk logged recovery does not provide the ability to restore the database to a point in time and records only enough information to roll back the transaction.

Only specific operations are marked as bulk logged such as `BULK INSERT`, `SELECT INTO`, and `BULK INSERT`, to name a few. A common misconception is that the bulk logged recovery model will not cause the log file to grow, which is untrue.

The following code demonstrates that bulk operations do still cause the transaction log file to grow with a database in the bulk logged recovery model:

```
USE master;
GO

IF EXISTS (SELECT * FROM sys.databases WHERE name = 'Logging')
BEGIN
DROP DATABASE Logging;
CREATE DATABASE Logging;
END
GO

ALTER DATABASE Logging
SET RECOVERY BULK_LOGGED;
GO

USE Logging;
GO
```

```
CREATE TABLE Currency(
CurrencyCode CHAR(3) NOT NULL,
Name CHAR(500) NOT NULL,
ModifiedDate CHAR(500) NOT NULL);
GO

BACKUP DATABASE Logging
TO DISK =  'C:\Apress\Logging.bak';
GO

SELECT type_desc,
           size AS size
FROM sys.database_files
WHERE type_desc = 'LOG';
GO

SELECT name,
           log_reuse_wait_desc
FROM sys.databases
WHERE database_id = DB_ID('Logging');
GO
```

```
type_desc  size
---------  ----
LOG        98

name      log_reuse_ wait_desc
-------   --------------------
Logging   NOTHING
```

```
BULK INSERT Logging.dbo.Currency
   FROM  'C:\Apress\Currency.dat'
   WITH
      (
         FIELDTERMINATOR = ',',
         ROWTERMINATOR = '\n'
      );
GO

BULK INSERT Logging.dbo.Currency
   FROM  'C:\Apress\Currency.dat'
   WITH
      (
         FIELDTERMINATOR = ',',
         ROWTERMINATOR = '\n'
      );
GO
```

```
BULK INSERT Logging.dbo.Currency
   FROM  'C:\Apress\Currency.dat'
   WITH
      (
         FIELDTERMINATOR = ',',
         ROWTERMINATOR = '\n'
      );
GO

BULK INSERT Logging.dbo.Currency
   FROM  'C:\Apress\Currency.dat'
   WITH
      (
         FIELDTERMINATOR = ',',
         ROWTERMINATOR = '\n'
      );
GO
--26
BULK INSERT Logging.dbo.Currency
   FROM  'C:\Apress\Currency.dat'
   WITH
      (
         FIELDTERMINATOR = ',',
         ROWTERMINATOR = '\n'
      );
GO

SELECT type_desc,
           size AS size
FROM sys.database_files
WHERE type_desc = 'LOG';
GO

SELECT name,
           log_reuse_wait_desc
FROM sys.databases
WHERE database_id = DB_ID('Logging');
GO
```

```
type_desc  size
---------  ----
LOG        136

name       log_reuse_ wait_desc
-------    --------------------
Logging    LOG_BACKUP
```

The results show that a database in bulk logged recovery mode will cause the log file to grow even when using bulk operations.

26-5. Performing a Differential Backup

Problem

To ensure that a recovery can be made as quickly as possible, you want a backup that will contain all the changes in a database since the last full backup.

Solution

A differential backup contains all the changes made since the last full backup. A backup/restore strategy can use as many differential backups as desired, and since a differential contains all the changes from the last full, this can speed up the restoration process.

```
BACKUP DATABASE AdventureWorks2012
TO DISK =  'C:\Apress\AdventureWorks2012.dif'
WITH DIFFERENTIAL;
GO
```

How It Works

The differential backup statement is almost identical to a full backup statement, with the exception of the `WITH DIFFERENTIAL`. A differential backup will contain all changes in a database since the last full backup, which means that a full backup must already exist before a differential can be taken. Differential backups can speed the restoration process since, unlike log file backups, only the most recent differential backup needs to be restored.

Although a differential backup can speed up the restoration process, it is important to understand the mechanics of the backup. Consider a backup strategy that utilizes a full backup at 12 p.m. and a differential every two hours thereafter. The further away in time the differential backup gets from the full backup, the larger, based on activity, that backup would be. The 2 p.m. differential would contain all the changes from 12 p.m. to 2 p.m., the 4 p.m. differential would contain all the changes from 12 p.m. to 4 p.m., and so on.

Figure 26-2 illustrates the overlap of data that can be contained within a differential backup.

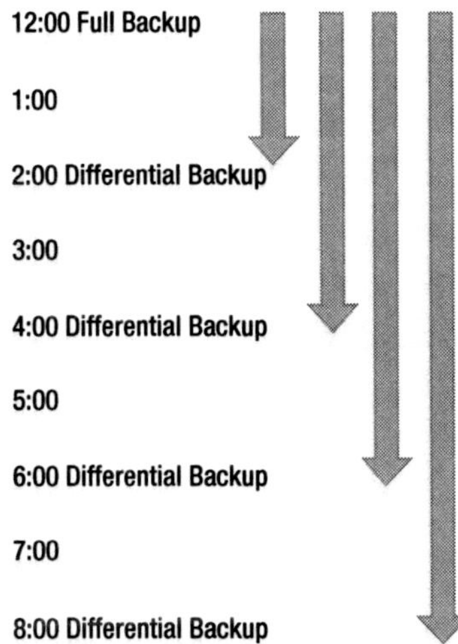

***Figure 26-2.** Differential backup timeline*

This figure shows that the space needed to maintain multiple differential backups may become prohibitive for a high OLTP database, and the resources needed to create the backup can result in degradation of performance as the differential backup grows.

26-6. Backing Up a Single Row or Table

Problem

Several incidents have required that only a specific row or table be restored and not the entire database.

Solution #1: Restore Rows from a Backup

Backup granularity within SQL Server starts with the database and then the filegroup and finally the file. Unless a table resides on its own filegroup, the backup statement does not natively support this functionality, but you can use several workarounds to meet this need.

To demonstrate how a full database backup can be used to restore a single row, I've created a database with a single table called Person using a SELECT INTO statement.

```
USE master;
GO

IF EXISTS (SELECT * FROM sys.databases WHERE name = 'Granular')
BEGIN
DROP DATABASE Granular;
END
CREATE DATABASE Granular;
GO

USE Granular;
GO

SELECT BusinessEntityID,
         FirstName,
         MiddleName,
         LastName
INTO People
FROM AdventureWorks2012.Person.Person;
GO

SELECT TOP 6 *
FROM People
ORDER BY BusinessEntityID;
GO
```

Executing the previous query will create the Granular database and populate the People table with the result of the SELECT statement from the Person.Person table from AdventureWorks2012.

```
BusinessEntityID    FirstName    MiddleName    LastName
----------------    ---------    ----------    --------
1                   Ken          J             Sánchez
```

```
2                Terri      Lee         Duffy
3                Roberto    NULL        Tamburello
4                Rob        NULL        Walters
5                Gail       A           Erickson
6                Jossef     H           Goldberg
```

Once the database is created and the table populated, a backup is created, and a single row is deleted in the following code:

```
BACKUP DATABASE Granular
TO DISK = 'C:\Apress\Granular.bak';
GO

DELETE People
WHERE BusinessEntityID = 1;
GO

SELECT TOP 6 *
FROM People
ORDER BY BusinessEntityID;
GO
```

Executing the previous query creates a full backup and deletes the person with a business entity ID of 1, as illustrated in these results:

```
BusinessEntityID FirstName  MiddleName  LastName
---------------- ---------  ----------  --------
2                Terri      Lee         Duffy
3                Roberto    NULL        Tamburello
4                Rob        NULL        Walters
5                Gail       A           Erickson
6                Jossef     H           Goldberg
7                Dylan      A           Miller
```

To be able to restore the single deleted row, the backup must be restored with a different name, and the row can then be restored using an INSERT statement.

```
USE master;
GO

RESTORE DATABASE Granular_COPY
FROM  DISK = 'C:\Apress\Granular.bak'
WITH MOVE N'Granular' TO 'C:\Program Files\Microsoft SQL Server\MSSQL11.MSSQLSERVER
\MSSQLSERVER\DATA\Granular_COPY.mdf',
MOVE N'Granular_log' TO N'C:\Program Files\Microsoft SQL Server\MSSQL11.MSSQLSERVER
\MSSQL\DATA\Granular_log_COPY.ldf';
GO
```

```
USE Granular;
GO

INSERT People
SELECT BusinessEntityID,
        FirstName,
        MiddleName,
        LastName
FROM AdventureWorks2012.Person.Person
WHERE BusinessEntityID = 1;
GO

SELECT TOP 6 *
FROM People
ORDER BY BusinessEntityID;
GO
```

The results of the previous query show that the row was restored:

```
BusinessEntityID    FirstName    MiddleName    LastName
----------------    ---------    ----------    ----------
1                   Ken          J             Sánchez
2                   Terri        Lee           Duffy
3                   Roberto      NULL          Tamburello
4                   Rob          NULL          Walters
5                   Gail         A             Erickson
6                   Jossef       H             Goldberg
```

How It Works

The process behind this method is fairly self-evident. The database backup being restored with a different name provides the ability to use a SELECT statement from the restored table. Several issues may complicate this method, such as a column that is an IDENTITY, replication, or triggers on the affected table.

Another concern is the size of the database. If the database size is 1TB, space needs to be available to restore the database, and the data and log files should be placed on separate disks from the production database to reduce disk I/O during the restore.

Solution #2: Restore Rows from a Database Snapshot

Restoring an entire database to recover lost rows or tables can be overly burdensome and definitely can be considered overkill. Another method is to utilize a database snapshot as a means of backing up "state" data. A database snapshot is created on a user database from within an instance of SQL and works on a "write" on change. After creating a database snapshot, disk space is reserved for the snapshot that is equal to the reserved space of the data files of the user database. The disk space reserved for the snapshot remains completely empty until a data page from the user database is modified or deleted. Once this change occurs the original data page is written to the database snapshot preserving the data as it appeared at the point in time of the snapshot being taken.

The following code will create a database called Original and populate it with a SELECT INTO statement from the AdventureWorks2012 database and then create a database snapshot from the Original database called Original_SS.

```
USE master;
GO

IF EXISTS (SELECT * FROM sys.databases WHERE name =
'Original')
BEGIN
DROP DATABASE Original;
END
CREATE DATABASE Original;
GO

USE Original;
GO

SELECT BusinessEntityID,
        FirstName,
        MiddleName,
        LastName
INTO People
FROM AdventureWorks2012.Person.Person;
GO

CREATE DATABASE Original_SS ON
( NAME = Original, FILENAME =
'C:\Program Files\Microsoft SQL Server\MSSQL11.MSSQLSERVER\MSSQL\DATA\ Original _SS.ss' )
AS SNAPSHOT OF Original;
GO

USE Original;
GO

SELECT name,
        type_desc,
        size
FROM sys.database_files;
GO

USE Original_SS;
GO

SELECT name,
        type_desc,
        size
FROM sys.database_files;
GO
```

The results of the previous query show that the Original and Original_SS databases were created and that the file sizes are identical.

```
name          type_desc    size
------------  ---------    ----
Original      ROWS         520
Original_log  LOG          168

name          type_desc    size
------------  ---------    ----
Original      ROWS         520
Original_log  LOG          168
```

Despite the results showing that the database snapshot has both a data file and a log file, there is in fact only a single file. Browsing the directory of the snapshot will show that a single file; the `.ss` extension represents the database snapshot, as illustrated in Figure 26-3.

Original.mdf	4,160 KB	5/31/2012 4:40 PM	SQL Server Databa...
Original_log.ldf	1,344 KB	5/31/2012 4:40 PM	SQL Server Databa...
Original_SS.ss	4,160 KB	5/31/2012 4:40 PM	SS File

***Figure 26-3.** Database snapshot file compared to data file*

Upon creating a database snapshot, the single snapshot file is completely empty and is used only as a placeholder. Data pages are added to the snapshot file as changes occur within the original database. This means that when directly querying the database snapshot, the requested 8KB data pages have not been modified since the snapshot was taken the data pages are being returned from the original database.

The following query is directly querying the `Original_SS` database, but because no changes have been made, the query is actually being returned from the `Original` database:

```
USE Original_SS;
GO

SELECT *
FROM People
WHERE LastName = 'Abercrombie';
GO
```

The results show the original values of people with the last name of Abercrombie.

```
BusinessEntityID  FirstName  MiddleName  LastName
----------------  ---------  ----------  -----------
295               Kim        NULL        Abercrombie
2170              Kim        NULL        Abercrombie
38                Kim        B           Abercrombie
```

Updating the last name from Abercrombie to Abercromby will cause the original data page to be written to the database snapshot, while the `Original` database writes the updated value. The following query updates all people with the last name Abercrombie and then queries both the `Original` and `Original_SS` databases to show the different values:

```
USE Original;

UPDATE People
SET LastName = 'Abercromny'
WHERE LastName = 'Abercrombie';
GO

SELECT *
FROM People
WHERE LastName = 'Abercrombie';
GO

USE Original_SS
GO

SELECT *
FROM People
WHERE LastName = 'Abercrombie';
GO;
```

```
(0 row(s) affected)

BusinessEntityID   FirstName   MiddleName   LastName
----------------   ---------   ----------   -----------
295                Kim         NULL         Abercrombie
2170               Kim         NULL         Abercrombie
38                 Kim         B            Abercrombie
```

The results show that once the `Original` database was updated, the last name of Abercrombie was updated, and no results were returned. Querying the snapshot database, `Original_SS`, shows all affected records have been written to the snapshot.

The snapshot can be used to revert the records to their original state by using a nonequi join on the desired columns.

```
USE Original;
GO

UPDATE People
SET LastName = ss.LastName
FROM People p JOIN Original_SS.dbo.People ss
ON p.LastName <> ss.LastName
AND p.BusinessEntityID = ss.BusinessEntityID;
GO
```

```
SELECT *
FROM People
WHERE LastName = 'Abercrombie';
GO
```

```
(3 row(s) affected)

BusinessEntityID  FirstName  MiddleName  LastName
----------------  ---------  ----------  -----------
295               Kim        NULL        Abercrombie
2170              Kim        NULL        Abercrombie
38                Kim        B           Abercrombie
```

How It Works

The results show that for all records in the Original database's People table where the BusinessEntityID matches the Original_SS database's Peoples table, the BusinessEntityID and LastName column values do not match. The net result is that the changes made to the last name are reverted to the values that are stored in the database snapshot, restoring them to the values at the time of the snapshot.

Although this chapter focuses on backups, it is important to know that a database snapshot can be used to restore a database, which is referred to as *reverting* the database. Reverting a database is also typically much faster than doing a full restore because the only thing that needs to be done is to revert the data pages from the snapshot to the original data files. The following code shows how to revert the Original database from the Original_SS snapshot:

```
USE master;

RESTORE DATABASE Original
FROM DATABASE_SNAPSHOT = 'Original_SS';
GO
```

26-7. Backing Up Data Files or Filegroups

Problem

Your database size is so large that it is prohibitive to complete a full database backup on a daily basis.

Solution #1: Perform a File Backup

It can become burdensome to maintain an effective and efficient backup procedure in very large databases (VLDBs) because of the time it takes to perform a full backup and the amount of space required. Rather than a full backup, backups can be made of the data files individually. This can be demonstrated by creating a database with multiple files and filegroups.

```
CREATE DATABASE BackupFiles CONTAINMENT = NONE
 ON  PRIMARY
( NAME = N'BackupFiles', FILENAME = N'C:\Program Files\Microsoft SQL Server\MSSQL11.MSSQLSERVER
\MSSQL\DATA\BackupFiles.mdf' , SIZE = 4096KB , FILEGROWTH = 1024KB ),
```

```
 FILEGROUP [Current]
( NAME = N'CurrentData', FILENAME = 'C:\Program Files\Microsoft SQL Server\MSSQL11.MSSQLSERVER\
MSSQL\DATA\CurrentData.ndf' , SIZE = 4096KB , FILEGROWTH = 1024KB ),
 FILEGROUP [Historic]
( NAME = N'HistoricData', FILENAME = 'C:\Program Files\Microsoft SQL Server\MSSQL11.MSSQLSERVER\
MSSQL\DATA\HistoricData.ndf' , SIZE = 4096KB , FILEGROWTH = 1024KB )
 LOG ON
( NAME = N'BackupFiles_log', FILENAME = 'C:\Program Files\Microsoft SQL Server\MSSQL11.
MSSQLSERVER\MSSQL\DATA\BackupFiles_log.ldf' , SIZE = 1024KB , FILEGROWTH = 10%);
GO
ALTER DATABASE [BackupFiles] SET RECOVERY FULL;
GO
```

To back up a single file from a database, simply use the BACKUP DATABASE command and specify the files to back up.

```
BACKUP DATABASE BackupFiles
FILE = 'HistoricData'
TO DISK =  'C:\Apress\Historic.bak';
GO
```

Solution #2: Perform a Filegroup Backup

Sometimes a filegroup contains multiple files that need to be backed up in a single backup set. This is accomplished easily enough using the BACKUP DATABASE command and specifying the filegroup to be backed up.

```
BACKUP DATABASE BackupFiles
FILEGROUP = 'Historic'
TO DISK =  'C:\Apress\HistoricGroup.bak';
GO
```

How It Works

Backing up a file or filegroup works the same as a full database backup other than that it provides a more focused granular approach to the specific filegroup or file in the database. Either method can be employed to reduce the amount of time and space required for a full database backup.

It is critical to fully plan a database design if this backup/recovery method is going to be used to ensure that the entire database can be restored to a point in time and remain consistent. Consider placing one table on a file that references another table on a separate file. If either file had to be restored and referential integrity was violated because of the point in time of the restoration, this can cause a great deal of work to be able to restore the database to a consistent and valid state.

Always also remember that the primary file/filegroup must be backed up because it contains all of the system tables and database objects.

26-8. Mirroring Backup Files

Problem

You want to ensure that multiple backups are written to different disks/tapes without affecting the backup media set or having to manually copy the backup files.

Solution

SQL Server 2005 Enterprise edition introduced the MIRROR TO clause, which will write the backup to multiple devices.

```
BACKUP DATABASE AdventureWorks2012
TO DISK =  'C:\Apress\AdventureWorks2012.bak'
MIRROR TO DISK = 'C:\MirroredBackup\AdventureWorks2012.bak'
WITH
   FORMAT,
   MEDIANAME = 'AdventureWorksSet1';
GO
```

■ **Tip** Make sure that the Apress and MirroredBackup folders exist on the C: drive or change the path in the previous query.

How It Works

During the backup, using MIRROR TO will write the backup to multiple devices, which ensures that the backup file resides on separate tapes or disks in case one should become corrupt or unusable. There are several limitations to using the MIRROR TO clause, the first being that it requires the Developer or Enterprise edition. The mirrored devices must be the same type, meaning you cannot write one file to disk and the other to tape. The mirrored devices must be similar and have the same properties. Insufficiently similar devices will generate the error message 3212.

26-9. Backing Up a Database Without Affecting the Normal Sequence of Backups

Problem

An up-to-date backup needs to be created that will not affect the normal sequence of backups.

Solution

Using the BACKUP command and specifying WITH COPY_ONLY will create the desired backup but does not affect the backup or restore sequence.

```
BACKUP DATABASE AdventureWorks2012
TO DISK =  'C:\Apress\AdventureWorks2012COPY.bak'
WITH COPY_ONLY;
GO
```

How It Works

The only difference in the backup process when using WITH COPY_ONLY is that the backup will have no effect on the backup or restore procedure for a database.

■ **Caution** If COPY_ONLY is used with a transaction log backup, the transaction log will not be truncated once the backup is complete. If COPY_ONLY is used with a differential backup, the COPY_ONLY will be ignored, and a differential backup will be created.

26-10. Querying Backup Data

Problem

You have to create a programmatic way to return backup information.

Solution

The msdb database maintains all of the backup history in the system tables. The system tables backupfile, backupfilegroup, backupmediafamily, backupmediaset, and backupset contain the full history of database backups as well as the media types and location. These tables can be queried to return information on any database backup that has occurred.

The following query will return the database name, the date and time the backup began, the type of backup that was taken, whether it used COPY_ONLY, the path and file name or device name, and the backup size ordering by the start date in descending order.

```
USE msdb;
GO
SELECT database_name,
           CONVERT(DATE, backup_start_date) AS date,
           CASE type
             WHEN 'D' THEN 'Database'
             WHEN 'I' THEN 'Differential database'
             WHEN 'L' THEN 'Log'
             WHEN 'F' THEN 'File or filegroup'
             WHEN 'G' THEN 'Differential file'
             WHEN 'P' THEN 'Partial'
             WHEN 'Q' THEN 'Differential partial'
             ELSE 'Unknown'
           END AS type,
           physical_device_name
FROM backupset s JOIN backupmediafamily f
ON s.media_set_id = f.media_set_id
ORDER BY backup_start_date DESC;
GO
```

```
Your results may vary
```

```
database_name        date        type               physical_device_name
-------------------  ----------  -----------------  ----------------------------------------
AdventureWorks2012   2012-06-01  Database           C:\Backups\AdventureWorks2012COPY.bak
AdventureWorks2012   2012-06-01  Database           C:\Backups\AdventureWorks2012.bak
AdventureWorks2012   2012-06-01  Database           C:\MirroredBackup\AdventureWorks2012.bak
BackupFiles          2012-06-01  File or filegroup  C:\Backups\HistoricGroup.bak
BackupFiles          2012-06-01  File or filegroup  C:\Backups\Historic.bak
Granular             2012-05-31  Database           C:\Backups\Granular.bak
```

The results show the most recent backups in descending order by the date the backup was taken.

How It Works

Whenever a backup is taken of a database, it is recorded in the `msdb` database. The system tables that record this information are made available to query. This information can be used for a number of different purposes including automating restoration of a database.

CHAPTER 27

Recovery

By Jason Brimhall

Chapter 26 discussed one of the most critical responsibilities of a SQL Server professional: backing up your data. In this chapter, I will discuss the second half of that very important topic: recovering your data. It is not enough to simply create a backup of the data; you need to also regularly restore your data to test the reliability of the backups.

This chapter will discuss how to restore a database from a backup file. A restore operation copies all data, log, and index pages from the backup media set to the destination database. The destination database can be an existing database (which will be overlaid) or a new database (where new files will be created based on the backup). After the restore operation, a "redo" phase ensues, rolling forward committed transactions that were happening at the end of the database backup. After that, the "undo" phase rolls back uncommitted transactions.

This next set of recipes will demonstrate database restores in action.

27-1. Restoring a Database from a Full Backup

Problem

You have created a full backup of your database. Now you want to test the backup to ensure it is a good backup.

Solution

Use the RESTORE command to restore a database from a full database backup. Unlike a BACKUP operation, a RESTORE is not always an online operation—for a full database restore, user connections must be disconnected from the database prior to restoring over the database. Other restore types (such as filegroup, file, or page) can allow online activity in the database in other areas aside from the elements being restored. For example, if filegroup FG2 is getting restored, FG3 can still be accessed during the operation.

Note Online restores are a SQL Server Enterprise Edition feature.

In general, you may need to restore a database after data loss because of user error or file corruption or because you need a second copy of a database or are moving a database to a new SQL Server instance.

The following is simplified syntax for the RESTORE command:

```
RESTORE DATABASE { database_name | @database_name_var } [ FROM<backup_device>[ ,... n ] ] [
WITH ] [Option Name ] [,... n]
```

The RESTORE DATABASE command also includes several options, many of which I'll demonstrate in this chapter.

The first example in this recipe is a simple RESTORE from the latest backup set on the device (in this example, two backup sets exist on the device for the TestDB database, and you want the second one). For the demonstration, I'll start by creating two full backups on a single device.

```
USE master
;
GO

Declare @BackupDate Char(8) = Convert(Varchar,GetDate(),112)
    ,@BackupPath Varchar(50);

Set @BackupPath = 'C:\Apress\TestDB_' + @BackupDate + '.BAK';

BACKUP DATABASE TestDB
TO DISK = @BackupPath;
GO
-- Time passes, we make another backup to the same device
USE master;
GO

Declare @BackupDate Char(8) = Convert(Varchar,GetDate(),112)
    ,@BackupPath Varchar(50);

Set @BackupPath = 'C:\Apress\TestDB_' + @BackupDate + '.BAK';

BACKUP DATABASE TestDB
TO DISK = @BackupPath;
GO
```

Now the database is restored using the second backup from the device (notice that the REPLACE argument is used to tell SQL Server to overlay the existing TestDB database).

```
USE master;
GO

Declare @DeviceName Varchar(50);

Select @DeviceName = b.physical_device_name
    From msdb.dbo.backupset a
        INNER JOIN msdb.dbo.backupmediafamily b
        ON a.media_set_id = b.media_set_id
    Where a.database_name = 'TestDB'
        And a.type = 'D'
        And Convert(Varchar,a.backup_start_date,112) = Convert(Varchar,GetDate(),112);

RESTORE DATABASE TestDB
FROM DISK = @DeviceName
WITH FILE = 2, REPLACE;
GO
```

This returns the following output (your results may vary):

```
Processed 4384 pages for database 'TestDB', file 'TestDB' on file 2.
Processed 2 pages for database 'TestDB', file 'TestDB_log' on file 2.
RESTORE DATABASE successfully processed 4386 pages in 10.742 seconds (3.189 MB/sec).
```

In this second example, a *new* database is created by restoring from the TestDB backup, creating a new database called TrainingDB. Notice that the MOVE argument is used to designate the location of the new database files.

```
USE master;
GO

Declare @DeviceName Varchar(50);

Select @DeviceName = b.physical_device_name
    From msdb.dbo.backupset a
        INNER JOIN msdb.dbo.backupmediafamily b
        ON a.media_set_id = b.media_set_id
    Where a.database_name = 'TestDB'
        And a.type = 'D'
        And Convert(Varchar,a.backup_start_date,112) = Convert(Varchar,GetDate(),112);
RESTORE DATABASE TrainingDB
FROM DISK = @DeviceName
WITH FILE = 2,
MOVE 'TestDB' TO 'C:\Apress\TrainingDB.mdf',
MOVE 'TestDB_log' TO 'C:\Apress\TrainingDB_log.LDF';
GO
```

This restore operation results in the following (your results may vary):

```
Processed 4384 pages for database 'TrainingDB', file 'TestDB' on file 2.
Processed 2 pages for database 'TrainingDB', file 'TestDB_log' on file 2.
RESTORE DATABASE successfully processed 4386 pages in 8.210 seconds (4.173 MB/sec).
```

In the last example for this recipe, the TestDB database is restored from a striped backup set. First, I create a backup set that will be used to perform the restore of a striped backup set.

```
USE master;
GO
/* The path for each file should be changed to a path matching one
That exists on your system. */
BACKUP DATABASE TestDB
TO DISK = 'C:\Apress\Recipes\TestDB_Stripe1.bak'
    , DISK = 'D:\Apress\Recipes\TestDB_Stripe2.bak'
    , DISK = 'E:\Apress\Recipes\TestDB_Stripe3.bak'
    WITH NOFORMAT, NOINIT,
NAME = N'TestDB-Stripe Database Backup',
SKIP, STATS = 20;
GO
```

Now, I will perform the restore of the striped backup set.

```
USE master;
GO
/* You should use the same file path for each file as specified
in the backup statement. */
RESTORE DATABASE TestDB
FROM DISK='C:\Apress\Recipes\TestDB_Stripe1.bak'
    , DISK='D:\Apress\Recipes\TestDB_Stripe2.bak'
    , DISK='E:\Apress\Recipes\TestDB_Stripe3.bak'
    WITH FILE=1, REPLACE;
GO
```

This restore operation results in the following (your results may vary):

```
Processed 152 pages for database 'TestDB', file 'TestDB' on file 1.
Processed 1 pages for database 'TestDB', file 'TestDB_log' on file 1.
RESTORE DATABASE successfully processed 153 pages in 0.657 seconds (1.907 MB/sec).
```

How It Works

In the first example, the query began by setting the database to the `master` database. This is because a full `RESTORE` is not an online operation and requires that there be no active connections to the database that is being restored in order to run.

The `RESTORE` was for the `TestDB` database, and it overlaid the current database with the data as it existed at the end of the second backup set on the backup device created from this command.

```
Declare @BackupDate Char(8)=Convert(Varchar,GetDate(),112)
    ,@BackupPath Varchar(50);

Set @BackupPath='C:\Apress\TestDB_'+@BackupDate+'.BAK';
```

Prior to running the `RESTORE` command, I needed to query the `msdb` database to determine the name of the backup device since I created it dynamically based on the current date. The following query shows how to find the name of that backup device:

```
Declare @DeviceName Varchar(50);

Select @DeviceName=b.physical_device_name
    From msdb.dbo.backupset a
        INNER JOIN msdb.dbo.backupmediafamily b
            ON a.media_set_id=b.media_set_id
    Where a.database_name='TestDB'
        And a.type='D'
        And Convert(Varchar,a.backup_start_date,112)=Convert(Varchar,GetDate(),112);
```

Having retrieved the name of the backup device, I can now restore the database using the following `RESTORE` command while specifying over which database to restore:

```
RESTORE DATABASE TestDB
```

The next line of this example designated the location of the backup device.

```
FROM DISK=@DeviceName
```

The last line of this example designated which backup set from the backup device should be used to RESTORE from (you can use RESTORE HEADERONLY to see what backup sets exist on a backup device).

```
WITH FILE=2, REPLACE
```

Any data that was updated since the last backup will be lost, so it is assumed in this example that data loss is acceptable and that data as of the last backup is desired. In the second example, a new database was created based on a RESTORE from another database. The example is similar to the previous query, only this time the MOVE command is used to designate where the new database files should be located (and the new database name is used as well).

```
MOVE 'TestDB' TO 'C:\Apress\ TrainingDB.mdf,
MOVE 'TestDB_log' TO 'C:\Apress\TrainingDB_log.LDF'
```

RESTORE FILELISTONLY can be used to retrieve the logical name and physical path of the backed-up database.

■ **Tip** The RESTORE...MOVE command is often used in conjunction with database migrations to different SQL Server instances that use different drive letters and directories.

In the last example of the recipe, the TestDB was restored from a striped backup set. FROM DISK was repeated for each disk device in the set.

```
USE master;
GO
RESTORE DATABASE TestDB
FROM DISK='C:\Apress\Recipes\TestDB_Stripe1.bak'
    , DISK='D:\Apress\Recipes\TestDB_Stripe2.bak'
    , DISK='E:\Apress\Recipes\TestDB_Stripe3.bak'
    WITH FILE=1, REPLACE;
GO
```

In each of these examples, the database was restored to a recovered state, meaning that it was online and available for users to query after the redo phase (and during/after the undo phase). In the next few recipes, you'll see that the database is often *not* recovered until a differential or transaction log backup can be restored.

27-2. Restoring a Database from a Transaction Log Backup

Problem

You need to restore a database to a predetermined time that is after the last full backup.

Solution

You can perform transaction log restores in conjunction with a full backup by using the RESTORE LOG command. Transaction log restores require an initial full database restore, and if you're applying multiple transaction logs, they must be applied in chronological order (based on when the transaction log backups were generated). Applying transaction logs out of order, or with gaps between backups, isn't allowed. The syntax for restoring transaction logs is RESTORE LOG instead of RESTORE DATABASE; however, the syntax and options are the same.

For this demonstration, the TrainingDB created in the previous recipe will be used (if it doesn't exist, we will create it).

```
USE master;
GO
IF NOT EXISTS (SELECT name FROM sys.databases
WHERE name='TrainingDB')
BEGIN
CREATE DATABASE TrainingDB;
END
GO
-- Add a table and some data to it
USE TrainingDB
GO
SELECT *
INTO dbo.SalesOrderDetail
FROM AdventureWorks2012.Sales.SalesOrderDetail;
GO
```

This database will be given a full backup and two consecutive transaction log backups.

```
USE master;
GO

Declare @BackupDate Char(8)=Convert(Varchar,GetDate(),112)
    ,@BackupPath Varchar(50);
Set @BackupPath='C:\Apress\TrainingDB_'+@BackupDate+'.BAK';

BACKUP DATABASE TrainingDB
TO DISK=@BackupPath;
GO
BACKUP LOG TrainingDB
TO DISK='C:\Apress\TrainingDB_20120430_8AM.trn';
GO
-- Two hours pass, another transaction log backup is made
BACKUP LOG TrainingDB
TO DISK='C:\Apress\TrainingDB_20120430_10AM.trn';
GO
```

The previous RESTORE examples have assumed that there were no existing connections in the database to be restored over. However, in this example, I demonstrate how to kick out any connections to the database prior to performing the RESTORE.

```
USE master;
GO
-- Kicking out all other connections
ALTER DATABASE TrainingDB
SET SINGLE_USER
WITH ROLLBACK IMMEDIATE;
GO
```

Next, a database backup and two transaction log backups are restored from backup.

```
USE master;
GO
```

```
Declare @DeviceName Varchar(50);

Select @DeviceName=b.physical_device_name
    From msdb.dbo.backupset a
        INNER JOIN msdb.dbo.backupmediafamily b
            ON a.media_set_id=b.media_set_id
    Where a.database_name='TrainingDB'
        And a.type='D'
        And Convert(Varchar,a.backup_start_date,112)=Convert(Varchar,GetDate(),112);
RESTORE DATABASE TrainingDB
FROM DISK=@DeviceName
WITH NORECOVERY, REPLACE;
RESTORE LOG TrainingDB
FROM DISK='C:\Apress\ TrainingDB_20120430_8AM.trn'
WITH NORECOVERY, REPLACE

RESTORE LOG TrainingDB
FROM DISK='C:\Apress\ TrainingDB_20120430_10AM.trn'
WITH RECOVERY, REPLACE
```

This results in the following (your results will vary):

```
Processed 5880 pages for database 'TrainingDB', file 'TrainingDB' on file 1.
Processed 3 pages for database 'TrainingDB', file 'TrainingDB_log' on file 1.
RESTORE DATABASE successfully processed 5883 pages in 8.140 seconds (5.645 MB/sec).
Processed 0 pages for database 'TrainingDB', file 'TrainingDB' on file 1.
Processed 2819 pages for database 'TrainingDB', file 'TrainingDB_log' on file 1.
RESTORE LOG successfully processed 2819 pages in 1.494 seconds (14.741 MB/sec).
RESTORE LOG successfully processed 0 pages in 0.072 seconds (0.000 MB/sec).
```

In this second example, I'll use STOPAT to restore the database and transaction log as of a specific point in time. To demonstrate, first a full backup will be taken of the TrainingDB database.

```
USE master;
GO
BACKUP DATABASE TrainingDB
TO DISK='C:\Apress\TrainingDB_StopAt.bak';
GO
```

Next, rows will be deleted out of the table, and the current time after the change will be queried.

```
USE TrainingDB;
GO
DELETE dbo.SalesOrderDetail
WHERE ProductID=776;
GO
SELECT GETDATE();
GO
```

This query returns the following (your results will vary):

```
2012-04-30 22:17:11.563
```

Next, a transaction log backup is performed.

```
BACKUP LOG TrainingDB
TO DISK = 'C:\Apress\TrainingDB_20120430_2022.trn';
GO
```

This results in the following:

```
Processed 17 pages for database 'TrainingDB', file 'TrainingDB_log' on file 1. BACKUP LOG
successfully processed 17 pages in 0.031 seconds (4.158 MB/sec).
```

The database is restored from backup, leaving it in NORECOVERY so that the transaction log backup can also be restored.

```
USE master;
GO
RESTORE DATABASE TrainingDB
FROM DISK = 'C:\Apress\TrainingDB_StopAt.bak'
WITH FILE = 1, NORECOVERY,
STOPAT = '2012-04-30 22:17:10.563';
GO
```

Next, the transaction log is restored, also designating the time prior to the data deletion.

```
RESTORE LOG TrainingDB
FROM DISK = 'C:\Apress\TrainingDB_20120430_2022.trn'
WITH RECOVERY,
STOPAT = '2012-04-30 22:17:10.563';
GO
```

The following query confirms that you have restored just prior to the data deletion:

```
USE TrainingDB;
GO
SELECT COUNT(*)
FROM dbo.SalesOrderDetail
WHERE ProductID = 776;
GO
```

This query returns the following:

```
228
```

How It Works

In the first example for this recipe, the TrainingDB database was restored from a full database backup and left in NORECOVERY mode. Being in NORECOVERY mode allows other transaction log or differential backups to be applied. In this example, two transaction log backups were applied in chronological order, with the second using the RECOVERY option to bring the database online.

The second example in the recipe demonstrated restoring a database as of a specific point in time. Point-in-time recovery is useful for restoring a database prior to a database modification or failure. The syntax was similar to the first example, only the STOPAT was used for both RESTORE DATABASE and RESTORE LOG. Including the STOPAT for each RESTORE statement makes sure that the restore doesn't recover past the designated date.

27-3. Restoring a Database from a Differential Backup

Problem

As a part of your backup strategy, you have implemented differential backups. You now need to restore the database to a point in time after the last full database backup, taking advantage of the differential backups that have been taken.

Solution

You will use the RESTORE DATABASE command. The syntax for differential database restores is identical to full database restores, only full database restores must be performed *prior* to applying differential backups. When restoring the full database backup, the database must be left in NORECOVERY mode. Also, any transaction logs you want to restore must be done *after* the differential backup is applied, as this example demonstrates.

First, however, I'll set up the example by performing a full, differential, and transaction log backup on the TrainingDB database.

```
USE master;
GO
BACKUP DATABASE TrainingDB
TO DISK='C:\Apress\TrainingDB_DiffExample.bak';
GO
-- Time passes
BACKUP DATABASE TrainingDB
TO DISK='C:\Apress\TrainingDB_DiffExample.diff'
WITH DIFFERENTIAL;
GO

-- More time passes
BACKUP LOG TrainingDB
TO DISK='C:\Apress\TrainingDB_DiffExample_tlog.trn';
GO
```

Now, I'll demonstrate performing a RESTORE, bringing the database back to the completion of the last transaction log backup.

```
USE master;
GO
-- Full database restore
RESTORE DATABASE TrainingDB
FROM DISK='C:\Apress\TrainingDB_DiffExample.bak'
WITH NORECOVERY, REPLACE;
GO
-- Differential
RESTORE DATABASE TrainingDB
FROM DISK='C:\Apress\TrainingDB_DiffExample.diff'
WITH NORECOVERY;
GO
-- Transaction log
RESTORE LOG TrainingDB
FROM DISK='C:\Apress\TrainingDB_DiffExample_tlog.trn'
WITH RECOVERY;
GO
```

This returns the following (your results will vary):

```
Processed 5880 pages for database 'TrainingDB', file 'TrainingDB' on file 1.
Processed 3 pages for database 'TrainingDB', file 'TrainingDB_log' on file 1.
RESTORE DATABASE successfully processed 5883 pages in 0.443 seconds (2.831 MB/sec).
Processed 40 pages for database 'TrainingDB', file 'TrainingDB' on file 1.
Processed 2 pages for database 'TrainingDB', file 'TrainingDB_log' on file 1.
RESTORE DATABASE successfully processed 42 pages in 0.069 seconds (4.860 MB/sec).
RESTORE LOG successfully processed 0 pages in 0.070 seconds (0.000 MB/sec).
```

How It Works

Differential backups capture database changes that have occurred since the last full database backup. Differential restores use the same syntax as full database restores, only they must always follow a full database restore (with NORECOVERY) first. In this recipe, the database was initially restored from a full database backup, then followed by a restore from a differential backup, and then lastly a restore from a transaction log backup. The differential RESTORE command was formed similarly to previous RESTORE examples, only it referenced the differential backup file. On the last restore, the RECOVERY option was designated to make the database available for use.

27-4. Restoring a File or Filegroup

Problem

You have a database with multiple filegroups. You need to restore one of the filegroups.

Solution

Restoring a file or filegroup uses virtually the same syntax as a full database restore, except you also use the FILEGROUP or FILE keyword. To perform a restore of a specific read-write file or filegroup, your database must use either a full or bulk-logged recovery model. This is required because transaction log backups must be applied after restoring a file or filegroup backup. In SQL Server, if your database is using a simple recovery model, only read-only files or read-only filegroups can have file/filegroup backups and restores.

To set up this recipe's example, I will create the VLTestDB database if it doesn't exist after which a filegroup backup is taken for the VLTestDB database.

```
USE master;
GO
If Not Exists (Select name from sys.databases where name='VLTestDB')
Begin
CREATE DATABASE VLTestDB
ON PRIMARY
     ( NAME=N'VLTestDB',FILENAME=N'c:\Apress\VLTestDB.mdf'
    ,SIZE=4072 KB , FILEGROWTH=0 ),
FILEGROUP FG2
     ( NAME=N'VLTestDB2', FILENAME=N'c:\Apress\VLTestDB2.ndf'
    , SIZE=3048 KB , FILEGROWTH=1024 KB )
    ,( NAME=N'VLTestDB3', FILENAME=N'c:\Apress\VLTestDB3.ndf'
    , SIZE=3048 KB , FILEGROWTH=1024 KB )
LOG ON
     ( NAME=N'VLTestDBLog', FILENAME=N'c:\Apress\VLTestDB_log.ldf'
    , SIZE=1024 KB , FILEGROWTH=10 %);
```

```
Alter DATABASE VLTestDB
Modify FILEGROUP FG2 Default;

END
GO

USE master;
GO
BACKUP DATABASE VLTestDB
FILEGROUP = 'FG2'
TO DISK = 'C:\Apress\VLTestDB_FG2.bak'
WITH NAME = N'VLTestDB-Full Filegroup Backup',
SKIP, STATS = 20;
GO
```

Time passes, and then a transaction log backup is taken for the database.

```
BACKUP LOG VLTestDB
TO DISK = 'C:\Apress\VLTestDB_FG_Example.trn';
GO
```

Next, the database filegroup FG2 is restored from backup, followed by the restore of a transaction log backup.

```
USE master;
GO
RESTORE DATABASE VLTestDB
FILEGROUP = 'FG2'
FROM DISK = 'C:\Apress\VLTestDB_FG2.bak'
WITH FILE = 1, NORECOVERY, REPLACE;
RESTORE LOG VLTestDB
FROM DISK = 'C:\Apress\VLTestDB_FG_Example.trn'
WITH FILE = 1, RECOVERY;
GO
```

This returns the following (your results may vary):

```
Processed 8 pages for database 'VLTestDB', file 'VLTestDB2' on file 1.
Processed 8 pages for database 'VLTestDB', file 'VLTestDB3' on file 1.
RESTORE DATABASE ... FILE=<name> successfully processed
16 pages in 0.048 seconds (2.604 MB/sec).
Processed 0 pages for database 'VLTestDB', file 'VLTestDB2' on file 1.
Processed 0 pages for database 'VLTestDB', file 'VLTestDB3' on file 1.
RESTORE LOG successfully processed 0 pages in 0.062 seconds (0.000 MB/sec).
```

How It Works

Filegroup or file backups are most often used in very large databases, where full database backups may take too long to execute. With filegroup or file backups comes greater administrative complexity, because you'll have to potentially recover from disaster using multiple backup sets (one per filegroup, for example).

In this recipe, the VLTestDB database filegroup named FG2 was restored from a backup device and left in NORECOVERY mode so that a transaction log restore could be applied. The RECOVERY keyword was used in the transaction log restore operation in order to bring the filegroup back online. In SQL Server Enterprise Edition, filegroups other than the primary filegroup can be taken offline for restores while leaving the other active filegroups available for use (this is called an ONLINE restore).

27-5. Performing a Piecemeal (PARTIAL) Restore

Problem

You have a database with multiple filegroups that needs to be recovered. You need to recover the primary filegroup in addition to any filegroups critical to the business based on a predetermined priority (you may recover certain filegroups at your leisure).

Solution

The PARTIAL command can be used with the RESTORE DATABASE command to restore secondary filegroups in a piecemeal fashion. This variation of RESTORE brings the primary filegroup online, letting you then restore other filegroups as needed later. If you're using a database with a full or bulk-logged recovery model, you can use this command with read-write filegroups. If the database is using a simple recovery model, you can use PARTIAL only in conjunction with read-only secondary filegroups.

In this example, the VLTestDB is restored from a full database backup using the PARTIAL keyword and designating that only the PRIMARY filegroup be brought online (and with filegroups FG2 and FG3 staying offline and unrestored).

First, to set up this example, the primary and FG2 filegroups in the VLTestDB are backed up.

```
USE master;
GO
BACKUP DATABASE VLTestDB
FILEGROUP = 'PRIMARY'
TO DISK = 'C:\Apress\VLTestDB_Primary_PieceExmp.bak';
GO
BACKUP DATABASE VLTestDB
FILEGROUP = 'FG2'
TO DISK = 'C:\Apress\VLTestDB_FG2_PieceExmp.bak';
GO
```

After that, a transaction log backup is performed.

```
BACKUP LOG VLTestDB
TO DISK = 'C:\Apress\VLTestDB_PieceExmp.trn';
GO
```

Next, a piecemeal RESTORE is performed, recovering just the PRIMARY filegroup.

```
USE master;
GO
RESTORE DATABASE VLTestDB
FILEGROUP = 'PRIMARY'
FROM DISK = 'C:\Apress\VLTestDB_Primary_PieceExmp.bak'
WITH PARTIAL, NORECOVERY, REPLACE;
RESTORE LOG VLTestDB
```

```
FROM DISK='C:\Apress\VLTestDB_PieceExmp.trn'
WITH RECOVERY;
GO
```

The other filegroup, FG2, now contains unavailable files. You can view the file status by querying sys.database_files from the VLTestDB database.

```
USE VLTestDB;
GO
SELECT name,state_desc
FROM sys.database_files;
GO
```

This query returns the following:

```
Name            state_desc
-----------     ----------------
VLTestDB        ONLINE
VLTestDBLog     ONLINE
VLTestDB2       RECOVERY_PENDING
VLTestDB3       RECOVERY_PENDING
```

How It Works

In this recipe, the VLTestDB was restored from a full backup, restoring just the PRIMARY filegroup. The WITH clause included the PARTIAL keyword and NORECOVERY so that transaction log backups can be restored. After the transaction log restore, any objects in the PRIMARY filegroup will be available, and objects in the secondary filegroups are unavailable until you restore them at a later time.

For very large databases, using the PARTIAL keyword during a RESTORE operation allows you to prioritize and load filegroups that have a higher priority, making them available sooner.

27-6. Restoring a Page

Problem

You have discovered that a few data pages have become corrupted in the database. You need to recover the corrupted pages.

Solution

SQL Server provides the ability to restore specific data pages in a database using a FULL or BULK_LOGGED recovery model via the PAGE argument. In the rare event that a small number of data pages become corrupted in a database, it may be more efficient to restore individual data pages than the entire file, filegroup, or database.

The syntax for restoring specific pages is similar to restoring a filegroup or database, only you use the PAGE keyword coupled with the page ID. Bad pages can be identified in the msdb.dbo.suspect_pages system table, can be identified in the SQL error log, or can be returned in the output of a DBCC command.

To set up this example, a full database backup is created for the TestDB database.

```
USE master;
GO
BACKUP DATABASE TestDB
```

```
TO DISK='C:\Apress\TestDB_PageExample.bak';
GO
```

Next, a restore is performed using the PAGE argument.

```
USE master;
GO
RESTORE DATABASE TestDB
PAGE='1:8'
FROM DISK='C:\Apress\TestDB_PageExample.bak'
WITH NORECOVERY, REPLACE;
GO
```

This query returns the following:

```
Processed 1 pages for database 'TestDB', file 'TestDB' on file 1. RESTORE DATABASE ...
FILE=<name>successfully processed 1 pages in 0.470 seconds (0.016 MB/sec).
```

At this point, any differential or transaction log backups taken after the last full backup should also be restored. Since there were none in this example, no further backups are restored.

Next, and this is something that departs from previous examples, a new transaction log backup must be created that captures the restored page.

```
BACKUP LOG TestDB
TO DISK='C:\Apress\TestDB_PageExample_tlog.trn';
GO
```

This query returns the following:

```
Processed 2 pages for database 'TestDB', file 'TestDB_log' on file 1. BACKUP LOG
successfully processed 2 pages in 0.840 seconds (0.014 MB/sec).
```

To finish the page restore process, the latest transaction log taken after the RESTORE...PAGE must be executed with RECOVERY.

```
RESTORE LOG TestDB
FROM DISK='C:\Apress\TestDB_PageExample_tlog.trn'
WITH RECOVERY;
```

How It Works

In this recipe, a single data page was restored from a full database backup using the PAGE option in the RESTORE DATABASE command. Like restoring from a FILE or FILEGROUP, the first RESTORE leaves the database in a NORECOVERY state, allowing additional transaction log backups to be applied prior to recovery.

27-7. Identifying Databases with Multiple Recovery Paths

Problem

You want to find any backups that have been created that are not used in your RESTORE process.

Solution

Use the sys.database_recovery_status catalog view. Multiple recovery paths are created when you recover a database from backup using point-in-time recovery or when you recover a database without recovering the latest differential or chain of log backups. When there are backups created that you do not use in your RESTORE process, you create a fork in the recovery path.

This recipe demonstrates how to use the sys.database_recovery_status catalog view to get information about a database with more than one recovery path. In the first step, I will create a new database and give it a full database backup, create a table and some rows, and finish up with a transaction log backup.

```
USE master;
GO
IF NOT EXISTS (SELECT name FROM sys.databases WHERE name='RomanHistory')
BEGIN
CREATE DATABASE RomanHistory;
END
GO
BACKUP DATABASE RomanHistory
TO DISK='C:\Apress\RomanHistory_A.bak';
GO

USE RomanHistory;
GO
CREATE TABLE EmperorTitle
(EmperorTitleID int NOT NULL PRIMARY KEY IDENTITY(1,1), TitleNM varchar(255));
GO

INSERT Into EmperorTitle (TitleNM)
    VALUES ('Aulus'), ('Imperator'), ('Pius Felix'), ('Quintus');
BACKUP LOG RomanHistory
TO DISK='C:\Apress\RomanHistory_A.trn';
GO
```

Next, I'll query the sys.database_recovery_status catalog view to get information about the database at this point (column aliases are used to shorten the names for presentation in this book).

```
USE msdb;
GO
SELECT LastLSN=last_log_backup_lsn ,Rec_Fork=recovery_fork_guid
    ,Frst_Fork=first_recovery_fork_guid ,Fork_LSN=fork_point_lsn
FROM sys.database_recovery_status
WHERE database_id=DB_ID('RomanHistory');
GO
```

This query returns the following (your values will vary):

LastLSN	Rec_Fork	Frst_Fork	Fork_LSN
18000000010900001	D020752F-1085-49F6-A848-21C9EDBFF290	NULL	NULL

Notice that the first_recovery_fork_guid and fork_point_lsn columns are NULL. This is because I have not created a fork yet in my recovery path. The last_log_backup_lsn tells me the LSN of the most recent log backup, and the recovery_fork_guid shows the current recovery path in which the database is active.

■ **Tip** A log sequence number (LSN) uniquely identifies each record in a database transaction log.

Next, I will perform a few more data modifications and another transaction log backup.

```
USE RomanHistory;
GO
INSERT Into EmperorTitle (TitleNM)
    VALUES ('Germanicus'), ('Lucius'), ('Maximus'), ('Titus');
GO
BACKUP LOG RomanHistory
TO DISK='C:\Apress\RomanHistory_B.trn';
GO
```

I'll now go ahead and RESTORE the database to a prior state (but not to the latest state).

```
USE master;
GO
RESTORE DATABASE RomanHistory
FROM DISK='C:\Apress\RomanHistory_A.bak'
WITH NORECOVERY, REPLACE;
RESTORE DATABASE RomanHistory
FROM DISK='C:\Apress\RomanHistory_A.trn'
WITH RECOVERY, REPLACE;
GO
```

Now if I reissue the previous query against sys.database_recovery_status, I will see that both the fork_point_lsn and first_recovery_fork_guid columns are no longer NULL.

```
USE msdb;
GO
SELECT LastLSN=last_log_backup_lsn ,Rec_Fork=recovery_fork_guid
    ,Frst_Fork=first_recovery_fork_guid ,Fork_LSN=fork_point_lsn
FROM sys.database_recovery_status
WHERE database_id=DB_ID('RomanHistory');
GO
```

This query returns the following (your results will vary):

LastLSN	Rec_Fork	Frst_Fork	Fork_LSN
18000000010900001	F18522D8-6FDB-40BE-AB99-047DE4280F40	D020752F-1085-49F6-A848-21C9EDBFF290	18000000010900001

How It Works

The sys.database_recovery_status catalog view allows you to see whether multiple recovery forks have been created for a database.

In this recipe, I made one full database backup and two transaction log backups. If I restored the database using all three of the backups, I would have remained in the same recovery path. However, instead, I restored only the first full backup and first transaction log backup, putting the database into recovery before restoring the second transaction log. By recovering prematurely, I brought the database online into a second recovery path.

CHAPTER 28

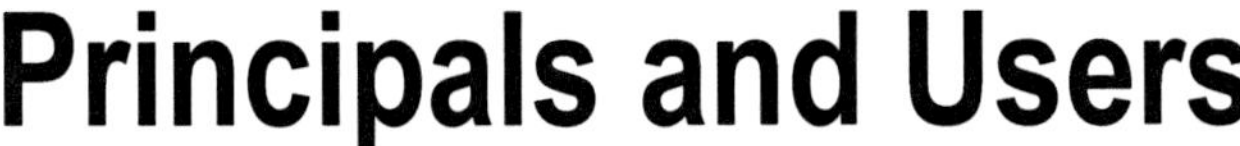

Principals and Users

by Jason Brimhall

Microsoft uses a set of terminology to describe SQL Server security functionality, which separates the security architecture into the following:

- *Principals:* These are objects (for example, a user login, a role, or an application) that may be granted permission to access particular database objects.
- *Securables:* These are objects (a table or view, for example) to which access can be controlled.
- *Permissions:* These are individual rights, granted (or denied) to a principal, to access a securable object.

Principals are the topic of this chapter, and securables and permissions are discussed in the next chapter. Principals fall into three different scopes:

- *Windows principals* are principals based on Windows domain user accounts, domain groups, local user accounts, and local groups. Once added to SQL Server and given permissions to access objects, these types of principals gain access to SQL Server based on Windows Authentication.
- *SQL Server principals* are SQL Server-level logins and fixed server roles. SQL logins are created within SQL Server and have a login name and password independent of any Windows entity. Server roles are groupings of SQL Server instance-level permissions that other principals can become members of, inheriting that server role's permissions.
- *Database principals* are database users, database roles (fixed and user-defined), and application roles—all of which I'll cover in this chapter.

I'll start this chapter with a discussion of Windows principals.

Windows Principals

Windows principals allow access to a SQL Server instance using Windows Authentication. SQL Server allows you to create Windows logins based on Windows user accounts or groups, which can belong either to the local machine or to a domain. A Windows login can be associated with a domain user, local user, or Windows group. When adding a Windows login to SQL Server, the name of the user or group is bound to the Windows account. Windows logins added to SQL Server don't require separate password logins; in that case, Windows handles the login authentication process.

When users log on to SQL Server using Windows Authentication, their current user account must be identified as a login to the SQL Server instance, or they must belong to a Windows user group that exists as a login.

Windows logins apply only at the server operating system level: you can't grant Windows principals access to specific database objects. To grant permissions based on Windows logins, you need to create a database user and associate it with the login. You'll see how to do this when I discuss database principals.

When installing SQL Server, you are asked to decide between Windows-only and mixed authentication modes. Whichever authentication method you choose, you can always change your mind later. Microsoft Windows Authentication allows for tighter security than SQL Server logins, because security is integrated with the Windows operating system, local machine, and domain, and because no passwords are ever transmitted over the network.

28-1. Creating a Windows Login

Problem

Your SQL Server instance is configured for mixed mode authentication. Now you need to add a Windows principal as a login within that instance.

Solution

Use the CREATE LOGIN command to add a Windows group or login to the SQL Server instance. When using mixed authentication mode, you can create your own database logins and passwords within SQL Server.

The abridged syntax for creating a login from a Windows group or user login is as follows:

```
CREATE LOGIN login_name
FROM WINDOWS
[ WITH DEFAULT_DATABASE = database
| DEFAULT_LANGUAGE = language ]
| CERTIFICATE certname ASYMMETRIC KEY asym_key_name
```

Table 28-1 describes the arguments of this command.

Table 28-1. *CREATE LOGIN Arguments*

Argument	Description
login_name	This option defines the name of the Windows user or group.
DEFAULT_DATABASE = database	This option specifies the default database context of the Windows login, with the master system database being the default.
DEFAULT_LANGUAGE = language	This option specifies the default language of the Windows login, with the server default language being the login default if this option isn't specified.
CERTIFICATE certname	This option allows you to bind a certificate to a Windows login.
ASYMMETRIC KEY asym_key_name	This option binds a key to a Windows login. See Chapter 19 for more information on keys.

In this recipe, I assume you already have certain Windows accounts and groups on the local machine or in your domain. This example creates a Windows *login* on the SQL Server instance, which is internally mapped to a Windows user.

```
USE master;
GO
CREATE LOGIN [ROIS\Frederic]
FROM WINDOWS
WITH DEFAULT_DATABASE=AdventureWorks2012,
DEFAULT_LANGUAGE=English;
GO
```

In the second example, a new Windows login is created, based on a Windows group. This is identical to the previous example, except that you are mapping to a Windows group instead of a Windows user.

```
USE master;
GO
CREATE LOGIN [ROIS\DuMonde]
FROM WINDOWS
WITH DEFAULT_DATABASE=AdventureWorks2012;
GO
```

How It Works

This recipe demonstrated adding access for a Windows user and Windows group to the SQL Server instance. In the first example, CREATE LOGIN designated the Windows user in square brackets.

```
CREATE LOGIN [ROIS\Frederic]
```

On the next line, the WINDOWS keyword was used to designate that this is a new login associated to a Windows account.

```
FROM WINDOWS
```

Next, the default database and languages were designated in the WITH clause.

```
WITH DEFAULT_DATABASE=AdventureWorks2012, DEFAULT_LANGUAGE=English
```

In the second example, I demonstrated how to add a Windows group to SQL Server, which again requires square brackets in the CREATE LOGIN command.

```
CREATE LOGIN [ROIS\DuMonde]
```

The FROM WINDOWS clause designated that this was a Windows group, followed by the default database.

```
FROM WINDOWS
WITH DEFAULT_DATABASE=AdventureWorks2012
```

When a Windows group is associated to a SQL Server login, it enables any member of the Windows group to inherit the access and permissions of the Windows login. Therefore, any members of this group will also have access to the SQL Server instance without explicitly having to add each Windows account to the SQL Server instance separately.

28-2. Viewing Windows Logins

Problem

You need to report on all Windows principals that have been added as logins in a SQL Server instance.

Solution

You can view Windows logins and groups by querying the `sys.server_principals` system catalog view. This example shows the name of each Windows login and group with access to SQL Server, along with the security identifier (`sid`). Each principal in the system catalog view has an `sid`, which helps uniquely identify it on the SQL Server instance.

```
USE master;
GO
SELECT name, sid
FROM sys.server_principals
WHERE type_desc IN ('WINDOWS_LOGIN', 'WINDOWS_GROUP')
ORDER BY type_desc;
GO
```

This returns the following results (your own results will vary):

```
name                                          sid
BUILTIN\Administrators                        0x01020000000000052000000020020000
ROIS\SQLServerMSSQLUser$ROIS$FREDERIC         0x0106000000000005500000000732B9753646EF90356745
ROIS\SQLServerMSFTEUser$ROIS$FREDERIC         0x0106000000000005500000000732B9753646EF90356745
ROIS\SQLServerSQLAgentUser$ROIS$FREDERIC      0x0106000000000005500000000732B9753646EF90356745
ROIS\DuMonde                                  0x0106000000000005500000000732B9753646EF91356745
NT AUTHORITY\SYSTEM                           0x010100000000000512000000
ROIS\Administrator                            0x0106000000000005500000000732B9753646EF90356845
ROIS\George                                   0x0106000000000005500000000732C9753646EF90356745
```

How It Works

In this recipe, I demonstrated how to query Windows logins on the SQL Server instance using the `sys.server_principals` system catalog view. This view actually allows you to see other principal types too, which will be reviewed later in the chapter.

28-3. Altering a Windows Login

Problem

You have discovered that a Windows login in your SQL Server instance is configured for the wrong default database. You need to change the default database for this login.

Solution

Once a Windows login is added to SQL Server, it can be modified using the ALTER LOGIN command (this command has several more options that are applicable to SQL logins, as you'll see reviewed later in the chapter). Using this command, you can perform tasks such as the following:

- Changing the default database of the login
- Changing the default language of the login
- Enabling or disabling a login from being used

The abridged syntax is as follows (arguments similar to CREATE LOGIN):

```
ALTER LOGIN login_name { ENABLE | DISABLE
WITH
DEFAULT_DATABASE = database DEFAULT_LANGUAGE = language }
```

In the first example, a Windows login (associated with a Windows user) is disabled from use in SQL Server. This prevents the login from accessing SQL Server and, if connected, ceases any further activity on the SQL Server instance.

```
USE master;
GO
ALTER LOGIN [ROIS\Frederic] DISABLE;
GO
```

This next example demonstrates enabling this account again.

```
USE master;
GO
ALTER LOGIN [ROIS\Frederic] ENABLE;
GO
```

In this example, the default database is changed for a Windows group.

```
USE master;
GO
ALTER LOGIN [ROIS\DuMonde]
    WITH DEFAULT_DATABASE = master;
GO
```

How It Works

In the first example, a Windows login was disabled using ALTER LOGIN and the login name.

```
ALTER LOGIN [ROIS\Frederic]
```

Following this was the DISABLE keyword, which removes this account's access to the SQL Server instance (it removes the account's access but still keeps the login in the SQL Server instance for the later option of reenabling access).

```
DISABLE
```

The second example demonstrated reenabling access to the login by using the ENABLE keyword.

The third example changed the default database for a Windows group. The syntax for referencing Windows logins and groups is the same—both principal types are designated within square brackets.

```
ALTER LOGIN [ROIS\DuMonde]
```

The second line then designated the new default database context for the Windows group.

```
WITH DEFAULT_DATABASE=master
```

28-4. Dropping a Windows Login

Problem

An employee has changed departments and no longer needs access to a SQL Server instance. You need to remove the employee's login.

Solution

In this recipe, I'll demonstrate dropping a login from the SQL Server instance entirely by using the DROP LOGIN command. This removes the login's permission to access the SQL Server instance. If the login is currently connected to the SQL Server instance when the login is dropped, any actions attempted by the connected login will no longer be allowed. The syntax is as follows:

```
DROP LOGIN login_name
```

The only parameter is the login name, which can be a Windows or SQL login (demonstrated later in the chapter), as this recipe demonstrates.

```
USE master;
GO
-- Windows Group login
DROP LOGIN [ROIS\DuMonde];
-- Windows user login
DROP LOGIN [ROIS\Frederic];
GO
```

How It Works

This recipe demonstrated the simple DROP LOGIN command, which removes a login from SQL Server. If a login owns any securables (see the next chapter for more information on securables), the DROP attempt will fail. For example, if the ROIS\Frederic login had been a database owner, an error like the following would have been raised:

```
Msg 15174, Level 16, State 1, Line 3
Login 'ROIS\Frederic' owns one or more database(s).
Change the owner of the database(s) before
dropping the login.
```

28-5. Denying SQL Server Access to a Windows User or Group

Problem

You need to temporarily prevent a group of users from connecting to a SQL Server instance.

Solution

Use the DENY CONNECT SQL command to deny a Windows user or group access to SQL server. Here's an example:

```
USE master;
GO
DENY CONNECT SQL TO [ROIS\Francois];
GO
```

To allow access again, you can use GRANT.

```
USE master;
GO
GRANT CONNECT SQL TO [ROIS\Francois];
GO
```

How It Works

This section is a sneak preview of Chapter 29, where GRANT and DENY will be explained in more detail. In a nutshell, the GRANT command grants permissions to securables, and DENY denies permissions to them. Use DENY CONNECT to restrict the Windows user or group login from accessing a SQL Server instance the next time a login attempt is made. In both GRANT CONNECT and DENY CONNECT, it is assumed that the Windows user or group already has a login in SQL Server. Keep in mind that there are limitations to which logins you can deny permissions to. For example, if you try to DENY CONNECT to your own login with the following code:

```
DENY CONNECT SQL TO [ROIS\Administrator]
```

you will see the following warning:

```
Cannot grant, deny, or revoke permissions to sa, dbo, information_schema, sys, or yourself.
```

SQL Server Principals

Windows Authentication relies on the underlying operating system to perform authentication (determining who a particular user is), which means that SQL Server performs the necessary authorization (determining what actions an authenticated user is entitled to perform). When working with SQL Server principals and SQL Server authentication, SQL Server itself performs both authentication and authorization.

As noted earlier, when using mixed authentication mode, you can create your own login and passwords within SQL Server. These SQL logins exist only in SQL Server and do not have an outside Windows user/group mapping. With SQL logins, the passwords are stored within SQL Server. These user credentials are stored in SQL Server and are used to authenticate the user in question and to determine her appropriate access rights.

Because the security method involves explicit passwords, it is inherently less secure than using Windows Authentication alone. However, SQL Server logins are still commonly used with third-party and non-Windows operating system applications. SQL Server *has* improved the password protection capabilities by enabling Windows-like password functionality, such as forced password changes, expiration dates, and other password policies (for example, password complexity), with Windows Server 2003 and newer.

As with Windows logins, SQL Server logins apply only at the server level; you can't grant permissions on them to specific database objects. Unless you are granted membership to a fixed server role such as sysadmin, you must create database users associated to the login before you can begin working with database objects.

As in previous versions of SQL Server, SQL Server supports principals based on both individual logins and server roles, which multiple individual users can be assigned to.

28-6. Creating a SQL Server Login

Problem

You need to create a SQL login for a user that does not have a Windows login.

Solution

To create a new SQL Server login, use the CREATE LOGIN command.

```
CREATE LOGIN login_name
[WITH PASSWORD=' password ' [ HASHED ] [ MUST_CHANGE ],
SID=sid],
DEFAULT_DATABASE=database,
DEFAULT_LANGUAGE=language,
CHECK_EXPIRATION={ ON | OFF},
CHECK_POLICY={ ON | OFF},
CREDENTIAL=credential_name ]
```

Table 28-2 describes the arguments of this command.

Table 28-2. *CREATE LOGIN Arguments*

Argument	Description
login_name	This is the login name.
' password ' [HASHED] [MUST_CHANGE]	This is the login's password. Specifying the HASHED option means that the provided password is already hashed (made into an unreadable and secured format). If MUST_CHANGE is specified, the user is prompted to change the password the first time the user logs in.
SID=sid	This explicitly specifies the sid that will be used in the system tables of the SQL Server instance. This can be based on a login from a different SQL Server instance (if you're migrating logins). If this isn't specified, SQL Server generates its own sid in the system tables.
DEFAULT_ DATABASE=database	This option specifies the default database context of the SQL login, with the master system database being the default.
DEFAULT_ LANGUAGE=language	This option specifies the default language of the login, with the server default language being the login default if this option isn't specified.
CHECK_EXPIRATION= {ON | OFF},	When set to ON (the default), the SQL login will be subject to a password expiration policy. A password expiration policy affects how long a password will remain valid before it must be changed. This functionality requires Windows Server 2003 or newer.

(continued)

Table 28-2. (*continued*)

Argument	Description
CHECK_POLICY={ ON | OFF},	When set to ON (the default), Windows password policies are applied to the SQL login (for example, policies regarding the password's length, complexity, and inclusion of nonalphanumeric characters). This functionality requires Windows Server 2003 or newer.
CREDENTIAL=credential_name	This option allows a server credential to be mapped to the SQL login. See Chapter 37 for more information on credentials.

This example first demonstrates how to create a SQL Server login with a password and a default database designated.

```
USE master;
GO
CREATE LOGIN Pipo
WITH PASSWORD='BigTr3e',
DEFAULT_DATABASE=AdventureWorks2012;
GO
```

Assuming you are using Windows Server 2003 or newer, as well as mixed authentication, the recipe goes on to create a SQL login with a password that must be changed the first time the user logs in. This login also is created with the CHECK_POLICY option ON, requiring it to comply with Windows password policies.

```
USE master;
GO
CREATE LOGIN Marcus
WITH PASSWORD='ChangeMe' MUST_CHANGE
, CHECK_EXPIRATION=ON
, CHECK_POLICY=ON;
GO
```

How It Works

The first example in this recipe demonstrated creating a SQL login named Pipo. The login name was designated after CREATE LOGIN.

```
CREATE LOGIN Pipo
```

The second line designated the login's password.

```
WITH PASSWORD=' BigTr3e',
```

The last line of code designated the default database that the login's context would first enter after logging into SQL Server.

```
DEFAULT_DATABASE=AdventureWorks2012
```

The second SQL login example demonstrated how to force a password to be changed on the first login by designating the MUST CHANGE token after the password.

```
CREATE LOGIN Marcus
WITH PASSWORD='ChangeMe' MUST_CHANGE ,
```

This password policy integration requires Windows Server 2003, as did the password expiration and password policy options also designated for this login.

```
CHECK_EXPIRATION=ON, CHECK_POLICY=ON
```

28-7. Viewing SQL Server Logins

Problem

During an audit, a request has been submitted to you to provide a list of all SQL logins.

Solution

Again, you can view SQL Server logins (and other principals) by querying the `sys.server_principals` system catalog view.

```
USE master;
GO
SELECT name, sid
FROM sys.server_principals
WHERE type_desc IN ('SQL_LOGIN')
ORDER BY name;
GO
```

This returns the following results:

```
name                                 sid
##MS_PolicyEventProcessingLogin##    0x812190CA1F613649AAA462AE02A3BBB4
##MS_PolicyTsqlExecutionLogin##      0x3632F962FE66F7449F4467B8B36F6F94
Helen                                0xAA7CFE96239C164CA7BA3D10E68882D3
Medusa                               0x1063EBB4A91E7D4795A19FBEA6CD0138
Pathos                               0x61E42C794BBFA34E9913F9006666D5FE
Pipo                                 0xF54D817AA1DE8A4781745DC7758A532E
sa                                   0x01
```

How It Works

This recipe's query returned the name and `sid` of each SQL login on the SQL Server instance by querying the `sys.server_principals` catalog view.

28-8. Altering a SQL Server Login

Problem

You need to change the password for a SQL Server login.

Solution

Use the ALTER LOGIN command. Once a login is added to SQL Server, it can be modified using the ALTER LOGIN command. Using this command, you can perform several tasks:

- Change the login's password
- Change the default database or language
- Change the name of the existing login without disrupting the login's currently assigned permissions
- Change the password policy settings (enabling or disabling them)
- Map or remove mapping from a SQL login credential
- Enable or disable a login from being used
- Unlock a locked login

The syntax arguments are similar to CREATE LOGIN (I'll demonstrate usage in this recipe).

```
ALTER LOGIN login_name { ENABLE | DISABLE
WITH PASSWORD = ' password '
[ OLD_PASSWORD = ' oldpassword '
| [ MUST_CHANGE | UNLOCK ] ]
DEFAULT_DATABASE = database
DEFAULT_LANGUAGE = language
NAME = login_name
CHECK_POLICY = { ON | OFF }
CHECK_EXPIRATION = { ON | OFF }
CREDENTIAL = credentialjiame I NO CREDENTIAL }
```

In the first example of this recipe, a SQL login's password is changed from BigTr3e to TwigSlayer.

```
USE master;
GO
ALTER LOGIN Pipo
WITH PASSWORD = 'TwigSlayer'
OLD_PASSWORD = 'BigTr3e';
GO
```

The OLD_PASSWORD option designates the current password that is being changed; however, sysadmin fixed server role members don't have to know the old password in order to change it.

This second example demonstrates changing the default database of the Pipo SQL login.

```
USE master;
GO
ALTER LOGIN Pipo
WITH DEFAULT_DATABASE = [AdventureWorks2012];
GO
```

This third example in this recipe demonstrates changing both the name and password of a SQL login.

```
USE master;
GO
ALTER LOGIN Pipo
WITH NAME = Patmos, PASSWORD = 'AN!celIttul@isl3';
GO
```

Changing the login name instead of just dropping and creating a new one offers one major benefit: the permissions associated to the original login are not disrupted when the login is renamed. In this case, the Pipo login is renamed to Patmos, but the permissions remain the same.

How It Works

In the first example of this recipe, ALTER LOGIN was used to change a password designating the old password and the new password. If you have sysadmin fixed server role permissions, you only need to designate the new password. The second example demonstrated how to change the default database of a SQL login. The last example demonstrated how to change a login's name from Pipo to Patmos, as well as change the login's password.

28-9. Managing a Login's Password

Problem

You have multiple users that are unable to log in to SQL Server. You would like to check the password settings for these users.

Solution

Use the LOGINPROPERTY function to retrieve login policy settings.

SQL Server provides the LOGINPROPERTY function to return information about login and password policy settings and state. Using this function, you can determine the following qualities of a SQL login:

- Whether the login is locked or expired
- Whether the login has a password that must be changed
- Bad password counts and the last time an incorrect password was given
- Login lockout time
- The last time a password was set and the length of time the login has been tracked using password policies
- The password hash for use in migration (to another SQL instance, for example)

This function takes two parameters: the name of the SQL login and the property to be checked. In this example, I want to return properties for logins to determine whether the login may be locked out or expired.

```
USE master;
GO
SELECT p.name, ca.IsLocked, ca.IsExpired, ca.IsMustChange, ca.BadPasswordCount,
ca.BadPasswordTime, ca.HistoryLength,
ca.LockoutTime,ca.PasswordLastSetTime,ca.DaysUntilExpiration
    From sys.server_principals p
        CROSS APPLY (SELECT IsLocked=LOGINPROPERTY(p.name, 'IsLocked') ,
        IsExpired=LOGINPROPERTY(p.name, 'IsExpired') ,
        IsMustChange=LOGINPROPERTY(p.name, 'IsMustChange') ,
        BadPasswordCount=LOGINPROPERTY(p.name, 'BadPasswordCount') ,
        BadPasswordTime=LOGINPROPERTY(p.name, 'BadPasswordTime') ,
        HistoryLength=LOGINPROPERTY(p.name, 'HistoryLength') ,
```

```
        LockoutTime = LOGINPROPERTY(p.name, 'LockoutTime') ,
        PasswordLastSetTime = LOGINPROPERTY(p.name, 'PasswordLastSetTime') ,
        DaysUntilExpiration = LOGINPROPERTY(p.name, 'DaysUntilExpiration')
    ) ca
    WHERE p.type_desc = 'SQL_LOGIN'
        AND p.is_disabled = 0;
GO
```

In SQL 2012, the PasswordHashAlgorithm property has been added. This property returns the algorithm used to hash the password. In this next example, I want to demonstrate this new property for the LOGINPROPERTY function.

```
USE master;
GO
SELECT p.name,ca.DefaultDatabase,ca.DefaultLanguage,ca.PasswordHash
    ,PasswordHashAlgorithm = Case ca.PasswordHashAlgorithm
        WHEN 1
        THEN 'SQL7.0'
        WHEN 2
        THEN 'SHA-1'
        WHEN 3
        THEN 'SHA-2'
        ELSE 'login is not a valid SQL Server login'
        END
    FROM sys.server_principals p
    CROSS APPLY (SELECT PasswordHash = LOGINPROPERTY(p.name, 'PasswordHash') ,
        DefaultDatabase = LOGINPROPERTY(p.name, 'DefaultDatabase') ,
        DefaultLanguage = LOGINPROPERTY(p.name, 'DefaultLanguage') ,
        PasswordHashAlgorithm = LOGINPROPERTY(p.name, 'PasswordHashAlgorithm')
    ) ca
    WHERE p.type_desc = 'SQL_LOGIN'
        AND p.is_disabled = 0;
GO
```

This query returns the following:

name	DefaultDatabase	DefaultLanguage	PasswordHash	PasswordHashAlgorithm
sa	master	us_english	0x0200...	SHA-1
Patmos	AdventureWorks2012	us_english	0x0200...	SHA-1
Helen	AdventureWorks2012	us_english	0x0200...	SHA-1
Pathos	AdventureWorks2012	us_english	0x0200...	SHA-1
Titan	AdventureWorks2012	us_english	0x0200...	SHA-1

How It Works

LOGINPROPERTY allows you to validate the properties of a SQL login. You can use it to manage password rotation, for example, checking the last time a password was set and then modifying any logins that haven't changed within a certain period of time.

You can also use the password hash property in conjunction with CREATE LOGIN and the hashed_password HASHED argument to re-create a SQL login with the preserved password on a new SQL Server instance.

In each of the examples, I queried the sys.server_principals catalog view and then used a CROSS APPLY with a subquery that utilized the LOGINPROPERTY function.

```
FROM sys.server_principals p
CROSS APPLY (SELECT PasswordHash=LOGINPROPERTY(p.name, 'PasswordHash') ,
    DefaultDatabase=LOGINPROPERTY(p.name, 'DefaultDatabase') ,
    DefaultLanguage=LOGINPROPERTY(p.name, 'DefaultLanguage') ,
    PasswordHashAlgorithm=LOGINPROPERTY(p.name, 'PasswordHashAlgorithm')
) ca
```

This method was used so I could retrieve information about multiple SQL logins at once. Rather than pass each login name into the first parameter of the LOGINPROPERTY function, I referenced the outer catalog view, sys.server_principals. This allows me to retrieve the properties for multiple logins simultaneously.

To limit the query to just SQL Server logins, I added the following in the WHERE clause:

```
WHERE p.type_desc='SQL_LOGIN'
    AND p.is_disabled=0;
```

I aliased the CROSS APPLY subquery and used the aliases to reference the columns I needed to return in the SELECT clause.

```
SELECT p.name,ca.DefaultDatabase,ca.DefaultLanguage,ca.PasswordHash
        ,PasswordHashAlgorithm=Case ca.PasswordHashAlgorithm
        WHEN 1
        THEN 'SQL7.0'
        WHEN 2
        THEN 'SHA-1'
        WHEN 3
        THEN 'SHA-2'
        ELSE 'login is not a valid SQL Server login'
        END
```

Here, you will also see that I utilized a case statement. This was done to render the output more easily understood than the numeric assignments of those values.

28-10. Dropping a SQL Login

Problem

After an audit, you discover that a login exists that should have been removed some time ago. You now need to remove that login.

Solution

Use the DROP LOGIN command to remove SQL logins.

This recipe demonstrates dropping a SQL login from a SQL Server instance by using the DROP LOGIN command.

The syntax is as follows:

```
DROP LOGIN login_name
```

The only parameter is the login name, which can be a Windows (as demonstrated in earlier in this chapter) or SQL login, as this recipe demonstrates:

```
USE master;
GO
DROP LOGIN Patmos;
GO
```

How It Works

This recipe demonstrated the simple DROP LOGIN command, which removes a login from SQL Server. The process is simple; however, if a login owns any securables (see the next chapter for information on securables), the DROP attempt will fail. For example, if the Patmos login had been a database owner, an error like the following would have been raised:

```
Msg 15174, Level 16, State 1, Line 3
Login 'Patmos' owns one or more database(s).
Change the owner of the database(s) before dropping the login.
```

28-11. Managing Server Role Members

Problem

You have a new user account that you need to create. Upon creation of this account, the user needs to be added to the diskadmin fixed server role.

Solution

To add a login to a fixed server role, use ALTER SERVER ROLE.

Fixed server roles are predefined SQL groups that have specific SQL Server-scoped (as opposed to database- or schema-scoped) permissions assigned to them. Prior to SQL Server 2012, you could not create new server roles; you could only add or remove membership to such a role from other SQL or Windows logins. With SQL Server 2012, you can now create a user-defined server role.

The sysadmin fixed server role is the role with the highest level of permissions in a SQL Server instance. Although server roles are permissions based, they have members (SQL or Windows logins/groups) and are categorized by Microsoft as principals.

The syntax to add a member to a fixed server role is as follows:

```
ALTER SERVER ROLE server_role_name
    ADD MEMBER server_principal
```

The first parameter (server_role_name) is the fixed server role to which you are adding the login. The second parameter (server_principal) is the login name to add to the fixed server role.

In this example, the login Titan is created and then added to the sysadmin fixed server role.

```
USE master;
GO
CREATE LOGIN Apollo WITH PASSWORD = 'De3pd@rkCave';
GO
```

```
ALTER SERVER ROLE diskadmin
    ADD MEMBER [Apollo];
GO
```

To remove a login from a fixed server role, use ALTER SERVER ROLE. The syntax is almost identical to adding a server_principal.

```
ALTER SERVER ROLE server_role_name
    DROP MEMBER server_principal
```

This example removes the Apollo login from the sysadmin fixed role membership.

```
USE master;
GO
ALTER SERVER ROLE diskadmin
    DROP MEMBER [Apollo];
GO
```

How It Works

Once a login is added to a fixed server role, that login receives the permissions associated with the fixed server role. ALTER SERVER ROLE was used to add a new login to a fixed role membership; ALTER SERVER ROLE was also used to remove a login from a fixed role membership.

Adding SQL or Windows logins to a fixed server role should never be done lightly. Fixed server roles contain far-reaching permissions, so as a rule of thumb, seek to grant only those permissions that are absolutely necessary for the job at hand. For example, don't give sysadmin membership to someone who just needs SELECT permission on a table.

28-12. Reporting Fixed Server Role Information

Problem

You need to report on all users who are members of the sysadmin fixed server role.

Solution

You can execute the system stored procedure sp_helpsrvrolemember or query the sys.server_role_members catalog view.

Fixed server roles define a grouping of SQL Server–scoped permissions (such as backing up a database or creating new logins). Like SQL or Windows logins, fixed server roles have a security identifier and can be viewed in the sys.server_principals system catalog view. Unlike SQL or Windows logins, fixed server roles can have members (SQL and Windows logins) defined within them that inherit the permissions of the fixed server role.

To view a list of fixed server roles, query the sys.server_principals system catalog view.

```
USE master;
GO
SELECT name
FROM sys.server_principals
WHERE type_desc = 'SERVER_ROLE';
GO
```

This query returns the following:

```
name
public
sysadmin
securityadmin
serveradmin
setupadmin
processadmin
diskadmin
dbcreator
bulkadmin
```

You can also view a list of fixed server roles by executing the sp_helpserverrole system stored procedure.

```
USE master;
GO
EXECUTE sp_helpsrvrole;
GO
```

This query returns the following:

```
ServerRole                      Description
sysadmin                        System Administrators
securityadmin                   Security Administrators
serveradmin                     Server Administrators
setupadmin                      Setup Administrators
processadmin                    Process Administrators
diskadmin                       Disk Administrators
dbcreator                       Database Creators
bulkadmin                       Bulk Insert Administrators
```

Table 28-3 details the permissions granted to each fixed server role.

Table 28-3. *Server Role Permissions*

Server Role	Granted Permissions
sysadmin	GRANT option (can GRANT permissions to others), CONTROL SERVER
setupadmin	ALTER ANY LINKED SERVER
serveradmin	ALTER SETTINGS, SHUTDOWN, CREATE ENDPOINT, ALTER SERVER STATE, ALTER ANY ENDPOINT, ALTER RESOURCES
securityadmin	ALTER ANY LOGIN
processadmin	ALTER SERVER STATE, ALTER ANY CONNECTION
diskadmin	ALTER RESOURCES
dbcreator	CREATE DATABASE
bulkadmin	ADMINISTER BULK OPERATIONS

To see the members of a fixed server role, you can execute the sp_helpsrvrolemember system stored procedure.

```
EXECUTE sp_helpsrvrolemember 'sysadmin'
```

This returns the following results (your results will vary):

```
ServerRole      MemberName                                      MemberSID
sysadmin        sa                                              0x01
sysadmin        NT AUTHORITY\SYSTEM                             0x010100000000000512000000...
sysadmin        BUILTIN\Administrators                          0x010200000000000520000000...
sysadmin        ROIS\SQLServerMSSQLUser$ROIS$FREDERIC           0x010500000000000515000000...
sysadmin        ROIS\SQLServerMSFTEUser$ROIS$FREDERIC           0x010500000000000515000000...
sysadmin        ROIS\Administrator                              0x010500000000000515000000...
sysadmin        ROIS\SQLServerSQLAgentUser$ROIS$FREDERIC        0x010500000000000515000000...
```

Alternatively, to see the members of a fixed server role, you can query the sys.server_role_members catalog view.

```
USE master;
GO
SELECT SUSER_NAME(SR.role_principal_id) AS ServerRole
        , SUSER_NAME(SR.member_principal_id) AS PrincipalName
        , SP.sid
    FROM sys.server_role_members SR
    INNER JOIN sys.server_principals SP
        ON SR.member_principal_id=SP.principal_id
    WHERE SUSER_NAME(SR.role_principal_id)='sysadmin';
GO
```

This returns the following results (your results will vary):

```
ServerRole      MemberName                                      MemberSID
sysadmin        sa                                              0x01
sysadmin        NT AUTHORITY\SYSTEM                             0x010100000000000512000000...
sysadmin        BUILTIN\Administrators                          0x010200000000000520000000...
sysadmin        ROIS\SQLServerMSSQLUser$ROIS$FREDERIC           0x010500000000000515000000...
sysadmin        ROIS\SQLServerMSFTEUser$ROIS$FREDERIC           0x010500000000000515000000...
sysadmin        ROIS\Administrator                              0x010500000000000515000000...
sysadmin        ROIS\SQLServerSQLAgentUser$ROIS$FREDERIC        0x010500000000000515000000...
```

How It Works

You can query the system catalog view sys.server_principals in order to view fixed server roles, or you can use the sp_helpsrvrole system stored procedure to view descriptions for each of the roles. To view members of a role (other principals), use the sp_helpsrvrolemember system stored procedure or query the sys.server_role_members catalog view. The next recipe will show you how to *add* or *remove* other principals to a fixed server role.

Database Principals

Database principals are the objects that represent users to which you can assign permissions to access databases or particular objects within a database. Where logins operate at the server level and allow you to perform actions such as connecting to a SQL Server, database principals operate at the database level and allow you to select or manipulate data, to perform DDL statements on objects within the database, and to manage users' permissions at the database level. SQL Server recognizes four types of database principals:

- *Database users:* Database user principals are the database-level security context under which requests within the database are executed and are associated with either SQL Server or Windows logins.
- *Database roles:* Database roles come in two flavors, fixed and user-defined. Fixed database roles are found in each database of a SQL Server instance and have database-scoped permissions assigned to them (such as SELECT permission on all tables or the ability to CREATE tables). User-defined database roles are those that you can create yourself, allowing you to manage permissions to securables more easily than if you had to individually grant similar permissions to multiple database users.
- *Application roles:* Application roles are groupings of permissions that don't allow members. Instead, you can "log in" as the application role. When you use an application role, it overrides all of the other permissions your login would otherwise have, giving you only those permissions granted to the application role.

In this section, I'll review how to modify, create, drop, and report on database users. I'll also cover how to work with database roles (fixed and user-defined) and application roles.

28-13. Creating Database Users

Problem

A SQL login has been created, and now you want that login to have access to a database.

Solution

Once a login is created, it can then be mapped to a database user. A login can be mapped to multiple databases on a single SQL Server instance—but only one user for each database it has access to. Users are granted access with the CREATE USER command. The syntax is as follows:

```
CREATE USER user_name [ FOR
{ LOGIN login_name
| CERTIFICATE cert_name
I  ASYMMETRIC KEY asym_key_name
} ] [ WITH DEFAULT_SCHEMA=schema_name ]
```

Table 28-4 describes the arguments of this command.

Table 28-4. CREATE USER Arguments

Argument	Description
user_name	This defines the name of the user in the database.
login_name	This defines the name of the SQL or Windows login that is mapping to the database user.
cert_name	When designated, this specifies a certificate that is bound to the database user. See Chapter 19 for more information on certificates.
asym_key_name	When designated, this specifies an asymmetric key that is bound to the database user.
schema_name	This indicates the default schema that the user will belong to, which will determine what schema is checked first when the user references database objects. If this option is unspecified, the dbo schema will be used. This schema name can also be designated for a schema not yet created in the database.

In this first example of the recipe, a new user called Apollo is created in the TestDB database.

```
USE master;
GO
IF NOT EXISTS (SELECT name FROM sys.databases
    WHERE name='TestDB')
BEGIN
    CREATE DATABASE TestDB
END
GO
USE TestDB;
GO
CREATE USER Apollo;
GO
```

In the second example, a Windows login is mapped to a database user called Doe with a default schema specified.

```
USE TestDB;
GO
CREATE USER Helen
FOR LOGIN [ROIS\Helen]
WITH DEFAULT_SCHEMA=HumanResources;
GO
```

How It Works

In the first example of the recipe, a user named Apollo was created in the TestDB database. If you don't designate the FOR LOGIN clause of CREATE USER, it is assumed that the user maps to a login with the same name (in this case, a login named Apollo). Notice that the default schema was not designated, which means Apollo's default schema will be dbo.

In the second example, a new user named Helen was created in the AdventureWorks2012 database, mapped to a Windows login named [ROIS\Helen] (notice the square brackets). The default schema was also set for the Helen login to HumanResources. For any unqualified object references in queries performed by Helen, SQL Server will first search for objects in the HumanResources schema.

28-14. Reporting Database User Information

Problem

You want to query to find more information about a database user.

Solution

You can report database user (and role) information for the current database connection by using the sp_helpuser system stored procedure. The syntax is as follows:

```
sp_helpuser [ [ @name_in_db= ] ' security_account ' ]
```

The single, optional parameter is the name of the database user for which you want to return information. Here's an example:

```
USE TestDB;
GO
EXECUTE sp_helpuser 'Apollo';
GO
```

This returns the following results:

```
UserName    RoleName    LoginName    DefDBName    DefSchemaName    UserID    SID
Apollo      public      Apollo       master       dbo              5         0x3057F4EEC4F07A46...
```

How It Works

The sp_helpuser system stored procedure returns the database users defined in the current database. From the results, you can determine important information such as the user name, login name, default database and schema, and user's security identifier. If a specific user isn't designated, sp_helpuser returns information on all users in the current database you are connected to.

28-15. Modifying a Database User

Problem

You want to modify the default schema for a database user.

Solution

You should use the ALTER USER command. You can rename a database user or change the user's default schema by using the ALTER USER command.

The syntax is as follows (argument usages are demonstrated in this recipe):

```
ALTER USER user_name

WITH NAME = new_user_name DEFAULT_SCHEMA = schema_name
```

In this first example of this recipe, the default schema of the Apollo database user is changed.

```
USE TestDB;
GO
ALTER USER Apollo
WITH DEFAULT_SCHEMA = Production;
GO
```

In the second example of this recipe, the default schema for a principal based on a Windows group is changed.

```
USE [master]
GO
CREATE LOGIN [ROIS\SQLTest] FROM WINDOWS
WITH DEFAULT_DATABASE = [TestDB];
GO
USE [TestDB]
GO
CREATE USER [ROIS\SQLTest]
FOR LOGIN [ROIS\SQLTest];
GO
ALTER USER [ROIS\SQLTest]
WITH DEFAULT_SCHEMA = Production;
GO
```

In the last example of this recipe, a database user name is changed.

```
USE TestDB;
GO
ALTER USER Apollo
WITH NAME = Phoebus;
GO
```

How It Works

The ALTER USER command allows you to perform one of two changes: renaming a database user or changing a database principal's default schema. The first example changed the default schema of the Apollo login to the Production schema. The second example changed the default schema of the ROIS\SQLTest principal. In SQL Server 2012, you can now modify the default schema for principals mapped to a Windows group, certificate, or asymmetric key. The last example renamed the database user Apollo to Phoebus.

28-16. Removing a Database User from the Database

Problem

While maintaining a SQL Server instance, you have found a database user exists for a login that was removed the prior month. You want to now remove this database user.

Solution

Use the DROP USER command to remove a user from the database. The syntax is as follows:

```
DROP USER user_name
```

The user_name is the name of the database user, as this example demonstrates:

```
USE TestDB;
GO
DROP USER Phoebus;
GO
```

How It Works

The DROP USER command removes a user from the database but does not impact the Windows or SQL login that is associated to it. Like DROP LOGIN, you can't drop a user that is the owner of database objects. For example, if the database user Phoebus is the schema owner for a schema called Test, you'll get an error like the following:

```
Msg 15138, Level 16, State 1, Line 2
The database principal owns a schema in the database, and cannot be dropped.
```

28-17. Fixing Orphaned Database Users

Problem

You have restored a database to a different server. The database users in the restored database have lost their association to the server logins. You need to restore the association between login and database user.

Solution

When you migrate a database to a new server (by using BACKUP/RESTORE, for example), the relationship between logins and database users can break. A login has a security identifier, which uniquely identifies it on the SQL Server instance. This sid is stored for the login's associated database user in each database that the login has access to. Creating another SQL login on a different SQL Server instance with the same name will not re-create the same sid unless you specifically designated it with the sid argument of the CREATE LOGIN statement.

For this recipe, we will create an orphaned user. This is done by first creating a login and a user. Then drop the login and re-create it, leaving the user untouched.

```
USE AdventureWorks2012;
GO
If not exists (select name from sys.server_principals
            where name='Apollo')
Begin
CREATE LOGIN Apollo
WITH PASSWORD='BigTr3e',
DEFAULT_DATABASE=AdventureWorks2012;
End
```

```
GO
If not exists (select name from sys.database_principals
            where name='Apollo')
Begin
CREATE USER Apollo;
END
DROP LOGIN [APOLLO];
CREATE LOGIN Apollo
WITH PASSWORD='BigTr3e',
DEFAULT_DATABASE=AdventureWorks2012;
GO
```

The following query demonstrates the link between Login and User by joining the sys.database_principals system catalog view to the sys.server_principals catalog view on the sid column in order to look for orphaned database users in the database.

```
USE AdventureWorks2012;
GO
SELECT dp.name AS OrphanUser, dp.sid AS OrphanSid
FROM sys.database_principals dp
LEFT OUTER JOIN sys.server_principals sp
    ON dp.sid=sp.sid
WHERE sp.sid IS NULL
    AND dp.type_desc='SQL_USER'
    AND dp.principal_id>4;
GO
```

This query returns the following (your results will vary):

```
OrphanUser        OrphanSid
Apollo            0x40C455005F34E44FB95622488AF48F75
```

If you RESTORE a database from a different SQL Server instance onto a new SQL Server instance—and the database users don't have associated logins on the new SQL Server instance—the database users can become "orphaned." If there are logins with the same name on the new SQL Server instance that match the name of the database users, the database users still may be orphaned in the database if the login sid doesn't match the restored database user sid.

Beginning with SQL Server 2005 Service Pack 2, you can use the ALTER USER WITH LOGIN command to remap login/user associations. This applies to both SQL and Windows accounts, which is very useful if the underlying Windows user or group has been re-created in Active Directory and now has an identifier that no longer maps to the generated sid on the SQL Server instance.

The following query demonstrates remapping the orphaned database user Sonja to the associated server login:

```
USE TestDB;
GO
ALTER USER Apollo WITH LOGIN=Apollo;
GO
```

The next example demonstrates mapping a database user ([Phoebus]) to the login [ROIS\Phoebus] (assuming that the user became orphaned from the Windows account or the sid of the domain account was changed because of a drop/re-create outside of SQL Server):

```
USE TestDB;
GO
ALTER USER [Phoebus]
WITH LOGIN=[ROIS\Phoebus];
GO
```

This command also works with remapping a user to a new login—whether or not that user is orphaned.

How It Works

In this recipe, I demonstrated querying the `sys.database_principals` and `sys.server_principals` catalog views to view any database users with an sid that does not exist at the server scope (no associated login `sid`). I then demonstrated using `ALTER USER` to map the database user to a login with the same name (but different `sid`). I also demonstrated how to remap a Windows account in the event that it is orphaned using `ALTER USER`.

■ **Tip** In previous versions of SQL Server, you could use the `sp_change_users_login` stored procedure to perform and report on `sid` remapping. This stored procedure has been deprecated in favor of `ALTER USER WITH LOGIN`.

28-18. Reporting Fixed Database Roles Information

Problem

You need to provide a list of database roles and associated members per role.

Solution

To view role membership, you can use `sp_helprolemember`.

Fixed database roles are found in each database of a SQL Server instance and have database-scoped permissions assigned to them (such as `SELECT` permission on all tables or the ability to `CREATE` tables). Like fixed server roles, fixed database roles have members (database users) that inherit the permissions of the role.

A list of fixed database roles can be viewed by executing the `sp_helpdbfixedrole` system stored procedure.

```
USE TestDB;
GO
EXECUTE sp_helpdbfixedrole;
GO
```

This returns the following results:

```
DBFixedRole            Description
db_owner               DB Owners
db_accessadmin         DB Access Administrators
db_securityadmin       DB Security Administrators
db_ddladmin            DB DDL Administrators
db_backupoperator      DB Backup Operator
db_datareader          DB Data Reader
db_datawriter          DB Data Writer
db_denydatareader      DB Deny Data Reader
db_denydatawriter      DB Deny Data Writer
```

To see the database members of a fixed database role (or any user-defined or application role), you can execute the `sp_helprolemember` system stored procedure.

```
USE TestDB;
GO
EXECUTE sp_helprolemember;
GO
```

This returns the following results (the member `sid` refers to the `sid` of the login mapped to the database user):

```
DbRole                MemberName     MemberSid
db_backupoperator     Phoebus        0x010500000000000515000000527A777BF094B3850F
db_datawriter         Phoebus        0x010500000000000515000000527A777BF094B3850F
db_owner              dbo            0x01
```

How It Works

Fixed database roles are found in each database on a SQL Server instance. A fixed database role groups important database permissions together. These permissions can't be modified or removed. In this recipe, I used `sp_helpdbfixedrole` to list the available fixed database roles.

```
EXECUTE sp_helpdbfixedrole;
```

After that, the `sp_helprolemember` system stored procedure was used to list the members of each fixed database role (database users), showing the role name, database user name, and login `sid`.

```
EXECUTE sp_helprolemember;
```

As with fixed server roles, it's best not to grant membership to them without assurance that all permissions are absolutely necessary for the database user. Do not, for example, grant a user `db_owner` membership when only `SELECT` permissions on a table are needed.

The next recipe shows you how to add or remove database users to a fixed database role.

28-19. Managing Fixed Database Role Membership

Problem

You have been given a list of new users that need to be added to specific roles within the database.

Solution

To associate a database user or role with a database role (user-defined or application role), use the `ALTER ROLE` command. The syntax is as follows:

```
ALTER ROLE database_role_name
ADD MEMBER database_principal
```

The first parameter (database_role_name) is the role name, and the second parameter (database_principal) is the name of the database user.

To remove the association between a database user and role, you will also use the ALTER ROLE command.

```
ALTER ROLE database_role_name
DROP MEMBER database_principal
```

The syntax for removing a database user is similar to adding a user to a role. To remove a user, you need to use the keyword DROP in lieu of ADD.

This first example demonstrates adding the database user Helen to the fixed db_datawriter and db_datareader roles.

```
USE TestDB
GO
If not exists (select name from sys.database_principals
       where name='Apollo')
Begin
CREATE LOGIN Apollo
WITH PASSWORD='BigTr3e',
DEFAULT_DATABASE=TestDB;
CREATE USER Apollo;
END
GO
ALTER ROLE db_datawriter
    ADD MEMBER [APOLLO];
ALTER ROLE db_datareader
    ADD MEMBER [APOLLO];
GO
```

This second example demonstrates how to *remove* the database user Apollo from the db_datawriter role.

```
USE TestDB;
GO
ALTER ROLE db_datawriter
    DROP MEMBER [APOLLO];
GO
```

How It Works

This recipe began by discussing ALTER ROLE, which allows you to add a database user to an existing database role. The database user Apollo was added to db_datawriter and db_datareader, which gives the user cumulative permissions to SELECT, INSERT, UPDATE, or DELETE from any table or view in the AdventureWorks2012 database.

```
ALTER ROLE db_datawriter
    ADD MEMBER [APOLLO];
ALTER ROLE db_datareader
    ADD MEMBER [APOLLO];
GO
```

The first parameter (database_role_name) was the database role, and the second parameter (database_principal) was the name of the database user (or role) to which the database role is associated.

After that, ALTER ROLE was used to remove Apollo's membership from the db_datawriter role.

```
ALTER ROLE db_datawriter
    DROP MEMBER [APOLLO];
GO
```

28-20. Managing User-Defined Database Roles

Problem

You have several users that require the same permissions within a database. You want to reduce the administration overhead with managing the permissions for this group of users.

Solution

Create a user-defined database role. User-defined database roles allow you to manage permissions to securables more easily than if you had to individually grant the same permissions to multiple database users over and over again. Instead, you can create a database role, grant it permissions to securables, and then add one or more database users as members to that database role. When permission changes are needed, you have to modify the permissions of only the single database role, and the members of the role will then automatically inherit those permission changes.

Use the CREATE ROLE command to create a user-defined role in a database.

The syntax is as follows:

```
CREATE ROLE role_name [ AUTHORIZATION owner_name ]
```

The command takes the name of the new role and an optional role owner name. The owner name is the name of the user or database role that owns the new database role (and thus can manage it).

You can list all database roles (fixed, user-defined, and application) by executing the sp_helprole system stored procedure.

```
USE TestDB;
GO
EXECUTE sp_helprole;
GO
```

This returns the following abridged results (the IsAppRole column shows as a 1 if the role is an application role and 0 if not):

```
RoleName        RoleId         IsAppRole
public          0              0
db_owner        16384          0
...             ...            ...
```

Once a database role is created in a database, you can grant or deny it permissions as you would a regular database user (see the next chapter for more on permissions). I will demonstrate granting permissions to a database role in a moment.

If you want to change the name of the database role, *without* also disrupting the role's current permissions and membership, you can use the ALTER ROLE command, which has the following syntax:

```
ALTER ROLE role_name WITH NAME = new_name
```

The command takes the name of the original role as the first argument and the new role name in the second argument.

To drop a role, use the DROP ROLE command. The syntax is as follows:

```
DROP ROLE role_name
```

If a role owns any securables, you'll need to transfer ownership to a new owner before you can drop the role.

In this example, I'll create a new role in the AdventureWorks2012 database.

```
USE AdventureWorks2012;
GO
CREATE ROLE HR_ReportSpecialist AUTHORIZATION db_owner;
GO
```

After being created, this new role doesn't have any database permissions yet. In this next query, I'll grant the HR_ReportSpecialist database role permission to SELECT from the HumanResources.Employee table:

```
Use AdventureWorks2012;
GO
GRANT SELECT ON HumanResources.Employee TO HR_ReportSpecialist;
GO
```

To add Apollo as a member of this new role, I execute the following:

```
Use AdventureWorks2012;
GO
If not exists (select name from sys.server_principals
                                where name='Apollo')

Begin
CREATE LOGIN Apollo
WITH PASSWORD='BigTr3e',
DEFAULT_DATABASE=AdventureWorks2012;
End
GO
If not exists (select name from sys.database_principals
                                where name='Apollo')

Begin
CREATE USER Apollo;
END
GO
EXECUTE sp_addrolemember 'HR_ReportSpecialist', 'Apollo';
GO
```

If later I decide that the name of the role doesn't match its purpose, I can change its name using ALTER ROLE.

```
Use AdventureWorks2012;
GO
ALTER ROLE HR_ReportSpecialist WITH NAME=HumanResources_RS;
GO
```

Even though the role name was changed, Apollo remains a member of the role. This last example demonstrates dropping a database role.

```
Use AdventureWorks2012;
GO
DROP ROLE HumanResources_RS;
GO
```

This returns an error message, because the role must be emptied of members before it can be dropped.

```
Msg 15144, Level 16, State 1, Line 1
The role has members. It must be empty before it can be dropped.
```

So, the single member of this role is then dropped, prior to dropping the role.

```
Use AdventureWorks2012;
GO
EXECUTE sp_droprolemember 'HumanResources_RS', 'Apollo';
GO
DROP ROLE HumanResources_RS;
GO
```

How It Works

The CREATE ROLE command creates a new database role in a database. Once created, you can apply permissions to the role as you would a regular database user. Roles allow you to administer permissions at a group level—allowing individual role members to inherit permissions in a consistent manner instead of applying permissions to individual users, which may or may not be identical.

This recipe demonstrated several commands related to managing user-defined database roles. The sp_helprole system stored procedure was used to list all database roles in the current database. CREATE ROLE was used to create a new user-defined role owned by the db_owner fixed database role.

```
CREATE ROLE HR_ReportSpecialist AUTHORIZATION db_owner
```

I then granted permissions to the new role to SELECT from a table.

```
GRANT SELECT ON HumanResources.Employee TO HR_ReportSpecialist
```

The Apollo user was then added as a member of the new role.

```
EXECUTE sp_addrolemember 'HR_ReportSpecialist', 'Apollo'
```

The name of the role was changed using ALTER ROLE (still leaving membership and permissions intact).

```
ALTER ROLE HR_ReportSpecialist WITH NAME = HumanResources_RS
```

The Apollo user was then dropped from the role (so that I could drop the user-defined role).

```
EXECUTE sp_droprolemember 'HumanResources_RS', 'Apollo'
```

Once emptied of members, the user-defined database role was then dropped.

```
DROP ROLE HumanResources_RS
```

28-21. Managing Application Roles

Problem

You have an application that requires limited permissions in a database. Any user using this application should use the permissions of the application over their individual permissions. You need to create a database principal for this application.

Solution

You should create an application role. An application role is a hybrid between a login and a database role. You can assign permissions to application roles in the same way that you can assign permissions to user-defined roles. Application roles differ from database and server roles, however, in that application roles *do not allow members*. Instead, an application role is *activated* using a password-enabled system stored procedure. When you use an application role, it overrides all of the other permissions your login would otherwise have.

Because an application role has no members, it requires a password for the permissions to be enabled. In addition to this, once a session's context is set to use an application role, any existing user or login permissions are nullified. Only the application role's permissions apply.

To create an application role, use `CREATE APPLICATION ROLE`, which has the following syntax:

```
CREATE APPLICATION ROLE application_role_name
WITH PASSWORD = ' password ' [ , DEFAULT_SCHEMA = schema_name ]
```

Table 28-5 describes the arguments of this command.

Table 28-5. *`CREATE APPLICATON ROLE` Arguments*

Argument	Description
`application_role_name`	The name of the application role
`password`	The password to enable access to the application role's permissions
`schema_name`	The default database schema of the application role that defines which schema is checked for unqualified object names in a query

In this example, a new application role name, `DataWareHouseApp`, is created and granted permissions to a view in the `AdventureWorks2012` database.

```
USE AdventureWorks2012;
GO
CREATE APPLICATION ROLE DataWareHouseApp
WITH PASSWORD = 'mywarehouse123!', DEFAULT_SCHEMA = dbo;
GO
```

An application role by itself is useless without first granting it permissions to do something. So, in this example, the application role is given `SELECT` permissions on a specific database view.

```
-- Now grant this application role permissions
USE AdventureWorks2012;
GO
GRANT SELECT ON Sales.vSalesPersonSalesByFiscalYears
TO DataWareHouseApp;
GO
```

The system stored procedure `sp_setapprole` is used to enable the permissions of the application role for the current user session. In this next example, I activate an application role and query two tables.

```
USE AdventureWorks2012;
GO
EXECUTE sp_setapprole 'DataWareHouseApp', -- App role name
    'mywarehouse123!' -- Password
        ;
GO
-- This query Works
```

```
SELECT COUNT(*) FROM Sales.vSalesPersonSalesByFiscalYears;
-- This query Doesn't work
SELECT COUNT(*) FROM HumanResources.vJobCandidate;
GO
```

This query returns the following:

```
-----------
14

(1 row(s) affected)

Msg 229, Level 14, State 5, Line 7
SELECT permission denied on object 'vJobCandidate',
database 'AdventureWorks2012', schema
'HumanResources'.
```

Even though the original connection login was for a login with sysadmin permissions, using sp_setapprole to enter the application permissions means that only that role's permissions apply. So, in this case, the application role had SELECT permission for the Sales.VSalesPersonSalesByFiscalYears view, but not the HumanResources.vJobCandidate view queried in the example.

To revert to the original login's permissions, you must close out the connection and open a new connection.

You can modify the name, password, or default database of an application role using the ALTER APPLICATION ROLE command.

The syntax is as follows:

```
ALTER APPLICATION ROLE application_role_name WITH NAME = new_application_role_name
PASSWORD = ' password '
DEFAULT_SCHEMA = schema_name
```

Table 28-6 shows the arguments of the command.

Table 28-6. *ALTER APPLICATION ROLE Arguments*

Parameter	Description
new_application_role_name	The new application role name
password	The new application role password
Schema_name	The new default schema

In this example, the application role name and password are changed.

```
USE AdventureWorks2012;
GO
ALTER APPLICATION ROLE DataWareHouseApp
WITH NAME = DW_App, PASSWORD = 'newsecret!123';
GO
```

To remove an application role from the database, use DROP APPLICATION ROLE, which has the following syntax:

```
DROP APPLICATION ROLE rolename
```

This command takes only one argument, the name of the application role to be dropped. Here's an example:

```
USE AdventureWorks2012;
GO
DROP APPLICATION ROLE DW_App;
GO
```

How It Works

This recipe demonstrated how to do the following:

- Create a new application role using `CREATE APPLICATION ROLE`
- Activate the role permissions using `sp_setapprole`
- Modify an application role using `ALTER APPLICATION ROLE`
- Remove an application role from a database using `DROP APPLICATION ROLE`

Application roles are a convenient solution for application developers who want to grant users access *only through an application.* Savvy end users may figure out that their SQL login can also be used to connect to SQL Server with other applications such as Microsoft Access or SQL Server Management Studio. To prevent this, you can change the login account to have minimal permissions for the databases and then use an application role for the required permissions. This way, the user can access the data only through the application, which is then programmed to use the application role.

CHAPTER 29

Securables, Permissions, and Auditing

by Jason Brimhall

In the previous chapter, I discussed principals, which are security accounts that can access SQL Server. In this chapter, I'll discuss and demonstrate securables and permissions. *Securables* are resources that SQL Server controls access to through permissions. Securables in SQL Server fall into three nested hierarchical scopes. The top level of the hierarchy is the *server scope,* which contains logins, databases, and endpoints. The *database scope,* which is contained within the server scope, controls securables such as database users, roles, certificates, and schemas. The third and innermost scope is the *schema scope,* which controls securables such as the schema itself, and objects within the schema such as tables, views, functions, and procedures.

Permissions enable a principal to perform actions on securables. Across all securable scopes, the primary commands used to control a principal's access to a securable are GRANT, DENY, and REVOKE. These commands are applied in similar ways, depending on the scope of the securable that you are targeting. GRANT is used to enable access to securables. DENY explicitly restricts access, trumping other permissions that would normally allow a principal access to a securable. REVOKE removes a specific permission on a securable altogether, whether it was a GRANT or DENY permission.

Once permissions are granted, you may still have additional business and compliance auditing requirements that mandate tracking of changes or knowing which logins are accessing which tables. To address this need, SQL Server introduces the SQL Server Audit object, which can be used to collect SQL instance- and database-scoped actions that you are interested in monitoring. This audit information can be sent to a file, the Windows Application event log, or the Windows Security event log.

In this chapter, I'll discuss how permissions are granted to a principal at all three securable scopes. In addition to permissions, this chapter also presents the following related securable and permissions recipes:

- How to manage schemas using CREATE, ALTER, and DROP SCHEMA
- How to report allocated permissions for a specific principal by using the fn_my_permissions function
- How to determine a connection's permissions to a securable using the system function HAS_PERMS_BY_NAME, as well as using EXECUTE AS to define your connection's security context to a different login or user to see their permissions, too
- How to query all granted, denied, and revoked permissions using sys.database_permissions and sys.server_permissions
- How to change a securable's ownership using ALTER AUTHORIZATION

- How to provide Windows external resource permissions to a SQL login using CREATE CREDENTIAL and ALTER LOGIN
- How to audit SQL instance- and database-level actions using the SQL Server Audit functionality

This chapter starts with a general discussion of SQL Server permissions.

Permissions Overview

Permissions apply to SQL Server objects within the three securable scopes (server, database, and schema). SQL Server uses a set of common permission names that are applied to different securables (and at different scopes) and imply different levels of authorization against a securable. Table 29-1 shows those permissions that are used for multiple securables (however, this isn't the exhaustive list).

Table 29-1. *Major Permissions*

Permission	Description
ALTER	Enables the grantee the use of ALTER, CREATE, or DROP commands for the securable. For example, using ALTER TABLE requires ALTER permissions on that specific table.
AUTHENTICATE	Enables the grantee to be trusted across database or SQL Server scopes.
CONNECT	Enables a grantee the permission to connect to SQL Server resources (such as an endpoint or the SQL Server instance).
CONTROL	Enables all available permissions on the specific securable to the grantee, as well as any nested or implied permissions within (so if you CONTROL a schema, for example, you also control any tables, views, or other database objects within that schema).
CREATE	Enables the grantee to create a securable (which can be at the server, database, or schema scope).
IMPERSONATE	Enables the grantee to impersonate another principal (login or user). For example, using the EXECUTE AS command for a login requires IMPERSONATE permissions. In this chapter, I'll cover how to use EXECUTE AS to set your security context outside of a module.
TAKE OWNERSHIP	Enables the grantee to take ownership of a granted securable.
VIEW	Enables the grantee to see system metadata regarding a specific securable.

To report available permissions in SQL Server, as well as view that specific permission's place in the permission hierarchy, use the sys.fn_builtin_permissions system catalog table function. The syntax is as follows:

```
    sys.fn_builtin_permissions
( [  DEFAULT | NULL ] | empty_string |
APPLICATION ROLE | ASSEMBLY | ASYMMETRIC KEY |
CERTIFICATE | CONTRACT | DATABASE |
ENDPOINT | FULLTEXT CATALOG| LOGIN |
MESSAGE TYPE | OBJECT | REMOTE SERVICE BINDING |
ROLE | ROUTE | SCHEMA | SERVER | SERVICE |
SYMMETRIC KEY | TYPE | USER | XML SCHEMA COLLECTION )
```

Table 29-2 describes the arguments of this command.

Table 29-2. *fn_builtin_permissions Arguments*

Argument	Description
DEFAULT | NULL | empty_string	Designating any of these first three arguments results in all permissions being listed in the result set.
APPLICATION ROLE | ASSEMBLY | ASYMMETRIC KEY | CERTIFICATE | CONTRACT | DATABASE | ENDPOINT | FULLTEXT CATALOG| LOGIN | MESSAGE TYPE | OBJECT | REMOTE SERVICE BINDING |ROLE | ROUTE | SCHEMA | SERVER | SERVICE | SYMMETRIC KEY | TYPE | USER | XML SCHEMA COLLECTION	Specify any one of these securable types in order to return permissions for that type.

In addition to the permission name, you can determine the nested hierarchy of permissions by looking at the covering_permission_name (a permission within the same class that is the superset of the more granular permission), parent_class_desc (the parent class of the permission—if any), and parent_covering_permission_name (the parent covering permission—if any) columns in the result set, which you'll see demonstrated in the next recipe.

29-1. Reporting SQL Server Assignable Permissions

Problem

You want to list the available permissions within SQL Server.

Solution

To view the available permissions within SQL Server and explain their place within the permissions hierarchy, you should use the system function sys.fn_builtin_permissions. In this first example, I'll return all permissions, regardless of securable scope:

```
USE master;
GO

SELECT class_desc, permission_name, covering_permission_name, parent_class_desc,
parent_covering_permission_name
    FROM sys.fn_builtin_permissions(DEFAULT)
    ORDER BY class_desc, permission_name;

GO
```

This returns the following (abridged) result set:

class_desc	permission_name	covering_permission_name	parent_class_desc	parent_covering_permission_name
APPLICATION ROLE	ALTER	CONTROL	DATABASE	ALTER ANY APPLICATION ROLE
APPLICATION ROLE	CONTROL		DATABASE	CONTROL
APPLICATION ROLE	VIEW DEFINITION	CONTROL	DATABASE	VIEW DEFINITION
...				
SERVER	ALTER ANY DATABASE	CONTROL SERVER	...	...
...				
XML SCHEMA COLLECTION	REFERENCES	CONTROL	SCHEMA	REFERENCES
XML SCHEMA COLLECTION	TAKE OWNERSHIP	CONTROL	SCHEMA	CONTROL
XML SCHEMA COLLECTION	VIEW DEFINITION	CONTROL	SCHEMA	VIEW DEFINITION

The next example shows only the permissions for the schema securable scope:

```
USE master;
GO

SELECT permission_name, covering_permission_name, parent_class_desc
    FROM sys.fn_builtin_permissions('schema')
    ORDER BY permission_name;
GO
```

This returns the following result set:

permission_name	covering_permission_name	parent_class_desc
ALTER	CONTROL	DATABASE
CONTROL		DATABASE
CREATE SEQUENCE	ALTER	DATABASE
DELETE	CONTROL	DATABASE
EXECUTE	CONTROL	DATABASE
INSERT	CONTROL	DATABASE
REFERENCES	CONTROL	DATABASE
SELECT	CONTROL	DATABASE
TAKE OWNERSHIP	CONTROL	DATABASE
UPDATE	CONTROL	DATABASE
VIEW CHANGE TRACKING	CONTROL	DATABASE
VIEW DEFINITION	CONTROL	DATABASE

How It Works

The sys.fn_builtin_permissions system catalog function allows you to view available permissions in SQL Server.

The first example in this recipe, sys.fn_builtin_permissions, was used to display all permissions by using the DEFAULT option. The first line of code referenced the column names to be returned from the function.

```
SELECT class_desc, permission_name, covering_permission_name, parent_class_desc,
parent_covering_permission_name
```

The second line referenced the function in the FROM clause, using the DEFAULT option to display all permissions.

```
FROM sys.fn_builtin_permissions(DEFAULT)
```

The last line of code allowed me to order by the permission's class and name,

```
ORDER BY class_desc, permission_name;
```

The results displayed the securable class description, permission name, and covering permission name (the *covering permission name* is the name of a permission class that is higher in the nested permission hierarchy). For example, for the APPLICATION ROLE class, you saw that the CONTROL permission was a child of the DATABASE class and ALTER ANY APPLICATION permission, but it was not subject to any covering permission in the APPLICATION ROLE class (because CONTROL enables all available permissions on the specific securable to the grantee, as well as any nested or implied permissions within).

```
class_desc       permission_     covering_permission_    parent_class_   parent_covering_
                 name            name                    desc            permission_name
...
APPLICATION      CONTROL                                 DATABASE        CONTROL
ROLE
...
```

For the OBJECT class, you can see that the ALTER permission is a child of the SCHEMA parent class and ALTER permission. Within the OBJECT class, the ALTER permission is also a child of the covering CONTROL permission (as seen in the covering_permission_name column).

```
class_desc       permission_     covering_permission_    parent_class_   parent_covering_
                 name            name                    desc            permission_name
...
OBJECT           ALTER           CONTROL                 SCHEMA          ALTER
...
```

For the SERVER class and ALTER ANY DATABASE permission, the covering permission for the SERVER class is CONTROL SERVER. Notice that the SERVER class does *not* have a parent class and permission.

```
class_desc       permission_     covering_permission_    parent_class_   parent_covering_
                 name            name                    desc            permission_name
...
SERVER           ALTER ANY       CONTROL SERVER
                 DATABASE
...
```

The second example in this recipe returned permissions for just the schema-securable class. The first line of code included just three of the columns this time.

```
SELECT permission_name, covering_permission_name, parent_class_desc
```

The second line included the word *schema* in order to show permissions for the schema-securable class.

```
FROM sys.fn_builtin_permissions('schema')
```

The results were then ordered by the permission name.

```
ORDER BY permission_name;
```

Permissions that control database objects contained within a schema (such as views, tables, and so on) were returned. For example, you saw that the DELETE permission is found within the schema scope and is covered by the CONTROL permission. Its parent class is the DATABASE securable.

```
permission_name          covering_permission_name          parent_class_desc
...
DELETE                   CONTROL                           DATABASE
...
```

Running this query, you will also see a new permission that has been added in SQL Server 2012. This new permission is CREATE SEQUENCE. The CREATE SEQUENCE permission is required for a user to create a sequence object within a database.

```
permission_name          covering_permission_name          parent_class_desc
...
CREATE SEQUENCE          ALTER                             DATABASE
...
```

Server-Scoped Securables and Permissions

Server-scoped securables are objects that are unique within a SQL Server instance, including endpoints, logins, and databases. Permissions on server-scoped securables can be granted only to server-level principals (SQL Server logins or Windows logins) and not to database-level principals such as users or database roles.

At the top of the permissions hierarchy, server permissions allow a grantee to perform activities such as creating databases, logins, or linked servers. Server permissions also give you the ability to shut down the SQL Server instance (using SHUTDOWN) or use SQL Profiler (using the ALTER TRACE permission). When allocating permissions on a securable to a principal, the person doing the allocating is the *grantor,* and the principal receiving the permission is the *grantee.*

The abridged syntax for granting server permissions is as follows:

```
GRANT Permission [ , ...n ] TO grantee_principal [ , ...n ] [ WITH GRANT OPTION ] [ AS
grantor_principal ]
```

Table 29-3 describes the arguments of this command.

Table 29-3. GRANT Arguments

Argument	Description
`Permission [ , ...n ]`	You can grant one or more server permissions in a single GRANT statement.
`TO grantee_principal [ , ...n ]`	This is the grantee, also known as the principal (SQL Server login or logins), who you are granting permissions to.
`WITH GRANT OPTION`	When designating this option, the grantee will then have permission to grant the permission(s) to other grantees.
`AS grantor_principal`	This optional clause specifies where the grantor derives its right to grant the permission to the grantee.

To explicitly *deny* permissions on a securable to a server-level principal, use the DENY command.

The syntax is as follows:

```
DENY permission [ , ...n ]
TO grantee_principal [ , ...n ]
[  CASCADE ]
[  AS grantor_principal ]
```

Table 29-4 describes the arguments of this command.

Table 29-4. DENY Arguments

Argument	Description
`Permission [ , ...n ]`	This specifies one or more server-scoped permissions to deny.
`grantee_principal [ , ...n ]`	This defines one or more logins (Windows or SQL) that you can deny permissions to.
`CASCADE`	When this option is designated, if the grantee principal granted any of these permissions to others, those grantees will also have their permissions denied.
`AS grantor_principal`	This optional clause specifies where the grantor derives his right to deny the permission to the grantee.

To *revoke* permissions on a securable to a principal, use the REVOKE command. Revoking a permission means you'll neither be granting nor denying that permission; REVOKE *removes* the specified permission(s) that had previously been either granted or denied.

The syntax is as follows:

```
REVOKE [ GRANT OPTION FOR ] permission [ , ...n ]
FROM<grantee_principal>[ , ...n ]
[ CASCADE ]
[ AS grantor_principal ]
```

Table 29-5 describes the arguments of this command.

Table 29-5. REVOKE Arguments

Argument	Description
GRANT OPTION FOR	When specified, the right for the grantee to grant the permission to other grantees is revoked.
Permission [, ...n]	This specifies one or more server-scoped permissions to revoke.
grantee_principal [, ...n]	This defines one or more logins (Windows or SQL) to revoke permissions from.
CASCADE	When this option is designated, if the grantee principal granted any of these permissions to others, those grantees will also have their permissions revoked.
AS grantor_principal	This optional clause specifies where the grantor derives its right to revoke the permission to the grantee.

The next set of recipes demonstrates some administrative tasks related to server-scoped securables.

29-2. Managing Server Permissions

Problem

You have a login in SQL Server to which you need to grant server-scoped permissions.

Solution

In this first example of this recipe, the SQL login Apollo is granted the ability to use the SQL Profiler tool to monitor SQL Server activity. This permission is given with the WITH GRANT OPTION, so Apollo can also GRANT the permission to others. Keep in mind that permissions at the server scope can be granted only when the current database is master, so I start the batch by switching database context.

```
USE master;
GO
/*
-- Create recipe login if it doesn't exist
*/
IF NOT EXISTS (SELECT name FROM sys.server_principals WHERE name='Apollo')
BEGIN
CREATE LOGIN [Apollo]
    WITH PASSWORD=N'test!#1', DEFAULT_DATABASE=[AdventureWorks2012], CHECK_EXPIRATION=OFF,
CHECK_POLICY=OFF
END;

GRANT ALTER TRACE TO Apollo
WITH GRANT OPTION;
GO
```

In this second example, the Windows login [ROIS\Frederic] (you will need to substitute this login for a login that exists on your system) is granted the permissions to create and view databases on the SQL Server instance:

```
USE master;
GO
GRANT CREATE ANY DATABASE, VIEW ANY DATABASE TO [ROIS\Frederic];
GO
```

In this next example, The Windows login [ROIS\Frederic] is denied the right to execute the SHUTDOWN command:

```
USE master;
GO
DENY SHUTDOWN TO [ROIS\Frederic];
GO
```

In the last example, the permission to use SQL Profiler is revoked from Apollo (leaving the login with the only the permissions that were in place prior to the previous example), including any other grantees he may have given this permission to as well:

```
USE master;
GO
REVOKE ALTER TRACE FROM Apollo
CASCADE;
GO
```

How It Works

Permissions on server-scoped securables are granted using GRANT, denied with DENY, and removed with REVOKE. Using these commands, one or more permissions can be assigned in the same command, as well as allocated to one or more logins (Windows or SQL).

This recipe dealt with assigning permissions at the server scope, although you'll see in future recipes that the syntax for assigning database and schema permissions is very similar.

29-3. Querying Server-Level Permissions

Problem

You need to identify server-scoped permissions associated with a SQL login.

Solution

You can use the sys.server_permissions catalog view to identify permissions at the SQL instance level. In this recipe, I will query all permissions associated with a login named TestUser2. To start, I'll create the new login.

```
USE master;
GO
CREATE LOGIN TestUser2
WITH PASSWORD='abcdelllllll!';
GO
```

Next, I'll grant a server-scoped permission and deny a server-scoped permission.

```
USE master;
GO
DENY SHUTDOWN TO TestUser2;
GRANT CREATE ANY DATABASE TO TestUser2;
GO
```

Querying sys.server_permissions and sys.server_principals returns all server-scoped permissions for the new login created earlier.

```
USE master;
GO
SELECT p.class_desc, p.permission_name, p.state_desc
    FROM sys.server_permissions p
    INNER JOIN sys.server_principals s
        ON p.grantee_principal_id=s.principal_id
    WHERE s.name='TestUser2';
GO
```

This query returns the following:

```
class_desc          permission_name            state_desc
SERVER              CONNECT SQL                GRANT
SERVER              CREATE ANY DATABASE        GRANT
SERVER              SHUTDOWN                   DENY
```

Even though I explicitly executed only one GRANT and one DENY, just by virtue of creating the login, I have implicitly granted the new login CONNECT permissions to the SERVER scope.

How It Works

In this recipe, I queried sys.server_permissions and sys.server_principals in order to return the server-scoped permissions associated with the new login I created. In the SELECT clause, I returned the class of the permission, the permission name, and the associated state of the permission.

```
SELECT p.class_desc, p.permission_name, p.state_desc
```

In the FROM clause, I joined the two catalog views by the grantee's principal ID. The grantee is the target recipient of granted or denied permissions.

```
FROM sys.server_permissions p
    INNER JOIN sys.server_principals s
        ON p.grantee_principal_id=s.principal_id
```

In the WHERE clause, I designated the name of the login I wanted to see permissions for.

```
WHERE s.name='TestUser2';
```

Database-Scoped Securables and Permissions

Database-level securables are unique to a specific database and include several SQL Server objects such as roles, assemblies, cryptography objects (keys and certificates), Service Broker objects, full-text catalogs, database users, schemas, and more.

You can grant permissions on these securables to database principals (database users, roles). The abridged syntax for granting database permissions is as follows:

```
GRANT permission [ , ...n ]
TO database_principal [ , ...n ]
[ WITH GRANT OPTION ] [ AS database_principal ]
```

Table 29-6 describes the arguments of this command.

Table 29-6. *GRANT Arguments*

Argument	Description
`permission [ , ...n ]`	This specifies one or more database permissions to be granted to the principal(s).
`database_principal [ , ...n ]`	Defines the grantees to whom the permissions should be granted.
`WITH GRANT OPTION`	When designating this option, the grantee has permissions to grant the permission(s) to other grantees.
`AS database_principal`	This optional clause specifies where the grantor derives its right to grant the permission to the grantee. For example, if your current database user context does not have permission to `GRANT` a specific permission but you have an `IMPERSONATE` permission on a database user that does, you can designate that user in the `AS` clause.

To *deny* database-scoped permissions to a grantee, the `DENY` command is used. The abridged syntax is as follows:

```
DENY permission [ , ...n ]
TO database_principal [ , ...n ] [ CASCADE ]
[ AS database_principal ]
```

Table 29-7 describes the arguments of this command.

Table 29-7. *DENY Arguments*

Argument	Description
`permission [ , ...n ]`	This specifies one or more database-scoped permissions to deny.
`<database_principal>[ , ...n ]`	This defines one or more database principals to deny permissions for.
`CASCADE`	When this option is designated, if the grantee principal granted any of these permissions to others, those grantees will also have their permissions denied.
`AS database_principal`	This optional clause specifies where the grantor derives its right to deny the permission to the grantee.

To *revoke* database-scoped permissions to the grantee, the REVOKE command is used. The abridged syntax is as follows:

```
REVOKE permission [ , ...n ]
FROM< database_principal> [ , ...n ]
[ CASCADE ]
[ AS database_principal]
```

Table 29-8 describes the arguments of this command.

Table 29-8. *REVOKE Arguments*

Argument	Description
database_permission [, ...n]	This specifies one or more database-scoped permissions to revoke.
< database_principal> [, ...n]	This defines one or more database principals to revoke permissions from.
CASCADE	When this option is designated, if the grantee principal granted any of these permissions to others, those grantees will also have their permissions revoked.
AS database_principal	This optional clause specifies where the grantor derives its right to revoke the permission to the grantee.

29-4. Managing Database Permissions

Problem

You need to alter database-scoped permissions for a database user.

Solution

You should use GRANT, DENY, and REVOKE to alter database-scoped permissions for a database user.

Starting off this recipe, I'll set up the logins and users if they don't already exist or haven't already been created earlier in the chapter:

```
USE master;
GO
/*
-- Create DB for recipe if it doesn't exist
*/
IF NOT EXISTS (SELECT name FROM sys.databases WHERE name = 'TestDB')
BEGIN
CREATE DATABASE TestDB
END
GO
/*
Create recipe login if it doesn't exist
*/
IF NOT EXISTS (SELECT name FROM sys.server_principals WHERE name = 'Phantom')
BEGIN
```

```
CREATE LOGIN [Phantom]
    WITH PASSWORD=N'test!#23', DEFAULT_DATABASE=[TestDB], CHECK_EXPIRATION=OFF,
CHECK_POLICY=OFF
END;
GO

USE TestDB;
GO
/*
-- Create db users if they don't already exist
*/
IF NOT EXISTS (SELECT name FROM sys.database_principals WHERE name='Apollo')
BEGIN
CREATE USER Apollo FROM LOGIN Apollo
END;
GO
IF NOT EXISTS (SELECT name FROM sys.database_principals WHERE name='Phantom')
BEGIN
CREATE USER Phantom FROM LOGIN Phantom
END;
GO
```

This first example demonstrates granting database permissions to the Apollo database user in the TestDB database:

```
USE TestDB;
GO
GRANT ALTER ANY ASSEMBLY, ALTER ANY CERTIFICATE TO APOLLO;
GO
```

This second example demonstrates denying permissions to the Phantom database user:

```
USE TestDB;
GO
DENY ALTER ANY DATABASE DDL TRIGGER TO Phantom;
GO
```

The last example demonstrates revoking database permissions to connect to the TestDB database from the Phantom user:

```
Use TestDB;
GO
REVOKE CONNECT FROM Phantom;
GO
```

How It Works

This recipe demonstrated how to grant, revoke, or deny database-scoped permissions to database principals. As you may have noticed, the syntax for granting database-scoped permissions is almost identical to server-scoped permissions. Schema-scoped permissions are also managed with the same commands, but with slight variations.

Before reviewing how to manage schema permissions, in this next recipe I'll demonstrate how to manage schemas in general.

29-5. Querying Database Permissions

Problem

You want to list the database-scoped permissions for a database user.

Solution

You can use the sys.database_permissions catalog view to identify permissions in a database. In this recipe, I will query all permissions associated with a user named TestUser in the AdventureWorks2012 database. To start, I'll create the new login and user.

```
USE master;
GO
CREATE LOGIN TestUser WITH PASSWORD='abcdelllllll!'
USE AdventureWorks2012;
GO
CREATE USER TestUser FROM LOGIN TestUser;
GO
```

Next, I'll grant and deny various permissions.

```
USE AdventureWorks2012;
GO
GRANT SELECT ON HumanResources.Department TO TestUser;
DENY SELECT ON Production.ProductPhoto TO TestUser;
GRANT EXEC ON HumanResources.uspUpdateEmployeeHireInfo TO TestUser;
GRANT CREATE ASSEMBLY TO TestUser;
GRANT SELECT ON Schema::Person TO TestUser;
DENY IMPERSONATE ON USER::dbo TO TestUser;
DENY SELECT ON HumanResources.Employee(BirthDate) TO TestUser;
GO
```

I'll now query the sys.database_principals to determine the identifier of the principal.

```
USE AdventureWorks2012;
GO
SELECT principal_id
FROM sys.database_principals
WHERE name='TestUser';
GO
```

This query returns the following results (if you are following along with this recipe, keep in mind that your principal identifier may be different):

```
principal_id
5
```

Now I can use the principal ID of 5 with the grantee principal ID in the sys.database_ permissions table (I could have integrated the prior query into this next query, but I've separated them in order to give a clearer picture of what each catalog view does).

```
Use AdventureWorks2012;
GO
SELECT
    p.class_desc,
    p.permission_name,
    p.state_desc,
    ISNULL(o.type_desc,'') type_desc,
    CASE p.class_desc
    WHEN 'SCHEMA'
    THEN schema_name(major_id)
    WHEN 'OBJECT_OR_COLUMN'
    THEN CASE
        WHEN minor_id=0
        THEN object_name(major_id)
        ELSE (SELECT
        object_name(object_id)+'.'+name
        FROM sys.columns
        WHERE object_id=p.major_id
        AND column_id=p.minor_id) END
    ELSE '' END AS object_name
FROM sys.database_permissions p
LEFT OUTER JOIN sys.objects o
    ON o.object_id=p.major_id
WHERE grantee_principal_id=5;
GO
```

This query returns the following:

class_desc	permission_name	state_desc	type_desc	object_name
DATABASE	CONNECT	GRANT		
DATABASE	CREATE ASSEMBLY	GRANT		
OBJECT_OR_COLUMN	SELECT	GRANT	USER_TABLE	Department
OBJECT_OR_COLUMN	SELECT	DENY	USER_TABLE	Employee.BirthDate
OBJECT_OR_COLUMN	EXECUTE	GRANT	SQL_STORED_ PROCEDURE	uspUpdateEmployee Hire Info
OBJECT_OR_COLUMN	SELECT	DENY	USER_TABLE	ProductPhoto
SCHEMA	SELECT	GRANT		Person
DATABASE_PRINCIPAL	IMPERSONATE	DENY		

How It Works

This recipe demonstrated querying system catalog views to determine the permissions of a specific database user. I created the login and user and then granted and denied various permissions for it.

After that, I queried `sys.database_principals` to determine the ID of this new user.

Walking through the last and more complicated query in the recipe, the first few columns of the query displayed the class description, permission name, and state (for example, GRANT or DENY):

```
SELECT
p.class_desc,
p.permission_name,
p.state_desc,
```

The type description was actually taken from the sys.objects view, which I used to pull information regarding the object targeted for the permission. If it is NULL, I return no characters in the result set.

```
ISNULL(o.type_desc,'') type_desc,
```

The next expression was the CASE statement evaluating the class description. When the class is a schema, I return the schema's name.

```
CASE p.class_desc WHEN 'SCHEMA'
THEN schema_name(major_id)
```

When the class is an object or column, I nest another CASE statement.

```
WHEN 'OBJECT_OR_COLUMN' THEN CASE
```

If the minor ID is zero, I know that this is an object and not a column, so I return the object name.

```
WHEN minor_id=0
THEN object_name(major_id)
```

Otherwise, I am dealing with a column name, so I perform a subquery to concatenate the object name with the name of the column.

```
ELSE (SELECT
object_name(object_id)+'.'+
name FROM sys.columns
WHERE object_id=p.major_id AND column_id=p.minor_id) END ELSE '' END AS object_name
```

I queried the permissions with a LEFT OUTER JOIN on sys.objects. I didn't use an INNER join because not all permissions are associated with objects—for example, the GRANT on the CREATE ASSEMBLY permission.

```
FROM sys.database_permissions p
LEFT OUTER JOIN sys.objects o
    ON o.object_id=p.major_id
```

Lastly, I qualified that the grantee has the ID of the user I created. The grantee is the recipient of the permissions. The sys.database_permissions also has the grantor_principal_id, which is the grantor of permissions for the specific row. I didn't want to designate this—rather, I just wanted the rows of permissions granted to the specified user:

```
WHERE grantee_principal_id=5;
```

Schema-Scoped Securables and Permissions

Schema-scoped securables are contained within the database securable scope and include user-defined data types, XML schema collections, and objects. The object securable also has other securable object types within it, but I'll review this later in the chapter.

As of SQL Server 2005, users are separated from direct ownership of a database object (such as tables, views, and stored procedures). This separation is achieved by the use of schemas, which are basically containers for database objects. Instead of having a direct object owner, the object is contained within a schema, and that schema is then owned by a user.

One or more users can own a schema or use it as their default schema for creating objects. What's more, you can apply security at the schema level. This means any objects within the schema can be managed as a unit, instead of at the individual object level.

Every database comes with a dbo schema, which is where your objects go if you don't specify a default schema. But if you want to create your own schemas, you can use the CREATE SCHEMA command.

The abridged syntax is as follows:

```
CREATE SCHEMA schema_name [AUTHORIZATION owner_name ]
```

Table 29-9 describes the arguments of this command.

***Table 29-9.** CREATE SCHEMA Arguments*

Argument	Description
schema_name	This is the name of the schema and the schema owner.
owner_name	The owner is a database principal that can own one or more schemas in the database.

To remove an existing schema, use the DROP SCHEMA command. The syntax is as follows:

```
DROP SCHEMA schema_name
```

The command takes only a single argument: the name of the schema to drop from the database. Also, you can't drop a schema that contains objects, so the objects must be either dropped or transferred to a new schema.

Note See Recipe 30-2 for a review of using ALTER SCHEMA to transfer schema ownership of an object.

Like with server- and database-scoped permissions, permissions for schemas are managed using the GRANT, DENY, and REVOKE commands.

The abridged syntax for granting permissions on a schema is as follows:

```
GRANT permission [ , ...n ] ON SCHEMA :: schema_name
TO database_principal [ , ...n]
[ WITH GRANT OPTION ][ AS granting_principal ]
```

Table 29-10 describes the arguments of this command.

***Table 29-10.** GRANT Arguments*

Argument	Description
Permission [, ...n]	This specifies one or more schema permissions to be granted to the grantee.
schema_name	This defines the name of the schema the grantee is receiving permissions to.
database_principal	This specifies the database principal permissions recipient.
WITH GRANT OPTION	When designating this option, the grantee has permissions to grant the schema permission(s) to other grantees.
AS granting_principal	This optional clause specifies where the grantor derives its right to grant the schema-scoped permission to the grantee.

To deny schema-scoped permissions to a grantee, the DENY command is used. The abridged syntax is as follows:

```
DENY permission [ , ...n ] ON SCHEMA :: schema_name TO database_principal [ , ...n ]
[ CASCADE ]
[ AS denying_principal ]
```

Table 29-11 describes the arguments of this command.

Table 29-11. *DENY Arguments*

Argument	Description
Permission [, ...n]	This specifies one or more schema-scoped permissions to deny.
schema_name	This defines the name of the schema where permissions will be denied.
database_principal [, ...n]	This specifies one or more database principals to deny permissions for.
CASCADE	When this option is designated, if the grantee principal granted any of these permissions to others, those grantees will also have their permissions denied.
AS denying_principal	This optional clause specifies where the grantor derives its right to deny the permission to the grantee.

To revoke schema-scoped permissions to the grantee, the REVOKE command is used. The abridged syntax is as follows:

```
REVOKE [ GRANT OPTION FOR ]
permission  [ , ...n ]
  ON SCHEMA :: schema_name
{ TO | FROM } database_principal [ ,  ...n ]
  [  CASCADE ] [ AS principal ]
```

Table 29-12 describes the arguments of this command.

Table 29-12. *REVOKE Arguments*

Argument	Description
Permission [, ...n]	This specifies one or more schema-scoped permissions to revoke.
schema_name	This defines the name of the schema of which the permissions will be revoked.
database_principal[, ...n]	This specifies one or more database principals to revoke permissions for.
CASCADE	When this option is designated, if the grantee principal granted any of these permissions to others, those grantees will also have their permissions revoked.
AS principal	This optional clause specifies where the grantor derives its right to revoke the permission to the grantee.

29-6. Managing Schemas

Problem

A new project is starting. Many new objects are to be created for this project. Prior to creating those objects, you need to create a schema that will own the new objects. You will also need to associate a user to this new schema.

Solution

You should use the CREATE SCHEMA command to create a new schema. When associating a user to a schema, you should use the ALTER USER command.

In this recipe, I'll create a new schema in the TestDB database called Publishers.

```
USE TestDB;
GO
CREATE SCHEMA Publishers AUTHORIZATION db_owner;
GO
```

I now have a schema called Publishers, which can be used to contain other database objects. It can be used to hold all objects related to publication functionality, for example, or used to hold objects for database users associated to publication activities.

To start using the new schema, use the schema.object_name two-part naming format.

```
USE TestDB;
GO
CREATE TABLE Publishers.ISBN (ISBN char(13) NOT NULL PRIMARY KEY, CreateDT datetime NOT NULL
DEFAULT GETDATE());
GO
```

This next example demonstrates making the Publishers schema a database user's default schema. For this example, I'll create a new SQL login in the master database.

```
USE master
GO
CREATE LOGIN Florence
WITH PASSWORD=N'testl23',
DEFAULT_DATABASE=TestDB,
CHECK_EXPIRATION=OFF,
CHECK_POLICY=OFF;
GO
```

Next, I'll create a new database user in the TestDB database.

```
USE TestDB;
GO
CREATE USER Florence FOR LOGIN Florence;
GO
```

Now I'll change the default schema of the existing database user to the Publishers schema. Any objects this database user creates by default will belong to this schema (unless the database user explicitly uses a different schema in the object creation statement).

```
USE TestDB;
GO
ALTER USER Florence WITH DEFAULT_SCHEMA=Publishers;
GO
```

Chapter 30 reviews how to transfer the ownership of an object from one schema to another using ALTER SCHEMA. You'll need to use this in situations where you want to drop a schema. For example, if I tried to drop the Publishers schema right now, with the Publishers.ISBN table still in it, I would get an error warning me that there are objects referencing that schema. This example demonstrates using ALTER SCHEMA to transfer the table to the dbo schema prior to dropping the Publishers schema from the database.

```
USE TestDB;
GO
ALTER SCHEMA dbo TRANSFER Publishers.ISBN;
GO
DROP SCHEMA Publishers;
GO
```

How It Works

Schemas act as a container for database objects. Unlike when a database user owns objects directly, a database user now can own a schema (or, in other words, have permissions to use the objects within it).

In this recipe, CREATE SCHEMA was used to create a new schema called Publishers. A new table was created in the new schema called Publishers.ISBN. After that, a new login and database user was created for the TestDB database. ALTER USER was used to make that new schema the default schema for the new user.

Since a schema cannot be dropped until all objects are dropped or transferred from it, ALTER SCHEMA was used to transfer Publishers.ISBN into the dbo schema. DROP SCHEMA was used to remove the Publishers schema from the database.

29-7. Managing Schema Permissions

Problem

A new user in your environment needs to be granted certain permissions on a schema that owns several objects.

Solution

You need to use the GRANT, DENY, and REVOKE commands using the ON SCHEMA option.

In this next set of examples, I'll show you how to manage schema permissions. Before showing you this, though, I would like to quickly point out how you can identify which schemas exist for a particular database. To view the schemas for a database, you can query the sys.schemas system catalog view. This example demonstrates listing the schemas that exist within the AdventureWorks2012 database:

```
USE AdventureWorks2012;
GO
SELECT s.name SchemaName, d.name SchemaOwnerName
FROM sys.schemas s
INNER JOIN sys.database_principals d
ON s.principal_id=d.principal_id
ORDER BY s.name;
GO
```

This returns a list of built-in database schemas (the fixed database roles dbo, guest, sys, and INFORMATION_SCHEMA) along with user-defined schemas (Person, Production, Purchasing, Sales, HumanResources).

```
SchemaName              SchemaOwnerName
db_accessadmin          db_accessadmin
db_backupoperator       db_backupoperator
db_datareader           db_datareader
db_datawriter           db_datawriter
db_ddladmin             db_ddladmin
db_denydatareader       db_denydatareader
db_denydatawriter       db_denydatawriter
db_owner                db_owner
db_securityadmin        db_securityadmin
dbo                     dbo
guest                   guest
HumanResources          dbo
INFORMATION_SCHEMA      INFORMATION_SCHEMA
Person                  dbo
Production              dbo
Purchasing              dbo
Sales                   dbo
sys                     sys
```

Within the AdventureWorks2012 database, I'll now demonstrate assigning permissions on schemas to database principals. In this example, the database user TestUser is granted TAKE OWNERSHIP permissions to the Person schema, which enables the grantee to take ownership of a granted securable.

```
USE AdventureWorks2012;
GO
GRANT TAKE OWNERSHIP ON SCHEMA ::Person TO TestUser;
GO
```

In the next example, I'll grant the database user TestUser multiple permissions in the same statement, including the ability to ALTER a schema, EXECUTE stored procedures within the Production schema, or SELECT from tables or views in the schema. Using the WITH GRANT OPTION, TestUser can also grant other database principals these permissions.

```
USE AdventureWorks2012;
GO
GRANT ALTER, EXECUTE, SELECT ON SCHEMA ::Production TO TestUser
WITH GRANT OPTION;
GO
```

In this next example, the database user TestUser is denied the ability to INSERT, UPDATE, or DELETE data from any tables within the Production schema.

```
USE AdventureWorks2012;
GO
DENY INSERT, UPDATE, DELETE ON SCHEMA ::Production TO TestUser;
GO
```

In the last example of this recipe, TestUser's right to ALTER the Production schema or SELECT from objects within the Production schema is revoked, along with the permissions she may have granted to others (using CASCADE).

```
USE AdventureWorks2012;
GO
REVOKE ALTER, SELECT ON SCHEMA ::Production TO TestUser CASCADE;
GO
```

How It Works

Granting, denying, or revoking permissions occurs with the same commands that are used with database- and server-scoped permissions. One difference, however, is the reference to ON SCHEMA, where a specific schema name is the target of granted, denied, or revoked permissions. Notice, also, that the name of the schema was prefixed with two colons (called a *scope qualifier*). A scope qualifier is used to scope permissions to a specific object type.

Object Permissions

Objects are nested within the schema scope, and they can include tables, views, stored procedures, functions, and aggregates. Defining permissions at the schema scope (such as SELECT or EXECUTE) can allow you to define permissions for a grantee on all objects within a schema. You can also define permissions at the object level. Object permissions are nested within schema permissions, schema permissions within database-scoped permissions, and database-scoped permissions within server-level permissions.

The abridged syntax for granting object permissions is as follows:

```
GRANT permission ON
[ OBJECT :: ][ schema_name ]. object_name [ ( column [ , ...n ] ) ]
TO<database_principal>[ , ...n ]
[ WITH GRANT OPTION ] [ AS database_principal ]
```

Table 29-13 shows the arguments of this command.

Table 29-13. *GRANT Arguments*

Argument	Description
permission [, ...n]	This specifies one or more object permissions to be granted to the grantee.
[OBJECT ::][schema_name]. object_name [(column [, ...n])]	This defines the target object (and if applicable, columns) for which the permission is being granted.
database_principal	This specifies the database principal that is the permissions recipient.
WITH GRANT OPTION	When designating this option, the grantee has permissions to grant the permission(s) to other grantees.
AS database_principal	This optional clause specifies where the grantor derives its right to grant the permission to the grantee.

To deny object permissions to a grantee, the DENY command is used. The abridged syntax is as follows:

```
DENY permission [ , ...n ] ON
[ OBJECT :: ][ schema_name ]. object_name [ ( column [ , ...n ] ) ] TO<database_principal>
[ , ...n ] [ CASCADE ] [ AS<database_principal> ]
```

Table 29-14 describes the arguments of this command.

Table 29-14. *DENY Arguments*

Argument	Description
[OBJECT ::][schema_name].object_ name [(column [, ...n])]	This specifies the target object (and if applicable, columns) for which the permission is being denied.
< database_principal>[, ...n]	This specifies one or more database principals for whom permissions will be denied.
CASCADE	When this option is designated, if the grantee principal granted any of these permissions to others, those grantees will also have their permissions denied.
AS database_principal	This optional clause specifies where the grantor derives its right to deny the permission to the grantee.

To revoke object permissions to the grantee, the REVOKE command is used. The abridged syntax is as follows:

```
REVOKE [ GRANT OPTION FOR ] permission [ , ...n ]
ON [ OBJECT :: ][ schema_name ]. objectjame [ ( column [ , ...n ] ) ] FROM<database_
principal>[ , ...n ] [ CASCADE ] [ AS<database_principal> ]
```

Table 29-15 describes The arguments of this command.

Table 29-15. *REVOKE Arguments*

Argument	Description
GRANT OPTION FOR	When this option is used, the right to grant the permission to other database principals is revoked.
permission [, ...n]	This specifies one or more object permissions to be revoked from the grantee.
[OBJECT ::][schema_name]. object_name [(column [, ...n])]	This defines the target object (and if applicable, columns) for which the permission is being revoked.
< database_principal>[, ...n]	This specifies one or more database principals to revoke permissions from.
CASCADE	When this option is designated, if the grantee principal granted any of these permissions to others, those grantees will also have their permissions revoked.
AS database_principal	This optional clause specifies where the grantor derives its right to revoke the permission to the grantee.

29-8. Managing Object Permissions

Problem

After having defined permissions at the schema scope, you have determined that you need to define additional permissions for a specific set of tables.

Solution

Like server-level, database-scoped, and schema-scoped permissions, you can use GRANT, DENY, and REVOKE to define permissions on specific database objects.

In this recipe, I grant the database user TestUser the permission to SELECT, INSERT, DELETE, and UPDATE data in the HumanResources.Department table.

```
USE AdventureWorks2012;
GO
GRANT DELETE, INSERT, SELECT, UPDATE ON HumanResources.Department TO TestUser;
GO
```

Here, the database role called ReportViewers is granted the ability to execute a procedure, as well as view metadata regarding that specific object in the system catalog views.

```
USE AdventureWorks2012;
GO
CREATE ROLE ReportViewers
GRANT EXECUTE, VIEW DEFINITION ON dbo.uspGetManagerEmployees TO ReportViewers;
GO
```

In this next example, ALTER permission is denied to the database user TestUser for the HumanResources.Department table.

```
USE AdventureWorks2012;
GO
DENY ALTER ON HumanResources.Department TO TestUser;
GO
```

In this last example, INSERT, UPDATE, and DELETE permissions are revoked from TestUser on the HumanResources.Department table:

```
USE AdventureWorks2012;
GO
REVOKE INSERT, UPDATE, DELETE ON HumanResources.Department TO TestUser;
GO
```

How It Works

This recipe demonstrated granting object permissions to specific database securables. Object permissions are granted by designating the specific object name and the permissions that are applicable to the object. For example, EXECUTE permissions can be granted to a stored procedure, but not SELECT permissions.

Permissions can be superseded by other types of permissions. For example, if the database user TestUser has been granted SELECT permissions on the HumanResources.Department table but has been denied permissions on the HumanResources schema itself, TestUser will receive the following error message when attempting to SELECT from that table, because the DENY overrides any GRANT SELECT permissions.

```
Msg 229, Level 14, State 5, Line 2
SELECT permission denied on object 'Department', database 'AdventureWorks2012', schema
'HumanResources'.
```

Managing Permissions Across Securable Scopes

Now that I've reviewed the various securable scopes and the methods by which permissions can be granted to principals, in the next set of recipes I'll show you how to report and manage the permissions a principal has on securables across the different scopes.

29-9. Determining Permissions to a Securable

Problem

You want to see the permissions your connection has on a securable.

Solution

With SQL Server's nested hierarchy of securable permissions (server, database, and schema), permissions can be inherited by higher-level scopes. Figuring out what permissions your current login/database connection has to a securable can become tricky, especially when you add server or database roles to the equation.

Understanding what permissions your database connection has added to a securable can be determined by using the HAS_PERMS_BY_NAME function. This system scalar function returns a 1 if the current user has granted permissions to the securable and returns 0 if not.

The syntax for this function is as follows:

```
HAS_PERMS_BY_NAME ( securable , securable_class , permission [ , sub-securable ] [ , sub-
securable_class ] )
```

Table 29-16 describes the arguments for this function.

Table 29-16. *Has_perms_by_name Arguments*

Parameter	Description
securable	The name of the securable that you want to verify permissions for.
securable_class	The name of the securable class you want to check. Class names (for example, DATABASE or SCHEMA) can be retrieved from the class_desc column in the sys.fn_builtin_permissions function.
permission	The name of the permission to check.
sub-securable	The name of the securable subentity.
sub-securable_class	The name of the securable subentity class.

This example demonstrates how to check whether the current connected user has permissions to ALTER the AdventureWorks2012 database:

```
USE AdventureWorks2012;
GO
SELECT HAS_PERMS_BY_NAME ('AdventureWorks2012', 'DATABASE', 'ALTER');
GO
```

This returns 0, which means the current connection *does not have* permission to ALTER the AdventureWorks2012 database.

```
0
```

This next query tests the current connection to see whether the Person.Address table can be updated or selected from by the current connection:

```
USE AdventureWorks2012;
GO
SELECT UpdateTable=CASE HAS_PERMS_BY_NAME ('Person.Address', 'OBJECT', 'UPDATE') WHEN 1 THEN '
Yes' ELSE 'No' END ,
SelectFromTable=CASE HAS_PERMS_BY_NAME ('Person.Address', 'OBJECT', 'SELECT') WHEN 1 THEN 'Yes'
ELSE 'No' END;
GO
```

This query returns the following:

```
UpdateTable      SelectFromTable
Yes              No
```

How It Works

The HAS_PERMS_BY_NAME system function evaluates whether the current connection has granted permissions to access a specific securable (granted permissions either explicitly or inherently through a higher-scoped securable). In both examples in this recipe, the first parameter used was the securable name (the database name or table name). The second parameter was the securable class, for example, OBJECT or DATABASE. The third parameter used was the actual permission to be validated, for example, ALTER, UPDATE, or SELECT (depending on which permissions are applicable to the securable being checked).

29-10. Reporting Permissions by Securable Scope

Problem

You want to provide a list of all permissions for the currently connected user.

Solution

You can report on all permissions for the currently connected user by using the fn_my_permissions function.

In this recipe, I'll demonstrate using the fn_my_permissions function to return the assigned permissions for the currently connected principal. The syntax for this function is as follows:

```
fn_my_permissions ( securable , 'securable_class')
```

Table 29-17 describes the arguments for this command.

Table 29-17. *fn_my_permissions Arguments*

Argument	Description
securable	The name of the securable to verify. Use NULL if you are checking permissions at the server or database scope.
securable_class	The securable class that you are listing permissions for.

In this first example, I demonstrate how to check the server-scoped permissions for the current connection.

```
USE master;
GO
SELECT permission_name
FROM sys.fn_my_permissions(NULL, N'SERVER')
ORDER BY permission_name;
GO
```

This returns the following results (this query example was executed under the context of sysadmin, so in this case, all available server-scoped permissions are returned):

```
ADMINISTER BULK OPERATIONS
ALTER ANY CONNECTION
ALTER ANY CREDENTIAL
ALTER ANY DATABASE
ALTER ANY ENDPOINT
ALTER ANY EVENT NOTIFICATION
ALTER ANY LINKED SERVER
ALTER ANY LOGIN
ALTER RESOURCES
ALTER SERVER STATE
ALTER SETTINGS
ALTER TRACE
AUTHENTICATE SERVER
CONNECT SQL
CONTROL SERVER
CREATE ANY DATABASE
CREATE DDL EVENT NOTIFICATION
CREATE ENDPOINT
CREATE TRACE EVENT NOTIFICATION
EXTERNAL ACCESS ASSEMBLY
SHUTDOWN
UNSAFE ASSEMBLY
VIEW ANY DATABASE
VIEW ANY DEFINITION
VIEW SERVER STATE
```

If you have IMPERSONATE permissions on the login or database user, you can also check the permissions of another principal other than your own by using the EXECUTE AS command. Chapter 19 demonstrated how to use EXECUTE AS to specify a stored procedure's security context. You can also use EXECUTE AS in a stand-alone fashion, using it to switch the security context of the current database session. You can then switch back to your original security context by issuing the REVERT command.

The simplified syntax for EXECUTE AS is as follows:

```
EXECUTE AS { LOGIN | USER }='name' [ WITH { NO REVERT } ]
```

Table 29-18 describes the arguments of this command.

Table 29-18. EXECUTE AS Abridged Syntax Arguments

Argument	Description
{ LOGIN | USER }='name'	Select LOGIN to impersonate a SQL or Windows login or USER to impersonate a database user. The name value is the actual login or user name.
NO REVERT	If NO REVERT is designated, you cannot use the REVERT command to switch back to your original security context.

To demonstrate the power of EXECUTE AS, the previous query is reexecuted, this time by using the security context of the Apollo login.

```
USE master;
GO
EXECUTE AS LOGIN=N'Apollo'
GO
SELECT permission_name
FROM sys.fn_my_permissions(NULL, N'SERVER')
ORDER BY permission_name;
GO
REVERT;
GO
```

This returns a much smaller list of server permissions, because you are no longer executing the call under a login with sysadmin permissions.

```
CONNECT SQL
VIEW ANY DATABASE
```

This next example demonstrates returning database-scoped permissions for the Apollo database user:

```
USE TestDB;
GO
EXECUTE AS USER=N'Apollo';
GO
SELECT permission_name
FROM sys.fn_my_permissions(N'TestDB', N'DATABASE')
ORDER BY permission_name;
GO
REVERT;
GO
```

This query returns the following:

```
ALTER ANY ASSEMBLY
ALTER ANY CERTIFICATE
CONNECT
CREATE ASSEMBLY
CREATE CERTIFICATE
```

In this next example, permissions are checked for the current connection on the `Production.Culture` table, this time showing any subentities of the table (meaning any explicit permissions on table columns):

```
USE AdventureWorks2012;
GO
SELECT subentity_name, permission_name
FROM sys.fn_my_permissions(N'Production.Culture', N'OBJECT')
ORDER BY permission_name, subentity_name;
GO
```

This returns the following results (when the `subentity_name` is populated, this is a column reference):

```
subentity_name          permission_name
                        ALTER
                        CONTROL
                        DELETE
                        EXECUTE
                        INSERT
                        RECEIVE
                        REFERENCES
CultureID               REFERENCES
ModifiedDate            REFERENCES
Name                    REFERENCES
                        SELECT
CultureID               SELECT
ModifiedDate            SELECT
Name                    SELECT
                        TAKE OWNERSHIP
                        UPDATE
CultureID               UPDATE
ModifiedDate            UPDATE
Name                    UPDATE
                        VIEW CHANGE TRACKING
                        VIEW DEFINITION
```

How It Works

This recipe demonstrated how to return permissions for the current connection using the `fn_my_permissions` function. The first example used a `NULL` in the first parameter and `SERVER` in the second parameter in order to return the server-scoped permissions of the current connection.

```
FROM sys. fn_my_permissions(NULL, N'SERVER')
```

I then used `EXECUTE AS` to execute the same query, this time under the `Apollo` login's context, which returned server-scoped permissions for his login.

```
EXECUTE AS LOGIN=N'Apollo';
GO
REVERT;
GO
```

The next example showed database-scoped permissions by designating the database name in the first parameter and DATABASE in the second parameter.

```
FROM sys.fn_my_permissions(N'TestDB', N'DATABASE')
```

The last example checked the current connection's permissions to a specific table.

```
FROM sys.fn_my_permissions(N'Production.Culture', N'OBHECT')
```

This returned information at the table level *and* column level. For example, the ALTER and CONTROL permissions applied to the table level, while those rows with a populated entity_name (for example, CultureID and ModifiedDate) refer to permissions at the table's column level.

29-11. Changing Securable Ownership

Problem

A database user needs to be removed. The database user owns objects within the database. You need to change the owner of the objects owned by this user in order to remove the user from the database.

Solution

As described earlier in the chapter, objects are contained within schemas, and schemas are then owned by a database user or role. Changing a schema's owner does not require the objects to be renamed. Aside from schemas, however, other securables on a SQL Server instance still do have direct ownership by either a server- or database-level principal.

For example, schemas have database principal owners (such as database user), and endpoints have server-level owners, such as a SQL login.

Assuming that the login performing the operation has the appropriate TAKE OWNERSHIP permission, you can use the ALTER AUTHORIZATION command to change the owner of a securable.

The abridged syntax for ALTER AUTHORIZATION is as follows:

```
ALTER AUTHORIZATION
ON [ <entity_type> :: ] entity_name
TO { SCHEMA OWNER | principaljiame }
```

Table 29-19 describes the arguments for this command.

Table 29-19. *ALTER AUTHORIZATION Arguments*

Argument	Description
entity_type	This designates the class of securable being given a new owner.
entity_name	This specifies the name of the securable.
SCHEMA OWNER | principal_name	This indicates the name of the new schema owner or the name of the database or server principal taking ownership of the securable.

In this example, the owner of the HumanResources schema is changed to the database user TestUser:

```
USE AdventureWorks2012;
GO
ALTER AUTHORIZATION ON Schema::HumanResources TO TestUser;
GO
```

In this second example, the owner of an endpoint is changed to a SQL login. Before doing so, the existing owner of the endpoint is verified using the sys.endpoints and sys.server_principals system catalog views.

```
USE AdventureWorks2012;
GO
SELECT p.name OwnerName
FROM sys.endpoints e
INNER JOIN sys.server_principals p
ON e.principal_id=p.principal_id
WHERE e.name='ProductWebsite';
GO
```

This query returns the following (your results will vary):

```
OwnerName
ROIS\Owner
```

Next, the owner is changed to a different SQL login.

```
USE AdventureWorks2012;
GO
ALTER AUTHORIZATION ON Endpoint::ProductWebSite TO TestUser;
GO
```

Reexecuting the query against sys.server_principals and sys.endpoints, the new owner is displayed.

```
OwnerName
TestUser
```

■ **Note** If the ProductWebSite endpoint does not exist and you attempt to change the owner to TestUser as done in this recipe, you will receive the following error:

Cannot find the endpoint 'ProductWebSite', because it does not exist or you do not have permission.

How It Works

This recipe demonstrated how to change object ownership. You may want to change ownership when a login or database user needs to be removed. If that login or database user owns securables, you can use ALTER AUTHORIZATION to change that securables owner prior to dropping the SQL login or database user.

In this recipe, ALTER AUTHORIZATION was used to change the owner of a schema to a different database user and the owner of an endpoint to a different SQL login (associated to a Windows account). In both cases, the securable name was prefixed by the :: scope qualifier, which designates the type of object you are changing ownership of.

29-12. Allowing Access to Non-SQL Server Resources

Problem

You have a SQL login that must have access to a share on the operating system.

Solution

In this chapter, I've discussed permissions and securables within a SQL Server instance; however, sometimes a SQL login (not associated to a Windows user or group) may need permissions outside of the SQL Server instance. A Windows principal (a Windows user or group) has implied permissions outside of the SQL Server instance, but a SQL login does not, because a SQL login and password are created inside SQL Server. To address this, you can bind a SQL login to a Windows credential, giving the SQL login the implied Windows permissions of that credential. This SQL login can then use more advanced SQL Server functionality, where outside resource access may be required. This credential can be bound to more than one SQL login (although one SQL login can be bound only to a single credential).

To create a credential, use the CREATE CREDENTIAL command.

The syntax is as follows:

```
CREATE CREDENTIAL credential_name WITH IDENTITY=' identityjiame '
[ , SECRET=' secret ' ] [ FOR CRYPTOGRAPHIC_PROVIDER cryptographic_provider_name ]
```

Table 29-20 describes the arguments for this command.

Table 29-20. *CREATE CREDENTIAL Arguments*

Argument	Description
credential_name	The name of the new credential
identity_name	The external account name (a Windows user, for example)
secret	The credential's password
cryptographic_provider_name	The name of the Enterprise Key Management (EKM) provider (used when associating an EKM provider with a credential)

In this example, a new credential is created that is mapped to the ROIS\Owner Windows user account.

```
USE master;
GO
CREATE CREDENTIAL AccountingGroup
WITH IDENTITY=N'ROIS\AccountUser',
SECRET=N'mypassword!';
GO
```

Once created, the credential can be bound to existing or new SQL logins using the CREDENTIAL keyword in CREATE LOGIN and ALTER LOGIN.

```
USE master;
GO
ALTER LOGIN Apollo
WITH CREDENTIAL=AccountingGroup;
GO
```

How It Works

A credential allows SQL authentication logins to be bound to Windows external permissions. In this recipe, a new credential was created called AccountingGroup. It was mapped to the Windows user ROIS\AccountUser and given a password in the SECRET argument of the command. After creating the credential, it was then bound to the SQL login Apollo by using ALTER LOGIN and WITH CREDENTIAL. Now the Apollo login, using credentials, has outside-SQL Server permissions equivalent to the ROIS\AccountUser Windows account.

Auditing Activity of Principals Against Securables

SQL Server Enterprise edition offers the native capability to audit SQL Server instance- and database-scoped activity. This activity is captured to a target data destination using a *Server Audit* object, which defines whether the audit data is captured to a file, to the Windows Application event log, or to the Windows Security event log. A Server Audit object also allows you to designate whether the SQL Server instance should be shut down if it is unable to write to the target. Once a Server Audit object is created, you can bind a Server Audit Specification or Database Audit Specification object to it. A *Server Audit Specification* is used to define which events you want to capture at the SQL Server instance scope. A *Database Audit Specification* object allows you to define which events you want to capture at the database scope. Only one Server Audit Specification can be bound to a Server Audit object, whereas one or more Database Audit Specifications can be bound to a Server Audit object. A single Server Audit object can be collocated with a Server Audit Specification and one or more Database Audit Specifications.

In the next few recipes, I will demonstrate how to create a Server Audit object that writes event-captured data to a target file. I will then demonstrate how to associate SQL instance-level and database-scoped events to the audit file, and I'll demonstrate how to read the audit data contained in the binary file.

29-13. Defining Audit Data Sources

Problem

A new requirement from the security department will require that auditing be enabled on SQL Server. Knowing that auditing will be required and that more specific requirements are forthcoming, you want to start setting up auditing while waiting for these requirements.

Solution

The first step in configuring auditing for SQL Server Enterprise edition is to create a Server Audit object. This is done by using the CREATE SERVER AUDIT command. The syntax for this command is as follows:

```
CREATE SERVER AUDIT audit_name
    TO { [ FILE (<file_options>[, ...n]) ] | APPLICATION_LOG | SECURITY_LOG }
     [  WITH ( <audit_options>[, ...n] ) ]
}
[ ; ]
<file_options>::=
{
    FILEPATH='os_file_path'
     [, MAXSIZE={ max_size { MB | GB | TB } | UNLIMITED } ]
     [, MAX_ROLLOVER_FILES=integer]
     [, RESERVE_DISK_SPACE={ ON | OFF } ]
}
<audit_options>::=
{
    [ QUEUE_DELAY=integer ]
    [, ON_FAILURE=CONTINUE | SHUTDOWN ]
    [, AUDIT_GUID=uniqueidentifier ]
}

<predicate_expression>::=
{
    [NOT ]<predicate_factor>
    [ { AND | OR } [NOT ] { <predicate_factor> } ]
    [, ...n ]
}

<predicate_factor>::=
    event_field_name { = | < > | !=|>|>= |<|<= } { number | ' string ' }
```

Table 29-21 describes the arguments for this command.

Table 29-21. *CREATE SERVER AUDIT Arguments*

Argument	Description
audit_name	This specifies the user-defined name of the Server Audit object.
FILE (<file_options>[, ...n])] |	This designates that the Server Audit object will write events to a file.
APPLICATION_LOG	This designates that the Server Audit object will write events to the Windows Application event log.
SECURITY_LOG	This designates that the Server Audit object will write events to the Windows Security event log.
FILEPATH	If FILE was chosen, this designates the OS file path of the audit log.
MAXSIZE	If FILE was chosen, this argument defines the maximum size in megabytes, gigabytes, or terabytes. UNLIMITED can also be designated.

(continued)

Table 29-21. (*continued*)

Argument	Description
MAX_ROLLOVER_FILES	If FILE was chosen, this designates the maximum number of files to be retained on the file system. When 0 is designated, no limit is enforced.
RESERVE_DISK_SPACE	This argument takes a value of either ON or OFF. When enabled, this option reserves the disk space designated in MAXSIZE.
QUEUE_DELAY	This value designates the milliseconds that can elapse before audit actions are processed. The minimum and default value is 1,000 milliseconds.
ON_FAILURE	This argument takes a value of either CONTINUE or SHUTDOWN. If SHUTDOWN is designated, the SQL instance will be shut down if the target can't be written to.
AUDIT_GUID	This option takes the unique identifier of a Server Audit object. If you restore a database that contains a Database Audit Specification, this object will be orphaned on the new SQL instance unless the original Server Audit object is re-created with the matching GUID.
predicate_expression	New to SQL Server 2012, this option is used to determine whether an event should be processed. This expression has a maximum size of 3,000 characters.
event_field_name	Name of the field that you want to filter as the predicate source.
number	Any numeric type. Limited only by physical memory and any number too large for a 64-bit integer.
'string'	ANSI or Unicode string used by the predicate compare. Implicit conversions are not permitted. Passing the wrong type will result in an error.

In this recipe, I will create a new Server Audit object that will be configured to write to a local file directory. The maximum size I'll designate per log will be 500 MB, with a maximum number of 10 rollover files. I won't reserve disk space, and the queue delay will be 1 second (1,000 milliseconds). If there is a failure for the audit to write, I will not shut down the SQL Server instance.

```
USE master;
GO
CREATE SERVER AUDIT LesROIS_Server_Audit TO FILE
( FILEPATH='C:\Apress\',
MAXSIZE=500 MB,
MAX_ROLLOVER_FILES=10,
RESERVE_DISK_SPACE=OFF) WITH ( QUEUE_DELAY=1000,
ON_FAILURE=CONTINUE);
GO
```

To validate the configurations of the new Server Audit object, I can check the sys.server_audits catalog view.

```
USE master;
GO
SELECT audit_id,type_desc,on_failure_desc
    ,queue_delay,is_state_enabled
FROM sys.server_audits;
GO
```

This query returns the following:

```
audit_id        type_desc       on_failure_desc        queue_delay     is_state_enabled
65536           FILE            CONTINUE               1000            0
```

As you can see from the `is_state_enabled` column of `sys.server_audits`, the Server Audit object is created in a disabled state. Later, I'll demonstrate how to enable it in the "Querying Captured Audit Data" recipe, but in the meantime, I will leave it disabled until I define Server and Database Audit Specifications associated with it.

To see more details around the file configuration of the Server Audit object I just created, I can query the `sys.server_file_audits` catalog view.

```
USE master;
GO
SELECT name,
log_file_path,
log_file_name,
max_rollover_files,
max_file_size
FROM sys.server_file_audits;
GO
```

This returns the following result set (reformatted for presentation purposes):

```
Column                  Result
name                    LesROIS_Server_Audit
log_file_path           C:\Apress\
log_file_name           LesROIS_Server_Audit_AE04F81A-CC5C-42 F7-AE23-BD2C31D7438E.sqlaudit
max_rollover_files      10
max_file_size           500
```

In this next recipe, I will create a new Server Audit object that will be configured similar to the prior recipe. This time, I want to take advantage of the `predicate_expression` available in SQL Server 2012. In this example, I will demonstrate a `predicate_expression` to filter for events occurring in the `AdventureWorks2012` database and the `Sales.CreditCard` table. If there is a failure for the audit to write, I will not shut down the SQL Server instance.

```
USE master;
GO
CREATE SERVER AUDIT LesROIS_CC_Server_Audit TO FILE
     ( FILEPATH='C:\Apress\',
    MAXSIZE=500 MB,
    MAX_ROLLOVER_FILES=10,
    RESERVE_DISK_SPACE=OFF) WITH ( QUEUE_DELAY=1000,
    ON_FAILURE=CONTINUE)
WHERE database_name='AdventureWorks2012' AND schema_name='Sales'
  AND object_name='CreditCard' AND database_principal_name='dbo';
GO
```

I confirmed the creation of this Server Audit Object with the following script:

```
USE master;
GO
SELECT name,
```

```
log_file_path,
log_file_name,
max_rollover_files,
max_file_size,
predicate
FROM sys.server_file_audits;
GO
```

This returns the following result set (reformatted for presentation purposes):

Column	Result
name	LesROIS_CC_Server_Audit
log_file_path	C:\Apress\
log_file_name	LesROIS_CC_Server_Audit_6E934469-D6A1-4B83-86D7-BA5E6C13C00D.sqlaudit
max_rollover_files	10
max_file_size	500
predicate	([database_dname]='AdventureWorks2012' AND [schema_name]='Sales' AND [object_name]='CreditCard' AND [database_principal_name]='dbo')

How It Works

The first recipe demonstrated how to create a Server Audit object that defines the target destination of collected audit events. This is the first step in the process of setting up an audit. Walking through the code, in the first line I designated the name of the Server Audit object.

```
CREATE SERVER AUDIT LesROIS_Server_Audit
```

Since the target of the collected audit events will be forwarded to a file, I designated `TO FILE`.

```
TO FILE
```

Next, I designated the file path where the audit files would be written (since there are rollover files, each file is dynamically named—so I just used the path and not an actual file name).

```
( FILEPATH='C:\Apress\',
```

I then designated the maximum size of each audit file and the maximum number of rollover files.

```
MAXSIZE=500 MB, MAX_ROLLOVER_FILES=10,
```

I also chose not to reserve disk space (as a best practice, you should write your audit files to a dedicated volume or LUN where sufficient disk space can be ensured).

```
RESERVE_DISK_SPACE=OFF)
```

Lastly, I designated that the queue delay remain at the default level of 1,000 milliseconds (1 second) and that if there was a failure to write to the target, the SQL Server instance will continue to run (for mission-critical auditing, where events *must* be captured, you may then consider shutting down the SQL instance if there are issues writing to the target file).

```
WITH ( QUEUE_DELAY=1000,
ON_FAILURE=CONTINUE)
```

In the second recipe, I demonstrated the use of the `predicate_expression` option that is new to SQL Server 2012.

```
WHERE database_name='AdventureWorks2012' AND schema_name='Sales'
  AND object_name='CreditCard' AND database_principal_name='dbo';
```

After creating the new Server Audit object, I used sys.server_audits to validate the primary Server Audit object settings and sys.server_file_audits to validate the file options.

In the next recipe, I'll demonstrate how to capture SQL instance-scoped events to the Server Audit object created in this recipe.

29-14. Capturing SQL Instance–Scoped Events

Problem

You have just received more detailed requirements from the security department about what to audit in SQL Server. You now know that you need to audit events that are instance-scoped.

Solution

A Server Audit Specification is used to define what SQL instance-scoped events will be captured to the Server Audit object. The command to perform this action is CREATE SERVER AUDIT SPECIFICATION, and the syntax is as follows:

```
CREATE SERVER AUDIT SPECIFICATION audit_specification_name
FOR SERVER AUDIT audit_name
{
{ ADD ( { audit_action_group_name } )
} [, ---n] [ WITH ( STATE={ ON | OFF } ) ] }
```

Table 29-22 describes the arguments for this command.

Table 29-22. *CREATE SERVER AUDIT SPECIFICATION Arguments*

Argument	Description
audit_specification_name	This specifies the user-defined name of the Server Audit Specification object.
audit_name	This defines the name of the preexisting Server Audit object (target file or event log).
audit_action_group_name	This indicates the name of the SQL instance-scoped action groups. For a list of auditable action groups, you can query the sys.dm_audit_actions catalog view.
STATE	This argument takes a value of either ON or OFF. When ON, collection of records begins.

In this recipe, I will create a new Server Audit Specification that will capture three different audit action groups. To determine what audit action groups can be used, I can query the sys.dm_audit_actions system catalog view:

```
USE master;
GO
SELECT name
FROM sys.dm_audit_actions
WHERE class_desc='SERVER'
AND configuration_level='Group'
ORDER BY name;
GO
```

This returns the following abridged results:

```
name
APPLICATION_ROLE_CHANGE_PASSWORD_GROUP
AUDIT_CHANGE_GROUP
BACKUP_RESTORE_GROUP
BROKER_LOGIN_GROUP
DATABASE_CHANGE_GROUP
DATABASE_MIRRORING_LOGIN_GROUP
DATABASE_OBJECT_ACCESS_GROUP
...
DBCC_GROUP
FAILED_LOGIN_GROUP
LOGIN_CHANGE_PASSWORD_GROUP
LOGOUT_GROUP
...
SERVER_OBJECT_PERMISSION_CHANGE_GROUP
SERVER_OPERATION_GROUP
SERVER_PERMISSION_CHANGE_GROUP
SERVER_PRINCIPAL_CHANGE_GROUP
SERVER_PRINCIPAL_IMPERSONATION_GROUP
SERVER_ROLE_MEMBER_CHANGE_GROUP
SERVER_STATE_CHANGE_GROUP
SUCCESSFUL_LOGIN_GROUP
TRACE_CHANGE_GROUP
```

In this recipe scenario, I would like to track any time a DBCC command was executed, BACKUP operation was taken, or server role membership change was performed.

```
USE master;
GO
CREATE SERVER AUDIT SPECIFICATION LesROIS_Server_Audit_Spec FOR SERVER AUDIT
LesROIS_Server_Audit
ADD (SERVER_ROLE_MEMBER_CHANGE_GROUP),
ADD (DBCC_GROUP),
ADD (BACKUP_RESTORE_GROUP) WITH (STATE=ON);
GO
```

Once the Server Audit Specification is created, I can validate the settings by querying the sys.server_audit_specifications catalog view.

```
USE master;
GO
SELECT server_specification_id,name,is_state_enabled
FROM sys.server_audit_specifications;
GO
```

This query returns the following:

```
server_specification_id        name                         is_state_enabled
65536                          LesROIS_Server_Audit_Spec    1
```

I can also query the details of this specification by querying the sys.server_audit_specification_details catalog view (I use the server specification ID returned from the previous query to qualify the following result set):

```
USE master;
GO
SELECT server_specification_id,audit_action_name
FROM sys.server_audit_specification_details
WHERE server_specification_id=65536;
GO
```

This query returns the following:

```
server_specification_id         audit_action_name
65536                           SERVER_ROLE_MEMBER_CHANGE_GROUP
65536                           BACKUP_RESTORE_GROUP
65536                           DBCC_GROUP
```

The entire auditing picture is not yet complete since I have not yet enabled the Server Audit object (LesROIS_Server_Audit). Before I turn the Server Audit object on, I will also add a Database Audit Specification object, and then I'll demonstrate actual audit event captures and how to query the audit log.

How It Works

In this recipe, I demonstrated how to create a Server Audit Specification that defines which SQL instance-scoped events will be captured and forwarded to a specific Server Audit object target (in this case, a file under C:\Apress).

I started the recipe first by querying sys.dm_audit_actions to get a list of action groups that I could choose to audit for the SQL Server instance. The sys.dm_audit_actions catalog view actually contains a row for all audit actions—at both the SQL instance and database scopes. So, in the WHERE clause of my query, I designated that the class of audit action should be for the SERVER and that the configuration level should be for a group (I'll demonstrate the nongroup action-level configuration level in the next recipe).

```
WHERE class_desc='SERVER' AND
configuration_level='Group'
```

Next, I used the CREATE SERVER AUDIT SPECIFICATION command to define which action groups I wanted to track. The first line of code designated the name of the new Server Audit Specification.

```
CREATE SERVER AUDIT SPECIFICATION LesROIS_Server_Audit_Spec
```

The next line of code designated the target of the event collection, which is the name of the Server Audit object.

```
FOR SERVER AUDIT LesROIS_Server_Audit
```

After that, I designated each action group I wanted to capture.

```
ADD (SERVER_ROLE_MEMBER_CHANGE_GROUP),
ADD (DBCC_GROUP),
ADD (BACKUP_RESTORE_GROUP)
```

Lastly, I designated that the state of the Server Audit Specification should be enabled upon creation.

```
WITH (STATE=ON)
```

In the next recipe, I'll demonstrate how to create a Database Audit Specification to capture database-scoped events. Once all of the specifications are created, I'll then demonstrate actual captures of actions and show you how to read the Server Audit log.

29-15. Capturing Database-Scoped Events

Problem

You have just learned that you need to audit some database-scoped events.

Solution

A Database Audit Specification is used to define what database-scoped events will be captured to the Server Audit object. The command to perform this action is CREATE DATABASE AUDIT SPECIFICATION, and the abridged syntax is as follows (it does not show action specification syntax—however, I'll demonstrate this within the recipe):

```
CREATE DATABASE AUDIT SPECIFICATION audit_specification_name {
[ FOR SERVER AUDIT audit_name ] [ { ADD (
{ <audit_action_specification> | audit_action_group_name } )
} [, ---n] ] [ WITH ( STATE={ ON | OFF } ) ] }
```

Table 29-23 shows the arguments for this command.

Table 29-23. *CREATE DATABASE AUDIT SPECIFICATION Arguments*

Argument	Description
audit_specification_name	This specifies the user-defined name of the Database Audit Specification object.
audit_name	This defines the name of the preexisting Server Audit object (target file or event log).
audit_action_specification	This indicates the name of a auditable database-scoped action. For a list of auditable database-scoped actions, you can query the sys.dm_audit_actions catalog view.
audit_action_group_name	This defines the name of the database-scoped action group. For a list of auditable action groups, you can query the sys.dm_audit_ actions catalog view.
STATE	This argument takes a value of either ON or OFF. When ON, collection of records begins.

In this recipe, I will create a new Database Audit Specification that will capture both audit action groups and audit events. *Audit action groups* are related groups of actions at the database scope, and *audit events* are singular events. For example, I can query the sys.dm_audit_actions system catalog view to view specific audit events against the object securable scope (for example, tables, views, stored procedures, and functions) by executing the following query:

```
USE master;
GO
SELECT name
FROM sys.dm_audit_actions
WHERE configuration_level='Action'
AND class_desc='OBJECT'
ORDER BY name;
GO
```

This returns a result set of atomic events that can be audited against an object securable scope.

```
name
DELETE
EXECUTE
INSERT
RECEIVE
REFERENCES
SELECT
UPDATE
```

I can also query the sys.dm_audit_actions system catalog view to see audit action groups at the database scope.

```
USE master;
GO
SELECT name
FROM sys.dm_audit_actions
WHERE configuration_level='Group'
AND class_desc='DATABASE'
ORDER BY name;
GO
```

This returns the following abridged results:

```
name
APPLICATION_ROLE_CHANGE_PASSWORD_GROUP
AUDIT_CHANGE_GROUP
BACKUP_RESTORE_GROUP
DATABASE_CHANGE_GROUP
DATABASE_OBJECT_ACCESS_GROUP
DBCC_GROUP
SCHEMA_OBJECT_ACCESS_GROUP
SCHEMA_OBJECT_CHANGE_GROUP
SCHEMA_OBJECT_OWNERSHIP_CHANGE_GROUP
SCHEMA_OBJECT_PERMISSION_CHANGE_GROUP
```

In this recipe scenario, I would like to track any time an INSERT, UPDATE, or DELETE is performed against the Sales.CreditCard table by *any* database user. I would also like to track whenever impersonation is used within the AdventureWorks2012 database (for example, using the EXECUTE AS command).

```
USE AdventureWorks2012;
GO
CREATE DATABASE AUDIT SPECIFICATION AdventureWorks2012_DB_Spec
    FOR SERVER AUDIT LesROIS_Server_Audit
    ADD (DATABASE_PRINCIPAL_IMPERSONATION_GROUP)
    , ADD (INSERT, UPDATE, DELETE ON Sales.CreditCard BY public)
WITH (STATE=ON);
GO
```

I can validate the settings of my Database Audit Specification by querying the sys.database_audit_specifications system catalog view.

```
USE AdventureWorks2012;
GO
SELECT database_specification_id,name,is_state_enabled
FROM sys.database_audit_specifications;
GO
```

This query returns the following:

```
database_specification_id       name                           is_state_enabled
65536                           AdventureWorks2012_DB_Spec     1
```

For a detailed look at what I'm auditing for the new Database Audit Specification, I can query the sys.database_audit_specification_details system catalog view (I'll walk through the logic in the "How It Works" section).

```
USE AdventureWorks2012;
GO
SELECT audit_action_name, class_desc, is_group
,ObjectNM=CASE
    WHEN major_id>0 THEN OBJECT_NAME(major_id, DB_ID()) ELSE 'N/A' END
FROM sys.database_audit_specification_details
WHERE database_specification_id=65536;
GO
```

This query returns the following:

```
audit_action_name        class_desc              is_group        ObjectNM
DATABASE_PRINCIPAL_      DATABASE                1               N/A
IMPERSONATION_GROUP
DELETE                   OBJECT_OR_COLUMN        0               CreditCard
INSERT                   OBJECT_OR_COLUMN        0               CreditCard
UPDATE                   OBJECT_OR_COLUMN        0               CreditCard
```

Although the Database Audit Specification is enabled, I have still not enabled the overall Server Audit object. I'll be demonstrating that in the next recipe, where you'll also learn how to query the captured audit data from a binary file.

How It Works

In this recipe, I demonstrated how to create a Database Audit Specification that designated which database-scoped events would be captured to the Server Audit object. To perform this action, I used the CREATE DATABASE AUDIT SPECIFICATION command. I started by changing the context to the database I wanted to audit (since this is a database-scoped object).

```
USE AdventureWorks2012;
GO
```

The first line of the CREATE DATABASE AUDIT SPECIFICATION command designated the user-defined name, followed by a reference to the Server Audit object I would be forwarding the database-scoped events to.

```
CREATE DATABASE AUDIT SPECIFICATION AdventureWorks2012_DB_Spec FOR SERVER AUDIT
LesROIS_Server_Audit
```

After that, I used the ADD keyword followed by an open parenthesis, defined the audit action group I wanted to monitor, and then entered a closing parenthesis and a comma (since I planned on defining more than one action to monitor).

```
ADD (DATABASE_PRINCIPAL_IMPERSONATION_GROUP),
```

Next, I designated the ADD keyword again, followed by the three actions I wanted to monitor for the Sales.CreditCard table.

```
ADD (INSERT, UPDATE, DELETE
ON Sales.CreditCard
```

The object-scoped actions required a reference to the database principal for which I wanted to audit actions. In this example, I wanted to view actions by all database principals. Since all database principals are by default a member of public, this was what I designated:

```
BY public)
```

After that, I used the WITH keyword followed by the STATE argument, which I set to enabled.

```
WITH (STATE=ON) GO
```

I then used the sys.database_audit_specifications to view the basic information of the new Database Audit Specification. I queried the sys.database_audit_specification_details catalog view to list the events that the Database Audit Specification captures. In the first three lines of code, I looked at the audit action name, class description, and is_group field, which designates whether the audit action is an audit action group or individual event.

```
SELECT audit_action_name, class_desc, is_group,
```

I used a CASE statement to evaluate the major_id column. If the major_id is a nonzero value, this indicates that the audit action row is for a database object, and therefore I used the OBJECT_NAME function to provide that object's name:

```
,ObjectNM=CASE
    WHEN major_id>0 THEN OBJECT_NAME(major_id, DB_ID()) ELSE 'N/A' END
```

In the last two lines of the SELECT, I designated the catalog view name and specified the database specification ID (important if you have more than one Database Audit Specification defined for a database, which is allowed).

```
FROM sys.database_audit_specification_details
WHERE database_specification_id=65536;
```

Now that I have defined the Server Audit object, Server Audit Specification, and Database Audit Specification, in the next recipe, I'll demonstrate enabling the Server Audit object and creating some auditable activity and then show how to query the captured audit data.

29-16. Querying Captured Audit Data

Problem

After enabling auditing on your SQL Server Instance, you now need to report on the audit data that has been captured.

Solution

With the auditing solution provided through the previous recipes, you will need to use the fn_get_audit_file function.

The previous recipes have now built up to the actual demonstration of SQL Server's auditing capabilities. To begin the recipe, I will enable the Server Audit object created a few recipes ago. Recall that I had defined this Server Audit object to write to a binary file under the C:\Apress folder. To enable the audit, I use the ALTER SERVER AUDIT command and configure the STATE option.

```
USE master;
GO
ALTER SERVER AUDIT [LesROIS_Server_Audit] WITH (STATE=ON);
GO
```

Now I will perform a few actions at both the SQL Server scope and within the AdventureWorks2012 database in order to demonstrate the audit collection process. I've added comments before each group of statements so that you can follow what actions I'm trying to demonstrate.

```
USE master;
GO
/*
-- Create new login (not auditing this, but using it for recipe)
*/
CREATE LOGIN TestAudit WITH PASSWORD='C83D7F50-9B9E';
GO
/*
-- Add to server role bulkadmin
*/
EXECUTE sp_addsrvrolemember 'TestAudit', 'bulkadmin';
GO
/*
-- Back up AdventureWorks2012 database
*/
BACKUP DATABASE AdventureWorks2012 TO DISK='C:\Apress\Example_AW.BAK';
GO
/*
-- Perform a DBCC on AdventureWorks2012
*/
DBCC CHECKDB('AdventureWorks2012');
GO
/*
-- Perform some AdventureWorks2012 actions
*/
USE AdventureWorks2012
GO
/*
-- Create a new user and then execute under that
-- user's context
*/
CREATE USER TestAudit FROM LOGIN TestAudit
EXECUTE AS USER='TestAudit'
/*
-- Revert back to me (in this case a login with sysadmin perms)
*/
REVERT;
GO
/*
-- Perform an INSERT, UPDATE, and DELETE -- from Sales.CreditCard
*/
```

```
INSERT Into Sales.CreditCard (CardType, CardNumber,ExpMonth,ExpYear,ModifiedDate)
    VALUES('Vista', '8675309153332145',11,2003,GetDate());
UPDATE Sales.CreditCard SET CardType='Colonial'
    WHERE CardNumber='8675309153332145';
DELETE Sales.CreditCard
    WHERE CardNumber='8675309153332145';
GO
```

Now that I have performed several events that are covered by the Server Audit Specification and Database Audit Specification created earlier, I can use the fn_get_audit_file table-valued function to view the contents of my Server Audit binary file. The syntax for this function is as follows:

```
fn_get_audit_file ( file_pattern,
    { default | initial_file_name | NULL },
    { default | audit_record_offset | NULL } )
```

Table 29-24 describes the arguments for this command.

Table 29-24. *fn_get_audit_file Arguments*

Argument	Description
file_pattern	Designates the location of the audit file or files to be read. You can use a drive letter or network share for the path and use the single asterisk (*) wildcard to designate multiple files.
{default | initial_file_name | NULL }	Designates the name and path for a specific file you would like to begin reading from. Default and NULL are synonymous and indicate no selection for the initial file name.
{default | audit_record_offset | NULL }	Designates the buffer offset from the initial file (when initial file is selected). Default and NULL are synonymous and indicate no selection for the audit.

In this first call to the fn_get_audit_file function, I'll look for any changes to server role memberships. Notice that I am using the sys.dm_audit_actions catalog view in order to translate the action ID into the actual action event name (you can use this view to find which event names you need to filter by).

```
USE master;
GO
SELECT af.event_time, af.succeeded,
af.target_server_principal_name, object_name
FROM fn_get_audit_file('C:\Apress\LesROIS_Server_Audit_*', default, default) af
INNER JOIN sys.dm_audit_actions aa
    ON af.action_id=aa.action_id
WHERE aa.name='ADD MEMBER'
    AND aa.class_desc='SERVER ROLE';
GO
```

This returns the event time, success flag, server principal name, and server role name.

```
event_time                  succeeded      target_server_principal_name    object_name
2012-04-25 15:06:54.702     1              TestAudit                       bulkadmin
```

In this next example, I'll take a look at deletion events against the Sales.CreditCard table.

```
USE master;
GO
SELECT af.event_time,
af.database_principal_name
FROM fn_get_audit_file('C:\Apress\LesROIS_Server_Audit_*', default, default) af
INNER JOIN sys.dm_audit_actions aa
    ON af.action_id=aa.action_id
WHERE aa.name='DELETE'
    AND aa.class_desc='OBJECT'
    AND af.schema_name='Sales'
    AND af.object_name='CreditCard';
GO
```

This query returns the following:

```
event_time                     database_principal_name
2012-04-25 15:13:24.542        dbo
```

The fn_get_audit_file function also exposes the SQL statement when applicable to the instantiating event. The following query demonstrates capturing the actual BACKUP DATABASE text used for the audited event:

```
USE master;
GO
SELECT event_time, statement
FROM fn_get_audit_file('C:\Apress\LesROIS_Server_Audit_*', default, default) af
INNER JOIN sys.dm_audit_actions aa
    ON af.action_id=aa.action_id
WHERE aa.name='BACKUP'
    AND aa.class_desc='DATABASE';
GO
```

This returns the event time and associated BACKUP statement text:

```
event_time                     statement
2012-04-25 15:07:29.482        BACKUP DATABASE AdventureWorks2012 TO DISK =
                               'C:\Apress\Example_AW.BAK'
```

The last query of this recipe demonstrates querying each distinct event and the associated database principal that performed it, along with the target server principal name (when applicable) or target object name:

```
USE master;
GO
SELECT DISTINCT
aa.name,
database_principal_name,
target_server_principal_name,
object_name
FROM fn_get_audit_file('C:\Apress\LesROIS_Server_Audit_*', default, default) af
INNER JOIN sys.dm_audit_actions aa
    ON af.action_id=aa.action_id;
GO
```

This returns the various events I performed earlier that were defined in the Server and Database Audit Specifications. It also includes audit events by default—for example, AUDIT SESSION CHANGED.

name	database_principal_name	target_server_principal_name	object_name
ADD MEMBER	dbo	TestAudit	bulkadmin
AUDIT SESSION CHANGED			
BACKUP	dbo		AdventureWorks2012
DBCC	dbo		
DELETE	dbo		CreditCard
IMPERSONATE	dbo		TestAudit
INSERT	dbo		CreditCard
UPDATE	dbo		CreditCard

How It Works

I started this recipe by enabling the overall Server Audit object using the ALTER SERVER AUDIT command. After that, I performed several SQL instance- and database-scoped activities—focusing on events that I had defined for capture in the Server and Database Audit Specifications bound to the LesROIS_Server_Audit audit. After that, I demonstrated how to use the fn_get_audit_file function to retrieve the event data from the binary file created under the C:\Apress directory.

■ **Note** I could have also defined the Server Audit object to write events to the Windows Application or Windows Security event log instead, in which case I would not have used fn_get_audit_file to retrieve the data, because this function applies only to the binary file format.

Each query to fn_get_audit_file I also joined to the sys.dm_audit_actions object in order to designate the audit action name and, depending on the action, the class description. Here's an example:

```
...
FROM fn_get_audit_file('C:\Apress\LesROIS_Server_Audit_*', default, default) af
INNER JOIN sys.dm_audit_actions aa
    ON af.action_id=aa.action_id
WHERE aa.name='ADD MEMBER'
    AND aa.class_desc='SERVER ROLE';
...
```

In the next and last recipe of this chapter, I'll demonstrate how to manage, modify, and remove audit objects.

29-17. Managing, Modifying, and Removing Audit Objects

Problem

Your corporate auditing requirements for SQL Server have changed. Now you need to modify the existing audit objects.

Solution

To modify existing audit objects, you should use the `ALTER SERVER AUDIT SPECIFICATION`, `ALTER SERVER AUDIT`, or `ALTER DATABASE AUDIT SPECIFICATION` command.

This recipe will demonstrate how to add and remove actions from existing Server and Database Audit Specifications, disable Server and Database Audit Specifications, modify the Server Audit object, and remove audit objects from the SQL instance and associated databases.

To modify an existing Server Audit Specification, I use the `ALTER SERVER AUDIT SPECIFICATION` command. In this first query demonstration, I'll remove one audit action type from the Server Audit Specification I created in an earlier recipe and also add a new audit action.

Before I can modify the specification, however, I must first disable it.

```
USE master;
GO
ALTER SERVER AUDIT SPECIFICATION [LesROIS_Server_Audit_Spec] WITH (STATE=OFF);
GO
```

Next, I will drop one of the audit actions.

```
USE master;
GO
ALTER SERVER AUDIT SPECIFICATION [LesROIS_Server_Audit_Spec]
DROP (BACKUP_RESTORE_GROUP);
GO
```

Now I'll demonstrate adding a new audit action group to an existing Server Audit Specification.

```
USE master;
GO
ALTER SERVER AUDIT SPECIFICATION [LesROIS_Server_Audit_Spec]
ADD (LOGIN_CHANGE_PASSWORD_GROUP);
GO
```

To have these changes take effect and resume auditing, I must reenable the Server Audit Specification.

```
USE master;
GO
ALTER SERVER AUDIT SPECIFICATION [LesROIS_Server_Audit_Spec]
WITH (STATE=ON);
GO
```

To modify the audit actions of a Database Audit Specification, I must use the `ALTER DATABASE AUDIT SPECIFICATION` command. Similar to Server Audit Specifications, a Database Audit Specification must have a disabled state prior to making any changes to it.

```
USE AdventureWorks2012;
GO
ALTER DATABASE AUDIT SPECIFICATION [AdventureWorks2012_DB_Spec]
WITH (STATE=OFF);
GO
```

This next query demonstrates removing an existing audit event from the Database Audit Specification I created earlier.

```
USE AdventureWorks2012;
GO
ALTER DATABASE AUDIT SPECIFICATION [AdventureWorks2012_DB_Spec]
```

```
DROP (INSERT ON [HumanResources].[Department] BY public);
GO
```

Next, I demonstrate how to add a new audit event to the existing Database Audit Specification.

```
USE AdventureWorks2012;
GO
ALTER DATABASE AUDIT SPECIFICATION [AdventureWorks2012_DB_Spec]
ADD (DATABASE_ROLE_MEMBER_CHANGE_GROUP);

GO
```

To have these changes go into effect, I need to reenable the Database Audit Specification.

```
USE AdventureWorks2012;

GO
ALTER DATABASE AUDIT SPECIFICATION [AdventureWorks2012_DB_Spec]
WITH (STATE=ON);
GO
```

To modify the Server Audit object, I use the ALTER SERVER AUDIT command. Similar to the Server and Database Audit Specification objects, the Server Audit object needs to be disabled before changes can be made to it. In this next example, I demonstrate disabling the Server Audit, making a change to the logging target so that it writes to the Windows Application event log instead, and then reenabling it.

```
USE master;
GO
ALTER SERVER AUDIT [LesROIS_Server_Audit] WITH (STATE=OFF);
ALTER SERVER AUDIT [LesROIS_Server_Audit] TO APPLICATION_LOG;
ALTER SERVER AUDIT [LesROIS_Server_Audit] WITH (STATE=ON);
```

Once the target is changed, audit events are now forwarded to the Windows Application event log. For example, if I execute a DBCC CHECKDB command again, I would see this reflected in the Windows Application event log with an event ID of 33205. The following is an example of a Windows Application event log entry:

```
Audit event: eventjtime:2012-04-25 18:17:49.4704464
sequence_number:1
action_id:DBCC
succeeded:true
permission_bitmask:0
is_column_permission:false
session_id:57
server_principal_id:263
database_principal_id:1
target_server_principal_id:0
target_database_principal_id:0
object_id:0
class_type:DB
session_server_principal_name:ROIS\Administrator
server_principal_name:ROIS\Administrator
Server_principal_sid:0105000000000005150000006bb13b36a981eb9a2b3859a8f4010000
database_principal_name:dbo
target_server_principal_name:
target_server_principal_sid:
target_database_principal_name:
server_instance_name:ROIS\Frederic
```

```
database_name:AdventureWorks2012
schema_name:
object_name:

statement:DBCC CHECKDB('AdventureWorks2012') additional_information:
```

To remove a Database Audit Specification, I need to disable it and then use the `DROP DATABASE AUDIT SPECIFICATION`, as demonstrated next:

```
USE AdventureWorks2012;
GO
ALTER DATABASE AUDIT SPECIFICATION [AdventureWorks2012_DB_Spec] WITH (STATE=OFF);
DROP DATABASE AUDIT SPECIFICATION [AdventureWorks2012_DB_Spec];
GO
```

To remove a Server Audit Specification, I need to disable it and then use the `DROP SERVER AUDIT SPECIFICATION` command.

```
USE master;
GO
ALTER SERVER AUDIT SPECIFICATION [LesROIS_Server_Audit_Spec] WITH (STATE=OFF);
DROP SERVER AUDIT SPECIFICATION [LesROIS_Server_Audit_Spec];
GO
```

Finally, to drop a Server Audit object, I need to first disable it and then use the `DROP SERVER AUDIT` command, as demonstrated next:

```
USE master;
GO
ALTER SERVER AUDIT [LesROIS_Server_Audit] WITH (STATE=OFF);
DROP SERVER AUDIT [LesROIS_Server_Audit];
GO
```

Any binary log files created from the auditing will still remain after removing the Server Audit object.

How It Works

This recipe demonstrated several commands used to manage audit objects. For each of these existing audit objects, I was required to disable the state prior to making changes. I used `ALTER SERVER AUDIT SPECIFICATION` to add and remove audit events from the Server Audit Specification and `DROP SERVER AUDIT SPECIFICATION` to remove the definition from the SQL Server instance.

I used `ALTER DATABASE AUDIT SPECIFICATION` to add and remove audit events from the Database Audit Specification and `DROP DATABASE AUDIT SPECIFICATION` to remove the definition from the user database. I used `ALTER SERVER AUDIT` to modify an existing Server Audit object—changing the target logging method from a binary file to the Windows Application event log instead. Lastly, I used `DROP SERVER AUDIT` to remove the Server Audit object from the SQL Server instance.

CHAPTER 30

Objects and Dependencies

by Wayne Sheffield

Almost everything in a database is an object; this includes tables, constraints, views, functions, stored procedures, and data types. Inevitably, there will come a time when you need to work on these at the object level: from renaming, to moving to a different schema, to determining dependencies between objects. This chapter covers maintaining and working with database objects at the object level.

30-1. Changing the Name of a Database Object

Problem

You need to change the name of an object in a database.

Solution

Utilize the system stored procedure sp_rename to rename an object in the database.

```
CREATE TABLE dbo.Test
       (
        Column1 INT,
        Column2 INT,
        CONSTRAINT UK_Test UNIQUE (Column1, Column2)
       );
GO
EXECUTE sp_rename 'dbo.Test', 'MyTestTable', 'object';
```

Executing the procedure returns the following caution message:

```
Caution:  Changing any part of an object name could break scripts and stored procedures.
```

How It Works

Using the sp_rename system stored procedure, you can rename table columns, indexes, tables, constraints, and other database objects.

The syntax for sp_rename is as follows:

```
sp_rename [ @objname = ] 'object_name' , [ @newname = ] 'new_name'
  [ , [ @objtype = ] 'object_type' ]
```

The arguments of this system stored procedure are described in Table 30-1.

Table 30-1. *sp_rename Parameters*

Argument	Description
object_name	The name of the object to be renamed
new_name	The new name of the object
object_type	The type of object to rename: column, database, index, object, and userdatatype

This example begins by creating a new table called dbo.Test, and then the system stored procedure sp_rename is used to rename the table:

```
EXECUTE sp_rename 'dbo.Test', 'MyTestTable', 'object';
```

Notice that the first parameter uses the fully qualified object name (schema.table_name), whereas the second parameter just uses the new table_name. The third parameter uses the object type of object.

Next, let's change the name of Column1 to NewColumnName:

```
EXECUTE sp_rename 'dbo.MyTestTable.Column1', 'NewColumnName', 'column';
```

Executing the procedure returns the following caution message:

```
Caution:  Changing any part of an object name could break scripts and stored procedures.
```

The first parameter used the schema.table_name.column_name to be renamed and the second parameter is the new name of the column. The third parameter used the object type of column.

In this next example, we build and then rename an index:

```
CREATE INDEX IX_1 ON dbo.MyTestTable (NewColumnName, Column2);
GO
EXECUTE sp_rename 'dbo.MyTestTable.IX_1', 'IX_NewIndexName', 'index';
```

The first parameter used the schema.table_name.index_name parameter. The second parameter used the name of the new index. The third used the object type of index.

When you successfully run sp_rename, you will receive the following caution message:

```
Caution:  Changing any part of an object name could break scripts and stored procedures.
```

In this next example, we create a new database, and then rename it:

```
CREATE DATABASE TSQLRecipes;
GO
SELECT name
FROM  sys.databases
WHERE  name IN ('TSQLRecipes', 'TSQL-Recipes');
GO
EXECUTE sp_rename 'TSQLRecipes', 'TSQL-Recipes', 'database';
SELECT name
FROM  sys.databases
WHERE  name IN ('TSQLRecipes', 'TSQL-Recipes');
GO
```

These statements produce the following results and messages:

```
name
-----------
TSQLRecipes

The database name 'TSQL-Recipes' has been set.
name
------------
TSQL-Recipes
```

In this final example, we build a user-defined data type, and then rename it.

```
CREATE TYPE dbo.Age
FROM TINYINT NOT NULL;
SELECT name
FROM  sys.types
WHERE  name IN ('Age', 'PersonAge');
EXECUTE sp_rename 'dbo.Age', 'PersonAge', 'userdatatype';
SELECT name
FROM  sys.types
WHERE  name IN ('Age', 'PersonAge');
```

These statements produce the following results and messages:

```
name
----
Age

Caution: Changing any part of an object name could break scripts and stored procedures.
name
---------
PersonAge
```

In a real-life scenario, in conjunction with renaming an object, you'll also want to ALTER any view, stored procedure, function, or other programmatic object that contains a reference to the original object name. I demonstrate how to find out which objects reference an object later on in this chapter in Recipe 30-3.

30-2. Changing an Object's Schema

Problem

You need to move an object from one schema to another.

Solution

You can use the ALTER SCHEMA statement to move objects from one schema to another:

```
CREATE TABLE Sales.TerminationReason
       (
        TerminationReasonID INT NOT NULL
                            PRIMARY KEY,
        TerminationReasonDESC VARCHAR(100) NOT NULL
       );
GO
ALTER SCHEMA HumanResources TRANSFER Sales.TerminationReason;
GO
DROP TABLE HumanResources.TerminationReason;
GO
```

How It Works

The ALTER SCHEMA command takes two arguments: the first being the schema name you want to transfer the object to, and the second is the object name that you want to transfer. In the above example, a table is created in the Sales schema, and it is then moved into the HumanResources schema, and finally deleted.

30-3. Identifying Object Dependencies

Problem

You need to see what objects a specified object depends upon, or what objects depend upon a specified object.

Solution

Query the sys.sql_expression_dependencies object catalog view to identify dependencies between objects.

How It Works

SQL Server provides methods for identifying object dependencies within the database, across databases, and across servers (using linked server four-part names). This following example demonstrates the use of the sys.sql_expression_dependencies object catalog view to identify dependencies in several scenarios.

I begin by checking for the existence of two databases, and dropping them if they exist. Next, I create two new databases and some new objects within them in order to demonstrate the functionality:

```
USE master;
GO
IF DB_ID('TSQLRecipe_A') IS NOT NULL
   DROP DATABASE TSQLRecipe_A;
```

```
IF DB_ID('TSQLRecipe_B') IS NOT NULL
   DROP DATABASE TSQLRecipe_B;

-- Create two new databases
CREATE DATABASE TSQLRecipe_A;
GO
CREATE DATABASE TSQLRecipe_B;
GO

-- Create a new table in the first database
USE TSQLRecipe_A;
GO
CREATE TABLE dbo.Book
       (
        BookID INT NOT NULL
                   PRIMARY KEY,
        BookNM VARCHAR(50) NOT NULL
       );
GO

-- Create a procedure referencing an object
-- in the second database
USE TSQLRecipe_B;
GO
CREATE PROCEDURE dbo.usp_SEL_Book
AS
SELECT BookID,
       BookNM
FROM   TSQLRecipe_A.dbo.Book;
GO
```

A stored procedure has been created that references a table in another database. Now if I wish to view all objects that the stored procedure depends on, I can execute the following query against sys.sql_expression_dependencies (I elaborate on the columns shortly):

```
SELECT referenced_server_name,
       referenced_database_name,
       referenced_schema_name,
       referenced_entity_name,
       is_caller_dependent
FROM   sys.sql_expression_dependencies
WHERE  OBJECT_NAME(referencing_id) = 'usp_SEL_Book';
```

This query returns one row (results pivoted for formatting):

```
referenced_server_name  NULL
referenced_database_name TSQLRecipe_A
referenced_schema_name  dbo
referenced_entity_name  Book
is_caller_dependent    0
```

Now create another stored procedure that references an object that doesn't yet exist (which is an allowable scenario for a stored procedure and this is a common practice). For example:

```
USE TSQLRecipe_B;
GO
CREATE PROCEDURE dbo.usp_SEL_Contract
AS
SELECT ContractID,
       ContractNM
FROM   TSQLRecipe_A.dbo.Contract;
GO
```

In versions of SQL Server before SQL Server 2008, dependencies on nonexistent objects weren't tracked. Subsequent versions corrected this behavior. You can issue the following query to check on the dependencies of `usp_SEL_contract`:

```
USE TSQLRecipe_B;
GO
SELECT referenced_server_name,
       referenced_database_name,
       referenced_schema_name,
       referenced_entity_name,
       is_caller_dependent
FROM   sys.sql_expression_dependencies
WHERE  OBJECT_NAME(referencing_id) = 'usp_SEL_Contract';
```

This query returns one row (results pivoted for formatting):

```
referenced_server_name    NULL
referenced_database_name  TSQLRecipe_A
referenced_schema_name    dbo
referenced_entity_name    Contract
is_caller_dependent       0
```

Even though the object `TSQLRecipe_A.dbo.Contract` does not yet exist, the dependency between the referencing stored procedure and the referenced table is still represented.

This recipe demonstrates how to determine object dependencies using the `sys.sql_expression_dependencies` catalog view. In the `SELECT` statement, five columns are referenced. The first four columns, `referenced_server_name`, `referenced_database_name`, `referenced_schema_name`, and `referenced_entity_name` will contain the value utilized for each part of the four-part qualified name. If that particular value isn't specified when the referencing object is created, it will be `NULL`. The fifth column, `is_caller_dependent`, indicates whether the object reference depends on the person executing the module. For example, if the object name is not fully qualified, and an object named `T1` exists in two different schemas, the actual object referenced would depend on the person calling the module and the execution context.

30-4. Identifying Referencing and Referenced Entities

Problem

You are making changes to a database object, and you need to examine all other objects that are either referencing this object, or are referenced by this object.

Solution

Utilize the `sys.dm_sql_referenced_entities` and `sys.dm_sql_referencing_entities` Dynamic Management Functions.

How It Works

The `sys.dm_sql_referenced_entities` and `sys.dm_sql_referencing_entities` Dynamic Management Functions are used to identify referenced and referencing objects. The `sys.dm_sql_referenced_entities` Dynamic Management Function, when provided with the referencing object name, returns a result set of objects being referenced. The `sys.dm_sql_referencing_entities` Dynamic Management Function, when provided the name of the object being referenced, returns a result set of objects referencing it. Notice that these two Dynamic Management Functions are named very similiarly, so ensure that you are using the proper function.

Let's go to an example to see how these Dynamic Management Functions work. This first section creates a database, and within that database a table, view, and stored procedure where the view and stored procedure reference the table:

```
USE master;
GO
IF DB_ID('TSQLRecipe_A') IS NOT NULL
   DROP DATABASE TSQLRecipe_A;
GO
CREATE DATABASE TSQLRecipe_A;
GO
USE TSQLRecipe_A;
GO
CREATE TABLE dbo.BookPublisher
       (
        BookPublisherID INT NOT NULL
                            PRIMARY KEY,
        BookPublisherNM VARCHAR(30) NOT NULL
       );
GO
CREATE VIEW dbo.vw_BookPublisher
AS
SELECT BookPublisherID,
       BookPublisherNM
FROM   dbo.BookPublisher;
GO
CREATE PROCEDURE dbo.usp_INS_BookPublisher
       @BookPublisherNM VARCHAR(30)
```

```
AS
INSERT dbo.BookPublisher
       (BookPublisherNM)
VALUES (@BookPublisherNM);
GO
```

To find all of the objects that are referenced by the dbo.vw_BookPublisher view, run the following query:

```
SELECT referenced_entity_name,
       referenced_minor_name
FROM   sys.dm_sql_referenced_entities('dbo.vw_BookPublisher', 'OBJECT');
```

This query returns the following result set:

```
referenced_entity_name  referenced_minor_name
----------------------  ---------------------
BookPublisher           NULL
BookPublisher           BookPublisherID
BookPublisher           BookPublisherNM
```

Notice that this function shows one row for the table referenced in the view, as well as two rows for each column referenced within the view.

The first parameter passed to this function is the name of the object that is referencing other objects. The second parameter designates the type of entities to list. The choices are OBJECT, DATABASE_DDL_TRIGGER, and SERVER_DDL_TRIGGER. In this case, OBJECT is the proper choice, and the result is the name of the referenced table and specific columns used in the SELECT clause of the view.

To find all of the objects that are referencing the dbo.BookPublisher table, run the following query:

```
SELECT referencing_schema_name,
       referencing_entity_name
FROM   sys.dm_sql_referencing_entities('dbo.BookPublisher', 'OBJECT');
```

This query returns the following result set:

```
referencing_schema_name  referencing_entity_name
-----------------------  -----------------------
dbo                      usp_INS_BookPublisher
dbo                      vw_BookPublisher
```

As you can see, both the view and the stored procedure that reference the table are returned.

The first parameter passed to this function is the name of the object that you want to find all other objects that reference it. The second parameter designates the class of objects to list. The choices are OBJECT, TYPE, XML_SCHEMA_COLLECTION, and PARTITION FUNCTION. In this case, OBJECT is the proper choice, which results in the view and stored procedure being listed in the output.

30-5. Viewing an Object's Definition

Problem

Now that you have identified the objects that are referencing an object, or that are referenced by an object, you need to view the definition of those objects.

Solution 1

Utilize the OBJECT_DEFINITION function to view the definition of an object:

```
SELECT OBJECT_DEFINITION(OBJECT_ID('dbo.usp_INS_BookPublisher'));
```

This query returns the following result set:

```
-------------------------------------------
CREATE PROCEDURE dbo.usp_INS_BookPublisher
    @BookPublisherNM varchar(30) AS
INSERT dbo.BookPublisher (BookPublisherNM)
VALUES (@BookPublisherNM);
```

Solution 2

Query the sys.all_sql_modules DMV and examine the definition column.

```
SELECT definition
FROM   sys.all_sql_modules AS asm
WHERE  object_id = OBJECT_ID('dbo.usp_INS_BookPublisher');
```

This query returns the following result set:

```
definition
-------------------------------------------
CREATE PROCEDURE dbo.usp_INS_BookPublisher
       @BookPublisherNM VARCHAR(30)
AS
INSERT dbo.BookPublisher
       (BookPublisherNM)
VALUES (@BookPublisherNM);
```

How It Works

In the first solution, the OBJECT_DEFINITION function accepts an object_id of an object, and it returns the Transact-SQL code that defines the specified object. In the above example, the object_id was obtained with the OBJECT_ID function; this function is described in the next recipe.

The OBJECT_DEFINITION function can also be used to determine the code of system objects. For example, you can reveal the code that makes up the sys.sp_depends system stored procedure with this query:

```
SELECT OBJECT_DEFINITION(OBJECT_ID('sys.sp_depends'));
```

This query returns the following (abridged) result set:

```
create procedure sys.sp_depends --- 1996/08/09 16:51
@objname nvarchar(776)          -- the object we want to check
as
...
select @dbname = parsename(@objname,3)

if @dbname is not null and @dbname <> db_name()
        begin
                raiserror(15250,-1,-1)
                return (1)
        end
...
```

In the second example, the definition of the view is retrieved from the sys.all_sql_modules Dynamic Management View (DMV). The view's object_id is used to filter the results to just this view.

Note that if the object that you pass in is encrypted, or if you don't have permission to view this object, you will have a NULL returned instead. This following example creates an encrypted view, and then attempts to retrieve the definition with each of the above solutions:

```
IF OBJECT_ID('dbo.EncryptedView', 'V') IS NOT NULL
   DROP VIEW dbo.EncryptedView;
GO
CREATE VIEW dbo.EncryptedView
WITH ENCRYPTION
AS
SELECT 1 AS Result;
GO

SELECT OBJECT_DEFINITION(OBJECT_ID('dbo.EncryptedView'));

SELECT definition
FROM   sys.all_sql_modules AS asm
WHERE  object_id = OBJECT_ID('dbo.EncryptedView');
```

These queries return the following results:

```
----
NULL

definition
---------
NULL
```

30-6. Returning a Database Object's Name, Schema Name, and Object ID

Problem

You know an object's name, and need to get its object_id (or you know an object's object_id, and need to get its schema name and the name of the object).

Solution 1

Utilize the OBJECT_ID, OBJECT_NAME, and OBJECT_SCHEMA_NAME functions:

```
SELECT object_id,
       OBJECT_SCHEMA_NAME(object_id) AS SchemaName,
       OBJECT_NAME(object_id) AS ObjectName
FROM   sys.tables
WHERE  object_id = OBJECT_ID('dbo.BookPublisher', 'U');
```

This query returns the following result set:

```
object_id   SchemaName  ObjectName
---------   ----------  -------------
245575913   dbo         BookPublisher
```

Note that you will most likely return a different object_id value.

Solution 2

Query the underlying system views directly:

```
SELECT t.object_id,
       s.name AS SchemaName,
       t.name AS ObjectName
FROM   sys.tables AS t
       JOIN sys.schemas AS s
            ON t.schema_id = s.schema_id
WHERE  s.name = 'dbo'
       AND t.name = 'BookPublisher';
```

This query returns the same result set:

```
object_id  SchemaName ObjectName
---------  ---------- -------------
245575913  dbo        BookPublisher
```

How It Works

In Solution 1, the OBJECT_ID function accepts a schema-qualified object name, and returns the object_id for this object. This function also has an optional second parameter, which is the type of object. In the above example, the type of 'U' was specified, which is the type for a USER TABLE.

The OBJECT_NAME function accepts an object_id, and returns the nonqualified name of the specified object. The OBJECT_SCHEMA_NAME function accepts an object_id, and returns the name of the schema of the specified object. Both of these functions have an optional second parameter (not used in the above example), which is the database_id of the database to be searched. If the database_id is not passed in, these functions will utilize the current database.

All of these functions will return a null if the specified object does not exist, or if the user does not have permissions on the object. Additionally, the OBJECT_ID function will return a null if a spatial index is specified.

In Solution 2, the sys.tables and sys.schemas system views are queried directly to return the same information. This solution also provides the opportunity to perform wildcard searches with the LIKE operator.

Index

A

B

C

D

E

F

G

H

I, J, K

L

M

N

O

P

S

T

U

V

W

X, Y, Z

CPSIA information can be obtained at www.ICGtesting.com
Printed in the USA
LVOW111158080513

332773LV00033B/119/P

9 781430 242000